MW01120458

System Administration 1

Infrastructure Planning and Design	Chapters 1, 3
Installation/Setup	Chapter 2
Maintenance and Operations	Chapters 3, 4
System Security	Chapters 4, 5
Troubleshooting	Chapters 4, 10

System Administration 2

Installation/Setup Competencies	Chapter 6
Maintenance and Operations	Chapter 9
System Security	Chapters 7, 8
Troubleshooting	Chapter 10

Application Development 1

Create Forms	Chapters 12, 13
Create Views	Chapter 14
Create Agents	Chapter 21
Create Actions	Chapter 15
Create Hotspots	Chapters 15, 16
Create Application Documentation	Chapter 16
Troubleshooting Application Problems	Chapter 24

Application Development 2

Architect Applications	Chapter 11
Create Forms	Chapters 18, 19
Create Views	Chapter 20
Creating Agents/Actions	Chapter 21
Maintaining Application Designs	Chapter 22
Securing Applications	Chapters 16, 23
Troubleshooting Application Problems	Chapter 24

CATHY BANNON
DENNIS MAIONE

CLP

TRAINING GUIDE

LOTUS NOTES

New
Riders

CLP Training Guide: Lotus Notes

By Cathy Bannon and Dennis Maione

Published by:
Que Publishing
201 West 103rd Street
Indianapolis, IN 46290 USA

©1998 by Que Publishing

International Standard Book Number: 0-7897-1505-8

Library of Congress Catalog Card Number: 97-80668

2000   99   98   97   4   3   2

Interpretation of the printing code: The rightmost double-digit number is the year of the book's printing; the rightmost single-digit, the number of the book's printing. For example, a printing code of 97-1 shows that the first printing of the book occurred in 1997.

Composed in New Baskerville and MCPdigital by Macmillan Computer Publishing

Printed in the United States of America

President	*Richard K. Swadley*
Publisher	*Don Fowley*
Associate Publisher	*David Dwyer*
Executive Editor	*Mary Foote*
Managing Editor	*Sarah Kearns*
Indexing Manager	*Ginny Bess*

Acquisitions Editor
Nancy Maragioglio

Development Editor
Nancy Warner

Software Development Specialist
Steve Flatt
Marjorie Kramer

Production Editor
Kate Shoup Welsh

Copy Editors
Jennifer Clark
Julie MacLean
Audra McFarland
Kris Simmons

Indexer
Cheryl A. Jackson

Technical Reviewer
Adam Gerhard

Editorial Coordinators
Mandie Rowell
Katie Wise

Resource Coordinator
Deborah Frisby

Editorial Assistant
Jen Chisholm

Cover Designer
Nathan Clement

Book Designer
Glenn Larsen

Copy Writer
David Reichwein

Production Team Supervisor
Victor Peterson

Production Team
Darlena Murray
Daniela Raderstorf
Megan Wade
Pamela Woolf

Dedications

Cathy Bannon   This book is dedicated to Peter, Kate, Grace, and Kane.

Dennis Maione   To my wife, Debra, for her strength and support. To Emma, Alexander, and Noah for understanding that Daddy was working again tonight.

Acknowledgments

Cathy Bannon   I want to thank both Nancy Maragioglio and Nancy Warner, without whose assistance I could not have completed this book. I would also like to thank Tom Papagiannopoulous for his recommendation and encouragement. I cannot thank my family enough for their support and interest during this "first book" experience.

About the Author

Cathy Bannon is an independent trainer for Lotus Notes. She became a certified trainer in 1993 with the Notes release 3 version and has specialized in the systems administration area. She worked for IBM for 10 years before leaving to pursue an independent path. Bannon has a Bachelor of Commerce from University of Windsor. She can be reached at cbannon@pcs.mb.ca.

Dennis Maione lives in frosty Winnipeg, Canada, which is a good thing because he has time to write books instead of lying on beaches and enjoying fun and sun. He is a certified Lotus professional in both system administration and application development, and is a certified Lotus instructor.

Dennis spends his free time at home sleeping (ask his wife!) when he isn't reading to his kids, watching Star Trek, or responsibly helping his wife with a myriad of household tasks.

Tell Us What You Think!

The staff of Macmillan Computer Publishing is committed to bringing you the very best in computer reference material. Each Macmillan Computer Publishing book or application is the result of months of work by authors and staff who research and refine the information it contains.

As part of this commitment to you, Macmillan Computer Publishing invites your input. As a reader, you are the most important critic of and commentator on our books. We value your opinion and want to know what we're doing right, what we could do better, what areas you'd like to see us publish in, and any other words of wisdom you're willing to pass our way. You can help us make strong books that meet your needs and give you the computer guidance you require. Please let us know if you enjoy this software, if you have trouble with the information and examples presented, or if you have a suggestion for the next version.

Please note, however: Macmillan Computer Publishing's staff cannot serve as a technical resource during your preparation for the Certified Lotus Professional certification exams or for questions about software- or hardware-related problems. Please refer to the documentation that accompanies the Lotus product or to the applications' help systems.

If you have a question or comment about any Macmillan Computer Publishing product, there are several ways to contact Macmillan Computer Publishing. We will respond to as many people as we can. Your name, address, or phone number will never become part of a mailing list or be used for any purpose other than to help us continue to bring you the best study materials possible. You can write us at the following address:

Macmillan Computer Publishing
Attn: Publisher—Certification
201 W. 103rd Street
Indianapolis, IN 46290

If you prefer, you can fax Macmillan Computer Publishing at (317) 581-4663. You also can send e-mail to Macmillan Computer Publishing at the following Internet address:

```
certification@mcp.com
```

If you have access to the World Wide Web, check out our site at

```
http://www.mcp.com.
```

Contents at a Glance

Table of Contents

Part I: System Administration

Part II: System Administration

11   Introduction to Application Development Components   437

Introduction

CLP Training Guide: Lotus Notes is designed for advanced end-users, service technicians, developers, and system administrators who are considering certification as a CLP (Certified Lotus Professional). This book tests your ability to administer, develop, and troubleshoot systems that incorporate Lotus Notes, as well as your ability to provide technical support to users of Lotus Notes.

Who Should Read This Book?

This book is designed to help advanced users, service technicians, and network administrators who are working toward Lotus certification prepare for the Certified Lotus Professional exams. This book is your one-stop shop. Everything you need to know to pass the exam is here. You do not *need* to take a class in addition to buying this book to pass the exam, but you might benefit from doing so.

This book also can help advanced users, developers, and administrators who are not studying for the Certified Lotus Professional exams but who are looking for a single-volume reference on Lotus Notes.

How This Book Helps You

This book takes you on a self-guided tour of all the areas covered by the Lotus exams and teaches you the specific skills you need to achieve your certification. You'll also find helpful hints, tips, real-world examples, and exercises. Specifically, this book is set up to help you in the following ways:

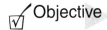 **Objective** ▶ This book is organized by two major exam areas and exam objectives. Every objective you need to know for the exam is covered in this book; a margin icon, like the one in the margin here, will help you quickly locate these objectives.

▶ Pre-chapter quizzes appear at the beginning of each chapter to test your knowledge of the objectives contained within that chapter. If you already know the answers to those questions, you can make a time-management decision accordingly.

▶ You'll find plenty of questions at the end of each chapter to test your comprehension of material covered within that chapter. An answer list follows the questions, so you can check yourself. These practice test options will help you decide what you already understand and what requires extra review on your part. The CD-ROM also contains a sample test engine that will give you an accurate idea of what the test is really like.

You'll also get a chance to practice for the certification exam using the test engine on the accompanying CD-ROM. The questions on the CD-ROM provide a more thorough and comprehensive look at what your certification exams really are like.

The Certified Lotus Professional (CLP) Program

Many users, developers, and system administrators want to earn recognition as a technical professional through the Lotus certification process. Certification ensures that individuals have been trained properly and meet Lotus' requirements for administering and developing Lotus products. Lotus recognizes the following levels of certification worldwide for Lotus Notes release 4 certification. The following information can be found on the Lotus Web site at http://www.lotus.com/home.nsf/tabs/education:

▶ Application Developer—This level is directed toward individuals responsible for building multiple Notes database applications that automate workflow between several departments.

Expertise in application architecture, development, security, and documentation is required.

▶ Principal Application Developer—This level is directed toward individuals responsible for building enterprisewide solutions to business problems. The ability to expand business solutions in one or more of the following ways is required:

  ▶ By expanding Notes solution capabilities through object-oriented scripting

  ▶ By extending Notes solutions to the Web using Domino

  ▶ By creating desktop solutions through object-oriented scripting

▶ System Administrator—This level is directed toward individuals experienced in Notes server installation and configuration, server monitoring and statistics, server maintenance and operations, certification, managing multiple Notes domains, and controlling Notes communications.

▶ Principal System Administrator—This level is directed toward individuals who have achieved system administrator status while proving their expertise in integrating additional product technology.

▶ Certified Lotus Specialist—This level is directed toward individuals who wish to demonstrate specialized technical product knowledge at a base level for Lotus Domino, Notes, cc:Mail, or SmartSuite. CLS certification requires successful completion of one exam developed and maintained by Lotus. Lotus recognizes the following exams for achieving CLS status:

  ▶ Domino Web Development and Administration

  ▶ Developing LotusScript Applications for SmartSuite using 1-2-3 '97

  ▶ Notes R4 Application Development 1

The Notes R4 Application Development 1 certification exam is directed toward individuals responsible for building a single Notes database application, including enhancing and modifying the application to incorporate increasingly advanced Notes features and functionality. Accomplished individuals will have expertise in creating forms, views, agents, actions, hotspots, and application documentation, and in troubleshooting application problems.

▶ Notes R4 System Administration 1

The Notes R4 System Administration 1 certification exam is directed toward individuals experienced in setting up, operating, and maintaining Notes/Domino servers and client workstations. The competencies measured are infrastructure, planning and design, server installation/setup, maintenance and operations, systems security, and troubleshooting.

▶ cc:Mail R6 System Administration 1

How Do I Become Certified?

You must successfully complete each level of certification in a series of exams developed and maintained by Lotus. The following lists the requirements for each certification level.

Lotus Notes release 4 certification	Lotus Notes release 4 examinations
CLS Application Development or System Administration	Application Development 1 or System Administration 1
CLP Application Developer	Application Development 1 System Administration 1 Application Development 2
CLP Principal	Application Development 1

Lotus Notes release 4 certification	Lotus Notes release 4 examinations
Application Developer	System Administration 1 Application Development 2
	Electives (one required): *Lotus Script in Notes for Application Developers
	*Developing Domino Applications for the Web (for Notes Developers)
	*Developing Lotus Script Applications for SmartSuite Using 1-2-3 '97
	*Domino Web Development and Administration
CLP System Administrator	Application Development 1 System Administration 1 System Administration 2
CLP Principal	Application Development 1
System Administrator	System Administration 1
	Electives (one required): *Administrating Specialized Tasks for Domino 4.5 *cc:Mail R6 System Administration

Exam Information

All exams for Lotus' certification programs are administered by two independent testing vendors:

> ▶ Sylvan Prometric Testing Centers, located worldwide, allow flexibility in scheduling needed exams, as well as times and locations. For more information about Sylvan Prometric Testing Centers, call 800-74-LOTUS (800-745-6887). Outside North America, contact your local Lotus Education office for the location of the nearest Sylvan Prometric Regional Service Center.

> ▶ CATGlobal is currently rolling out select centers worldwide. Look for full worldwide coverage in early 1998. For more information about the center nearest you, visit the CATGlobal Web site at www.catglobal.com.

Understanding What the Lotus Notes Exam Covers

Lotus professional certification demonstrates a broad depth of knowledge in Lotus Notes and cc:Mail and earns you recognition as a technical professional.

To accomplish your certification goals, Lotus has developed a set of competencies associated with job tasks to be measured, which are represented in either exam format. Exam questions are then structured to test your ability to perform these tasks. The competency areas provide you with direction on which topics you may need to study, or you may attempt to extrapolate how a specific competency is used to formulate a possible exam question. The exam competencies are summarized in the following sections.

System Administration 1

Five basic competency areas are measured by the System Administration 1 certification exam:

- ▶ Infrastructure planning and design
- ▶ Installation/setup
- ▶ Maintenance and operations
- ▶ System security
- ▶ Troubleshooting

Application Development 1

Seven basic competency areas are measured by the Application Development 1 certification exam:

- ▶ Creating forms

- ▶ Creating views

- ▶ Creating agents

- ▶ Creating actions

- ▶ Creating hotspots

- ▶ Creating application documentation

- ▶ Troubleshooting application problems

System Administration 2

Four basic competency areas are measured by the System Administration 2 certification exam:

- ▶ Install/Setup Competencies

- ▶ Maintenance and Operations

- ▶ System Security

- ▶ Troubleshooting

Application Development 2

Seven basic competency areas are measured by the Application Development 2 certification exam:

- ▶ Architect applications

- ▶ Creating forms

- ▶ Creating views

- ▶ Creating agents/actions

- ▶ Maintaining application designs

- ▶ Securing applications

- ▶ Troubleshooting application problems

Hardware and Software Needed

As a self-paced study guide, much of the book expects you to use Lotus Notes and follow along through the exercises while you learn. Lotus designed Notes to operate in a wide range of actual situations, and the exercises in this book encompass that range.

System Administration Requirements

The computer configurations for the system administration portion of this book are described as follows:

- ▶ A PC with an Intel 80486 or Pentium Processor

- ▶ An operating system capable of running your version of Lotus Notes (Windows 95, Windows NT, OS/2)

- ▶ 16MB minimum free hard disk space, 24MB or greater recommended

- ▶ 150MB minimum server hard disk space, 300MB or greater recommended

- ▶ VGA (or Super VGA) video adapter

- ▶ VGA (or Super VGA) monitor

- ▶ Mouse or equivalent pointing device

- ▶ Two-speed (or faster) CD-ROM drive

- ▶ Network Interface Card (NIC) (if networked, though not necessary)

- ▶ Notes server (if available, though not necessary)

Application Development Requirements

The computer configurations for the application development portion of this book are described as follows:

- A PC with an Intel 80486 or Pentium Processor

- An operating system capable of running your version of Lotus Notes (Windows 95, Windows NT, OS/2)

- 8MB of RAM for Windows 95 and OS/2, 16MB of RAM for Windows NT

- 30MB (or more) free hard disk space

- 3.5-inch, 1.44-MB floppy drive

- VGA (or Super VGA) video adapter

- VGA (or Super VGA) monitor

- Mouse or equivalent pointing device

- Two-speed (or faster) CD-ROM drive

- Network Interface Card (NIC) (if networked, though not necessary)

- Notes server (if available, though not necessary)

Tips for the Exam

Each Notes exam consists of 40–60 multiple-choice questions (with one or multiple answers). Each test has a specific time limit assigned. The time limit will be adequate for most candidates to complete the exam.

The tests are computerized and allow you to answer questions or mark particular questions to return to. In addition, you can always go back and review any questions you have answered. Questions will be direct and related to a certain topic or will be based upon a given scenario in which the candidate must gather pertinent information.

The exams are in a closed-book format. This means that no notes, calculators, or computers will be allowed. A blank sheet of paper will be provided to you at the exam, though you must return it when you complete the exam.

After the exam is finished, the score will immediately be displayed on the screen. A printout of the score will also be given to each candidate. You must pass a certain percentage of questions, which you will be informed of at the onset of the exam. The Lotus Education department will be forwarded the scores within five business days.

Remember the following tips as you prepare for the Lotus certification exams:

▶ Read all the material—Lotus has been known to include material not specified in the objectives. This course has included additional information not required by the objectives in an effort to give you the best possible preparation for the examination, and for the real-world network experiences to come.

▶ Complete the exercises in each chapter—All Lotus Notes exams are experience-based, and require you to have used the product in a real environment. Exercises for each objective are placed at the end of each chapter to give you a taste of that experience; it is recommended that you complete each one and understand how and why each did what it did.

▶ Complete all the questions in the "Review Questions" sections—they will help you remember key points. The questions are fairly simple, but be warned: Some questions may have more than one answer.

Note

Although this book is designed to prepare you to take and pass the Lotus Notes certification exam, there are no guarantees. Read this book, work through the exercises, and take the practice assessment exams.

When taking the real certification exam, make sure you answer all the questions before your time limit expires. Do not spend too much time on any one question. If you are unsure about an answer, answer the question as best you can and mark it for later review when you have finished all the questions.

Instead of leaving an answer blank (never a good idea), eliminate all definitely incorrect answers, and take a "best guess"
at the choices you have left. Good luck.

Remember, the object is not to pass the exam; it is to understand
the material. After you understand the material, passing is simple.
Knowledge is a pyramid; to build upward, you need a solid foundation. The Lotus Notes Certification program is designed to
ensure that you have that solid foundation.

P a r t 1

System Administration

Introduction to Notes System Administration Components

This chapter helps you prepare for the exam by covering the following objectives:

√ Objectives

▶ Why do companies use Notes?

▶ What is a Notes infrastructure?

▶ Functions of Notes server and Notes client

▶ Functions of a Notes administrator

▶ Notes basic architectural components

▶ Notes domains

▶ Notes named networks

▶ Certifier IDs

▶ Public Address Book

Test Yourself! Before reading this chapter, test yourself to determine how much study time you will need to devote to this section.

1. When planning for the installation of Notes, what are the three architectural Notes components you should be concerned about?

2. What is the certifier ID used for?

3. What does the Public Address Book represent?

4. For Notes servers to be in the same Notes named network, they must meet what conditions?

Answers are located at the end of the chapter...

Understanding Why Companies Use Notes

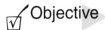 Objective   Before jumping into the functionality of Notes, you should understand why a company might choose to employ Notes in its day-to-day operations. Following is an example of a fictional company called *Bean*. This example illustrates various requirements within the company and why Notes was a logical choice.

Following a Company Example

The IS manager at Bean has been asked to determine which system would best meet Bean's newly stated requirements. Bean, a company that buys and sells coffee beans, is located in four areas:

▶ Toronto

▶ Chicago

▶ Boston

▶ New York

Bean's headquarters are in New York, and it has a mainframe that keeps track of inventory, sales, accounting, and personnel. Each of Bean's locations has a local area network (LAN) that allows the central storage of files as well as basic messaging to occur. Reports from the mainframe are downloaded on a weekly basis and available on the network file server. Some sales-reporting tools have been developed in Lotus 1-2-3 and WordPerfect, but users often get confused with different file formats. There has been some dissatisfaction with the current system from the end users, and a task force has been organized to gather information about desired functions from the users and to format these into requirements. Figure 1.1 diagrams the Bean company's current system and topology.

Figure 1.1

Bean's pre-Notes system and topology.

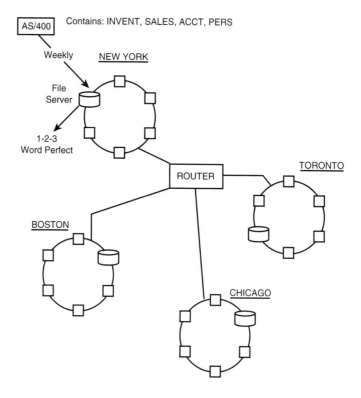

The task force has made recommendations for what the Bean company needs to implement. They are as follows:

▶ Users need easier access to HQ information on a daily basis dealing with inventory, sales, shipping, and so on.

▶ Field people need better tools to manage their clients with information concerning the following:

  ▶ History tracking and documentation.

  ▶ Sales plan.

  ▶ Client profiles.

  ▶ Travel plans.

  ▶ Project management.

  ▶ Electronic mail is required.

▶ Tools and formats currently used in Lotus 1-2-3 and Word-Perfect for expenses, forecasting, and reporting should be incorporated into the new system as opposed to being re-invented.

▶ Field people want to have all information with them when they are away from the office and disconnected from the network.

The IS manager has evaluated several systems and determined that Notes will meet all of the task force's stated requirements:

▶ Notes has many strong functional tools for importing and exporting data to and from relational databases.

▶ Notes has an easy developmental process for creating databases used for gathering and sharing information.

▶ Notes' replication process is a strong system for the distribution and sharing of information across the company.

▶ Notes mail has more-than-adequate tools for Bean's mail requirements.

▶ Notes supports current standards for the embedding and linking of objects that will greatly reduce learning curves for users.

The IS manager has looked at the security components and is satisfied that the information will remain secure. The following lists how the Bean company system and topology will function after Notes has been installed:

1. The New York Notes server imports information from the mainframe at 6:00 a.m. into the Notes company report databases and client databases.

2. The New York server replicates with the Toronto, Boston, and Chicago Notes servers at 6:30 a.m. to send all mainframe information to them.

3. By 7:00 a.m., all servers have the same information in the replica copies of their databases and are in sync.

4. Mail within the Notes named network is delivered immediately. Mail across the Notes named networks is scheduled to go eight times a day.

5. Replication is set to occur between servers three times a day: 7:00 a.m., 12:00 p.m., and 7:00 p.m..

6. Remote users are set up with replica copies of the databases they need on their laptops. They edit and enter data during their tasks and average two replications a day with their home servers and send and receive mail.

7. At 9:30 p.m., Notes servers export information to the mainframe to update relational databases.

The implementation of these steps will allow all information flowing from the mainframe to the Notes servers and information from the Notes servers to other Notes servers to meet the requirements of the users for timely and relevant information. Mail will also be delivered in a timely fashion.

Comparing the Use of Notes

The following lists reasons why you should use Notes:

▶ It is a strong functional system for information distribution (it creates replica copies of databases).

▶ The replication process brings distributed information where changes have been made back in sync.

▶ Remote users can benefit from taking replica copies of databases with them on their laptops and using the replication process with servers to update and receive information.

▶ The database development tools are easy to use, fast, and powerful.

▶ Notes has strong integration capabilities with both relational databases and standard objects.

▶ Notes has a strong security model.

▶ Notes has a full-function mail system.

The following lists reasons why you might not want to use Notes:

▶ Notes databases are not relational. If you need the capabilities of data management from relational databases, do not use Notes.

▶ Notes does not support record locking and, with its distributed format, it does not support applications where information needs to be centrally stored (for example, information pertaining to withdrawals and deposits for a banking account).

Understanding the Notes Infrastructure

Objective

The term *infrastructure* suggests a framework on which a system relies, such as the road systems that allow us to use our cars to get to our destinations. Notes also requires a framework to allow it to get its information to the desired destination. Replication requires information to transfer from one server to another; mail-routing requires a method of delivering mail. Notes is not capable of doing this on its own; it requires an infrastructure based on an operating system that tells it how to interact with the computer and a networking system that directs how information travels. Figure 1.2 diagrams Bean's infrastructure, which contains two LANs connected by a router.

Figure 1.2

Bean's infrastructure of two LANs connected by a router.

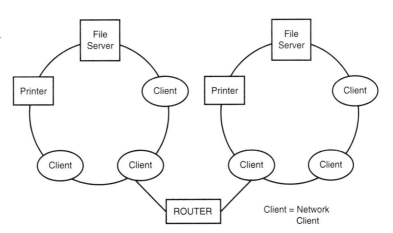

Suppose the Bean company has decided to install Notes so it can share and distribute database information and send and receive mail. Figure 1.3 diagrams how Bean's LANs look now:

Figure 1.3

Bean's new net-work topology after it has added Notes.

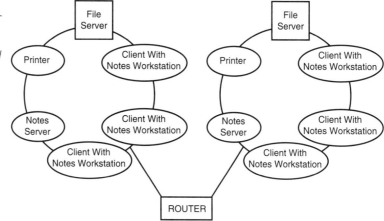

Notice that after the Notes system has been installed, there is a new node on each LAN: the Notes servers. The existing clients are now running a new application—the Notes client. As long as the disk and memory requirements are adequate and the network capacity can handle the new traffic generated by Notes, no new machines, with the exception of the Notes servers, would need to be added to these LANs.

The Notes server and the network file server are often mistaken one for the other, but they perform very distinct and separate functions. Notes is simply another application that runs on an operating system across a network. Although it is possible to run your Notes server application on a network file server, this approach is not recommended for two reasons:

▶ Notes has strong security enforced at various layers, but if users could gain access to the Notes database files through the network file servers, they would be circumventing the Notes security system.

> ▶ Possible performance degradation on one or both systems—
> In growing and changing environments, it can be difficult to
> gauge the system requirements for Notes servers as well as
> for network file servers. It is more difficult to identify and
> isolate performance problems when the Notes server and
> the file server are the same machine.

Operating Systems and Networking Protocol

A Notes system is not a standalone; it requires an infrastructure in order for it to function. Specifically, the following is required:

▶ An operating system

▶ At least one network protocol

Without these, Notes won't operate.

The following figures show the operating systems that currently support Notes and the network protocols with which Notes interfaces. Figure 1.4 shows the server system requirements and Figure 1.5 shows the client system requirements.

Figure 1.4

Server system requirements.

Certified Operating System							
Protocol Support		AIX 4.1.3	HP-UX 10.01	OS/2 Warp	Solaris 2.4	Windows 95	NetWare	Windows NT 3.51
	Apple Talk	No	No	Yes	No	No	Yes	Yes
	SPX	Yes	Yes	Yes	Yes	Yes	Yes	Yes
	SPX II	No	Yes	No	Yes	No	Yes	Yes
	NetBios/ NetBeui	No	No	Yes	No	Yes	No	Yes
	TCP/IP	Yes	Yes	Yes	Yes	Yes	Yes	Yes
	Vines	No	No	Yes	No	No	No	Yes
	X.PC	Yes	Yes	Yes	Yes	Yes	Yes	Yes

Figure 1.5

Client system requirements.

Protocol Support	Certified Operating System						
	HP-UX	AIX	Macintosh System 7.1, 7.5	OS/2 Warp and Warp Connect	Solaris	Windows 3.1 and Workgroup 3.11	Windows 95
Apple Talk	No	No	Yes	No	No	No	No
SPX	Yes	Yes	No	Yes	Yes	Yes	Yes
SPX II	Yes	No	No	No	Yes	No	No
NetBios/ NetBeui	No	No	No	Yes	No	Yes	Yes
TCP/IP	Yes	Yes	Yes	Yes	Yes	Yes	Yes
Vines	No	No	No	Yes	No	Yes	Yes
X.PC	Yes	Yes	Yes	Yes	Yes	Yes	Yes

A company will usually have decided on these two systems before purchasing Notes, and many times it will have multiple operating systems and networks companywide. One of Notes' strengths is that it will accommodate multiple systems and allow the sharing of Notes databases and mail to be sent across the organization.

If your company has multiple systems, you will need to be aware of the implications of Notes named networks and multiple protocol machines, which are covered in Chapter 2, "Server and Client Setup."

This was the Bean infrastructure before Notes was installed:

▶ Operating system for servers: Windows NT

▶ Operating system for workstations: Windows 95

▶ Network protocols: SPX and TCP/IP

Here is the Bean infrastructure now that Notes is installed (refer to Figures 1.1 and 1.2):

▶ Operating system for servers: Windows NT

▶ Operating systems for workstations: Windows 95

▶ Network protocols: SPX and TCP/IP

Working with Notes' Server and Client Functions

In Notes, you could be working with three different components:

▶ The server session

▶ The workstation session

▶ The server's workstation session

Let's look at what each of these different components will do. Some of the most common functions performed by the server session are:

▶ Share Notes databases for client access.

▶ Store user mail files.

▶ Accept mail and perform database replication with clients.

▶ Act as a dial-in server for remote users.

▶ Enforce security for databases by requiring that users and other servers have a certified ID file and sufficient rights in the database Access Control Lists and Public Address Book.

▶ Run mail and fax gateways and run add-in programs and custom server tasks from clients for delivery. The server session also plans the route for initiates delivery.

▶ Perform both database replication and mail routing with other servers.

▶ Act as entry point for clients to the Internet.

 Tip

Remember that Notes servers *are not* network file servers.

The workstation session functions can

▶ Access databases on its hard drive or on the Notes servers.

▶ Have multiple sessions open to multiple Notes servers.

▶ Have replica copies of databases on its hard drives and replicate periodically with the servers.

▶ Create and send mail to the server for delivery. The workstation session can also receive mail from the server in the mail database.

▶ Dial in to the server as a remote user and access the database or replicate with the server and send mail.

▶ Create its own personal databases.

The server workstation session functions can

▶ Act much the same as the workstation function, but the ID in use is the server's, not the administrator of the server's.

▶ Not be used to send or receive mail because mail functions are not enabled.

▶ Be used to override some Access Control Levels and to change settings or data inadvertently.

It is very important to understand what the server sessions can do, both the server and its workstation function.

Organizing Functions of Notes Administrators

 Objective

As can be supposed, administrators have a very important role in the Notes system. The administrator functions are often divided among groups of administrators. You might have a few administrators who are in charge of creating certifier IDs, other administrators who can create only user IDs, and others who can create only server IDs. There are many tools in Notes that can be used to limit the power of an administrator.

Although there is an administrator field on the Server document in the Public Address Book, its only function is to allow the use of the remote console. The real power of how the Notes system operates is in the Public Address Book and the access to use the certifier ID files.

These rights to the Public Address Book and certifier IDs are given automatically to the first administrator through the first-server setup process, but are never automatically given again. An organization must decide which access rights will be given to which administrator and implement these rights accordingly. There are no automatic or even suggested groupings for this; it is up to each organization.

The following is a list of administrator functions:

- ▶ Planning and implementing the security for the information held in Notes.

- ▶ Planning and implementing the replication strategy that will allow the timely sharing of information.

- ▶ Planning and implementing mail routing to deliver mail in a timely fashion.

- ▶ Setting up (initial) servers and users, and recertification if necessary.

- ▶ Planning and implementing a hierarchical naming scheme.

- ▶ Planning and implementing cross-certification to allow secure communication between different organizations.

- ▶ Providing for and supporting remote user dial in.

- ▶ Implementation of statistics collection and monitoring on the server.

Utilizing Notes' Basic Architectural Components

 Objective

Notes uses basic components to organize itself. *Domains* is a term used to identify all entities listed in a Public Address Book. When you belong to a Notes organization, you hold a certificate in common with all other entities who belong to the organization. If you understand these components and others discussed in this section, the planning, development, and maintenance of your Notes system will go smoothly.

Using Notes Domains

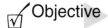

Suppose you want to reach Michael Vincent at Bean. You haven't been given a telephone number or office location. To find him, you go to the closest Bean location and ask to see the company directory. There you find his phone number, street address, e-mail address, and fax number. Also, by looking through the Bean directory, you can see how many offices Bean has, who its directors are, and how it is organized.

In Notes, a domain is very similar to this: It is a database that identifies all the entities who work at a company and how they are organized.

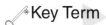

By definition, all entities (servers and users) in a Notes domain share the same Public Address Book. Therefore, if two or more servers are listed in the same Public Address Book, they are considered to be in the same domain.

Most organizations have only one domain (that is, one Public Address Book), but sometimes organizations have multiple domains (multiple Public Address Books). Chapter 8, "Working with Domains," explores the possible reasons for using multiple domains in detail. Most organizations use a single domain for the following reasons:

▶ A single domain provides more efficient mail addressing and routing because the mailer and router have to check only one Public Address Book.

▶ It's easier for administrators to control one Public Address Book.

Using the Certifier ID

The certifier ID is like the stamp of approval for the checks issued by a company. Should someone get a hold of this stamp, he or she could produce facsimiles of the checks and authorize them with an approved stamp.

When you present your ID for approval in Notes (which must happen each time you communicate with a server), the ID is checked for an authentic certificate. This certificate was generated and assigned by the certifier ID.

When you register your first Notes server, one of the special files that gets created is the certifier ID file. Its default filename is `cert.id`, but you can change the filename to whatever you want (doing so does not affect the contents of the file).

The purpose of the certifier ID file is to stamp each entity that gets created in Notes, whether it be a server or a user with a certificate. So each server ID file and user ID file contains a certificate for the organization given to it by the certifier ID. The name of this certificate is whatever the organization was called during first-server setup. Figure 1.6 shows an example of a certifier ID.

Figure 1.6

The certifier ID is used to stamp the user and server IDs upon creation to ensure that they receive a valid certificate.

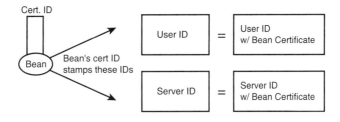

Using Notes Named Networks

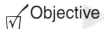

The legal division of Bean is located in Boston. That division has its procedures and standards defined for its purposes. The marketing division of Bean is located in New York; that division, too, has its own procedures and standards. In certain situations, information must be transferred between marketing and legal—but neither department gets the information in the format it wants. So one person is charged with knowing both divisions and getting information back and forth in the correct manner.

In Notes, the legal server is running SPX as its network protocol and the marketing server is running TCP/IP. When the Notes legal server wants to talk to the Notes marketing server, it can't communicate because the marketing server does not use the same protocol. To resolve this, one of the servers must be configured to speak both protocols (SPX and TCP/IP).

A Notes named network is a group of Notes servers that all speak the same protocol and have some type of constant communication. When all the Notes servers are using the same protocol and they have a connection to talk over, there is no problem with replication or mail routing occurring at any time.

In Figure 1.7, Bean has grouped the Manhattan LAN (M1) and the Queens LAN (Q1) as one Notes named network. This meets the requirements of both servers running the same protocol and being constantly connected. Bean has called the Notes named network SPX_NY to indicate the protocol and the location of the servers.

Figure 1.7

An example of a Notes named network as a group of Notes servers.

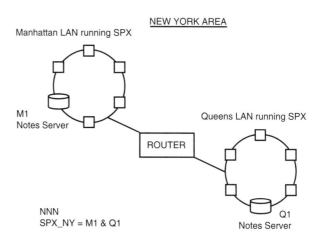

If the servers do not speak the same protocol, they cannot be in the same Notes named network; a multiprotocol server that can communicate with and between servers will have to created (see Figure 1.8).

Figure 1.8

An example of a Notes named network that doesn't speak the same protocol.

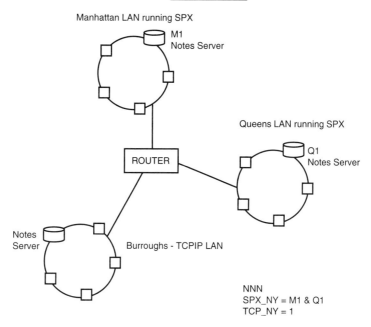

NEW YORK AREA

Manhattan LAN running SPX

M1
Notes Server

Queens LAN running SPX

Q1
Notes Server

ROUTER

Notes
Server

Burroughs - TCPIP LAN

NNN
SPX_NY = M1 & Q1
TCP_NY = 1

In the example shown in Figure 1.8, you must have two Notes named networks because even though all the servers have a constant type of connection, all are not speaking the same protocol. Two protocols are being used so, at a minimum, there must be two Notes named networks.

You run two protocols on one of the Notes servers so it can speak both protocols. Let's pick the B1 server; it will be able to talk to both M1 and Q1. The protocol software must be installed and the B1 server must be set to recognize both protocols. The network topology will still be the same, but the Notes named network definition will now be:

```
Notes Named Networks
SPX_NY = M1 + Q1 + B1
TCP_NY = B1
```

The following summarizes Notes named network restrictions:

▶ All servers in the Notes named network must use the same network protocol.

▶ There must be a constant connection between the servers in the Notes named network on the same LAN or bridged/routed WAN.

Following are features of a Notes named network:

▶ Mail routing occurs automatically between servers in the same Notes named network. This is not the case where servers are in separate Notes named networks; mail routing must be scheduled by the Administrator.

▶ When users select File Database | Open | Server | Other , they will see a list of all the other available servers that exist in the same Notes named network as their home server. If users want to see other servers in their organization, they must type the name of the server in the dialog box.

▶ Each server must be running a particular protocol. For example, a server running SPX cannot communicate through a network wire with a server running a different protocol (such as TCP/IP) on a different Notes named network; servers running different protocols cannot be on the same Notes named network.

▶ A server can run multiple protocols. For example, a server running both SPX and TCP/IP must, by definition, belong to multiple Notes named networks; when the server is running multiple protocols, it can communicate with any other server running any of its protocols.

Note

Remember that serial communications, independent of protocols, are available for server connection.

Here are some guidelines for deciding where to organize your servers within a Notes named network (provided they meet the restrictions mentioned previously):

▶ Where there will be significant amounts of mail sent between two or more servers, put both servers in the same Notes named network.

▶ Where users will be accessing databases across several servers, group the servers in the same Notes named network.

▶ To be able to route mail across network wires between two separate Notes named networks using different protocols, install multiple protocols on one server that will be the conduit between the two Notes named networks.

When naming your Notes named network, keep some guidelines in mind. Many companies name their Notes named network after the protocol the network is using and its physical location. For example a Notes named network located in Chicago running SPX would be `SPX_Chicago`.

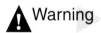
Warning

When you register a server, the default for the Notes named network to which it will belong is `Network1`. If you do not change this, all your servers will belong to this one Notes named network even if they do not share a constant connection or the same protocol.

Using the Public Address Book

Objective

The domain is like a company directory. So if the domain equals the Public Address Book, it follows that the Public Address Book equals the company directory. This is true in that the Public Address Book lists and identifies all the entities in its Notes system much like a company directory identifies all entities in its organization.

But the Public Address Book goes beyond that. Also contained in the Public Address Book are specifics as to when one server will exchange information with another server as well as who will use a server as a passthru to obtain information, what tasks each server is responsible for, and when each server performs those tasks. So not only is the Public Address Book a company directory, it also defines how and when the company does its work.

The Public Address Book in Notes identifies all the people and servers and where they can be reached. It also identifies when mail will be transferred from Notes named network to Notes named network, when servers will replicate, which database they will replicate, what add-in programs to run, and who doesn't belong to a company and is denied access.

Key Term

The Public Address Book is *the* most important database to administrators of a Notes system. It contains all the data which defines the system and how the system works. Almost every subject covered in the remaining chapters relate to the Public Address Book on some level. Whenever security is talked about in relation to Notes, keep in mind how you are going to secure your Public Address Book.

Here is a list of the views and documents available in the Public Address Book, as shown in Figure 1.9:

▶ Group view with Group documents, which identify groups of users or servers.

▶ Location view with Location documents, which provide user-setup information.

▶ People view with Person documents, which provide information about users.

▶ Server (related) views, which provide the following:

  ▶ Certificate view with Certifier documents describing each certifier.

  ▶ Cluster view with Server documents (not yet implemented).

  ▶ Configuration view with Server Configuration documents containing information about server settings.

  ▶ Connection view with Connection documents describing the connection information between servers for replication and mail routing.

▶ Deny Access groups with Group documents specified as deny only use.

▶ Domain view with Domain documents describing Notes domains, adjacent and nonadjacent, as well as non-Notes domains.

▶ License view with Person documents, showing licenses used in the registration process.

▶ Mail in Databases view with Mail in Database documents describing databases enabled to receive documents through mail functions.

▶ Mail Users view with Person documents.

▶ Network view with Server documents grouped by network.

▶ Program view with Program documents detailing scheduled server programs.

▶ Server view with Server documents detailing information about each server.

▶ Setup Profile view with Profile documents, which assist in the registration of users.

▶ V3 Stats and Events with Monitor documents, which were created in release 3 of Notes.

Some of these documents will be integral to the creation of your Notes system: the Person documents, the Server documents, the Connection documents, and so on. You will explore other documents as you fine-tune your Notes system and develop standards (for example, by creating Setup Profile documents to assist in registering your users).

Figure 1.9

The views available in Bean's Public Address Book.

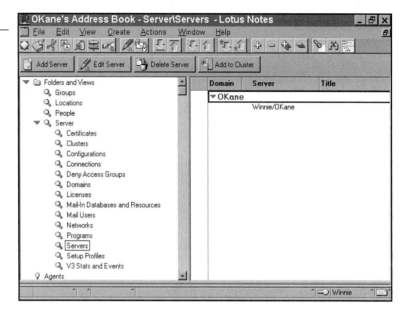

Exercises

In this lab exercise, you will review a fictional company's implementation of Notes and provide solutions for its setup scenarios.

Exercise 1.1

General Mufflers has decided to implement Notes. This company already has LANs in its four regional operations. It will use Notes to collect and distribute information as well as to handle its mail. General Muffler's Notes installation will be on the following machines:

- ▶ It will install Notes on four servers and 300 clients in the Toronto region. Two of these servers use the TCP/IP protocol and two use the SPX protocol.

- ▶ Notes will be installed on three servers and 200 clients in Montreal. All servers use the TCP/IP protocol.

- ▶ Notes will be installed on two servers and 100 clients in Calgary. Both servers use the SPX protocol.

- ▶ Notes will be installed on one server and 40 clients in Winnipeg. The server uses the TCP/IP protocol.

The LAN in Toronto is connected to the LAN in Montreal by a router. All other LAN connections are via asynchronous dial up.

Scenario A

Based on this scenario, how many Notes named networks would you create, how would you name them, and how would you group them? List reasons.

Scenario B

Based on your Notes named networks, how would you ensure that servers running on different protocols were capable of communicating?

Note: General Mufflers has decided to call its domain `General Mufflers` and its organization `GM1`.

Scenario C

What would the name of General Muffler's Public Address Book be?

Scenario D

What would General Muffler's president, William Okane's, hierarchical name be? (Assume you registered him with the organization certifier ID.)

Solution A

Winnipeg would be one Notes named network. A good naming convention in Notes is to use the location of the Notes named network and the protocol it is running (for example, `Winnipeg_TCPIP`). Calgary (`Calgary_SPX`) would be another Notes named network.

Toronto has two SPX servers and, because they are running a protocol different from the other two Toronto servers, they must be in their own Notes named network (`Toronto_SPX`). Toronto's other two servers must be in a separate Notes named network, but they could be in the same network as the two servers in Montreal because they are constantly connected by the router and running the same protocol—TCP/IP. Before you decide whether to place the two SPX servers in Toronto in the same Notes named network as the servers in Montreal, consider the following:

- ▶ Do you want the users in Montreal to see the servers in Toronto when they select File | Database | Open and vice versa?

- ▶ Do you want mail delivered automatically or on a schedule?

Here are your options:

- ▶ One Notes named network (`TorMtl_TCPIP`) that includes the TCP/IP servers in both Toronto and Montreal.

- ▶ Two Notes named networks, one for Toronto (`Toronto_TCPIP`) and one for Montreal (`Montreal_TCPIP`).

The total number of Notes named networks would be either four or five.

Solution B

Servers running different protocols in different Notes named networks can't communicate because they are "speaking different languages." To resolve this, one of the servers in either Notes named network must be enabled to run multiple protocols. This multiprotocol server would be the conduit between the two Notes named networks running different protocols.

With the Notes named networks for Calgary and Winnipeg, there is no concern because they will communicate asynchronously. In Toronto, however, you have two Notes named networks, each running different protocols. You could add the SPX protocol to one of the servers in the `Toronto_TCP IP` Notes named network. That server would then belong to both Notes named networks and would be the conduit between them. The other option is to take one of the servers in the SPX Notes named network and add the TCP/IP protocol to it. Whichever way you do it, the conduit would also be used to communicate with the SPX servers in Montreal.

Solution C

The name of the Public Address Book would be "General Muffler's Public Address Book." The name of the Public Address Book reflects the name of the domain.

Solution D

William Okane's hierarchical name would be `William Okane/GM1`. Whatever the organization is called is what the organization unit identifier will stamp when a hierarchical name is created.

Review Questions

1. True or false: A domain as identified in Notes follows the same format as your network domain.

2. The advantages of people and servers being in the same Notes named network are (include the fact that):

   a. Mail delivery is automatic.

   b. Replication is automatic.

   c. You see all servers in the domain when you select File | Database | Open.

3. Servers can be in the same Notes named network only if:

   a. They use the same operating system.

   b. They are in same building.

   c. They are constantly connected and use the same network protocol.

   d. They use the same network protocol and connect as needed.

4. True or false: Servers are put into a default Notes named network at registration time.

5. The main function of a Notes server is to

   a. Act as a mail server.

   b. Update database catalogs.

   c. Share database information.

6. Name two reasons to implement Lotus Notes.

   a. Security

   b. Relational databases

   c. Mail function

   d. Replication

7. Name three Notes sessions.

    a. Server

    b. Domain

    c. Server workstation

    d. Workstation

8. True or false: A network file server is an essential part of a Notes system.

9. True or false: If your company has LANs running multiple protocols, this must be changed before you can implement Notes.

10. Identify the functions of the workstation session (circle all that apply):

    a. To access databases on the server

    b. To initiate replication with the server

    c. To send mail across the network

    d. To create personal databases

11. True or false: All administrators have equal rights in Notes.

12. True or false: To be identified as an administrator, your name must be in Administrator field in the Server document. This will give you certain rights to the Public Address Book.

13. True or false: The domain name and organization name must be the same.

14. True or false: One of the reasons companies use Notes databases is because of their support of record locking.

Review Answers

1. False. A Notes domain is a separate from any network domain component. A Notes domain is represented by the

Public Address Book. For more information, refer to the section titled "Using Notes Domains."

2. A. Replication is never automatic. When you are in a Notes named network, you see all servers in that network when you select File | Database | Open. For more information, refer to "Using Notes Named Networks."

3. C. For more information, refer to "Using Notes Named Networks."

4. True. For more information, refer to "Using Notes Named Networks."

5. C. Notes was developed to share database information. For more information, refer to the section titled "Working with Notes' Server and Client Functions."

6. A and D. Notes does not support relational databases and, although its mail functionality is very good, Notes is much more than just a mail application. For more information, refer to the section titled "Understanding Why Companies Use Notes."

7. A, C, and D. For more information, refer to the section titled "Working with Notes' Server and Client Functions."

8. False. Network file servers are not used within the Notes environment. For more information, refer to "Working with Notes Server and Client Functions."

9. False. For more information, refer to "Using Notes Named Networks."

10. A, B, and D. For more information, refer to "Working with Notes' Server and Client Functions."

11. False. For more information, refer to the section titled "Organizing Functions of Notes Administrators."

12. False. For more information, refer to "Organizing Functions of Notes Administrators."

13. False. For more information, refer to the section titled "Using Notes Domains."

14. False. For more information, refer to the section titled "Comparing the Use of Notes."

Answers to Test Yourself Questions at Beginning of Chapter

1. When planning for the installation of Notes, you should consider how you will be implementing the domain, organization, and the Notes named networks. When you plan your implementation of these three components, you will reduce the implementation time for the creation of your Notes environment and greatly reduce the need for changes in the future. For more information, refer to the section titled "Introduction to Notes' System Administration Components."

2. The certifier ID is used for registering users and servers and defining an organization. To access a server, a certificate must be presented and verified. The certificate is created by the certifier ID. For more information, refer to the section titled "Using the Certifier."

3. One Public Address Book contains all the information about one domain. For more information, refer to the section titled "Using Notes Domains."

4. For Notes servers to be in the same Notes named network, they must be constantly connected and must be sharing a common network protocol. For more information, see the section titled "Using Notes Named Networks."

C h a p t e r

Server and Client Setup

This chapter will introduce you to the following objectives:

 Objectives

- ▶ Designing a hierarchical naming scheme

- ▶ Choosing North American or international IDs

- ▶ Setting up the first server

- ▶ Seeing the results of setting up the first server

- ▶ Understanding the Notes.ini file

- ▶ Understanding server startup

- ▶ Understanding the server console and the remote console

- ▶ Setting up the administrator's workstation

- ▶ Viewing the Administration panel

- ▶ Registering additional servers

- ▶ Setting up additional servers

- ▶ Registering users

- ▶ Setting up users

- ▶ Setting up network and COM ports

Test Yourself! Before reading this chapter, test yourself to determine how much study time you will need to devote to this section.

1. When registering users, what are the methods available to you in Notes?

2. Is the process for server setup the same for all servers?

3. What are the limitations for hierarchical naming?

4. Where are all settings for the server contained in the Server Configuration document found?

5. What type of access must you have to register servers?

6. Where must you make any change to the ports on a server?

Answers are located at the end of the chapter...

This chapter will introduce you to the basic setup procedures and settings you will encounter when installing your Notes system. The more knowledgeable you are about the setup criteria and intended results, the more efficient and smooth your installation will be.

In addition, this chapter will take you through the process of planning and setting up your first servers and clients. This chapter will introduce you to

▶ Understanding and implementing hierarchical naming

▶ Setting up your first server and first client (administrator)

▶ The registration process for remaining servers and clients

▶ Port setup for server communication

Designing a Hierarchical Naming Scheme

 Objective

Hierarchical names, although derived from X.500 standards, can be compared to the naming conventions of various cultures. For example, the Irish O'Kanes, O'Malleys, and O'Roukes indicate what county a person comes from; in this way, Peggy O'Kane is differentiated from Peggy O'Rouke. The French were given to attaching the function of the person to his or her name, so that Jean Boulanger (the baker) could be differentiated from Jean DuBois (the woodcutter).

Hierarchical naming sort of combines these two methods and gives you a system in which each person has his or her "name;" attached to each name is an organization identifier that tells you what company he or she belongs to and unit identifiers that tell you what he or she does. So if Kathy Schiller works for Acme Corporation and is in the Sales department, in Notes she would be known as

```
Kathy Schiller/Sales/Acme
```

The hierarchical naming system was not used in the first releases of Notes; it was first implemented in release 3. Before that the naming convention was *flat*, meaning that in Notes versions 1 and

2, if a user's name was "John Breen," his name in Lotus Notes would be

```
John Breen
```

This is how he would have been referred to in access control lists and mail and security rights.

When you set up the first server in releases 3 and 4, you automatically get set up in a hierarchical system. Nonetheless, Notes has maintained backwards compatibility, so you can create a flat certifier, recertify your first server, and define the rest of your organization as flat.

In the hierarchical system, every user and every server not only has a common name (as they did in the flat system), they also have at minimum an organization identifier. At maximum, every user and server can have four other organizational unit identifiers and a country code. It's up to the people planning the hierarchical naming system to decide.

For example, suppose John Breen works for Bean, a fictional company that sells coffee beans. Bean's planners have decided to name their Notes entities (people and servers) with a common name and organization identifier. In the hierarchical system, John Breen would now be known in Notes as

```
John Breen/Bean
```

This is how his name should be typed for all mail, access control lists, and security fields. (Notes does have some shortcuts in mail that allow you to enter a short name.)

Now suppose the planners for the Bean organization decided that this naming method was not detailed enough, so they implemented the identification of two organizational units: by group and by region. So John Breen, who works in Sales in the Toronto region, is now known in Notes as

```
John Breen/Sales/TO/Bean
```

The Components of Hierarchical Naming

Table 2.1 lists all the components available for implementation in an organization's naming scheme.

Table 2.1

Possible naming components.

Component	Description	Characters
Common name (CN)	The person's full first and last names or the server name. This component is required.	80 maximum
Organizational unit name (OU)	Typically a department or location name. Notes allows the use of as many as four organizational units in each distinguished name. This component is optional.	32 per OU
Organization name (O)	Typically the company name. Try to keep it short. This component is required.	3 minimum to 64 maximum
Country (C)	Two-letter abbreviation for the country from the ISO standards. This component is optional.	2

So in the case of John Breen/Sales/TO/Bean, the components would be as follows:

Common name for user (CN) = John Breen

Organizational unit (OU2) = Sales

Organizational unit (OU1) = TO

Organization (O) = Bean

In this example, the country code has not been used and only two of four possible organizational units have been used.

Notes stores all hierarchical names in a *canonical* format and displays them in an *abbreviated* format. The canonical format for John Breen is

```
CN=John Breen/OU=Sales/OU=TO/O=Bean
```

The abbreviated format is

```
John Breen/Sales/TO/Bean
```

Notes uses an internal routine to transfer the format of stored canonical names into abbreviated format for display and vice versa.

Note

Knowing the definitions of *canonical format* and *abbreviated format* and the differences between them can be very important for the exam.

Understanding Hierarchical Names

Before you look at the mechanics of creating hierarchical names, let's examine some reasons for implementing hierarchical naming and some of the advantages and disadvantages. Two main reasons for implementing hierarchical naming are

▶ So you can distinguish between same-named individuals in the same company. For example, suppose that two men named John Breen work at Bean: one in Sales and the other in Accounting. In the flat naming system, the administrator would have to alter their names so they would be different. How would people trying to reference them know which was which? In the hierarchical system, they would be known as

```
John Breen/Sales/Bean
```

```
John Breen/Acct/Bean
```

This system makes it much easier to determine who is who.

▶ So you can associate an organization with an individual. As indicated in Table 2.1, the two required components are CN and O. So in the hierarchical system, a user's or server's name must be followed by a slash and an organization identifier. Suppose that two organizations, let's say Bean and Reef (a fictional coffee-mug maker) determine that they need to communicate, and each organization employs someone named John Breen. In the flat naming scheme, this would create confusion, mail problems, and possible security breaches. But in the hierarchical naming system, John Breen would be known as

```
John Breen/Bean
```

```
John Breen/Reef
```

These are two very distinct names that allow no confusion between them. In this way, hierarchical naming provides a method for distinguishing all the people in your organization from like people in other organizations that you might communicate with.

Key Term

Hierarchical names are also referred to as *fully-distinguished* names.

Although there are a few disadvantages to implementing hierarchical naming, they are outweighed by the following advantages:

▶ Fully distinguished names—Each individual and server in the company can be distinguished from same-named individuals in the company through the use of organizational unit identifiers (OUs). These can be based on departments, regions, or other classifications.

▶ Improved security—Requiring organization identifiers (Os) in the naming convention eliminates the possibility of a same-named individual from another company that communicates with yours gaining unauthorized access to databases and servers.

▶ More efficient communications—IDs that contain multiple flat certificates take slightly longer to complete the process known as authentication.

▶ The decentralization of user certification—organizational unit certifiers can be distributed to regional administrators, who then have the tools to register people only in their organizational unit.

▶ The use of the administration process—This new process, introduced with Notes release 4, facilitates the renaming or recertification of users. This process works only with hierarchical names.

The following are disadvantages of hierarchical naming:

▶ It requires more up-front planning—Before jumping in and registering all your users, give some careful thought as to all the possible components available to you. Try to keep the components as short as possible, but remember that you need the ability to distinguish users and servers from each other. Keep in mind how your company has changed in the past and might in the future, and consider how your naming convention will accommodate these changes.

▶ It requires users and administrators to have knowledge of the method used to distinguish users and servers—When a system is implemented, try to make it as logical as possible so that it is obvious to all people who have to choose between same-named people or servers.

The following are suggestions for hierarchical naming:

▶ Use the most common method employed by the company to distinguish people (perhaps by region and department), and make sure that identifier is not likely to change.

▶ The hierarchical names should work from left to right with the smallest denominator leading up to the largest denominator. For example, with the hierarchical name `John Breen/Sales/CR/Bean`, John Breen is an individual (the smallest denominator) who works in the Sales department of the central region in the Bean company (the largest denominator).

► Don't forget that your servers will also have hierarchical names. You must decide how you are going to group your servers. Will you place them in the region or department in which they are located, or will you give them their own organizational unit? Many companies find it easier to group their servers in their own organizational units.

► Although four organizational units are available for implementation, it is suggested that at a maximum you only use three and leave the fourth for the occasion in which two like-named individuals are in the same department. For example, suppose there are two Jenny Kanes in the Promo/Sales/CR/Bean organizational unit. In this case, the fourth organizational unit identifier would be used to differentiate between these two. If one of the Jenny Kanes was an Administrator and the other was Director, this is how you might distinguish their names using the fourth organizational unit:

```
Jenny Kane/Adm/Promo/Sales/CR/Bean
```

```
Jenny Kane/Dir/Promo/Sales/CR/Bean
```

► Don't forget that although Notes is getting better about allowing users to select names from the Public Address Book, there are occasions in which you will have to type the entire name. Try to keep the components as short as possible, but remember that you must have at least three characters in the organization (O) component.

► Some multinational companies use the countries in which they are operating as their top-level organizational unit identifier instead of using country codes. So a company such as IBM might choose to have the following organizational units:

```
Sales/US/IBM
```

```
Sales/UK/IBM
```

Creating a Hierarchical Naming Scheme

Suppose that Bean has decided to implement Notes. The company must decide how it will name its people and its servers given its environment and the components of hierarchical naming. Suppose its environment is as follows (divided into four groups):

▶ South America group—This group buys coffee beans and ships them to the group that is selling them.

▶ Africa group—This group buys coffee beans and ships them to the group that is selling them.

▶ U.S. group—This group is responsible for selling beans and distributing them to purchasers.

▶ Canada group—This group is responsible for selling beans and distributing them to purchasers.

Create your own scheme for Bean and see how it compares to what it decided to do.

Bean's organization identifier will be Bean. Bean will use the countries/continents in which it operates as its first organizational unit identifier like so:

```
US/Bean

CA/Bean

SA/Bean

AF/Bean
```

Under each of the country/continent identifiers, Bean will further distinguish by department. Departments include Sales (Sales), Distributing (Dist), and Purchasing (Purch):

```
Sales/US/Bean

Dist/US/Bean

Sales/CA/Bean

Dist/CA/Bean

Purch/SA/Bean

Dist/SA/Bean
```

```
Purch/AF/Bean

Dist/AF/Bean
```

Each person who works in the specified department will be registered with the appropriate components.

Servers will be grouped in their own identifiers (OU1 = SVR) and further defined by mail (M), database (DB), or hub (H) like so:

```
M/SVR/Bean

DB/SVR/Bean

H/SVR/Bean
```

Here are the mechanics of how organization certifier ID and organizational unit certifier IDs are created and how you register people and servers with them. This process is covered again when the first server is set up and in more detail in Chapter 6, "Administration Tools."

When the first server is set up, the cert.id/organization certifier file is automatically created and saved to the install drive. This file is essential for the initial setup of a Notes environment, and is used to stamp the initial server ID with a certificate and create the hierarchical name. One of the questions asked when the first server is set up is what is your organization's name? Whatever you type here will be used as your organization identifier and will provide the organization certificate.

For example, suppose your organization is the United Grain Growers, and you type it as such during setup of the first server. If the common name of the first server is Silo1, the hierarchical name of your server will be

```
Silo1/United Grain Growers
```

This is a bit long, especially if you are going to add other organizational unit identifiers. Try to use some abbreviation of your organization's name when you type it in during setup of the first server. When you are setting up the first server, whatever you type for the organization's name will automatically be assigned as the domain name as well. This can be changed under advanced options if you want your domain name to be different from your organization name.

After your organization certifier is created, you can use this certifier ID to create all the other certifiers. In the example of the Bean organization, how many certifiers would exist? If your answer is 17, you are right. Only eight of these would be used to register users and three would be used to register servers. The other six would be used only to create the organizational units that exist below them.

Using Hierarchical Names

Hierarchical names are used for the following purposes:

▶ Mail

▶ Access control lists

 Caution

> When Access Control Lists are created and only common names are used, any user who tries to access the database with the common name will be allowed in. For example, `Bev Breen/Pers/HQ/Acme`, who has access to a salary database, has been listed as only `Bev Breen` in the Access Control List. When `Bev Breen/Maint/South/Acme` tries to access this database, she will be allowed in because her common name is listed in the Access Control List.

▶ Readers fields and Authors fields

▶ Console commands

▶ Group entries

Hierarchical names are not used for:

▶ Group names

▶ Domain names

When you want to reference all the names in a certain organizational unit, you can place an asterisk in front of the identifier and the field will execute for all names that have been certified with the specific identifier. For example, suppose you want to specify in a server document that only a specific group has access to that server. In the Access server field, you could enter

```
*/Legal/Acme
```

In this case, all users with the identifier /Legal/Acme would have access to this server. You cannot use the asterisk method of identification for mail-delivery purposes. Notes is not enabled to deliver mail using this address method.

Comparing North American and International IDs

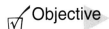 Objective

When registering people or servers, one of the choices you have besides name, expiration date, registration server, and so on is whether the license will be North American or international.

Because of government regulations, a restriction is imposed on using certain security methods outside of North America. Lotus Notes uses the dual-key RSA Cryptosystem to encrypt data when the person or server doing the encrypting has a North American license. It is illegal to use this encryption system outside of North America. If data becomes encrypted by a person who has a North American license, it can be decrypted only by a person who holds the correct key and who has a North American license. If the person attempting to decrypt the data has an International license, he or she will be unable to do so. However, data encrypted by a user or server with an International license can be decrypted by a person holding the correct key and having a North American license because the International encryption employs a shorter-length key.

If you are required to share encrypted data with people or servers outside of North America, an International license should be used to encrypt the data. The drawback is that the method of encryption for the International license is considered less secure than the dual-key RSA Cryptosystem.

Software Installation

When you install the software, there will be minimal differences between the platforms that Notes operates under. The installation procedure gives the option of performing a standard installation with all components or a subset of the installation programs. Suppose, for example, that you are not interested in installing the help databases or the sample databases and templates; you could choose to deselect these. If you choose to perform a choice-by-choice component selection, remember that you need the following components for a workable server:

▶ Notes server

▶ Notes client

▶ Required program datafiles

▶ Personal datafiles

Setting Up the First Server

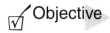 Only when you have done all your planning should you begin the setup of your first server. Think of this planning as laying the cornerstone of your building. Each of the following should occur:

▶ A hierarchical naming scheme should be established.

▶ Whether North American or International licenses will be used should be established.

▶ You should understand your operating systems and network protocols and how Notes will work with them.

▶ You should develop a plan for organizing your Notes named network and how to name the network.

▶ You should decide on your domain and organization name.

▶ A communication scheme for server connection should be established.

▶ A communication scheme for remote users should be established.

▶ Server settings and functions should be specified.

▶ User settings and functions should be specified.

Now you are ready to begin setup:

1. Click the Notes icon to invoke the dialog box shown in Figure 2.1.

Figure 2.1

Installing the first server in your new Notes system.

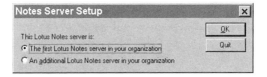

2. In this instance, select the The First Lotus Notes Server in Your Organization option (you will set up additional servers later). This invokes the First Server Setup dialog box (see Figure 2.2).

Figure 2.2

Settings for setup of the first server.

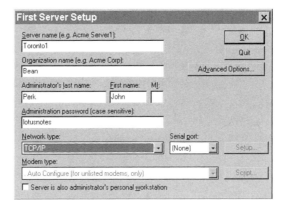

The following describes each option in the dialog box, along with how the input will affect how your Lotus Notes organization is set up:

▶ Server name—This is the common name of the server. When naming servers or users, never enter what you know the fully distinguished name will be. Instead, enter the common name (CN) component of the name. When the ID is created, the rest of the distinguished name will be added by the system.

 Tip

When naming servers, avoid using the following symbols:

▶ ( )

▶ @

▶ \ and /

▶ =

▶ +

When naming a server, try to use a continuous name. If you choose to use a name with spaces, you must remember to type the server's name in quotation marks when you are using the server console. Also, have a consistent method for naming your servers (for example, a physical location or function identifier). This naming method should be considered at the same time you develop your hierarchical naming scheme.

▶ Organization name—This is your company name. Whatever name you enter here will be used as your organization identifier (O) in your hierarchical naming scheme. This name will also be used, by default, as your domain name (this can be changed).

Remember that this name will appear in every name that gets created for users and servers because the O component is required. Try to keep this name short because fully distinguished names tend to be long. Also remember that the minimum number of characters you use for an O identifier is three.

▶ Administrator's last name, first name, MI—During first-server setup, the administrator's name is entered in the Administrator field of the server document, and the user ID for the administrator is created. Simply type the common name of the administrator, but give some thought as to whether you really want to use middle initials in the common name. As mentioned earlier, the distinguished names are long enough and hopefully specific enough to make the use of middle initial occasional.

▶ Administration password (case-sensitive)—This password does double duty as the password used for the user.id for the administrator and also as the password for the certifier ID, which will be created. The default here is a minimum of eight characters. Both of these passwords can be changed after creation.

▶ Network type—Under Notes release 4, this option is now context-sensitive. Based on the operating system on which you installed Notes, the appropriate network protocols will be presented as choices.

▶ Serial port—The default is none, but this option will be set after first-server setup.

▶ Modem type—Notes is provided with modem command files, which tell it how to communicate with your modems in the specific serial ports. This is where you can choose one if you have specified a serial port in the previous input box.

▶ Server is also administrator's personal workstation—It is possible to set up the system so that the client session that runs on most servers is configured as the administrator's personal client session (in other words, his or her mail file, log file, and so on are put on the desktop). However this setup is not recommended for performance and security reasons. With the right Access Control Levels and remote server console, there are very few reasons the administrator need be physically at the server.

3. Click the Advanced Options button to look at the advanced server setup options (see Figure 2.3).

Figure 2.3

The Advanced Server Setup Options dialog box.

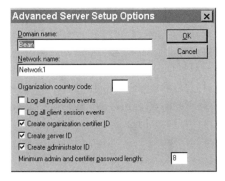

The following describes each option in the dialog box along with how the advanced input will affect how your Lotus Notes organization is set up:

▶ Domain name—As before, what you enter as your organization name will default to the domain name. In most Notes systems, these two components are called the same name, so this is not a problem. Remember that a domain name appears in the Public Address Book and an organization name is your top-level identifier and certifier in the creation of names and certificates. Having multiple domains or organizations will be discussed in Chapter 6.

▶ Network name—This refers to what you will call your Notes named network. The default is Network1. Change this option to reflect whatever guidelines you will be using for naming your Notes named networks (such as network protocol and physical location).

▶ Log all replication events—If this box is checked, the start and end of replication events will be recorded in the Notes log and displayed on the console.

▶ Log all client session events—If this box is checked, client session events will be recorded in the Notes log and displayed on the console.

▶ Create organization certifier ID—You must check this box for the creation of a new Notes system. You would deselect this box only if you were using an existing cert.id file.

▶ Create server ID—Deselect this box only if you are setting up your server with an existing `server.id` file.

▶ Create administrator ID—Deselect this box only if you have an existing user ID for the administrator.

▶ Minimum admin and certifier password length—The default is `8`. It's recommended that you leave it as such or go higher because the more characters there are in a password, the harder it is to guess.

4. After you have made all your choices and click the OK buttons, your first server will be set up. Information boxes will appear to let you know what the process is doing as the server is set up.

Results of Setup

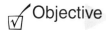

Here are the results of the setup process:

▶ The organization certifier ID is created—In my example, it would be for the organization Bean. This certifier ID, or `cert.id`, will be written to the installation drive under the `Notes/Data` directory. You can rename this file (for example `bean.id`). This would help identify it as the organization certifier ID. This is an extremely important file for later use because it is the file in which you will need to register all future servers, users, or additional organizational unit certifiers. You should make several backup copies of this file, remove it from the first server hard drive (with no possible retrieval), and think about implementing multiple passwords for this ID. Should this file ever get lost or fall into the wrong hands, you would have to create a new certifier and recertify all existing users and servers with it: not an appealing prospect. The certifier ID will be further discussed in Chapter 5, "Security."

▶ Server ID is created—In my example, it would be for the server `Toronto1`. This server ID is called `server.id` and is written to the installation drive under the `Notes/Data` directory. This file can also be renamed if you want. This file has the information about `Toronto1` concerning its distinguished name, its certificate, the expiration date of its certificate, license, and so on. It would be akin to a passport. When the server starts up, the ID is used to identify which server it is; when the server wants to connect to another server, it must present its ID so its name and certificate can be verified. Without a server ID, a server will not be able to start up.

▶ Public Address Book is created—This database is called `names.nsf` and is written to the `Notes/Data` directory. From installation there are a number of template files that are then used to build databases. This is how the Public Address Book is created, from the template that resides in the `Notes/Data` directory. This template is called `pubnames.ntf`. The database is customized from the information given in the setup dialog boxes. The domain name becomes the name of the Public Address Book; Bean's Address Book and the documents in Table 2.2 will be found there.

Table 2.2

Documents found in Public Address Book.

Document name	Description of documents
Server document	Details server name, administrator, what Notes named network it belongs to, and so on.
Person document	Creates a person document for the administrator with his or her name, home server, and mail server.
Group documents	Two group documents automatically create one called `LocalDomainServers`. Every server that is registered is automatically added to this group.
Certifier document	Shows the registration of the certifier creation.

The `names.nsf` database is your most important database. Be sure you know it in detail.

First-server setup also results in the following:

▶ The administrator ID is created—In the Beans example, the user ID for Pedro Grind is created, but isn't written to the hard drive as the other two IDs are. The ID is instead stored as an attachment on the Person document for Pedro Grind in the Public Address Book. The user ID is used for the same purpose as a server ID; when a user starts up, the ID is used for Notes to identify the correct distinguished name and is used for connection purposes to determine whether the user has the correct certificate.

▶ The administrator mail file is created—The `mail.nsf` for the administrator is created and put in the `notes/data/mail` directory.

▶ The log database is created—`log.nsf` is created from a template. Its purpose, as you will explore later, is to keep track of all the activities of the server. This is a very important database for the administrator to be aware of and work with.

▶ `Notes.ini` is customized—The `Notes.ini` file starts out as either two or three lines from the installation process. After setup, it is customized with the specific parameters taken from the information given in the dialog boxes as well as further general parameters.

Table 2.3 summarizes the results of server setup.

Table 2.3

First-server setup results summary.

Created	Description
Certifier ID	The `cert.id` file, which will be needed for all future registration and certification.
Server ID	Contains hierarchical name, license, and certificate for the first server.
Administrator ID	Contains hierarchical name, license, and certificate for the first user.

continues

Table 2.3   Continued

Created	Description
names.nsf	Public Address Book for the domain.
log.nsf	Keeps track of all server activity.
Documents in Public Address Book	Server document, Group document, Person document (for administrator), Certifier document.
Notes.ini	Customized with settings from setup. Can be further customized with direct editing or server configuration documents from Public Address Book.

÷Viewing Notes.ini

Objective

Here is an example of the Notes.ini file after installation, but before server setup:

```
[Notes]
Directory=c:\notes\data
Kittype=2
```

Here is an example of the Notes.ini file after server setup:

```
[Notes]
Directory=c:\notes\data
Kittype=2
WinNTIconPath=c:\notes\data\W32
$$HasLANPort=1
Preferences=2148011121
Passthru_LogLevel=0
Console_LogLevel=2
VIEWIMP1=Lotus 1-2-3
Worksheet,0,_IWKSV,,.WKS,.WK1,.WR1,.WRK,.WK3,.WK4,
VIEWIMP3=Structured Text,0,_ISTR,,.LTR,.CGN,.STR,
VIEWIMP4=Tabular Text,0,_ITAB,,.PRN,.RPT,.TXT,.TAB,
VIEWEXP1=Lotus 1-2-3 Worksheet,0,_XWKS,,.WKS,.WK1,.WR1,.WRK,
VIEWEXP3=Structured Text,0,_XSTR,,.LTR,.CGN,.STR,
```

```
VIEWEXP4=Tabular Text,1,_XTAB,,.LTR,.RPT,.CGN,.TAB,
EDITIMP1=ASCII Text,0,_ITEXT,,.TXT,.PRN,.C,.H,.RIP,
EDITIMP2=MicrosoftWord RTF,0,_IRTF,,.DOC,.RTF,
EDITIMP3=Lotus 1-2-3
Worksheet,0,_IWKSE,,.WKS,.WK1,.WR1,.WRK,.WK3,.WK4,
EDITIMP4=Lotus PIC,0,_IPIC,,.PIC,
EDITIMP5=CGM Image,0,_IFL,,.GMF,.CGM,
EDITIMP6=TIFF 5.0 Image,0,_ITIFF,,.TIF,
EDITIMP7=BMP Image,0,_IBMP,,.BMP,
EDITIMP8=Ami Pro,0,_IW4W,W4W33F/V0,.SAM,
EDITIMP17=WordPerfect 5.x,0,_IW4W,W4W07F/V1,.DOC,
EDITIMP22=PCX Image,0,_IPCX,,.PCX,
EDITIMP28=Binary with Text,0,_ISTRNGS,,.*,
EDITIMP29=WordPerfect 6.0/6.1,0,_IW4W,W4W48F/V0,.WPD,.WPT,.DOC,
EDITIMP30=Excel 4.0/5.0,0,_IW4W,W4W21F/V4C,.XLS,
EDITIMP31=Word for Windows 6.0,0,_IW4W,W4W49F/V0,.DOC,
EDITIMP32=GIF Image,0,_IGIF,,.GIF,
EDITIMP33=JPEG Image,0,_IJPEG,,.JPG,
EDITEXP1=ASCII Text,2,_XTEXT,,.TXT,.PRN,.C,.H,.RIP,
EDITEXP2=MicrosoftWord RTF,2,_XRTF,,.DOC,.RTF,
EDITEXP3=CGM Image,2,_XCGM,,.CGM,.GMF,
EDITEXP4=TIFF 5.0 Image,2,_XTIFF,,.TIF,
EDITEXP5=Ami Pro,2,_XW4W,W4W33T/V0,.SAM,
EDITEXP14=WordPerfect 5.1,2,_XW4W,W4W07T/V1,.DOC,
EDITEXP21=WordPerfect 6.0,2,_XW4W,W4W48T/V0,.DOC,
EDITEXP22=WordPerfect 6.1,2,_XW4W,W4W48T/V1,.WPD,.WPT,.DOC,
EDITEXP23=Word for Windows 6.0,2,_XW4W,W4W49T/V0,.DOC,
DDETimeout=10
```

```
NAMEDSTYLE0=0200426173696300000000000000000000000000000000000000000000000000000
➡0000000001010100000A000000000000000100A0050000A005000000000000000000000000
➡00000000000000000000000000000000000000000000000000000000000000000000000000000
➡00000000
NAMEDSTYLE1=02004275606C065740000000000000000000000000000000000000000000000000
➡0000000001010100000A0000000000000000080700000807000000000000000000000000000
➡0000000000000000000000000
NAMEDSTYLE2=02004865616C6696E65000000000000000000000000000000000000000000000000
➡0000000001010101010B0C000000000000000100A0050000A005000000000000000000000000
➡00000000000000000000000000000000000000000000000000000000000000000000000000000
➡00000000
```

```
$$$OpenSpecial=NotesNIC, InterNotes
$$$NotesNIC=CN=Home/OU=Notes/O=NET, welcome.nsf, Notes NIC Wel-
come, Notes
➡Network Information Center on the Internet
$$$InterNotes=,web.nsf,Web Navigator, Local InterNotes Web Navi-
gator Database
```

```
ServerTasks=Replica,Router,Update,Stats,AMgr,Adminp,Sched,CalConn
ServerTasksAt1=Catalog,Design
ServerTasksAt2=UpdAll,Object Collect mailobj.nsf
ServerTasksAt5=Statlog
7TCPIP=TCP, 0, 15, 0
LAN0=NETBIOS, 0, 15, 0
SPX=NWSPX, 0, 15, 0
COM1=XPC,1,15,0,
COM2=XPC,2,15,0,
COM3=XPC,3,15,0,
COM4=XPC,4,15,0,
COM5=XPC,5,15,0,
Ports=TCPIP
DisabledPorts=LAN0,SPX,COM1,COM2,COM3,COM4,COM5
LOG_REPLICATION=0
LOG_SESSIONS=0
KeyFilename=server.id
CertificateExpChecked=c:\notes\data\server.id 07/21/97
ZONE_SET=1
Timezone=6
DST=1
CertifierIDFile=c:\notes\data\cert.id
MailServer=CN=Toronto1/O=Bean
Domain=Bean
Admin=CN=Pedro Grind/O=Bean
TemplateSetup=1
Setup=49
ServerSetup=7
ECLSetup=3
StackedIcons=1
DESKWINDOWSIZE=15 27 420 288
MAXIMIZED=1
WinNTIconCommonConfig=Universal
WinNTIconSize=2
WinNTIconPos=2
WinNTIconHidden=0
WinNTIconRect=-1 -1 641 25
Win32InfoboxPos=2 110
FileDlgDirectory=C:\notes
```

Table 2.4 examines how certain lines in the Notes.ini file affect
how the server will run.

Table 2.4

Specific Notes.ini *file lines.*	
Line in Notes.ini	Purpose of line and parameters
Kittype=2	The 2 indicates that this will be a server type. A 1 would indicate that it is a user (client) type.
KeyFilename=server.id	This tells the server which ID to reference for proper names and certificates.
Domain=Bean	This specifies the server's domain.
Admin=Pedro Grind/Bean	This specifies the name of the administrator of the server.
ServerTasks=Replica,Router, Update,Stats,AMgr,Adminp, Sched,Calconn	These are the tasks that the server will begin on startup. If you would like to change these tasks, you can edit Notes.ini and restart the server.
ServerTasksAt1=Catalog, Design ServerTasksAt2= UdpAll,Object Collect mailobj.nsf ServerTasks-At5=Statlog	These are the tasks that will run at the time specified, 1 being 1 a.m. and so on. These are editable.
ZONE_SET=1 Timezone=6DST=1	These lines specify which time zone the server is observing and whether to observe daylight savings time (1 equals yes).
Console Loglevel=2	This determines the level of information that gets written to the console, 0 being no information and 4 being where full trace information is displayed.
EDITIMP3=Lotus 1-2- Worksheet,0,_IWKSE,,.WKS,. WK1,.WR1,.WRK,.WK3,.WKR	This allows the importation of 1-2-3 documents into Notes documents.
Ports=TCPIP	This displays all the ports that are enabled for this particular server.

Table 2.4 shows just a few of the lines in the Notes.ini file. The default Notes.ini does not use all the possible settings. To further manage your server, you can directly edit Notes.ini and add or remove settings for your server. It is recommended, however, that you make any setting changes by editing the Server Configuration document or the Server document in the Public Address Book.

These two documents cover the majority of the settings applicable to a server. Each Server document is specific to a server, but Server Configuration documents can apply to a specific server, a group of servers, or all servers in the domain. Should a server setting be specified in two different Server Configuration documents, the most specific document takes precedence. For example, if there is a Server Configuration document for all servers in the domain specifying that SharedMail=2 and a Server Configuration document for server A specifying that SharedMail=0, the more specific document, the one for server A, will take precedence.

Server document settings are more applicable to security. Should you make any direct edits to Notes.ini and the settings are already specified in the Server Configuration document or the Server document, the direct edits will be overwritten by the fields in the documents. You can also use the Set Configuration console command to immediately change the Notes.ini setting for a single server. Using this console command will not only make the setting change, it will also check for the existence of a Server Configuration document with this setting; if there is, it will update the document.

Starting Up the Server

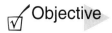 Objective

After you have received the message that your server setup is complete, you can start your server by double-clicking the Notes Server icon. Before you do this, let's look at how the server operates (see Figure 2.4).

As shown in the diagram, Notes operates with an operating system and a network protocol. Notes interfaces with these two systems to accomplish its tasks. The main task of a Notes server is to allow the sharing of Notes databases. To do this and to carry out database management, replication, mail routing, and so on, it must run other tasks such as Indexer, Replica, and Logger.

Figure 2.4

Layers with which the server operates.

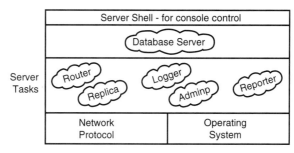

Notes Server

As indicated in the Notes.ini file, these tasks can be scheduled to run at startup or at certain times in the day. Some tasks, such as Replica, must be run at all times so that when a request for replication comes in, the server can perform it. Some tasks, such as Design, which updates databases from templates, need to be run only once a day.

Double-click the server icon now to start up the server.

Using Console Commands

The server shell is used for console commands, so administrators can directly control the server, start and stop tasks, and monitor the server.

Table 2.5 lists the commands you can use at the server console. The hot key for each command is underlined.

Table 2.5

Server console commands.

Console command	Description
Broadcast	Sends the message to active users of the server.
Drop	Drops or closes the user session; can indicate username or specify ALL.
Exit	Shuts down the server.
Help	Displays a list of server commands.

continues

Table 2.5. Continued

Console command	Description
Load	Begins a specified server task.
Pull	Begins a replication process that brings new data in from the target server.
Push	Begins a replication process that sends new data from the source.
Quit	Shuts down the server (same as Exit).
Replicate	Begins replication process that brings new data from the target and sends data from the source.
Route	Sends mail from the mail.box on the current server to the mail.box on the destination server.
Set Configuration	Adjusts/creates settings in the server's Notes.ini file.
Set Secure	Password-protects the server console. You cannot use the Load, Tell, Exit, Quit, or Set Configuration commands after console is secured.
Set Stat	Resets statistics that are numeric additive.
Show Configuration	Lists the current Notes.ini settings.
Show Directory	Shows all databases in the Notes data directory.
Show Diskspace	Displays diskspace on the server.
Show Memory	Displays memory status for the server.
Show Port	Displays port status for the specified port on the server.
Show Schedule	Displays a list of all scheduled tasks and the next time they will run.
Show Server	Displays information about the server.
Show Statistics	Displays a complete list of statistics.

Console command	Description
Show Tasks	Displays information about the server and lists all active tasks on a server.
Show Users	Shows users who have sessions with the server, databases used, and elapsed time.
Tell	Issues a command to a specified server task. This command is commonly used to stop individual tasks without quitting the server.

The following are some examples of commands and their results.

The broadcast Command

```
> broadcast "Server Toronto1 will be down in 10 minutes for 20
minutes"
07/30/97 04:51:59 PM BROADCAST from Toronto1/Bean: Server
Toronto1 will be down in 10 minutes for 20 minutes
```

The Sh server Command

```
> Sh server

Lotus Notes r Server (release 4.1 for Windows/32) 07/30/97
09:16:15 PM

Server name:            Toronto1/Bean
Server directory:       c:\notes\data
Elapsed time:           00:01:06
Transactions/minute:    Last minute: 0; Last hour: 0; Peak: 0
Peak # of sessions:     0 at
Transactions:           0
Shared mail:            Not enabled
Pending mail:  0        Dead mail:  0
```

The sh port com2 Command

```
> sh port com2

Waiting for incoming call

Counts since the beginning of the last connection:
```

```
0 User messages sent
0 User messages received
0 User bytes sent
0 User bytes received
0 Retransmitted packets
0 CRC errors detected
0 Port errors detected
```

Two console commands relate specifically to the tasks that the server is able to run, such as `Replicate` for replication or `Router` for mail routing. These two commands are `Load` and `Tell`. To start the replication and routing tasks, the commands would be:

```
Load Replicate

Load Router
```

Here is an example of the results from these commands:

```
> load replica
07/30/97 05:06:22 PM  Database Replicator started
> load router
07/30/97 05:06:27 PM  Mail Router started for domain BEAN
```

To stop the replication tasks, the command would be

```
Tell Replicate Quit
```

The server has the capability (given the adequate resources) to run many tasks at once. To see the tasks that are running at a given time on the server, the console command is

```
Show Tasks
```

Here is an example of the results from this command:

```
> show tasks

    Task                Description

Database Server     Perform console commands
Database Server     Listen for connect requests on COM2
Database Server     Idle task
```

```
Admin Process      Idle
Agent Manager      Executive '1': Idle
Agent Manager      Idle
Indexer            Idle
Router             Idle
Replicator         Idle
```

As you can see from this server, the `Database Server` task is running. This is one task that you do not load and do not quit. It is always running when the server is up. The other tasks are loaded because of the following line in `Notes.ini`:

```
SERVERTASKS=
```

Table 2.6 shows the possible tasks that the server could run.

Table 2.6

Possible server tasks to run.

Program name	Description of program
AdminP	Starts the administration process that monitors for name changes and implements changes.
AMGR	Allows agents to be run as per schedule.
Chronos	Updates full-text indexes that are marked to be updated hourly, daily, or weekly.
Catalog	Updates catalog.nsf with new databases that have been added to the server.
Compact	Compacts databases that have 10 percent or more of whitespace. Removes deletion stubs.
Fixup	Checks and repairs databases that have been corrupted. Removes documents that have been corrupted from databases.
Design	Updates the design of server databases based on their templates.
Event	Allows the collection of events and reports them.
Updall	Updates all views and full-text indexes.

continues

Table 2.6 Continued

Program name	Description of program
Object	Stores managers that perform maintenance on databases and mail files that use shared mail.
Replica	Allows the replicator to function through a schedule or through direct commands at the console.
Reporter	Creates file statistic reports
Router	Allows the transfer of mail from one server to another through schedules or through the direct console command.
Stalog	Records activity for every database to the Notes log.
Stats	Responds to the Show Statistics command.

Let's try to load a few of these tasks and see the results. Here is an example:

```
> tell router quit
07/30/97 09:20:36 PM  Router: Shutdown is in progress
07/30/97 09:20:37 PM  Mail Router shutdown
load fixup
Database fixup process started
Performing consistency check on ...(all database and templates)
Database fixup process shutdown
```

Using the Remote Console

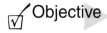 As will be mentioned many times, it is best to get in the habit of managing the server from the remote console. There is nothing you can't do from the remote console, with the exception of starting the server and perhaps changing some ACLs. Access the remote console by selecting File I Tools Server Administration I Remote Console. Figure 2.5 shows the Remote Console dialog box.

Figure 2.5

*The Remote
Console dialog
box.*

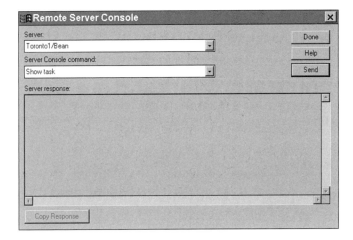

It is very important to understand how administrators receive the right to remotely control the server. A Notes user could just as easily get to the remote console and try to enter a command for a server. So where is it specified who can control the server from a remote console? There is an `Administrator` field on each Server document. The name(s) or group name(s) listed in this field identify who can use the remote console to control each server.

Many companies create an `Administrator` group or a subset `Administrator` group. That way, if an administrator is ill or unavailable, the server can still be controlled remotely. Of course, you can't forget hierarchical names; the correct hierarchical name must be in the `Administrator` field in the Server document or you will receive an `Unauthorized` error message.

One of the drawbacks of using the remote console is that the feedback is not always identical to what you would see sitting in front of the server console, especially for replica and routing commands. On the whole, most Notes servers will be behind locked doors and might be some distance from where the administrator works; therefore, the remote console will prove to be useful.

Note   There is no other use for the `Administrator` field in the Server document. Its only purpose is to allow the use of the remote console to control the server.

Before you can use the remote console, you must set up the administrator's Notes client.

Administrator Workstation Setup

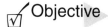 **Objective**

From the first-server setup, you know that the administrator's ID was created and put on a Person document, which was also created in the Public Address Book as an attachment. You also know that the administrator's mail file was created. So now you are ready to set up the administrator's workstation:

1. Double-click the Notes icon and the dialog box shown in Figure 2.6 will appear. From this point, the user can indicate his or her connection to a server, which will be one of the following:

   ▶ Network connection (via LAN)

   ▶ Remote connection (via modem)

   ▶ Network and remote connections

   ▶ No connection to a server

   In this dialog box, the user can also indicate whether he or she has his or her user.id file on a local drive or diskette so that setup process need not retrieve it from a Person document.

Figure 2.6

Choosing the connection to the server and location of the user.id *file.*

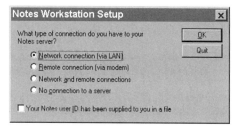

2. The most common choice for user setup is Network connection (with the user ID not being supplied in a file). After you select this option, you will be presented with the dialog box shown in Figure 2.7, which asks for information pertaining to setup.

Figure 2.7

Setting up the administrator workstation using a network connection.

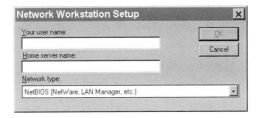

The following describes the fields the user is asked to complete to accomplish setup:

▶ Your user name—This is the hierarchical name of the person who will be using this workstation.

▶ Home server name—This is the hierarchical name of the registration server in which the user's ID resides.

▶ Network type—This is the network protocol on which the user's machine will be running (hopefully the same as his or her home server).

The following lists the results of the setup process:

▶ The user ID gets detached from the Person document, copied to the hard drive of the workstation, and placed in the Notes/data directory.

▶ Database icons for the Public Address Book and the user's mail file (both of which reside on the user's home server) are put on the user's desktop.

▶ A Personal Address Book, names.nsf, is created for the user on his or her hard drive and a database icon is put on his or her desktop. names.nsf is also created in the Notes\data directory as well.

▶ Location documents are put in the Personal Address Book.

▶ Notes.ini gets customized for his or her workstation.

Although the administrator for the first server is really just a regular user with certain special rights (such as remote control of the server), a few access rights are given to this administrator that are not automatically given to any other user, even future administrators for additional servers:

▶ Manager access to the Public Address Book and access to all roles (very powerful).

▶ Manager designation in the server log database, `log.nsf`.

3. After the setup process is complete, the administrator should test the remote console to ensure that he or she can access his or her mail file.

4. The next step is for the administrator to register the other Notes servers in the organization.

Using the Administration Panel

New to release 4, all the tools an administrator could possibly use to manage his or her Notes system have been gathered in one panel. To reach this panel, select `File | Tools | Server Administration`.

From here you will have access to registration, the remote console, the Public Address Book, the log databases, Certifier, Mail, and so on. This is a very efficient interface for an administrator, but you still need the correct rights to execute any of these functions.

For those who know how to accomplish functions in release 3 but can't seem to find where they are in release 4, there is a release 3 menu finder under Help on the menu bar.

Additional Notes Server Registration

To be able to register anything, whether it be a server or a user, the person attempting to do it must have two things:

▶ Access to a certifier ID. Without this, no certificate can be placed in the ID, and no ID is valid without a certificate. Access to a certifier ID provides physical access, either on a hard drive (not recommended unless the drive is totally secured and backup of it is in a protected location) or on a diskette, but you must also know the password to access the certifier ID.

▶ Sufficient access rights to the Public Address Book to create a Person or Server document. If a person or a server is not identified in the Public Address Book, Notes doesn't know it exists.

What are sufficient rights to create documents in the Public Address Book? Did you know you could be specified as a manager and still not be able to create documents? In release 4 of Notes, the Public Address Book's Access Control List has been modified to include roles (see Figure 2.8). If a user does not have the specific role assigned to him or her, that user cannot create Person or Server documents.

Figure 2.8

Roles in the access Control List of the Public Address Book.

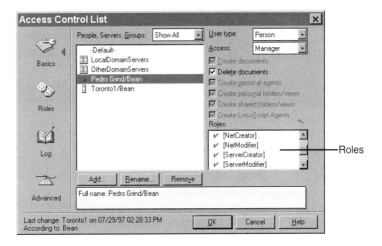

After a user has access to the proper certifier ID and the correct role assignment, he or she can begin registration. To do this, select File | Tools | Server Administration | Server | Register Server.

After you correctly answer the question "Do you have a license for this registration?," you will be asked to provide a certifier ID and its password. You will then see the dialog box shown in Figure 2.9.

Figure 2.9

Beginning the server registration process.

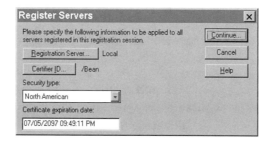

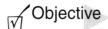

Additional Server Setup

Objective

The dialog box in Figure 2.9 is new to release 4. Its purpose is for the registration of multiple servers. This dialog box allows you to answer the questions once and have those answers apply to all the servers you will be registering. The fields in this dialog box are as follows:

- ▶ Registration Server—This is the server to which the Server and Connection documents will be written. As I mentioned, all registration should be done at the administrator's workstation; therefore, the choice should not be Local or the documents will be written to the administrator's Personal Address Book. Change this option to reflect the server that will be storing the ID file.

- ▶ Certifier ID—This is the certifier you chose at the beginning of the registration process. If you've made a mistake here, you can change to another certifier ID. Whatever you see after the slash is what will be appended to the common name of the server.

- ▶ Security type—Indicate your license choice: North American or International. Remember that North American licenses use the dual-key Cryptosystem for encryption, a more secure method than the one used by the International license. Refer to Chapter 1, "Introduction to Notes System Administration Components," for more information.

- ▶ Certificate expiration date—Every time you register a server, you must enter a date for expiration. The default is 100 years for a server, but you can change that if you want, perhaps for pilot servers.

These are the basic registration facts about your server. Figure 2.10 shows the Basics section of the Register Servers dialog box.

Figure 2.10

Basic information about the server for registration purposes.

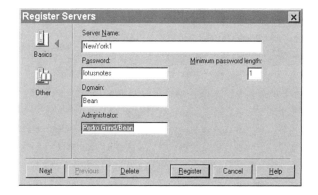

The following explains the fields in the Basics section of the Register Servers dialog box:

▶ Server Name—The common name of the server. Remember to develop a scheme for naming your servers and to keep your server names short. If you put a space in the name, you must enclose the server name in quotes when referencing it at the server console.

▶ Password—You do not want to have passwords associated with servers because if the server machine goes down and then restarts you don't want the Notes servers to wait for someone to enter a password. There are other methods for securing the server, which will be covered later. However, if you choose to attach the server ID to the Server document in the Public Address Book, which is what most do, you must have a password attached to the ID. You can remove the password as soon as you set the server up.

▶ Domain—The system gets the domain name from the organization specified in the certifier ID. Only change this if your domain is different from your organization.

▶ Administrator—This translates to the Administrator field in the Server document. As mentioned in the section about the remote console, the user whose name is listed in this field will be able to use the remote console to control this server. Remember to use hierarchical names.

Let's look at the Other section of the Register Servers dialog box, shown in Figure 2.11, to see what else you can specify.

Figure 2.11

The Other section allows you to provide additional information pertaining to server registration.

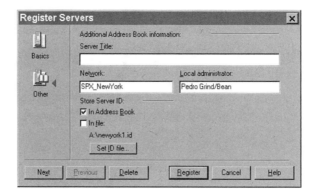

The following explains the fields of the Other section:

▶ Server Title—A field in the Server document that provides an opportunity to give a name to the server that is more descriptive than what the common name might provide. Note that this name does not become part of the server's hierarchical name.

▶ Network—A very important field in the Server document. Contents of this field will be the Notes named network to which this server will belong. Whoever is registering this server must understand the naming scheme for Notes named networks.

▶ Local administrator—This will translate to a field on the Server document that is new to release 4. It is at the very bottom of the document under the section called "Administration." This is different from the Administrator field (which gives remote console rights) in that its purpose is to control who has edit capabilities for this Server document. This is a security measure implemented in the document. As you can imagine, the power to edit the Server document, which controls how the server operates, can be far-reaching.

▶ Store Server ID—In most cases, the server ID will be stored as an attachment to the Server document. Alternatively, you can save the server.id file to a diskette or somewhere on a hard drive. If you save it as an attachment to the Server document, you have no choice in the initial filename; it will be called server.id (this can be changed later, after the server is set up). If you choose to save to file, you have the option of modifying the filename before saving it.

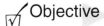
Objective

After the correct information has been entered, click the Register button. The results of the setup are as follows:

▶ server.id is created—server.id will be added to the Server document as an attachment or in a file as you specified.

▶ The Server document is created—This document is written to the Public Address Book of the registration server.

▶ The Server name is added to the group LocalDomainServer— This is written to the Public Address Book of the registration server.

▶ The Server document is added to several views in the Public Address Book, including the Licenses and Network views.

Additional Server Setup

After the server(s) have been registered, the setup process can begin at the actual server:

1. Double-click the Notes icon on the server, not the Server icon, to invoke the dialog box shown in Figure 2.12.

Figure 2.12

Notes set up choices for additional servers.

2. In this case, select the An Additional Notes Server in Your Organization option and click OK. This invokes the dialog box shown in Figure 2.13.

3. The following fields must be completed:

▶ New server name—The hierarchical name of the server that has been registered.

▶ Server name in the Get Domain Address Book from area—Hierarchical name of the server in which the new server was registered.

▶ Network type—The network protocol this server is running.

Figure 2.13

The Additional Server Setup dialog box is for setup information pertaining to additional servers.

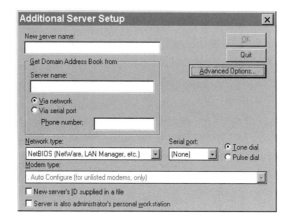

4. After these fields have been completed, the setup choice is made and the following events occur:

▶ server.id is copied to server's hard drive—Notes takes the attachment from the registration server's Server document and copies the file to the additional server's hard drive. The attachment is then removed from the Server document in the Public Address Book.

▶ A replica of the Public Address Book is taken—A replica of names.nsf is taken from the registration server and put on the additional server.

▶ A server log is created for the additional server—A server log, log.nsf, is created for the additional server.

▶ Connection documents are created in the additional server's Public Address Book—Because Notes took the replica of the Public Address Book from the registration server, it assumes that these two servers will be communicating and a connection document is created, although it is marked disabled.

▶ The server's Notes.ini file is customized—As per the information in the registration process and the setup, Notes.ini is customized and set up with certain defaults.

Did you notice that nowhere in the process of registering or setting up the additional server did the administrator ID, Person document, or mail file get created? Nor did any certifier ID get created.

Additional Server Startup

Now that the servers have been set up, they are ready to start up. Double-click the Notes Server icon, and you should see the additional servers start up, just as you saw the first server start up.

 Caution   Many people assume that the first server has additional capabilities or rights beyond the additional servers. This not true. The first server gets the Public Address Book created on it, but once the additional servers are set up, they are equal in that they all have replicas of the Public Address Book. If you want to think about power or rights in Notes, think about rights to the Public Address Book and access to certifier ID's.

Registration of Users

 Objective   You now have your servers set up and running. You have one user whose ID was created during first-server setup, and you are now ready to register your remaining users. Remember that the same requirements that had to be met for server registration hold true here as well:

▶ You must have access to the certifier ID, which will stamp the user ID.

▶ You must have access rights to create a new Person document in the Public Address Book.

After you are sure you have these two things, you are ready to start registration:

1. Select File | Tools | Server Administration | People | Register Person. You will be prompted to answer the same questions as when the servers were being registered:

   Do you have the license for this new user?

   What is the certifier and the password for the certifier?

2. After you supply the correct information, the Register Person dialog box, shown in Figure 2.14, is presented.

Figure 2.14

The Register Person dialog box is where you provide information for the registration of a user.

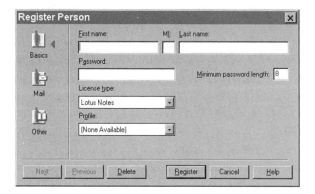

The Register Person dialog box contains the following fields:

▶ First name, MI, Last name—This should be the common name of the user. The fully distinguished name will be created by the certifier ID file and recorded in the user.id file.

▶ Password—You'll have to tell the user what password you have used for him or her to do his or her setup.

▶ License type—Three different license types are available in Notes. Lotus Notes allows full-function rights; Lotus Notes Desktop allows all functions except design functions; Lotus Notes Mail allows users access only to mail functions and four other specified databases.

▶ Profile—The Person document has many specific user settings such as which Internet server the user employs, the user's dial-in server and the phone number, the user's passthru server, and so on. If you create a User

Profile document identifying these settings, you can then refer to it here in the registration process and the settings will be entered in the Person document during registration. This User Profile document can make registration a more efficient task for the administrator and the user.

After you have entered these fields, the registration is ready to begin. These results will occur:

▶ The user ID is created—The User ID file is created with a valid certificate. It is stored as an attachment in the Person document. The User ID can also be stored as a file.

▶ The Person document is created—The Person document is stored in the Public Address Book with `user.id` as an attachment.

▶ The user mail file is created—As per the specified home server, the mail file for the user is created.

If you have a great number of users to register and many of the fields will be the same, you might find it more efficient to register your users through a text file.

Use any text editor and use one line per user. Each line can have the following information separated by a semicolon; if you don't want to enter anything for a particular field, just remember that each semicolon represents a field and use the proper number of semicolons. The only required fields are `Lastname`, `Firstname`, and `password`:

```
Lastname;Firstname;MiddleInitial;organization;password;IDfiledirectory;
➥IDfilename;homeservername;mailfiledirectory;mailfilename;location;
➥comment;forwarding address
```

A sample registration line might be

```
Breen;Bev;;;lotusnotes;;;Toronto1;;;;;;
```

where all I want to enter is the name, password, and home server.

Using this method for multiple users is similar to using it for individual users:

1. Select File | Tools | Server Administration | People | Register Person.

2. From here, continue in the same way as when you entered an individual user. Just remember that the registration settings are going to apply for all users in the text file.

User Setup and Results

Objective

After the registration process is complete, the user is ready to set up his or her Notes workstation. After double-clicking the Notes icon, the user will see the Workstation Setup dialog box. The fields in this dialog are as follows:

▶ Name—This is the fully distinguished name of the user.

▶ Home Server—This is the fully distinguished name of the server in which the user's ID is located as an attachment.

▶ Network Protocol—If the user is attached to a LAN, this is the protocol he or she is using to talk to his or her home server.

Some differences might occur if the ID is stored other than as an attachment. In this case, you must give the user the ID or let them know where it is located. Also, if the user is setting up remotely, you must give him or her the name of the home server as well as the phone number for dial-in.

Results of the user setup process are as follows:

▶ user.id is copied to the user's workstation—The user.id attachment is taken from the Person document and copied to the user's workstation; it is written to the Notes/data directory.

▶ Notes.ini is customized— Like the servers, each workstation also has a Notes.ini file that specifies certain defaults of how the workstation will operate.

▶ A Personal Address Book is created—A Personal Address Book that mimics a subset Public Address Book is created and the user can create or modify documents to simplify how he or she connects with people and servers.

▶ The desktop is modified—Three database icons are created. One icon leads the user to the Public Address Book on his or her home server. A second icon leads the user to the mail database on his or her home server. The third icon leads the user to his or her Personal Address Book.

Network and Communication Port Setups

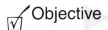 Objective

When setting up a server, it is typical to set it up using one network protocol. If additional protocols are needed in the server's configuration, they are usually added after the server is set up and successfully running on the initial protocol. Most communication port settings are also set after the server is set up.

Network Ports

After successfully setting up the server using the initial network protocol, you might need to add a protocol for multiple protocol servers, delete a protocol that is no longer needed, or modify an existing protocol. To modify, add, or delete any of your server's ports, select File | Tools | User Preferences | Ports at the server workstation. This invokes the Ports section of the User Preferences dialog box, shown in Figure 2.15.

Figure 2.15

The Ports section of the User Preferences dialog box enables you to work with network ports.

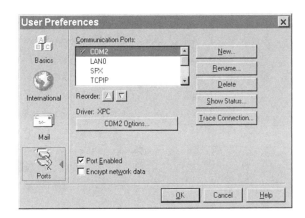

Caution

Be sure your server session is down. Otherwise, your port changes will not take effect. Also make sure you have the proper drivers and interface cards installed before you begin.

When Notes connects, it will search for a port over which it can communicate. It will use the same protocol the next time it communicates. Should that port not work, Notes will look through the list of ports and choose the next one in order of how they are listed. You can use the Reorder buttons to change the order in which the ports are listed. If you have specified a port for the server to use in a Connection document for replication or mail, that port will take precedence.

Caution

Before you leave this dialog box, make sure you have enabled the correct ports.

After you finish enabling your port(s), follow these additional steps to ensure that the server(s) recognizes them. Access the Server document in the Public Address Book and do the following:

1. Enter the port name on the Server document.

2. Enter the Notes named network to which this server will belong with this port.

Tracing Network Connections

Notes provides you with a tool to test your server's connection to other servers. This administrative tool is not available under the Server Administration panel; it is available only from the server client session. From this session, select File | Tools | User Preferences | Ports | Trace Connection. From this dialog box, enter the name of the destination server for which you want to test the connection.

After you have entered the destination server, click Trace; Notes will collect the full trace information and display it in the dialog box. The Log Options selection at the bottom of the dialog box allows you to select what level of detail (if any) you want saved to the Notes log (see Figure 2.16). This does not affect what is being shown in the dialog box, only what is being saved to the Notes log. In the event the connection is unsuccessful, the remaining servers are listed in the Remaining Path box in the Trace Connections dialog box.

Fig 2.16

Tracing the network connections to another server.

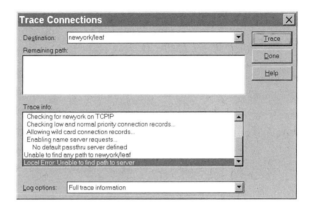

Note

Remember, the Trace Network Connection feature is not available from the Server Administration panel. At the server client session, you must select Ports from User Preferences. Then choose the network port you want to test and click Trace.

Communication Ports

There are many issues to consider before deciding on your modem configurations for your servers:

▶ Explore your options for methods remote users will employ to dial into Notes servers:

Serial communication

Call into LAN and access Notes server via LAN

Use Microsoft RAS to access LAN and Notes server

▶ Determine how many remote users one server will support

▸ Assess the user's tolerance for busy signals

▸ Determine whether users will stay remotely connected to work online with the server or whether users will primarily use replication with the server

To set up a communications port, you choose the same path as for network port; again, you only do this when the server is down. Select the communications ports you want to enable and click Com*X* Options, with *X* being the specific port. Figure 2.17 shows additional setup options.

Figure 2.17

Communication port settings.

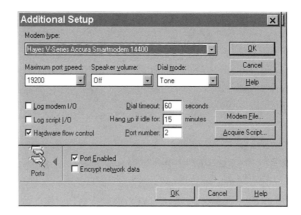

This is where you will specify the modem file that Notes will use to interface with your modem. All the modem files listed here are in the subdirectory notes\data\mdm. If your modem is not listed here, Lotus and see whether it has a modem file for your specific modem or whether you can create one of your own. This is where you also specify the other settings for your modem.

Congratulations! You now have a working Notes system. Here is a recap of the steps for the Notes system setup:

1. Plan the hierarchical naming scheme and decide whether you want to use the North American or International license type.

2. Plan your network organization and decide on any multi-protocol machines.

3. Decide on an organization name and domain name.

4. Install all Notes software.

5. Set up the first server.

6. Secure the `cert.id` file.

7. Start the server.

8. Set up the administrator's workstation.

9. Register other servers.

10. Set up other serves.

11. Register users.

12. Set up users.

13. Set up additional ports for servers and users.

The actual registration and setup of servers and users should be a simple fill-in-the-blanks exercise if you have done all of the necessary planning. Be aware of all the options and restrictions that Notes gives you; be aware of the requirements of your company and implement accordingly.

Servers and workstations are very easy to break down and set up; things that *can't* be re-created if they are lost or destroyed are IDs. You can make new ones that have the same names, but they won't have the same keys. Your hierarchical naming scheme should involve consensus, as it will be used across the company.

The real power in controlling and extending the Notes system comes from rights to the Public Address Book and access to the certifiers.

Exercises

Notes software for servers should be installed on your machine. The following two icons should be available:

▶ Lotus Notes

▶ Lotus Notes Server

The instructions are being given for Notes release 4.1 on Windows 95, assuming that there is no LAN adapter card and that TCP/IP is not installed.

In this exercise you will go through the setup and results of the first server in your fictional organization. Seeing and testing different scenarios is the best way to become familiar and confident in the results of certain operations. Should you have access to networked machines for these exercises, please extend the scope of the exercise to take advantage of your equipment setup.

Exercise 2.1

To begin setting up the first server, do the following:

1. Double-click the Lotus Notes icon, not the Lotus Notes Server icon. The server cannot be started until it is set up.

2. Choose the First Server in your Organization option (see the following input information).

Server name	Toronto1
Organization name	Bean
Administrator's last name	Grind
First name	Pedro
Middle initial	(none)
Password	lotusnotes
Network type	(none)

Serial port	(none—will set up later)
Modem type	(none—will set up later)
Server is also administrator's personal workstation	Do not check this (until you really understand the difference between a client session and a server client session, this is too confusing).

3. Under Advanced Options, enter the following:

Domain	Leave the domain as Bean.
Notes named network	Change to TorArea_SPX.

Leave all other choices at the default.

4. Click OK to return to the main dialog and click OK to create the first server.

Use the following checklist to verify the completion of first server setup:

❏ Check to see whether there are two ID files in the Notes/data directory: server.id and cert.id.

❏ Open the Notes.ini file and review its settings.

❏ Back in the server client session, open the Public Address Book. Look at the Person document for Pedro Grind. See whether his user.id is attached at the bottom of the document.

❏ Open the Server document for Toronto1. See how the hierarchical names for the server and for Pedro have the organization identifier Bean.

❏ Open the Certificates view and see the Bean certificate.

continues

Exercise 2.1   Continued

❏ Look at the ACL for the Public Address Book and see the
   default, groups, and settings for Pedro and for Toronto1.

❏ Verify that a Notes log (log.nsg) has been created for Toron-
   to1.

❏ Look at the Public Address Book and see the two groups
   created: LocalDomainServers and OtherDomainServers.

Exercise 2.2

In this exercise you are ready to begin registering your other servers.

1. Select File I Tools I Server Administration I Servers I Register
   Server.

2. You will be asked whether you have a license for the registration. Answer yes. If you have left your certifier ID on the
   hard drive, Notes will find it and prompt you for the password associated with it. Should you have prudently removed
   the certifier ID, you will be prompted for the certifier ID
   itself and then for the password associated with it. Leave the
   choices and click Continue.

3. Under Basics, enter the following information:

Server name	NewYork1
Password	lotusnotes (this can be removed later)
Domain	Leave as Bean
Administrator	Leave as Pedro Grind/Bean (this will be the contents of the Administrator field for this server document)

4. Go to Other and enter the following information:

Server title	Leave this blank

Network name	NYArea_TCP
Local administrator	Leave as Pedro Grind/Bean (this will be the contents of the Administrator field)
Store Server ID	Leave this set to the In Address Book option, which means that the server.id file will be put as an attachment in the server document

5. Click Register.

Use the following checklist to verify that your server was registered:

❑ The Server document was created in the Public Address Book.

❑ The correct administrator's name was put in the Administrator field.

❑ server.id was created and is attached to the Server document.

❑ The server name was added to the group LocalDomainServers.

Congratulations! You have registered your second server.

Exercise 2.3

This exercise will begin with the creation of a user profile, which you will use in your user registration process. To create the user profile, go to Bean's address book, server view, setup profiles:

1. Click the Add Setup Profile button in the bar at the top and enter the following information:

Profile name	Toronto
Internotes server	Toronto1/Bean

continues

Exercise 2.3   Continued

Default passthru server	Toronto2/Bean
Area code	905
Phone number	876-3456

2. Close and save the document.

You will now register a user. Follow the same procedure as you did for servers, but with a few differences:

1. Select File | Tools | Server Administration | People | Register Person.

2. Choose Yes to license. Again, Notes will find the certifier ID if there is one in the data directory.

3. Enter the password for the certifier ID. Notice that the default for the expiration date is two years for a user versus 100 years for a server. Both of these dates can be changed if needed.

4. Click Continue.

5. Enter the following information in the dialog box:

First name	John
MI	(none)
Last name	Valdez
Password	lotusnotes
License type	Lotus Notes
Profile	Toronto

6. Click Mail. Leave all defaults. The assumption is that the registration is occurring at the server in this exercise. Registration would usually be occurring at the administrator's workstation and the home server would have to be defined by name and not simply as local.

7. Click Other and leave all defaults.

8. Click Register.

Use the following checklist to verify completion:

❏ The Person document was created in the Public Address Book.

❏ `user.id` was created and was included as an attachment in the Person document.

❏ Setup profile `Toronto` was identified in the Person document.

❏ The mail file was created on the home server.

❏ The mail server was identified in the Person document.

The information in the profile will be used to create the Location documents for the person when he or she is set up and his or her Personal Address Book is created. Congratulations! You have registered a user.

Exercise 2.4

In this exercise you will verify your server setup by starting the server and observing the process. Click the Lotus Notes Server icon to start the server; here's what should happen:

1. Databases should be scanned.

2. The replicator should be started.

3. The router should be started for the domain `Bean`.

4. The index update process should be started.

5. The agent manager should be started.

6. The database server should be started.

The server is now up and running, ready to serve any database session, execute any replicate commands, and send and receive

continues

mail. Let's enter a few console commands and see what the server will do:

▶ Show Tasks—This command should provide you with information about your server and all tasks it is currently running.

▶ Show Stats—This command will provide you with statistical information about the server. This is the command used in requesting the Remote Statistics document in the statistics and events database.

▶ Tell Replica Quit—This command closes the replication task on the server.

▶ Show Tasks—You should now see that the replication task is not running.

▶ Load Replica—This command starts the replication running on the server.

▶ Set Secure lotusnotes—This command will invoke console security. After entering this command, enter Tell Replica Quit. You should receive the message This command is not permitted when console security is in effect. To clear the console security, enter the Set Secure lotusnotes command.

▶ Show Disk X—This command will display the amount of space, in bytes, available on the drive specified.

Review Questions

1. Hierarchical naming is based on which of the following:

    a. X.2500 standards

    b. X.500 standards

    c. X.400 standards

2. True or false: Hierarchical naming has always been used in Notes.

3. True or false: At a minimum, a user must have a common name in hierarchical naming.

4. In a hierarchical name users can have at a maximum:

    a. CN, 4 OUs, 1 O, and 1 C

    b. CN, 3 OUS, 1 O

    c. CN, 2 OUS, 1 O

5. True or false: The maximum number of characters for an organization identifier is 64, and there is no minimum.

6. `CN=John Breen/OU=Sales/OU=TO/O=Bean` is called:

    a. The canonical format

    b. The abbreviated format

7. What are the reasons for implementing hierarchical naming schemes? Choose all that apply.

    a. For allocating each user to an organization

    b. For identifying people within an organization

    c. Because they are easy to change

8. True or false: Servers do not use hierarchical names.

9. True or false: When you enter names in the ACL, it does not let you enter only common names.

10. Hierarchical names are used for which of the following?

    a. Mail

    b. ACL

    c. The name of groups

    d. Domain names

11. The difference between a North American and an International license is:

    a. The encryption system

    b. The language

    c. The user interface

12. True or false: When setting up the first server, you should be sure to enter a hierarchical name in the dialog box asking for the server name.

13. True or false: During first-server setup, what you enter for the organization name will default to the domain name and cannot be changed.

14. True or false: The certifier ID is very important, but if it ever gets lost or destroyed it can always be re-created.

15. The Public Address Book is called by what filename?

    a. `PAB.nsf`

    b. `names.nsf`

    c. `dir.nsf`

16. True or false: The `Notes.ini` file is noneditable and the settings are controlled only through the Public Address Book.

17. True or false: Anyone who is in a group called `Administrators` in the Public Address Book can operate the remote consoles of all servers.

18. True or false: Your name is not listed in any Administrator field on any server document. You have access to the certifier ID, and you have rights to created documents in the Public Address Book. You can register a server.

19. True or false: Each time a server is registered, the administrators defined in the registration also get their `user.id` created.

20. The default expiration date for a user is

    a. One year

    b. Two years

    c. Three years

    d. Six years

21. The methods capable of changing the settings in the `Notes.ini` are

    a. Via a direct edit of `Notes.ini`

    b. Via the Server Configuration document

    c. Via the Set Configuration command at the server console

22. True or false: `Kittype=1` in the `Notes.ini` file indicates a workstation.

Review Answers

1. B. For more information, refer to the section titled "Designing a Hierarchical Naming Scheme."

2. False. Hierarchical naming was introduced in Notes release 3. For more information, refer to "Designing a Hierarchical Naming Scheme."

3. False. At a minimum, a user must have a common name as well as an organization identifier. For more information, refer to "Designing a Hierarchical Naming Scheme."

4. A. For more information, refer to "Designing a Hierarchical Naming Scheme."

5. False. Although it is true that the maximum number of characters is 64, there is a minimum of 3. For more information, refer to "Designing a Hierarchical Naming Scheme."

6. A. Canonical format lists the identifier component as well as the contents. For more information, refer to "Designing a Hierarchical Naming Scheme."

7. A and B. Hierarchical naming schemes can be difficult to change if they were not planned well. For more information, refer to "Designing a Hierarchical Naming Scheme."

8. False is correct. Servers and users both use hierarchical names. For more information, refer to "Designing a Hierarchical Naming Scheme."

9. False is correct. Although it is considered a security breach to only use common names in the ACL, it is allowed as Notes still supports flat naming (non-hierarchical). For more information, refer to "Designing a Hierarchical Naming Scheme."

10. A and B. Group names are subjective names, as are domain names (although most domain names are the same as their corresponding organization name). For more information, refer to "Designing a Hierarchical Naming Scheme."

11. A. The encryption system used by the North American license is protected by law against export outside of North America. For more information, refer to "Designing a Hierarchical Naming Scheme."

12. False. Notes will take care of adding the correct component to the common name to create the full hierarchical name. For more information, refer to "Setting Up the First Server."

13. False. Domain names can be changed to be different from the corresponding organization names. For more information, refer to "Setting Up the First Server."

14. False. The certifier ID, when created, has keys associated with its certificates. These keys can never be re-created—it doesn't matter whether you call your new certifier ID by the same organization name, the certificate key is your security. For more information, refer to "Setting Up the First Server."

15. B. For more information, refer to "Setting Up the First Server."

16. False. Notes.ini is editable and server settings can be controlled though it as well as through the Public Address Book. For more information, refer to "Viewing the Notes.ini."

17. False. The field to allow a user to operate the remote console for a server is the `Administrator` field in the Server document in the Public Address Book. For more information, refer to "Using the Remote Console."

18. True. You do not need to be listed as the administrator to register a user. For more information, refer to "Registration of Users."

19. False. The only time an administrator is registered at the same time as a server is for the first server. For all other servers, the administrator must be registered separately. For more information, refer to "Additional Notes Server Registration."

20. B. For more information, refer to "Registration of Users."

21. A. B. C.

22. True. `Kittype=2` indicates that it is a server type. For more information, refer to "Viewing `Notes.ini`."

Answers to Test Yourself Questions at Beginning of Chapter

1. Notes does not have a method to do multiple registration of users without using a text file with the registration information. For more information, refer to "Registration of Users."

2. No, first-server setups are different from additional server setups. For more information, refer to "First Server Setup."

3. Hierarchical names are limited to the common name, four organizational units, one organization, and one country. For more information, refer to "Designing a Hierarchical Naming Scheme."

4. To register servers you must have the ServerCreator role in the Public Address Book and access to the certifier ID. For more information, refer to the section titled "Additional Notes Server Registration."

5. Although there is information about ports in the server document, making changes to, disabling, or enabling a port must be done from the User Preferences dialog box at the server workstation. For more information, refer to the section titled "Network and Communication Port Setup."

Chapter

Replication

This chapter will introduce you to the following objectives:

 Objectives

- ▶ Different types of replication
- ▶ Replication topologies
- ▶ The effect of the access control level on replication
- ▶ Server commands for replication
- ▶ Scheduling replication
- ▶ Passthru for replication
- ▶ Settings for replication
- ▶ Workstation-to-server replication

Test Yourself! Before reading this chapter, test yourself to determine how much study time you will need to devote to this section.

1. What is the first step of the replication process?

2. How many Connection documents must there be to start replication between two servers?

3. Which replication method requires the fewest Connection documents and is the most secure?

4. The same field in a document has been edited in two replica copies of a database. What will Notes do when replication occurs?

Answers are located at the end of the chapter...

server A (BA). Replication then continues, with servers B and C replicating. The result is that server B gets the information from servers A and C (BAC) and server C gets the information from server B (CBA). This process continues until all servers have the information from all other servers (ABCD), at which point the replication process between all servers is complete.

Figure 3.1

An example of end-to-end replication.

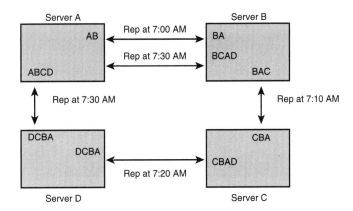

There are several advantages as well as several disadvantages to this system. Disadvantages include the following:

▶ Suppose that server B does not use the legal database, but A, C, and D do. Even though server B doesn't use that database, it must still carry the database so that it can accept the changes and pass them on.

▶ The Access Control Level must be the same for every server. If server B is considered unsecure and the Access Control Level is set accordingly (at reader level), server B will not be able to pass any manager changes from server A to server C.

The following are advantages to this system:

▶ This system will work well with a small number of servers.

▶ This system does not require a large number of Connection documents.

Mesh Replication

With mesh replication, every server in the system either receives a call for replication or places a call for replication with every other server (see Figure 3.2).

Figure 3.2

An example of mesh replication.

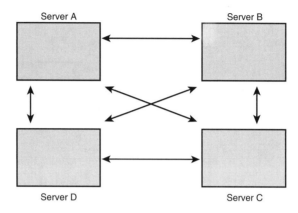

When you get more than four servers, using mesh replication will quickly result in too many calls being made. This can be very confusing. But some advantages of mesh replication are that, unlike with end-to-end replication, if one server goes down, all other servers still replicate. Also, unlike with end-to-end replication, theAccess Control Levels for each server can be different and still allow all changes to get through. Each server does not have to contain all databases.

Hub-to-Spoke Replication

In hub-to-spoke replication, one server is designated as the hub (see Figure 3.3). Either the hub or the spoke servers can initiate replication. The hub is responsible for having replica copies of all relevant databases on it and it must have manager rights to all databases. The spokes require the databases only their users need; the Access Control List will reflect the needed rights for individual spoke servers. This is the preferred method of replication for most environments for the following reasons:

▶ Spokes need not contain databases that their users do not require

▶ The required Connection documents are not excessive

▶ Access Control Levels for all spokes need not be set to manager

Figure 3.3

An example of hub-to-spoke replication.

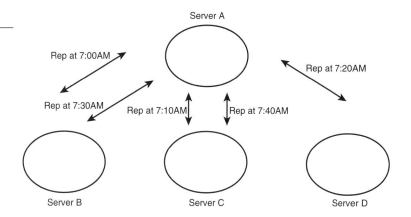

In Figure 3.3, server A is the hub server. Each time it replicates with a server, it receives the replication information from the server and passes its own replication information to the spoke server. When server A replicates with server B at 7 a.m., the result is that server A then has the replication information from server B (AB) and server B has the replication information from server A (BA). The hub then passes information from the first spoke to the second spoke it replicates with, and so on until all servers have the replication information from all other servers.

The Mechanics of Replication

Replication methods can vary, but the mechanics of replication do not. A process is followed so that administrators can understand that process and determine exactly what happens during replication.

Creating Replica Copies

The very first step in the replication process is the creation of replica copies of the database on the various servers. Although many administrators forget about this step, it is critical because if no replica copies of the database exist, the replication process cannot occur. With the exception of a few databases, namely the Public Address Book and a few others, this does not happen automatically. A conscious decision must be made and steps followed to create a replica copy of a database on a server or servers.

There are three ways to create copies of a database:

▶ Create a replica of the database by selecting File I Replication I New Replica.

▶ Create a copy of the database by selecting File I Database I New Copy.

▶ Use the operating system to copy the database.

All of these methods create copies of the database and allow you to change the title or even the filename of the database. The databases will look identical and the contents of the databases will be the same. Nonetheless, if the databases are not *replica* copies of each other (that is, if their replica IDs are not identical), then the databases will never replicate with each other.

Replica copies of a database have identical replica Ids. A replica ID is an alphanumeric identifier assigned to each database file by Notes. You can determine the replica ID of a database by selecting the Information tab of the Properties for Database dialog box (see Figure 3.4).

Figure 3.4

The Information tab of the Properties for Database dialog box lists the replica ID.

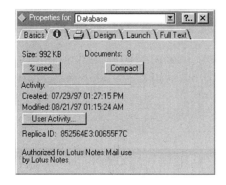

Although all the methods for creating copies of databases listed previously will work, only the first and third methods create replica copies. The second method (selecting File | Database | New Copy) creates a copy of the database with a completely different replica ID. The third method (using the operating system to create a copy of the database) creates a replica copy because the replica ID is part of the NSF file, and copies of the NSF file automatically incorporate the replica ID.

 Tip

You will often receive calls from users telling you that although they can replicate with the server, they do not see the new documents from the server, nor are their documents going up to the server. The first thing you should do is compare the replica IDs of the databases. Replication will not occur if the replica IDs are different. Because there is no way to alter the replica ID, you must copy and paste documents the user created into a new replica copy of the database and delete the nonreplica database.

Comparing, Adding, Skipping, Merging, or Creating Conflicts

After the replica copies are made, Notes is ready to begin the replication process. This process can produce one of five possible actions in relation to documents after they have been compared:

▶ A new document is added.

▶ A document is deleted and a deletion stub is added.

▶ The document is skipped.

▶ The document is updated or merged.

▶ A conflict is created.

The information within the database determines what action Notes takes. This information is available from the document itself, or from the Field Properties dialog box. Table 3.1 illustrates how Notes uses this information to determine what action to take.

Table 3.1

Information about the Document Properties Information box.

Information	Location	Replication Use
Document identification number	Properties for Document box on Information tab (see Figure 3.5)	Used to compare to target to see whether it contains this document
Document creation date	Properties for Document box on Information tab (see Figure 3.5)	Compare to last successful replication date
Document modification date	Properties for Document box on Information tab (see Figure 3.5)	Compare to last successful replication date
Document sequence number	Properties for Document box on Information tab (see Figure 3.5)	Compare against base sequence number of target
Field sequence number	Properties for Document box on Field tab (see Figure 3.6)	Determines which fields have been modified in the document
Replication history	File l Replication l History (see Figure 3.7)	Is compared against creation or modification date

Figure 3.5

The Information tab of the Properties for Document dialog box lists the creation date, modified date, document ID, and document sequence number.

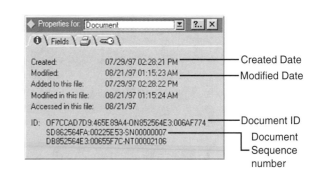

Figure 3.6

The Fields tab of the Properties for Document dialog box lists the field-sequence number.

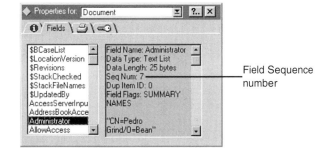

Field Sequence number

Figure 3.7

The replication history for a database.

A simplified version of the replication process explains how Notes compares, skips, adds, deletes, merges, and creates conflicts. After Notes compares the history, date, and time of the last successful replication with the modified dates on the documents, one of the following occurs:

- ▶ If the modified or creation date is earlier than the last successful replication, the document is skipped.

- ▶ For all documents having a later creation or modified date, Notes does the following:

  - ▶ If the document identification number is not found in the target, the document is added to the target.

  - ▶ If a deletion stub (an identifier specifying the deletion of a document) is found for the document ID, the document is deleted in the target and the deletion stub is added.

  - ▶ If the document has been modified, Notes compares the base document sequence numbers on both the source and the target.

▶ If only one document sequence number has been changed, the unchanged document is updated.

▶ If both base document sequence numbers are changed, Notes checks whether merging is enabled. If merging is not enabled, Notes creates a Conflict document. If merging is enabled, Notes checks the field-sequence number on both the source and the target. If different fields have been changed, Notes merges the fields into a new document. If the same fields have been changed, Notes creates a Conflict document.

Field-Level Replication

New to release 4 of Notes is automatic field-level replication. In earlier releases, the whole content of the changed document would have been transferred; field-level replication allows replication to occur on the field, rather than document, level. To illustrate, Figure 3.8 depicts a document with three fields: Field 1 is 30KB, field 2 is 100KB, and field 3 is 2MB. Server A has a document change involving field 1; when replication occurs with server B, only the contents of field 1 are passed over.

Figure 3.8

An example of field-level replication in Notes.

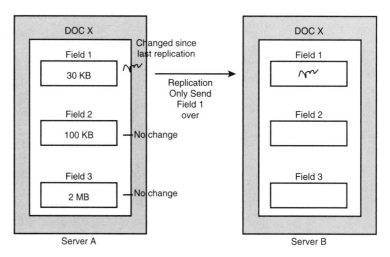

The field-sequence number assists Notes in determining what to replicate. When a document has been modified since the last replication, Notes determine which fields to replicate by examining the sequence numbers of the fields, whereas in previous releases, all fields would have been replicated even if only one field had been modified. Notice in Figures 3.9 and 3.10 that the sequence numbers of two fields in the same document are different. Only fields with a sequence number higher than the base sequence number, in this case 2, would be considered for replication.

Figure 3.9

The Server PhoneNumber *property in the Properties for Document dialog box.*

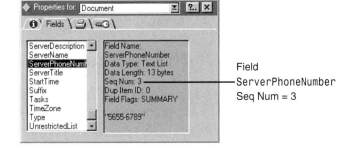

Field ServerPhoneNumber Seq Num = 3

Figure 3.10

The AreaCode *property in the Properties for Document dialog box.*

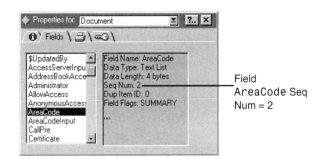

Field AreaCode Seq Num = 2

Replication Conflicts

As I mentioned, there is no record-locking in Notes; therefore, there is nothing to prevent the same document on different replica copies of a database from being changed (if the access control level allows it). When (if) these two replica copies exchange documents, Notes will recognize both documents and save both, but will classify one of them as a conflict.

You're probably wondering how Notes decides which document gets saved as the document and which gets saved as the conflict. Notes identifies the loser, or conflict, as the document with the fewest edits; if this factor is equal in both documents, the least-recently modified document is identified as the conflict.

How do conflicts get resolved? It is usually up to the owner of a database to resolve conflicts, but as the system administrator, you might be responsible for resolving conflicts in the Public Address Book. Here is the procedure for resolving conflicts:

1. Compare the two documents to determine how they are different. If this is not evident, look at the Properties for Document dialog box to see the field-sequence levels. After you have looked at the documents, decide whether to delete one of them or merge their contents.

2. If you want to delete the conflict, do so. If you want to save the conflict and delete the "winner," open the conflict, make some type of edit to it, and then save the document. This will change it from the conflict to the document.

3. If you want to merge the documents, copy and paste the conflict to the document and then delete the conflict.

 Note
When designing the database, the database developer must consider the fact that Notes does not support record-locking. If your database consistently experiences numerous conflicts, this might indicate an incorrect application of access rights within the database.

Field Merging

Developers can use many tools to limit the creation of conflicts. One such tool of which you, as a system administrator, should be aware is the Merge Replication Conflict function, which can be enabled by an application developer. If two different fields in a document are changed on two replica copies of a database, the fields will be merged into the same document (see Figure 3.11).

Figure 3.11

An example of field-merging during replication.

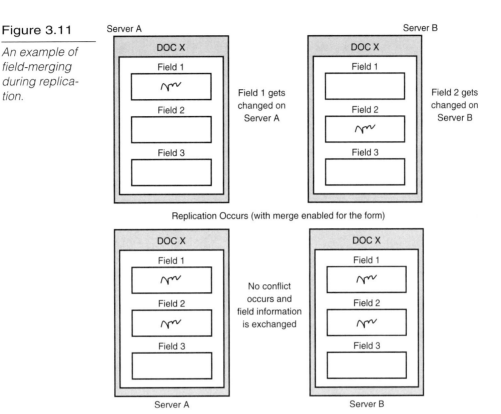

Be aware that this function does not resolve all conflicts. In the event that the same field gets changed in a document on two different replica copies, Notes will not merge the contents of the same field. Notes will create a replication conflict to identify that the same field has been changed and, through a manual process, someone must decide what to do with the contents of the field (see Figure 3.12).

Field-merging is not automatic; it must be turned on in the Form Properties dialog box. If field-merging is not enabled, replication conflicts will occur even when two different fields have been changed in the same document.

Figure 3.12

An example of field-merging during replication and conflict.

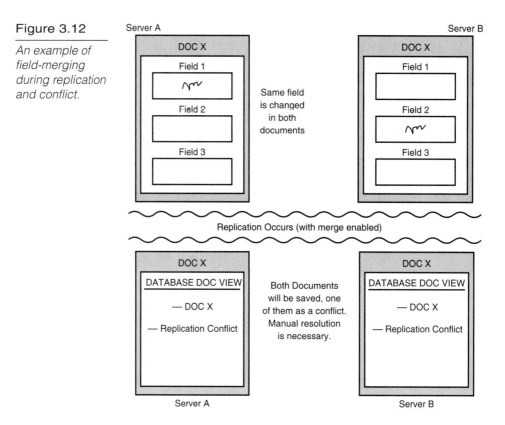

The Server-Replication Task

The server-replication task involves a fair amount of overhead from the server and the replication task keeps careful track of what it does. In Notes, replication can be set up as a two-way or a one-way process; in all, four different types of replication can be run:

▶ Pull-pull

▶ Pull-push

▶ Push-only

▶ Pull-only

Pull-Pull Replication

In pull-pull replication, the initiating server (A) calls server B and uses its replication thread to pull changes from server B's databases. This process also wakes server B's replication thread; server B's replication thread then pulls changes from server A. Both replication threads are working and involved in the process and the events from the process are written in the Notes log (see Figure 3.13).

Figure 3.13

Server A initiates pull-pull replication with server B.

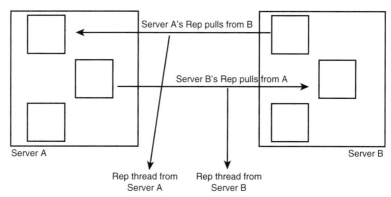

Server A initiates Pull Pull Replication

Server A's Rep pulls from B

Server B's Rep pulls from A

Server A

Server B

Rep thread from
Server A

Rep thread from
Server B

Pull-Push Replication

This process involves only the replication thread from the initiating server. Server A calls server B to begin replication; server A's replication thread pulls documents from server B, and server A's database-server thread pushes its changed documents to server B. Server B's Replica task does not get involved in this process (see Figure 3.14).

Figure 3.14

Server A initiates pull-push replication with server B.

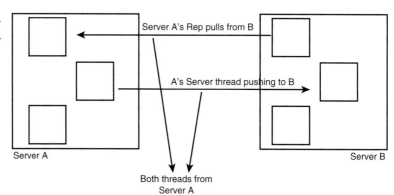

Server A initiates Pull Push Replication

Server A's Rep pulls from B

A's Server thread pushing to B

Server A

Server B

Both threads from
Server A

Push-Only Replication

In push-only replication, server A calls server B, and its database server thread pushes changed documents to server B. As shown in Figure 3.15, server A does not ask for and does not receive any changes from server B.

Figure 3.15

Server A initiates push-only replication with server B.

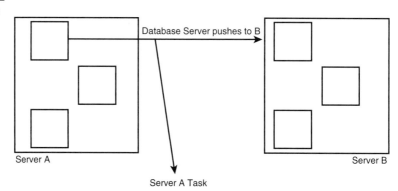

Server A initiates Push Only Replication

Database Server pushes to B

Server A

Server B

Server A Task

Pull-Only Replication

In pull-only replication, server A calls server B, and server A's Replica task pulls from server B. Server A does not send or ask server B to pull any of its changed documents (see Figure 3.16).

Figure 3.16

Server A initiates pull-only replication with server B.

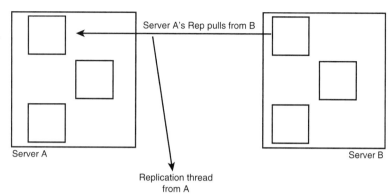

Server A initiates Pull Only Replication

Server A's Rep pulls from B

Server A

Server B

Replication thread
from A

Note

The advantage of using pull-push replication over pull-pull replication is that with pull-push, you can consolidate the overhead of replication on one server instead of involving both servers in replication, as is the case with pull-pull. The disadvantage is that although the replication process does a very complete job of logging itself and picking up where it left off if any disruptions happen, the database-server thread that does the pushing does not and will start over from the beginning.

How to Start Replication

As with most Notes processes, there are many ways to start replication. As discussed in Chapter 2, "Server and Client Setup," one of the tasks that runs on a server is the `Replica` task. This task must be running before replication can proceed. When a Notes server is set up, the `Notes.ini` file is customized, and one of the default lines is

```
ServerTasks=Replica,Router,Update,Stats,AMgr,Adminp
```

These are the tasks that begin every time the server starts up, so if you haven't modified your `Notes.ini` or executed a `TELL ROUTER QUIT` command, your server should be running the `Replica` task. To confirm this, execute a `SHOW TASK` command to determine whether `Replica` is running.

After you make sure `Replica` is running, tell the server to replicate with another server. Although there are five different ways you can do this, this section concentrates on only the first two because they are the methods used primarily for servers (the other three methods are used primarily for users, but they could be used at the server workstation):

▶ Via the server console commands

▶ Via the Connection documents in the Public Address Book

▶ Via the replicator workspace page

▶ Via File | Replication | Replicate

▶ Via stacked icons with pop-up menus

Server Console Commands

After you have made sure your server is running the `Replica` task, you are ready to ask the server to replicate. At the console, type the following:

```
Replicate servername filename
```

Where *servername* is the hierarchical name of the server you want to replicate with. *filename* is optional; if you do not specify a filename, all files with identical replica IDs will replicate. When you use the `Replicate` command, you are asking the server to perform pull-push replication. Two other commands that you can use at the console are:

```
Pull servername filename
```

```
Push servername filename
```

with pull and push operating as explained in the section titled "Server Replication Tasks."

Scheduling Replication

You probably don't want to spend a lot of your time sitting at the console telling the server to replicate. Instead, you can implement a replication schedule with Connection documents that indicate when a server will replicate with another server. The important thing is to plan your schedule first, considering these criteria:

- ▶ Who will initiate the call?

- ▶ What type of replication will be used? Pull-push, pull-pull, push-only, or pull-only?

- ▶ When will replication occur?

- ▶ What databases do you want replicated at what time?

After you have thought about these questions, you will implement your decisions through a document in the Public Address Book called the Connection document. To create a Connection document in the Public Address Book, you need, at a minimum, `author access to the database` status and the `Net Creator` role in the Access Control List. Table 3.2 examines the Connection document, and discussing some of the available fields.

Table 3.2

Fields available in the Connection document.

Field name	Description of field
Connection Type	There are nine choices available to indicate how this server will connect to the other server. These choices are LAN, dial-up modem, passthru server, remote LAN server, X.25, SMPT, X.400, cc:Mail, and SNA.
Source Server	This is the server that will initiate the call.
Destination Server	Sometimes referred to as the *target* server. This is the server the source server will be calling.

continues

Table 3.2 Continued

Field name	Description of field
Use the ports	A server might have several ports to communicate over. Indicate which one will be used.
Source/Destination Domain	Use these only if the domains for the two servers are different.
Call at Times	There are three possible ways to specify when to call: a range of times, a specific time, or multiple specific times. When configured to attempt connection over a range of times, say 8 a.m. to 10 p.m., Notes will attempt to make the connection at 8 a.m. If the connection cannot be made, Notes will try again. If the connection fails again, Notes will increase the interval in subsequent attempts using an algorithm, but it will keep trying to connect until the end of time range is reached (in this case, 10 a.m.). If a connection is not reached before the end of the time range, Notes will stop trying until the next day. When configured to attempt connection at a specific time, say 8 a.m., Notes will attempt to connect at 8 a.m. If the connection fails, Notes will try again, with each attempt having a longer interval, for a maximum period of 60 minutes. After this time expires, Notes will stop attempting and will not execute the connection until the next day. When configured to attempt connection at multiple specified times, Notes will use the same logic as when configured to connect at one specified time, but will apply it to each specific time listed in the Call At field.
Repeat Interval	This applies only to a range of times, and the replication occurs again at the interval specified after the last successful replication.

Field name	Description of field
Days of the Week	Will suspend the schedule for the days of the week not indicated.
Tasks	You can create a Connection document only for replication, you can create one only for mail routing, or you can create one to address both tasks at once.
Route at Once If/ Routing Cost	Both of these fields relate only to mail routing and have nothing to do with replication.
Replicate Database of:	Each database has in its Properties dialog box under Replication settings (select Other | Scheduled Replication Priority) the following choices: High, Medium, and Low. These settings indicate the priority of the database replication.
Replication Type	Here you select which type of replication to execute. As discussed earlier in this chapter in the section titled "Server-Replication Tasks," the following replication types are available: pull-push, pull-pull, pull-only, and push-only.
File/Directory to Replicate	If you want to indicate which database is to be replicated by specifying a filename in a directory, do so in this field.
Replication Time Limit	Sometimes replication can take much longer than anticipated, which means that subsequent servers on the replication schedule are overlooked. To prevent this, you can indicate the maximum time a server can use to replicate. At the time of next replication, it will take up exactly where it left off.
Owners and Administrators	These two fields, which are author-type fields, indicate who can modify/edit this document. If you are in the Access Control List as an author but your name is not in this field for this document, you will not be able to edit it.

Replication Settings

Each replica copy of a database has settings that identify how it will replicate with other servers. In fact, two replica copies might have completely different replication settings. Although both might be valid settings, this can cause replication problems. To look at the replication settings for a database, select the database, then select File | Replication | Settings; this invokes the Replication Settings For Database dialog box.

Some very functional uses of the replication settings include

▶ The capability to execute replication through subsets of views and folders

▶ The capability to replicate only certain documents through formulas

The latter is accomplished via the Space Savers section of the Replication Settings for Database dialog box (shown in Figure 3.17). From here, you can also indicate that you want to remove documents with a certain creation or modified date (these documents are not deleted; they are only removed from your replica copy of the database).

Figure 3.17

The Space Saver panel of the Replication Settings for Database dialog.

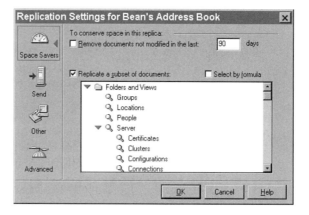

In the Send panel of the Replication Settings for Database dialog, shown in Figure 3.18, you can indicate whether to send local modifications or deletions through the process of replication.

Figure 3.18

The Send panel of the Replication Settings for Database dialog box.

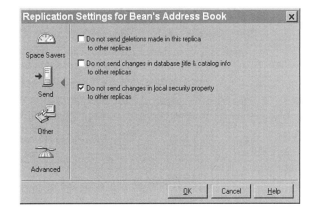

In the Other panel of the Replication Settings for Database dialog, shown in Figure 3.19, you have following options:

▶ You can disable replication for this database. If you know there is some corruption or problem with the database, you can turn off replication until the problem is resolved.

▶ You can identify what priority this database is in relation to the Connection documents and the Scheduled Replication Priority field. The default is Medium.

▶ You can specify that you want to replicate only documents with a certain creation or modified date. This can help you conserve disk space.

▶ If you plan to publish a database on CD-ROM, you can specify the publishing date. That way, when replication occurs with the original database, a full replication is not performed.

Figure 3.19

The Other panel of the Replication Settings for Database dialog box.

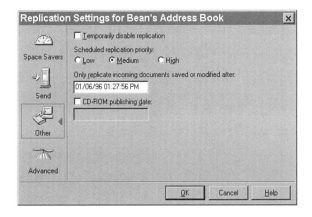

In the Advanced panel of the Replication Settings for Database dialog box, shown in Figure 3.20, you can select to replicate by subset or by formula for hubs and spokes (see Figure 3.20).

Figure 3.20

The Advanced panel of the Replication Settings for Database dialog box.

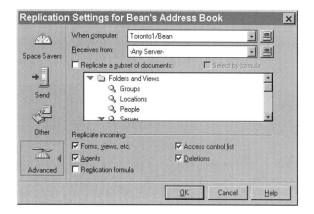

Each replication between hub and spokes can be governed by a specific formula so that only the relevant information is sent to the spokes. This is referred to as selective replication. Selective replication is beneficial in terms of how long the replication process takes as well as how much disk space a database will occupy, as illustrated in Figure 3.21.

Figure 3.21

The Advanced replication settings for a database.

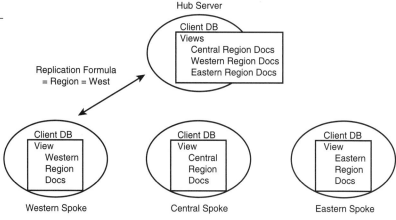

The Advanced panel enables you to indicate whether you want to replicate the following:

- ▶ Access Control List

- ▶ Forms and views

- ▶ Deletions

- ▶ Agents

- ▶ Replication formulas

With the exception of the Replication Formulas option, all these selections are usually turned on. This configuration essentially indicates that if the server with which you are replicating has the Access Control Level rights, you will accept any changes involving these options in the replication process.

Nonetheless, there are some situations where you might want to disable these selections. For example, if my server is a hub and I never want to accept Access Control List changes from my spoke servers, I would disable the acceptance of incoming Access Control List changes during replication. However, I would make sure that all my spoke servers had this option enabled so they could accept my hub's Access Control List changes. Plan how you want to replicate these database components and implement your replication setting accordingly.

 Note   Remember that indexes are not replicated. Each server is responsible for building and maintaining both view indexes and full-text indexes.

Replication History

Each database keeps a history of when it last successfully replicated with a server. This is a major factor in replication because only documents with time stamps later than the last successful replication will be considered for the current replication. There is an option to clear the history so that when replication occurs, a full comparison between all documents transpires. Clearing the history is necessary when you have resolved an Access Control List problem that was limiting document replication.

Suppose server A replicates with server B. By some error, server B is listed in server A's Access Control List as author. During replication, no edited documents are passed to A because the Access Control List won't allow it. You discover the problem and resolve it; server B is now listed as manager in server A's Access Control List, but when you replicate again, the documents still don't flow to A. This is because replication has been occurring successfully for the last two days, based on what the Access Control List said to do. Documents with a time stamp older than the last successful replication are not considered. This is why the documents are still not being exchanged during replication.

To resolve this, you can clear the replication history by selecting File | Replication | History and then clicking Clear (see Figure 3.22). If you clear the history, Notes will compare all document IDs, find the out-of-sequence documents, and bring over the edited documents.

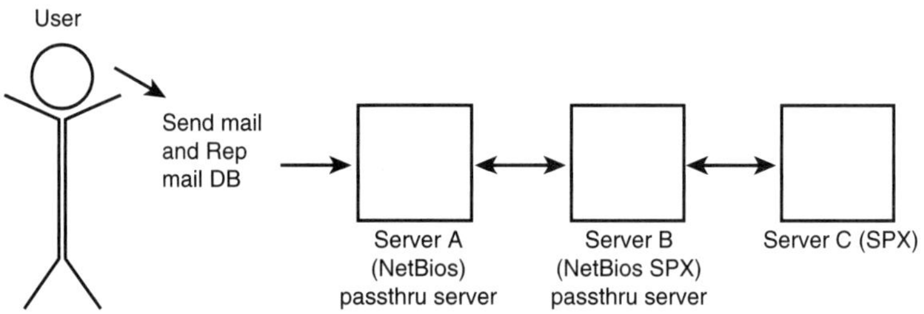

Figure 3.22

The replication history for a database.

ACL Rights

Access Control List (ACL) rights are a vital part of the replication process. The important concept to understand is that users enter changes on a server replica copy and the servers replicate with each other. In reality, the server is responsible for sending the users' changes to all other servers. It makes sense, then, that the server must have equal or greater rights as compared to its highest Access Control Level user so that the server can pass that user's changes.

Suppose server A is listed as editor in the Access Control List and user X is manager. User X makes a change in the Access Control List. Server A accepts the change because user X is listed as manager, but when server A replicates with server B, server B will not accept the change from server A because server A is listed as editor.

This concept applies not only to Access Control List rights, but also to other security devices such as author and reader fields, which are discussed in Chapter 5, "Security." If a database creator uses these fields, he or she must make sure that the appropriate server name or group is included so servers can read documents and transfer edits.

When dealing with Access Control List rights on the server and with replication, it is important to understand that each server respects its own Access Control List and will accept only those documents that its Access Control List permits. For example, suppose that replica copies of the client database exist on servers A and B, but that the Access Control Lists on the servers are different:

▶ Server A's Access Control List says that server B is listed as editor and that server A is listed as manager.

▶ Server B's Access Control List says that both servers A and B are listed as manager.

Figure 3.23

Server A's Access Control List is different from server B's.

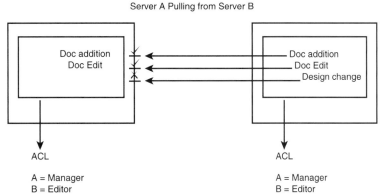

When server A pulls from server B, it will allow only editor-level changes because its Access Control List says that's the level at which B is permitted to perform; when server B pulls from server

A, it will allow manager-level changes because its Access Control List says that's the level at which A is permitted to perform (see Figure 3.23).

If a server is receiving documents during replication, it checks its own Access Control List to see whether the server sending the documents is allowed to make the changes. The receiving server does not check the Access Control List of the sending server.

Note

The only exception to this is if a server has been configured to replicate incoming Access Control List (File l Replication l Settings l Advanced l Replicate Incoming l Access Control List). In this case, the first thing to be replicated is the Access Control List itself, and then the documents are replicated according to the new Access Control List.

Table 3.3 summarizes what a server will pull from another server given their Access Control Level status.

Table 3.3

Access Control Level impact on replication.

Server A's Access Control List	Server A will accept from Server B
Server B = manager	Access Control List changes, design changes; document edits, additions, and deletions
Server B = designer	Design changes; document edits, additions, and deletions
Server B = editor	Document edits, additions, and deletions
Server B = author	Document additions
Server B = reader	Nothing
Server B = depositor	Document additions
Server B = no access	Nothing

Deletion Stubs

When a user with sufficient rights deletes a document, a deletion stub is created in the database. When replication occurs, this deletion stub is passed to the target server, where the deletion occurs as well. In this way, the document is deleted across all replica copies of the database. Two things to be aware of are

- ▶ Suppose someone deletes a document on one replica copy and another user edits the same document on another replica copy at a later time. When replication occurs, the edit takes precedence over the deletion because the edit occurred after the deletion.

- ▶ Deletion stubs are purged regularly (if they weren't, they would use too much space). The purge criteria (specifically, the Remove Documents Not Modified in the Last *x* Days check box) are located in the Space Savers panel of the Replication Settings for Database dialog box (refer to Figure 3.17).

The default setting for the Remove Documents Not Modified in the Last *x* Days field is 90 days. The purge interval is one third the value of the one specified in this field. If the field indicates 90 days, then all deletion stubs older than 90 days will be purged every 30 days. That means you could have deletion stubs as old as 59 days, because if the deletion stub purge occurred when a document was 29 days old, it would be another 30 days before another deletion stub purge would occur. To ensure that you receive deletion stubs from a database, be sure to replicate within the purge interval.

Multiple Replicators

New to release 4 is the server's capability to run multiple (a maximum of 10) replicators. But be careful; each replicator consumes at least 3MB of memory and is very processor and I/O intensive. Multiple replicators allow a server to replicate with two different servers at the same time. If server A calls server B at 8 a.m. and begins a replication that takes 15 minutes, it can also call server C at 8:05 and begin replicating with it. In earlier releases, server A would have had to put server C in a queue, which can hold only five requests, and wait for the Replica task to finish with server B. Running multiple Replica tasks on the server does not allow you to complete replication more quickly on a single server, but it does help when you have replication requests from or to multiple servers.

There are three ways to enable multiple replicators, but before you use one of these methods, you should make sure that you really need multiple replicators and have the resources to run them. The three methods are as follows:

▶ In the Server Configuration document in the Public Address Book, you can specify how many Replica tasks you want to run, with a maximum of 10 (in practice, you will probably need fewer than 10).

▶ At the server console, you can type `LOAD REPLICA`. Each time you type this, another `Replica` task will be loaded. To see how many `Replica` tasks you have running, type `SHOW TASKS`. To shut down the Replica tasks on the server, type `TELL REPLICA QUIT`. Unfortunately, this command shuts down all replica threads; there is no way to specify that only one or two threads be shut down.

▶ You can edit your `Notes.ini` file to indicate several Replica tasks like so:

```
ServerTasks=Replica,Replica,Replica,Router,Update,Stats,AMgr,Adminp
```

Restoring Purged Documents

When a document has been removed from the database because of corruption, it does not create a deletion stub; therefore, the next time the database replicates, it will recognize that it does not have the document and will retrieve it. But if replication occurs before the corruption is detected and removed, it's possible that the document will be corrupted (and removed using Fixup, covered in Chapter 2, "Server and Client Setup") across all replica copies of the database. Unfortunately, there is no way to directly restore only one document that has been deleted in a database.

Instead, you must restore the database itself from a backup copy, and then copy and paste the document from that backup.

Workstation-to-Server Replication

So far, you've covered replication topics relating only to server-to-server replication, but a large part of Notes' functionality is through workstation-to-server replication. It is important to understand that even though this is called *replication* and accomplishes what you understand replication to be, it does *not* involve the Replica task on the server. Instead, it functions simply as a read and write to the database according to the replication history and the rights of the user and server. Although this form of replication is logged in the user's `log.nsf` as a replication event, it is not logged in the server's `log.nsf` as such because it does not involve the server's replicator.

There are four ways to replicate in this way:

▶ Via the Connection document in the personal address book.

▶ Via stacked icons.

▶ Via the replicator page in the workspace.

▶ From within the database or after selecting the database from the workspace, select File | Replication | Replicate.

Unlike with a server, there is no console available at the workstation level to issue a replication command. Nonetheless, users have available to them many of the same tools as servers. All the settings covered earlier in the chapter in the section titled "Replication Settings" are valid for users as well as for servers.

Users must be aware of their Access Control Level. If the Access Control Level is not locally enforced, the user can enter his or her local replica copy as `manager`, and can accomplish tasks in the database that the server will not accept when replication occurs. This can be confusing for users; they believe something is wrong with replication, but in fact, the server is simply obeying its Access Control List.

Users can schedule their replications as servers do; the difference is that users must have both a Location document and a Connection document, whereas servers use only a Server Connection document. The user's Location document specifies the replication tasks and the Connection document specifies how to connect with the server. Figure 3.24 shows the fields on the Location document that deal with replication. As you might have noticed, these fields are very similar to the fields on the Server Connection document; in fact, they are used for the same purpose.

Fig 3.24

Replication fields on the user's Location document.

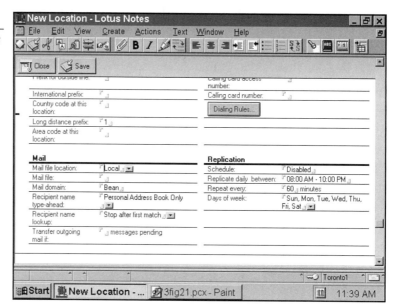

Using Passthru for Replication

Passthru is a wonderful tool for replication. It eliminates the need for multiple calls to servers and can be as useful for server-to-server replication as for workstation-to-server replication.

Server-to-Server Passthru

Can you think of a situation where two Notes servers could not connect with each other to replicate over a LAN or a WAN? How about if they were running different protocols? If this were the case, and if these two servers were the only ones using a database, then in the past you would have had to put a replica copy of the database on a multiprotocol server that would serve as the intermediary for replication (see Figure 3.25).

Figure 3.25

Using B as intermediary server for replication between A and C.

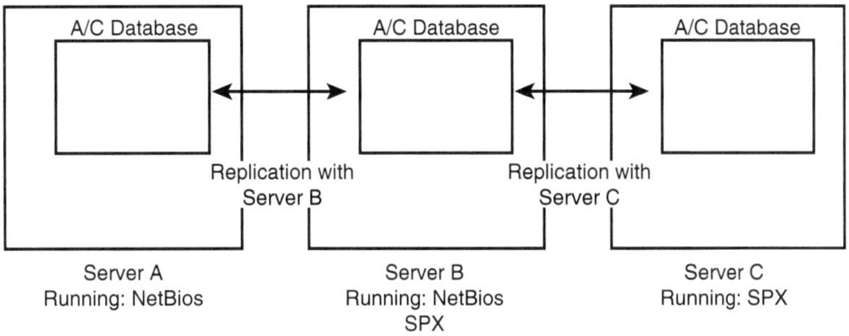

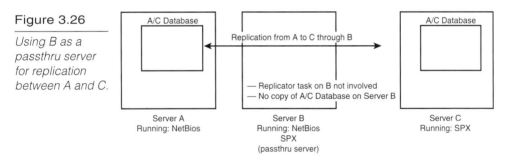

With passthru, you can simply identify the multiprotocol machine as the passthru. It does not have to replicate with server A and then with server C to get the changes to both. Instead, server B would operate as a translator, allowing server A to replicate with server C (see Figure 3.26).

Figure 3.26

Using B as a passthru server for replication between A and C.

To enable this process, create a Connection document in the Public Address Book that identifies the connection as passthru and specifies server A as the source, server C as the destination, and server B as the passthru (see Figure 3.27).

When server A goes to replicate with server C as per the schedule, it will know to connect with server B first, and will send and receive the replication information through server B. At no time does server B require any of the databases that server A and server C are replicating, nor is server B's replicator involved.

Figure 3.27

*A sample
passthru Connec-
tion document.*

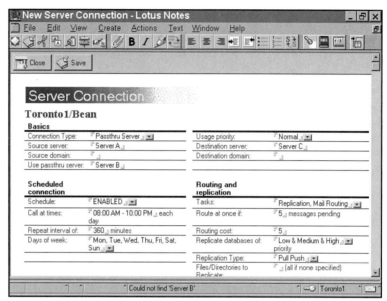

To fully enable passthru, you must configure the Connection documents as well as modify the appropriate Server documents. Table
3.4 examines the fields in the Server document in which you are
interested.

Table 3.4

Server document fields relating to passthru.

Field name	Description
Access this server	By default, this field is blank, meaning that no one can access this server using pass-thru. Using the previous example, unless this field was changed in server C's Server document, server A would never be able to access server C, no matter what the Connection document said.
Route through	By default, this field is blank, meaning that no one can use this server as a route to reach a final destination. Using the previous example, this field would have to be filled out for server B's Server document to indicate that server A could use it as a route to another server.

Field name	Description
Cause calling	If the destination server can be reached only through a phone call, this field must indicate who can cause the passthru server to call the destination server. If the destination server can be reached through a network wire, this field has no impact. If the field is blank, no one is allowed to cause a phone call to occur.
Destinations allowed	This field is for the intermediary server; it dictates which server the intermediary server can reach as a destination for the server asking for a passthru. Using the previous example, this field would tell server B which server it can reach as a destination. The difference here is that the default, which is blank, allows all. So if you leave this field blank, server B can reach any server (except for Cause calling). But if you enter only one server name in this field, all other servers are excluded. When entering specific allowable destinations, make sure you include all the servers you want to allow as destinations.

Using the previous example, you would have to modify the Server documents for both server B and server C in relation to these fields.

Workstation-to-Server Passthru

Like servers, users can use passthru to great advantage. Not only can users use one multiprotocol server to talk to other servers running different protocols, they can use passthru in a modem scenario. In this scenario, one server has the modem pool and acts as the call-in server. The user can then reach other servers (for example, for mail and replication purposes) through this passthru server instead of having to dial each server.

In the past, if a company kept its mail on one server and its databases on another, any remote user trying to get his or her mail and to replicate his or her databases had to make two calls. With passthru, one server (the one with the modem pool) can reach the mail and the database servers. When users call in to get their mail and to replicate their databases, they call only the passthru; the connection to the other destinations is accomplished via mail and replication requests.

To make this work, you must enable the appropriate

- Connection document(s)

- Location document(s)

- Server document(s)

To recap, suppose that user X is remote and wants to get his mail and replicate his databases. The Notes environment has a pass-thru server (multiprotocol), a mail server (running NetBios), and a database server (running SPX). Perform the following for this scenario to execute:

1. The Location document must be configured. Let's assume the user is at home and using his home Location document. The user must indicate on this document where his home server is (that is, where his mail file is) as well as what server, if any, is being used as the passthru. The Location document allows for schedules for replication and criteria for mail transfer. Notice there is no field for connection information (that is, what number to call to get to the passthru server).

2. The Connection document must be configured. This Connection document tells the workstation session the phone number of the passthru server. The connection type will be dial-up modem and not passthru because the passthru server has already been identified in the Location document.

3. Server documents must be configured. If server A is to be used as the passthru for user X to get to server B and server C, then the Server documents for all three need to be modified:

- Server A's Server document needs to indicate who can route through.

▶ Server B's and server C's Server documents need to indicate who can access this server using passthru.

The other two fields relating to passthru are not needed here; there is no phone call to get from A to B or C, and the Destinations Allowed option allows all, and you don't want to restrict it right now.

After these steps have been taken, user X will be able to use server A as its passthru to servers B and C (see Figure 3.28).

Figure 3.28

User X using passthru for mail and replication.

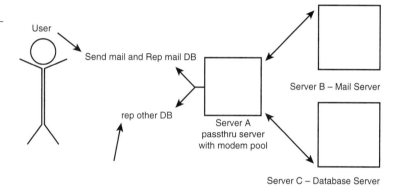

Of course, you might encounter other scenarios. Let's take a look at two more to get the idea of how you can use passthru. In the next scenario, user X is trying to get to his mail, but he's been told that server A is down for the next two hours. He's told that he can use server D as a temporary passthru and is given the phone number to call. With this information, he can create two documents in his personal address book and then get his mail and replicate his databases:

▶ A Connection document specifying that server D is a passthru server to get to server B.

▶ A Connection document specifying the phone number to call to get to server D.

User X will not have to modify his home Location document because Notes checks for passthru Connection documents before it looks at the default passthru server in the Location document. After server A is back up and running, user X can remove these documents from his personal address book and go back to his default. Of course, in order for this scenario to work properly, the Server documents for servers D, B, and C would have to reflect the correct entries in the Route Through and Access this Server field.

The third scenario has user X using server A as his passthru, but his mail file is now on server C, which is running a different protocol from server A. Server B, which is multiprotocol, can be used as a passthru for server A to get to server C (see Figure 3.29).

Figure 3.29

A passthru scenario using two passthru hops.

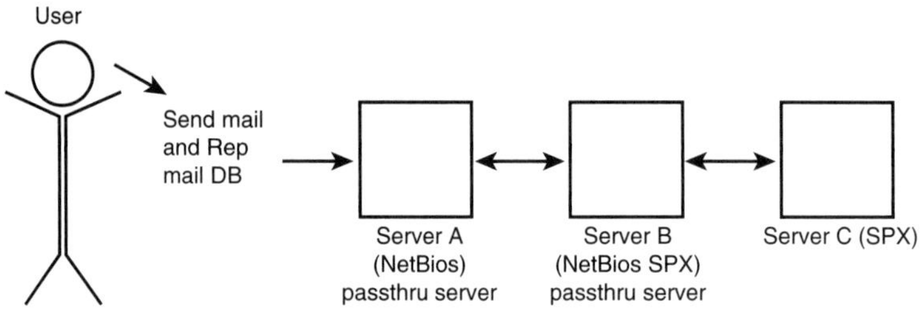

The Location document for user X now specifies that user's passthru server still as server A, but his mail server is specified as C. His Connection document stays the same (it has the phone number to get to server A). In the Public Address Book, there will be a Connection document of type passthru that tells server A to use server B as a passthru to get to server C.

When user X tries to get to server C, his Location document will see that his passthru server is A, look at his Connection document on how to get to A, and dial A. Server A will then look at its Public Address Book to see how it can connect to server C. The passthru Connection document will indicate that server B is used to get to server C, and user X will then be connected with server C. As usual, all the Server documents must contain the appropriate entries in the Route Through and Access this Server fields.

As demonstrated by these scenarios, there are many ways that passthru can be used. Remember, though, that the maximum hop using passthru is 10 (although it is unlikely that you will use that many).

Making Sense of It All

Replication can be affected by many settings in your Notes environment. When replication is not proceeding according to plan, you should be aware of how to implement monitors for replication. This is covered in Chapters 6, "Administration Tools," and 9, "Server and System Monitoring."

A great part of the efficiency and security of database replication belongs to the application developer through the creation of the Access Control List, the management of Author and Reader fields, and the ability to merge replication conflicts for the form. If these are not implemented properly, it will likely be reported as a replication problem. Ensure that you understand how these database functions are used to assist you in the resolution of replication anomalies.

The replication scheme is entirely up to administrators. You must decide what is appropriate and acceptable for your users and system, and implement accordingly. Remember: The most important database to any administrator is the Public Address Book. You must ensure that it is replicated to all servers and that its security is maintained. Your users are also typically involved in the replication process. Plan how you want your users to replicate as carefully as you do your servers.

Exercises

These exercises will explore the various ways of creating copies of databases and the differences between them. You will also examine some of the factors involved in replication.

To begin, let's create a sample database to work with:

1. Select File | Database | New.

2. Under template, choose Discussion (R4). The title of the database will be Discussion.

3. Click OK. You now have a new database on your server.

Let's look at the database properties:

1. Select File | Database | Properties.

2. Go to the Information tab. Here you will see the replica ID associated with your new database.

3. Close your Properties dialog box.

Let's create two other copies of the database and see what replica IDs they are given:

1. Escape out to the workspace and select the Discussion database.

2. Select File | Replication | New Replica. In this dialog box, change the filename of the new database to Disrep.nsf.

3. Click OK to create the new replica copy.

In most setups, the replica copies of a database will be stacked, and there will be a tiny box (sometimes referred to as a *hinkie minkie*) with a downward indicator in the upper-right corner. Using this allows you to flip between your pointer, taking you to various replica copies of databases.

To help you differentiate between your copies, let's show the file names:

1. Click View, then, holding down the Shift key, click Show Server Names.

2. Use the procedure listed previously to see the replica IDs for both databases; they should be the same (if they weren't the same, they would not be stacked).

Let's make another copy of this database:

1. Select File | Database | New Copy.

2. Change the title to Copy Discussion (filename: Copydis.nsf).

3. Click OK. You should immediately see that the Database icon is not stacked.

Verify the replica ID to ensure that it is different from that of the original and the replica copies.

Exercise 3.2

Let's go back to your original database and create a new main topic:

1. After creating the document, take a look at the document properties (select the document, then select File | Document Properties). The Information tab will provide dates associated with the document, and in the lower part will be the ID number. Included in the ID number is the sequence number (in the second line toward the right side). The sequence number of your newly created document should be 1.

2. Click the Fields tab, then click each of the fields in the document. You should see that the sequence numbers of the fields are all 1 as well.

3. Now edit one field of the document you just created, save the changes, and close the document.

continues

Exercise 3.2 Continued

4. Look at the document properties again. On the first tab, you should see that the sequence number of the document is now 2.

5. Go to the Field tab. You should see that the fields you have changed have a sequence number of 2, but that the unchanged fields still have a sequence number of 1. This tells Notes which fields have been updated so that field-level replication can occur.

To allow replication merging to take place, let's alter the design of your database:

1. When in the database, select Views | Designs, and then select the Forms and Main Topic options.

2. When in the form, select File | Document Properties, which invokes the Form Properties dialog.

3. At the bottom of the first tab in this dialog box, you will see the Merge Replication Conflicts option. By enabling this, you allow different-fields edits to merge during replication (same-field edits will still produce a replication conflict).

Note that because you have only one machine, you cannot actually perform the replication process in this exercise. If you have the equipment, try this with multiple machines.

Review Questions

1. True or false: When replication occurs, the servers build a table of the database file names to determine which databases to replicate.

2. A document in a database has been corrupted and deleted from the database. To get it back, you must:

    a. Retrieve it from another database.

    b. Restore it.

c. Restore a backup copy of the database and perform a copy-and-paste operation.

3. Hub-and-spoke replication requires the Access Control List to reflect the following:

a. All servers must be listed as manager.

b. All servers must, at minimum, be editor.

c. There are no Access Control List requirements for hub-and-spoke replication.

4. True or false: One of the disadvantages of end-to-end replication is that if one of the servers is down, replication will be hindered.

5. What is the maximum number of replicators you can run on a server?

a. 4

b. 8

c. 10

6. Using the command TELL REPLICA QUIT will:

a. Stop last replicator started.

b. Give you a list of replicators and ask you which one to shut down.

c. Stop all replicators.

7. Selective formula replication allows you to selectively replicate:

a. Access Control Lists

b. Indexes

c. Views

d. All of the above

8. Two new features in replication are field-level replication and field merging. Which of the following is true?

    a. Both are automatic features.

    b. Both must be enabled in order to work.

    c. Field-level replication is automatic, and field merging must be enabled.

9. When you use REP at the console, the replication method is

    a. pull-push

    b. pull-pull

    c. push-only

    d. pull-only

10. To see how many replicators are running, execute the command

    a. SHOW TASKS

    b. SHOW SERVER

11. True or false: With pull-pull replication, only one server's replicator is doing the work.

12. How many requests can a replicator queue hold?

    a. 2

    b. 3

    c. 5

    d. 10

13. True or false: The purpose of multiple replicators is to decrease replication time between two servers.

14. True or false: Deletion stubs are not passed through replication. They are valid only in the database in which they are created in.

15. Deletion stubs are purged

    a. Every day

    b. When replication occurs

    c. Every 90 days

    d. At one-third of the value of the Remove Documents Not Modified in the Last *x* Days field

16. Servers identify replica copies through

    a. File names

    b. Database titles

    c. Replica IDs

17. True or false: With merge fields turned on, there could still be conflicts.

18. True or false: Notes does not support record-locking in its databases.

19. True or false: Field-sequence numbers can be equal to or less than the document sequence number.

20. For a server to pass a user's document creation and edits, the servers must be listed in the Access Control List as _____, at a minimum.

    a. manager

    b. editor

    c. author

Review Answers

1. False. Filenames are not important in determining what databases to replicate. Notes uses the replica ID associated with the database to determine whether two databases have identical replica IDs. For more information, see the section titled "The Mechanics of Replication."

2. C. Although A might work, it's possible that the corruption could have spread to a replica copy. There is no method of simply restoring a document; you must restore the database and then copy and paste the document. For more information, see the section titled "Restoring Purged Documents."

3. C. Each spoke can have an individualized Access Control Level because it is not responsible for passing anything to another server. For more information, see the section titled "Methods of Replication."

4. True. In end-to-end replication, each server is an integral part of the replication process. For more information, see "Methods of Replication."

5. C. For more information, see the section titled "Multiple Replicators."

6. C. For more information, see "Multiple Replicators."

7. C. Access Control Lists are not part of the selective formula replication process even though they are in the Advanced section of Replication Settings, and indexes are not replicated. For more information, see the section titled "Replication Settings."

8. C. For more information, see "The Mechanics of Replication."

9. A. For more information, see "The Mechanics of Replication."

10. A. More information, see the section titled "How to Start Replication."

11. False. With pull-pull replication, each server's replicator is involved. For more information, see "Methods of Replication."

12. C. For more information, see "Multiple Replicators."

13. False. Multiple replicators are used so a server can replicate with more than one other server in a shorter period of time.

The time spent with each server will be the same. For more information, see "Multiple Replicators."

14. False. Deletion stubs are passed through the replication process. For more information, see the section titled "Deletion Stubs."

15. D. For more information, see "Deletion Stubs."

16. C. For more information, see the section titled "Creating Replica Copies."

17. True. When two or more users edit the same field on a document, even if merge is turned on, there will be a conflict. For more information, see the section titled "Comparing, Adding, Skipping, Merging, or Creating Conflicts."

18. True. For more information, see the section titled "Replication Conflicts."

19. True. A document sequence number indicates how many times the document has been edited; a field-sequence number is the number of times a field has been edited. For more information, see "Comparing, Adding, Skipping, Merging, or Creating Conflicts."

20. B. For more information, see the section titled "ACL Rights."

Answers to Test Yourself Questions at Beginning of Chapter

1. The first step of the replication process is to make a replica copy of the database. Replication cannot occur unless there are replica copies of the database on the servers. For more information, see the section titled "Creating Replica Copies."

2. For replication to occur, only one Connection document is needed where both the `Replica task` and what type or replica is to take place are specified. For more information, see the section titled "Scheduling Replication."

3. Hub-and-spoke replication requires the fewest connection documents and is the most secure. Although mesh replication is secure and does not require that all servers listed as `manager`, it requires many more documents than hub-to-spoke would. For more information, see the section titled "Methods of Replication."

4. Notes will save both documents, and call the one with the fewest edits the Conflict document. Notes uses the number of edits to determine which document will be the Conflict document. If this number is the same for both documents, Notes then uses the time factor, selecting the least-recently modified document as the conflict. For more information, see the section titled "Comparing, Adding, Skipping, Merging, or Creating Conflicts."

Chapter

Mail

This chapter deals with all aspects of mail functions within Notes. User interaction is usually very high with regards to mail, and it behooves all administrators to fully understand how Notes manages their users' mail, including the following:

 Objectives

- ▶ Components of mail in Notes

- ▶ How mail gets delivered in Notes

- ▶ How shared mail works in Notes

- ▶ Administering shared mail in Notes

- ▶ Administering mail in Notes

- ▶ Remote users and their mail

- ▶ Mail security in Notes

- ▶ Troubleshooting mail

Test Yourself! Before reading this chapter, test yourself to determine how much study time you will need to devote to this section.

1. What method of encryption is used to encrypt mail?

2. True or false: The first router determines the entire path of a mail message and each subsequent router must do the same.

3. When the setting is `Shared_Mail=1`, when will messages be stored in the Shared Mail database?

4. To route mail between two Notes named networks, does the system require one or two Server Connection documents?

Answers are located at the end of the chapter...

Before beginning this chapter, you should have basic knowledge of how a user interacts with Notes using mail. You should know how to create a mail message, how to create replica copies of mail databases, how to start replication with a server, and how to send mail remotely. You should also understand the concept of Notes named networks and restrictions that apply to them.

This chapter will introduce you to the basic components of Notes and the network infrastructure on which Notes depends, including

▶ Basic components of the mail system in Notes

▶ How mail works across Notes named networks and domains

▶ How shared mail works within Notes

▶ Users' mail files

Understanding Mail Components

The mailing system in Notes houses three basic components. Each of these components plays an integral part; without each component, mail would not be delivered. These three components are

▶ Mailer

▶ mail.box

▶ Router

Using Mailer

Mailer is the workstation software that enables users to compose and send mail messages. Even though the server has a workstation session, if you select Create | Mail, you will see the message None Available. The Mail Create option will appear only on a user workstation session.

The mailer is also responsible for implementing Soundex, which will not allow a user to send a mail message within the domain to someone who is not identified in the Public Address Book. In release 4, the mailer also offers a type-ahead function; after you enter a few letters of the recipient's name, mailer finishes it for you. Each user's Location document has a field that specifies what address books to check for the type-ahead function. This setting is also definable under File | Tools | User Preferences | Mail | Local Address Books. Soundex is available to users only when they are connected to a server.

Using `mail.box`

`mail.box` is a special database that relates to both servers and users. For now, I will discuss it as it relates to servers. Think of this mail component as a mail box. Its sole use is to accept mail from users. The mail is then picked up by the router, which determines the path to the mail's final destination. The `mail.box` database is on every server that is running a router task, but you won't be able to see it under File | Database | Open because it does not have an `.nsf` extension. You can add it to the server's workspace by typing the filename `mail.box` in the Filename dialog box. You will be able to access it only if your name is in the ACL or if you are sitting at the server's workstation. When `mail.box` gets created for a particular server, it creates an ACL with the server's name in it as `manager`; the administrator of the server is also entered in the ACL as `manager`. Should a message be in `mail.box` because it is awaiting delivery or because it has dead-mail status, you will not be able to read the mail message. The only available information relates to the sender and recipients. If it is dead mail, you can determine what the problem is, fix it, return to `mail.box`, select the messages, and then select Action | Release Dead Messages.

The `mail.box`'s ACL will list `depositor` by default. Leave this as is; you want all other servers to be able to deposit mail here.

Using the Router

The router is a server task. It does not run on the workstation. Each server must be running a router task or it will be unable to deliver mail. As with the replicator, when the server is set up, one of the default lines in `Notes.ini` reads:

```
ServerTasks=Replica,Router,Update,AMgr,Adminp
```

Unless you modify your `Notes.ini` or enter `TELL ROUTER QUIT` at the server console, you will have the router task running on your server. To verify this, run a `SHOW TASK` command at the console. The router's job is to pick up mail from `mail.box` on the server and determine where it should go to get to its final destination. Often, the mail will have to go through several servers before it reaches its destination.

Although each server's router is responsible for determining the complete path, once a router sends a message to the next hop, the next router determines what it considers to be the best path. How do routers determine this? It's all from the Public Address Book. Each router receives all its information from this database. The Public Address Book contains the following information:

▶ The recipient's mail server

▶ The name of recipient's mail file (`jjones.nsf`) and the directory that contains it

▶ What servers are in what Notes named networks

▶ If servers are in different Notes named networks, what the connections are between them

▶ Cross-domain connections

The router considers this information and more to determine what it should do with the mail it finds in the `mail.box`. To allow the routers to do their jobs, the Public Address Book should always be up to date with correct connections and locations.

Delivering Mail

Having covered the three components of mail within Notes, let's see how they act together in certain scenarios.

Key Terms

> Mail is delivered immediately when it is sent to a mail server in the same Notes named network. There is no need for any Server Connection document or route command. Mail sent outside of a Notes named network will require a Server Connection document or a route command before being sent on.

Mail Sent on the Same Server

Suppose that John and Judy have their mail files on the same server. John sends Judy a mail message. Here is the sequence of events:

1. John uses his mailer to create and send the message to the `mail.box` on his mail server. Soundex verifies that Judy is a valid recipient.

2. The router on John's mail server looks in the `mail.box` and sees a message to Judy. The router checks Judy's Person document in the Public Address Book; it determines that her mail file is on this server, and ascertains the mail file's filename. It then deposits the mail in Judy's mail file.

Mail Sent Within the Same Notes Named Network

Judy's mail file is on server A. John's mail file is on server B. Servers A and B are in the same Notes named network. When Judy sends a mail message to John, the sequence of events is as follows:

1. Judy uses her mailer to compose the message, which ensures that John's is a valid name in the Notes domain, and deposits the message in her mail server's `mail.box`.

2. The router on Judy's mail server checks the `mail.box` and sees that the recipient of the message therein is John. The router checks the Public Address Book to see where John's mail server is and what his mail file is. It sees that server B is John's mail server and that it is in the same Notes named network as server A. The router does not wait for any Server Connection document; it sends the mail immediately to server B and deposits it in server B's `mail.box`.

3. The router on server B checks the `mail.box`, sees that the recipient of the message therein is John (whose mail file is on server B), and deposits the message into John's mail file (see Figure 4.1).

Figure 4.1

Mail being delivered in the same Notes named network.

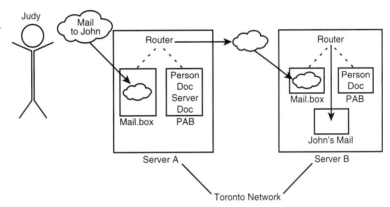

Mail Sent Outside the Notes Named Network

John is now going to send a message to Kyle. John's mail server is server B on the `Toronto` network and Kyle's mail server is server N in the `NewYork` network. Here is the sequence of events:

1. John uses his mailer to create and send the message to his mail server's `mail.box`. Soundex is used to ensure that Kyle's is a valid name in the domain before the mail is deposited in the `mail.box`.

2. The router on server A looks in the `mail.box` and finds a message for Kyle. When the router checks the Public Address

Book, it determines that Kyle's mail server is server N, and that server N is in the NewYork network.

3. The router then looks for a Server Connection document for some type of path from the Toronto network to the New-York network. It sees that server C in the Toronto network calls server M in the NewYork network.

   The router on server B determines that the route will be to server C to server M to server N. Because server M is in the same Notes named network as server N, it can transfer the mail message after it has received it from server C. The router on server B has determined that this is the shortest, most cost-effective method of delivering the mail. It takes the first step of sending the mail to the mail.box on server C.

4. The router on server C examines the mail in the mail.box and goes through the same procedure as the router on server B did. Hopefully, it will come up with the same route as the server B router did, because both should be working from the same Public Address Book. The next step is to send the message from the Toronto network (server C) to the New-York network (server M). This requires a Server Connection document. Server C's router waits for the Server Connection document to execute and sends the mail to server M.

5. The router on server M examines the message in its mail.box and sees that the recipient's mail file is on server N. Server N is in the same Notes named network as server M, so the message is sent right over to the mail.box on Server N.

6. The router on server M examines the message in its mail.box, sees that the recipient's mail file is local, and deposits the message there (see Figure 4.2).

Figure 4.2

Mail being delivered from outside of a Notes named network.

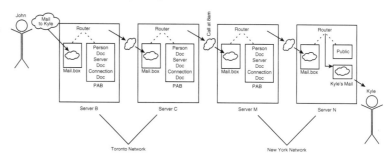

Mail Sent from Outside of a Notes Domain

Kyle, who is in the Bean domain, must send a message to Lydia in the Leaf domain. Cross-certification exists between the two domains, and there is a connection from server N in the Bean domain to server X in the Leaf domain. Here is the sequence of events:

1. Kyle creates a message with his mailer. Soundex does not check the name because the recipient is not in the Bean domain. Kyle then deposits the message in his mail server's mail.box.

2. The router on server N examines the mail.box and sees that the recipient's name indicates a different domain. The router then looks for a Server Connection document in the Public Address Book for the shortest, cheapest way to get to the domain Leaf. It sees that there is a connection from server M, which is in the same Notes named network as server N, to server X in the Leaf domain. Server N sends the message to server M's mail.box.

3. The router on server M examines its mail.box, and sees a message for someone in the domain Leaf. It reviews the Public Address Book and finds a Server Connection document to server X in Leaf domain. It waits for the connection to execute and sends the message to server X.

4. Server X's router examines the mail.box and checks Leaf's Public Address Book to see where Lydia resides. Server X then sends the message to Lydia's mail server (see Figure 4.3).

Figure 4.3

Mail being delivered outside of a Notes domain.

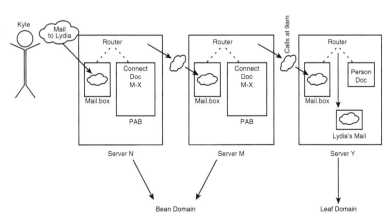

Documents in the Public Address Book

As you can gather from the previous examples, the importance of the Public Address Book in the delivery of mail cannot be stressed enough. It is the source of information for all the routers. Information in the Public Address Book must be correct; if it is out of sync, you will be plagued with mail problems. Keep your Public Address Book clean and correct and make sure all the routers are singing from the same songbook.

Let's take a look at some of the documents from the Public Address Book and see how they help the router.

The Person Document

The Person document (an example of which is shown in Figure 4.4) is extremely important to mail delivery. Let's review the fields that affect mail (see Table 4.1).

Table 4.1

Pertinent Public Address Book fields.	
Field name	Importance to router
Mail server	Tells the router on which server the person's `mail file` resides
Mail system	Tells the router whether the person is using a system for mail other than Notes.
Mail file	Tells the router where on the mail server `mail file` is located and what the actual filename of the mail database is
Domain	Indicates to the router the domain of the person's mail server

Server Documents

After the router determines the server location of the recipient's mail file, it must turn to the Server document (an example of which is shown in Figure 4.5) for more information. Remember: Notes immediately delivers mail within the same Notes named network. if the router determines that the mail server for the recipient is in the same Notes named network, it delivers it immediately. If the mail server for the recipient is elsewhere, the router then looks for a Server Connection document between servers.

Figure 4.4

The Person document in the Public Address Book.

Figure 4.5

A Notes named network identified in the Server document.

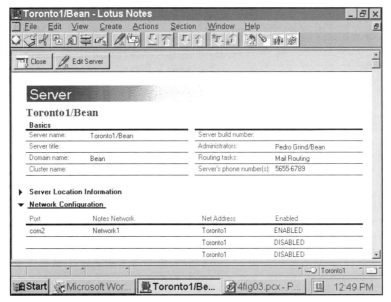

The Server Connection Document

From the Server documents, the router sees that two servers exist in different Notes named networks (see Figure 4.6). The router then checks to see whether there is a Server Connection document between these two servers (see Figure 4.7). This Server Connection document specifies that when Toronto1/Bean has one mail message pending, it will initiate a connection with NewYork1/Bean and send the mail on. Let's look at other fields that relate to mail in the Server Connection document and consider how those fields affect mail delivery:

- ▶ Call at Times—There are three possible ways to enter the times at which the Notes attempts to connect:

  - ▶ A range of times (for example, 8 a.m. to 10 p.m.)—In this case, Notes will attempt to connect at 8 a.m.; should this connection fail, Notes will try again. If the connection fails again, Notes will increase the interval between subsequent attempts using an algorithm to determine the intervals. Connection attempts will occur until the end of time range is reached, and will restart the following day.

  - ▶ A specific time (for example, 8 a.m.)—In this case, Notes will attempt to connect at 8 a.m.; failing this, it will try again, increasing the interval between subsequent attempts, for a maximum of 60 minutes. After this period expires, Notes will stop attempting until the next day.

  - ▶ Multiple specific times (for example, 8 a.m., 11 a.m., 5 p.m.)—With multiple specific times, Notes will use the same logic as with one specific time, but will apply it to each time listed in the Call at Times field.

  - ▶ Repeat Interval—Applies only to a range of times. If you enter a specific time or multiple specific times, repeat will not execute.

  - ▶ Route At Once If—This field enables you to force the connection so that mail can be delivered. It indicates the number of mail messages in the `mailbox` needed to force a connection. (Low-priority mail is counted to reach this number, but is not sent.)

▶ Routing Cost—There might be multiple paths to the final destination; the router's job is to find the least costly method. It does this by using information from the Routing Cost field. For example, suppose a path involves three connections with costs of 1, 5, and 1. The total cost of this path is 7. If the least-costly path fails, a cost of 1 is added for each failed attempt. As soon as the adjusted cost reaches the same level as the next least-costly path, the second path is tried. The cost can be a value between 1 and 10, with 10 being the most expensive and 1 being the least expensive. When you create a LAN Connection document, Notes enters as the default a value of 1, and a dial-up modem connection gets a value of 5. These values are arbitrary. Someone with knowledge of the actual cost of communication (for example, whether the leased line is at a flat rate, the speed of the modem connection, and so on) should assign the costs. This field should not be modified by every local administrator.

Figure 4.6

Notes named networks identified.

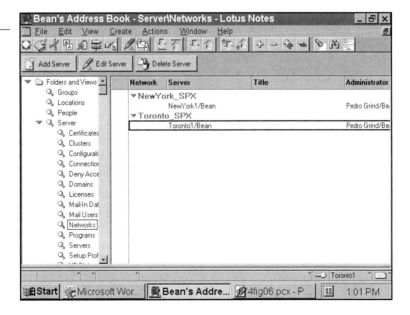

Figure 4.7

Server Connection document for mail routing.

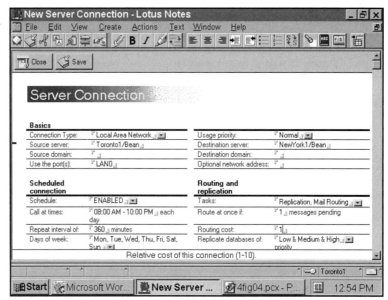

Key Terms

The Server Connection document just mentioned tells the router that `Toronto1/Bean` has a way of sending mail to `NewYork1/Bean`. Although many people assume that the same Server Connection document will work when `NewYork1/Bean` has mail that must be sent to `Toronto1/Bean`, this is not the case. For mail to be sent from `NewYork1/Bean` to `Toronto1/Bean`, there must be a Server Connection document specifying this. With replication, Server Connection documents can specify pull-pull or pull-push, either of which would have documents flowing in both directions. Mail, however, is different. There must be a Server Connection document for both directions.

Creating a Mail Topology

Let's look at a detailed Bean environment and a suggested mail topology, and review the logic of it (see Figure 4.8).

The four identified Server Connection documents will accomplish all the mail delivery for the `Bean` domain. You know servers in the same Notes named network do not need Server Connection documents. Because servers in the same Notes named networks route mail automatically, it makes sense to have one of the Notes named network servers act as the conduit for mail going in or out of the Notes named network.

Figure 4.8

The **Bean** *domain's mail topology.*

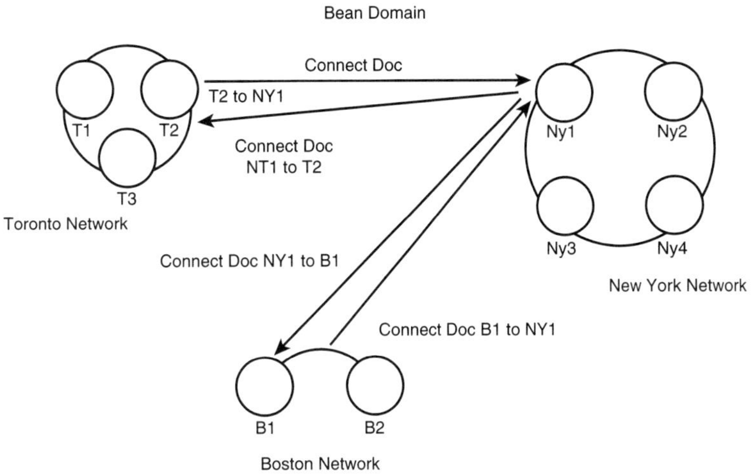

Shared Mail in Notes

Shared mail (sometimes referred to as *single copy object store,* or *SCOS*) is a space saver for your mail servers. Most mail users are notorious hoarders, and tend to drive administrators wild with disk-space concerns. Shared mail can alleviate these concerns if a large number of the mail messages exist in multiple users' mail files. Shared mail is not a compressor; it simply recognizes that two or more recipients exist on the same mail server, puts the contents of the mail in the shared database, and puts the header information in each recipient's mail. This header information also contains a pointer to the content information that is in the shared database. That the message is shared is transparent to users; they see no indication of this when reading their mail (see Figure 4.9).

Understanding Shared Mail Methods

Before discussing how to enable shared mail (it is not automatic), let's explore the methods available for shared mail.

Figure 4.9

Shared mail in Notes.

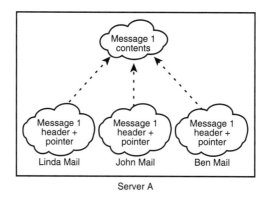

Server A

Shared_Mail=1

`Shared_Mail=1` dictates that if a server receives a mail message, the server will immediately put the message into the first recipient's `mail.nsf`. Notes will then determine whether there are additional recipients. If not, the mail stays in the user's `mail.nsf`, and is never placed in the shared mail database. If, however, Notes determines that there is another recipient, it will replace the entire message in the first user's `mail.nsf` with a header, copy the message to the shared mail database, and put the header information, with a pointer, in the additional recipient's `mail.nsf`.

Key Terms

> `Shared_Mail=1` affects only the delivery, not the transfer, of mail across various servers. It will put the contents of the message into shared mail only if there is more than one recipient on the server (see Figure 4.10).

Shared_Mail=2

With `Shared_Mail=2`, the router receiving mail does the following:

1. Mail is put directly into the shared mail database.

2. The router then determines whether any recipients, even just one, exist on this server.

3. If so, the router puts the header information with a pointer into each recipient's `mail.nsf`.

4. If there are no recipients on this server, the router erases the mail from the shared mail database.

5. If the router finds that there are additional servers in the path, it passes the message to the next server.

Figure 4.10

An example of `Shared_Mail=1`.

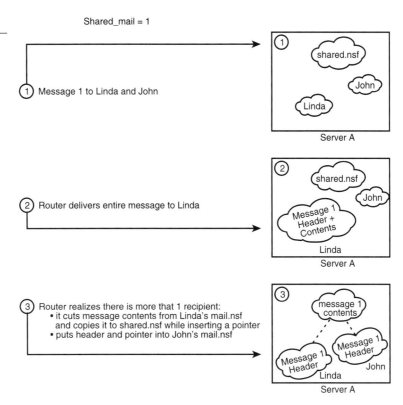

Shared_mail = 1

① Message 1 to Linda and John

② Router delivers entire message to Linda

③ Router realizes there is more that 1 recipient:
 • it cuts message contents from Linda's mail.nsf and copies it to shared.nsf while inserting a pointer
 • puts header and pointer into John's mail.nsf

🔑 **Key Terms**

`Shared_Mail=2` affects both the delivery and the transfer of mail across multiple servers and will store mail in the shared mail database even for just one recipient on the server (see Figure 4.11).

Enabling Shared Mail

There are various ways to enable shared mail:

▶ Via the Server Configuration document (in the Public Address Book)

▶ Via Notes.ini

▶ Via console commands

Figure 4.11

An example of
SharedMail=2.

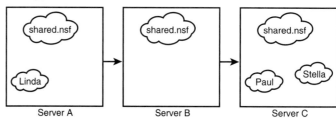

① Message 1 to Linda, Paul, & Stella.
Delivery path = Server A to Server B to Server C.

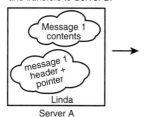

② Router delivers contents of the message to shared.nsf
on Server A and header and pointer in Linda's mail
and transfers to Server B.

③ Router on Server B delivers contents of the message to shared.nsf and realizes there
is no recipient for this server, it then transfers this message on to Server C.

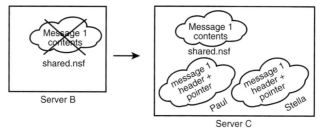

④ Router on server erases contents from shared.nsf. Router on Server C delivers the
message contents to shared.nsf and the header and pointers to Paul and Stella.

Enabling Shared Mail Via the Server Configuration Document

To enable shared mail via the Server Configuration document, do the following:

1. Create or modify a Server Configuration document in the Public Address Book and click the Set/Modify Parameters button.

2. From the Items list, select SHARED_MAIL and enter the value (see Figure 4.12).

The creation of the Configuration document and the selection of parameters for shared mail will not execute immediately; it depends on how busy the server is. Nonetheless, it should take only a few minutes. The result of this process is the creation of a `mailobj.nsf` file and a shared mail database named, by default, `mailobj1.nsf`.

Enabling Shared Mail Via `Notes.ini`

Within the `Notes.ini` file, `Shared_Mail=integer` can be 0 (none), 1 (shared mail for delivery only with multiple recipients), or 2 (shared mail for delivery and transfer for one or more recipients).

Figure 4.12

Enabling shared mail in the Server Configuration document.

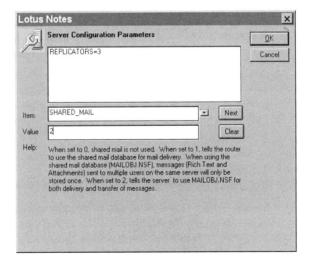

Any changes to Notes.ini will execute only after the server is brought down and back up again. The result of this method will be the creation of a mailobj.nsf file and a shared mail database named mailobj1.nsf by default.

Enabling Shared Mail Via the Server Console

At the server console, enter the following command:

```
TELL ROUTER USE shared.nsf
```

where *shared.nsf* is the name of the database file. Any filename can be used; it is not limited to mailobj1.nsf. Results of this command are the creation of the shared.nsf and mailobj.nsf files, and the Notes.ini's SHARED_MAIL parameter is set to 2.

Reviewing Results of Enabling Shared Mail

After shared mail is enabled by any of the methods discussed previously, two items will be created:

▶ mailobj.nsf—Although this file has an .nsf extension, it is really only a text file that points the router to the shared.nsf file. Anytime you specify via the TELL ROUTER USE command that a new shared.nsf file be used, mailobj.nsf will be updated to point the router to the new shared.nsf.

▶ mailobj1.nsf—This is the shared mail database, which is a secure Notes database with no views. mailobj1.nsf is a default name; I recommend that you change this name to reflect a method you will use to manage your shared mail databases. It is unlikely that you will always use only one shared mail database. As your needs grow, you will want to make this database available for existing pointers, and you will create a new database to store incoming shared mail. Depending on the size of your shared mail, you might want to name your database by month and server name. When you use the first two methods of enabling shared mail, the default name of the database is mailobj1.nsf, which you can change afterward. When you use the third method (the server console command), you can indicate the desired shared mail database name when shared mail is enabled.

Security in Shared Mail

A valid concern when using shared mail is the security afforded to users. The only way to create a shared mail database is by using one of the three methods described previously or by directing the router via the `TELL ROUTER USE newshared.nsf` command to use a new shared mail database. The `shared.nsf` that gets created in this case has no views, and none can be added. This database is inaccessible by all users, even when sitting at the server workstation using the server ID. Only the server can access it (and a server can access it only as a server, not as a server client). The shared database is encrypted so that only the server ID can read it.

Using Server Console Commands for Shared Mail

There are many console commands that you can use to manage shared mail. Before looking at these, let's examine a few scenarios you might encounter when administering shared mail.

Scenario 1

Suppose that Message 1 is in the shared mail database and three users have pointers to it. User 1 deletes the message from her mail file, but two other users still have pointers to it; the message does not get deleted from the shared database. The next day, the two remaining users delete the message from their mail files, but the message *still* does not get deleted from the shared database. To purge messages that have no pointers from databases, the `COLLECT` task must run on the server. By default, this task is set in the `Notes.ini` to run at 2 a.m. every day:

```
ServerTasksAt1=Catalog,Design
ServerTasksAt2=UpdAll,Object Collect mailobj.nsf
ServerTasksAt5=Statlog
```

If you want to force the purging of obsolete shared messages, you can type the following at the console:

```
LOAD OBJECT COLLECT shared.nsf
```

You can also use the OBJECT COLLECT command against user mail files to delete any header files that point to content that is no longer there. This should not happen often.

Scenario 2

Linda Pratt is moving to another location, and her mail file will now exist on another server. Her present mail server is using Shared_Mail=2. These steps must be followed to ensure that Linda's mail file is moved correctly:

1. All of Linda's shared messages must be unlinked from her present shared databases. To unlink Linda's shared messages, execute the following command:

   ```
   LOAD OBJECT UNLINK MAIL/Lpratt.nsf
   ```

   This will unlink all Linda's shared messages from all shared mail databases used on her mail server (see Figure 4.13).

Figure 4.13

Unlinking Linda Pratt's mail messages.

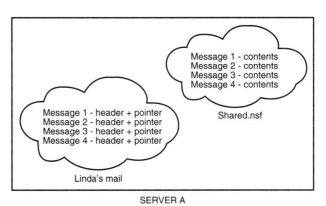

2. Linda's message-based mail file will have to be sent to her new mail server. Several methods can be used to move `Lpratt.nsf` to the new server. Use whatever options are available to you as an administrator. You can perform this task by e-mailing the file, by making replica copies of the file on the other server, or by making Linda responsible for getting the file to her new administrator.

3. Linda's message-based mail file must be linked to the shared mail on her new mail server. After the new administrator puts Linda's mail file on the server, he must link it to his shared mail database (because he is set up for `SharedMail=2`) using the following command:

```
LOAD OBJECT LINK MAIL/Lpratt.nsf
```

This command would link all of Linda's messages to the current shared mail database of the new mail server that Linda is now using (see Figure 4.14).

Figure 4.14

Linking Linda Pratt's file to a shared mail database.

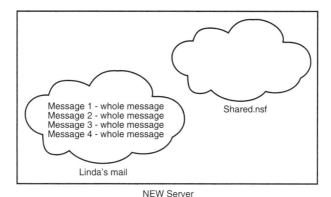

NEW Server

LOAD OBJECT LINK MAIL/PRATT.NSF

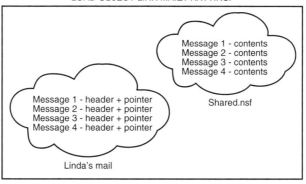

Scenario 3

You want to amalgamate the shared mail databases from the past three months into one shared database. Let's assume that all your mail users' files are in the `mail` subdirectory, the current shared mail database is `Mar97.nsf`, with `Jan97.nsf` and `Feb97.nsf` shared mail databases still being used for links created in January and February. Suppose you want to have all shared mail for the first quarter be in `Mar97.nsf` (see Figure 4.15). You would enter the following command at the console:

```
LOAD OBJECT LINK -RELINK MAIL/ MAR97.NSF
```

This command would take into consideration all the mail files under the subdirectory `mail`. Every message linked to `Jan97.nsf` or `Feb97.nsf` would be relinked to `Mar97.nsf`. Any messages in the mail file that are unlinked at the time of this command would also be linked to `Mar97.nsf`.

The `LINK -RELINK` command addresses mail linked to a specific database that you want to relink to another. The `LINK` command, as mentioned previously, links only those messages that do not have a current link.

Scenario 4

Suppose you want to find out whether a user's mail file is shared. If you want to determine a users' status as to shared mail, you can enter at the console:

```
LOAD OBJECT INFO usermail.nsf
```

You can also ask for information on the shared mail database with either of the following console commands:

```
LOAD OBJECT INFO shared.nsf
```

```
LOAD OBJECT INFO -FULL shared.nsf
```

The `-FULL` parameter provides a table of statistics and writes it to `statrep.nsf`, which is covered in Chapter 9, "Server and System Monitoring."

Figure 4.15

Relinking Linda Pratt's mail messages to another shared mail database.

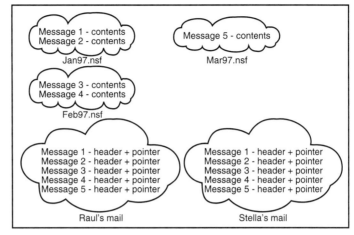

LOAD OBJECT LINK-RELINK MAIL/MAR97.NSF

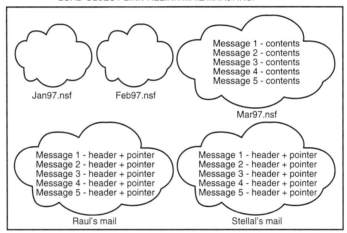

Table 4.2 reviews the console commands for shared mail.

Table 4.2

Shared mail console commands.

Console command	Description
LOAD OBJECT LINK mail.nsf shared.nsf	This command acts against the mail-file specified, or you can specify a mail directory and it will act against all mail files in the directory. The function of this command is to create

continues

Table 4.2 Continued

Console command	Description
	a link in the specified `shared.nsf` for all messages that do not have a link.
`LOAD OBJECT LINK -RELINK mail.nsf shared.nsf`	This command not only creates a link for all messages that do not currently have one, it also takes all messages that do have links and changes the link to the `shared.nsf` indicated in your command.
`LOAD OBJECT UNLINK`	This command removes all links. The contents information is returned to the database(s). You can use this command against a `mail.nsf` or a `shared.nsf`. In either case, all shared mail is returned to message-based mail.
`LOAD OBJECT COLLECT`	This command can be used against `mail.nsf` or `shared.nsf`. Its purpose in both cases is to identify any header or content information that has no valid link. After it identifies such a header or such content, it removes it from the database.
`LOAD OBJECT INFO`	This command can be used as a command for `mail.nsf` or `shared.nsf`, and will display basic information about the object store if it is one.
`LOAD OBJECT SET -NEVER usermail.nsf`	This command will exclude the specified `usermail.nsf` from shared mail.
`LOAD OBJECT RESET -NEVER usermail.nsf`	This command will remove the exclusion and include the user in shared mail.

Exceptions to Shared Mail

Even if you have `Shared_Mail=2`, messages will still be saved to an individual's mail file when:

- ▶ The user encrypts incoming mail—Shared mail will store encrypted outgoing mail.

- ▶ The user saves mail—When a user saves mail before or when sending it, the router never sees the message; therefore, the router can't place the message in the shared database. If the a user wanted to place the message in the shared database, she would have to CC: herself.

- ▶ The user makes replica copies of her `mail.nsf`—As soon as a user makes a replica copy of her database, all her shared content is copied to her replica. This makes sense because a remote user won't have access to the shared database on the server.

- ▶ The user edits and saves the message—When a user edits a message, its contents are being changed. So when the new message is saved, it is not seen by the router and not put in the shared database.

Shared Mail Database Backup

A main concern when sharing mail content among multiple users is to ensure that you have a backup plan. Because the shared mail database is open and active most of the time, your backup facility must accommodate open files. At minimum, you should back up the shared mail database once a day; in reality, you'll probably want to back it up two or three times a day.

User's Mail File and Shared Mail

Users whose mail files are on servers using shared mail will not be aware of the fact. Their mail will appear to them no different from message-based mail. The links that direct their headers to the appropriate contents will be transparent, even if different headers point to contents in different `shared.nsf` databases. Users would become aware of shared mail if one of the shared mail databases was deleted or corrupted and the contents of their mail messages not found.

Administering Mail in Notes

Users will come to you with concerns and problems related to their mail databases. As an administrator, you will be responsible for ensuring the quick delivery of messages. The following tools will enable you to monitor and resolve mail problems.

Quotas and Limits

Quotas and limits on databases are discussed in detail in Chapter 6, "Administration Tools," but it is important to note here that mail databases are exceptions to these rules. Even if you put a quota on a mail database and the quota is reached, it will not prevent Notes from accepting mail for users. Although the quota will prevent users from saving mail, users can circumvent this by mailing to themselves.

Dead and Pending Mail

As an administrator, you should be concerned if you have any dead mail sitting in the `mail.box` or if you have unusual amounts of pending mail. *Dead mail* refers to messages that cannot be delivered and about which a delivery-failure notice cannot be sent. Dead mail is quite serious in that the sender is not aware her mail was not delivered. When messages fail due to invalid recipient names, the message goes back to the sender with a note as to why the message wasn't delivered; this is not considered dead mail.

Pending mail is all a function of how you set your mail schedules. You might have a large number of pending messages going to Germany because you choose to send to Germany only once a day. Should you find large amounts of mail pending for a server to which you have a flat-rate leased line, you might want to reconsider what you enter in the Route at Once field in the Server Connection document.

High- and Low-Priority Mail

When a user creates a mail message, he or she is offered the choices in the Delivery Options dialog box (see Figure 4.16).

Figure 4.16

High, medium, and low priority mail delivery options.

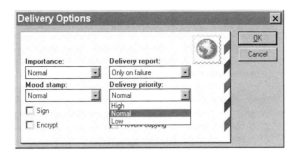

These priorities are of great interest to you, the administrator, because they affect how the mail will be delivered:

- ▶ High—This selection overrides the scheduled Server Connection document and forces the connection to send this piece of mail. Of course, if your scheduled connection is set to ROUTE AT ONCE IF 1, this will not be a problem. Otherwise, you have the option of disabling mail priority through a Notes.ini setting of MailDisablePriority=1.

- ▶ Medium—This selection indicates that the mail will go at the regular scheduled time or when ROUTE AT ONCE IF is reached.

- ▶ Low—By default, low priority mail is automatically sent only between 12 a.m. and 6 a.m.; the trick here is to create a Server Connection document between Notes named networks for this time range or to modify the existing Server Connection documents to include this range of time. If you fail to do this, low priority mail will sit in the mail.box and not be delivered. Your other option is to use a setting in the Notes.ini that specifies a different time range for low priority mail (for example, MailLowPriorityTime=20:00-22:00), and have a Server Connection document that address this range. Remember, this must be a range; you cannot specify a single time.

Note

These priority levels apply only to mail that is being sent outside a Notes named network; mail sent within a Notes named network is sent immediately, unless classified as low priority. Low priority mail is, by default, routed only between midnight and 6 a.m. within the same Notes Named Network.

Troubleshooting Mail Problems

Notes provides a new tool, Mail Trace, for determining where mail roadblocks exist. Find this tool under File I Tools I System Administration I Mail I Send I Mail Trace (see Figure 4.17).

Figure 4.17

Sending Mail Trace in Notes.

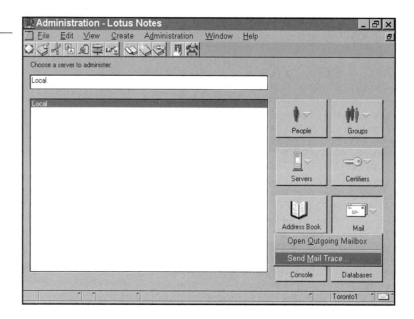

Mail Trace undergoes the same process as delivering a message, but stops short of leaving a message in the intended recipient's mail file. Your options are to receive information from each router or from only the last router (which is usually the source of the problem). The trace report is then delivered to your mail file (see Figure 4.18).

Figure 4.18

Mail Trace input.

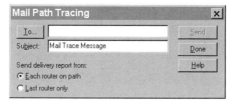

One annoying thing about this otherwise great tool is that if you have a certain schedule for mail delivery, there is no way to force the trace by specifying it as high priority; the trace will occur only at normal priority.

Remote Users and Mail

As an administrator, you should be familiar with all the components that a remote user would employ to ensure that Notes mail and its functions operate for them. One of the new features that users will notice is the Location documents in their personal address books. These default Location documents are created when the user is set up. They are meant to simplify the Notes environment so that when a user changes her physical location, she can set up her corresponding Notes settings by choosing the correct Location document.

Creating Replica Copies

Before a user can walk away from the server and expect to be able to create, send, or receive mail, she must create a replica copy of her `mail.nsf` for her laptop. Without this local replica copy, the user will have no access to her mail and will not be able to read, respond to, or create mail. Have the user select her server mail file and select File | Replication | New Replica | Immediately before she leaves the office or separates from the server.

Location and Server Connection Documents

There is a Location document for every possible Notes environment and then some. You might find it convenient to delete some of the defaults, which are as follows:

▶ Office (Network)

▶ Travel (Modem)

▶ Island (Disconnected)

▶ Home (Modem)

The remote user must also have the correct Server Connection documents to connect to the mail server identified in the Location document. These documents are discussed in the section about passthru replication in Chapter 3, "Replication."

The Replicator Page

The replicator page enables remote users to set their replication parameters based on their location. If the remote user is working at home for the next week, he can set up a schedule for mail and replication in his Location document. If the user is traveling, replication and mail can be done on an as-needed basis, and only certain databases will be replicated.

Getting New Mail While Remote

Replication of a remote user's mail file will allow him to receive mail delivered to his mail server. Replication will send him all mail that has been delivered to the server copy of his `mail.nsf`. However, replication of his `mail.nsf` will do nothing to send the mail he has created remotely.

Sending Mail While Remote

When a remote user is attached to no server, a `mail.box` database, similar to the one on mail servers, is created on the user's workstation. The user then starts creating mail and sending it, but because he is not attached to any server, the mail is deposited in his `mail.box`. After he is connected to a server, he will either initiate or be prompted to send his outgoing mail (in his `mail.box`) to the server's `mail.box`. After the mail is transferred to the server's `mail.box`, the router takes over and sends the mail to its destination.

Shared Mail

When users are working with a local replica copy of their `mail.nsf`, none of the messages on that copy are shared because they are not attached to the server. This does not mean that the messages on the server's copy of the `mail.nsf` are no longer shared, just that after you make a local replica copy, you are taking the whole message (the header as well as the content) with you.

Using Remote Encryption and Name and Address Type-Ahead

Encryption and name and address type-ahead are available only if you have the Person document of the person to whom you want to encrypt or whose name you want to check. There are two ways that remote users can make Person documents available to themselves:

▶ In the Public Address Book, select the Person document and copy and paste it to the personal address book.

▶ Select the Public Address Book on the server and select File | Replication | Make a New Replica | Replication Settings. Under Space Savers, click Replicate a Subset Of and choose People.

Mail Security in Notes

Users must feel that their mail is safe. As an administrator, you should be able to explain their choices to them at different levels of security. Let's examine how users can send secure mail, protect received mail, and defend their local replica copies of their mail files.

Notes users have two keys, based on the RSA cryptosystem dual-key system, assigned to their user ID:

▶ Private key—Anything encrypted with private key can be decrypted only with the public key. This key is located in the user ID file.

▶ Public key—Anything encrypted with the public key can be decrypted only with the private key. This key is located in the user ID file and Person document in the Public Address Book.

For example, suppose I want to send an encrypted message to Linda. To do so, I enable the Encrypt check box in the Delivery Options dialog box (refer to Figure 4.16). The Notes system retrieves the public key from Linda's Person document. Notes then encrypts the mail message using this key before sending it to my server's `mail.box`. This encrypted mail message might cross several servers before arriving at Linda's mail server. Regardless of where it is, the only key able to decrypt this message is Linda's private key. The location of Linda's private key is in her user ID file, which is hopefully password-protected.

If you don't have access to the Person documents, you can't encrypt a mail message (for example, when you are remote with no immediate access to the Public Address Book). When remote users want to encrypt, they must either take a replica copy of the Public Address Book (preferably a subset of it containing only the Person documents) with them or copy and paste the relevant Person documents to their Personal Address Book.

When a user wants to protect her own incoming mail, she can enable encryption in her Person document. When a user wants to encrypt all mail that she sends or saves, she can do so through the Mail tab of the User Preferences dialog box. Simply select the Encrypt Sent Mail, Encrypt Saved Mail, and Sign Mail options (see Figure 4.19).

Figure 4.19

Settings for encrypting all sent or saved mail.

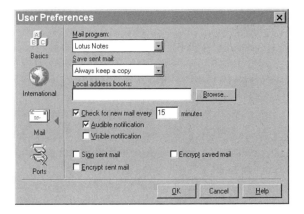

In this dialog box, the user has the option of signing the mail she sends. This is not a scanned-in picture of the user's signature; rather, it is a signal of the sender's private key. When the recipient receives the mail, the private key is decrypted with the sender's public key from the Public Address Book. The message box at the bottom will read `Signed by Username on SignedDate`. The data in the mail itself is not encrypted. Signing is a method of verifying and trusting who sent you the message. This trust is established because the public key can decrypt the private key of the sender. Signing can also be done on each individual message throughout the Delivery Options dialog box.

Note

> The dual-key RSA cryptosystem just described is used for encryption and decryption for mail. A different method, *single-key encryption*, is used for field and network-data encryption. In the single-key method, the same key is used to decrypt and encrypt the data.

Users will approach you with concerns about the security of their mail. The following two sections provide information to illustrate the importance of the user ID file and of security relating to mail files.

The user ID File Is Lost

If a user loses his user ID file, he will have lost his certificate(s), keys, and hierarchical name. Without these things, he will have no access to servers; if he has encrypted his local replica database copies, he will have no access to them either.

What can you, as an administrator, do for such a user? The best thing is to have a backup copy of his user ID. If you don't have one, you can re-create it. The user can be given the same name and certificate, meaning that he can access his servers again and all databases in which his name is listed. However, you cannot re-create the user's private key. Without the private key, any encrypted mail in his `mail.nsf` is lost.

Access to Users' Mail Files

When a user mail file is created, the ACL lists the user and his mail server as `manager`. All others are defined as `no access`. Administrators are not allowed access to mail file. However, the server copy of the mail file can be read by anyone gaining local access to the server, and the user's local copy of his mail file can be read by someone gaining access to his machine. Two new functions, available in release 4, pertain to securing both the server copy and the user's local replica copy of the mail file:

▶ The local encryption of database

▶ The enforcement of a consistent ACL across all replica copies of the database

Both of these functions are covered in detail in Chapter 5, "Security."

Exercises

Users are very interested in their mail. As system administrator, the better versed you are about your mail system, the more your users will appreciate you. The Notes mail system uses a router server task to deliver the mail. The router gets all the information it needs to do its job from the Public Address Book. Person, Server, and Server Connection documents are the most relevant. Shared mail can be very beneficial to your system if a large number of users share mail messages. Mail monitoring is covered in Chapter 9, and enabling cross-certification for mail purposes is covered in Chapter 7, "Naming Conventions and Certification." For now, let's review some exercises that will help you better grasp the information you learned in this chapter.

Exercise 4.1

In this exercise, you will cover mail routing. Make sure your server is up and the router task is running, then complete the following steps:

1. From the server's client session, open Pedro's mail file by selecting File | Database | Open. Choose the `mail` subdirectory, and then choose Pedro's mail file. Select the "Open" button.

2. After you are in Pedro's mail file, create a new memo. Remember that you are the server sending this mail, not Pedro.

3. In the To field, enter Pedro's name and send the mail.

4. You will see the message `mail submitted for delivery` in the status bar.

5. Going back out to the default view, you will see the mail message delivered. The sender is identified as `Toronto1`.

Exercise 4.2

In this exercise, you will enable shared mail and examine the results of doing so. Message-based mail (that is, every user receives

continues

his own copy of the message in the mail file) is the default. In this lab, you are going to change your server to `Shared_Mail=2`. Follow these steps:

1. At the server console, enter `TELL ROUTER USE Jan98.nsf`. This will accomplish three things:

   ▶ It will update the `Notes.ini` to `Shared_Mail=2`.

   ▶ It will create the `mailobj1` pointer file.

   ▶ It will create the shared mail database, `Jan98.nsf`.

2. Check your server to verify that these three things occurred.

`Shared_Mail=2` is now enabled for your server. Unfortunately, because you have only one server, you cannot experiment with sending mail to multiple users across different servers.

Review Questions

1. True or false: John sends an encrypted message to Peter, whose mail server is using `Shared_Mail=2`. The server receives the message and, even though it's encrypted, puts it in the shared mail database.

2. True or false: Peter decides to encrypt his incoming mail. His server still stores the mail in the shared mail database.

3. `Shared_Mail=2` is on all servers (A, B, C, and D). A message is sent; it travels from A to B to C to D. The recipients of the message exist on D. How many shared mail databases will this message be written to?

   a. 1

   b. 2

   c. 3

   d. 4

4. `SharedMail=1` affects

   a. Transfer

   b. Delivery

   c. Transfer and delivery

5. What does it mean when you sign a mail message?

   a. The recipient will see a signature.

   b. The recipient will see the message `This message was signed by` *username on signed date* in the message box.

   c. The recipient will see the message `Trust this information.`

6. What is signing used for?

   a. Data security

   b. Source trust

   c. Path trust

7. True or false: `mailobj.nsf` is the name of the default shared mail database.

8. Enabling shared mail can be done in what document?

   a. The Server document

   b. The Server Configuration document

   c. The Server Connection document

9. To link all messages for Peter, who has been using shared mail to a specific shared mail database (`Mar97.nsf`), which command would you use?

   a. `LOAD OBJECT LINK MAIL/PETER.nsf Mar97.nsf`

   b. `LOAD OBJECT RELINK MAIL/PETER.nsf Mar97.nsf`

   c. `LOAD OBJECT LINK -RELINK MAIL/PETER.nsf MAR97.NSF`

10. True or false: There is no way to exclude users from shared mail if you have your server set to

    SharedMail=2.

11. After all users have deleted their pointers to a message, how are the contents removed?

    a. Automatically

    b. LOAD OBJECT UNLINK

    c. LOAD OBJECT COLLECT

    d. LOAD OBJECT DELETE

12. Server Connection documents contain Call At fields in which you can enter a range of times. If the connection is not made on the first attempt, what will Notes do?

    a. Try to connect every 15 minutes.

    b. Keep trying for 60 minutes, increasing the length of time between each subsequent attempt.

    c. Keep trying for the entire range, increasing the length of time between each subsequent attempt.

13. All encryption keys are kept secure in the user ID file. Suppose a user loses his ID and there is no backup. If you re-create a new user ID file, the user will

    a. Never be able to access his mail file again

    b. Never be able to read his encrypted mail

14. A router gets all its information for delivery from

    a. The Public Address Book

    b. mail.box

    c. The mailer

15. Routers determine the path to the next server. What are Server Connection documents used for?

    a. Delivery across Notes named networks

    b. Delivery within Notes named networks

    c. Delivery across domains

16. True or false: If the Route at Once level is reached and low-priority mail is in `mail.box`, it will be sent as well.

17. `SharedMail` is set at `2`. A user receives a mail message addressed only to her, and it is stored in the shared mail database. The users edits the message. What happens to the edited message?

    a. It is stored in the shared mail database.

    b. It is removed from the shared mail database and put in the user's mail file.

18. True or false: The administrator has set a quota on all users' mail files. Although user A has reached his limit, when he receives a new message, it is accepted.

19. True or false: Routing costs are fixed. All LAN connections must be `1` and all dial-ups must be `5`.

20. True or false: Routing costs help servers determine how to send mail within Notes named networks.

Review Answers

1. True. When an encrypted message enters the shared mail database, it will remain there. However, when a user decides to encrypt mail he or she has received, it is put in the user's mail file. For more information, refer to the section titled "Shared Mail."

2. False. Once the user decides to encrypt the message, it becomes different from all others and is put in the user's mail file. For more information, refer to "Shared Mail."

3. D. Each time a message is received and shared mail is enabled, the message is deposited in the shared mail database and then deleted if no recipients are found on the server. For more information, refer to "Shared Mail."

4. B. With SharedMail=1, mail is stored in the shared mail database only if there are at least two recipients. If there is only one (or no) recipient, the message is never written to the shared mail database. This is in contrast to SharedMail=2, which affects both the transfer and delivery of mail. For more information, refer to "Shared Mail."

5. B. Signing a mail message verifies who sent the message. For more information, refer to the section titled "Mail Security in Notes."

6. B. Signing verifies the source of the message; it illustrates that the message came from who it said it did. For more information, refer to "Mail Security in Notes."

7. False. The default name of the shared mail database is mailobj1.nsf. For more information, refer to "Shared Mail."

8. B. The Server Configuration document can specify SharedMail=(0,1,or 2). For more information, refer to the section titled "Enabling Shared Mail."

9. C. RELINK links all messages, linked or unlinked, to the new shared mail database. The RELINK command must be used in conjunction with the LINK command. For more information, refer to "Shared Mail."

10. False. You can use the command LOAD OBJECT SET -NEVER usermail.nsf. For more information, refer to "Shared Mail."

11. C. The COLLECT task purges obsolete messages from the shared mail database. For more information, refer to "Shared Mail."

12. C. Notes will try for the entire duration of the range, and will increase the length between each attempt. For more information, refer to the section titled "The Server Connection document."

13. B. All parts of the user ID file can be re-created except the private key. Without the private key, decryption of the messages is impossible. For more information, refer to the section titled "Mail Security in Notes."

14. A. All the documents in the Public Address Book let the router know how to deliver a message. For more information, refer to the section titled "Using the Router."

15. A and C. No Server Connection documents are needed for delivery within a Notes named network; delivery is automatic. For more information, refer to the section titled "Delivering Mail."

16. False. Low priority mail will be sent only at the default time and if a Server Connection document is in the Public Address Book. For more information, refer to the section titled "High and Low Priority Mail."

17. B. The user is altering the document and saving it; saved documents do not get put in the shared mail database. For more information, refer to the section titled "Exceptions to Shared Mail."

18. True. Even if the quota is reached on a mail file, the message will be accepted. For more information, refer to the section titled "Administering Mail in Notes."

19. False. The numbers for the Cost field can be anything from 1 to 10 (lowest to highest). For more information, refer to the section titled "The Server Connection document."

20. False. No Server Connection documents are needed to send mail within Notes named networks. For more information, refer to the section titled "Delivering Mail."

Answers to Test Yourself Questions at Beginning of Chapter

1. Notes uses a dual-key method for encryption of mail. The public key of the recipient is used to encrypt the message, and the private key of the recipient is used for decryption. For more information, see "Mail Security in Notes."

2. Yes. Each router is responsible for determining the message's full path. For more information, see "Using the Router."

3. Messages for two or more users are stored in the shared mail database. For more information, see "`Shared-Mail=1.`"

4. Unlike replication, where one Server Connection document can issue a two-way replication task, mail needs to see a Server Connection document for each direction the mail takes (that is, from server A to server B and from server B to server A). For more information, see "The Server Connection Document."

C h a p t e r

Security

5

This chapter will introduce you to the different types of security in Notes:

 Objectives

- ▶ Physical

- ▶ Validation and authentication

- ▶ Server access

- ▶ ACL

- ▶ Database design security

- ▶ Encryption

Test Yourself! Before reading this chapter, test yourself to determine how much study time you will need to devote to this section.

1. What is the authentication process invoked for?

2. What are databases secured with?

3. Does network encryption use the dual-key system?

4. Will the Access Control List accept common-name components independent of the full hierarchical name?

5. How is additional Public Address Book security provided?

6. To protect access to a server, would you enforce authentication?

Answers are located at the end of the chapter...

Security is addressed in every aspect of Notes—from user Ids and access to servers and databases to encryption and mail issues. Each Notes component is secured using an appropriate system. Later chapters discuss other aspects of Notes security: Chapter 6, "Administration Tools," further addresses security features with recertification; Chapter 7, "Naming Conventions and Certification," discusses cross-certification; and Chapter 9, "Server and System Monitoring," covers monitoring for security breaches.

Before you begin this chapter, you should understand how Access Control Levels are used to protect databases, and you should understand the security factors in a database.

Understanding the Lotus Notes Security Levels

Six main levels of security are used within Notes. These six levels are grouped by the sequence in which they are applied. Remember in the old TV series *Get Smart*? When Maxwell Smart, Agent 66 for Control, entered HQ, he had to pass through a series of secure doors. No door was opened for him until he gained access to the previous one. You can think of Notes security in the same way. The six major levels of security are

- ▶ Physical
- ▶ Validation and authentication
- ▶ Server access
- ▶ ACL
- ▶ Database design security
- ▶ Encryption

After you review all the levels of security (see Figure 5.1), you will see that Notes can be very secure. But depending on how you configure Notes, it also can be *un*secure. As you read about the levels, I will point out the defaults, which are set for an open system. If you want your Notes environment to be extremely secure, review all the security functions discussed in this and other security-related chapters of this book, and ensure that the defaults are reset to your specifications.

Figure 5.1

The security levels in Notes.

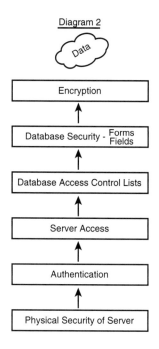

Diagram 2

Physical Security

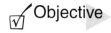 Objective

The physical security of the Notes server is of paramount importance. The Notes server must be locked in a room with limited physical access to ensure against circumvention. Just as you wouldn't allow anyone access to your file servers or routers, you should protect your Notes servers. You can also use the following console command to secure your servers:

Set Secure

This command protects your server by not allowing the use of the commands LOAD, TELL, SET CONFIG, or EXIT. The command is imperfect, though, as it doesn't prevent any of your database files from being copied from the server. There is also the chance of exposure with this security measure in that the password protection is identified in the Notes.ini. Someone could open the Notes.ini and delete the setting line. They could then restart the server and have full access. The Set secure *password* security feature is useful, but employ it with knowledge of its limitations.

SET SECURE *password*

Depending on the operating system on which the Notes server is running, you can invoke the OS security mechanisms to protect Notes databases and server files. Remember, however, that the chance of exposure here comes through the operating system's access to both database and server-file information.

Validation and Authentication

 Every time users attempt to reach a server, they must validate and authenticate. The same is true when servers attempt to access each other. Although you will often hear both these processes referred to as *authentication*, you should remember that both validation and authentication are involved each time an entity attempts server access.

Think of the authentication process as resembling a family reunion. Suppose, for example, you arrive at the reunion for the descendants of Napoleon. Before you are accepted, you must prove that you belong. You must pass two tests to prove this:

▶ You must provide a certificate that proves who you are—You bring the notarized birth certificates of every member of the direct line between Napoleon's son and you.

▶ You must possess a genetic key shared among all descendants— You, like the other members of Napoleon's family, have the ability to decipher Napoleon's battle plan for the Battle of the Pyramids.

In Notes, you also must prove who you are; like the members of Napoleon's family, Notes demands that you possess the key to decipher an encryption test presented by the server.

Before you begin the process of validation and authentication, you should examine the contents of your user ID file by choosing File, Tools, User ID, and then entering the correct password. You can then examine:

▶ Hierarchical username

▶ License

▶ Certificate(s)

- ▶ Public key associated with the ID

- ▶ Private key associated with the ID

- ▶ Encryption key(s) for databases (optional)

A hierarchical user file contains only one hierarchical certificate, which identifies your "line of descent" within the organization. A key is associated with each level of the hierarchical name. When you authenticate with a server, the following occurs (this example assumes that you and the server belong to the same organization; I discuss how to authenticate when you belong to different organizations in Chapter 7):

1. You present the certificate containing your line of descent along with the keys associated with each level.

2. The server examines each of the keys beginning with the key you have in common: the one associated with the organization level.

3. When the server trusts the common key (the organization-level key), it uses that key to check and trust each of the following keys until it finally arrives at your key, checks it, and trusts it.

The authentication process is now complete; the server trusts your public key. It now wants to validate your public key:

1. The server chooses a random number and encrypts it using your trusted public key.

2. The server sends this encrypted number to you. You must decrypt the number using your private key and send the number back to the server.

3. If the correct number is returned, you are accepted.

Server Access

 The next step in your examination of security levels is to determine whether the servers allow you access. Just because you have

passed an authentication test does not mean you get immediate access to the server. Access restrictions to the server are identified in the Server document in the Public Address Book. The Restrictions and Security sections of the Server document are shown in Figure 5.2.

Figure 5.2

The server access control sections of the Server document.

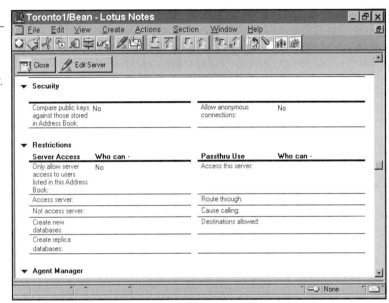

Even though each field is fairly self-explanatory, there are blank fields that can be confusing. In some cases, a blank field allows everyone access; in other cases, a blank field allows no one access. It is important, therefore, to understand what you are allowing when you leave the field blank. These fields and their descriptions are as follows:

▶ Only Allow Server Access to Users Listed in This Address Book—Although some administrators assume that if they remove a user's Person document from the Public Address Book, they remove that person's access to the servers, this is not the case. A user with a valid user ID can authenticate with the server. After he or she has authenticated, the next step is for the server to check the Server document. If this field is set to Yes, the server compares the name of the user to the names in the Person document. If there is no Person document for this user, the user will be denied access to the server. The default is No.

▶ Access Server—This field specifies who can access this server by name (users, servers, and groups). Caution: As soon as you put names in this field, those users become the only ones who can access the server. A blank field allows access to all but does not override authentication or other security fields. The default is blank.

▶ Not Access Server—This field overrides the Access Server field if the same name is found in both fields. Even if users authenticate with the server, they are denied access. I strongly suggest that you create a group called Terminated and keep this group name in this field for all servers. A blank field, which is the default, denies no one.

▶ Create New Databases—This field specifies who can put a new database on the server. Incredibly, a blank field, which is the default, allows all who gain access to put a database on the server. This is one field you probably want to change right away; you should decide whether you want designers or administrators to be responsible for putting databases on the servers.

▶ Create Replica Databases—This field specifies who can put replica databases on the server. A blank field (the default) indicates that no one—not even the server—can put replica copies on the servers. In most cases, this is the job of the administrator.

Although Notes is getting better at caching field contents and updating the cache when fields change, there are still certain fields in which Notes.ini does not reflect changes unless the server is brought down and back up again.

Using Group Names

This section discusses the use of group names versus usernames in relation to Server document security fields. Group names can and should be used in any field relating to users or servers. This suggestion applies not only to fields in the Server document but also to Access Control Lists (ACLs) and other document fields related to users.

The following example illustrates how I've handled group names versus server names. Suppose that Bill Vincent of the Bean organization has been transferred from the Marketing department in Toronto to the HQ department in New York. This transfer involves a hierarchical name change for Bill, which is addressed through the administration process (covered in Chapter 6).

How do I address all the database ACLs and field contents where Bill is listed? In his new group HQ, Bill is allowed higher access to certain databases; he also has special rights in some of the security fields in the New York network. The Marketing department, on the other hand, wants Bill removed from some of its internal databases.

This would have been a daunting task if I had used Bill's username in all these locations. Luckily, when building my Notes environment, I decided to create groups for all my departments and subgroups within departments if needed. I then used these group names in the ACLs and the security fields in various documents. Now when someone transfers in or out of a department (group), only the group document needs to be changed (the member is either added or deleted). Nothing else needs to be done. So in this case, I can take Bill out of the Marketing group and add him as `Bill Vincent/HQ/Bean` to the HQ group. Very simple! See Figure 5.3 for a sample group document.

Figure 5.3

A sample group document.

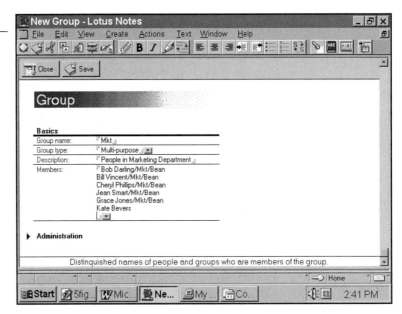

 Note Although group names are not hierarchical, you should put the hierarchical name of the users or servers in the Members field.

Using Wildcards

In addition to using groups to simplify your security procedures, you can use the wildcard (*) feature. Although using the word "wild" in connection with security might make you nervous, I think you will find this feature useful.

Suppose that in the marketing database (Mkt.nsf), the Access Control Level for the Marketing department should be author. You can set this by putting the group name Mkt in the ACL as author, or you can put */Mkt/Bean in the ACL as author. This tells the Mkt.nsf that *anyone* who identifies Bean as the organization and Mkt as the first organizational unit in his or her hierarchical name is allowed access as author. This wildcard feature can also be used in any of the security or restrictions fields on the Server document including the Access Server field. For example, you can enter */Bean in this field to allow entrance to only those users who have Bean identified as an organization in their hierarchical names. Wildcard naming is a benefit of using hierarchical naming. You can then use organization identifiers or even organizational unit identifiers in ACLs and access fields.

 Note

Wildcards cannot be used for mail-addressing purposes. Notes has not enabled this as a mail function—its use could be too far-reaching and end up creating mail where it is not intended.

Understanding the Access Control List

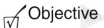 **Objective**

After users pass the authentication level and server access fields, they are in the server and looking for specific databases. It is only at this point that the Access Control Lists for each database come into play. Each database has its own ACL. Each user who attempts to access the database is judged against the ACL. A user's access level to a database must be set in each separate database ACL—the user cannot have a "global" access level set for all databases. Table 5.1 examines the options available in the ACL.

Table 5.1

Available ACL options.

Level	Functions available
manager	A manager has all the rights of the levels below it and, in addition, is the only one who can change the ACL and delete the database.
designer	A designer has all the rights of the levels below it and is also allowed to create/edit/delete all aspects of the database design, including views, forms, and fields.
editor	An editor has all the rights of the levels below it and, in addition, can edit/delete documents he or she did not create.
author	An author has the right to create documents, and to edit and delete documents for which he or she is listed as an author in the Authors type field on the document. Authors can read all documents.

continues

Table 5.1   Continued

Level	Functions available
reader	Readers can only read documents. They have no creation capability.
depositor	Depositors can create and save documents, but cannot read or edit their documents. The depositor option is best used in databases in which you are interested in capturing information but not sharing it (for example, with voting, user-feedback, and mailbox databases).
no access	No access to the database at all.

These access levels are fairly straightforward, but you should be aware of additional settings that can modify how these levels act. For example, Linda Pratt is identified in the ACL as manager, but I have removed her right to delete documents. You want at least one manager to be able to delete documents, but denying a certain manager the right to delete documents might provide a needed level of security. Take another look at the levels and see what you can modify for each one (see Table 5.2).

Table 5.2

Possible modifications to access levels.

Access level	Possible modifications in the ACL
manager	You can deny the manager the ability to delete documents.
designer	You can deny the designer the ability to delete documents and create LotusScript agents.
editor	You can deny the editor the ability to delete documents and create personal agents, personal folders/views, shared folders/views, and LotusScript agents.

Access level	Possible modifications in the ACL
author	You can deny the author the ability to create and delete documents and to create personal agents, personal folders/views, and LotusScript agents.
reader	You can deny the reader the ability to create personal agents, personal folders/views, and LotusScript agents.

Most of the modifications make sense and can provide additional security. There is some confusion, though, over denying the author the ability to create documents. Why would you identify a user as an author but not allow that user to create any documents? When you answer this question in the context of a database such as the Public Address Book, however, it makes more sense. For example, as the owner of the Public Address Book, I might choose to list each person as the author of his or her Person document so that he or she can edit certain fields. I never want these users to create new documents or be able to delete their Person documents, so I remove these capabilities in their author settings.

Identifying User Types

As well as defining who is a manager, designer, editor, and so forth, you can identify in the ACL the type of users that the manager, designer, and editor are. For example, suppose you have a group called admins that lists the top-level administrators. They are in the ACL of the Public Address Book as managers. Suppose further that someone then creates a user ID with the name admins. If this user gains access to the server and then to the Address Book, his or her name, admins, would match the entry in the ACL with the level manager. If you specified the group admins as a person group, however, the ACL would not allow the user admins in at the group setting. For added security, all your ACL entries should be identified by type (see Figure 5.4). If you leave the ACL entry as unspecified, the ACL will not discriminate; it will match by person, server, or group.

Figure 5.4

Specifying user types in the Access Control List.

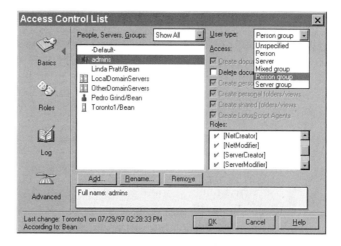

Ways to Access Server Databases

You can open a database while sitting at the server machine by selecting File | Database | Open. This invokes the dialog box shown in Figure 5.5. This dialog box contains a minimum of two choices: Local and *Server Name* (the name of the server at which you are sitting).

Figure 5.5

Accessing the databases locally or through the server at the server client station.

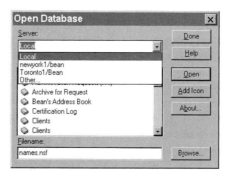

When you see the Local and *Server Name* choices at a user workstation, it makes sense because you are searching for your own local data directory or for a specific server name. But when you are sitting at a server, choosing either option invokes the same list of databases. The difference between going into a server's databases through the local data directory versus through the actual server name is that when you choose the Local option and open the database, you are circumventing the ACLs.

For example, suppose that Toronto1/Bean has a personnel database and the ACL lists Toronto1/Bean as editor. You can circumvent the ACL by opening selecting File | Database | Open | Local | Personnel; this gives you manager-level access to the database. If you select File | Database | Open | Toronto1/Bean | Personnel to open the database, you get editor-level access to the database.

Caution   Be aware of how you open a database. You might think you have a higher level of access than the ACL allows you in replication. There is a new Local Enforcement of ACL option that does not allow the circumvention of ACLs. This topic is covered later in this chapter in the section titled "Local Enforcement of the ACL."

ACL Defaults

After the user has authenticated with the server and passed the server access control settings, he or she is ready to begin searching for databases. ACLs are the protectors of the database in that the users of the database are allowed to perform only the functions that the ACL specifies. Typically, the database developer or manager creates the ACL. As system administrator, your job involves protecting the server and databases connected to the administration of Notes environments. This responsibility involves securing these administrative databases by enforcing effective ACLs. After you become knowledgeable about securing databases using ACLs, you should ensure that your database developers and managers are aware of the capabilities and limitations of ACLs.

As system administrator, the Database ACL which concerns you the most is the ACL for the Public Address Book. This database is automatically created at first-server setup. The ACL for this database is created by default; Table 5.3 shows the default ACL created for Bean's Public Address Book.

Table 5.3

The default ACL of Bean's Public Address Book.	
Name	Level
Default	author
LocalDomainServers	manager
OtherDomainServers	reader
First server to be created	manager
First administrator to be created	manager

The ACL specifies the first server and the first administrator as managers. Two groups are also identified in the ACL: Local-DomainServers and OtherDomainServers. These two groups are created automatically when the Public Address Book is created. Every server registered in the domain automatically gets added to LocalDomainServers. LocalDomainServers are added to the ACL as a server group type and are given manager-level access with all rights. OtherDomainServers is also created automatically, but you must add servers outside your domain to this group. They are given reader-level access as a server group type, and have no other rights.

If the ACL does not identify you by name or group, you get the level of access secified by the -Default- level. Refer to Figure 5.6, which shows that the default for entrance to the Public Address Book is the author level. This setting might surprise you; when you consider the importance of this database with regards to the administration of Notes, you realize that you would not want just anyone to be able to create documents. But if you look more closely at this setting, you will see that the right to create documents has been removed. Anyone who gets the -Default- level of access to the database is allowed to read and edit the documents for which they are specified as authors in the Author field.

When a person is registered in Notes, a Person document is created. During creation, the person's name is automatically put into the Owner field, identifying him or her as the author of this document. Any person registered in Notes, therefore, is automatically given author status in his or her Person document.

Caution

> I strongly recommend a more secure ACL for a database that is as important as the one shown in Figure 5.6. In scenarios such as the one depicted, I feel more comfortable making the default `no access`. I then must determine which access levels I want certain people to be. One possibility is to specify `*\Bean` in the ACL as `author` with no document-creation rights. Doing so prevents people outside my domain from reading my Public Address Book.

Rules of Enforcement

Conflicts in the ACL might occur. For example, you might find users listed in the ACL multiple times and at different levels, or a user might be listed individually at one level and in a group at another level. How should these conflicts be handled? Here are some guidelines for ACL conflicts:

▶ If a user is listed twice, once as an individual and once in a group, the level for the individual listing overrides the level of the group listing. For example, suppose that `Linda Pratt/Bean` is listed as `author` in the ACL, and as `editor` in the Marketing group, of which she is a member. Linda receives author-level access because her individual setting takes precedence over her group setting.

▶ An individual cannot be listed twice in the ACL.

▶ If an individual is listed in more than one group, that user is granted the access at the highest group level. For example, suppose that Kate has been transferred from the Marketing group to the Productions department. She has been added to the `productions` group, which has `reader`-level rights, but has not been deleted from the `marketing` group, which has author-level rights. Linda receives the `author` setting when she opens the database.

Hierarchical Names in the ACL

One of the reasons for implementing hierarchical names is to ensure secure access to databases. When an ACL decides how you are to enter the database, it compares your username to the names in its list and to the names of the members of the groups in its list. When the ACL specifies that `Linda Pratt/Bean` is the manager of the database, the `user.id` file accessing the database *must* contain the username `Linda Pratt`. So not only is `Linda Pratt/Bean` accepted as manager, `Linda Pratt/Leaf` would be as well (Leaf is a company with which the Bean organization does some business, but with which Bean does not want to share all information). If you list only common names in the ACL, anyone with a given common name in his or her ID will be allowed access, no matter what organization or organizational unit that user is from.

Using only the common name in the ACL constitutes a breach of security. Remember: Hierarchical naming enables you to have multiple people with the same names in your organization because you can *individualize* them using organizational units and secure them using an organization identifier. If you forget to use full hierarchical names in the ACL, you allow anyone who has the common name indicated in the ACL to enter the database. That makes it possible for someone from another company, who you have cross-certified at an OU level, to create a `user.id` with a known name from your company and go exploring (see Figure 5.6).

Figure 5.6

Using common names in the Access Control List.

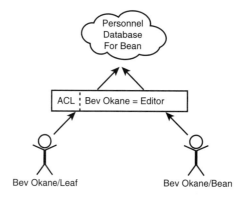

Local Enforcement of the ACL

The default access level for local database access at the client or server is manager. Suppose a user takes a replica copy of a database home with her on her laptop, opens the database, and beings to work. She realizes that she can edit documents on the server to which she was denied access, and makes changes on these documents. She then replicates to the server when she returns to the office, and complains to her administrator because the changes did not replicate.

Of course, the changes do not replicate because the server's ACL for the database did not recognize the user's right to change these documents, and refused the edits, despite the fact that the user had manager-level access when she worked on the replica copy on her laptop. To prevent this confusion, you should specify on each database ACL that the ACL is enforced at the local level (see Figure 5.7). This means that users will access the database on their local drive at the same level as on the server's copy of the database.

Figure 5.7

This dialog box is invoked when a user attempts to access a database that has been configured to locally enforce the Access Control Level.

Roles in the Access Control List

Using roles is a convenient way to assign database rights to users and servers already identified in the ACL. However, a role assignment cannot override the ACL level. For example, if I create a role in my database that allows a user to create an approval document, I can assign the role to someone who has only reader status, but that user would not be able to create documents.

As a system administrator, you should be aware of how role assignments work in the Public Address Book (see Table 5.4). To view these roles in the Access Control List, refer to Figure 5.4.

Table 5.4

Public Address Book assigned roles.

Role name	Purpose of role
GroupCreator	Only users assigned the GroupCreator role can create group documents in the Public Address Book.
GroupModifier	Authors assigned the GroupModifier role can modify group documents. Users with editor-level access and higher can modify group documents without being assigned the GroupModifier role.
NetCreator	Only users assigned the NetCreator role can create documents—with the exception of Person, Server, and Group documents—in the Public Address Book. Authors can modify the Person, Server, and Group documents only if they have the roles needed to modify those documents.
NetModifier	Authors assigned the NetModifier role can modify documents—with the exception of Person, Server, and Group documents—in the Public Address Book. Authors can modify the Person, Server, and Group documents only if they have the roles needed to modify those documents. Users with editor-level access and higher can modify documents without being assigned the NetModifier role.
ServerCreator	Only users assigned the ServerCreator role can create Server documents.
ServerModifier	Authors assigned the ServerModifier role can modify Server documents. Users assigned editor-level access and higher can modify Server documents without being assigned the ServerModifier role.
UserCreator	Only users assigned the UserCreator role can create a Person document.

Role name	Purpose of role
UserModifier	Authors assigned the UserModifier role can modify Person documents. Users with editor-level rights and higher can modify Person documents without being assigned the UserModifier role.

Through the use of these roles, an administrator can have author-level access in the Public Address Book and yet be limited to creating only group documents. Another administrator, also having author-level status in the ACL, can be assigned the UserCreator role. This would enable that administrator to create Person documents, but be restricted from creating any other type of document.

The creator roles need to be assigned even if the user is a manager in the ACL. You only need to assign modifier roles if the user is listed solely at the author level. Users with editor-level rights and higher automatically receive modifier rights.

Database Security Options

 Objective

In addition to the ACL and the roles that can be assigned in it, many other security functions are available to protect the information in the database:

- ▶ Forms and views have settings that can enhance or restrict creation and viewing capabilities.

- ▶ Authors and Readers fields can be implemented in the documents to afford additional control over individual documents.

- ▶ Encryption of fields in documents, local encryption of the entire database, and network encryption can be implemented to increase security.

Forms and Views

When creating the database, the designer is capable of implementing two types of restrictions (see Figure 5.8):

- ▶ Form reading—The application of the restriction in the "Form read access list" applies to all levels of the ACL, from Reader up to Manager. If the user isn't listed in this list, they cannot read the document at all. The only exception to this rule is that if the user is listed in an Authors field on the document, they can also read the document, even if they aren't in the Form Read Access List. The Form Read Access List restricts the reading for all levels in the ACL.

- ▶ Form creating—This restriction can remove creation rights for users assigned author status or higher unless the users are listed as creators in the form-creating restriction list.

Figure 5.8

Form security options for read and create restrictions.

View restrictions are available in the Properties for View dialog box under the Security tab (see Figure 5.9).

Figure 5.9

The available view-restriction options.

Think of the view-restriction options as convenience factors for users who don't need to see certain views. But from a security standpoint, don't depend on the view restrictions to prevent users from reading documents because most users can create their own private views to see all documents to which they have access.

Authors and Readers Fields

Within forms, certain field types can specify authors and readers for the document as a refinement, or enhancement, of the ACL, not as a way of overriding the ACL. These field types include the Authors and Readers fields. Any individual, group, or role listed in the Authors field on a document can edit the document, as long as they have Author access in the database ACL. Anybody with Editor access or higher in the ACL automatically gets editing privileges to all documents which they can read. Readers fields, however, are more restrictive. A document with a Readers field allows only users or servers whose names are in the field to read the document. A person can be listed as manager in the ACL, but if his or her name is not in the Readers field, that person cannot see the document. Using these two types of fields on a form is the most effective way to limit edit and read access to documents.

Directory Links

Notes allows the use of directory links, which allow the use of areas of disk that are not directly under the Notes\Data directory. Through the creation of a text file (with a .dir extension) that contains the path of the link, Notes will present the link as a subdirectory of Notes\Data when the user selects File | Database | Open. For example, if you have space in a directory called Sales in the root directory of the C: drive and you want to store a Notes database there, you would create a directory link file, Sales.dir, and save it in the Notes\Data directory. The contents of the file would be C:\Sales. When users select File | Database | Open, they will see a dialog box in which the Sales directory, which is really under the C: root, is shown as being under Notes\Data.

You can also use the directory link files as a security method by entering in them the group names or usernames for the people or servers you want to have access to the databases in the directory. To enable this, enter a second line in the directory link file identifying the group names or usernames. For example, if you want the database in the `Sales` directory to be available only to members of the `Sales` group, the contents of the `Sales.dir` file would be as follows:

```
C:\Sales
Sales
```

Only the people or servers identified in the directory link file would see and have access to this directory link.

Encryption

Notes uses different methods of encryption for different purposes:

▶ In database encryption, the fields in a database are encrypted.

▶ Local encryption refers to the encryption of an entire database.

▶ Network encryption refers to the encryption of database information crossing network wires.

Database-Field Encryption

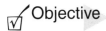 Objective

Fields in documents can be encrypted with a key. Keys relating to field encryption are incorporated into user IDs. Keys can be sent to users who you want to be able to read the encrypted fields, and those users then incorporate the key into their user IDs.

 Note

This method of encryption differs from the dual-key system used for mail-encryption purposes. With mail, one key (the public key) is used to encrypt and another key (the private key) is used to decrypt. In database-field encryption, the same key is used for encrypting as well as decrypting.

Local Encryption of Databases

If a user loses a laptop containing replica copies of databases, you want to be able to prevent whomever finds (or steals) the laptop from opening Notes and examining the information (this can be dangerous if the user's access level is high). To address this, Notes allows users to create locally encrypted databases so that anyone attempting to look at a Notes database would need the password to the user's `user.id` file. Local encryption is not the default when copies or replica copies are made; the user must enable it by selecting File | Replication | New Replica | Encryption (this invokes the dialog shown in Figure 5.10).

Figure 5.10

Local database encryption choices.

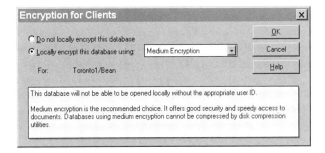

The user is given three choices for local database encryption:

▶ Strong—This setting offers maximum security, but it takes a little longer to open than the medium and weak modes. When this option is enabled, the database cannot be compressed.

▶ Medium—When this setting is enabled, documents open a bit more quickly than they do in strong mode, but this setting provides less security. When this option is enabled, the database cannot be compressed.

▶ Simple—This setting offers minimum security, but requires little overhead. When this option is enabled, the database can be compressed.

Databases can be locally encrypted after you create the replica or database copy; simply select File | Database | Properties | Encryption, enable the Locally Encrypt This Database Using radio button, enter the level of encryption you want to implement, and click OK.

Local encryption of a database differs from field encryption in that with local encryption, you will be granted access to the database if you provide the correct password. With field encryption, however, you must have the correct keys in your `user.id` to see the contents of the fields.

Network Encryption

Both users and servers can set preferences so that information traveling out of their ports is encrypted. Doing so prevents eavesdropping on the network wire and, thus, protects sensitive information. The information is encrypted only while traveling across the network; it is decrypted as soon as it reaches another Notes port. To enable network encryption, select File | Tools | User Preferences | Ports. Choose the port and the Encrypt Network Data option. Do this for every port for which you want to enable network encryption. This method of encryption uses the single-key system.

User Protection

The user.id file, which allows users to access servers and databases, must not be compromised. If it is, so too is the security of the servers and databases. A user's local or replica database copies must also be protected. As an administrator, you should always enforce the use of passwords with `user.id` files. The other method of protection involves forcing users to log off whenever they are away from their systems to prevent the unauthorized access of databases and servers.

`user.id` Password Protection

When a user is registered, the administrator can specify a password requirement and demand that a minimum number of characters be used. Doing so protects the Notes environment from anyone who manages to take a copy of the `user.id` file or gain access to it. If the `user.id` file is password-protected, there is less danger of the `user.id` file being used by an unauthorized source.

Notes has implemented the following functions to ensure the safety of your password:

▶ Time delay—Every time an incorrect password is entered, the response time is increased. Hopefully your intruder is as impatient as he is nosy.

▶ Anti-spoofing—Have you noticed that when you type your password, hieroglyphics appear on the left side of the Enter Password screen? Their purpose is to protect your password from being caught by a capture program. When the capture program runs, it looks like your password entry for Notes, but in reality it is capturing and sending your password to someone else. Memorizing the pattern of the hieroglyphics can help you detect when someone attempts to gain your password through a capture program; if you notice that the hieroglyphics are wrong when you start typing your password, you know that someone has tried to break in. If this happens to you, stop typing your password and alert your system administrator immediately.

User Logoff

Suppose you have authenticated with a server and have been working in a sensitive database. You walk away from your desk for a quick break, and are yanked into a meeting. Anyone who subsequently sits down at the vacated desk can act like you; he or she can browse databases, read mailfiles, or even send mail! Thankfully, you, the user, can protect yourself in two ways:

▶ The F5 key—Press the F5 key when you move away from your workstation. F5 performs a logoff operation and clears private user information. Anyone who tries to browse the database or resume your work at the workstation after you leave is asked for your user.id password.

▶ Automatic logoff—In the User Preferences dialog, you can configure the workstation to automatically log off after a specified number of minutes of inactivity. Before you can resume your Notes session, you must provide your user.id password.

> Many people assume that the use of multiple passwords helps protect a `user.id` file. Although it is possible to enable multiple passwords for a `user.id` file—or even a `server.id` file—it does not make sense to do so. Multiple passwords are useful for certifier IDs, but generally speaking, you, as an individual user, are responsible for only your `user.id`; therefore only a single password is required.

There are certain things that you, as an administrator, can do to ensure the security of servers and databases:

▶ Enforce the use of passwords.

▶ Educate your users as to the changing of their password and User Preferences settings.

After you have informed your users of the security standards in your organization, it becomes their job (as well as yours) to keep information secure.

Multiple Password ID Protection

Notes can assign multiple passwords to any type of ID file, including `user.id`, `server.id`, and `cert.id` files. The purpose of assigning multiple passwords is to divide the trust among two or more people. Think of it this way: To access a safety-deposit bank in a box, two keys—the bank's and the owner's—are needed. Likewise, in Notes, you can require two or more users to provide passwords before access is granted. For example, to access an ID file, you can require that a certain number of users type their passwords.

Although you can do so, using this system for a `user.id` file makes little sense. After all, you don't want to have to ask another user to enter his or her password every time you want to use your ID. Likewise, using multiple passwords for `server.id` files makes little sense. As a rule, servers don't have passwords. If your server crashes at 2 a.m. and then comes back up, you don't want the server to have to pause during startup to prompt for a password.

The multiple-password system is really intended for your certifier IDs, which are used to create user IDs and server IDs. Anyone with access to these certifier IDs can create—and even mimic existing—IDs containing valid certificates. Indeed, suppose someone with sole access to a certifier ID left the company with a copy of it in his or her possession! In such a case, you might experience some exposure; implementing multiple passwords eliminates this scenario. By assigning multiple passwords, you are ensuring that two or more people must enter their passwords before access to the certifier ID is granted. You are dividing your trust. To assign multiple passwords to a certifier ID, complete the following steps:

1. Select Tools | System Administration | Certifier IDs | Edit Multiple Passwords.

2. Choose the certifier ID to which you want to assign the multiple passwords; you must have password access to the certifier to do this. This invokes the screen shown in Figure 5.11.

Figure 5.11

Enter multiple passwords for the certifier ID.

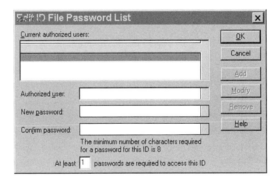

3. Add the name of the user (this need not be the hierarchical name; it can be any name the user chooses) and then type and confirm the password associated with that user.

4. Indicate the minimum number of passwords required to access this certifier ID. This process removes the original password associated with the certifier ID.

When you try to access the certifier ID, you will be presented with the dialog box shown in Figure 5.12.

Figure 5.12

Access to the certifier ID using multiple passwords.

Exercises

The following lab exercises cover testing the Access Control List and adding multiple passwords. Exercise 1 combines information you learned in this chapter with information from Chapter 2, "Server and Client Setup."

Exercise 5.1

In this exercise, you will enable your single server to use a protocol to communicate between the server session and the client session. The end result of the exercise will be that when you select File | Database | Open, two options will be available to you: Local and *Server Name*. Being able to trick the server will assist you in some of the exercises in this book.

One way to achieve this is to enable TCP/IP as your port in Notes, create an IP address in Windows, and create a host file to refer Notes to the TCP/IP address. If you have available to you a network or another way of creating the communication path, you do not need to perform the steps in this lab. Otherwise, complete the following steps:

1. Make sure your server is down.

2. In the client session, select File | Tools | User Preferences | Ports.

3. Select TCP/IP, and then click Enable.

4. Go to the Server view of the Public Address Book, and then go into the Server document for Toronto1/Bean.

5. Edit the document in the Network Configuration section.

6. In the Port field, enter TCPIP.

7. Make sure this port is set as Enabled.

8. In the Net Address field for TCP/IP, enter the TCP/IP address for your machine.

continues

9. To find this address, go to a DOS prompt in the `window` subdirectory and type the command `winipcfg`. (The above command is for use with Windows 95. If using Windows NT, type `ipconfig`.)

10. If you don't have an IP address, select My Computer | Control Panel | Network.

11. Select TCP/IP and then choose Properties.

12. Go to IP Address tab.

13. If you are running a standalone machine, enter your own IP address, and then use the same address in your Notes Server document.

14. Shut down your applications and restart your machine for this to take effect.

When you start your Notes server and server client session, you can access your server through its Notes name (for example, `Toronto1/Bean`) instead of through the Local option.

Exercise 5.2

In this exercise, you will examine the Access Control List used to protect a database. Due to the assumption that you have only one available server, you must ensure that the server session is running and is accessible through the server name, not just through the Local option.

First, you must detach the `user.id` from the Person document so you can switch to `John Valdez/Bean`. To detach the user ID, complete the following steps:

1. Go to John Valdez's Person document in Bean's Public Address Book.

2. Go to the bottom of the document, where you will see the `user.id` attachment.

3. Double-click the attachment and choose Detach.

4. Rename the file `JValdez.id`.

5. Detach it to the `Notes\Data` directory.

Before you switch to John Valdez's ID, you must add him to the ACL of Bean's Public Address Book. To do this, complete the following steps:

1. Select Bean's Public Address Book and select File | Database | Access Control.

2. From the Basics panel, choose Add, and click the Person icon.

3. Select John Valdez from the list, click Add, and then click OK (depending on who or what was selected when you added John Valdez, he will be added at the same level).

4. Ensure that `John Valdez/Bean` is set to `Author` in the Access field and to `Person` in the User Type field. Make sure he has no options checked for Document Create, Document Delete, and so on, and that no roles are selected for him.

5. Now you will switch to John Valdez's ID and access Bean's Public Address Book. To switch to John's ID, select File | Tools | Switch User ID, and select `JValdez.id` from the `Notes/Data` directory. Provide the password; you are now John Valdez.

6. Access Bean's Public Address Book and try to create a Person document, a Program document, and a Group document. You will receive the following message:

   `You are not authorized to add XXX documents to this database.`

   Even though John has author-level access, he is not allowed to create documents for two reasons:

   ▶ The Document Create option is not checked in the Public Address Book.

continues

▶ He is not assigned the role needed for the creation of certain documents.

7. To allow John to create documents, you must:

   A. Give him the ability to create documents. To do this, you must switch to the `server.id` to change the ACL. Go to Bean's Public Address Book and change the ACL to indicate that `John Valdez/Bean` has Document Create rights.

   B. Assign him the `NetCreator` role. While you are in the ACL and have `John Valdez/Bean` selected, click the `NetCreator` and `NetModifier` roles.

   These two settings will allow John Valdez to create and modify all documents—except Person, Server, and Group documents—in the Public Address Book.

8. Switch back to John Valdez's ID and attempt to create documents in the Public Address Book. Note that you cannot create Person, Server, or Group documents.

9. To finish the exercise, give John the roles to allow him to create Person, Server, and Group documents:

   A. Switch to the `server.id` and change the ACL of the Public Address Book to give John the appropriate roles.

   B. Switch back to John Valdez's ID and attempt to add a Group document. You will now be able to.

Exercise 5.3

In this exercise, you will add multiple passwords to your certifier ID, and will gain understanding about the process and logic behind this function. If you did Exercise 1 in Chapter 2, you should have your `cert.id` file in your `Notes\Data` directory. In this exercise, you will change the password associated with this file (`lotus-notes`).

1. Select File | Tools | Server Administration, and click the Certifiers icon. Choose Edit Multiple Passwords.

2. For the Choose ID for Multi Password Management option, select your `cert.id` file.

3. Enter your original password for Bean (`lotusnotes`). You will be presented with the Edit ID File Password List dialog box.

4. Enter a name, enter eight-character password two times, and click Add. Repeat these actions for additional users.

5. Enter 2 in the At Least *X* Passwords Are Required To Access This ID field.

Following are examples of names and passwords. Notice that these names are not hierarchical. Notes does not check the user ID when the passwords are entered, so there is no need to enter the hierarchical name:

Name: John Valdez   Password: `carpools`

Name: Frederick Stone   Password: `stoneages`

After you enter these names with their passwords (while keeping in mind that in the real world, each user would enter his or her own password without revealing it to others) and click OK, the original password associated with the `cert.id` file will be gone, and you will need two passwords to access the `cert.id` file. Try this:

1. Click the Certifiers icon in the Server Administration panel try to edit multiple passwords for the `cert.id` file.

2. You will see a dialog box indicating that two passwords are needed to access this ID, and you will see a list of authorized users. Enter the two passwords, and you will be granted access to the ID.

Review Questions

1. True or false: System administrators have the right to change the ACLs of databases on their servers.

2. What is the default access for the Public Address Book?

   a. no access

   b. reader

   c. author

3. True or false: Within a database's ACL, you can create authors who have no rights to create or delete documents.

4. Which type of encryption is used within Notes?

   a. RSA dual-key cryptosystem.

   b. Multiple encryption systems are used.

5. What is authentication?

   a. The process of validating and authenticating your public key.

   b. The process of checking your public key against the public key in the Public Address Book.

   c. The process of ensuring that you have a Person document in the Public Address Book.

6. In an ACL, Jenny is listed twice, once as herself (she has author-level rights) and once in a group (the group has editor-level rights). What access does Jenny have in the database?

   a. author

   b. manager

   c. editor

   d. no access

7. True or false: Roles are used to assign certain rights to people, groups, and servers already in the ACL. If a user is listed as `manager` in the Public Address Book and you want that person to be able to create Server documents, you must assign the `ServerCreator` role to that person.

8. True or false: If you want a person who is has `manager`-level rights in the ACL to be able to modify the Server documents, you must assign that person the `ServerModifier` role.

9. True or false: Field encryption uses the RSA dual-key cryptosystem.

10. True or false: A document in the database has a Readers field containing the usernames `Bob` and `Peggy`. If server A has manager-level access in the database, it will be able to read the documents.

11. True or false: A user cannot choose network encryption; only a server can.

12. Which of the following depicts the correct sequence of security levels?

    a. Server access, authentication, database ACL, encryption

    b. Authentication, server access, database ACL, encryption

    c. ACL, server access, authentication, encryption

13. Anti-spoofing involves which of the following?

    a. Hieroglyphics that change when you type your password

    b. A delayed password with each incorrect entry

14. What is the ability to apply multiple passwords useful for?

    a. User IDs

    b. Certifier IDs

    c. Both of the above

15. True of false: If John Smith/Personnel/Bean is listed as John Smith and has manager rights in the Salary database, John Smith/Maintenance/Bean will be able to access that database as manager.

16. Match the component of the hierarchical name with its respective benefit:

A. Organization component

1. Handles same-named individuals in the company

B. Organizational unit

2. Acts as a security identifier component for your company.

17. What is the Public Address Book default ACL level for all servers in the group OtherDomainServers?

a. no access

b. reader

18. True or false: The authentication process checks the public key in the ID file against the public key in the Public Address Book.

19. Using wildcards, you can identify users and servers by:

a. Organization components

b. Organizational unit components

c. Both of the above

20. You can use wildcards in which of the following?

a. The ACL

b. Fields in documents

c. Mail addressing

Review Answers

1. False. Only managers of the database have access to change the ACL of that database. If all the security options are not enforced and system administrators have physical access to the servers, administrators can change the ACLs, but this is not the way Notes is meant to be implemented. For more information, refer to the section titled "Understanding the Access Control List."

2. C. For more information, refer to the section titled "ACL Defaults."

3. True. These types of authors would be allowed to edit any documents having Authors fields in which the author is identified. For more information, refer to the section titled "Understanding the Access Control List."

4. B. RSA dual-key is used for authentication and mail encryption, but single-key encryption is used for field encryption. For more information, refer to the section titled "Encryption."

5. A. B and C can be enforced as security options, but they are not the process of authentication. For more information, refer to the section titled "Validation and Authentication."

6. A. Individual listings always override listings of a member in a group. For more information, refer to the section titled "Understanding the Access Control List."

7. True. It doesn't matter what level users have (they could be `manager`); if they don't have the role assigned to them for document creation (`ServerCreator`), they will not be authorized to create document. For more information, refer to the section titled "Roles in the Access Control List."

8. False. The `ServerModifier` editing role must be assigned only if the person is an author. Users with editor-level access and higher will automatically receive the right to edit. For more information, refer to the section titled "Roles in the Access Control List."

9. False. Field encryption uses single-key encryption. For more information, refer to the section titled "Encryption."

10. False. It doesn't matter if a user or a server is listed as `manager` in the ACL; if the document has a Readers field and the user's or server's name is not in that field, that user or server will not be able to read the document. If a server cannot read a document, it cannot replicate it either. For more information, refer to the section titled "Authors and Readers Fields."

11. False. Both users and servers can choose to encrypt information they send over the network wire. For more information, refer to the section titled " Network Encryption."

12. B. For more information, refer to the section titled "Understanding the Lotus Notes Security Levels."

13. A. The hieroglyphics change as the password is typed, so a user will know when a capture program is trying to spoof the user into providing his or her password. For more information, refer to the section titled "`user.id` Password Protection."

14. B. You want to divide the trust among several users for the certifier IDs, which are vital to your security. User IDs, however, are for single users; it would be counterproductive to apply multiple passwords because it would make it impossible for mobile users to access their `user.id` files. For more information, refer to the section titled "Multiple Password ID Protection."

15. True. When only common names are identified in the ACL, any user or server with the common name can access the database at the identified level. For more information, refer to the section titled "Understanding the Access Control List."

16. A-2, B-1. Organization components ensure that all users and servers in an organization share an ancestral certificate, which enables authentication. Organizational unit components help allow for same-named people in the naming scheme. For more information, refer to the section titled "Validation and Authentication."

17. B. Any server in the group `OtherDomainServers` will be allowed `reader` access to your Public Address Book unless you change your ACL. For more information, refer to the section titled "ACL Defaults."

18. False. The authentication process checks the common ancestral certificate keys against each other and uses the trusted key to check all other keys down the line until it arrives at a trust of the individual's key. It then checks this key against the user's private key. The checking of the public key in the ID against the public key in the Public Address Book is done through a field in the Server document, not the authentication process. For more information, refer to the section titled "Validation and Authentication."

19. C. A wildcard in Bean could be `*/Bean`, meaning anyone from the Bean organization, or `*/Tor/Bean`, meaning anyone from the Toronto region in the Bean organization. For more information, refer to the section titled "Using Wildcards."

20. A and B. Notes is not configured to handle wildcard-addressed mail. For more information, refer to the section titled "Using Wildcards."

Answers to Test Yourself Questions at Beginning of Chapter

1. The authentication process is invoked for every entity attempting access. Authentication occurs automatically each time a server or user tries to access a server, no matter where the server or user is from. For more information refer to the section titled "Validation and Authentication."

2. The Access Control list is used for each database created, and the encryption and special fields are optional. For more information, refer to the section titled "Database Security Options."

3. No, network encryption does not use the dual-key system. Instead, network encryption uses the single-key system for encryption and decryption. For more information, refer to the section titled "Network Encryption."

4. Even though you are using a hierarchical organization, Notes does not force the use of hierarchical names in the Access Control List. It will accept common names and evaluate users against only the common-name portion. For more information, refer to the section titled "Hierarchical Names in the ACL."

5. User types, roles, and local enforcement of the Access Control List can be used to increase the security of the Public Address Book. For more information, refer to the section titled "Understanding the Access Control List."

6. Authentication is only the first step in the protection of a server; instead of being something to enforce, it is automatic. You can further protect the server by using the security and restriction fields on the Server document. For more information, refer to the section titled "Server Access."

Chapter

Administration Tools

This chapter will introduce you to tools and processes that will assist you in your job as administrator. These tools include the following:

 Objectives

> ▶ The administration process
>
> ▶ The Server Administration panel
>
> ▶ Registration and recertification tools
>
> ▶ Database tools
>
> ▶ Mail tools
>
> ▶ Server logs
>
> ▶ Database catalogs and libraries

Test Yourself! Before reading this chapter, test yourself to determine how much study time you will need to devote to this section.

1. Which databases does the administration process require to be able to function?

2. To begin and complete a RENAME process through the administration process, what do you need?

3. What is the difference between a database catalog and a library?

4. Do only administrators have access to the Server Administration panel?

5. Mail activity is logged in which view(s) in the log.nsf?

6. After the initial size of a database has been chosen, can it be changed later via the Database icon in the Server Administration panel?

Answers are located at the end of the chapter...

To begin this chapter, you should have read all previous chapters and understood the concepts of Notes servers, clients, and their infrastructure. You should also completely understand the processes of replication and mail routing.

This chapter is invaluable for administrators because it discusses processes, such as the administration process, that automate tasks that were previously manual. This chapter also discusses in detail the Server Administration panel, which centralizes the tools (such as databases, tracers, registration processes, and server logs) that administrators use in their daily work.

Understanding the Administration Process

The usefulness of the administration process will not be fully obvious to you when you first set up your Notes environment. The real benefit of this process is revealed after you complete setup and changes must be made.

Suppose that in your hierarchical naming scheme, you have decided to organize your people by department. Terry Jones, who is in Sales, is recognized in Notes as `Terry Jones/Sales/Bean`. Terry then receives a promotion to a position in the Marketing department, and his hierarchical name must be changed to `Terry Jones/Mkt/Bean`.

But wait. It's not enough to change Terry's name in his `user.id` file. Consider all the places Terry is mentioned in Notes under his old name—the Access Control Lists, the Person document in Public Address Book, the Group documents, and the Readers and Authors fields. First you have to remember all the places where Terry's name has been used, and then you must find them. This can be a daunting task, especially when you consider the number of changes the average organization generates. This is where the administration process comes in. Its functions are as follows:

▶ It automates name changes in the `user.id`.

▶ It automates name changes in the Person document in the Public Address Book.

▶ It automates name changes in Group documents.

▶ It automates name changes in the ACL of all databases having Server Administrators defined.

▶ It deletes users, servers, or groups from Notes.

▶ It converts flat names to hierarchical names.

▶ Recertifies users and servers

▶ Creates replicas of multiple databases

▶ Enables password checking during authentication

Although the administration process will convert *flat* names to hierarchical names, all other administration processes will work only on hierarchical names.

The administration process does not, at this time, change the contents of Authors or Readers fields, although it is slated to do so for release 4.5.

Setting Up the Administration Process for Notes

To implement the administration process, certain databases must be created and certain server processes must be started. In addition, each database must have allocated to it an administration server. Three databases are required for most administration processes:

▶ The administration requests database (admin4.nsf)—This database is automatically created when the server starts. When a server is set up, the Notes.ini line SERVERTASKS= defaults to

SERVERTASKS=REPLICA,ROUTER,UPDATE,STATS,AMGR,ADMINP

As you'll remember from server setup, this line in the Notes.ini specifies what server tasks begin on server setup. You'll notice that the last task listed in the line is ADMINP; this is the administration process task. When the server runs for the first time, the ADMINP process runs and automatically creates an admin4.nsf, the administration requests database. Every server that runs the ADMINP task will create an admin4.nsf, and it is important to note all instances of admin4.nsf in a domain will be replica copies.

▶ The certification log (certlog.nsf)—The administration process can process no requests without a certification log database. This database is *not* created automatically; you must create it manually from the Certification Log database template and name it certlog.nsf. The purpose of this database is to keep track of the certification processes.

▶ The Public Address Book (names.nsf)—The Public Address Book is the database where the requests for most administration processes are made for users, servers, and groups. When in the view for users, servers, or groups, a person with appropriate access can select the Actions option from the menu bar and start a request for an administration process. Figure 6.1 illustrates the choices an administrator sees in the Public Address Book.

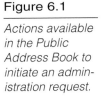

Figure 6.1

Actions available in the Public Address Book to initiate an administration request.

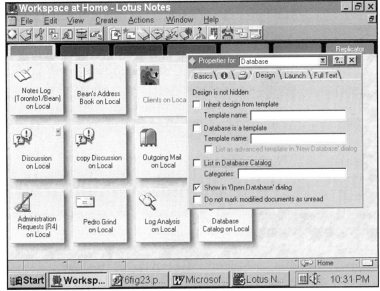

Note

A few administration requests involve other databases:

▶ DeleteStatistics Monitors in Address Book—Use this request document to remove any statistics documents that have been put in or transferred to the address book by mistake.

▶ Copy Server's Certified Public Key—This document is actually created by the server when it realizes its public key is invalid or has been corrupted. The administration process copies new public key information into the Server document.

▶ Place Server's Notes Build Number into Server Doc— This document is created by the server when it realizes its build number is incorrect; this document issues a request for the Administration Process to copy the server's build number into the Server document.

Understanding Access to Start and Complete the Administration Process

Certain access is needed to initiate a request for administration, and other rights are needed to fulfill and distribute that request. To be able to request a rename or rectification, or a conversion from a flat name to a hierarchical one, a user will need author access to certlog.nsf (the certification log database) and admin4.nsf (the administration requests database). Without these, the user cannot create the request or certification documents needed to start the process.

The initiation of the request is only the beginning. To complete the process, the user must accept the name change in his or her user.id. When the user accepts, additional administration requests are created until the entire process is completed. The first request is always to rename, recertify, remove, and so on, a user, server, or group in the Public Address Book. To do this, the ADMINP process must run against the Public Address Book database; but how many replica copies of the Public Address Book are out there, and is the `ADMINP` process going to run on the Public Address Book on each of the servers containing a replica copy? The answer is no. Only one server will run the `ADMINP` process against its replica copy of the Public Address Book. After the server has processed the required changes, it passes the change through the process of replication (see Figure 6.2).

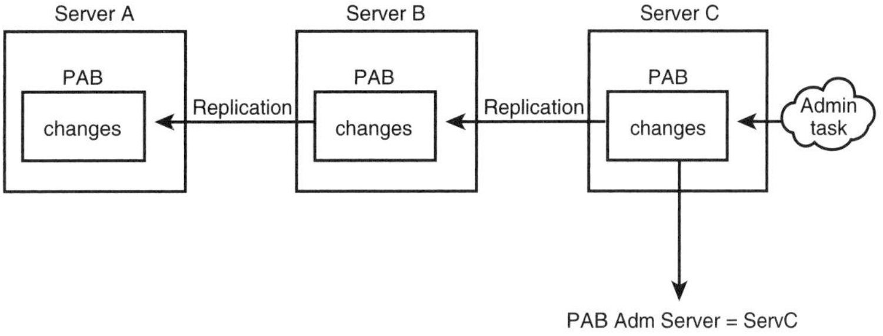

Figure 6.2

One server runs the administration request against the Public Address Book and then replicates to other servers.

Now that you understand that only one server is responsible for running the administration requests, how do you decide which server runs it and where do you indicate what server is responsible? When determining which server runs the administration process, try to estimate the number of changes you have and ensure that running the process won't affect the performance of the server you select. Some companies use their hub servers to run the `ADMINP` process because the purpose of those servers is to disseminate change through replication. You indicate which server is responsible through the ACL of the database. Each ACL has an Advanced screen (shown in Figure 6.3) that identifies the administration server for this database. There is room to indicate only one server.

There is one other way to specify the administration server for a database; I'll cover this method when discussing the Server Administration panel.

Figure 6.3

The Administration Server setting in the Access Control List.

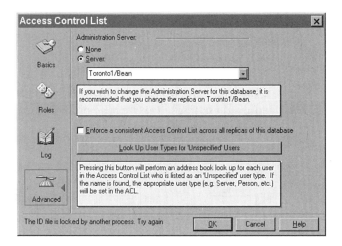

Understanding the Administration Process as a Server Task

The server task `ADMINP` was discussed briefly at the beginning of the chapter; let's go over this process in more detail to understand how it works and how you, the administrator, can control it. The function of the `ADMINP` process, which runs at certain intervals, is to check the `admin4.nsf`, the administration requests database, for any requests. If there are requests, the server checks whether it is listed as the administration server for any of the databases it contains. When it determines that it is the administration server, it then processes the request. These parameters can be set in the Server Configuration document in the Public Address Book. Three parameters can be set in the Server Configuration document:

▶ `ADMINPINTERVAL`—This is the interval, in minutes, that a server will wait before looking for administration requests to process. The default is 60 minutes if no entry is found in the Server Configuration document.

▶ `ADMINPMODIFYPERSONDOCUMENTSAT`—This is the specific time (in 24-hour format) that the `ADMINP` process will modify the Person documents in the Public Address Book. The default is 12 a.m. if there is no entry in the Server Configuration document.

▶ `Name_Change_Expiration_Days`—This is the number of days before a name change will expire and have to be reissued. The default is 21, the maximum is 60, and the minimum is 14.

These settings in the Server Configuration document also get written to the Notes.ini.

Controlling the Administration Process From the Server Console

You can use several commands from the server console to control how and when the administration process occurs. Following are some of those commands:

- ▶ LOAD ADMINP—This command tells the ADMINP process to look for and act upon requests.

- ▶ TELL ADMINP QUIT—This command halts the ADMINP process, and no requests will be acted upon.

- ▶ TELL ADMINP PROCESS PEOPLE—This command forces the ADMINP process to scan admin4.nsf for new and modified requests to update Person documents in the Public Address book.

- ▶ TELL ADMINP PROCESS NEW—This command forces the ADMINP process to look for and run requests in admin4.nsf.

Remember: The server's ADMINP process will act only on databases for which it is the administration server. It will not act against databases that list other servers as the administration server or databases with no administration server at all.

Changing a Name Using ADMINP

Suppose that Pedro Grind was the administrator created when the first server was set up. His name was automatically Pedro Grind/Bean because Bean was the first and only certifier available at the time. Suppose further that you have decided that Pedro will be identified by his geographical location as well as by his organizational identifier. You can use the administration process to make this change and disseminate it through the organization:

1. Request the change from the Public Address Book. Do so by selecting the Person document for Pedro from the People view in the Public Address Book and selecting Actions | Rename Person from the menu bar.

Caution

Administrators will not have the authority to accomplish this unless they have `editor`-level access to the administration requests database and the certification log database. They will also need access to the certifier ID they will use to rename the person.

2. After you've asked to rename the person, you have three choices:

   ▶ Change Common Name—You can ask to rename the common-name portion of the hierarchical name (this is useful if the person whose name you're changing got married or legally changed his or her name).

   ▶ Upgrade to Hierarchical—You can choose to upgrade the user to a hierarchical name if he or she has a flat name.

   ▶ Request Move to New Certifier—You can change which certifier provides the user with his or her certificate.

   The third option is what you want for Pedro Grind. He currently holds a certificate from Bean, but you want his certificate to come from Tor/Bean, a descendant of Bean.

3. You are asked if you have the access to Pedro's old certifier. After you supply it and the password, a Move User's Name in Hierarchy request document is put in the administration requests database and is available under three views:

   ▶ Request by Activity

   ▶ Request by Server

   ▶ Name Move Request

4. When looking at the document in the Name Move Request view, go to the Action menu and select Complete Move for Selected Entries.

5. You will be asked for the new certifier under which Pedro Grind will now operate. After you have provided this

information, the new certification will be logged in the administration requests and certification log databases. A new request, Initiate Rename in Address Book, will be put in the administration requests database (see Figure 6.4). This request will ask that the Person document be amended to reflect the new name.

Figure 6.4

After the name move has been completed, a request to move the user's name hierarchy is entered.

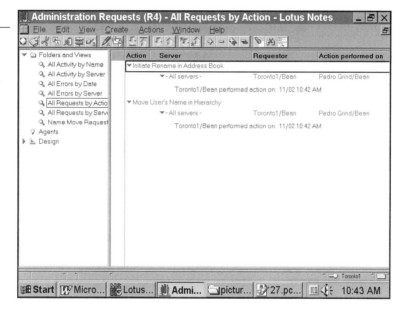

6. The name move request will be processed and logged in the certification log and administration requests databases. The next time Pedro Grind attempts to access the server, he will be asked if he wants to accept his new name.

7. When Pedro accepts his new name, his user.id will change to reflect his new hierarchical name as well as the new certificate his user.id will contain.

8. After Pedro has received his new certificate and it has been logged, the ADMINP server task will run on the administration server for the Public Address Book and process the new request to Rename in the Public Address Book. The completed action is logged in the administration requests database, and the results can also be seen in Pedro's Person document (see Figure 6.5).

Figure 6.5

Pedro's Person document reflects his old and new names.

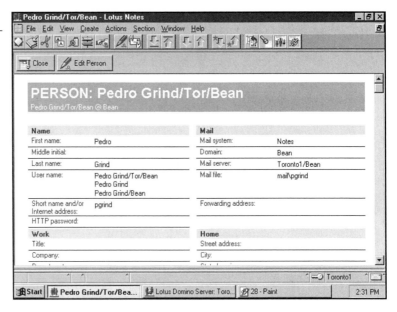

9. After the user has accepted his new name and his Person document has been changed, two new requests are sent to the administration requests database for all servers that are *administration servers* of databases (see Figure 6.6):

   ▶ Rename Person in Address Book—Unlike the Initiate Rename in Address Book request, which affects only the Person document, the Rename Person in Address Book affects all other documents in which the person is referenced in the PAB.

   ▶ Rename Person in Access Control List—This request changes all instances in the ACLs of Pedro Grind/Bean to Pedro Grind/Tor/Bean.

   Each server that is the administration server of a database is responsible for running these requests. After the documents in the PAB and the Access Control Lists have been changed, the changes are then passed to all other replica copies of these databases through replication.

Figure 6.6

The Rename Person in Address Book and Rename Person in Access Control List requests and the logging of the server that performed the action.

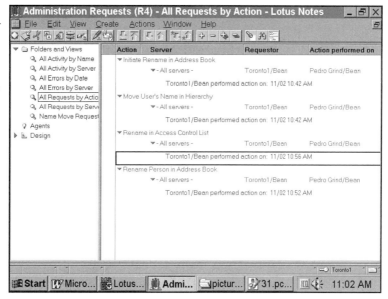

Reviewing Results of ADMINP

The final results of the administration process are as follows:

1. The renaming of the person is initiated in the Public Address Book, and a request is logged to `admin4.nsf`.

2. Users accept their new names and certificates.

3. Documents in the Public Address Book are updated with new names.

4. Access Control Lists are updated with new names.

Understanding the Administration Requests Database

Let's look at the database that contains the request for administrative changes. In this database, seven views are available; the following three main ones are each available in two different formats:

▶ Activity by name and by server

▶ Errors by date and by server

▶ Request by action and by server

When a request gets posted to `admin4.nsf`, the only place you will see it is in the Request view; after the request is acted on by the `ADMINP` process, a document logging the action will be created and shown in both the Request and Activity views. Only if the action was not executed will you see the document in the Errors view. The fourth view, Name Move Request, must be used to complete a move where you are issuing a new certificate.

Request documents are not created in the Administration Requests database; they are typically started in the Public Address Book with a request to rename, delete, or recertify a user or server. When the request is posted in the administration requests database, the `ADMINP` process runs on a server, looks for requests for actions, acts on any found requests, and logs their activity in the administration requests database.

Using the Administrative Process with Manual Methods

Although administrators can use the administration process to help them complete their tasks, it might be valuable to use (or at least understand) the manual method of changing a user or server ID through renaming, through the use of new certificates, or through recertification. The manual method can involve using Notes mail or getting the user ID to the administrator in some other way. Typically, the user creates a safe copy of his or her user ID. The safe copy of the user ID contains only three things:

- ▶ Name
- ▶ License number
- ▶ Public key

The safe copy is sent to an administrator, who renews the safe copy's certificate, gives the safe copy a new name, or gives it a new certificate, and then sends the safe copy back to the user. The user then accepts the new information, and merges it into his or her active ID.

To create a safe copy, users must do the following:

1. Select File | Tools | User ID | Certificates | Request Certificate.

2. Enter the name of the administrator to receive the request.

When the administrator receives the request, the message will look like the one shown in Figure 6.7.

Figure 6.7

The administrator will certify the safe ID.

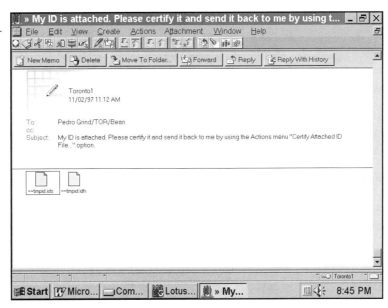

The administrator certifies the safe ID by filling in the Mail Certified ID dialog box, shown in Figure 6.8, and then sends the safe ID back to the requester.

Figure 6.8

Administrator mails the completed request to the requester.

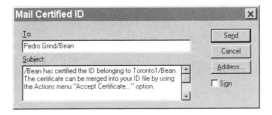

After the requester receives the safe copy in his mail, he can accept the certificate by selecting Actions | Accept Certificate (see Figure 6.9).

Figure 6.9

The user receives the mail containing the safe ID with the new certificate.

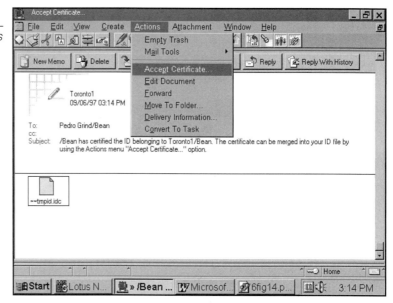

There is also a way to accomplish this without using Notes mail:

1. The user creates the safe copy by selecting File | Tools | User ID | More Options | Create Safe Copy.

2. The user employs any available method to get the safe copy to the administrator (Notes mail, the Internet, a courier, and so on).

3. After the administrator receives the safe copy, he or she selects File | Tools | Server Administration | Certifier | Certify ID File.

4. The administrator chooses the cert.id file he or she will use to recertify the safe copy, and then chooses the safe ID to which the certifier will be applied.

5. After applying the certifier, the administrator returns the safe ID to the user.

6. The user selects File | Tools | User ID | More Options | Merge a Copy.

7. The user specifies that the safe ID with the new certificate be merged into user.id.

When the administrator is recertifying the safe ID due to the expiration of the user's certificate, no Person document, Group documents, or Access Control Lists need to be changed because the person's name has not changed (his or her certificate has only been reissued). However, if this manual request involves a name change, then manual changes must also be applied to Person documents, Group documents, and all Access Control Lists in which the person or server has been identified.

Knowing the Server Administration Panel

The Server Administration panel is akin to a desktop organized specifically for Notes administrators. Every tool that you, as an administrator, need is available from this panel. Of course, you can use these tools to accomplish certain administrator tasks only if you have the appropriate rights or access to servers, databases, and ID files. Let's take a look at each of the main icons available in the panel.

Viewing or Creating People

To view the people who exist in the Public Address Book or create new ones, you have the following options:

- ▶ People View—Depending on what server you have selected from the list on the left, this option will take you to People view in the Public Address Book.

- ▶ Register Person—Selecting this option begins the registration process for a person. The administrator must have access to the correct certifier ID, the UserCreator role in Access Control List in the Public Address Book, and the right to create documents in the PAB and in the certification log (if there is one).

- ▶ Register from File—This option allows the specification of a file against which the registration process will run to batch-register users. The registration file format is identified in Chapter 2, "Server and Client Setup."

Viewing or Creating Groups

Groups can be viewed or created, as discussed next:

- ▶ Group View—Selecting this option takes you to Group view of the server you are administering.

- ▶ Create Group—This option allows the creation of groups in the Public Address Book if the administrator has access to create documents and is assigned the GroupCreator role.

Managing Servers

Clicking the Server icon enables you to manage your servers through the Public Address Book, and allows the registration of new servers. To manage the server through console commands, you must use the Console icon, which is discussed in the section titled "Using Console." The available options are as follows:

- ▶ Servers View—Selecting this option takes you to the Public Address Book (PAB) of the server you have selected; specifically, this option invokes the Server view, where you can view or edit the Server documents.

- ▶ Configure Servers—This option takes you to the PAB of the server you have selected; specifically, this option invokes the Configuration view, where you can edit or create a Configuration document for a server.

- ▶ Register Server—This option starts the registration process for a new server. You must have access to a certifier ID and the Certification log, the right to create documents in the PAB, and the ServerCreator role in the PAB.

- ▶ Log Analysis—Running a log analysis creates a database called Log Analysis (loga4.nsf) that uses the template loga4.ntf. This database is also referred to as the "results" database. After running the search for analysis criteria against the Server Log database (log.nsf), the log analysis puts documents that meet the search criteria in the results database. The results database can contain searches run against multiple servers. By default, when an analysis is run, it overwrites the previous analysis. To append to instead of overwrite the original analysis, you must indicate this from the Results Database dialog box, shown in Figure 6.10. select Log Analysis | Results Database, and enable the Append to this Database check box.

Figure 6.10

To avoid overwriting the previous log analysis, you must enable the Append to this Database check box.

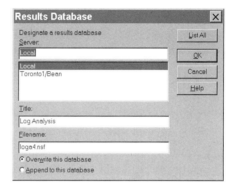

Using Certifiers

TheCertifier icon is crucial to the creation of the hierarchical system; it allows the upkeep of the system, and provides the ability to allow communication as needed between different organizations using cross certification. Cross certification and multiple organizational unit certifiers are not dealt with in detail here; for more information, see Chapter 7, "Naming Conventions and Certification." The Certifier options are as follows:

▶ Certify ID File—This choice allows an administrator who has access to a `user.id`, `server.id`, and Certifier ID file to recertify an existing user or server ID. A hierarchical name can contain only one certificate, so if an ID needs a new certificate or if the old certificate has expired and must be replaced, an administrator can do so from here.

▶ Cross Certify ID File—A cross certificate is a Certificate document that exists in the PAB and holds a key that allows cross communication between two separate organizations. You can create the cross certificate here to enable your end of the cross communication; the other organization must also create a cross certificate for the communication to occur. Cross communication cannot occur with only one cross certificate.

▶ Cross Certify Public Key—It is possible to issue a cross certificate using information from over the phone. For example, suppose you call a trustworthy member of the other organization and persuade him to tell you his organization's public key and exact name. You can type the information here and issue a cross certificate. The same is done for his organization; now you have cross certificates for communication.

▶ Edit Multiple Passwords—This process of replacing the original password with multiple passwords is covered in Chapter 5, "Security," in the section titled "Multiple Password ID Protection."

▶ Open Certification Log—Using this option links you to the certlog.nsf file (if you have created one). You can view the results of certifiers you have created or of any instances of new certification you have performed.

▶ Register Organizational Unit—For every level that exists below the top-level organization, you must create an organizational unit certifier. This new certifier, which will exist as a descendant of the organization, will be used to register all people or servers identified as belonging to it. After you have decided on the names of the levels below the organization, you can begin to register the organizational units. Chapter 7 covers this process in greater detail.

▶ Register Organization—You will probably never use this option. When you set up your first server, your organization certifier is created for you. The cert.id file contains the name of your organization, which was specified in the setup. You would need to use this option only if you changed your organization or if you created a second organization existing in your domain. This type of situation is covered in Chapter 8, "Working with Domains."

▶ Register Non-Hierarchical—Non-hierarchical, or flat, names identify only the common name of the user or server and the user and server IDs containing the certificate(s) of the non-hierarchical certifier. If you want your organization to be non-hierarchical (not recommended for security reasons), you must create a non-hierarchical certifier through this process and then register your people and servers using the non-hierarchical certifier ID. When you set up your first server, it automatically creates a hierarchical certifier ID. To create a non-hierarchical Notes environment, you must create (register) a non-hierarchical certifier, reregister your first server and administrator, and go from there.

Using the Address Book

Clicking the Address Book icon links you to the Public Address Book of the server with which you are working.

Using Mail

The Mail icon provides two options:

▶ Open Outgoing Mailbox—Select this option to open the `mail.box` of the server so you can identify pending and dead mail (if any).

▶ Send Mail Trace—Select this option to send a mail attempt (but not actually deliver a message to the recipient). A response will be returned to you, identifying the route and success of the delivery.

Using the Console

Click the Console icon to invoke the remote console (shown in Figure 6.11), which allows administrators with appropriate rights to remotely control the server as though they are sitting at the server workstation; the only thing you cannot do from the remote console is restart the server. One drawback of working from the remote console is that you sometimes get the message `No immediate server response`. This does not mean the command did not work; it simply means you're not seeing the same feedback information as you would sitting at the server. To get the feedback, you can look at the server log (`log.nsf`).

Figure 6.11

Remotely forcing the replication of the Public Address Book from Toronto1/Bean *to* NewYork1/Bean.

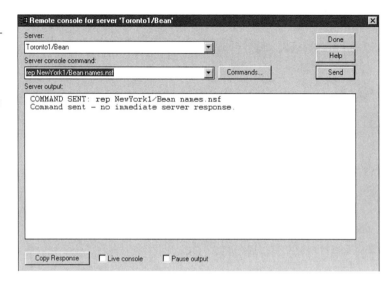

Using Databases

The Databases icon links you to tools to help you manage your databases on the server as well as to databases with information about servers and administration tasks. The options for managing server databases and accessing administrative databases are as follows:

▶ Open Log—Select this option to open the server log (log.nsf) for documents detailing all activity relating to the server tasks.

▶ Open Catalog—This database is not created automatically at server startup, but it will be created if the CATALOG server task runs or if an administrator uses the Database CATALOG template to create the database. The purpose of the database is to create a tool for users that allows them to search for databases, determine which servers they are on and who the managers are, and obtain a brief description of the database. No databases are listed in a database at creation time. The server task CATALOG must be run to update the database catalog with all the databases on the server. By default, the CATALOG task is in the Notes.ini and is to be run at 1 a.m. In all Database Properties boxes, you can specify that the database in the catalog not be included.

▶ Open Statistics—Chapter 9, "Server and System Monitoring," discusses the creation of server monitors and the statistics collected for a server. Selecting the Open Statistics option from the Server Administration panel links you to the database collecting statistics from a server and any events or alarms (statrep.nsf).

▶ Open Administration Requests—Selecting this option links you to the admin4.nsf database.

▶ Configure Statistics Reporting—Selecting this choice links you to the database defining the statistics and events available to monitor on a server(or servers), the events4.nsf database. In this database, you can create monitor documents to track events occurring on a server(s). This process is covered in detail in Chapter 9.

▶ Database Analysis—This is a very useful tool when you are trying to determine what has brought a database to its present situation. See Figure 6.12 for the list of various components you can request to be analyzed. The analysis components and the results of the database analysis are discussed at the end of this chapter.

Figure 6.12

You can request an analysis of these components for a database.

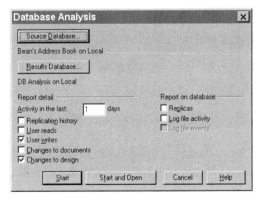

▶ Database Compact—The purpose of COMPACT, a server task discussed in Chapter 2, is to remove whitespace in the NSF file and thereby free disk space. Many servers use a Program document to control the execution of COMPACT with certain parameters on a scheduled basis. From the Server Administration panel, you can force COMPACT to run against a database if you have manager- or designer-level access. Be aware that the database cannot be in use when you do this, and the server needs enough space to copy the database to another location on the hard drive and then copy it back to its original location. To compact databases that are in use when the server is running (for example names.nsf and log.nsf), you must shut down the server first. If the server is not running, names.nsf and log.nsf can only be compacted if the adminstrator is sitting at the local server.

▶ Database Full Text Index—To create a full-text index is to create a number of files containing information about documents in the database. Users can then enter complex search criteria and search against the index, which returns documents meeting the criteria. The drawbacks to creating a full-text index are that it requires significant space on the hard drive, and that you will use processor time to update the index as the documents change. You must have manager- or designer-level access to create a full-text index for a database, and the administrator of the server might have some input as to disk space and processor time.

▶ Database Quotas—When a database is created, the designer can allocate the maximum size that database will reach. In release 4, the default is 1GB, with choices of 2GB, 3GB, or 4GB. After the size has been specified, it cannot be changed. In addition to imposing a size limit, you can also impose a quota, which is really an extra size restriction, and a threshold, which simply warns the administrator about the size. Figure 6.13 shows the Set Database Quotas dialog box, where you impose the quota and threshold. If a database quota is reached, it will not allow documents to be saved and users will see the message shown in Figure 6.14. If a database threshold is reached, the document will be saved and the user will see no message. As shown in Figure 6.15, a warning will be written to the Notes log (log.nsf), where the administrator can see it and take action if necessary.

Note

A quota can be applied against a mail database for a user; if the quota is reached, the user will still be able to receive messages, but he or she will be unable to save his or her own messages.

Figure 6.13

Imposing a quota or a threshold on a database.

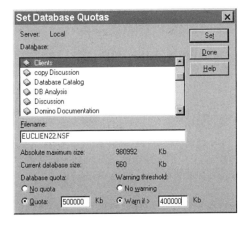

Figure 6.14

The user receives this message if the quota has been exceeded.

Figure 6.15

Message in Server Log database indicating database has exceeded their threshold. Users are not stopped saving their documents.

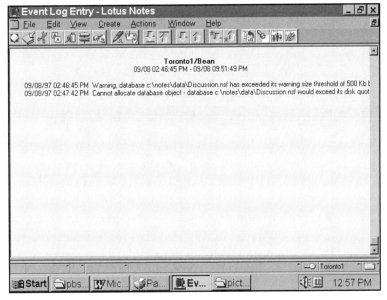

▶ Database Administration Server—From this chapter's discussion of the administration process, you know that only one server will run the administration requests against a database. The server is identified in the database's Access Control List as the administration server. This can be specified directly modifying the ACL under the Advanced option or it can be done from the Server Administration panel. Simply select File | Tools | Server Administration | Databases | Database Administration Server. This invokes the Set the Database Administration Server dialog box, shown in Figure 6.16.

Figure 6.16

Specifying the administration server of a database from the Server Administration panel.

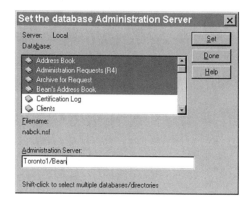

This covers all the choices available to you from icons in the Server Administration panel. The Administration choice in the menu bar also offers these choices, as well as offering the ID File option, which lets you examine an ID file.

Understanding the Notes Log—Server Log

Understanding the Notes log database is essential to understanding what your Notes server does. Everything the server does or is asked to do is logged here. As you can imagine, this database can get rather large. If you find that it provides too much or too little information for you, the settings can be changed in various ways, including through the Notes.ini file. Let's look at the database and the views it offers to understand the documents you will be exploring.

Understanding the log.nsf File

The log.nsf database is automatically created when the server is set up. If the database was for some reason deleted, it would re-create itself the next time the server started. You do not create documents in this database; the server activity forces the creation of a document to log its activity. Let's review the 10 views available in the `log.nsf`:

▶ Database Sizes—This view allows you to see the size and activity of all databases on the server. Use this view to examine unused space in a database or unused views.

▶ Database Usage—This view shows all sessions relating to a database, reads, writes, and replication. Use this view to check how a database is used and to look for replication issues.

▶ Mail Routing Events—Logging mail activity can be confusing because mail events are logged, by default, in two views: this one and Miscellaneous Events (the Phone Calls views can also be helpful if mail is transferred by phone). The Mail Routing Events view provides the most detail in relation to specific messages. If you want all mail routing events to be in one view (for example, Miscellaneous Events), you can set the `Notes.ini` file to:

```
Mail_Log_To_Miscevents = 1
```

If this setting is not indicated in the `Notes.ini` file, detailed mail activity is not logged in the Miscellaneous Events view. This setting can also be indicated in the Configuration document for the server. If you want to modify the level of detail appearing in your mail activity logging, you must specify the following setting in the `Notes.ini` file or Configuration document:

```
LogMailRouting = value (10,20,30 or 40)
```

The values in this setting are defined as follows:

▶ `10`—This value specifies that only errors, warnings, and major routing events be shown. Successful deliveries and transfers are not recorded.

▶ `20`—This value (the default) specifies that errors, warnings, major routing events, and successful deliveries and transfers be shown.

- ▶ 30—This value specifies that the events shown with the values 10 and 20, plus thread information, be displayed.

- ▶ 40—This value specifies that the events shown with the values 10, 20, and 30, plus transfer messages, message queues, and full document information for mail.box, be shown.

▶ Miscellaneous Events—This creates a document for every server startup and logs all high-level server activity for mail routing, replication, modem I/O, user registration, and so on. The use of this view does not mean information is not logged in more detail in other place.

▶ Phone Calls by Date—This view gives information about all calls the server makes and receives. Use this information to gauge the activity of a server and to help identify any problems with replication or mail involving phone calls.

▶ Phone Calls By User—This is the same as Phone Calls by Date, but the documents are listed by user.

▶ Replication Events—This view provides detailed information about each replication event (events where the Replica task was used to exchange information) involving the initiator, the time duration, and which documents were added, deleted, and modified.

▶ Sample Billing—This view shows the same information as the Usage views, but it's unsorted for easy transport to a spreadsheet program. This view can be used to help to determine what to charge for phone calls, network usage, database usage, and so on.

▶ Usage by Date—This view gives very specific information regarding the usage of a database, including what views were used, what documents were accessed and written, and network usage. This view shows totals by date and user/server.

▶ Usage by User—This view is the same as Usage by Date, but is sorted by user.

Notes.ini Settings Relating to log.nsf

The following setting in the Notes.ini (and in the Configuration document in the Public Address Book) affects how activities get logged to the log.nsf for a server:

```
Log=log.nsf, 1, 0, 7, 40000
```

where log.nsf is the filename of the log, 1 is the value for the log_option parameter, 0 is the value for the not_used parameter, 7 is the value for the days parameter, and 40000 is the value for the size parameter.

This setting, the default for server setup, tells the logger to write to log.nsf, log to the server console, and discard log documents after seven days, and that the log can contain a maximum of 40,000 words. These settings are described as follows:

- ▶ logfilename—The name of the server log.

- ▶ log_option—A setting of 1 specifies that the server logs to the console; a setting of 2 forces database fixup when the log.nsf is opened; a setting of 4 specifies that a full-document scan be performed.

- ▶ not_used—This parameter, which is not currently used, is always set to 0.

- ▶ days—This specifies the number of days log documents should be retained.

- ▶ size—This specifies the size of log text in Event documents.

Log_Mailrouting

This setting was covered when mail-routing events were discussed; the purpose of this setting is to control the level of detail being logged for mail events. Its syntax is as follows:

```
Log_Mailrouting = value (10, 20, 30, or 40)
```

The default is 20.

Log_Replication

The following determines whether replication events are logged to the console (1) or not (0):

```
Log_Replication = value (0 or 1)
```

When replication is started by a Connection document, this information is not displayed on the console if the setting is 0. During server setup, there is a choice under the Advanced Server Setup option to log replication; this is the same setting. It can be a bit confusing because it is often interpreted as a yes or no to the logging of all replication activity. This is not the case; this setting is specifically for logging to the console and the logging of the start and end of replication sessions.

Log_Sessions

Like Log_Replication, Log_Sessions is available under Advanced Server Setup. It controls whether user sessions are logged to the console as well as to the log.nsf, and whether individual sessions are recorded. When a user opens and interacts with a database, it is not displayed on the console unless Log_Sessions = 1.

Log_Task

Like Log_Replication and Log_Session, Log_Task specifies whether you want all task activity being logged to log.nsf to also be written to the console. The syntax of Log_Task is as follows:

```
Log_Task = value (0 or 1)
```

A value of 1 specifies that task activity be logged to console; a value of 0 specifies that task activity not logged to console.

Log_View_Events

The following specifies whether you want all view events logged to the log.nsf to also be written to the console:

```
Log_View_Events = value (0 or 1)
```

A value of 0 specifies that messages not be logged when views are rebuilt; a value of 1 specifies that messages be logged when views are rebuilt. If you are interested in knowing when views are rebuilt (perhaps because the view is becoming corrupted too often), you might want to enable this setting.

Mail_Log_to_MiscEvents

The following specifies whether you want detailed mail activity being logged to the Miscellaneous Events view. If you do not, it will be logged in the Mail Routing Events view.

```
Mail_Log_to_MiscEvents = value (0 or 1)
```

A value of 0 specifies that detailed mail events will not be displayed in the Miscellaneous Events view. A value of 1 specifies that mail events be displayed in the Miscellaneous Events view.

This setting was covered in the discussion about the Mail Routing Events view. If this setting is not included in the Notes.ini or the Configuration document, mail events are logged to the Mail Routing Events view by default. As an administrator, you specify your preference as to where mail events are logged.

Understanding Libraries

Databaselibraries can be created as a means of grouping related databases. As mentioned in the discussion about the Server Administration panel, a database catalog can be created, which keeps track of all databases and a server task called CATALOG can update that catalog. The purpose of the database catalog is to provide information about all databases on a server (or servers). A library database, on the other hand, provides information about only those databases that you publish to the library.

For example, your Sales department might find it useful to create a Sales library database to identify all databases that people in the Sales department might find useful. Likewise, the Marketing department might choose to create a Marketing library.

Creating a library is quite simple: Simply select
File | Database | New (use the database library template). To pub-
lish a database to the library, select the database you want pub-
lished, select File | Database | Publish, and select the library you
want it published to. Modify the Database document to briefly
discuss why users might want to access it.

When a user decides to access a database from the library, the
server uses the replica ID identified in the document to search for
the database. If the server can't find the database on the user's
home server, it looks at the catalog database to find a path to a
replica of the database on another server. Should a database be
moved from its original location in the library, Notes will have a
method to locate it; there is no need to update the Library document.

Aiding Database Maintenance

Several server tasks aid in the maintenance of databases. These
tasks help resolve corrupted documents and views, help minimize
disk-space requirements, and help keep designs, views, and full-
text indexes updated.

Using COMPACT

The COMPACT server process involves making a temporary copy of
the database, copying it back to the original location, and in the
process, removing any whitespace left by document or attachment
deletions. When a database is being compacted, it cannot be accessed by the users. The COMPACT server task can be used with parameters to involve only those databases having significant
whitespace. For example, the following command would compact
only those databases consisting of 15% or more whitespace:

```
LOAD COMPACT -s 15
```

Using UPDALL

The UPDALL server process involves updating indexes. As you probably know, Notes uses two types of indexes: view indexes and full-text indexes. All databases have view indexes, but not all databases have full-text indexes. Like most server programs, you can initiate UPDALL in a number of ways: from Notes.ini, manually from the console, or from a Program document in the Public Address Book. The UPDALL program has a number of switches that dictate how it will run:

-f	Updates full-text indexes, but does not update view indexes.
-s	Updates all full-text indexes that have immediate or hourly as an update frequency. Also performs scheduled update if a Program document exists for UPDALL.
-m	Does the same as -s, and no Program document is needed for scheduled updates.
-h	Updates full-text indexes with index-update frequencies of immediate or hourly.
-l	Updates all view and full-text indexes.
-x	Rebuilds full-text indexes.
-v	Updates database views only.
-r	Repairs database views.
database name -c	Rebuilds all views in the database.

If you include no arguments, UPDALL updates all full-text indexes and views in all databases on the server.

Using FIXUP

The FIXUP server task is perhaps misnamed; it is used to detect corruption in documents or views, but it does not fix the corruption. After FIXUP detects the corrupted view or document, it deletes it so the database can be used, but it leaves the task of restoring the deleted, corrupted document or view to you. FIXUP runs at server startup, but check only Notes.log, names.nsf, and mailobj.nsf. It stops running against other databases until the server is up and running. All FIXUP activity is logged in Notes.log. The following switches are available with FIXUP:

-l	Only logs the suspected corruption; does not delete at the time of FIXUP.
-v	FIXUP does not check views. This will shorten the FIXUP time.
-I	FIXUP checks only documents modified since the last FIXUP.
-n	This prevents FIXUP from deleting the corrupted document. Use this if you have no backup from which to restore and you want to try to salvage the document.

Understanding DESIGN

The design of a database will likely change over time as users request changes to views, forms, and so on, and as designers add new formulas for automation. If there is only one database in the Notes environment, this is no problem. However, with Notes' distributed environment, there could be 20 replica copies of the database. To simplify the process of propagating the design changes, the designer should make the change to the design template and let the DESIGN server task automatically make the changes to the database based on the design template. By default, DESIGN is run at 1 a.m. from Notes.ini:

```
SERVERTASKSAT1=CATALOG,DESIGN
```

Restoring Corrupted Documents

Should a document become corrupted, the FIXUP task will remove it so the database can be used; nonetheless, there remains the issue of reclaiming the removed document. There are two ways to do this:

▶ Check other replica copies to see whether they still have the document. If they do, replicate with the server to return the document to the database. If the corruption has already replicated, try the next option.

▶ Restore a backup copy of the database, open it, and copy and paste the document you are looking for. There is no method for restoring the *document*; you must restore the database and then the copy and paste.

Restoring Corrupted Views

Restoring views is similar to restoring documents: You can replicate a replica copy of the database with the server to retrieve the deleted view, or you can restore a backup copy of the database and copy and paste the view. If the view index is corrupt, there are other methods available to fix the problem:

1. Select the corrupted view from the database and press Shift+F9. This rebuilds the view index.

2. In the database, press Ctrl+Shift+F9. This rebuilds and updates all views.

3. Enter the following at the server console to repair database views:

```
LOAD UPDALL filename -r
```

Database Analysis

Database analysis allows you to request a search for specific activities occurring in the database over a number of days. The dialog box for this analysis (refer to Figure 6.13) always reverts to the default settings, with only User Writes and Changes to Design as choices. If you want to analyze the activity on the day of the analysis, you must enter 0 in the Activity in the Last *XX* Days field. The template used to create the database analysis is dba4.ntf, and the filename of the database it creates is dba4.nsf. Any time you perform an analysis on a database, the default is to overwrite the old information. If you want to append the new information to the old information, you must specify this before you start the analysis; simply select the Results Database dialog box and enable the Append to this Database check box.

When you choose to perform your analysis, you can select to receive information about the replication history of this database, user reads, user writes, and changes to documents (including deletions) and design. You can also choose to analyze other replica copies of this database on other servers by selecting Report on Database | Replicas. To receive activity information on the database contained in log.nsf, selectLog File Activity from Reports on Database. If you have chosen Log File Activity, you can also choose to receive event messages relating to the database contained in log.nsf. When you are concerned about a certain database, the database analysis tool is invaluable.

Exercises

You have covered many tools to assist you in your functions as administrator. The administration process is an excellent productivity tool. The various tools available to you in the Server Administration panel will no doubt be used in your everyday tasks.

Exercise 6.1

In this lab, you will change John Valdez's common name in his ID to Johnny Valdez. Before you begin the process, create an ID with the name `John Valdez`, create a group in the Public Address Book and add John's name to it, and put his name in the Access Control List for the Public Address Book as well. To change the name, complete the following steps:

1. Go to the People view of the Public Address Book and select John Valdez's Person document (don't enter the document, just select it from the view).

2. From the menu bar, select Actions|Rename Person|Change Common Name.

3. You are asked for the certifier ID; this is the same certifier ID you used to create the person (in this case, `cert.id`, which should still reside in your `Notes/Data` directory). Remember: You are changing nothing but the common name in the user ID.

4. Enter the password for the `cert.id`.

5. Enter the new first name (`Johnny`).

6. Click Rename. You will see the document being processed and you will receive the following message:

   ```
   1 entry processed and succeeded—see certifier log for
   details
   ```

   This indicates that the request document has been created in the administration requests database, and a Certification document has been created in `certlog.nsf`.

continues

7. Go to server console and type the following:

   ```
   TELL ADMINP PROCESS NEW
   ```

   The default for ADMINP to search for requests is 60 minutes, but you want to force it now.

8. Check the administration requests database; you will see under the All Requests by Action view that Toronto1/Bean has initiated rename in the address book.

9. Go to the People view of the address book and check John Valdez's Person document. You will see it has changed to Johnny Valdez in the view, but that both names are listed in the document. For further activity to occur, Johnny must accept his new name via his user.id.

Because you have only one machine, you are going to detach John's ID from his Person document, switch IDs at the server, and access the server using Johnny's ID. To do this, complete the following steps:

1. Go to Johnny's Person document, page down to the bottom, double-click the user.id, and choose Detach.

2. Detach it to the Notes/Data subdirectory as johnny.id.

3. Get out of the Person document and the Public Address Book database.

4. Select File | Tools | Switch IDs, and choose johnny.id.

5. Open a database on the server by specifying the server name, not by selecting the Local option. You will be asked whether you want to accept your new name, Johnny Valdez. Answer yes.

Now that you have accepted the new name in John's user.id, there is a new request document (Rename Person in Address Book) in the administration requests database. Continue by taking the following steps:

1. Switch to the `server.id` by selecting File | Tools | Switch ID | Back to `server.id`.

2. Return to the console and type the following:

   ```
   TELL ADMINP PROCESS NEW
   ```

   Activity documents are now logged in the administration database; they indicate that Johnny has been renamed in all relevant documents in the Public Address Book.

3. A request is then generated to rename in the Access Control List. Return to the server console and type the following:

   ```
   TELL ADMINP PROCESS ALL
   ```

   The Access Control Lists for the Public Address Book, and Johnny's mail database have been changed to reflect his new name. This is true only for databases for which `Toronto1/Bean` is listed as the administration server. Check his mail file to verify this.

The process is now complete; Johnny's name has been changed in his Person document, `user.id`, all relevant documents in the Public Address Book, and all Access Control Lists for which `Toronto1/Bean` is the administration server.

Review Questions

1. True or false: The administration process is started by default as a task on the server.

2. Which icon on the Server Administration panel do you use to register a new person?

   a. The Certifier icon

   b. The People icon

   c. The Address Book icon

3. Which icon on the Server Administration panel do you use to analyze the log database for a server?

 a. The Database icon

 b. The Server icon

 c. The Address Book icon

4. Which icon on the Server Administration panel do you use to register a server?

 a. The Certifier icon

 b. The Server icon

 c. The Remote Console icon

5. To analyze documents from a database, the server creates an analysis database using which of the following templates?

 a. log.ntf

 b. db.ntf

 c. dba4.ntf

 d. loga4.ntf

6. What view in the log.nsf database would you use to view high-level router activity?

 a. The Miscellaneous Events view

 b. The Mail Events view

 c. The Phone Calls view

7. You publish a database to a library from

 a. within the library

 b. the database to be published

 c. the Server Administration panel

8. Setting a quota on a database means that users will get which of the following general messages when their documents push the database past its quota:

    a. document cannot be saved

    b. document will be saved and message sent to manager

    c. no message

9. When renaming a user through the ADMINP process, a certification log is

    a. required

    b. optional

    c. automatically created

10. Which of the following commands would you enter at the console to force the server to process any new request in the administration requests database?

    a. LOAD ADMINP

    b. TELL ADMINP PROCESS NEW

    c. It can't be done. The ADMINP interval specifies when the request will be processed.

11. ADMINP runs on every server, so

    a. it can handle the requests for all databases it contains.

    b. it can handle requests for the database for which it is the administration server.

12. True or false: All databases are automatically assigned an administration server.

13. Catalog databases are

    a. created automatically by the server setup.

    b. created when the CATALOG server task runs at 1 a.m.

    c. created by a server administrator using the catalog template.

14. True or false: When a document in a database has been corrupted, the FIXUP task on the server will correct the corruption and restore the document.

15. By default, a database analysis by default will

    a. overwrite any existing analysis.

    b. append itself to an existing analysis.

16. What is the default filename when you create a database analysis?

    a. analyze.nsf

    b. dba4.nsf

17. The administration process will

    a. process flat names.

    b. only upgrade flat names to hierarchical names.

    c. recertify flat names.

18. Requests for renaming are entered from

    a. the Person icon in the server administration database.

    b. the Person document in the Public Address Book.

    c. the administration requests database.

19. The administration process will not

    a. upgrade flat names to hierarchical names.

    b. change Reader and Author fields.

    c. update Group documents.

20. Editing or adding multiple passwords to the certifier ID is done

    a. from the ID itself.

    b. from the Certifier icon in the Server Administration panel.

    c. from the certification log.

Review Answers

1. True. The default `Notes.ini` includes `ADMINP` as a startup server task. For more information, refer to the section titled "Understanding the Administration Process."

2. B. The Person icon is where you access the registration process for a person. For more information, refer to the section titled "Viewing or Creating People."

3. B. Log analysis for a particular server is available from this icon. For more information, refer to the section titled "Understanding the Notes Log—Server Log."

4. B. The Server icon is where you access the registration process for a server. For more information, refer to the section titled "Managing Servers."

5. C. For more information, refer to the section titled "Database Analysis."

6. A. High-level mail activity is logged to the Miscellaneous Events view. For more information, refer to the section titled "Understanding the `log.nsf` File."

7. B. The process is via File | | Database | Publish. For more information, refer to the section titled "Understanding Libraries."

8. A. The actual message is more detailed, but the document will not be saved. For more information, refer to the section titled "Using Databases."

9. A. Without a certification log, the request will not be created. The certification log must be created; this is not automatic. For more information, refer to the section titled "Understanding the Administration Process."

10. B. Using this command will force ADMINP to look for and process any request. For more information, refer to the section titled "Understanding the Administration Process as a Server Task."

11. B. The administration process of a server will only process requests against databases for which it is identified as the administration server. For more information, refer to the section titled "Understanding the Administration Process."

12. False. Some (for example, mail file), but not all, databases are automatically assigned an administration server. For more information, refer to the section titled "Understanding the Administration Process."

13. B and C. Both of these actions result in the creation of the database catalog. For more information, refer to the section titled "Using Databases."

14. False. The FIXUP task only deletes the corruption; because FIXUP does not create a deletion stub, the document can be retrieved through replication. For more information, refer to the section titled "Using FIXUP."

15. A. The default is always to overwrite the existing database. For more information, refer to the section titled "Database Analysis."

16. B. It uses the same name as the template from which it is created. For more information, refer to the section titled "Database Analysis."

17. B. Flat names must be upgraded to hierarchical names, which the administration process can do. For more information, refer to the section titled "Understanding the Administration Process."

18. B. Select the Person document from the People view, and choose Rename from Actions. For more information, refer to the section titled "Changing a Name Using ADMINP."

19. B. This function is not available in ADMINP at this point. For more information, refer to the section titled "Understanding the Administration Process."

20. B. From the Certifier icon, choose Edit Multiple Passwords. For more information, refer to the section titled "Using Certifiers."

Answers to Test Yourself Questions at Beginning of Chapter

1. The administration process requires the Administration Requests database, Public Address Book, and Certification Log databases to function. Without these three databases, the administration process will not complete. For more information, refer to the section titled "Understanding the Administration Process."

2. You need access to the original certifier ID with which the user was created, and you need to be able to create documents in both the Administration Requests database and the Certification Log database. For more information, refer to the section titled "Understanding the Administration Process."

3. A library lists all databases published to it, while a database catalog lists all databases on the server by name, replica ID, and manager. You publish a database to a library. For more information, refer to the section titled "Understanding Libraries."

4. No, everyone can access the Server Administration panel, but you can use the tools only if you have the appropriate access. For more information, refer to the section titled "Understanding the Server Administration Panel."

5. High-level routing activities are logged in the Miscellaneous Events view, and detailed-level activities are logged in the Mail Routing Events view. For more information, refer to the section titled "Understanding the log.nsf File."

6. No, once the database size has been chosen, it cannot be changed. For more information, refer to the section titled "Understanding the log.nsf File ."

C h a p t e r

Naming Conventions and Certification

This chapter introduces you to the following objectives:

▶ Hierarchical naming conventions

▶ Creating certifiers

▶ Cross certificates

▶ Flat naming conventions

Test Yourself! Before reading this chapter, test yourself to determine how much study time you will need to devote to this section.

1. A company decides to implement Notes and is going to use hierarchical naming. The company is organized by division (three) and each division by departments (four). It is going to use its company organization to implement hierarchical naming. How many certifier IDs, registered servers, and users will there be in total?

2. How many IDs were created for the creation of the hierarchical name Bev Breen/Promo/Sales/Acme?

3. Two servers belong to different organizations. The administrators of these servers want to enable communication, so they each edit the Server documents in the Public Address Book and put the server's name from the other organization in their Allow Access field. Will the servers be allowed to communicate?

4. To enable two servers to communicate and replicate, what is needed?

5. Cross certificates can be given at what levels?

6. When an organization decides not to communicate with a server to which it has given a cross certificate, it deletes the cross certificate from the Public Address Book. Is there a similar document for servers with flat names when the same procedure is followed for removing access?

Answers are located at the end of the chapter...

The purpose of this chapter is to make you fully comfortable with and knowledgeable of the hierarchical naming convention. You begin by reviewing why companies implement hierarchical naming and continue by exploring the methods of creating certifiers and certificates.

This chapter further explores the concept of hierarchical naming, which was discussed in some detail in Chapter 2, "Server and Client Setup." Before continuing, you should be comfortable and familiar with the information and concepts provided in the earlier chapter.

Using Hierarchical Naming

First, you will review the Bean organization scenario presented in earlier chapters to understand its situation and how it will use hierarchical naming (see Figure 7.1).

Figure 7.1

The Bean organization.

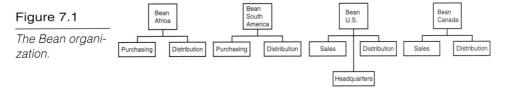

A brief summary of the Bean organization's operation is as follows: The South American and African groups buy coffee beans and ship them to the selling groups. The Canadian and U.S. groups are responsible for selling the beans and distributing them to purchasers. Table 7.1 lists the components available in the hierarchical system for your naming plan.

Table 7.1

Components of Hierarchical Naming.		
Component	Description	Characters
Common name (CN)	The person's full first and last names or the server name. Required component.	80 maximum

continues

Table 7.1 Continued

Component	Description	Characters
Organizational unit name (OU)	Typically a department or location name. Notes enables the use of up to four organization units in each distinguished name. Optional component.	32 per OU
Organization name (O)	Typically the company name. Try to keep it short. Required component.	3 min to 64 max
Country (C)	Two-letter abbreviation for the country from the ISO standards. Optional component.	2

Based on Bean's organization and the components available in hierarchical naming, Bean must decide how to name its servers and users. As was stressed in Chapter 2, planning is the key. As an administrator, you don't want to come back in six months to rename everyone because the original hierarchical naming plan was not logical. To avoid this inconvenience, take a look at each component to identify things you might want to consider:

▶ Common name—The first thing you want to decide is the use of the middle initial. Is it really necessary or will it make it more difficult to know the person's correct common name? For example, many people probably know that Mike Breen works in Accounting but don't know that his middle initial is V. Middle initials can help differentiate between people with the same name, but organizational units can be used for this purpose, too. You also must decide whether to use the common or formal version of a person's first name—Mike versus Michael, Bob versus Robert, Peggy versus Margaret.

▶ Organizational units—These identifiers are used to differentiate between same-named people in the organization and to further identify people in the organization—in other words, the department in which they work, the geographical location in which they are located, and so on. Although you can use a maximum of four organizational unit identifiers, Lotus recommends that you use only two. These components are optional, but many companies use at least two levels, the most common being the department the person works in and the physical location in which he resides.

▶ Organization identifier—This is a required component. To implement hierarchical naming, you must be identified as belonging to an organization. This can be seen literally in looking at the name Bill Vincent/Bean, but more important, it is identified in the user ID by the certificate containing the correct certifier key. This key identifies someone as being a "descendant" of the organization.

▶ Country code—This component is not required. Country codes are predefined, and the list is available in Appendix F of the *Lotus Notes Administrator's Guide*. These codes follow the International Standards Organization standards in ISO 3166. If you choose to use the country code component, the minimum three-character restriction in the Organization Identifier is lifted because there is no chance of confusing it with a country code.

Bean has decided that its organization identifier (O) will be Bean, and it will use the countries/continents it operates in as its first organizational unit identifiers (OU):

```
US/Bean
CA/Bean
SA/Bean
AF/Bean
```

These are organization identifiers, not country code components. Under each of the country/continent organizational identifiers, Bean further distinguishes by department—Sales (Sales), Distributing (Dist), and Purchasing (Purch):

```
Sales/US/Bean
Dist/US/Bean
Sales/CA/Bean
Dist/CA/Bean
Purch/SA/Bean
Dist/SA/Bean
Purch/AF/Bean
Dist/AF/Bean
```

Creating New Certifiers

Now that the organization identifier and the organizational units you will use to differentiate between the people in the organization exist, you are ready to create the certifier IDs to create the users and servers.

Creating the Organization Identifier

There are two methods available to create an organization identifier. The first is automatic and available in the setup of the first server. Remember that when you set up the first server, under Advanced Options, the setup process defaults to create three IDs:

▶ Server ID

▶ Organization certifier ID

▶ Administrator ID

Unless you deselect the certifier ID choice, you will enable the creation of an organization certifier ID file.

The second method to create an organization identifier is available from the administration panel (select File | Tools | Server Administration | Certifiers | Register Organization).

By using either of these two methods, you will register an organization identifier. The second method is used where a server or user already is set up—perhaps a test environment or another organization. When they set up a Notes environment, many consultants create certifiers ahead of time on their servers and bring them with them to do the setup.

Now you are at the second step, which is to create the organizational unit certifiers. Remember that you will not use the organization certifier to create any users or servers. Instead, it will be used to generate the next level of certifiers, the first-level organizational unit certifiers.

First-Level Organization Unit Certifiers

To create this first-level OU certifier, you require access to the organization certifier. Without the ancestor, you cannot create the descendant. There is only one process to create the OU: Select File | Tools | Server Administration | Certifiers | Register Organizational Unit.

As soon as you select Register Organizational Unit, you are asked to provide the organization certifier with which you will create the organizational unit certifier (see Figure 7.2).

Figure 7.2

Choose the organization certifier.

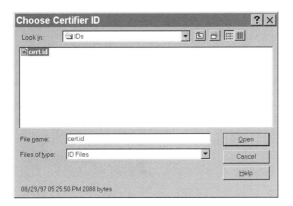

The following screen identifies the registration server—the server whose Public Address Book the certificate document will be written to. If it indicates local and you are sitting at your own work-station, the certificate document is written to your Personal Address Book; make sure you change it if you are sitting at a user station. Also identified is the certifier from which the organizational unit certifier is descending—in this case, Bean (see Figure 7.3).

You must provide the organizational unit name and the password to be associated with it. Do not provide any slashes with the organizational unit name. Notes inputs these. If you want to associate multiple passwords with the certifier, you must do this after it is created. If this certifier will be used to certify users and servers, provide an administrator name so that request for recertification is mailed directly to them.

Figure 7.3

Registration criteria for creating an organizational unit certifier.

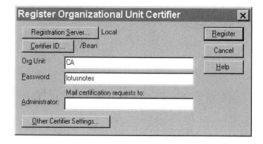

Under Other Certifier Settings, you can provide comments to reside in the certificate document to be created. You also can indicate what type of license you will invoke, relating to the encryption scheme you will be using. For the purposes here, you have chosen International because you are sending encrypted documents outside of North America (see Figure 7.4).

Figure 7.4

Choosing the license type for certifier.

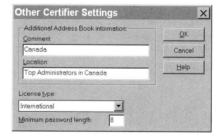

When you are ready to tell the system to register the certifier, it attempts to register it first to the A: drive. It does this for security reasons. Although you have specified a password for the certifier ID, saving it to a disk forces you to consider how you will secure the ID itself. You also should make several copies, which you will secure in a safe location. If you want to save the certifier to the hard drive, click Cancel and choose where to save it.

Two things result from this registration:

▶ The creation of the ID file, defining the organizational unit certifier. The filename should reflect the organization unit; in this case, the Canada organizational unit certifier is CA.id.

▶ A certificate document is created in the Public Address Book (see Figure 7.5).

Figure 7.5

The document specifying the registration of a certifier.

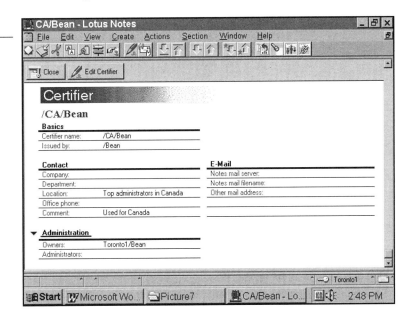

If you have created a certification log, the information about this certifier is also logged there.

Second-Level Organizational Unit Certifiers

Although you could continue to create the other three first-level organizational unit certifiers, you will continue to create the organizational unit certifiers until you are ready to register people or servers. Under the CA/Bean certifier, you want to identify three departments: Sales, Purchasing, and Distribution. Let's begin with Sales. Select File | Tools | Server Administration | Certifiers | Register Organizational Unit. When you are asked for the certifier ID, choose CA to achieve the end result of Sales/CA/Bean (see Figure 7.6).

Figure 7.6

The immediate intended ancestor of Sales in Bean for Canada.

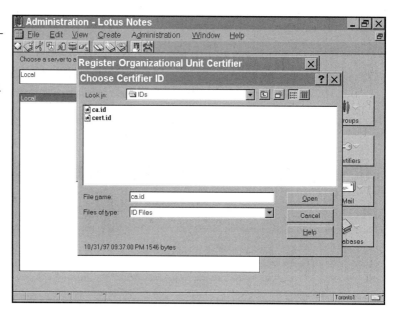

As you can see from Figure 7.7, the registration server is identified and can be changed if necessary. The ancestor certifier ID is identified, as well, and if you made a mistake with regards to the immediate ancestor, you can change this here by clicking Certifier ID. This enables you to choose another certifier ID as the immediate ancestor. After you've ensured that both these settings are correct, specify the name of the organizational unit—in this case, Sales. The password and the license type under Other Certifier Settings are input here.

Figure 7.7

Settings for certifier Sales in Bean for Canada.

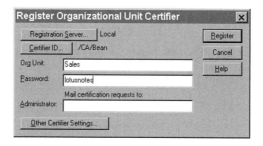

Two things result from this registration:

▶ The creation of a sales.id file, defining the organizational unit. To minimize confusion, try to name your ID files to reflect the contents. For example, the default file name is the organizational unit name, but in this case, you are going to have four sales departments, one for each country. Rename this file `SalesCA.id` to accurately reflect its contents.

▶ A Certifier document is created in the Public Address Book (see Figure 7.8).

Figure 7.8

*The document
specifying the
registration of
a certifier.*

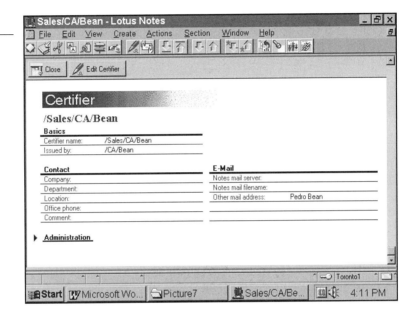

Follow the same process for the Purchasing and Distribution departments. It is best to keep the identifiers as short as possible—perhaps `Purch` for purchasing and `Dist` for distribution.

Registering the User

Now that you have registered three certifiers, you can create the others, making sure to always choose the correct certifiers as the certifier. With one organization certifier, there will be a total of 17 certifiers: four first-level certifiers and under each of these, three second-level certifiers. Only 12 of these will be used to register users, however.

To register Peggy Vincent, who works in the Sales department in Canada, use the `Sales/CA/Bean` certifier. To register John Breen in the Sales department in the United States, use the certifier `Sales/US/Bean` and so on.

Registering the Servers

A similar process for registering users is followed for servers, as well. Make sure the correct certifier ID is chosen so that the server receives the correct hierarchical name.

Working with Cross Certification

When a user or server tries to talk to a server and they are both descendants of the same ancestor—they all belong to the same organization—the default is allowed through the process of authentication. Remember from Chapter 5, "Security," though, that administrators can set their server documents to specify access or deny access even if the request comes from a user or server who has passed authentication. If a user or server tries to gain access to a server from another organization, Notes' default is to *not* allow access because authentication cannot occur. Administrators can, however, create cross certificates at various levels, which enable authentication.

There are two important features to be aware of when dealing with cross certificates:

▶ Cross means both directions. Each organization must have a cross certificate in its Public Address Book, saying that it has given a cross certificate to the other. If only one organization has granted a cross certificate, access is not given to either.

▶ Cross certificates can be given at one of four levels. When you consider the type of ID files created in Notes, there are basically four: organization IDs, organizational unit IDs (all four levels), server IDs, and user IDs. Each of these IDs can be given a cross certificate. In the following sections, you learn how to give and receive cross certificates.

Although certificates exist in your user and server IDs, cross certificates do not. Cross certificates exist in the Public Address Book, and for this reason they are also easy to remove should you decide you no longer want to communicate with an organization. If a cross certificate exists in another person's ID file, you can never remove it, because you do not have access to that person's ID file. Having the cross certificate in your Public Address Book means that if you change your mind about the cross certification, you need only to remove the document from your address book and access is denied.

Understanding the Cross Certificate Document

A cross certificate document contains a certificate from the ID, giving the cross certificate to the ID requesting it. If the Bean organization wants to cross-certify the Leaf organization, it would require the Leaf name and Leaf's public key. Bean would then create a document, giving this name with the associated public key a Bean certificate (see Figure 7.9). This certificate would reside in Bean's Public Address Book.

Figure 7.9

Bean's cross certificate for Leaf.

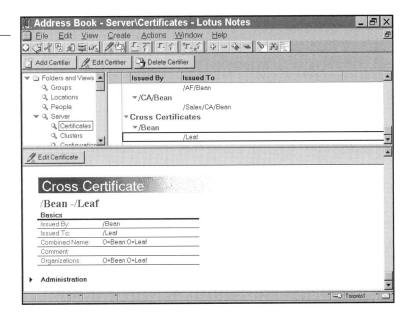

As you know, authentication is a two-way process. Each entity checks for a certificate it trusts. If one entity does not find the trust it requires, the deal is off, and there is no communication. The same is true for entities that do not share a common ancestral certificate. If Leaf tries to access Bean, Bean checks whether or not it has a cross certificate in its Public Address Book for Leaf, and Leaf also checks to see whether or not it has a cross certificate in its Public Address Book for Bean. Should one of the cross certificates be missing or expired, access is denied to both servers (see Figure 7.10).

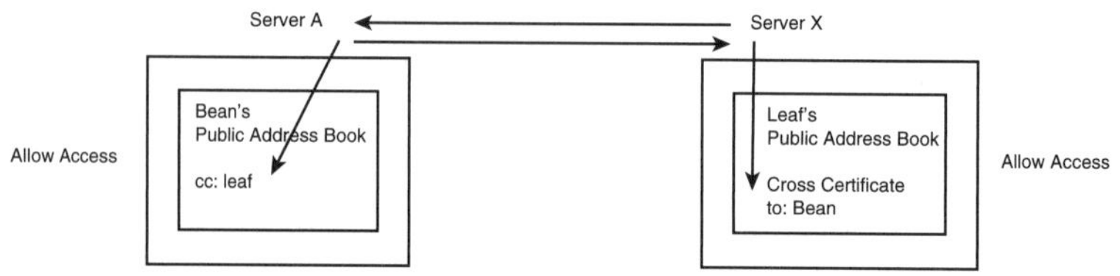

Figure 7.10

An example of cross certification.

Server A ← → Server X

Bean's Public Address Book
cc: leaf

Allow Access

Leaf's Public Address Book
Cross Certificate to: Bean

Allow Access

Different Levels of Issuing Cross Certificates

As mentioned previously, there are four different types of IDs in Notes: the organization certifier ID, the organizational unit certifier ID (all four levels of them), the server IDs, and the user IDs. A cross certificate can be issued to any one of these types of IDs. The lower the level at which you issue a cross certificate, the more secure. Issuing a cross certificate from Bean to Leaf (organization IDs) and vice versa, enables authentication for all entities holding a Leaf ancestral certificate to the Bean organization and access for all entities (servers and users) holding a Bean ancestral certificate to the Leaf organization. If, on the other hand, one Leaf server issues a cross certificate to one Bean server and vice versa, only these two servers can authenticate. Mail and replication can occur between only these servers, and information would flow between the two organizations with the minimum of cross certification.

 Note

Any type of cross certification in no way overrides any server access fields, Access Control Lists, or other security features of the databases (see Figure 7.11).

Figure 7.11

The role of cross certification in the security levels.

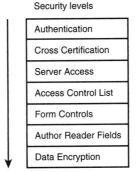

Security levels

| Authentication |
| Cross Certification |
| Server Access |
| Access Control List |
| Form Controls |
| Author Reader Fields |
| Data Encryption |

Organization Cross Certificate

Should Bean decide to issue a cross certificate at the organization level to Leaf, it would in effect be saying that any entity with a certificate from Leaf or a descendant of Leaf can access Bean. This method of cross certification is the most liberal. It is not recommended for most intercompany communication schemes. One example of a situation in which you might use organization-to-organization cross certification is where two companies have merged but have decided to keep their own naming schemes.

Organizational Unit Cross Certificate

In this situation, Bean has decided to issue a cross certificate at the organizational unit level. Leaf is organized by department, and its hierarchical names reflect this.

Leaf has issued its cross certificate to the Bean organization, but Bean only wants to enable Leaf's marketing department to access its servers. Bean then issues a cross certificate to Mkt/Leaf, so only entities containing a certificate from Mkt/Leaf are able to access Bean (see Figure 7.12). Organizational unit cross certification can help minimize the access you are conferring with your cross certificate. Should your decision be to cross-certify at the organizational unit level, implementing it at the lowest level is your most secure method.

Figure 7.12

Bean, enabling access to only organizational unit entities (Mkt/ Leaf).

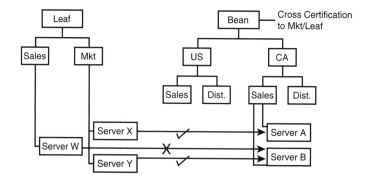

Bean Access Restricted to only Mkt/Leaf and below

Server ID Cross Certificate

Bean has decided to be even more stringent in its cross certification and cross-certify only a particular server. Only the server identified in the cross certificate can access Bean. Bean creates a cross certificate for the specific server and uses the server's public key to do so (see Figure 7.13).

Figure 7.13

Bean, restricting access to only server Y/Mkt/ Leaf.

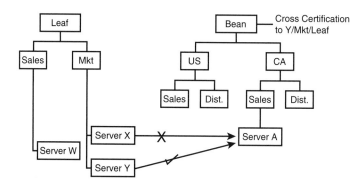

User ID Cross Certificate

As with a server ID, Bean can choose to cross-certify a user ID from Leaf so that only that user can access Bean. Bean creates a cross certificate document in the Public Address Book by using the user's public key (see Figure 7.14).

Figure 7.14

Bean enabling access to only a user.

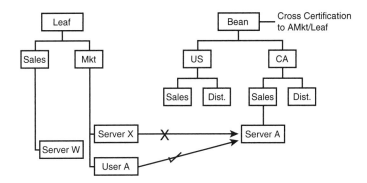

 Note

For a user to employ cross certification to access a server, the user must have the cross certificate in his or her *Personal Address Book*. In most cases, the users must copy and paste the document from the Public Address Book into their Personal Address Books.

Although you have been concentrating on Bean's issuing of cross certificates to Leaf at varying levels, Leaf must give Bean cross certificates, as well. Leaf's levels, however, do not have to match Bean's levels. If, for example, Bean grants a cross certificate to server A in Leaf, and Leaf grants a cross certificate to Bean as organization, then only server A can access the Bean organization, but all of Bean can access all of Leaf.

Methods of Creating Cross Certificates

There are various methods of creating cross certificates in Notes. They all, however, end up creating the same thing: a cross certificate document in the Public Address Book, identifying a name and associated public key with a certificate granted from a non-ancestral certifier.

On Demand

If you try to access a server from another organization, you are told that you are not allowed due to lack of a valid certificate and you are asked whether you would like to create a cross certificate for the server you are trying to reach. (This is a new feature to Notes release 4.) You also are warned at this time that you cannot complete your access to the server until the other organization's server (or a higher-level ID) grants you a cross certificate in its Public Address Book. To complete the "on demand" process, the other server tries to access your server, and if it responds positively to the creation of a cross certificate for your server, both servers can authenticate each other.

By Notes Mail

It might seem strange to suggest that you cross certify by mail when the servers can't communicate due to lack of cross certification. If Notes mail can be delivered through another organization to which you both have access, however, it is possible. Select File | Tools | User ID | Certificates | Request Cross Certificate (see Figure 7.15).

Figure 7.15

Requesting a cross certificate through Notes mail with the Request Cross Certificate button.

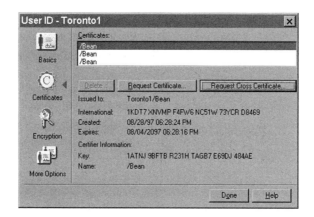

At this point, you are not forced to use the ID you have been examining. You can choose the ID that you want to receive the cross certificate (see Figure 7.16). The result of this operation is the creation of a safe copy of the ID, which is then inserted into a mail message.

You then choose whom the request is to be sent to and mail it (see Figure 7.17).

Figure 7.16

Choosing the ID to be cross-certified.

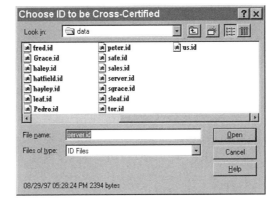

Figure 7.17

Mailing the request.

When the administrator receives the mail, he selects Actions|Cross Certify Attached ID File. To complete the action, the administrator must choose the ID he will use for cross certification and click Cross Certify. This completes the request and results in the creation of a cross certificate document in the Public Address Book. The same process is repeated in the other direction so that both organizations have the correct Cross Certificate documents.

Other Mail Methods

If you have no way of communicating by using Notes mail until you have achieved cross certification, you must employ some other method of getting a safe copy of the ID you want to cross-certify to the other organization. This process might involve the Internet, the postal service, or another organization. The objective here is to first create a safe copy of the ID. If the ID is to be cross certified or is a server or user ID, you can select File|Tools|User ID|More Options|Create Safe Copy. Specify the filename you want and where you want to save it.

If the ID to be cross-certified is an organization certifier or organizational unit certifier, you must select File | Tools | Server Administration | Administration | ID File, choose the ID file to examine (enter the password), click More Options, then select Create a Safe Copy (from here, it's the same as for a server or user ID).

After you create your safe copy, use whatever method is available to you to get the ID to the administrator in the other organization who will create the cross certificate for you. As soon as the administrator receives it, she selects File | Tools | Server Administration | Certifiers | Cross Certify ID File.

After choosing the ID file with which to create the certificate, the administrator specifies the safe ID file as the one containing the correct name and public key to receive the certificate. There is no need to return the safe ID, as the purpose of this exercise is to create a cross certificate in the Public Address Book of the organization to which the safe copy was sent.

Again, for cross certification to work, the process must be repeated in the other direction, as well.

By Phone

The optionto create the cross certificate over the phone, with the information given verbally, also exists. As mentioned previously, the information in a cross certificate contains the name and the public key associated with the name. The name and the public key are identified in the ID file and can be read and verbally transmitted to the person who is going to provide the cross certificate.

To examine a server or user ID, select File | Tools | User ID | Basics. Then, read the name and key information. Unfortunately, this can be a cumbersome and potentially error-prone method of creating a cross certificate.

Examples and Implications of Providing Cross Certificates

Now, examine a few examples of issuing cross certificates at various levels and the implications to your system security in doing so.

Organization Level

To begin with, before planning to provide a cross certificate at the organization level—in other words, Bean—you must have access and know the password to the certifier ID for Bean. You also must be able to create documents in the Public Address Book. Through whatever method used, you receive the name and public key of the ID you are going to cross-certify. When you cross-certify the ID, either through the System Administration panel or through actions available in the mail message, the first thing you must do is choose the ID who will grant the cross certificate.

After you have done this, the confirmation of the ID granting the certificate appears on the next screen; if you have made a mistake at this point, it can be changed by clicking Certifier and choosing the correct one (see Figure 7.18).

Figure 7.18

Verify that you've chosen the correct ID to grant the cross certificate.

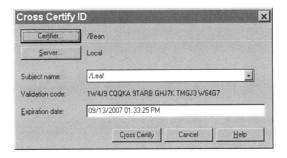

The organization ID granting the certificate is granting access to all IDs that are descendants of this certificate, which, in this case, is the entire Bean organization. This is quite a wide-ranging certificate to be granted. The ID you are granting the certificate in this scenario can be one of four types. Now, step through the scenario for an organization ID, granting a certificate to the different types of IDs (see Table 7.2).

Table 7.2

Results of Cross Certification	
Organization ID (Bean) granting certificate to:	**Results**
Organization ID	Bean would be granting access to all of its direct descendant entities—servers in Bean organization—because users can't communicate with other users. This access would be granted to all descendant entities of the organization to whom the cross certificate has been granted—Leaf. Any server or user who is a descendant of the Leaf certifier can authenticate all of Bean's servers. Again, this does not override any server access fields or Access Control Lists, or any security associated with databases.
Organizational unit ID	Bean is still the ID granting the certificate and, therefore, is still granting access to all of its descendants. However, it grants this access only to descendants of the organizational unit ID it is cross-certifying—Mkt/Leaf. The organization unit Sales/Leaf will not have access because it is not a descendant of Mkt/Leaf; it is a descendant of Leaf. If the certificate is granted to a lower level of organizational unit, again the certificate is valid only to descendants of the organizational unit and below, not above.
Server ID	Bean granting a certificate to a server ID enables only that server to access all entities descending from the Bean certificate.
User ID	Bean granting a certificate to a user enables only the user to access all servers in the Bean organization. The user must copy and paste the cross certificate into her Personal Address Book before she can access the Bean servers.

Organizational Unit Cross Certification

In the next case, the options remain the same, but instead of Bean (organization certifier) granting the cross certificate, US/Bean (organizational unit) grants the cross certificate (see Table 7.3).

Table 7.3

Results of Cross Certification

Organizational unit certifier (US/Bean) granting certificate to:	Results
Organization ID	The certifier, US/Bean, has given a certificate to Leaf, enabling access to all entities who have descended from US/Bean but denying access to other branches of descent from the Bean organization. All descendants from Leaf can use this certificate.
Organizational unit certifier	US/Bean has given a cross certificate to Mkt/Leaf. All descendants of Mkt/Leaf can access all descendants of US/Bean. Neither can access higher-level descendants or descendants from another line in Bean or Leaf.
Server ID	US/Bean gives a cross certificate to a server ID. The server receiving the certificate is able to access all descendants of US/Bean.
User ID	US/Bean gives a cross certificate to a user ID. Only the user can access all descendants of US/Bean.

Server Cross Certification

In Table 7.4, the results of a server ID granting a cross certificate are listed.

Table 7.4

Results of Cross Certification	
Server ID (Toronto1/Bean) granting certificate to:	Results
Organization ID	When a server grants a cross certificate to an organization ID, all descendants of the organization can access this server and this server only.
Organizational unit ID	When a server grants a cross certificate to an organizational unit, only descendants of the organizational unit can have access. All descendants from a higher certifier or another line of descent are not allowed.
Server ID	When one server grants a certificate to another server, only these two servers are granted access to each other. It has nothing to do with descendants, as a server ID cannot register other IDs. These two servers are then ready for authentication between the two organizations.
User ID	When a server grants a cross certificate to a user ID, only the user identified in the document is given access. The user must copy and paste the cross certificate document to his Personal Address Book for access to occur.

User Cross Certification

The fourth type of ID is the user ID, but it doesn't make sense for a user.id to grant a cross certificate, because users can't communicate with other users in Notes. You can access only a server. Of course, users can be granted certificates because they will be accessing servers.

Using Flat Naming Conventions

Although the default for Notes release 4 is a hierarchical setup, Notes will still support the flat naming convention. The flat naming system is typically a less-desirable system, mainly for security reasons. There are several important differences to be aware of if you make the decision to use, or stay with, flat naming. Many processes I have discussed in previous chapters are not available for flat naming.

Flat Names

Flat naming is very easy to differentiate from hierarchical. When examining the name in Notes, the name itself only shows a common name portion. There are no organizational unit identifiers; there are no organization identifiers. When you view a flat name, you have no idea to what company this person belongs, and there are no indicators as to what department or location he or she is affiliated with. When you use a flat certifier, you can create only flat names.

Flat names can contain multiple certificates. When their flat certifier ID creates them, users receive a certificate from that certifier. When they attempt to access a server, the authentication process executes and verifies that there is a certificate in common—both entities contain the same certificate or a certificate that they trust (see Figure 7.19).

Figure 7.19

Checking for a common certificate.

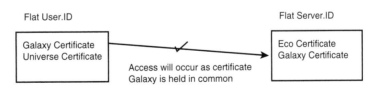

If a company has created an organization by using only one flat certifier, no problems will occur when entities try to access servers. If several flat certifiers were used, however, a user created with one certifier cannot access a server created with a different one, even though they belong to the same company. The user must then go through the process of obtaining the same certificate as the server he is trying to access. (I cover this process in the "Multiple Certificates" section.) At this point, it is important to understand that users and servers must have the *same* certificate (not a descendant) in their ID as the server they are trying to access. Cross certificates are not relevant to flat names; they are used only for hierarchical names.

Flat Certifier ID

Flat certifiers are completely unrelated to one another, which is their main difference from hierarchical certifiers. Each certificate conferred by a flat certifier is independent of any other. The function of a flat certifier is simply to confer a certificate to a server or user ID. The flat certifier does not make any changes to the name of the ID. Simply looking at the name of a user or server gives you no idea of the certificates it might contain and, therefore, the access capability it might have. To create a flat certifier, select File | Tools | System Administration | Certifiers | Register Non-Hierarchical.

Notice the difference between registering a non-hierarchical and an organization certifier. For non-hierarchical, you are not asked for any organization name, as this component is not used in flat naming, and you are not asked to specify any administrator name for mailing purposes because this system is not implemented with flat naming (see Figure 7.20).

Figure 7.20

Creating a non-hierarchical or flat certifier.

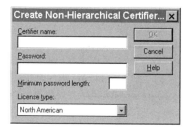

The process of registering users is identical whether you are using the flat certifier or hierarchical certifiers.

Multiple Certificates

Because a user requires the same certificate of the server it is trying to access, flat names must be capable of containing multiple certificates. Cross certification is not an option with flat naming. Cross certification was implemented with hierarchical naming and does not function with flat names. Next, examine the process a user or server follows to request a certificate for access and the process an administrator follows to confer a certificate.

Requesting Certificate

Your goal is to acquire a certificate in the user or server ID. The safest method of accomplishing this is to send the administrator who will be conferring the certificate a safe copy of the ID. It is not prudent to send an actual copy of the ID, as it contains all of the private keys and encryption keys that are used for security purposes. A safe copy of the ID contains only the name, license number, and public key (see Figure 7.21).

Figure 7.21

Contents of a safe copy of an ID.

Safe ID

Name
License
Public Key

Think of the safe copy as a delivery vehicle that you are using to pick something up. To create a safe copy of an ID, select File | Tools | User ID | More Options | Create Safe Copy.

After you create your safe copy, send it to the administrator who holds the flat certifier that you require. Her function is to grant the certificate to your safe copy and return it to you, after which you merge this additional certificate into your ID.

Granting Certificate to Safe Copy

You are the administrator of the flat certifier. You have received a mail message containing a safe copy of an ID and asking you to grant them a certificate. If you trust this mail message, select

File | Tools | System Administration | Certifiers | Certify ID File. Choose the flat certifier to grant the certificate and indicate the safe ID, which will receive this certificate to carry back. Mail the safe ID back to the requester.

Accepting the Certificate

The requester receives the safe copy and completes the following steps to incorporate the certificate into his ID. Select File | Tools | User ID | More Options | Merge a Copy.

The requester then chooses the safe ID to merge into his ID and is asked whether he wants to accept the certificate. By answering yes, his ID now contains the new certificate, as well as any previous certificates it contained. The requester is now ready to access the server.

Trusting Non-Hierarchical Certificates

As mentioned previously, cross certification does not apply to non-hierarchical names. For a non-hierarchical user or server to access a server, it must contain the same certificate as the server it is trying to access. When a server collects a certificate, it might then be vulnerable to access by other servers holding the same certificate.

Figure 7.22 shows that the Hatfield marketing server has received a Mackoy certificate, the Mackoy marketing server has received a Hatfield certificate, and both of the servers have turned trust off. Neither of the servers trusts the certificate it has requested, but it will present the certificate to the server to which it is trying to gain access. For example, the Hatfield/Mkt server does not trust the Mackoy certificate, but it presents the Mackoy certificate to the Mackoy/Mkt server when trying to access it, and because the Mackoy/Mkt servers trust its own certificate, one side of authentication occurs. For the other side of authentication, the Mackoy/ Mkt server presents its Hatfield certificate, which it does not trust, to the Hatfield/Mkt server, which does trust the Hatfield certificate. Authentication completes, and these two servers can now communicate. Each server is protected from access by other servers carrying the non-trusted certificate. Trust is turned on or off from within the ID information box.

Figure 7.22

Servers do not trust any certificate they have identified as non-trusted. They use them only to present for access, not to grant access.

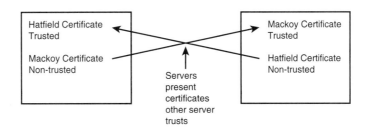

Another method for implementing communication with non-hierarchical names is to create a specific "outside company" flat certifier. Only servers designated to communicate with other servers outside the company hold this certificate, and this certificate is the one granted to outside servers wanting to communicate. Using this method does not expose all of the servers in the organization. This second method is inherently a more secure method of communication.

Communication Between Hierarchical Servers and Non-Hierarchical Servers

Communication between two hierarchical servers requires cross certification. Communication between two non-hierarchical servers requires common certificates. To implement communication between a hierarchical server and a non-hierarchical server, you cannot use cross certificates; instead, you must create a non-hierarchical certifier for the hierarchical environment. You then certify the server ID from the hierarchical environment with this new non-hierarchical certifier. The server ID would then contain one hierarchical certificate and one non-hierarchical certificate. The non-hierarchical company creates a safe copy of the server ID it will use and sends this through whatever method is available to the hierarchical company. The hierarchical company certifies this safe copy with the non-hierarchical certifier it has created. The safe copy is sent back to the non-hierarchical company. The server that will be merging this certificate into its ID is shut down. The ID merges the certificate, the server is restarted, and communication can then occur between the two servers. Both servers now contain a common certificate, even though one of the servers is a hierarchical server. This method of communication works only if one of the servers is non-hierarchical; should both servers contain hierarchical certificates as well as a non-hierarchical certificate in common, Notes ignores the non-hierarchical certificate and looks for cross certificates.

Administration Process

The Notes release 4 administration process can be used to upgrade flat names to hierarchical. Until this upgrade has taken place, none of the administration process requests can be used against non-hierarchical names. To upgrade non-hierarchical names, the request is generated from the Public Address Book. The name is selected and the administrator chooses Rename Person. Next, click upgrade to hierarchical. Choose the hierarchical certifier you will use and then upgrade (see Figure 7.23).

Figure 7.23

Upgrading to hierarchical.

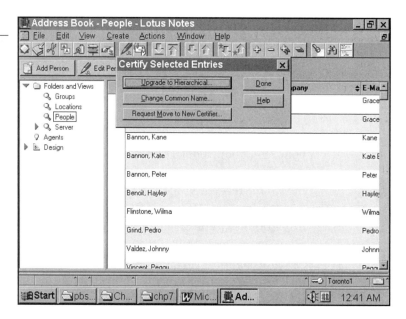

Exercises

In this chapter, you explored the complexities of the hierarchical naming conventions, how to use the naming components in your organization, and for what purposes. Without a grasp of these concepts, Chapter 8, "Working with Domains," would be very difficult to understand. As administrator, you want to take full advantage of Notes' communication capabilities without exposing your organization to any security breaches. Your full understanding of cross certification in a hierarchical environment and sharing certificates in a non-hierarchical environment is essential.

Exercise 7.1

You have decided that the next level in your hierarchical system below Bean is a geographical indicator. All of your people in Toronto will have the identifier TOR/Bean after their common names. In this lab, you will create the new organizational certifier ID and register a user with it. Complete the following steps:

1. Select File | Tools | Server Administration | Certifiers | Register Organizational Unit. If your cert.id is on your hard drive, Notes automatically uses this and asks for your password. As long as this is the correct cert.id, enter the password. Because you are working directly at the server, leave the registration server as local.

2. The certifier ID should indicate that you have chosen Bean; if this is not the case, click Certifier ID and choose the Bean cert.id.

3. Enter Tor as the new unit (don't use any slashes).

4. Enter lotusnotes as the password.

5. Enter Pedro Grind as the administrator.

6. Click Register.

7. When Notes prompts you to save to the A: drive, click Cancel and save the new organizational unit certifier ID to the Notes/Data directory.

continues

8. Notes defaults to saving the file with the same name as the unit (Tor.id).

You have now created a new certifier ID file, which you use to register a person who will be working in Toronto. Complete the following steps:

1. Select File | Tools | System Administration | People | Register Person. Answer Yes to the question about license.

2. If Notes prompts you for the password for the Bean ID, click cancel.

3. Notes prompts you to choose the certifier ID.

4. To register this person, choose the Tor.id file.

5. Enter the password for Tor.id.

6. Leave all information in this first dialog box as is.

7. Because you are working at the server, the registration server is local.

8. Certifier ID should be identified as TOR/Bean; if this is not the case, click Certifier ID and select Tor.id.

9. Click Continue.

10. Enter the name and password of the person you want to register.

11. Examine other choices, but leave all defaults as is.

12. Click Register.

13. On the status bar, you should see messages indicating that the ID file and mail file are being created and the certification log is being updated. Answer No to Do you want to register another person?

14. Go to the People icon and choose the People view.

You should be able to see the person document in the Public Address Book, and find the mail file created on the server.

Review Questions

1. To create a first level organizational unit certifier, you need which of the following?

   a. Access to the address book

   b. Access to the organization certifier ID

   c. Access to the server console

2. To register a person who will be identified by a first-level organizational unit certifier, you need which of the following?

   a. Access to only the first-level organizational unit certifier

   b. Access to both the first-level OU certifier and the O certifier

   c. A NetCreator role in the Public Address Book

3. Cross certificates are kept where?

   a. In the ID of the entity receiving the cross certificate

   b. In the Public Address Book

   c. In Cross Certificates under the Certifier icon in the Server Administration panel

4. True or false: Cross certificates can be issued only from server to server.

5. True or false: If cross certificates don't exist between two servers in different organizations, they can still send mail to each other.

6. To nullify a cross certificate, do which of the following?

   a. Change the field access in the cross certificate to no access.

   b. Remove the cross certificate from the Public Address Book.

   c. Remove the cross certificate from the Public Address. Book and make sure the other organization removes its cross certificate, too.

7. True or false: For cross certificates to work, they must be issued at the same level between two organizations.

8. True or false: Organization cross certificates mean only entities certified directly by the organization certifier can use the cross certificates.

9. When trying to access a server with whom you have a cross certificate, what message do you receive?

   a. You are not authorized to access this server.

   b. You are not authorized to access this server, would you like to issue a cross certificate for this server?

   c. You are not authorized to access this server, would you like to receive a cross certificate from this server?

10. True or false: When you want to request a cross certificate with another organization, you can send that organization a Notes mail message with your request along with your key.

11. True or false: When you send someone a safe copy of your ID for purposes of cross certification, your safe ID need not be sent back to you.

12. For two servers, one that is hierarchical and one that has flat naming to connect, which of the following is true?

    a. The hierarchical server must obtain a flat certificate.

    b. The flat server must obtain a hierarchical certificate.

13. Which of the following is true?

    a. Flat IDs can contain multiple certificates.

    b. Hierarchical IDs can contain multiple certificates.

    c. Both flat and hierarchical IDs (lowercase) can contain multiple certificates.

14. Which of the following is true?

    a. Hierarchical IDs can contain multiple hierarchical certificates.

    b. Hierarchical IDs can contain only one hierarchical certificate.

15. True or false: As soon as a flat ID contains a certificate, it must trust any other ID that contains the same certificate.

16. A safe copy of an ID contains which of the following?

    a. All ID information, password protected

    b. Name and all keys

    c. Name, license, and public key only

17. True or false: To enable authentication between two servers, one using a flat name and the other a hierarchical name, cross certificates cannot be used.

18. True or false: Two flat IDs having different certificates but belonging to the same domain can authenticate with each other.

Review Answers

1. A, B. Without the organization certifier ID and access to the Address Book, you cannot create a descendant, which is what the first-level organizational unit is. For more information, refer to the section titled "First-Level Organization Unit Certifiers."

2. A, C. You do not need the O certifier to register a user who will be identified as belonging to the first-level organizational unit. For more information, refer to the section titled "Registering the User." You do need the NetCreator role.

3. B. Organization certificates are kept in the user and server ID, but the cross certificates are kept in the Public Address Book. For more information, refer to the section titled "Working with Cross Certification."

4. False. Although it is very common for cross certificates to be issued at the server-to-server level, they can also be issued to organization IDs, organizational unit IDs, and user IDs. For more information, refer to the section titled "Working with Cross Certification."

5. False. Before any information can pass between servers, including mail, the servers must be able to authenticate. If the two servers are from different organizations, they must have cross certificates before this can occur. For more information, refer to the section titled "Working with Cross Certification."

6. B. When the cross certificate is removed from the Public Address Book (and the servers should be restarted so the cache is cleared), no access is granted. For more information, refer to the section titled "Working with Cross Certification."

7. False. The level at which the cross certificate is granted does not matter; the only condition is that there must be a cross certificate in each direction. For more information, refer to the section titled "Working with Cross Certification."

8. False. Any server or user certified directly by the organization certifier or any descendant of the organization certifier

will have access. For more information, refer to the section titled "Working with Cross Certification."

9. B. This is the new on-demand system for cross certification available in release 4 of Notes. Cross certificates are issued; they are not received. For more information, refer to the section titled "Working with Cross Certification."

10. False. If you don't have a cross certificate with an organization, its server will not accept any information, including mail, from you. For more information, refer to the section titled "Working with Cross Certification."

11. True. The information from the safe ID is incorporated into the cross certificate, which is created in its Public Address Book. The safe ID is no longer of any use to them, and you do not need it to access its server(s). For more information, refer to the section titled "Working with Cross Certification."

12. A. Flat IDs cannot contain hierarchical certificates. For more information, refer to the section titled "Using Flat Naming Conventions."

13. C. Both types of IDs can contain multiple certificates, but hierarchical IDs can contain only one hierarchical certificate and multiple flat certificates, and flat IDs can contain multiple flat certificates but no hierarchical certificates. For more information, refer to the section titled "Using Flat Naming Conventions."

14. B. Hierarchical IDs can contain only one hierarchical but multiple flat certificates. For more information, refer to the section titled "Using Flat Naming Conventions."

15. False. In the information box for an ID containing a flat certificate, "trust" can be turned off for flat certificates. For more information, refer to the section titled "Using Flat Naming Conventions."

16. C. Safe IDs are used for two main purposes: to provide information for the creation of cross certificates and to collect certificates to merge back into the ID. Only this limited information is needed for these functions. For more information,

refer to the sections titled "Using Flat Naming Conventions" and "Working with Cross Certification."

17. True. Cross certificates are valid only when both IDs are hierarchical. For more information, refer to section titled "Using Flat Naming Conventions."

18. False. Even if the IDs belong to the same domain, they are certified by different flat certifiers. There is no relationship between flat certifiers, and the IDs they certified cannot talk to one another. To communicate, they must share a common certificate. For more information, refer to the section titled "Using Flat Naming Conventions."

Answers to Test Yourself Questions at Beginning of Chapter

1. One organization ID, three first-level organizational unit IDs, and 12 second-level organizational unit IDs (three divisions with four departments each). Only the second-level OU IDs are used to register servers and people. For more information, see "Using Hierarchical Naming."

2. The organization certifier ID, first-level OU ID, second-level OU ID, and the user ID. For more information, see "Using Hierarchical Naming."

3. Before looking at the server document to see whether a user or server is allowed access, the server or user must pass authentication, or a cross certificate must exist for it. For more information, see "Working with Cross Certification."

4. For authentication to occur between two servers from different organizations, they each must have issued a cross certificate for the other. For replication, only one Connection document is needed. For more information, see "Working with Cross Certification."

5. Cross certificates can be given at organization, organizational units, server, and user levels. Cross certificates cannot be given to domains or country codes; they do not have IDs. For more information, see "Working with Cross Certification."

6. For a hierarchical server to communicate with a non-hierarchical server, it must create a non-hierarchical (flat) certificate, and each server must share a common certificate. These flat certificates reside in the server IDs. They cannot be removed unless you have access to the ID. To deny access to a server you have stamped with a valid certificate, you must put them in your deny access field in the Server document. For more information, see "Using Flat Naming Conventions."

Chapter

Working with Domains

This chapter examines how domains differ from organizations, as well as how these differences can affect the way a company implements Notes and how a company can implement Notes when mergers or splits of Notes domains or organizations occur. You learn how to do the following:

- ▶ Control domain access
- ▶ Control domain routing
- ▶ Merge and split domains
- ▶ Set up domain routing/replication

Test Yourself! Before reading this chapter, test yourself to determine how much study time you will need to devote to this section.

1. Can a domain contain multiple organizations?

2. You are a Notes user. Where is your domain identified?

3. Servers in adjacent, one-organization domains require cross certification to communicate. This is also true of servers in non-adjacent domains. Is this statement true? If not, why?

4. When using Cascading Public Address Books on a server, does a user have to identify the domain to which a recipient belongs?

Answers are located at the end of the chapter...

In all previous chapters except Chapter 7, "Naming Conventions and Certification," you have been working with one domain. Mail routing and replication have occurred between servers in one domain. Even with the process of authentication, you have been dealing mainly with entities that receive their certificate from the same ancestor. In this chapter, however, you examine heterogeneous environments—servers in different domains replicating and sending mail. In other words, users from one domain access a server in a different domain. You'll cover the following:

▶ Multiple domains and organizations

▶ Merging domains

▶ Splitting domains

▶ Requirements for connections to another domain

▶ Adjacent and non-adjacent domains

▶ Cascading address books

In Chapter 2, "Server and Client Setup," domains and organizations were discussed and defined. At this point, it is important that you fully understand what these terms mean. What are the limitations of a domain? What rights do users and servers inherit by being in the same organization? Chapters 2 and 6, "Administration Tools," cover the majority of this information, setting the stage for this section on working with domains.

Multiple Domains and Organizations

You know from Chapter 2 that a domain is the sum of the entities listed in a Public Address Book. Two servers or users listed in the same Public Address Book are considered to be in the same domain. Having a different certificate doesn't matter; an organization is composed of all the entities that descend from an organization certifier. An organization can be contained in one address book or it can span several address books, and a domain can contain multiple organizations. The following sections examine the three possible scenarios for domains and organizations.

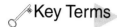

Key Terms

> To belong to an *organization*, your ID must contain a certificate from the organization certifier or a certificate from a descendant of the organization certifier.
>
> To belong to a *domain*, the Person or Server document must specify the domain's name in the domain field, and the documents must be in the same Public Address Book.

Single Domain/Single Organization

In this scenario, there is one Public Address Book, and everyone in it has a certificate that originates from the same ancestral certifier (see Figure 8.1.)

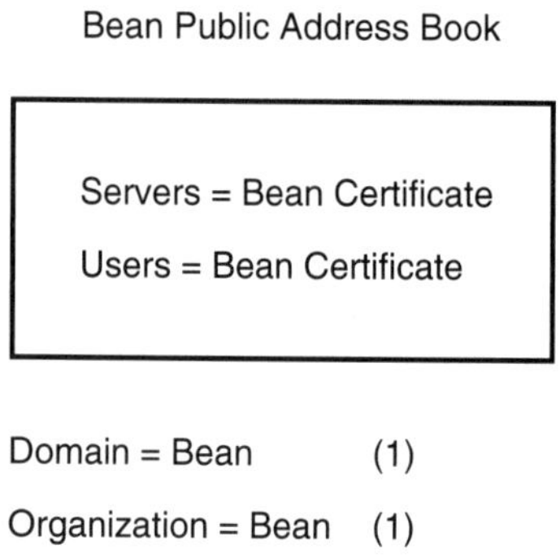

Figure 8.1

One Public Address Book with a common ancestral certificate.

Bean Public Address Book

Servers = Bean Certificate

Users = Bean Certificate

Domain = Bean   (1)

Organization = Bean   (1)

This is the most common scenario for a Notes environment. If the organization is not too large, having just one domain and one organization helps keep things simple and fairly easy to control.

Single Domain/Multiple Organization

Although there is only one Public Address Book in a single domain, within this one address book there are people and servers listed who have been certified by completely unrelated ancestors. Picture a scenario in which the Bean and Leaf organizations have merged. During the merger, they decide to consolidate their Notes operations and use only one address book. As a result, Server Y/Mkt/Leaf is in the same address book as Server A/Sales/US/Bean. For this scenario to function, a prerequisite is the creation of cross certificates so that a form of authentication can occur when users and servers from the same address book attempt to access servers with which they do not share a common ancestral certificate (see Figure 8.2).

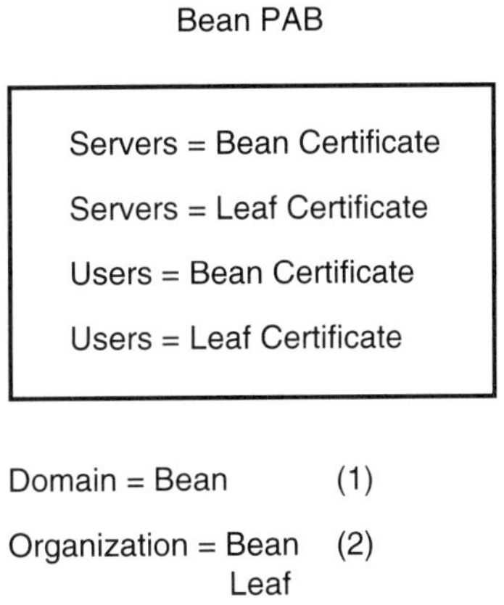

Figure 8.2

One Public Address Book with different ancestral certificates.

Bean PAB

```
Servers = Bean Certificate

Servers = Leaf Certificate

Users = Bean Certificate

Users = Leaf Certificate
```

Domain = Bean   (1)

Organization = Bean   (2)
                 Leaf

The concept of cross certificates, how they are granted, and their function was covered in Chapter 7. As mentioned in the preceding example, the merger scenario is one of the main reasons why people and servers listed in the same address book can have different ancestral certificates. Multiple divisions in a large corporation build up their Notes environments, and then they are ordered to merge. It is much simpler to merge all the Public Address Books into one and issue cross certificates than to go through the process of renaming and recertifying. This particular scenario really illustrates the function and definition of a domain; it demonstrates how Notes entities with completely unrelated certificates (in other words, organization) can exist together in the same Public Address Book.

Multiple Domains/Single Organization

In some Notes environments, the number of Person, Server, and even Connection documents is so large that the database itself is unwieldy. It becomes more manageable to split the Public Address Book into two or three logical domains. Yet, the same ancestral certificate certifies all entities identified in each of the domains (see Figure 8.3). If servers try to communicate from one domain to another, there is nothing in the authentication process to inhibit their communication. The same is true for users attempting to access servers in the other domains. This is completely the opposite scenario in single-domain, multiple organizations in which, even though entities were in the same domain, they required cross certificates to communicate because their certificates were from different organizations.

These last two scenarios should drive home the definition of domain versus organization. Domain is the Public Address Book to which you belong, and it is not listed anywhere in your ID. Organization is the certificate you carry in your ID and who it came from—in other words, the organization certifier ID.

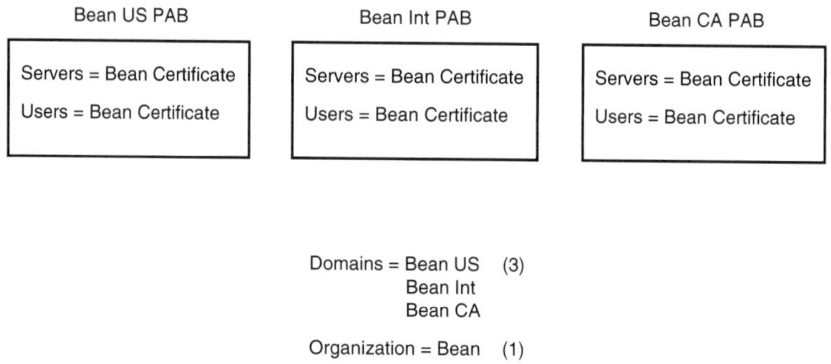

Figure 8.3

Multiple domains and one organization.

Bean US PAB	Bean Int PAB	Bean CA PAB
Servers = Bean Certificate Users = Bean Certificate	Servers = Bean Certificate Users = Bean Certificate	Servers = Bean Certificate Users = Bean Certificate

```
Domains = Bean US    (3)
          Bean Int
          Bean CA

Organization = Bean    (1)
```

Merging Domains

The topics of merging and splitting domains are not activities you engage in regularly. Nonetheless, it is important to understand the guidelines for accomplishing these procedures for the purpose of executing them, as well as to give you an in-depth understanding of the use of domains, where they are referenced, how you can alter these references, and so on. You also will become familiar with certificates, how they allow and disallow entities from communicating, and how to use cross certificates where needed.

Consider the following scenario: A merging of the companies from the earlier example, Bean and Leaf, has been proposed and will happen in a couple of months. You have been asked to develop a plan for merging the domains together. Both companies use

Notes for e-mail and distribute and gather data by using Notes databases. You must consider the following items:

▶ What cross certificates will be created to enable authentication?

▶ What `names.nsf` will be used in the final merge: Bean's or Leaf's?

▶ Who will be responsible for copying and pasting the documents from one Address Book to the other?

▶ What will be the procedure for replacing the old `names.nsf` with the new one?

▶ After the new Public Address Book works for one of the servers, how do you distribute the new address book to all other servers?

▶ What other databases use the domain name as a component?

▶ How will mail routing be implemented?

▶ What about a replication schedule?

After considering these issues and attempting a few options on test servers, you come up with the following recommendations:

▶ Cross certificates will be issued at the organization level, Bean to Leaf and Leaf to Bean. This allows authentication currently as if the entities were in the same organization.

▶ Server access fields, Access Control Lists, and database security will be dealt with as needed.

▶ Leaf's Public Address Book will be merged into Bean's.

▶ All of the relevant documents (see the following list) will be copied from `Leaf` and pasted into `Bean`. All references to the `Leaf` domain will be modified to refer to the `Bean` domain. The relevant documents are as follows:

▶ Server documents

▶ Connection documents (to implement mail routing and replication schemes)

▶ Domain documents

▶ Person documents

▶ Location documents

▶ Mail-in Database documents

▶ Group documents (`LocalDomainServers`, `OtherDomain-Servers`)

To merge two domains into one while maintaining two organizations, complete the following steps:

1. After the documents are added to Bean's address book and modified, a replica copy is placed on one of Leaf's servers; make sure that the filename does not start with the word `names`, because this confuses the server.

2. The server is brought down.

3. A backup copy of Leaf's address book is made in case something goes wrong and the server needs to be brought back up under Leaf.

4. The `domain =` line in the `Notes.ini` of the Leaf server being tested is changed to reflect the domain name `Bean`.

5. The Leaf address book, `names.nsf`, is removed from the data directory, and the Bean address book is put in the data directory with the filename `names.nsf`.

6. The server is brought back up. Note the startup message `Domain = Bean`.

   You now should be able to send a mail message from Leaf to a user in Bean without using the domain name.

7. The following databases in Leaf will be altered or replaced with the replica copies from Bean:

   ▶ `certlog.nsf`

   ▶ `admin4.nsf`

   ▶ `events4.nsf`

   ▶ `statrep.nsf`

After you successfully complete these steps for one server, use the same procedure to send the new Public Address Book to all Leaf servers:

1. All Bean servers receive the new Public Address Book through replication.

2. Users in both Bean and Leaf are advised of the new Public Address Book and told to replace any existing replica copy they may have on their disk.

After these steps are followed, you have merged two domains into one while maintaining two organizations. The entities from the separate organizations are capable of communicating with cross certification at the organization level.

Splitting Domains

Splitting domains is the reverse process of merging. You take the same documents from the Public Address Book and instead of changing the domain fields to reflect the same name, you change the domain fields to differentiate the domains. The certificates in the names are not changed, so authentication occurs between entities in the two domains without any need for cross certification.

If security is an issue, this must be addressed. However, there are many other tools with which to protect data: server access fields, the Access Control List for the databases, data encryption, and other database security features. These features will continue to protect the servers and the data until the decision is made to change them. Depending on whether or not security is an issue in the splitting of domains, you might want to add it to your list of procedures for splitting domains.

If security is a concern, treat it the same way you would an individual who has left the company. Use the administration process to remove an individual from the newly split Public Address Book, Access Control Lists, and groups, and add him or her to a terminated group specifically denied access to everything. Of course, to achieve the highest level of security, you should plan a new organization, create the certifiers, and recertify all users and servers.

Consider the following scenario: The merger with Leaf is canceled. Bean Canada is very upset with the way things have been handled. They have decided to break off from Bean U.S. in terms of directing their business, but they will continue to purchase products and participate in the distribution methods. Part of the agreement is that Bean Canada will now manage its own Notes environment. As a result, the domain must be split. You have been asked to consider the factors and suggest an implementation plan. The following are factors regarding Bean Canada:

▶ The names and certification will remain the same (security is not an issue).

▶ The following Server documents will be cut or copied from Bean's address book and pasted into the new Public Address Book that Bean Canada creates:

  ▶ Server documents

  ▶ Connection documents

  ▶ Domain documents

  ▶ Person documents

  ▶ Location documents

  ▶ Mail-in Database documents

  ▶ Group documents (`LocalDomainServers`, `OtherDomainServers`)

- The new domain name is BeanC.

- All documents listed previously must be modified to reference the new domain name.

- The Connection documents must be modified not only for domain name but also to reflect whatever mail routing and replication scheme Bean Canada has devised.

After the new address book has been created and modified, do the following:

1. Bring down one of the servers.

2. Back up the old address book.

3. Rename the new address book names.nsf.

4. Change the Domain= line in the Notes.ini to Domain=BeanC.

5. Start the server.

6. Follow the same procedure with another server.

7. Test communication between the two test servers with access, mail routing, and replication.

8. After success, continue this procedure with all servers in the BeanC domain. Advise all users who might have a replica copy of the old Bean address book to delete it and make a replica copy of the new address book.

The following databases should be deleted by the adminstrator on each server and will be re-created when loaded again:

- admin4.nsf

- events4.nsf

- statrep.nsf

Bean will delete certain documents from its Public Address Book and modify others, based on the mail routing or replication scheme:

> ▶ Server documents—All Server documents for servers in BeanC must be deleted.

> ▶ Connection documents—New Connection documents can be added, based on any new mail routing or replication. Existing documents can be kept but modified to reflect the new domain name for the BeanC servers.

> ▶ Domain documents—You can choose to create Domain documents for BeanC.

> ▶ Person documents—Delete all Person documents for people now in BeanC.

> ▶ Location documents—If there were location documents for Bean Canada's use, they can be deleted.

> ▶ Mail-in Database documents—Delete any Mail-in Database documents referencing servers in BeanC.

> ▶ Group document (LocalDomainServers, OtherDomainServers)— Remove servers in BeanC from LocalDomainServers and add them to OtherDomainServers or create a new group for them.

Communicating Between Domains

Although Bean and BeanC have split, they still will want to discuss and share many things. Also, even though Bean and Leaf did not merge, they have decided to operate jointly on some marketing objectives, so communication is a factor, too. How can you implement communication between these two domains?

Connection Documents and Cross Certification

Before you consider mail routing concerns and Domain documents, review the basics:

> ▶ For two servers that are not in the same Notes named network to send mail to one another, a Connection document is necessary. This Connection document specifies the mechanics of

how the two will talk. Will they talk across phone lines and if so, using what phone number? Or, will they talk across the network wire, and if so, using what port?

▶ If the two servers do not share an ancestral certificate—in other words, two different organization certifiers certified them—they will need cross certificates to authenticate.

Mail Routing Between Domains

Four types of domains exist in Notes:

▶ Foreign, which is usually some type of gateway into another system, fax, SMTP mail, and so on.

▶ Adjacent, which means there is a way of connecting between at least two servers in each domain.

▶ Non-adjacent, which means there is no connection method between two domains, but each of these two non-adjacent domains are adjacent to another common domain.

▶ Global domain, which is used for SMTP purposes (see Figure 8.4).

In the following sections, you learn about the implementation of communication between both adjacent and non-adjacent domains.

Communication Between Adjacent Domains

There is nothing too complicated about sending mail between two adjacent domains. As already mentioned, adjacent means that there is a method of communication between at least two servers in each domain. There must be Connection documents, and the servers must be able to authenticate, most likely through cross certificates.

When someone decides to send mail to a user in the adjacent domain, the Send To field in the mail message must contain the domain name (see Figure 8.4).

Figure 8.4

Identifying the domain name when sending mail outside of your domain.

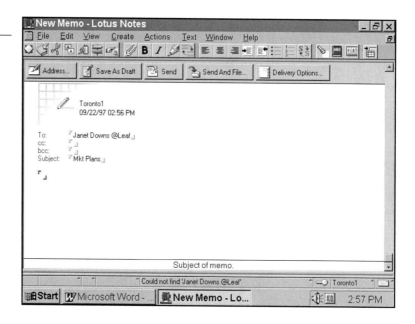

The Soundex on the server sending the mail does not check the validity of the name, because it doesn't have the Public Address Book of the other domain to check against. Instead, the router examines the recipient name and sees the domain to which it must go. The router then checks the Public Address Book to verify that there is a Connection document for one of its servers to send mail to a server in the destination domain. The router's job is to get the mail to that server, which then sends it over to the server in the destination domain at the scheduled time. As soon as the mail arrives at the destination domain, the router checks its Public Address Book to see where the recipient resides (see Figure 8.5).

Figure 8.5

Sending mail to another domain.

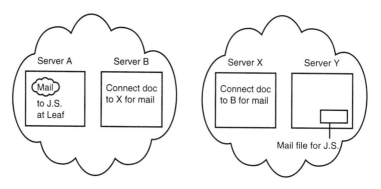

The steps involved in Figure 8.5 are as follows:

1. Server A/Bean's router sees that the domain destination for the mail message is Leaf.

2. Router finds a Connection document in the Public Address Book, identifying Server B/Bean as its connector to send mail to Server X/Leaf.

3. Server A/Bean's router sends message to Server B/Bean.

4. Server B/Bean's router sends mail over to Server X/Leaf at the scheduled time.

5. Server X/Leaf's router determines that J.S.'s mail file is on Server Y/Leaf from J.S.'s Person document in Leaf's Public Address Book and transfers it.

6. Server Y/Leaf delivers mail to the J.S. mail file.

The mail is then delivered to the recipient. There is no requirement to have an adjacent Domain document for this process to occur.

Connections Between Non-adjacent Domains

Non-adjacent domains imply that there is no Connection document between two domains; usually there would be no method for authentication even if they did connect. Consider the example in Figure 8.6: Bean has a connection method to BeanC, (Server B from Bean and Server M from BeanC have Connection documents) and a connection method to Leaf, (Server A from Bean and Server Y from Leaf have Connection documents). Bean shares an ancestral certificate with BeanC and has cross certificates with Leaf, so authentication is not a problem with either domain.

Although BeanC and Leaf do not have servers that communicate, mail can be delivered from BeanC to Leaf in one of two ways. The first way is by using only existing Connection documents:

1. Users from BeanC know that they can get a message to Bean. Many also know Bean can get messages to Leaf, so they address their mail messages with the path that the message will take to get to Leaf. In this case, the address is Recipient @Leaf @Bean.

2. The router from BeanC knows from its address book that it can get the message to the domain Bean. It doesn't worry about the second domain identified in the address. The router always addresses the right-most domain first.

3. After the message is delivered to Bean, the @Bean is stripped away and the router for the server in domain Bean now looks for a Connection document for a server in the domain Leaf. It finds it and delivers the message to the Server Y in Leaf.

4. The Leaf server's router then looks for the location of the recipient's mail file and completes the delivery.

Figure 8.6

Connection between two domains who don't have a connection—non-adjacent domains.

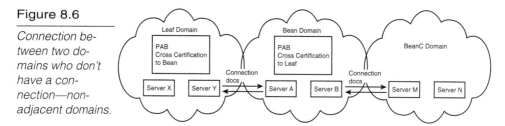

So even though BeanC and Leaf do not communicate directly— they are non-adjacent—mail still can be delivered through the intermediary (adjacent) domain Bean. I will discuss possible restrictions later in this chapter (see the section titled "Restricting Access from Other Domains").

The second way to deliver mail from BeanC to Leaf is by using Connection documents and Domain documents. To make life a little easier for users, a BeanC administrator can create a non-adjacent Domain document. This non-adjacent Domain document specifies mail intended for recipients in the domain Leaf, which will go through the domain Bean to get there. See Figure 8.7 for an example of the Domain document.

Figure 8.7

Specifying a route through an intermediary domain by using a non-adjacent Domain document.

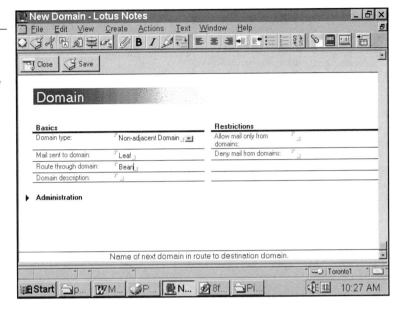

A BeanC user sending a message to a recipient in Leaf only has to put the domain of the recipient and not the explicit routing, as described in the preceding example. In this case the user should include Recipient @Leaf.

The router on servers in BeanC knows that any mail sent to Leaf domain is sent to Bean (it knows this from the non-adjacent Domain document in the Public Address Book). The router adds the domain Bean to the address and sends it there first; Bean then sends it to domain Leaf.

Restricting Access from Other Domains

Processing mail requires server resources. If your domain is an intermediary domain—other domains route mail through you to get to a final destination domain—you might decide to restrict this. You don't want your servers to become overloaded handling other people's mail. The fields in the Domain document for both adjacent and non-adjacent domains enable you to specify whom you will allow or deny. Figure 8.8 is an adjacent Domain document.

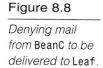

Figure 8.8

Denying mail from BeanC to be delivered to Leaf.

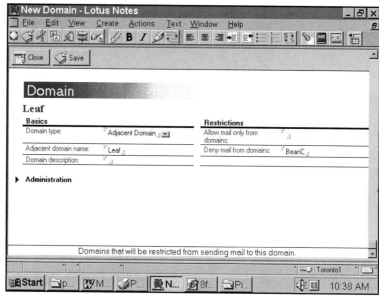

Consider the following scenario: You are the administrator responsible for mail routing in the Bean domain. After examining the mail delivered through your servers, you conclude that there are far too many messages going from BeanC to Leaf and vice versa. You decide to implement two Domain documents, one for adjacent domain BeanC and one for adjacent domain Leaf. You have decided to heavily restrict your acceptance of mail. In both documents in the field, you must specify Allow Mail Only From Domains, with their respective domain names. This measure is sometimes referred to as a firewall for messages trying to go through your domain. These same fields are available in non-adjacent Domain documents and are used for the same purpose.

Cascading Address Books

The Leaf and Bean companies are sending each other a lot of mail. Their work on the joint marketing plans is coming along. There are complaints, however, that mail has to be delivered two or three times because of incorrect recipient naming. When sending mail from one domain to another, there is no Soundex involved because most Notes environments can refer only to their own Public Address Book. As a result, the mail is sent with an error in the name, and after it is delivered to the `Leaf` domain, the recipient mail file cannot be found and the message is returned as undeliverable. The name has to be checked and the mail resent. This is very annoying!

As administrator, you can assist your users by obtaining either a subset replica copy of Leaf's Public Address Book, containing only people documents or an address book database with only people documents, containing mail information. After you have this database on your servers and are certain that you are replicating it with Leaf to update it, you are ready to give your users access to it so that they can address mail to Leaf correctly. Obviously when you put this database on your server(s), you do not give it the filename `names.nsf`. You might call it something like `leafbook.nsf`. You then reference this filename in your `Notes.ini` for each server who will use it. To do this, insert a line in your `Notes.ini` anywhere after the first four lines (if you do not already have one):

`Names=Names,leafbook`

This line tells the server (really the Soundex) what address books to check for name verification and specifically in what order to check them—from left to right (see Figure 8.9). Because the server (Soundex) checks from left to right, always put your domain's address book first. You should not indicate the `.nsf` extension in the `Names=` line in the `Notes.ini`.

Figure 8.9

Cascading ad-dress books on a server.

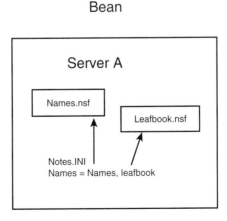

Bean

 **Key Term**

A server can have a *cascading* (multiple) address book, but only one can be named `names.nsf`, which is the address book of the domain to which the server belongs. All other address books must be renamed. To reference these address books for mail-addressing purposes, include these other domain address books in the server's `Notes.ini` in the line `Names=names,leafbook,rootbook,`*etc*.

Exercises

This chapter ends by increasing your comfort level in working with domains. Should you encounter a situation in which you must either merge or split an existing domain(s), you should feel comfortable enough with a domain to make changes to it. As mentioned previously, these are not functions you will do every day, but understanding your Public Address Book—your do-main—helps you become a better administrator. Now, try the following exercises to reinforce what you have learned.

Exercise 8.1

In this exercise, you create another address book for the domain `Leaf` and create several Person documents in this address book. You then modify the `Notes.ini` to have Toronto1/Bean search the multiple address books when you attempt to send mail from Pedro's mail file.

The first step is to create the Leaf Public Address Book:

1. Select File | Database | New.

2. Leave Server as local.

3. For the title, enter `Leaf's Address Book`.

4. For the filename, enter `leafbook.nsf`.

5. For the template, choose Public Address Book.

6. Click OK.

Now, create a few Person documents in Leaf's new address book:

1. Open Leaf's address book and go to the People view.

2. Click Add Person.

3. For your purposes, you need to fill in only four fields. You can use the following example or create one of your own:

continues

Exercise 8.1 Continued

First Name:	Margaret
Last Name:	Breen
Full Name:	Margaret Breen/Leaf
Domain:	Leaf

4. Save and exit this document and repeat to add one more person:

First Name:	Cordelia
Last Name:	Vincent
Full Name:	Cordelia Vincent/Leaf
Domain:	Leaf

You now have a very basic facsimile of Leaf's address book on your server. At this point, even if you try to create a mail message to any of these people in Leaf, your server will not check their names for you. To enable your server to check these names, you need to alter your Notes.ini file.

Now, shut the Notes sessions down, for both server and client:

1. Open your Notes.ini file and edit it to include the following line (it doesn't matter where the line is, as long as it's after the first four lines):

   `Names=names,leafbook`

2. Save and exit your Notes.ini file.

3. Restart your server and your server client.

4. Open Pedro Grind's mailfile by selecting File|Database|Open,|Mail (subdirectory)|Pedro Grind.

5. From within Pedro's mailfile, click New Memo.

6. In the To field type `Br`. Notes fills in the rest for you, and you see `Margaret Breen/Leaf` as soon as you go to the next field.

7. In the CC field, type `Cor`. Notes fills in the rest for your, and you see `Cordelia Vincent/Leaf`.

Your Notes Server can provide these names for you because you have told it to search the databases listed in the `Names=` line in the `Notes.ini` file, and it does this in left-to-right order. Of course, your domain's Public Address Book is always listed first, and it is the only one with the filename `Names.nsf`.

Review Questions

1. In the `A` domain, servers have different ancestral certificates. They will be capable of communicating if:

   a. Their Server documents are all in the same Public Address Book

   b. There are cross certificates for them.

   c. They have Connection documents.

2. How is a domain defined?

   a. Through the Server documents

   b. Through the Public Address Book

   c. Through the organization

3. Cross certificates can be issued for which of the following?

   a. Connection documents

   b. Server documents

   c. Any ID

   d. `cert.id` only

4. Which of the following is not considered a component in a hierarchical name?

   a. Country

   b. Common name

   c. Organization

   d. Domain

5. What is the main function of a Notes domain?

   a. Server management

   b. Connection document management

   c. Mail routing

6. After you merge two domains into one, you must do which of the following?

   a. Recertify all users with a new organization certifier

   b. Issue cross certificates to enable communication

   c. Create a new certifier for both domains

7. True or false: You can have two domains, both containing servers and users with the same ancestral certificate in a Notes environment.

8. If you are splitting a domain in two but communication is still required, you should do which of the following?

   a. Leave all the Server and Person documents in the old address book

   b. Delete the Server and Person documents that are going into the new domain from the old address book

9. You have split a one-organization domain into two domains. To make sure the server and users can still authenticate, you must do which of the following?

    a. Create cross certificates

    b. Do nothing

    c. Create a new group for the new domain and include them in the access fields in the Server documents

10. Domain names are not listed in which of the following documents?

    a. Person

    b. Server

    c. Connection

    d. Group

11. Cross certificates do which of the following?

    a. Perform a sort of authentication

    b. Perform a one-way authentication

    c. Override server-access fields

12. True or false: After you merge domains and put the new address books on the servers, the old domain servers automatically update their Notes.ini to reflect the new domain.

13. What is a domain to which you can indirectly connect called?

    a. A foreign domain

    b. An adjacent domain

    c. A non-adjacent domain

14. What is a gateway into another system that Notes can pass information to and from called:

    a. A non-adjacent domain

    b. A foreign domain

    c. A gateway domain

15. Multiple address books can be searched on your system by referencing them in the:

    a. Public Address Book

    b. `Notes.ini`

    c. Configuration document

16. Mail routing firewalls can be established through the use of which of the following?

    a. Fields on the Connection documents

    b. Fields on the Server documents

    c. Fields on the Domain documents

17. True or false: Users can send mail to non-adjacent domains without having Domain documents in the Public Address Book.

18. When users use explicit routing to send their mail, the domains to travel are indicated:

    a. In a right-to-left fashion, with the right-most domain being the first to be accessed

    b. In a left-to-right fashion, with the left-most domain being the first to be accessed

19. True or false: The deny and access fields on the adjacent Domain document and the non-adjacent Domain document are used for the same purposes.

20. To send mail to an adjacent domain, you need which of the following?

    a. A Domain document and a Connection document

    b. A Domain document

    c. A Connection document and possibly cross certificates

Review Answers

1. B. If servers have different ancestral certificates, they are from different organizations. For servers from different organizations to communicate, there must be cross certificates. For more information, refer to the section titled "Multiple Domains/Single Organization."

2. B. All entities (servers and users) defined in one Public Address Book are defined as being in one domain. For more information, refer to the section titled "Multiple Domains and Organizations."

3. C. A cross certificate can be issued to certifier IDs, server IDs, and user IDs. For more information, refer to the section titled "Multiple Domains and Organizations."

4. D. Domains are separate from organizations and are not identified in the hierarchical name. For more information, refer to the section titled "Multiple Domains and Organizations."

5. C. The Public Address Book is used for many things, but the main reason for specifying the entities in a PAB as part of a domain is to help in mail routing. For more information, refer to the section titled"Multiple Domains and Organizations."

6. B. The fastest and easiest way to enable communication is to issue cross certificates at a high level. For more information, refer to the section titled "Multiple Domains and Organizations."

7. True. This is an example of multiple domains, one organization. For more information, refer to the section titled "Multiple Domains/Single Organization."

8. B. A server or a person should only be identified once, in their domain's Public Address Book. The documents should be deleted from the old PAB and put in the new one. For more information, refer to the section titled "Multiple Domains/Single Organization."

9. B. The servers and users in the new domain still have the organization certificates in their IDs, so authentication occurs. For more information, refer to the section titled "Multiple Domains/Single Organization."

10. D. Group documents do not contain any domain fields. For more information, refer to the section titled "Merging Domains and Splitting Domains."

11. A. Cross certificates verify the public key of the entities asking for access against a valid certificate. For more information, refer to the section titled"Communicating Between Domains."

12. False. Updating the `Notes.ini` is needed but is not automatic. For more information, refer to the section titled "Merging Domains."

13. C. When you cannot send mail directly to a Domain X but instead must go through Domain Y, to whom you do have a direct connection, Domain X is called a non-adjacent Domain. For more information, refer to the section titled "Mail Routing Between Domains."

14. B. Fax gateways and such are called foreign domains in Notes. For more information, refer to the section titled "Mail Routing Between Domains."

15. B. The line `Names = names, leafbook, etc` in the `Notes.ini` identifies the cascading address books on a server. For more information, refer to the section titled "Cascading Address Books."

16. C. Fields on the Domain documents enable you to define from whom you do and do not receive mail . For more information, refer to the section titled "Mail Routing Between Domains."

17. True. As long as the sender fully identifies the recipient by domain and there is a Connection document between a server in each domain, the mail will be sent. For more information, refer to the section titled "Mail Routing Between Domains."

18. A. The mail is first sent to the domain on the far-right of the address. For more information, refer to the section titled "Mail Routing Between Domains."

19. True. These fields indicate mail to be allowed and disallowed. For more information, refer to the section titled "Mail Routing Between Domains."

20. C. The Connection document identifies the servers in each domain that connect, and the cross certificates ensure that they can communicate. For more information, refer to the section "Mail Routing Between Domains."

Answers to Test Yourself Questions at Beginning of Chapter

1. Yes. Organizations do not list domains, and domains are not split. For more information, see "Multiple Domains and Organizations."

2. The domain is identified in the Person document. Domain is not identified in the user ID file. For more information, see "Multiple Domains and Organizations."

3. This statement is false. Because servers in non-adjacent domains do not communicate with each other—they communicate through an intermediary server—no cross certification is necessary. For more information, see "Connections Between Non-adjacent Domains."

4. A user does not have to identify the domain to which a recipient belongs. The server goes through the cascading Public Address Books and returns the user's name with the domain identified, as well. See /"Cascading Public Address Books."

Chapter

Server and System Monitoring

This chapter will introduce you to the different monitoring tools available to you in Notes:

Objectives

▶ Setup statistics

▶ Setup events

▶ Setup monitoring

▶ Setup monitoring documents

▶ Monitor domain routing

▶ Monitor domain replication

▶ Troubleshoot using the Statistics and Event Monitor database

Test Yourself! Before reading this chapter, test yourself to determine how much study time you will need to devote to this section.

1. To run Notes' monitoring system, do both the REPORTER task and the EVENT task have to be running on the server?

2. Without the REPORTER or EVENT task running, does the server log.nsf receive any information?

3. Are trouble tickets created automatically when an event of fatal severity occurs, or must they be created by an administrator?

4. Which task is more server resource intensive, EVENT or REPORTER?

5. Where are message documents stored?

6. When composing an event monitor, under the field Event Types, what categories are you presented with?

Answers are located at the end of the chapter...

This chapter will take you through the tools available to assist in your maintenance of the server:

- ▶ Notes log

- ▶ Databases involved in monitoring

- ▶ Server processes involved in monitoring

- ▶ Statistics and events

- ▶ Statistics monitors

- ▶ Event monitors

- ▶ Trouble tickets

- ▶ Centralized monitoring

Events are different from statistics and the REPORT task is not a partner to the EVENT task. REPORT has only one method of notification and EVENT has four. Yet, they are all involved in the monitoring of the system. Be patient, understand the monitoring system included with Notes, and perhaps evaluate some third-party program to assist in monitoring your Notes system.

To understand the material presented in this chapter, it is necessary to have read about the server log database, log.nsf, which is one of the three databases involved in system monitoring (covered in Chapter 6, "Administration Tools"). I also discuss two new server tasks, REPORTER and EVENT, and you must be comfortable with the function of a server task, how to start it, its identification in the Notes.ini, and so on. Be prepared with this knowledge, and the subjects to be discussed should build on your foundation.

Monitoring Overview

A mother has a new baby. She must look after this new baby as well as her other tasks. She has determined she requires assistance in this matter. She will employ a nurse who will monitor the baby and report to her on all activities the baby performs. The nurse will chart the activities and let the mother know if the baby falls above or below any thresholds, so the mother may plan to take action. The nurse will also be responsible for alerting the mother as soon as possible of any serious events.

The nurse has three books do deal with:

▶ The log book where she writes down *everything* she observes the baby doing.

▶ The mother's book of guidelines where she has indicated specific thresholds and events along with appropriate actions.

▶ The baby event reporting book, where the nurse must chart any thresholds the baby has met, as well as any events that have occurred.

The nurse starts duty at five o'clock in the morning. She records in the log book that the baby wakes up at 5:30 a.m. She also records the changing of the diaper and any unusual contents. She reports the feeding of the baby at 6:00 a.m. and that the baby consumed five ounces of formula.

The nurse has recorded in the baby event and threshold book that the baby cried vigorously between 3:30 and 5:30 p.m. every day over the last week. After looking over the statistics, the mother determines the baby is colicky during this time. The solution is the baby must be taken for a walk from 3:30 to 5:30 p.m. The mother viewed a pattern she wants to change and has taken action to accomplish it.

The following day the nurse observes the baby is quite hot. The baby's temperature is taken and is found to be five degrees above the normal threshold. The nurse checks the guideline book and finds the mother's directions are to call her immediately, call the doctor, and meet at the hospital. This is an example of events occurring that require immediate notification.

With this method mapped out, the mother feels confident that she will be alerted in cases where a threshold has been exceeded or not met, and preventative action can then be taken. She also feels confident she will be alerted when events, which immedi-ate action, must be taken. The mother also has the log book to rely on for informative information on the baby's day-to-day activities.

Monitoring the Server

Let's compare this analogy to the Notes environment and the tools you are provided with to monitor the server(s). First of all, you have your baby, your precious server. This server is very im-portant to you, and you want to be aware of any potential prob-lems that may arise, as well as being made aware of any immediate problems in the server's activities. You could stand by the server every minute of every day and see that activities are initiated and completed successfully, or you could implement processes and databases that assist you in monitoring the server (baby).

The nurse would be analogous to the three processes that you use to assist you in monitoring the server:

▶ Server logging activity

▶ The REPORT task

▶ The EVENT task

Each of these processes accomplishes a specific activity, which monitors server activity and reports on thresholds or events. Each of these processes will be discussed in detail in the following sec-tions of this chapter.

The nurse has three books to deal with:

▶ The baby log book is analogous to the log.nsf database, which records all activity the server performs. There is no switch or setting to turn on or off to log this activity; it is automatic. If the log database is deleted, the server will re-create it. The same information used to log server activity is also used to complete the statistical documents and compare this to threshold settings as well as event monitors.

▶ The mother's book of guidelines with specific events and threshold is analogous to the statistics and event databases, events4.nsf. In the Statistics and Events database, you have the listing of all messages that can be set for threshold triggers and event triggers. This is also the database where you create the documents to specify your monitoring requirements.

▶ The Statistics Reporting database (statrep.nsf) that reports on thresholds exceeded, not exceeded, events, and other general statistics is analogous to the baby event reporting book the nurse works with. This book records the general statistics of your server and will log any alarms (thresholds met or not met) as well as any event situations that have been triggered from the documents in the Statistics and Events database. See Figure 9.1 for the database used in monitoring.

Figure 9.1

The database you use to monitor the Notes system.

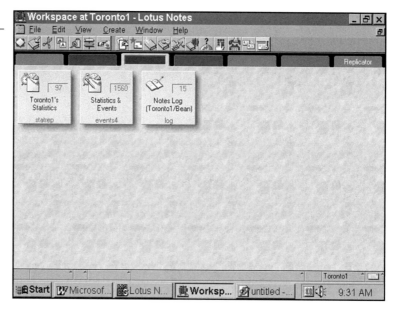

This completes your fairly high-level analogy. Each of the processes and databases I have referenced will be covered in the following sections. From experience, I have found these databases and processes to be confusing to users exposed to them for the first time. It sometimes helps to refer to this analogy as you go through the processes. If this analogy does not work for you, try to convert it to something that does.

Understanding the Processes Involved

There are two specific server processes directly involved in the reporting of statistics and thresholds and events: the EVENT task and the REPORT task. These server tasks have separate responsibilities and do not need to be used together. You will differentiate the responsibilities of these two tasks and how they interact with the Statistics and Events database (events4.nsf) and the server Statistics Reporting database (statrep.nsf). There is a third process, which cannot be started or stopped, and this process logs all activities the server attempts. This logging of all server activity is written to the server's log database log.nsf.

Be aware that there is no named process to start or stop the logging of server activity to the log database. This occurs by default.

The REPORT Task

You can initiate the REPORT task using the following command at the server console:

```
LOAD REPORT
```

When loaded for the first time, the REPORT task creates the following two databases if they do not already exist:

- ▶ The Statistics and Events database (events4.nsf)

- ▶ The Server Statistics Reporting database (statrep.nsf)

If documents relative to the monitoring process still exist in the Public Address Book as they did in release 3 of Notes, these documents will be copied over to the Statistics and Events database.

As you will see from the console when you enter the command to load REPORT, the default collection interval for statistics on a server is 60 minutes. This collection interval can be changed; you will examine the document used to change it in the following sections.

If you want the REPORT task to run at server startup, be sure to include REPORT in the Notes.ini in the SERVERTASKS= line. Every time the server starts, the REPORT task will run. That line should look as follows:

SERVERTASKS=REPORT

The purpose of the REPORT task is to collect statistics and then report them in the Statistics Reporting database (statrep.nsf). The REPORT task does this through the creation of Statistics documents, which are saved in statrep.nsf (see Figure 9.2). These statistics are saved as one of four types of documents:

▶ System

▶ Mail and Database

▶ Communications

▶ Network

Figure 9.2

Types of Statistics documents saved in Statistics Report view.

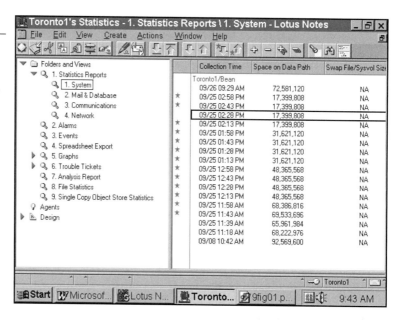

In the collection of statistics, the REPORT task also will be aware of statistics monitors. REPORT will report when thresholds have been reached. It will do this through the creation of alarm

documents, which will reside in the Statistics Reporting database
(statrep.nsf) after having been created by the REPORT task (see
Figure 9.3).

Figure 9.3

Alarm documents detailing thresholds reached, created by REPORTER.

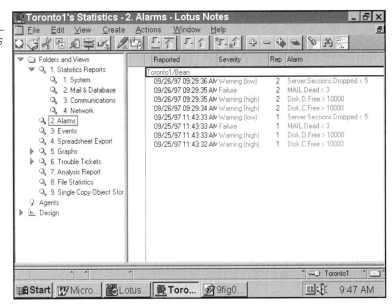

REPORTER creates two types of documents: Statistics documents and
Alarm documents (see Figure 9.4).

Figure 9.4

REPORTER *creating documents.*

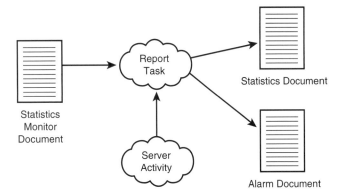

The EVENT Task

The EVENT task has a totally different function than the REPORT task.
The EVENT task has nothing to do with the monitoring and logging
of statistics for the server. The EVENT task is solely concerned with

monitoring event occurrences. This, of course, brings you to the definition of event. Events are defined in the Statistics and Events database. These are the default events, and they are grouped by function; that is, communication events, server events, mail events, and so on. You will see later that these events and their grouping can be modified. There are also two events that are not grouped but can be monitored singly because of their importance: the ACL change event monitors and the replication event monitors. These can be set individually per database.

Like the REPORT task, EVENT is not loaded by default—it can be a heavy user of memory. You can load EVENT directly at the console by typing LOAD EVENT. If the server is shut down and restarted, EVENT will have to be reloaded manually. Should you want EVENT to run whenever the server is running, edit the Notes.ini to include EVENT in the SERVERTASKS= line.

The first time EVENT is run on the server it will check to see if a Statistics Reporting database and a Statistics and Events database exist. EVENT will create these databases if they don't exist. Should any statistics and event views and documents still exist in the Public Address Book, they will be copied over to the Statistics and Events database. As part of the creation of the Statistics and Events database, EVENT will reference the list of servers in the Public Address Book and create Servers to Monitor documents in the Statistics and Events database for them.

Reviewing the Databases

In this section, you will look at the three databases that aid in monitoring your servers. There is an enormous amount of information available in each of these databases. You need to understand the type of information available to monitor, as well as the standard information that is generated, so that you can search for information to assist you in analyzing your system performance. The three databases covered are

- ▶ The Statistics and Events database (`events4.nsf`)

- ▶ The Statistics Reporting database (`statrep.nsf`)

- ▶ The log database (`log.nsf`)

The Statistics and Events Database (`events4.nsf`)

This database contains the documents that indicate the servers that will be monitored for both statistical thresholds and event occurrences, as long as `REPORTER` and `EVENT` are running on the servers. This database also contains the Statistics Monitor documents, which identify the statistic to monitor and the associated threshold, as well as the Event documents to monitor for events.

See Figure 9.5 for the views available in the Statistics and Events database.

Figure 9.5

Document viewing in the Statistics and Events database.

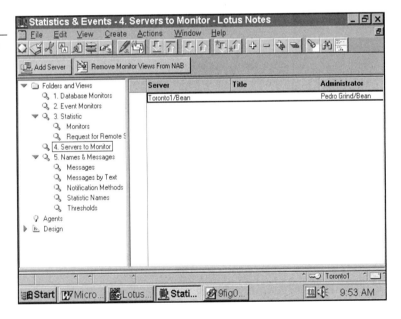

Let's go through each of the views and examine existing documents, default fields, and documents you should consider creating for your system monitoring.

View #5: Names and Messages

The Messages view represents all defined events in the Notes environment. As you can see from Figure 9.6, the events are grouped by function because the event reporting is function-based. You do not ask for a monitor of a particular event, you ask for a monitor for communication events with a severity of failure. These messages are useful to you as an administrator because when you create an event monitor for communications, by looking at these messages, you are aware of the exact events you will be asking to be monitored.

Figure 9.6

Partially collapsed view to illustrate events grouped by function and severity.

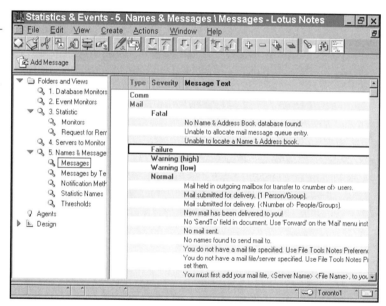

The Messages By Text view shows the same documents as listed in the previous view. They are presented in this format so that you can look for a particular event, view the document, and see what function and severity it is listed under.

The Notification Methods view lists the four common methods that you can use for notifying. Not all of these methods are available for all monitors. For example, with statistical monitors, the only notification method available is Logged to a Database, the database usually being the Statistics Reporting database.

The Statistics Names view lists all of the statistics you can monitor for a server. When you compose a statistics monitor, it uses the information from these documents to suggest thresholds, possible resolutions, values, and descriptions.

The Thresholds view is a subset of the Statistics Names view and lists only the Statistics documents that have thresholds indicated. For example, `X PC COM Speed Port` reports on the speed per unit of the port. This can be useful information for analyzing port performance, but it would not be useful to set a monitor with a threshold for this. Most statistical documents in this view would be used to create Statistics Monitor documents with; not all documents in the statistics view would be.

These five views under the Names and Messages heading are used for reference purposes by administrators who are interested in the type of monitors (both statistical and event) they can create, as well as reference documents for the system when monitor documents are created. Information from these messages is transferred to the monitor documents. If you, as an administrator, want to change certain fields in these documents, such as severity of the message, suggested possible actions, and so on, this can be done. If you have the rights to edit documents, you may change certain fields to alter the messages in these documents and, therefore, alter the information that would be passed on to the monitor documents when they are created.

View #4: Servers to Monitor

Under this view, you will find documents detailing the servers to monitor and their settings. Let's take a look at a server to monitor document (see Figure 9.7).

In this document, you can specify how often you want `REPORT` to generate Statistics documents, what default mail-in database this server will use, and how often an analysis report will be run for this server. You can find Analysis reports in the Statistics Reporting database under the Analysis Reporting view.

Figure 9.7

Monitor settings for the server Toronto1.

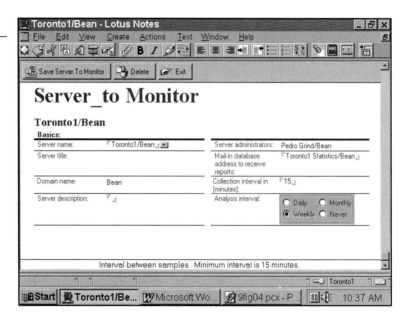

View #3: Statistics Monitor

Here you can view monitors other administrators might have created and, if you have sufficient access, you can create your own monitors for statistical information. Let's take a look at a Statistics Monitor document and review the fields and settings available (see Figure 9.8).

Figure 9.8

The Statistics Monitor document.

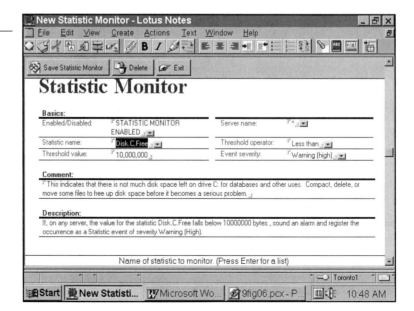

In choosing to create a statistics monitor, the only two default fields are the Enabled field, which is set to enable, and the Server Name field that has an asterisk. An asterisk indicates this monitor document will default to monitoring all servers. Of course, these two fields are entirely editable and can be changed so that the Statistic would be monitored only for one server, or a subset of all servers.

When you click the indicator in the Statistic Name field, a pop-up keyword list appears. This keyword list is built from the Threshold view under Names and Messages. Choosing the keyword to indicate the statistic you want to monitor fills in the remaining fields of the monitor document with the information from the Statistic document in the Names and Messages view. This information is suggested information and some fields can be edited; others have keyword lists you can choose from. Notice from this document there is no location for you to indicate how you should be notified of this statistic threshold being reached. When the REPORT task, using the statistical monitor, realizes a Threshold has been reached, its *only* option is to create an alarm document in the Statistic Reporting database.

Note

Requests for remote statistics will be covered in the "Centralized Reporting" section for the central collection of statistics.

View #2: Event Monitors

Take a look at the Event Monitor document in Figure 9.9. As mentioned previously, Event Monitor documents cover a function group, not individual events. Notice the title for the event monitor in Figure 9.9 is listed as Event Notification; this is an Event Monitor document, however.

Choose the function group you want to monitor from the Event Type field. Your choices are

▶ Comm/Net—Messages concerning communication or networks.

- ▶ Security—Messages concerning ID files, access rights, and ACLs.

- ▶ Mail—Messages relating to mail routing.

- ▶ Resource—Messages concerning machine-related resources.

- ▶ Miscellaneous—Messages not related to other functions, such as corrupted databases and documents.

- ▶ Server—Messages concerning server functionality and server information.

- ▶ Statistic—Messages concerning Statistic monitors. Remember that with Statistic monitors you have no notification choice; it is automatically sent as an alarm document to the Statistics Reporting database. If you want any Statistics documents for which thresholds have been reached to be mailed, you can do this by creating an event monitor that is really monitoring statistics of a certain severity level.

Figure 9.9

The Event Monitor document.

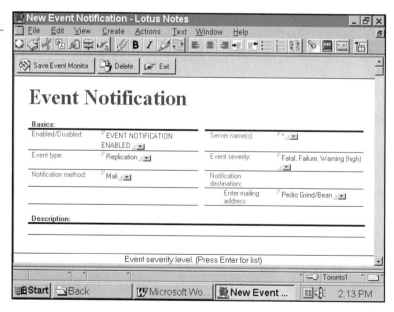

With event monitors, you do have a choice of how the monitor should notify. Let's review the choices available when creating the document:

▶ Mail—Notification of the alarm will be sent to the person you identify in the Mail Notification field via e-mail. Avoid using this method of notification for mail events. There is no use sending a notification by mail if there is a problem with mail.

▶ Log to database—This choice will send the event document to the database you identify in the Notification Destination field. This database must reside locally on the server that is monitored.

▶ Relay to another server—This choice will send the information to the server identified in the Notification Destination field, and the alarm document will be logged there. The restriction associated with this choice is the destination server, which must be in the same Notes named network or using the same protocol as the server who is monitored. This method of relaying information actually uses the network layer rather than the Notes application.

▶ SNMP Trap—This is an acronym for Simple Network Management Protocol, which is an industry standard network management protocol. If you use a third-party application, such as Notes View, you may choose this notification method to relay events. With the standard tools available, SNMP is not used.

▶ Severity—The Event Severity field indicates to the monitor document if there is a subgroup of the event function that you want to monitor. Under the Names and Messages view, you saw all events categorized by function and then subcategorized by severity. By looking at these documents, you can easily see all of the events you would be monitoring if you chose Security as your function and Fatal as your severity. Before choosing the severity level of your monitor, become familiar with the events in this group by looking at the documents in the Names and Messages view. If you are not happy with the severity assigned to certain documents, you can change them if you have the appropriate access.

Let's review the severity choices available and the general meaning assigned to them:

▶ Fatal—Indicates imminent system crashes.

▶ Failure—Indicates severe system failure that will not cause system crash.

▶ Warning (high)—Indicates function loss that will require administrator attention.

▶ Warning (low)—Indicates a loss of performance.

▶ Normal—These messages indicate status; these would not be appropriate for event monitors.

▶ All severity—Includes all of above severity messages.

View #1: Database Monitor

There are two types of database monitors: ACL and replication. Due to the importance of security and replication to the Notes environment, individual monitors can be created for these functions. In addition, these monitors will address individual databases, as the name indicates. Let's review each of these monitors for field definitions.

ACL Monitors

This monitor will report to the identified person any changes to the ACL of the indicated database. These changes can be manual, achieved through replication, or through a Notes API program; they will all be reported on. If you want an event document to also go to the Statistics Reporting database, you must have an event monitor of type security with whatever severity level you assigned to your ACL monitor (see Figure 9.10).

Figure 9.10

*Access Control
List Change
Monitor for*
`names.nsf`.

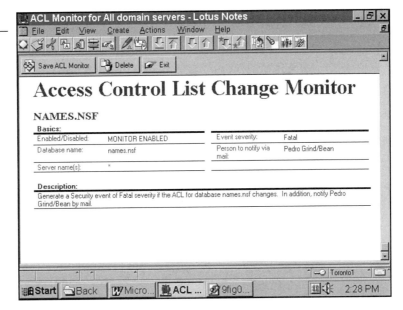

Figure 9.10

*Access Control
List Change
Monitor for*
`names.nsf`.

Replication Monitor

Replication monitors will advise administrators of failure to replicate. Administrators can specify the time interval they would like to be notified of. For example, if an organization has a schedule where `names.nsf` on each server should replicate twice a day, the administrator can create a monitor document to advise if replication does not occur in 24 hours. Obviously, this monitor would be used for critical Notes databases, both for the operation of the Notes environment as well as for the operation of the company. As with ACL monitors, if you want an event document to be created in the Statistics Reporting databases, you must have an Event Monitor document of type replication with the same severity level you applied to the replication monitor.

This concludes the review of the documents available from the Statistics and Events databases. You will be returning to this database to discuss the collections of statistics and events to a central location in the section "Centralized Reporting."

Statistics Reporting Database

Now that you have an understanding of message documents and monitor documents available in the Statistics and Events database, let's review the documents available to you in the Statistic Reporting database.

The majority of the documents in this database will not be created by administrators, but by the tasks running on the server, that is, the REPORT task and the EVENT task. Some documents will also be created by the settings in the servers to monitor document. For example, the setting of analysis will indicate whether an analysis report should be generated and how often.

For an example of the documents available in the Statistic Reporting database, examine the views displayed in Figure 9.11.

Figure 9.11

Views available from the Statistics Reporting database.

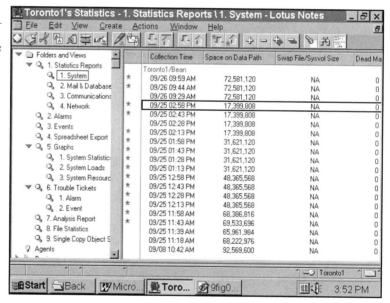

View #1: Statistics

This view provides access to the Statistics documents created by the REPORT task run on the server. The number of times the Statistics documents are generated per day is dictated by the Collection Interval field on the servers to monitor documents in the

Statistics and Event databases. The default is 60 minutes, but you may find that this is too frequent and change to a longer interval. Four types of Statistics documents are created:

- ▶ System

- ▶ Mail and database

- ▶ Communications

- ▶ Network

These documents are excellent for understanding what your system is busy doing and at what performance level it is doing it. The information from these documents is also used in other views to create load reports and simple graphs to help understand the system performance.

View #2: Alarms

This view provides documents detailing when the threshold of a Statistics monitor has been met. See Figure 9.12 to view an alarm document detailing a dead mail delivery threshold.

Figure 9.12

Dead Mail Alarm generated from a dead mail statistic threshold.

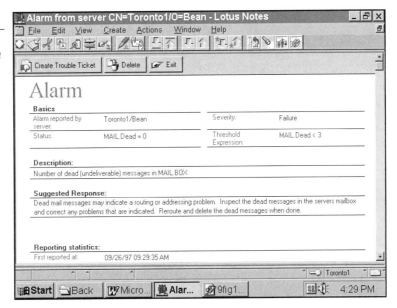

Typically, when you generate an alarm, action is necessary. Remember when a Statistics monitor is created, no notification method can be chosen by the author; the default in the alarm document is written to this database and appears in this view. To have a statistics alarm mailed for notification, it is necessary to create an event monitor for Statistics type and ensure it is the appropriate severity. Of course, the EVENT server task must be running for this to occur here.

View #3: Events

This view will display documents indicating where an event message has occurred. Remember that event monitors are not created for individual events but rather are grouped by function and severity. If you had created an event monitor asking to monitor replication events of severity levels fatal and failure, any occurrence of the replication events defined in these documents would generate an event alarm document here in the Statistics Reporting database.

View #4: Spreadsheet Export

Exporting information from multiple Notes documents into a spreadsheet is easiest done by displaying the information to be exported from a view. This view has been created specifically for this purpose. The most relevant information appears in columns in the view; when you export this to a spreadsheet, each column will be entered into a spreadsheet cell for each document.

View #5: Graphs

Under View #5, there are three subviews. Each of these views will use statistical information gathered through the REPORTER task and will display this information in a very basic kind of graph. The three different graph views are

▶ System Statistics

▶ System Performance

▶ System Resources

View #6: Trouble Tickets

Trouble tickets are created manually from the Statistics Reporting database; there is no automatic process to create these tickets. Trouble tickets are used for assigning a problem to a specific person. The trouble ticket can also be mailed to the person it is assigned to and saved as a trouble ticket document in this view. Trouble tickets can be used by administrators to assist in the assignment of problem resolution. There are two types of trouble tickets:

▶ Alarm (statistics) tickets

▶ Event tickets

Having opened any Event or Alarm documents, there is an action for creating a trouble ticket (see Figure 9.13).

Figure 9.13

Creation of an event trouble ticket.

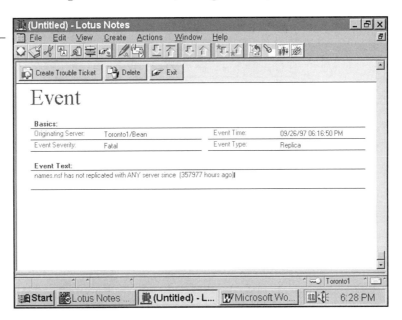

Having chosen this action, you are presented with the Event Trouble Ticket form in Figure 9.14.

In this form, the Ticket ID field is a generated number, and information concerning the event is transferred over to the trouble ticket from the Event or Alarm document. Before you save the document, you must identify the person this trouble ticket will be mailed to.

Figure 9.14

Creation of trouble ticket for an Event Alarm document.

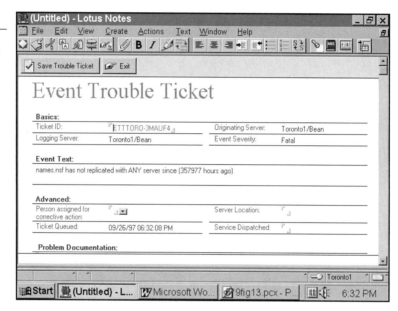

View #7: Analysis Report

Based on the Servers to Monitor document in the Statistics and Events database, an analysis will be run on the server. The report of this analysis will appear in this view of the Statistics Reporting database. It will display the averages, highs, and lows for reported statistics (see Figure 9.15).

View #8: File Statistics

This view shows information about each NSF and NTF file, that is, the database and template on the server. Each document will indicate the size, replica ID, and percent of used space (see Figure 9.16).

These reports will also indicate when the percentage used of the database drops below 70 percent, suggesting that you should compact the database at this point.

Figure 9.15

Analysis report for Toronto1/ Bean.

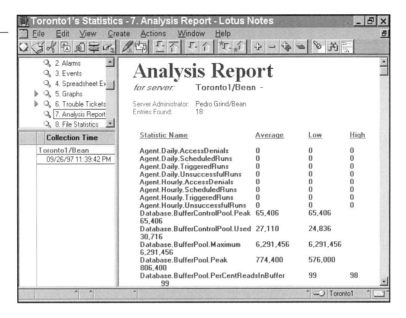

Figure 9.16

Information about databases and templates on the server.

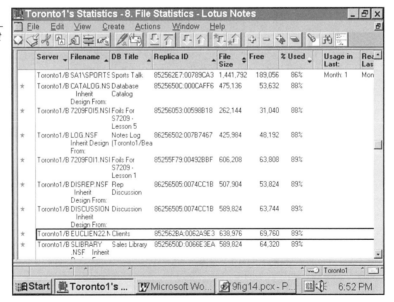

View #9: Single Copy Object Store Statistics

The documents in this view will advise you of the extent of message sharing in single copy object store. These statistics about the shared mail database are generated by the COLLECT task that runs at 2 a.m. by default (see Figure 9.17).

Figure 9.17

Shared Mail analysis run by the collect process.

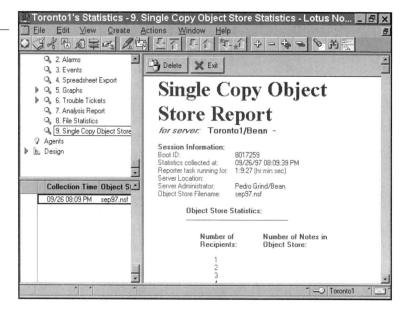

This completes the examination of the various views available in the Statistics Reporting database and the documents created by server tasks, and manual creation by administrators with the appropriate access to the database. The Statistics Reporting database is basically the repository database for statistical and event information including alarms and trouble tickets. This database also provides several views, which graphically display System Information.

Notes Log Database

The Notes log is the third database you will review. This database does not require any monitor documents to create information, nor does it require the loading of any special server tasks to generate information. All of the server processes and all activities write to the Notes log where the server processes are logged.

Let's go through the various views available in the Notes log (see Figure 9.18):

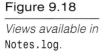

Figure 9.18

Views available in Notes.log.

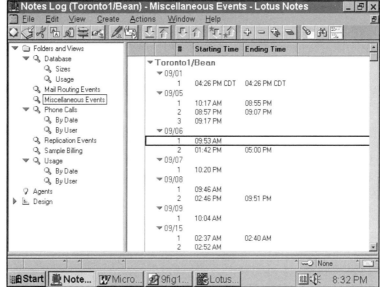

▶ Database Size—Shows the database size in KB as well as the percentage of space used and the weekly usage.

▶ Database Usage—Shows information concerning document use in the database, replication, and sessions.

▶ Mail Routing Events—Shows information concerning detailed routing activity.

▶ Miscellaneous Events—Shows all information that is not detailed in other views. This view has a document for each server startup time that details all activity until the server is shut down.

▶ Phone Calls by Date and Phone Calls by User—These two views show the same documents; they are simply sorted differently. These documents detail information about calls made and received by a server.

▶ Replication Events—A document is created for every replication event. The initiating server is identified, time of replication, databases replicated, and so on (see Figure 9.19). This does not contain information about user to server replication, as this process does not use the REPLICA task.

> ▶ Sample Billing—This view provides the same information as shown in Usage by Date and Usage by User. It is reformatted in this view to provide easy export to a spreadsheet for calculations to be made to charge users/servers for their personal usage.

> ▶ Usage by Date—This view provides information about sessions, lengths of sessions, databases opened, and number of transactions. Includes total by date and by user.

> ▶ Usage by User—This view has the same information as Usage by Date but is sorted by user name.

Figure 9.19

Replication document from `log.nsf`.

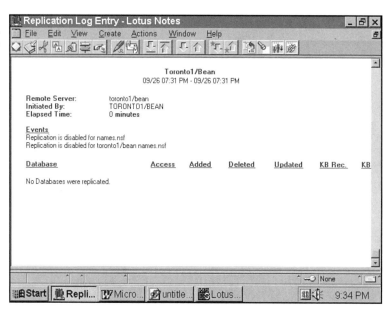

Notes provides a tool to assist in the analysis of a log database. As an administrator, this tool can be useful in determining what server processes have occurred and the results from them. This analysis tool is available from the System Administration panel and was covered in Chapter 6. Let's review this tool here as it is an integral part of your goal in system monitoring.

The Analysis tool is available via File|Tools|Server Administration. From the Administration panel, choose the server you want to analyze. Click the Server icon and choose Log Analysis. You will then see the Server Log Analysis dialog box (see Figure 9.20).

Figure 9.20

Analyzing the `log.nsf` *of* `Toronto1/Bean` *for all documents with the keyword router.*

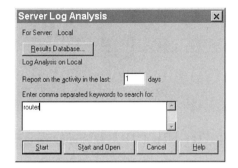

Always try to create the Results database you will be creating on your local drive. This will avoid a conflict between multiple administrators overriding each other's Results database. The default for a Results database overrides any existing Results database. Even if you change the defaults to append, at the next occurrence of creating a Results database, the default is back to overwrite. If you want to do multiple searches and append them together, click Results Database and choose Append to This Database; after indicating your search criteria, click Start. This executes the search but does not open the Results database. On your last search, click Start and Open; the search will execute and the Results database will open so you may view your analysis results.

The Results database has one view only, Log Events. This view is categorized by server and shows the date and time of events, their source, and the text of messages. Please note this view will not display times for server console messages.

The template used for creating the results database is LOGA4.NTF.

Centralized Reporting

All Statistic Reporting databases are replica copies, and eventually through the replication process, all events and statistical information will be contained in each replica copy of the database. This can be seen as a waste of disk space, as there is a method for relaying the information to one copy of the Statistics reporting database. This does not mean that individual servers are exempt from running the REPORTER or EVENT task. Each server wanting to create statistical information or monitor event occurrences must run these tasks. What the servers can do is relay their information to a central database. The notification methods are different for both the event monitoring and the statistics monitoring. Let's review how to create centralized reporting for each of these processes.

Centralizing Event Reporting

Create the Statistics Reporting database on the server you want to be the centralized collector. For all Event Monitor documents on this centralized server, specify the notification method as Log to Database. For all other servers, there are two options:

▶ If the servers use the same protocol as the collecting server, the notification message for their event monitors would indicate Relay to Other Server. This would then relay the information to the centralized collection server, creating the appropriate document in the Statistics Reporting database.

▶ If the servers are using different protocols, send the information to the centralized server. The notification method would be mail, and the notification destination would be the name of the Statistics Reporting database.

This database (statrep.nsf) would be removed from all of the noncollecting servers and a mail-in database document would be in the Public Address Book referencing the statrep.nsf on the collecting server.

Centralizing Statistics Reporting

With statistical reporting the notification default is that it is written to the Statistics Reporting database, statrep.nsf. To change this from writing it to your local Statistics Reporting database: after REPORT is run for the first time on the server, you will delete the database from all but the centralized server. You will then create a mail-in database document in the public address referencing the location of the *central* Statistics Reporting database.

There are other factors to consider in centralized reporting, as covered in the following three examples:

▶ Example 1—Because the Statistics Reporting database can grow very large, many companies either disable replication or only enable replication to the centralized databases and modify the *remove documents* setting under replication settings to an extremely short date for the noncentralized databases.

▶ Example 2—Although some aren't editable, many of the messages relating to Statistics and Events can be changed to better reflect the information your company would like to operate on. To customize an event message, you can modify such things as event severity, probable causes, and possible solutions.

▶ Example 3—In the Statistics and Events database, under View #3, *Statistics,* there is a view called Request for Remote Stats. In this view, you can create a request document. This request document identifies the server you want to collect statistics about and identifies who you would like this information to be mailed to (see Figure 9.21).

Figure 9.21

Creating request for remote stats in Statistics and Events database.

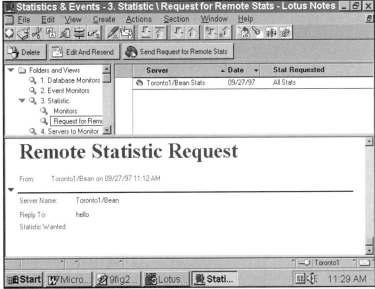

For this request to execute, neither the REPORT task nor the EVENT task needs to be running. This request document executes the STATS task on the server, collects the information into a mail document, and mails it to the group or individual identified in the Reply To field. Before this request can execute, there needs to be a Stat database created for the server. To create this database, you must enter the following command at the server console:

```
LOAD STATS -c
```

The argument *c* will create the server Stat database. Without this database, you will receive an error message when trying to send a request for remote stats.

When you send the request, the STATS task is run on the server, collected in a mail document, and mailed to the person in the Reply To field. The individual opens the mail file and sees the information collected by the STATS task.

Reviewing the Basic Monitoring Process

Use Figure 9.22 to review the basic monitoring process.

Figure 9.22

An example of the Notes' monitoring process.

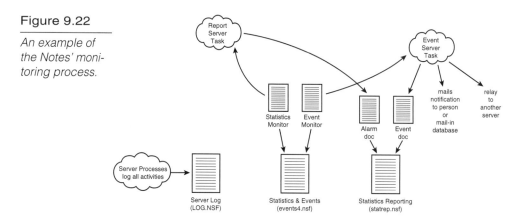

Your three processes are illustrated:

▶ Server process logging

▶ The REPORT task

▶ The EVENT task

The server process logging writes all server activity to the server log (log.nsf).

The REPORT task uses statistic monitor documents from the Statistics and Events database to decide when it should create a statistics alarm document. When it has to create one, its only option is to write this document to the statrep.nsf. If this database is on the local server, fine; if not, it looks in the public name and address book for a mail-in database document to see where it can send it to.

The EVENT task uses event monitors (including ACL and replication monitors) to decide when it should create an event alarm document. When it has to create one, it must consult the monitor document to see where it should send the notification to:

1. Mail (to a person or a mail-in database)

2. Relay to another server (as long as it is using the same protocol)

3. Log to a database (a local copy of statrep.nsf)

Exercises

Becoming aware of the monitoring options available to you is a large undertaking. The next step, of course, is *planning.* You, or the lead group of administrators in your organization, must decide on a strategy for monitoring your systems. There is no correct way to do this and there are many, many possible schemes. Much depends on what your criteria are, how large your systems are, who you will assign for checking for alarms, if trouble tickets are to be assigned, and more.

Exercise 9.1

In this lab, you will start both server tasks: EVENT and REPORT. You will then create some Statistics monitor documents, event monitors, and ACL monitors to see what you will be advised of. Begin by starting REPORT and EVENT:

1. At the server console enter LOAD REPORT. You should see the REPORT task starting and two databases being created: the events4.nsf (Statistics and Events) and the Statistics Reporting database (statrep.nsf). Views and documents will be copied over and a server to monitor document will be created in the events4.nsf database for Toronto1/Bean.

2. Open your client session and check to verify these databases now exist.

3. Now open the Statistics and Events databases and see that a Server to Monitor document has been created for Toronto1/Bean. Edit this document and change the reporting interval to 15 minutes for the purposes of this lab.

4. Go to the server session and enter LOAD EVENT at the console. Because the databases have already been created by the REPORT task, you will see a message that the event dispatcher has started and that is all.

While you wait for your 15-minute interval, create some monitor documents.

If you do not create any monitor documents at all, you will still receive a statistical report on the server every 15 minutes. These documents will appear in the statistics reporting database under the Statistics view. The following Statistics documents are generated: Communication, Network, System, Mail, and Database.

In the Statistics and Events database, you will begin by creating a statistics monitor document:

1. Go to the Statistics Monitors view.

2. Choose Add Statistics Monitor from the action bar.

3. In the Statistics monitor documents, click the arrow in the field Statistic Name. From the list presented, choose Disk C Free. This choice then completes the remainder of the document.

4. You only want to change the threshold field. Change the threshold field to Greater Than. This threshold would not make sense in a working environment. It is the simplest way to generate a statistics alarm in your lab.

5. Save this monitor.

You will now create an event monitor:

1. Go to the Statistics and Events database.

2. Go to the Event Monitors view.

3. Choose Add Event Monitor.

4. Choose Event Type Mail.

5. For Notification Method, choose Log to a Database.

6. For Event Severity, choose All Severities.

continues

You will now create a situation to generate an event and, therefore, create an alarm. Go to the Pedro Grind Mail database and create a new memo to Pebbles at Bedrock; send the message. Because you do not have a domain document for Bedrock and Toronto, and you do not have a Mail database to receive an error report, there will be an alarm generated for this event.

Now create an ACL monitor:

1. Go to the Database Monitors view and choose Add ACL Monitor.

2. In this document, put `names.nsf` in the field Database Names.

3. Put Pedro Grind in the Person to Notify by Mail field.

4. For the Severity field, enter Warning High.

To force this alarm, go to the Public Address Book and add a new person to be ACL. This will generate a message to Pedro informing him the ACL has been changed.

Review Questions

1. Which of the following describes a default characteristic of the `statrep.nsf` database?

   a. Purge interval of seven days

   b. Same replica ID

   c. One statistical view

2. `EVENT` and `REPORT` have been added to the `Server Tasks=`line in the `Notes.ini` file. What happens when the server is restarted?

   a. `event4s.nsf` and `statrep.nsf` are created.

   b. `event.nsf` and `stat.nsf` are created.

   c. Statistic documents are copied from `events.nsf` to `names.nsf`.

3. What would Larry do to view the results immediately of a Notes log analysis?

    a. Select Open

    b. Select Start and Open

    c. Select Start

4. Which views would be seen in the Results database of a Notes log analysis?

    a. Server name

    b. Date and Time

    c. Text of Messages

    d. Log Events

5. What databases are created the first time EVENT is loaded?

    a. Log.nsf, events4.nsf, and statrep.nsf

    b. events4.nsf

    c. events4.nsf and statrep.nsf

6. To specify how often REPORT will generate Statistics documents, you:

    a. Modify a field in the server configuration document.

    b. Modify a field in the Server document in the Public Address Book.

    c. Modify a field in the Servers to Monitor Document in events4.nsf.

7. A log result database view does not contain:

    a. Event time and date

    b. Server categorization

    c. Server source of events

    d. Time for server console messages

8. For event monitors to be acted upon, the following task must be running on the server:

   a. REPORTER

   b. EVENT

   c. REPORTER and EVENT

9. What is the name of the database where all server activity is logged?

   a. log.nsf

   b. log4a.nsf

   c. statrep.nsf

10. Where are high-level mail router events stored by default?

    a. Miscellaneous view

    b. Mail view

    c. Router events are not logged

11. In which view would you see detailed router activity?

    a. Mail Routing Events

    b. Miscellaneous

    c. Replication

    d. Database usage

12. What creates the statrep.nsf database?

    a. events4

    b. The REPORT or EVENT task

    c. REPORT task

13. To analyze the Notes log for multiple servers:

    a. Perform separate searches and for each search choose Results Database and Appended to This Database.

    b. Indicate the servers before you start the search.

14. Of these three notification methods, the one available to Statistic monitor documents is:

    a. Mail To

    b. Log to a Database

    c. Relay to Another Server

15. True or false: The message documents in the `events4.nsf` cannot be modified.

16. When relaying an event to another server, there needs to be:

    a. Common protocol between the two servers.

    b. Mail-in database document in the public address book.

Review Answers

1. B. Each server's Statistics Reporting database will be a replica copy. For more information, refer to the "Centralized Reporting" section.

2. A. These databases are created the first time `REPORT` or `EVENT` are run. For more information, refer to the "Monitoring Overview" section.

3. B. Start and Open will allow immediate viewing of the Log analysis. For more information, refer to the "Notes Log Database" section.

4. D. The Results database of a Notes log analysis will only offer this one view. For more information, refer to the "Notes Log Database" section.

5. C. Even if just the server task EVENT is loaded, both databases (events4.nsf and statrep.nsf) are created. For more information, refer to the "Monitoring Overview" section.

6. C. One of the fields in the Servers to Monitor document is Collection Interval. For more information, refer to the "Servers to Monitor" section.

7. D. This information is not generated in the Results database. For more information, refer to the "Notes Log Database" section.

8. B. To monitor an EVENT monitor, only the EVENT task needs to be running. For more information, refer to the "Monitoring Overview" section.

9. A. All server activity is logged to its log.nsf. For more information, refer to the "Notes Log Database" section.

10. A. High-level routing is logged to the Miscellaneous view. For more information, refer to the "Notes Log Database" section.

11. A. Detailed router activity is logged in the Mail Routing Events view. For more information, refer to the "Notes Log Database" section.

12. B. Either of these tasks will create the statrep.nsf. For more information, refer to the "Monitoring Overview" section.

13. A. For each search on each server, you must select Results Database and Append to This Database. For more information, refer to the "Notes Log Database" section.

14. B. With Statistic Monitor documents, you have no choice; they will be logged to a database. For more information, refer to the "Statistics and Events Database" section.

15. False. Certain fields in the message documents can be changed. For more information, refer to the "Centralizing Statistics Reporting" section.

16. A. Relay an Event notification uses the network layer so not only do the servers need to share a common protocol, they need to be on the same wire. For more information, refer to the "Event Monitors" section.

Answers to Test Yourself Questions at Beginning of Chapter

1. REPORT and EVENT are separate tasks; they do not need to run in conjunction. For more information, see "Understanding the Processes Involved."

2. The Server log, log.nsf, receives all the server activity information whether REPORT or EVENT are running or not. For more information, see "Understanding the Processes Involved."

3. Trouble tickets must be created manually. For more information, see "Trouble Tickets."

4. The EVENT task is much more server resource intensive than the REPORT task. For more information, see "Monitoring Overview."

5. Message documents are stored in the Statistics and Events database for reference and modification. For more information, see "Names and Messages."

6. You are presented with Comm/Net, Security, Mail, Replication, Resource, Miscellaneous, Server, and Statistics. For more information, see "Event Monitors."

Chapter 10

Troubleshooting System Administration Problems

In this chapter, I will cover the troubleshooting competency areas by discussing potential problems and providing reasons and solutions for some of the most common errors users and administrators run across. These problems will address the following areas:

 Objectives

- ▶ Setup
- ▶ Communication
- ▶ Replication
- ▶ Mail
- ▶ Security
- ▶ Cross certificates

Test Yourself! Before reading this chapter, test yourself to determine how much study time you will need to devote to this section.

1. What would cause the message Not authorized to access the server?

2. What would be the first thing you would examine if you received the message No route found to Domain X?

3. A document created in a database on server A is not being replicated to server B, but there is no problem with any other documents. Where you would look first to find a probable cause?

Answers are located at the end of the chapter...

This chapter will take you through all of the Notes functions covered in the previous chapters to explore your understanding of the impact of these functions. You will also review the use of administrative tools to assist in problem identification so you can implement the correct resolution.

This chapter introduces a potential problem for each of the troubleshooting areas and provides a common explanation of why the problem occurs and, if applicable, a solution. If troubleshooting tools are available to assist in the problem identification, they, too, are covered.

Troubleshooting User Problems

The following problems are common to users:

▶ Server access problems

▶ Server document problems

▶ Database access problems

▶ Database ACL problems

▶ ID problems

▶ Password problems

▶ Mail problems

These problems are covered in the sections that follow.

Server Access Problems

Problem: A user, who has been put in a group called *Terminated*, which is identified in the Access Control List as no access, still has access to the database. Why?

Reason & Solution: The user was also identified in the Access Control List individually as author. Individual listings take precedence over group listings. Therefore, even though the user was listed in ACL in the Terminated group with no access, his individual listing takes precedence and he is still allowed access to the database. Remove his individual listing from all database ACLs. For more information on ACLs, refer to the section titled "Understanding the Access Control List" in Chapter 5, "Security."

Server Document Problems

Problem: A user has the correct certificate and can authenticate the server, but when she tries to access the server, she is told she is not allowed. The user is not included in any Terminated groups. Why is the user not allowed to access the server?

Reason & Solution: The Server document has groups in the Access Server field, and this user is not listed in any of these groups. When you put any groups or users in this field, those groups or users become the only ones with access to the server. You will have to include the user in one of the groups that is given access. For more information on fields in the Server document, refer to the section titled "Server Access" in Chapter 5.

Database Access Problems

Problem: A user has access to a database, but when he opens it, there are no documents. The database seems empty.

Reason & Solution: The user has been given depositer access in the database's Access Control List. Depositors will never see any documents in a database; they will be allowed only to create and save a document. Change the user's ACL status if he must read documents as well. For more information on ACLs, refer to the section titled "Understanding the Access Control List" in Chapter 5.

Database ACL Problems

Problem: Administrators cannot register servers in the Public Address Book. An administrator who has the correct certifier ID file is given the error message You are not authorized to perform this operation during the registration process. Why?

Reason & Solution: An integral part of the server registration process is the creation of the Server documents in the Public Address Book. Even if the administrator has the correct certifier ID and is listed as manager in the Public Address Book, if he has not been assigned the correct role, he will not be able to perform the operation. To perform the operation of creating a server, the administrator must be assigned the role ServerCreator in the Access Control List. For more information, refer to the section titled "Roles in Access Control Lists" in Chapter 5.

Problem: You can no longer change the ACL at the server client session. Even though you are not listed as a manager, you have been able to change the ACL of a database by going to the server client session and accessing the database locally. Now when you go to the server, you are no longer able to do this. Why?

Reason & Solution: In the Access Control List of the databases, the servers have been identified as type *server*, and the Access Control List has been enforced locally. This prevents anyone who has access to the server client session from bypassing the Access Control List.

This feature is useful for users who have replica copies of databases on their local drive and want to avoid confusion as to their access control rights. You will have to go to a manager of the database and ask him or her to implement your ACL change—which is the correct procedure. For more information, refer to the section titled "Understanding the Access Control List" in Chapter 5.

ID Problems

Problem: A user has changed her name in her user ID and no longer has access to the server. What has happened?

Reason & Solution: When a user chooses File | Tools | User ID | More Options | Change Name and changes her name, she loses all her certificates. Without the right certificates, she will not be able to access any server. Users are warned about this when they change their names. To give the user back her certificates, you have to re-certify her with the correct certifier ID file. For more information on certificates, refer to the section titled "Validation and Authentication" in Chapter 5.

Password Problems

Problem: A user has forgotten his password and cannot use his user ID file. How can you get his password back?

Reason & Solution: You can't get his password back if he has changed it since you first issued it to him (and hopefully he has). Administrators should have backup copies of all IDs they create, along with knowledge of the passwords associated with those IDs. Send the user the backup copy with the password associated with it, and give him instructions how to change the password. If you don't have a backup copy of the IDs, you will have to re-create the ID. If the user had any encrypted mail, he will not be able to access it.

Mail Problems

These problems revolve around mail not being delivered.

Can't Send Mail to a Particular Domain

Problem: A user attempts to send mail to a user in another domain by using the correct address, but the sender receives a delivery failure notice telling him that no route to the domain was found.

Reason & Solution: In order for mail to be sent to a different domain and different organization, cross certification and a Connection document must be established between at least two servers. You will have to implement cross certification between the two organizations and create the appropriate Connection documents. For more information on communication between multiple domains, refer to the section titled "Communicating Between Domains" in Chapter 8, "Working with Domains."

Domain Document Problems

Problem: A user in the Bean domain wants to send mail to a user in the Leaf domain. The sender has the correct name and domain identifier, and a Domain document exists, but the mail is not delivered.

Reason & Solution: Even if the sender has the correct name for mail purposes and there is a Domain document, mail will not be delivered unless there is a Connection document between two servers in the two domains. The appropriate Connection document will have to be created (and cross certification must be implemented). For more information on communication between domains, refer to the section titled "Communicating Between Domains" in Chapter 8.

Passthru Server Access Problems

Problem: Mail is to be delivered from server A to server B through server C. Although the mail reaches server B, the mail is not delivered.

Reason & Solution: In the Server document for server B, under Restrictions | Passthru, the Access This Server field is blank. When this field is blank, no one is allowed to reach the server through passthru. To allow server access by way of passthru, enter in the Access This Server field LocalDomainServers. For more information on passthru, refer to the section titled "Using Passthru for Replication" in Chapter 3, "Replication."

Person Not Listed in Public Address Book

Problem: A mobile user creates a mail message, connects with the server, and sends the contents of his mail.box to the mail.box on the server. The next time the mobile user connects with the server and replicates his mail file, he finds a delivery failure notice telling him that the recipient of his message was not found in any address book. Why?

Reason & Solution: The Notes server's only way of delivering mail is by using the Person documents in the PAB. The recipient names on all messages have to exactly match the Person documents in the PAB. If there is the slightest misspelling, the names cannot be matched, and the message will be returned to the sender—who will then have to check the name against the PAB. Users can resolve this situation by taking a subset replica copy of the Public Address Book with just the Person documents with them. For more information on taking subset replica copies, refer to the section titled "Replication Settings" in Chapter 3.

Person Document Problems

Problem: An administrator is registering people, and the process seems to be complete: The administrator sees messages indicating that the IDs and Person documents were created. Yet when he looks in the Public Address Book, he finds no Person documents. Why?

Reason & Solution: During the registration process, the registration server was identified as local. Because The administrator was doing the registration at his own workstation, local refers to his own hard drive. Therefore, the Person document was written to his Personal Address Book, and not to the Public Address Book. The administrator should identify the *registration server* by name during the registration process instead of leaving it as local.

Person Record Removed from Public Address Book

Problem: A user mistakenly deletes her Person document from the PAB (she was given the rights to do so in the ACL). She does still have a valid certificate, though, so she has not been put in any terminated groups and can access all servers. However, when anyone tries to send her mail, they are told she can't be found in the PAB.

Reason & Solution: If for any reason a Person document is removed from the PAB—whether it be by the user herself if she has the access or by an administrator who has access—mail cannot be delivered to the user because the Person document is what the router uses to determine where to deliver mail. An administrator will have to re-create a Person document for this user in the Public Address Book.

Can't Send to or Receive from a Particular Person

Problem: User A cannot send a mail message to user B, nor can user A receive a mail message from user B.

Reason & Solution: The server that holds user B's mail file has limited its access server field to exclude user A's server, and user A's server has done the same to user B's server. Even though user A and user B can authenticate each other, the servers have specified in their Server documents that they will not communicate. Therefore, mail can't be sent or delivered between them. The Server documents will have to be changed so the servers can access each other and send and receive mail for their users. For more information on the restriction fields in the Server document, refer to the section titled "Server Access" in Chapter 5.

Remote Access File Problems

Problem: A remote user tries to access her server's mail file by using the Connection document in her Personal Address Book. The mail file is on a server she can access only through passthru. The user receives a message telling her a route to the destination server cannot be found.

Reason & Solution: The Public Address Book does contain the correct Passthru documents and passthru fields on the Server documents, but the user's Personal Address Book is missing a document. The user does have a Location document specifying her mail server and passthru server, but she is missing a Connection document giving the information on how to connect to her passthru server (its name, phone number, and type of connection). The user must create this document before she will be able to access her mailfile on her mail server. For more information on how users can implement passthru, refer to the section titled "Workstation to Server Passthru" in Chapter 3.

Can't Access Own Mail File

Problem: A user tries to access his mail file and is told he is not allowed access. The user had requested a name change through Notes mail and merged the safe ID he received back from his administrator. Why can't he access his mail?

Reason & Solution: When the administrator changed the user's name and gave him the correct certificate, the administrator forgot to change the user's name in the mail file's Access Control List. The administrator will have to modify the ACL to indicate the user's new name.

Troubleshooting Database Integrity Problems

The following problems concern application integrity:

▶ Database corruption problems

▶ Database consistency problems (copies versus replica copies)

▶ Reappearing deleted document problems

These problems are covered in the sections that follow.

Database Corruption Problems

Problem: Documents in a database are being corrupted fairly often. While fixup is removing the corrupted documents and allowing access to the database, what is causing this database corruption?

Reason & Solution: By looking in the log.nsf of the server, the administrator can see that the server has been crashing fairly often because of insufficient memory. Server crashes are the most common source of document corruption. Fix the cause of the server crashes—in this case by adding more memory—and the database corruption problems will lessen.

Database Consistency Problems (Copies versus Replica Copies)

Problem: During the replication process between a user and a server, documents are not being replicated. The user has created a replica copy of a database on her laptop. When she goes to replicate with her server, she doesn't receive documents from the server, nor are her documents sent to the server. Why?

Reason & Solution: In a situation in which no documents are being replicated, the first things to check are the replica IDs of the databases. Have the user perform these steps:

1. Click the replica copy.

2. Select File | Database.

3. Choose Properties.

4. Select the Information tab and read off the replica ID at the bottom.

You compare the replica ID she reads to the replica ID on the server's database. They are probably not the same. If not, have the user go through the correct procedure to make a replica copy of the database. For more information on making replica copies, refer to the section titled "Creating Replica Copies" in Chapter 3.

Reappearing Deleted Document Problems

Problem: A user deletes a document that he no longer needs in the database. Two weeks later, the user notices the document is back again. What happened? Why?

Reason & Solution: When a user deletes a document, a deletion stub is created to pass this deletion on to all other replica copies of the database. However, the deletion stub purge interval for this particular database is set at 10 days, and the replication schedule for this database is once every two weeks. By the time the replication occurs, the deletion stub has been purged. Because the replication process finds the document in one database and not the other, it adds the document to the database from which it appears to be missing. If you change the purge interval for deletion stubs to 20 days, the deleted documents will stop reappearing. For more information on purge intervals for deletion stubs, refer to the section titled "Deletion Stubs" in Chapter 3.

Troubleshooting Communications/Remote Communications Problems

The resolution of these problems—and indeed any problem relating to communication—is vital to the functioning of Notes.

 Note

Network Trace will be your primary tool for troubleshooting connection problems. As explained in the section titled "Tracing Network Connections" in Chapter 2, "Server and Client Setup," Network Trace is a tool available only at the server client Session under File I Tools I User Preferences I Ports I Trace Connection. This tool enables you to select the specific port about which you want information and to trace its attempt to connect to a specific destination.

Problem: Replication is scheduled to occur three times a day between two servers, but at best is happening only once a day. The other attempts are failing because of network problems.

Solution: To test the network path, do the following:

1. From the server or workstation that you want to test, choose File I Tools I User Preferences.

2. Click the Ports icon and select the port you want to test.

3. Click Trace Connection.

4. Select the server to which you want to connect, and then click Trace.

This will give you detailed information about the actual connection, which should enable you to identify and resolve your network problem.

Troubleshooting Application Problems

The following problems encompass a few of the scenarios you will encounter in a Notes environment:

- Administration process problems

- Document replication problems

- Access problems (ACLs)

These problems are covered in the sections that follow.

Administration Process Problems

Problem: An administrator goes through the administration process Actions | Rename Person through the PAB, but she keeps getting the message Entry Failed. The administrator has the correct IDs and the correct access in the ACL.

Reason & Solution: The administrator has all the correct tools and ACL rights to use the administration process, but the certification log with the filename certlog.nsf has not been created. Without the certification log, the administration process will not work. Create the certification log database using the certification log template (certlog.ntf), and name the file certlog.nsf. For more information on the administration process, refer to the section titled "Understanding the Administration Process" in Chapter 6, "Administration Tools."

Document Replication Problems

Problem: Not all documents are being replicated. A user created a document in a database, and he calls a colleague to discuss the contents. The colleague opens the database on her server but can't find the document. Why?

Reason & Solution: Because the creator of this document wanted only him and his colleague to see it, he put only their names in the Readers field. When the creator's server replicated with the colleague's server, the colleague's server could not read the document because the server was not specifically referenced in the Readers field. Therefore, the server could not replicate the document. To enable replication, the creator must include in the Readers field all servers involved in the replication process as well as the users who will read the document. For more information on Readers fields, refer to the sections titled "ACL Rights" in Chapter 3 and "Forms and Views" in Chapter 5.

Access Problems (ACLs)

Problem: A user with manager access in a database's ACL finds that her design changes and ACL changes to the database are not being passed on through replication.

Reason & Solution: The user's server has only editor access in the database's ACL and, therefore, is not capable of passing on this user's information. The server's ACL level will have to be changed to manager in order for it to pass on the user's changes, and the replication history will have to be cleared to allow all past changes to be sent on. For more information on ACLs and replication, refer to the section titled "ACL Rights" in Chapter 3.

Troubleshooting Mail Routing Problems

Mail routing is vital to user satisfaction. You must understand how to resolve potential problems such as the following, as well as how to use Mail Trace to troubleshoot routing problems:

▶ Dead/pending mail

▶ Shared/message-based mail problems

These problems, as well as how to use Mail Trace to troubleshoot routing problems, are covered in the sections that follow.

Dead/Pending Mail

Problem: When examining the `mail.box` of server A, the administrator consistently notices a large number of mail messages waiting to be delivered to server B. How can he fix this?

Reason & Solution: The administrator examines the Connection document for the mail routing task between server A and server B and notices that it has an extremely high number in the field labeled Route at Once if *XXXX* Mail Messages Pending. Although the schedule includes a range from 6 a.m. to 11 p.m. with a repeat interval of 60 minutes, in the Days of the Week field, only Saturday and Sunday are listed. The administrator changes the Days of the Week field to include all days and then lowers the value in the Route at Once field to `10`, and the problem is solved. For more information on the fields in the Connection documents, refer to the section titled "Connection Document" in Chapter 4, "Mail."

Using Mail Trace to Troubleshoot Routing Problems

Problem: A user complains to his administrator that his Notes mail is not being delivered. The intended recipients are telling the user they have not received his messages. What can the administrator do?

Reason & Solution: If the administrator knows the intended recipient's name, he can test the mail delivery route by using these steps at his own workstation:

1. Select File | Tools | Server Administration.

2. Click the Mail icon and choose Send Mail Trace.

3. Enter the mail address of the intended recipient.

4. Select Each Router on Path in the Send Delivery Report From field to receive a delivery report from each router on the path. Select Last Router Only in the Send Delivery

Report From field to receive a delivery report from only the last router.

5. Click Send.

The administrator will receive a trace report from the last router on the path or from each router, depending on his selection. The administrator can then determine whether the messages are really being delivered, and if not, where they are being stopped. For more information on Mail Trace, refer to the section titled "Troubleshooting Mail Problems" in Chapter 4.

Shared/Message-Based Mail Problems

Some of the shared/message-based mail problems include the following:

- ▶ Addressing problems

- ▶ Connection or Connection document problems

- ▶ Person document problems

- ▶ Group document problems

- ▶ Server document problems

- ▶ Server document/INI incompatibility problems

These problems are covered in the sections that follow.

Addressing Problems

Problem: A user sends a mail message to a person in another Notes domain. The message is returned saying No route found to the domain. There is a Connection document for mail, as well as cross certificates.

Reason & Solution: The user made a mistake in spelling the domain name. The domain name in the mail message must exactly match the domain name in the Connection document. Therefore, the user will have to correct the spelling of the domain name.

Connection or Connection Document Problems

Problem: Mail is not being sent when it should be. A user is sending mail to three recipients in three different Notes named networks. Two of the recipients receive the mail, but two days later, the third recipient has still not received his. Why?

Reason & Solution: Whenever mail must be delivered across Notes named networks, a Connection document must be created. Look at the Connection document between the sender's network and the Notes named network to which the mail was not delivered. The Route at Once If field is set to 15, and the Days of the Week field says only Monday and Friday. In addition, there are only five messages in the `mail.box` waiting to go to that particular Notes named network. To fix the problem, lower the setting in the Route at Once If field, and change the Days of the Week field to include all days. This will enforce the schedule every day and force an unscheduled connection if the Route at Once value is exceeded by the number of mail messages. For more information on the fields in the Connection document, refer to the section titled "Connection Document" in Chapter 4.

Person Document Problems

Problem: A user moves his mail file to another server, and he stops receiving mail.

Reason & Solution: When the mail file was moved, the administrator for the new server had to change the filename of the mailfile, but forgot to change its name in the Person document. Without the correct filename, the router cannot deliver mail to the user's mail database. The administrator will have to correct the information in the Person document so mail can be delivered correctly. For more information on mail delivery, refer to the section titled "Understanding Mail Components" in Chapter 4.

Group Document Problems

Problem: A user creates a mail message to send to a group named *Focus*, which is defined in the PAB. However, the members of the group never receive the message, nor does the sender get a delivery failure notice.

Reason & Solution: There is a person in the PAB called *Fred Focus.* The sender didn't look at the To field very closely, and the message was sent to Fred Focus. The name of the group will have to be changed.

Server Document Problems

Problem: Server E is not receiving mail from server D. However, server D can receive mail from server E.

Reason & Solution: Look at the Server document for server E. In the Access Server field under Restrictions, `LocalDomainServers` is listed. Because server D is not part of the `LocalDomainServers` group, server E is not allowing access to server D. To solve the problem, add server D to the group. For more information on server access, refer to the section titled "Server Access" in Chapter 5.

Server Document/INI Incompatibility Problems

Problem: When the Notes release 4 server starts up, it displays the incorrect release version of Notes.

Reason & Solution: When Notes release 4 was installed, a new `Notes.ini` file was created, but the `Notes.ini` from the Notes release 3 setup was never removed. Now, when the server starts up, it uses the wrong `Notes.ini` to initialize the server. You should back up and erase the old `Notes.ini`.

Troubleshooting Replication Problems

Without the correct operation of replication, information will not be shared. The following are some common replication problems:

▶ Field replication problems

▶ Connection document problems

▶ Replica ID problems

- ▶ ACL problems

- ▶ Purge interval problems

- ▶ Replication and merge conflict problems

These problems are covered in the sections that follow.

Field Replication Problems

Problem: An administrator finds many replication conflicts in a database. Looking into it, the administrator learns that many of the conflicts involve documents in which fields have been changed. Why?

Reason & Solution: To avoid conflicts when different fields are changed on the same document, you must modify the design of the database to enable Field Merge (it is not enabled at this point). Change this design setting on each form for which you want to enable Field Merge. For more information on merging during replication, refer to the section titled "Field Merging" in Chapter 3.

Connection Document Problems

Problem: An administrator finds that one particular database is not being replicated between two servers even though all other replica databases on these two servers are being processed by the replication task.

Reason & Solution: The administrator looks at the Connection document, specifying the schedule and the replication task, and finds that only high-priority databases are indicated in the Connection document. For the one database that's not being replicated, the Replication Setting is set to Medium priority. The administrator changes this setting to High, and the problem is solved. For more information on replication settings, refer to the section titled "Replication Settings" in Chapter 3.

Replica ID Problems

Problem: A mobile user creates a number of documents in her replica copy of a database. She then connects with the server and starts replication. However, the documents do not replicate between the two replica copies. Later, the user finds out that she did not make a replica copy; she made a database copy. The user then asks the administrator how to change the replica ID on her database so the database can become a replica copy.

Reason & Solution: The user cannot do that because the replica ID of a database cannot be edited. The only thing the administrator can do is copy and paste the new documents into the server's replica copy. The user should then delete her database copy and make a true replica copy of the server's database.

ACL Problems

Problem: A mobile user takes a replica copy of a database on the road with her. She edits, creates, and deletes documents. When she replicates with her server, only certain documents—the ones she created—get passed on to the server.

Reason & Solution: The ACL on this database specifies this user as author, but gives her no deletion capability. Because the user took a replica copy and accessed it locally without enforcing the ACL across all replica copies, she was able to enter locally as manager and make manager-type changes. However, the server will not accept those changes. The manager of this database can modify the ACL on this database so that the ACL will be enforced on all replica copies to prevent this problem. For more information on ACLs, refer to the section titled "ACL Rights" in Chapter 3.

Purge Interval Problems

Problem: An administrator wants deletion stubs to be purged every 10 days. In the database's replication settings, the Remove Documents Not Modified in the Last *XXX* Days field specifies 10. But, for some reason, deleted documents keep reappearing.

Reason & Solution: Notes calculates one-third of the value in the Remove Documents Not Modified in the Last *XXX* Days field, and it purges deletion stubs at that interval. Therefore, if an administrator wants deletion stubs to be purged every 10 days, she must enter 30 in the Remove Documents Not Modified in the Last *XXX* Days field. For more information, refer to the section titled "Deletion Stubs" in Chapter 3.

Replication and Merge Conflict Problems

Problem: Replication conflicts occur regularly in a particular database. An administrator suggests that the database's designer enable Field Merge for the forms in the database. The designer does so, and the number of conflicts drops, but conflicts still occur from time to time.

Reason & Solution: Even when Field Merge is enabled on a form, conflicts may still occur if two or more users change the same field on the same document. To further reduce the number of replication conflicts, the designer would have to change the design of the forms. For more information, refer to the section titled "Field Merge" in Chapter 3.

Troubleshooting Workstation Problems

The faster and easier it is for users to set up Notes, the happier they will be.

Problem: A user is trying to set up his workstation. The administrator tells him that his user ID file has been created and is available in the Public Address Book. When the user goes to set up, he enters all the correct information in the fields and clicks the UserID Supplied in a File option, but the setup cannot be completed.

Reason & Solution: The user misunderstood. Because the administrator said he has a user ID file, he assumed the Public Address Book is some directory he has access to. For the setup to be completed with the User ID Supplied in a File option, the user must have direct access to the ID file during the setup process. Having a user ID file stored in the Public Address Book does not qualify.

The user should not click the User ID Supplied in a File option when his user ID file is in the Public Address Book.

Troubleshooting Server Problems

These potential problems review the importance of the Server documents and Connection documents for Notes servers. The following are some common replication problems:

- ▶ Passthru server problems

- ▶ Improper Connection document problems

- ▶ Improper passthru server settings problems

These problems are covered in the sections that follow.

Passthru Server Problems

Problem: Server A attempts to access server D through a passthru server (server C), but it cannot make the connection.

Reason & Solution: The administrator researching the problem finds that the Route Through field for the passthru server is blank. By default, when this field is blank, this server cannot be used as a passthru server. To enable server A to use server C as a passthru server, the administrator would have to put server A's name in the Route Through field for server C. For more information, refer to the section titled "Using Passthru for Replication" in Chapter 3.

Improper Connection Document Problems

Problem: A Connection document for server A/Svr/Bean and server M/Svr/Bean is not functioning.

Reason & Solution: In the Connection document, the Source Server field reads server A, and the Destination Server field reads server M. The two servers cannot successfully connect because the names of the servers are incorrect. The correct entries are `server A/Svr/Bean` and `server M/Svr/Bean`. Modify the Connection document to reflect the correct hierarchical names of the servers.

Improper Passthru Server Settings Problems

Problem: Server A tries to access server Y through server X, but the connection is not successful.

Reason & Solution: The administrator finds that all of the Connection documents seem to be in order, but he sees that server X is still a Notes release 3 server. Notes release 3 servers cannot be used as passthru servers. The administrator will have to either use a release 4 server as the passthru server or upgrade server X to release 4.

Troubleshooting Compatibility Problems

Problem: Users ask for a replica copy of a database to be put on their server. Once they start using it, however, replication conflicts occur involving the documents they edit.

Reason & Solution: The server these users work on is a Notes release 3 server. The database was created by using a release 4 format and is designed to take advantage of merging fields. As soon as the replica copy of the database was put on the release 3 server, it reverted to release 3 format, which does not support Field Merge.

Troubleshooting—System Administration II

These are some common system administration problems:

▶ Statistics and Event Monitor database problems

▶ Domain routing mail delivery problems

▶ Mailfile access problems

- ▶ Mail delivery problems between domains

- ▶ Incomplete firewall problems between two domains

- ▶ Cascading address book problems

- ▶ Mail-in database problems

- ▶ Replication problems among domains using log analysis

- ▶ Database problems: using database analysis

- ▶ Network connection problems: using network tracing

- ▶ Authentication problems

These problems are covered in the sections that follow.

Statistics and Event Monitor Database Problems

Problem: When looking for the statistics report for a server, the administrator can see the statistics for all servers except server O.

Reason & Solution: Looking at the Statistics and Event Monitor database in the Servers to Monitor view, the administrator sees that there is no Monitor document for server O. To solve the problem, make sure that one of the Servers to Monitor documents includes server O. For more information on Servers to Monitor documents, refer to the section titled "The Statistics and Events Database" in Chapter 9, "Server and System Monitoring."

Domain Routing Mail Delivery Problems

Problem: Users are complaining that mail is taking too long to be delivered.

Reason & Solution: Create a statistics monitor to send an alarm when Mail Waiting exceeds 15 items. This will let the administrator know how often large amounts of mail are being held so she can modify the mail routing schedule accordingly. For more information on creating statistics monitors, refer to the section titled "View #3: Statistics Monitor" in Chapter 9.

Mailfile Access Problems

Problem: A user is no longer receiving mail when he replicates his local replica copy of his mail with his mail server.

Reason & Solution: In the user's `log.nsf` file under Replication, the administrator sees that the server has no access to the user's mailfile. When the administrator looks at the ACL of the user's mailfile, the server is no longer listed, nor is the group `LocalDomainServers`. The asdministrator adds them back to the ACL so the server can again begin delivering mail to the user's local replica copy. For more information, see "ACL Rights" in Chapter 3.

Mail Delivery Problems Between Domains

Problem: Users are complaining that mail they send to the domain called `Leaf` is not getting through.

Reason & Solution: Check the PAB to verify the existence of a Connection document and cross certificate between the two domains. In this case, cross certificate is missing, and communication cannot take place. Cross certificate must be implemented in order for mail to be exchanged. For more information, refer to the section titled "Communicating Between Domains" in Chapter 8.

Incomplete Firewall Problem Between Two Domains

Problem: The `Bean` domain is an intermediary between the `Leaf` domain and the `BeanC` domain. Mail from `BeanC` has been passing through `Bean` to get to `Leaf`. But `Bean` decides that it no longer wants to be an intermediary, so it modifies its domain documents for `Leaf` and `BeanC` to deny mail from `Leaf` to go through to `BeanC`, and vice versa. However, mail from a domain called `Branch` is still going through `BeanC` and then `Bean` to get to `Leaf`.

Reason & Solution: The domain documents have been modified to specify whom to disallow. But to prevent *any* mail from going through Bean, the administrator must fill in the Access Mail Only from Domain field in the Domain document as well as specify that only Bean will be allowed to send mail to its adjacent domains. For more information, refer to the section titled "Restricting Access from Other Domains" in Chapter 8.

Cascading Address Book Problems

Problem: Other domains' address books have been put on the server so users can search for correct addresses, but the server will let users search only its own domain PAB.

Reason & Solution: The Notes.ini file has not been modified. The Notes.ini contains a line indicating its own domain's Public Address Book. Modify this line to include any other Public Address Book the server may contain, such as Names = names.nsf, leafbook.nsf. For more information, refer to the section titled "Cascading Address Books" in Chapter 8.

Mail-In Database Problems

Problem: REPORT and EVENT are both running on server A, and there is a Server to Monitor document for server A as well. However, the statistics reports are not being generated in the Statistics database (statrep.nsf).

Reason & Solution: There is no mail-in document in the Public Address Book. Without this document, which identifies the filename and location of the statistics reporting depository for server A, the statistics report will not be written to it. For more information, refer to the section titled "Reviewing the Basic Monitoring Process" in Chapter 9.

Replication Problems Among Domains Using Log Analysis

Problem: Documents from two replica copies of a database are not being exchanged.

Reason & Solution: Use log analysis with the search criteria `Rep` and the database name. You find replication documents indicating that replication is taking place on a scheduled basis, but the ACL of the database does not allow access to one of the servers. The ACL will have to be changed to allow that access. For more information, refer to the section titled "Notes Log Database" in Chapter 9.

Database Problems: Using Database Analysis

Problem: A user reports that a number of documents have been deleted in the last two days, and she needs to know which documents were deleted.

Reason & Solution: Run a database analysis asking for document changes for the last two days to determine which documents were deleted. For more information, refer to the section titled "Using Databases" in Chapter 6.

Network Connection Problems: Using Network Tracing

Problem: Servers are not connecting according to their Connection document schedules.

Reason & Solution: When servers are not connecting and you need to troubleshoot, the best and quickest method of obtaining information about the problem is by way of Trace Connection in the User Preferences dialog box. To obtain this information from a server, you need to be at the server using a client session. From there, select File | Tools | User Preferences, select Ports, and then click Trace Connection.

In the dialog box that appears, indicate the destination server. Under Log, choose Whole Trace Information. This will provide you with the most complete information concerning the connection. This information will also be logged to the `log.nsf` under the Miscellaneous view. For more information, refer to the section titled "Tracing Network Connections" in Chapter 2.

Authentication Problems

Problem: A user can't access a server to which she has a cross certificate. A cross certificate has been issued at an organizational level between two organizations. But when the user tries to connect to a server in the other organization, she is refused. Why?

Reason & Solution: The cross certificate is valid, but when the user wants to present a cross certificate to a server, she must have the cross certificate in her Personal Address Book. Therefore, the user must copy and paste the cross certificate into her Personal Address Book. For more information, refer to the section titled "Working with Cross Certification" in Chapter 7, "Naming Conventions and Certification."

Troubleshooting Tools

To assist you in resolving any problems you might encounter in your Notes environment, these tools will provide you with information concerning what was attempted and any responses or error messages that were generated:

- ▶ log.nsf—This database contains all of the information for all activity a server performs. This is an excellent tool for determining what happened.

- ▶ Log analysis—This tool, available in the Server Administration panel, enables you to search the log.nsf using word and time criteria.

- ▶ Database analysis—This tool, available in the Server Administration panel, enables you to search a database for reads, writes, deletions, replications, and so on. It is a very useful tool for database-specific information.

- ▶ Replication settings—Replication seldom goes *wrong*. It typically does what it is told to do, which is why it's important to understand the replication settings.

▶ Replication history—This is a quick method of determining the last successful replication with another server.

▶ Mail Trace—Without having to send a message, this tool looks at the path and gives you detailed information on the route a message will take.

▶ Port Trace—This tool provides you with detailed information on the path and success of information going through a port on the server.

▶ EVENT—With the right Monitor documents, the EVENT task can advise you of particular situations you have identified.

▶ REPORT—With the right Monitor documents, the REPORT task can advise of any thresholds you have set and provide statistical reports on servers.

Despite all of these tools, many times you will not receive any errors as to events that occur because the system believes it is operating as it should. In such cases, you must be aware of how Notes operates and what mistakes you or a user might have made to produce what you consider to be erroneous operations.

Exercises

These exercises will take you through a few sample scenarios that you might come across in a Notes environment.

Exercise 10.1

A user wants to change his name (perhaps he goes by Bob instead of Robert). Complete the following steps:

1. You will be using Pedro's user ID for this exercise, so make a backup copy first so you can get his ID back after the exercise.

2. Make sure you are using Pedro's ID; if you're not, switch to it.

3. Select Tools | User ID | More Options | Change Name.

4. Enter a new common name, such as `Peter Grind`.

5. You will be told that changing the name will remove all certificates. Click Yes, and then click Done to close the window.

6. Choose File | Database | Open, and choose the server name—not local. You will not be allowed access to the server because you no longer have any certificates in your name.

7. Choose File | Tools | User ID | Certificates to verify your lack of certificates.

Exercise 10.2

In this exercise, you will change Pedro's Person document and send the router to a nonexistent mail file for Pedro. This will result in dead mail.

1. Go to Bean's Public Address Book and change Pedro's mail file name (originally `mail/pgrind.nsf`) to `mail\pdgrind.nsf`. This will direct the router to a nonexistent mail file.

2. Switch to Pedro's ID if you're not already using it.

3. Go to Pedro's mail file and create a memo to Pedro and send it.

4. Check Pedro's mail file. The message will not be delivered because the router has the wrong information.

5. To open the `mail.box`, select Server | File | Database | Open and type `mail.box` under Filename. You will see the message in the `mail.box`, but it will be identified as dead mail.

6. To fix the problem, edit Pedro's Person document to include the correct filename of the mailfile.

7. Open `mail.box`, choose Actions, Release Dead Messages.

Review Questions

1. A database is experiencing replication problems. To gather information to assist in problem resolution, you will use which of the following tools?

   a. Log analysis, with the search criteria of `replicate` and the database name

   b. Database analysis, with the search criteria of `replicate` and the database name

   c. Database analysis, selecting Replication History, Log File Activity, and Log File Events

2. Sever X is not generating statistics reports. To find out why, you would go first to:

   a. `log.nsf` for server X

   b. The Statistics and Events database

   c. The Statistics Reporting database

3. Two servers with a replication schedule are having problems. The replication is happening only every other day. What would you look at to help resolve the problem?

   a. The replication history of the database

   b. The Statistics Reporting database

   c. The Connection document for the replication schedule

4. An administrator calls you and explains that he is trying to implement passthru for a server. He has created all the correct Connection documents, but he cannot get the passthru to connect. What would you suggest he do?

   a. Do a trace connection through the port he identified in the Connection document.

   b. In the Server documents, check the contents of the fields in the Restriction area.

5. A user informs you that the mail message he sent yesterday has still not been received by the recipient. What tools do you use to investigate?

   a. Port | Trace Connection to verify the path you believe the message is taking

   b. Server Administration panel | Mail | Send Mail Trace

   c. Log analysis

Review Answers

1. C. If your replication problem is with one database, it makes sense to do a database analysis, which lets you search the log.nsf at the same time. For more information, refer to the section titled "Troubleshooting Tools."

2. B. The Server to Monitor documents are in this database, and the probable cause is that server X is not indicated. For more information, refer to the section titled "Troubleshooting—System Administration II."

3. C. You already know what the problem is, so the information in the statistics reporting and replication history is redundant. You need to resolve the problem, which is in the Connection document: It specifies only Mon, Wed, Fri in the Days of the Week field. For more information, refer to the section titled "Troubleshooting Replication Problems."

4. B. If they have already created the correct Connection documents, it is probably the fields in the Server Document under Restrictions that have been forgotten. For more information, refer to the section titled "Troubleshooting User Problems."

5. B. The simplest, most direct method of obtaining information about how a mail message is delivered is to do a mail trace directly to the recipient. This provides you with all the detailed information you require to identify problems that may exist. For more information, refer to the section titled "Troubleshooting Tools."

Answers to Test Yourself Questions at Beginning of Chapter

1. Lack of proper certification, Access and Deny fields in the Server document, and connection problems in reaching the server—all three could be the cause of the message. For more information, see "Troubleshooting Server Problems."

2. The message tells you it cannot find a route, which means there's a problem with the information contained in the Connection documents. For more information, see "Troubleshooting Mail Routing Problems."

3. When you are having problems with only one document, it is probably something in the document that's causing the problem. For example, if a Readers field does not have the server name in it, the server cannot read or replicate the document. For more information, see "Troubleshooting Application Problems."

P a r t 2

Application Development

Chapter 11

Introduction to Application Development Components

This chapter will introduce you to the following objectives:

 Objectives

- ▶ Understanding development
- ▶ Creating databases
- ▶ Understanding database elements
- ▶ Understanding the standard view

Test Yourself! Before reading this chapter, test yourself to determine how much study time you will need to devote to this section.

1. What is the main role of an application developer?

2. How does creation of a database from a template differ from creation of a database by copying?

3. Why would you encrypt a database and what are the implications of doing such a thing?

4. What are the maximum sizes for databases that you can specify when creating a new database?

5. If, in the New Database dialog box, you want to select a template but can't find the one you want, what can you do to find it?

Answers are located at the end of the chapter...

Application development encompasses many varied topics. It is essential that a well-rounded application developer understand these topics and when to use the tools and techniques that are part of each. This is essential both for the task of application development as well as for the AD exams.

Understanding Development

 Most of what any Notes user sees from day to day, as he interacts with Lotus Notes, has been created by an application developer. Set apart from the role of system administrator, application developers are responsible for the implementation of the potential of Notes to share information in organizations. Application developers take the ideas and wishful thinking of users and turn them into functioning applications. As a result, an awareness of the features of Notes and the fundamental design elements available for a developer is essential to anyone who carries the title Lotus Notes Application Developer.

Starting from the seed of an idea, an application developer builds an application piece by piece until it is ready for release into the user community—only to be changed over and over again as time progresses and his or her users become more sophisticated and less amazed by the power of the product. "We've seen" is the beginning of many sentences that the user community will utter, and it's your responsibility to have seen or at least be able to duplicate those functions.

The chapters that make up the application development section of this book are designed to introduce you to the building blocks of Lotus Notes application development. Of course, they also prepare you for the exams that you will take to prove that you've earned the right to be called a Certified Lotus Notes Application Developer.

The Application Development 1 and 2 exams cover a wide variety of application development topics. These topics are covered in the chapters that follow. The intent of these chapters is to give you a broad and deep understanding of the kinds of topics you will see on the exam and the kinds of information you will need to develop quality applications. As a result, in some cases, more detail is given than would be normally expected for exam preparation.

The topics covered in the Application Development chapters are roughly divided into two sections: those for AD1 and those for AD2. Although there is some overlap, it is intended that Chapters 11–16 cover AD1 topics and Chapters 17–23 cover AD2 topics; Chapter 24, "Troubleshooting Application Development Problems," covers topics that span both areas.

Application development begins with the creation of a database and progresses from there. To prepare for the AD1 exam, you need to be familiar with the ways you can create a database and some of the basic components found in databases. (See the section "Creating a Lotus Notes Database" later in this chapter.)

From the topic of database creation, you will move on to cover the design of the various elements. Of course, these elements are all included on the test to greater or lesser extents. Be prepared to understand the construction and properties of forms (see Chapter 12, "Creating Forms") and views (see Chapter 14, "Creating Views") because these are fundamental to all databases. As well, be prepared for elementary formulas (as least for the AD1 exam) and some of the most common @ Functions (see Chapter 13, "Introduction to Formulas").

In preparation to apply form knowledge, you need to understand how a form is created and named and its basic properties. You also need to know the fundamental form component: the field. Not only do you need to understand how to insert a field onto a form, you need to understand edit and data types and the values that these can take. You need to be comfortable creating fields, assigning data and edit types, and then dealing with the unique processing that is required in each.

In conjunction with forms and fields, you also need to understand basic @ Functions for the AD1 exam. This topic includes using @ Functions to manipulate editable fields as well as computed fields. In addition, you need to be able to apply formulas to view selections and column values. You need to apply this understanding of

@ Functions to the syntax of the functions in Chapter 13 because you might be asked to troubleshoot problems with functions that are presented to you.

Of course, you also need to understand what views are, how to create them, the kinds of views (shared versus personal), and how to design them. Understanding the basic concepts of views ensures that you know how and when to use them. In addition to understanding the properties of views themselves, you need to understand view design—that is, how to create view columns and how to populate those columns with values from fields, actions, and formulas.

Once you know how the major components of the Notes database are constructed, the AD1 exam will expect that you can also enhance those elements through the use of automation, navigators, security, and documentation. Although you will spend much of the exam answering questions regarding views, forms, databases, and formulas, do not neglect your understanding of the enhancements because you will be expected to understand how to apply them.

Automation is frequently accomplished through the use of actions and hotspots, buttons that can be clicked to invoke system commands or functions (see Chapter 15, "Creating Actions and Hotspots"). These buttons prove invaluable to an application developer in making his or her applications more user-friendly. For the exam, you need to be able to distinguish between an action button and a hotspot button, where they are used, and what they can do. In addition, you need to be aware of specific applications and the use of the @command class of functions, primarily because they are used in these buttons.

Navigators are not a large portion of the exam, but they are important to understand nonetheless (see Chapter 16, "Finalizing the Database"). Because navigators are new for Notes release 4, you might see questions that test your understanding of the new features. As well, features such as hotspots can be integrated into navigators, so navigators are a potential context for hotspot questions. Understand how navigators are constructed, the kind of components that they contain, and how they can be displayed and manipulated.

Although security is really a system administration topic, a good application developer understands the implications of security features on his or her application. AD1 expects that you understand database Access Control Lists (ACLs) and the level of access afforded by the different access levels. In addition, you should be familiar with how to open the ACL dialog box and how to manipulate the information on the Basics page (see Chapter 16).

The last topic for the AD1 section of this book (and for the AD1) is documentation (see Chapter 17, "Creating Application Documentation"). Like navigators, documentation is not covered in great detail on the exam, but a proper understanding of documentation methods is essential in understanding Notes. You need to understand what the built-in documentation facilities are and how you can use other tools to document forms and your applications in general.

The Application Development 2 exam covers some new topics (such as mail-enabling forms, creating and using agents, design, and templates) and goes into more depth in others (such as advanced formulas and advanced security).

For AD2, you need to understand formulas in depth and be able to draw on a wide variety of @ Functions and their syntaxes. This includes understanding how lists work and how you apply and manipulate lists in formulas and functions (see Chapter 18, "Advanced Formulas Part I"). In addition, you need to understand how to use the functions @DBColumn and @DBLookup, their syntax, and their application because they are included on the exam almost without fail (see Chapter 19, "Advanced Formulas Part II").

In addition to the general theory of formulas, you need to be able to use @MailSend in the context of enabling forms for mail (see Chapter 19). As a result, some understanding of the techniques for mail-enabling is also required. This includes the special reserved fields for mail-enabling as well as the formula and design techniques that are required for successfully implementing document routing in Notes.

Layout regions and subforms are important topics for exams as well (see Chapter 20, "Layout Regions and Subforms"). As with the navigators section, not a lot of questions are dedicated to layout regions; one reason might be that asking questions about areas of notes that are primarily graphical is difficult given the content of most multiple-choice exams. However, you need to understand layout regions because, like navigators, this is a new feature for Notes release 4, and you might be quizzed on it to judge your understanding of new features. Be sure that you know how fields react to being on a layout region and how the features of some data types (especially keywords) change.

Subforms are also an important part of application development and a good area for questions. Not only should you understand basic subform design, you should also know what subforms are for and how to use them. In addition, AD2 questions might also revolve around the use of formulas to insert subforms, and you need to understand the relationship between the subform formula and the insertion of the subform itself.

Understanding the function of agents is also essential to your understanding of AD2 topics (see Chapter 21, "Creating Agents"). Agents enhance your ability to automate applications. For the exam, you need to know the types of agents, how they can be triggered, what their parameters are, and what kinds of processes they can run. A basic understanding of how agent execution is controlled is also important; however, you do not need a deep understanding because this area crosses over into the realm of system administration.

The AD2 section comes to a close with a discussion of design finalizing and maintenance and security. When it comes to design finalizing, you need to understand the design template and how templates are created. You need to know what the .ntf extension means, how templates are defined by their use, not by their extension or intended function, and how replace and refresh work in the context of design maintenance and update (see Chapter 22, "Maintaining Application Designs").

Security is extremely important in Notes as a whole, and security that is internal to the design of your databases is also important in your rounded knowledge of application development (see Chapter 23, "Securing Applications"). Whereas AD1 expected you to understand the database-level security afforded by the ACL, AD2 expects you to understand security at the form, view, document, and field levels. This security is accomplished through the use of Access Control Lists, roles, readers and Authors fields, encryption, and signing. Know how each of these features contributes to overall security and the practical aspects of the implementation of each feature in your applications.

Woven throughout the AD1 and AD2 exams is the expectation that you understand troubleshooting. The capability to understand a problem, diagnose it, and then repair it in a short period of time is essential in the design process. Understanding troubleshooting is extremely important in the context of any exam where you have only a fixed time to prove that you have the knowledge necessary to pass. You can develop troubleshooting skills by understanding the major pitfalls that you might encounter (see Chapter 24). However, there is no substitute for understanding the correct ways to do things and then applying those techniques through experience in application development.

Part II, "Application Development," was designed to cover both the Lotus exam objectives and the correct techniques for applying these basic skills in the world outside the exam room. You will find tips, tricks, and information that is not tested on the exam but that you need to know to understand application development in Notes. This knowledge, in the end, will prepare you to prove that you really do know how application development is done.

The first thing that you need to be able to do in the design of a Lotus Notes application is create a new database.

Creating a Lotus Notes Database

 Objective

The Lotus Notes database is the container in which information is stored in Notes. Databases are the files that are created by a Notes application developer, allowing for information storage, retrieval, and sharing. To build an application, you must have at least one database.

There are three ways to create a Notes database: using a template, copying a currently existing database, and creating a blank database and building from scratch. The first two ways involve, by far, the least amount of work, but of course, you need to find templates or databases that are similar to what you want to create yourself.

In any of the three methods, you must provide some information as your new database is created:

▶ The location (whether the database is on your workstation or on a server and if on a server, which one)

▶ The title (the commonly used and referenced name)

▶ The filename (the actual reference to the database on your disk drive)

▶ Whether you want to encrypt the database when you create it (make it impossible for anyone else to access without your user ID and password)

▶ How big the database can get (1GB, 2GB, 3GB, or 4GB)

When you create a database from a template, you must tell Notes which template you are using, and when you copy an existing database, you must select the database icon from your workspace (the icon must be on the workspace first).

Creating a Notes database from scratch or from a template involves the following process:

1. From the File menu, choose Database | New.

2. Fill in the fields on the New Database dialog box. (See the section "Using the New Database Dialog Box" later in this chapter for details.)

3. Choose a template (the one called Blank if you are creating from scratch).

4. Click the OK button to initiate database creation.

Creating a Notes database by copying a current database involves a slightly different process:

1. Place the icon for the database you want to copy on your workspace using File | Database | Open.

2. Select the icon of the database you want to copy by clicking it once.

3. From the File menu, choose Database | New Copy.

4. Fill in the fields on the Copy Database dialog box. (See the section "Using the Copy Database Dialog Box" later in this chapter for details.)

5. Indicate which of the database elements you want to copy (design, documents, ACL) and whether you want to create a full text index for the new database.

6. Click the OK button to initiate the database copy.

Note

There are two cases where copying a database to get a new one to modify is not as easy as it sounds. The first case is where there is no design provided with the database. As part of maintaining the design, an application developer can choose to remove the design. In that case, there is no design to copy, so there will be no design elements in the new database to use and modify (see Chapter 22).

The second case is where you do not have at least `designer`-level access in the ACL of the source database. If you choose to copy the ACL as part of the elements of the database and the copy is going on a server, you will not be able to modify the database design (the new ACL will not allow you to). To make a copy without the ACL simply deselect the "Copy All" option in the dialog box.

The New Database dialog box has a number of features that require detailed explanation; the following section deals with the fields and choices in detail.

Using the New Database Dialog Box

The New Database dialog box (see Figure 11.1) can be divided into four main sections: names, encryption, size limit, and template. The names section allows you to specify the naming of your database; encryption allows you to indicate local database security levels; size limit allows you to specify the maximum database size; template allows you to base your design on a current design template.

Figure 11.1

The New Database dialog box allows you to create a new database.

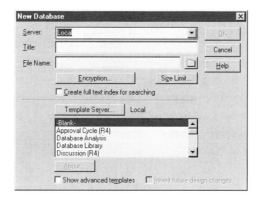

Names

The first name required is the server. The server is the place where the database file will reside and where users (including you) will open it. The server is either local, meaning that it is created on the hard drive of the machine where you are currently working, or is some other specified server name, such as Brazil/Bean.

To create a database anywhere other than your local machine, you must have permission from that server to do so; you do not need such permission to create local databases. This permission is set up in the Server document for that server, and that document is found in the Public Address Book for your organization. If you do not have the ability to create new databases on the server, you get an error message when you attempt to create any new database. If you get an error message, you (or someone with appropriate permissions to change server documents) must change the Server document for the server where you want to create the new database. This allows you to create new databases—which is done in the Create New Databases field in the Restrictions section of the appropriate server document.

The second name required is the database title. This title, which can be up to 32 characters long, will appear on the database icon when it is placed on the workspace and will appear in the database list when you open an existing database. Because this title is the name that most people will reference, it should be meaningful and descriptive of the database's function.

The last name required is the filename of the database. Because Lotus Notes is supported on many different operating system platforms, recommending names is difficult. To simplify naming, Lotus recommends in its documentation that you keep your names to the lowest common denominator, which is eight characters, no spaces, only underscores (_) or hyphens (–) to separate words, and either all uppercase or all lowercase. If, however, you know the naming conventions of the operating system and your Notes implementation consists of servers and workstations that all support the same naming conventions, then you can use any valid filename. For example, if your servers and workstations are all Windows 95 or Windows NT machines, then they all support long filenames and you are free to use 255-character filenames. If some of your workstations are Windows 3.11, then you might want to use eight-character filenames, but this choice is only significant if people reference the databases by the filename (which is not likely) because in that case, they will see the truncated eight-character names if they browse a long filename.

Of course, the filename also includes an extension in addition to the name itself. This extension should be either .nsf (for regular databases) or .ntf (if you are creating a template).

Notes expects that the database you are creating will be placed into the default Notes data folder on the server you specified in the server field (frequently, this is `C:\Notes\Data`). If that is the case, then you can simply enter the filename and Notes will take care of placing it into the correct folder, such as `newdb.nsf`. However, if the database you are creating does not belong in the default directory, you must provide additional information. If the database is placed in a subfolder of the default data folder, you need to provide only the additional information. For example, if you are placing the new database in the `Accounting` folder that is in the default data directory, you need only specify `Accounting\newdb.nsf`, and this database will be placed in `C:\Notes\Data\Accounting\newdb.nsf`. If the database is to be placed in a folder other than the default data folder or one of its subfolders, then you must provide the complete path, such as `C:\Accounting\newdb.nsf`.

Note

It is not recommended that you create databases in places other than in the default data folder because doing so makes locating that database more difficult. The database will not show up in the Open Database dialog box, and you will only be able to browse for it on the disk if you are looking for a local database and not a server database.

Encrypting Local Databases

Security on Notes databases is such that the Access Control List of a database ensures that information in server-based databases can be accessed only by people who have permission to access it. However, databases that are accessed locally—that is, by workstation software on the machine that has the database file —do not respect the ACL settings. This means that anyone with physical access to a machine with databases on it will be able, by default, to access any of the information held in any of those databases. To fix this security problem, one of the things you can do is locally encrypt databases as they are created. This local encryption comes in three strengths and results in a user being challenged for the password of the person who created and encrypted the database every time it is opened.

Note   The database can be encrypted only for one user ID. This means that regardless of how many people use the workstation where the database is located, only the one with the password to the ID used to encrypt will be able to open that database.

The encryption strengths are simple, medium, and strong. As you increase the strength, the encryption algorithm gets more complex, meaning that it will be more difficult to break the encryption code. However, there are two drawbacks to encryption. First, as the strength increases, so does the time required to open documents in the database because each document must be decrypted to show you the information contained in it. The second drawback is that all encryption strengths except simple will prevent you from using compression programs to shrink database size. To locally encrypt a database, follow this procedure:

1. From the New Database Dialog box or the Copy Database dialog box, click the Encryption button.

2. In the Encryption for dialog box (see Figure 11.2), choose the Locally Encrypt This Database Using radio button and select an encryption strength from the pull-down list.

Figure 11.2

The Encryption for dialog box allows you to set local database security through encryption.

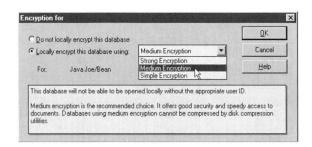

3. Click the OK button to exit to the New Database or Copy Database dialog box.

Setting Maximum Database Size Limits

At the time you create a database, you set the maximum size that a database can grow to. The maximum size can be 1GB, 2GB, 3GB, or 4GB. This setting prevents the database from growing larger than this indicated size. Although some documentation says that this size cannot be changed after it is set, the truth is that it cannot be changed easily. It can in fact be changed once it is set, but only through a server process called COMPACT, which must be run by a system administrator on a Notes server.

 Note

> The only difference between a database created with a maximum size of 1GB and one with a maximum size of 4GB is the size at which documents will be refused. Neither the initial size of the database nor the rate at which they grow with the addition of documents is affected by the maximum size.

To set the maximum size of a database at creation, follow this procedure:

1. From the New Database Dialog box or the Copy Database dialog box, click the Size Limit button.

2. In the Size Limit field on the Size Limit dialog box (see Figure 11.3), choose the maximum size required from the pull-down list.

Figure 11.3

The Size Limit dialog box allows you to set the maximum database size.

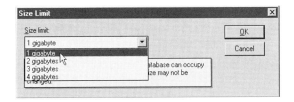

3. Click the OK button to exit to the New Database or Copy Database dialog box.

Using the Database Template

Creation of databases is often simpler if there is a pattern, or template, available upon which to base the design. Some templates are provided with an installation of Lotus Notes; others are created by application developers. (For more information on template creation and management, see Chapter 22.)

If you want to create a database that is based on the design of a template, then choose a template from the list provided; otherwise, choose Blank, which will create a database but not base it on a template.

If the template that you require is not in the template list provided, then select Show Advanced Templates to see additional templates. If the template is still not available, then you might have to change the template server—that is, look at a different Notes server to see its templates. Some templates are installed with the workstation software and others are installed with the server software. Furthermore, if templates have been created by application developers, then they might be on only one server. By choosing a different Notes server to look for templates, you might find the template you are looking for. To specify a template server, follow these steps:

1. From the New Database dialog box, click the Template Server button.

2. In the Template Servers dialog box (see Figure 11.4), choose a server from the pull-down list or type a server name in the text box to replace Local.

Figure 11.4

The Template Servers dialog box allows you to choose the server where a template is found.

3. Click the OK button to exit to the New Database dialog box.

The Copy Database dialog box has some features that differ from the New Database dialog box. These features are described in the next section.

Using the Copy Database Dialog Box

The Copy Database dialog box (see Figure 11.5) appears when you choose File | Database | New Copy. You use it to specify characteristics for a database created by copying the design (and perhaps the documents) from an existing database.

Figure 11.5

The Copy Data-base dialog box allows you to create a new copy of a data-base.

The specifications for Server, Title, File Name, Encryption, and Size Limit are the same as for the New Database dialog box, and I refer you to those sections in the previous discussion for details.

The Copy Database dialog box differs from the New Database dialog box in that the former's copy specifications replace the template specifications of the latter.

When specifying what to copy from the existing database, you can choose Database Design and Documents to copy both the design as well as all the documents or Database Design Only to ignore the documents and simply copy the design. You can also indicate whether you want the same Access Control List by selecting the Access Control List check box. If you do not select this, you will have to populate the ACL manually.

Finally, you can also create a full-text index for searching as the database is created by selecting the Create Full Text Index check box.

Understanding Database Elements

 Objective

Databases consist of a number of design elements. These elements, when taken together, form the structure in which documents are created and data is shared. If a database is created from a template or copied from another database, many of the design elements will already be present. However, if created from a blank template— from scratch—a database is basically a hollow shell, waiting to be filled with design structure.

The design elements that you can build into a Notes database are forms, views, folders, agents, subforms, shared fields, navigators, documentation documents, and the icon. Follow these steps to create a new element:

1. Open the database by double-clicking its icon on your workspace.

2. From the Create menu, choose Design and then pick the element you want to create.

Forms

The form is where data entry begins. You can think of the form as the starting point upon which a document is built, even though it really is more than that. A user will choose a form, a predesigned entry structure, in which to enter information. That information, when saved, becomes a document. When the document is opened for editing or viewing, it is usually opened using the same form that was used to create it, thus ensuring a consistent look to the information in the document.

Forms in Notes are designed, as a form on paper is designed, with text to indicate where one section begins and another ends and with areas labeled to accept certain information. These areas for recording information, known as fields, are named so that information can be accessed and displayed in the future.

Views

The view is how you, the application developer, give the users of a database ways to see the data without opening each individual document. A view is a list of documents and some or all of their fields. Views can be selective—that is, they can display some of the documents based on a criteria—or they can display all the documents in a database. Views can sort documents by certain fields, display only certain fields, and summarize information in numeric fields.

There can be many views in a database, each showing information in a different way or using different criteria. Not only can a developer create views for all users of the database to see, but the average user can also create his own views when the views designed by the developer don't suit him or when he needs a special way of seeing, sorting, or selecting the information.

Folders

Folders are like views in that they display documents found in a database. What makes them different is the way that documents are placed into these folders. Whereas the documents found in views relate to some selection criteria (or in the absence of selection criteria, all the documents in the database), folders by default contain no documents at all. To get a document into a folder, a user must put it there. In this way, a folder becomes a miscellaneous collection of documents, which are held together in some logical way in the mind of the user but might not have any specific criteria that a view could use to calculate membership.

Agents

Agents are automated programs that can repeat tasks on schedule or on specific system cues or that can run manually. These agents can perform complex or simple tasks. Basically, anything that a user can do manually, an agent can be created to perform automatically. This means that the chances for error in complex processes are reduced because the processes are done the same way every time. Moreover, by scheduling agents to run at specific intervals or after certain events happen, you ensure that an action is never forgotten.

Subforms

Subforms are aids to design efficiency. They are groups of fields and other design elements normally found on a form. You can create these groups and then insert them into new forms as they are required. This means that design time is reduced because subforms can be created and used over and over again. Subforms also reduce the time for updating forms because a change in a subform results in the change being propagated to all the forms that contain that subform.

Shared Fields

Shared fields are like subforms in that they are elements that can be created and then used in many places; however, they are unlike subforms in that they are single elements, rather than groups of elements. Shared fields are single-field design elements that cause the definition of a field to be created once and then inserted into many forms. These shared fields are likely to appear in many places. Like subforms, if the shared field is changed, its change is also propagated to all the places where the field was inserted.

Navigators

Navigators are the elements that allow users to see what views are available and that provide a user-friendly environment in which to work. Like the navigator on a ship or in an airplane, the navigator shows you where you can go and helps you get there. The default navigator is called *folders*, and it is simply a list of all the views and folders that are available in a database as well as the agents that a user can access. You can create graphical navigators that include bitmapped images and buttons that initiate actions, such as moving to a certain view.

Documentation Documents

Documentation documents allow you, the developer, to create documentation for your users. Two standard documents that have already been created for you, which you should populate with information, are the About Database document and the Using Database document. Through these documents, you can define what the database is all about, what it does, and who should use it. You can also provide detailed documentation on what each form is for, how each view works, each view's selection criteria, how the agents work, and each agent's triggers.

The Icon

The database icon is what the user first sees on the workspace. This picture is supposed to give a graphical interpretation of what the database does and make the database shortcut on the workspace easily recognizable. The icon is a standard design when a database is first created but can be modified. (See Chapter 16.)

Now that you have been introduced to all the elements that can be present in a database, look at the standard folders view, the place where you can access all of these elements.

Using the Standard (Folders) View

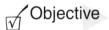 Objective

The standard, or folders, view is the view presented when a database is first opened. It is present in every database, but depending on how the database is designed, users might never see it. (See Figure 11.6.)

The standard view consists of two panes: On the left is the folders and views list, and on the right are the contents of whatever view is currently selected on the left. All the views and folders that the current user can access are listed at the top of the left side, and under that is the agents view, which can be selected to display the list of agents that the current user can see.

Figure 11.6

The standard view is present in every database.

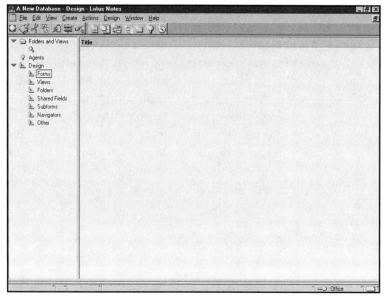

As a designer, you can see another group of views that others cannot; it is called the design view. This view allows you to see the categories of design elements and, upon your selecting any of the categories, to see the actual design elements that have been created. This list of design elements can be expanded or collapsed by clicking the twistie (the triangle) to the left of the design category.

Using the Design View

The design view is available by default only to database designers and managers; however, anyone who has higher than no access-level rights to the database in the ACL can see a list of the design elements by selecting View|Show|Design. Only those users with designer or manager access to the database will be able to modify these design elements. In some instances, the design itself might not be present due to special precautions taken by the designer to ensure design confidentiality. In that case, no one, no matter the access, will be able to view or modify the design (see Chapter 22). The design view contains a category for every major element that you can create except agents, which are available by clicking the Agents entry just above the design view header. The categories listed in the design list are Forms, Views, Folders, Shared Fields,

Subforms, Navigators, and Other. Most of these map exactly to the database elements described in the section "Database Elements" with the exception of Other. The Other category contains the Documentation documents as well as the database icon.

Exercises

This lab does not require you to copy any files from your CD-ROM as there are no prerequisites. You will create a database in which you can begin design of a customer and invoice tracking system (the lab scenario throughout the Application Development chapters of this book).

Exercise 11.1

1. From the File menu, choose Database | New. (See Figure 11.7.)

Figure 11.7

The completed New Database dialog box.

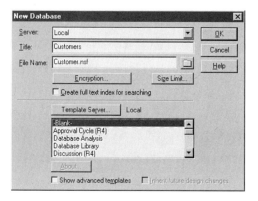

2. Leave the server name as Local, and in the Title field, type Customers.

3. In the filename field, type customer.nsf.

4. Leave all other characteristics at default—no local encryption, 1GB maximum size, Blank template—and click the OK button to create the database.

5. Exit the database when it opens.

Exercise 11.2

You will need two other databases as you complete the application you are building. The challenge is this:

1. Create a database called Invoices with a filename of Invoices.nsf and create another called Reference with a filename of Referenc.nsf.

Review Questions

1. Noah has an inventory database and wants to create another, almost identical database for archiving old inventory items. If he has no template available, what is his best method?

    a. Create a new database and copy the design elements from the old one into the new one.

    b. Select the inventory database, use File | Database | New Copy, and specify to copy database design and documents.

    c. Select the inventory database, use File | Database | New Copy, and specify to copy database design only.

    d. Select the inventory database and use File | Replication | New Replica to create a new database.

2. Alexander wants to ensure that the database he is creating can never become larger than 1GB. How can he do this at creation time?

    a. Specify a maximum size of 1GB in the Size Limit dialog box.

    b. Specify the maximum size of encrypted database as 1GB in the encryption properties.

    c. He can't restrict the maximum size at creation time.

    d. Send an e-mail at time of creation to all the users warning that they shouldn't put too many documents into the database.

3. Emma wants to ensure that the filename she is giving to her database is fully understandable by all users on all operating system platforms. What should she check about her filename?

    a. That it contains no more than 15 characters

    b. That it does not contain any spaces

    c. That it conforms to Windows 8.3 naming convention

    d. That it does not contain the word "snow"

4. What is the maximum number of characters that you can include in a database title?

    a. 10

    b. 32

    c. 255

    d. 8

5. Of the following, where does the database title not appear?

    a. In the database icon on the workstation

    b. In the Title field in the Database Properties dialog

    c. In a list of databases in the Open Database dialog box

    d. In a list of databases as presented by the Windows Explorer

6. Zeus created a new database by copying an existing one. However, when he goes into the ACL of the new one, all the users and groups that he created have disappeared. What did he do wrong at database creation?

    a. Nothing. There is no way to copy the ACL from one database to the other.

    b. He deselected the Access Control List check box in the Copy Database dialog box.

    c. He selected the Database design only radio button in the Copy Database dialog box.

    d. He specified an invalid filename and the ACL could not be copied.

Review Answers

1. C. The database that Noah wants to create is an exact duplicate of the one he already has. However, because he does not
   want to automatically archive all the existing documents, he
   will want to copy only the database's design, not the documents as well. For more information, refer to the section
   titled "Using the Copy Database Dialog Box."

2. A. In the New Database and Copy Database dialog boxes, you
   can specify a maximum size for the database from the Size
   Limit dialog box. You can access this dialog box by clicking
   the Size Limit button. For more information, refer to the
   section titled "Setting Maximum Database Size Limits."

3. C. For maximum usability, a database filename should take
   into account the lowest common denominator. The Windows 8.3 naming convention is the lowest common denominator: a maximum of eight characters in the filename, no
   spaces, only _ and – as punctuation, and a three-character
   extension. For more information, refer to the section titled
   "Names."

4. B. The maximum number of characters allowed in a database title is 32. For more information, refer to the section
   titled "Names."

5. D. The database title appears in all these places except in a
   list of files as presented by Explorer. This shows files on your
   hard drive and as such, can only display the database filename, not the title. For more information, refer to the section titled "Names."

6. B. In the Copy Database dialog box is a check box labeled
   Access Control List, which, when selected, ensures that the
   ACL for the source database is copied into the destination.
   This check box is selected by default, so Zeus must have in-
   advertently deselected it before he initiated the copy. For
   more information, refer to the section titled "Using the Copy
   Database Dialog Box."

Answers to Test Yourself Questions at Beginning of Chapter

1. The main role of an application developer is to design and implement Lotus Notes databases for the purpose of sharing information between people in an organization. Application developers also provide ongoing maintenance of databases that either they or others have created. For more information, refer to the section titled "Understanding Development."

2. Creation of a database from a template uses a database that was designed to be copied and never includes documents created in that template. Creation of a database by copying uses another database, usually one that users interact with as its basis, and the copy can include either the design only or the documents in addition to the design. For more information, refer to the section titled "Creating a Lotus Notes Database."

3. Encryption is performed to maintain local security on a database. You would encrypt because most of the security features for a database are bypassed when a database is accessed locally and you are concerned about people gaining access to the hard drive on your computer. The downside of encryption is that documents take a little longer to open, some encryption strengths do not support file compression, and only the person with the password to the user ID used to encrypt will be able to locally access the database. For more information, refer to the section titled "Encryption."

4. The maximum sizes are 1GB, 2GB, 3GB, and 4GB. This maximum can be increased to 4GB through the use of a server process called COMPACT. For more information, refer to the section titled "Setting Maximum Database Size Limits."

5. Templates can be different on different machines. If you cannot find the template you want, you can select a different template server by clicking the Template Server button. Once you choose a new server, you can browse the template list on that server. For more information, refer to the section titled "The Database Template."

Chapter 12

Creating Forms

This chapter introduces you to the following objectives:

Test Yourself! Before reading this chapter, test yourself to determine how much study time you will need to devote to this section.

1. What is a form name synonym (or alias), and how is it created?

2. What is the function of the form type Response?

3. How many field data types are there and what are they?

4. What is the function of static text on a form?

5. What is the relationship between a form and a document?

Answers are located at the end of the chapter...

The document is the fundamental unit of Notes storage in a database. Connected closely to the document are forms, the design element tied to a document that enables data entry, data display, and document editing.

Understanding Forms

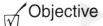Objective

The fundamental unit of data storage in a Notes database is the document. The primary method of document creation is through the use of forms. It is through the design of forms that the format of most documents in your databases is established. After forms are created, people using your databases have a vehicle through which to input their information.

When a document is first created with a form, Notes also creates a field on that document called Form, and in that field it places the name of the form that was used to create it. Frequently, the same form is always used to view, edit, and print that document. After the document has been created, however, there is no necessary relationship between the document and its creating form. Additional forms can be created that enable the viewing, editing, and printing of document information in different ways, and perhaps, with different styles. Just as a person can wear clothing that accentuates or hides one part of his or her body, so too can forms be changed to accentuate or hide different parts of a document. The document remains the same, although its appearance might change.

In addition, many forms can be used to input information into the same document. Just like a surgeon places a sheet over his or her patient that shows only that part of the patient that is to be operated on, so too can a form be coupled with a document to show only the fields necessary at the time or that need to be modified by the person editing the document.

It is important to maintain the distinction between forms and documents clearly in your mind. Documents are not forms, and forms are not documents. There is a relationship between the two, but no document is irreversibly connected to any form, and the form that enables you to view, edit, or print a document can be designed to change at any time and for any reason.

Form Types and Relationships

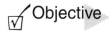 Objective

There are three kinds of forms: Document forms, Response forms, and Response-to-Response forms. These form types are used to create three kinds of documents: Document documents, Response documents, and Response-to-Response documents.

Documents of type Document can stand alone and do not require any other documents in your database in order to be created. In contrast, Responses cannot stand alone; they need a document of type Document to respond to. Response to Responses cannot stand alone either; they need either a type Document, a type Response, or a type Response-to-Response document to respond to in order to be created.

To illustrate, think of a conversation. You can initiate a conversation without previously having uttered a word to the other person. The initiation of a conversation is like a document of type Document. You can try as many conversation starters as you want until the other party becomes interested. So, you might say to a man in the park, "Nice weather, don't you think?" and then after pausing say, "Those shoes look quite comfortable," and finally say, "You are quite rude. I think I'll kick you in the leg!" Those three statements are your documents. After hearing your statements, the other party might choose to respond to you or might start a different conversation. If he says, "I've got a cat," then he is issuing a new document. However, if he says, "Yes they are, I bought them last week, and I love them," this is a response to your statement about his shoes. This response cannot happen without your original statement because your statement and his response are linked together. In the same way, a Notes Response document must be in response to a Notes Document document, or it cannot be created; the phrase "in response to" means that you have selected the document in a view, or opened the document, before you indicated that you wanted to create the response.

To continue the conversation, if you respond to the man's response with "Oh, where did you get them?" you are responding to him. In Notes, however, you have another level of response—the Response to Response. Now, whereas a Response document in Notes can respond only to a Document document, a Response to Response is a multipurpose document. A Response to Response can be issued in response to a Response, directly to a Document, or as a response to a Response to Response. In fact, if you want to continue the conversation and respond and respond and respond, each one in his turn, you must use Response-to-Response documents for each subsequent response.

These document types are used in many places in Notes. The most obvious and intuitive is in a discussion database in which many people have a discussion—one person begins a conversation and others join in by responding to the initial document or other people's responses or by starting their own discussions.

 Tip   You can look at an example of a typical discussion database by creating a new database, using the template `Discussion` (`R4`). This new database has all the form types, and you can see the interaction as you create new documents.

Less obvious might be a customer tracking database. Documents in this database might be the customers themselves. In this case, a Response document might keep track of individual people who were contact people for that customer (the relationship—the contacts—are responses to the customer). You can then progress down the hierarchy and envision letters, faxes, invoices, meeting records, and follow-up meetings, as being Response to Responses (in this case, a letter is issued to a contact—a response).

When a Response document is created, the parent of that new document is recorded as such—in other words, the fact that the document type Document is being responded to is noted. However, the connection does not enable dynamic interaction between the documents after the response is created. When the response is created, there might be a need to obtain information from the parent, and this can be done. On an ongoing basis, however, data exchange is not possible.

When a Response document is created, often you want to obtain certain values from its parent. In the previous example, when a contact is created in response to the customer document, you might want to get the customer name from the customer document and place it into the Contact document (the response). You do this because there is no easy way to reference the data in the parent document from the response, and as a result, the best option is to place that data into the response itself. Although there is no ongoing relationship between the data in the parent and the response, there is a one-time connection at the time of response creation. The process of obtaining and storing parent data into the response at creation is referred to as inheritance. As its name implies, inheritance of data is like the inheritance of genetic information from your parents. When you were conceived, you obtained genetic information from each of your parents. This genetic information remains the same regardless of any mutations that happen to your parents' genes after that point. In essence, what happens to their data does not affect yours. The same is true of the common data that a parent and its response share; they start out the same, but changing the data in one does not change the data in the other.

Inheriting data from a parent is a two-phase process: First, the Response or Response-to-Response form must be enabled for inheritance (see the section titled "Using the Defaults Tab" later in the chapter); second, the Response or Response-to-Response form must contain fields that are computed and that contain formulas referring to fields on the parent document.

Designing and Creating Forms

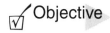 Forms contain a number of elements that enable users to input their data. In this chapter, we discuss two of those elements: *fields* and *static text*. Fields are the places in which the data is actually stored, and static text enables you to indicate to users what data is supposed to go into what fields and to otherwise label and annotate the form.

Before you actually create a form, sketch it out on paper; barring that, you should at least have a list of fields you want to place on the form and some idea how the form is to be laid out.

To create a form, do the following:

1. Open the database by double-clicking its icon on your work-space.

2. Select Create | Design | Form.

Now that the form has been created, you need to add the appropriate fields and text to it; first, however, you must understand the form design environment.

Using the Form Design Environment

The form design environment appears when you double-click and open a form from the forms list in the design view (see Figure 12.1). This environment consists of three panes (although usually only two show). Two panes are on the top and one is on the bottom. Each of these panes can be independently resized to enable design in any of the three areas. On the top is the form builder window—the area in which the form design actually occurs. This area is like a sketch pad on which you create your form's final look.

On the bottom is the design pane—the area in which formulas are created for calculating a variety of values, including values for computed fields (for more information, see Chapter 13, "Introduction to Formulas"). If you need this area to be larger or smaller, you can resize it by dragging its top border up or down. Its top border is the thick line that divides this pane from the form builder window.

The final pane is usually hidden. Its left-hand border can be seen on the right side of the form builder window, just to the right of the form builder window's vertical scroll bar. This pane can be opened by dragging the border to the left with your mouse or by selecting the Menu View, Action Pane (see Figure 12.2). This pane shows a list of actions that have been defined for this form, either by default or by a developer (for more information, see Chapter 15, "Creating Actions and Hotspots").

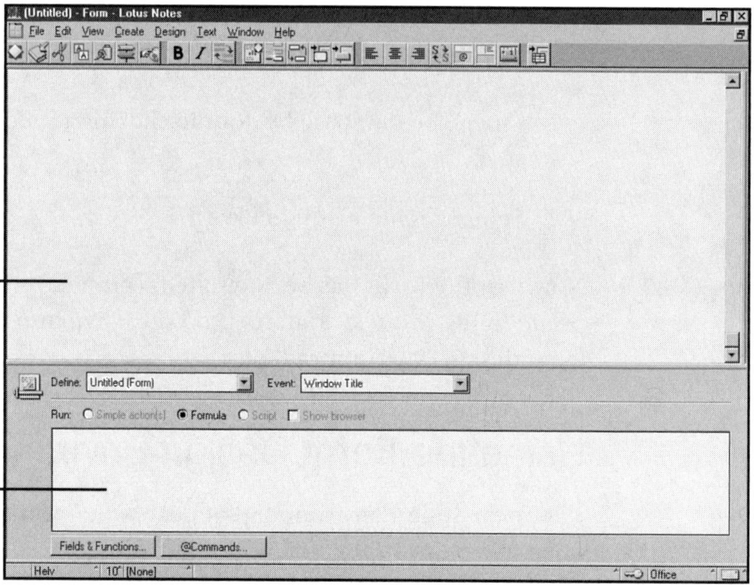

Figure 12.1

The form design environment.

Form builder window

Design pane

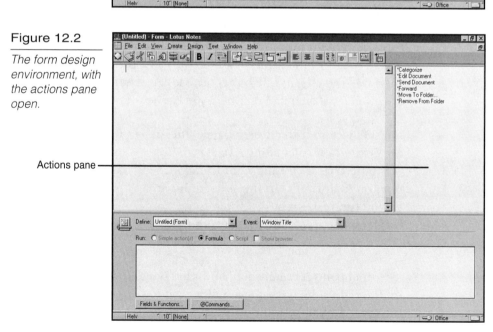

Figure 12.2

The form design environment, with the actions pane open.

Actions pane

Understanding Form Properties

Like other Notes objects, forms have properties that define their characteristics. These properties can be seen and set for a form by bringing up the Properties for Form dialog box. This dialog box can be brought up by clicking your right mouse button on any blank area in the form builder window and choosing Form Properties from the menu that appears. This Properties dialog box is divided into tabs: Basics, Defaults, Launch, Printing, and Security, which is the tab with the key on it (see Figure 12.3).

Figure 12.3

The Properties for Form dialog box enables you to set form properties.

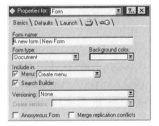

Using the Basics Tab

The Basics tab contains fields for information relating to the basic definition of the form. This includes name, form type, and color of the background.

The form name is the name that the users see in any menu system and that you see when you look at a list of forms from the standard view. Form names can be up to 64 characters long, after which you receive an error message indicating that the name is too long.

Two special features are built into form names: *synonyms* (sometimes called aliases) and *cascading menus*. Synonyms are names that are given to forms that users don't see but that you use to refer to a form in a formula. Synonyms are useful for two reasons: long names are inconvenient to work with, and users sometimes change their minds about what a form should be called, especially if its name appears in a menu. Synonyms can be used to alleviate both of these problems. If you have a form with a long name—for example, `Create a new Customer`—you can give it a synonym like `Customer`. In this way, you can save yourself some typing whenever you reference the form in formulas. Second, if the name changes, you will experience problems, especially if you have made reference to the old name in formulas. For example, the formula:

```
@Command([Compose];"Create a New Product Line")
```

can be used to create a new document by using a form called `Create a New Product Line`. However, say that you had used this formula in 20 different places and then your user community requests that you change the name of the form to `Define a Product Line`. This simple removal of a word from the form name requires you to modify all the formulas to reflect the new form name. In addition, any documents that were created when the form was called by the old name might not open anymore or might open by using the wrong form. To alleviate this difficulty, you can give the form a synonym to take the place of the form name that the users see in any formulas; this synonym will be the name that any documents look for when trying to get a form to open. This is advantageous because the user portion of a form name can change without changing the synonym—the portion that you are referencing.

A synonym is added to a form name by appending a ¦ (vertical bar) to the name, followed by the synonym name. For example, the new name for the form in the preceding example might be `Define a Product Line¦Products`, and you would always refer to the form by using its synonym, `Products`.

 Note   The left-most name is the descriptive name of the form that displays, while the right-most synonym is the name that is stored and referenced with formulas.

The second feature of the name is the capability to group and categorize names when users access the forms to create new documents. If you select the check box to the left of the property Include menu in: Menu (discussed later in this section), the name of the form appears in the Create menu, enabling users to create new documents based on this form. You can use special features of the form name to create cascading groups of form names that appear as submenus under the Create menu.

For example, I have a number of forms that create documents for managers to use and a number of forms that create documents for people from accounting to use. If I have five of each kind of form, I can place them all in a list under the Create menu. This can look quite sloppy, and because the names of forms are sorted alphabetically under the Create menu, it can be difficult to order them so that they are grouped together. Instead, I can create a cascading menu so that two groups appear under the Create menu—Management and Accounting—and the forms appear under each of those submenus. This can be accomplished by adding group names, followed by a \ (backslash) in front of the form name. If I have forms called `Create a New Invoice¦Invoice` and `Create a New Customer¦Customer` and those forms are both accounting forms, I can modify their names to be `Accounting\Create a New Invoice¦Invoice` and `Accounting\Create a New Customer¦Customer` (see Figure 12.4). As a result, users accessing the Create menu see an Accounting choice and when they choose it, they see two more choices. Observe that we also have added synonyms to these names so that we can refer to the forms by the names Invoice and Customer instead of the full names.

Note

When creating cascading menus, it is very important that the common parts of the names be exactly the same. If punctuation is different, if the groups are spelled differently, or even if there is an extra space before or after one of the words, the result will be unwanted groups. For example, if in the previous illustration, the second form were called `Accounting \Create a New Customer¦Customer` (note the extra space before the \), then two entries appear under the Create menu, one reading `Accounting` and the other reading `Accounting`.

Figure 12.4

Cascading menus increase usability and friendliness.

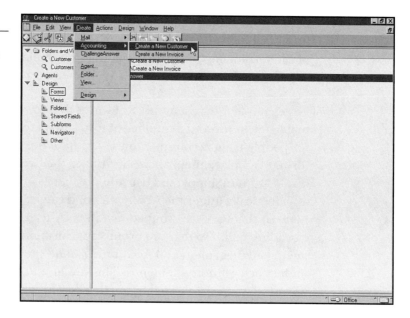

The Form type indicates how this form relates to other forms. Three form types can be chosen from the pull-down menu: Document, Response, and Response to Response. The background color field is a pull-down palette of colors that, when chosen, becomes the background color of the form. Be sure to choose colors that are not too bright or saturated, or your forms might irritate your user community. It is recommended that you use only light pastel colors.

There are two *include in* options: one to include a choice to create documents by using this form in a menu and the other to include this form in the search builder when creating searches for documents by using specific criteria. If you select the check box next to Menu, you can choose to either have the form's name appear directly under the Create menu or have the form's name appear in a dialog list box that is generated when the user chooses Other after choosing the Create menu.

 Tip

Forms are always ordered alphabetically in menus, which means that if you want forms to appear in a particular order, you must create unique beginnings for each form. For example, you might want to begin each form name with a number or a letter.

In addition, if the form name is set to appear in the Create menu, the first unique character will become the Accelerator key—by pressing the key combination Alt+C and then the accelerator, you can invoke the menu choice without using your mouse. These accelerator keys are always indicated in the menu with an underscore. For example, you might see a menu choice under the Create menu that appears like this: 1. Create a New Invoice. From the keyboard, you can press Alt+C+1, and a new Invoice document appears.

 Tip

If you place the form in the Other dialog box, cascading groups do not work. So, only use cascading options if you plan to place the form's name directly under the Create menu; otherwise, do not try to create cascading form menus.

If you select the check box next to Search Builder, this form appears in the list of forms presented when you create selection criteria, based on the form with which a document has been created.

The Versioning pull-down list enables you to select a versioning type, if versioning is required. Versioning enables you to save a new copy of the document every time a field is modified. Thus, you can ensure that a complete change-tracking mechanism is in place. The choices enable you to indicate whether new versions become responses, the old version's parent, or the old document's sibling. In other words, the new document remains the same document type as the old one was. In conjunction with the choice for versioning is the creation of new versions. Having chosen a versioning type, you can save a new version every time new changes are made or save a version only when requested by selecting File | New Version.

The check box labeled Anonymous Form enables you to create a form whose documents do not record the name of the person who created them. Usually, when a document is created, Notes maintains a hidden field called $UpdatedBy, which contains the names of all people who have modified the document since it was created. If the Anonymous Form check box is selected, the $UpdatedBy field will not be maintained.

Note

To preserve anonymity, ensure that there are no computed fields on your form that record the name of the author.

The check box labeled Merge Replication Conflicts is the last field on this Properties page. It enables you to reduce the number of replication conflicts for documents created with this form by ensuring that conflicts in replication are checked for at the field level. Normally, when Notes checks to see if a replication conflict has occurred, it checks to see if the same document has been modified in any way on two different replicas. If it has, then a replication conflict is the result. When this check box is selected, however, a conflict is only declared if the same field on two different replicas of the same document are changed. Therefore, if the value in the name field on one replica is changed and the value in the address field of another replica is changed, no replication conflict is declared; instead, the resulting document has both the address change and the name change reflected in it.

Using the Defaults Tab

The Defaults tab enables you to indicate a number of default or automatic settings that are applied to this form (see Figure 12.5).

Figure 12.5

The Properties for Form Defaults tab.

When selected, the Default Database Form check box indicates that this form is the default form for the database. This means that if documents arrive in this database that do not bear the name of a form in the database, this form is used to try and display the document's contents (for more information, see Chapter 19, "Advanced Formulas, Part II"). In contrast, if this option is not selected for any forms and a document arrives in this database that does not bear the name of a form in this database, that form will not open when double-clicked in a view.

 Note

Each database can have only one default form. By selecting the Default Database Form check box, you automatically make this form the only default; if another form was marked as default, its check box is now deselected.

When selected, the Store Form in Document check box indicates that when saved, any documents created by this form will save the document information, as well as the form definition. This can be useful when copying or mailing the document to another database that does not have the form used to create this document (for more information, see Chapter 19).

When selected, the Disable Field Exchange check box indicates that any field exchange that is configured for this form will not occur.

 Note

Field exchange is an advanced development technique that enables Lotus Notes fields to dynamically exchange data with OLE server applications. This technique is not covered on any AD1 or AD2 exam, and so it is not explained in detail here.

When selected, the Automatically Refresh Fields check box indicates that as each field value is entered, any computed values in other fields should be recalculated and displayed. Normally, only specific events cause refresh, such as saving a document or manually asking for refresh by pressing the F9 key.

Note Automatically refreshing fields can have a detrimental effect on document entry when there are a number of computed fields present on the document. Entry is slowed because re-calculation of these values is happening every time a new value is entered.

The next two check boxes relate to the inheritance of fields from one document to another. When selected, the Formulas Inherit Values from Selected Document check box enables one document to get values from the selected document when the new document was created. Frequently, this means that a response inherits values from its parent. For example, a document contains information for a customer. A Response document is to contain information for a customer contact, but some of the information, such as the address, is the same for the contact as for the customer's head office. In this case, you might want to inherit the address from the document to the response. Enabling this feature is the first step in getting the field value from the parent (for more information, see Chapter 13).

When selected, the field `Inherit Entire Selected Document Into Rich Text Field` enables you to take the entire contents of a parent document and place those contents into a rich text field on the response. This is what happens in Notes Mail when you reply with History or Forward a document. Rather than being inherited into a number of separate fields, the entire document is inherited into a single field.

When selected, the Automatically Enable Edit Mode check box causes the document to be edited when it is opened. Ordinarily, documents open in read mode and are then put into edit mode manually.

 Note For this automatic edit feature to work, the user opening the document has to have the ability to edit it as specified in the ACL for the database. In other words, the user must have author access to edit a document he or she creates or must have editor or higher access to edit documents other people create.

When selected, the Show Context Pane check box causes another field to appear to its right: a pull-down list containing the choices Parent and Document link. The context pane is a pull-up portion at the bottom of a document's display that can show part of the document that is the parent of the current response or is the document from which a document link opened the document you are currently looking at (see Figure 12.6). With this check box selected, when a document is opened, the context pane opens at the bottom of the document and the appropriate document is displayed.

Figure 12.6

A Response form with parent in a context pane.

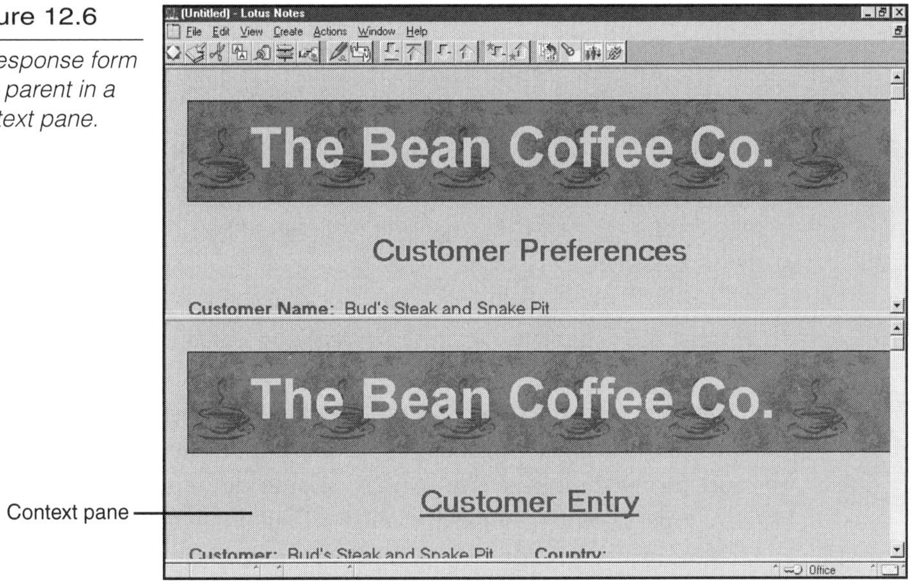

Context pane

When selected, the Present Mail Send Dialog check box causes a dialog box to appear, with mailing options for the document when it is saved (for more information, see Chapter 19).

Using the Launch Tab

The Launch tab enables you to specify which, if any, inserted document link is launched when the document is opened (see Figure 12.7). If you choose First Attachment from the pull-down list, then when opened, Notes attempts to launch the first attachment inserted into the document. If you choose First Document Link, Notes attempts to bring up the object (document, view, or database) linked to in any database. If you choose First OLE Object, Notes attempts to open the first OLE object inserted into the document. This carries on down the list of launch options.

Figure 12.7

The Properties for Form Launch tab.

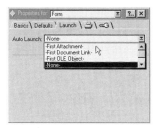

These Attachments, Document Links, and OLE objects can be items inserted into a rich text field by the author of the document, or they can be inserted into the design of the form by an application developer.

Using the Printing Tab

The Printing tab enables you to control how documents created with this form are printed—specifically, what their headers and footers look like (see Figure 12.8). Using the option buttons at the top of the tab, you can modify either the header or the footer. Then, by using a combination of text you type in and special formatting characters entered by clicking the buttons below the display window, you can format the information you want to be in your headers and footers. The codes you can use are as follows:

▶ &P prints the current page.

▶ &D prints the current date.

> ▶ &T prints the current time.

> ▶ ¦ changes the alignment of the text that follows to the next alignment in the list (starting from left and going to center and then to right).

> ▶ &W displays the name of the current database.

The font face, size, and style enable you to choose the formatting characteristics for your header and footer. Finally, when selected, the Print Header and Footer on First Page enables the printing of the header and footer on the first page, in addition to the subsequent ones.

Figure 12.8

The Properties for Form Printing tab.

Using the Security Tab

The Security tab enables you to define who is allowed to use this form to create documents, who is allowed to view the documents created with this form, what the default encryption key or keys are (for more information, see Chapter 23, "Securing Applications"), and whether documents created with this form can be printed, forwarded, or copied to the clipboard (see Figure 12.9).

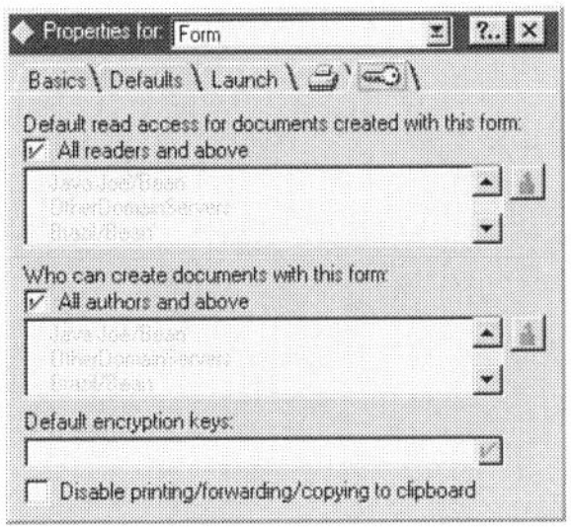

Figure 12.9

The Properties for Form Security tab.

When selected, the Disable Printing/Forwarding/Copying to Clipboard check box prevents the contents of the document from being reproduced through printing, forwarding by mail, or copying any or all of it to the clipboard for pasting elsewhere.

After all the desired form properties are set, you are ready to begin populating the form builder window with the form elements that display when documents are created—specifically text and fields.

Adding Static Text to Forms

 Objective

By default, the Form design environment is text-oriented, meaning that, like a word processor, all objects must be anchored to either one of the margins or to another object. In other words, if the current line is left-aligned, information must progress from left to right with characters in all the gaps.

Text is inserted by clicking the form builder window and typing. Text formats are changed through text properties. These properties can either be set first and then applied as text is typed or applied after text is typed by selecting the text, dragging it over with your mouse, and then setting the properties. Invoke the Properties for Text dialog box by selecting Text | Text Properties (see Figure 12.10). The properties in this dialog box are grouped by tabs:

> Font (AZ tab)
>
> Paragraph (lines tab)
>
> Page (paper with number)
>
> Hide-When (blind tab)
>
> Style (tag tab)

Because the only text properties covered on the exam deal with hiding, the other properties are dealt with in a cursory manner.

Figure 12.10

The Properties for Text dialog box enables you to change text properties.

The Font tab enables you to change the font characteristics of the text to which it is applied. This includes font face, point size, character style, and color.

The Paragraph tab enables you to change the characteristics for the paragraph in which the text to which you apply these properties is located (see Figure 12.11). These include paragraph alignment, indentation, numbering and bulleting, left margin, and inter- and intra-paragraph spacing.

Figure 12.11

The Properties for Text Paragraph tab.

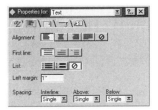

The Page tab enables you to change the characteristics for pagination, the page's right margin set for printing, and the position of tabs on the page (see Figure 12.12).

Figure 12.12

The Properties for Text Page tab.

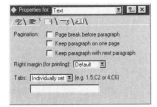

The Styles tab enables you to create, modify, apply, and delete formatting styles with respect to your text (see Figure 12.13).

Figure 12.13

*The Properties for
Text Styles tab.*

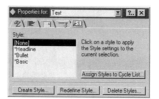

The Hiding tab is used to select the conditions under which the current paragraph disappears from view (see Figure 12.14). These conditions include when the document is being read (opened or previewed), when the document is being edited (opened or previewed), when the document is printed, when the document is copied to the clipboard, or under conditions as defined by a formula.

Figure 12.14

*The Properties for
Text Hiding tab.*

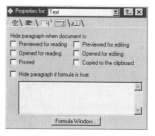

Note

It is important to note that the hiding characteristics apply to the entire paragraph in which the text is located. This means that if the hiding condition is true, the whole paragraph (including other text and fields) disappears, not just the text you selected when you applied these properties.

Tip

A number of the text properties can be applied by using shortcuts, either on the Text menu, in the SmartIcon set, or in the Status bar at the bottom of your screen. Check these places for a way to apply the formatting before you go to the Properties for Text dialog box.

Text does not enable the entering of information; it only annotates your form and indicates what information should be entered. To enter information into documents, you must first create fields on your form.

Adding Fields to Forms

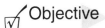Objective

Having already planned your form and the position of your text and fields, it should be a simple matter to insert the fields in the appropriate places. As with text, fields must be inserted in a place on the form in which they are anchored against something, like text, spaces, or the left side of the form. After a field has been inserted into a form, the properties must be set.

To create a new field, complete the following steps:

1. Position your insertion point at the place on the form at which the field is to be inserted.

2. From the Create menu, choose Field to insert a field; the Properties for Field dialog box appears.

As with text, the Field Properties dialog box has properties grouped in tabs (see Figure 12.15). The Basics tab contains the essential definition properties for the field, including name, data type, and edit type. Depending on the data type, there also are varying settings for display options (see the appropriate section under "Data Types"). At the bottom of this tab, there is also a check box labeled Allow multi-values. When selected, this check box enables you to specify that the field can contain multiple discrete values of the same type (for more information, see Chapter 18, "Advanced Formulas, Part I"). Selecting this check box also enables some multivalue selection options on the Options tab.

If you select an edit type of Computed or Computed for Display (see the sections to follow), you also see another check box at the bottom of this tab labeled Compute After Validation. When selected, this check box defers the calculation of a computed field until all the other fields have passed validation; in essence, this enables you to ensure that all the data that might be used to calculate a field's value is valid (as opposed to calculating a field's value and receiving an error because some other field, upon which this field's value is based, is not filled in or not filled in properly).

Figure 12.15

The Properties for Field dialog box enables you to set field properties.

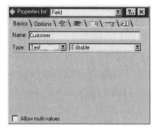

The Options tab contains properties for field-level help, form focus, multivalues, and security (see Figure 12.16). The field next to the label Help description is a text area in which you can type field-level help for your users. Any text typed into this box appears as a help message in the field help line at the bottom of the document when it is being edited.

Figure 12.16

The Properties for Field Options tab.

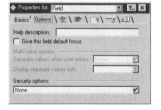

 Tip

Users can turn the field level help on and off by selecting View | Show | Field Help.

The amount of text that you can type here is virtually unlimited, but the amount displayed is limited to a single screen width, which varies with the resolution of the user's display.

The check box labeled Give This Field Default Focus enables you to indicate which field the insertion point is placed in when the document is created or edited.

Note   If you enable this check box for more than one field on a form, the field given default focus is the one closest to the top of the form, and if more than one field is on the same line, the one closest to the left is given focus.

If you selected the check box on the Basics tab labeled Allow multi-values, then you are able to set two values on the Options tab, both in the group labeled Multi-value options.

The Separate Values When User Enters pull-down list enables you to choose how a user enters multiple discrete values in a single field. By choosing one or more delimiters, you enable the user to type in multiple values, separated by any of the delimiters chosen.

The Display Separate Values With pull-down list enables you to choose how multiple values in this field are displayed. This can be different from the delimiter used to enter multiple values. For example, your users might want to enter a list of names, separating them with commas, but they might want the list presented with a single name on each line. You can choose New Line to achieve the result.

The Security Options pull-down list enables you to choose which, if any, encryption keys are used to encrypt this field, if encryption is enabled for the document (for more information on encryption, see Chapter 24).

The last five tabs (Font, Paragraph, Page, Hiding, and Style) are exactly the same as the last five tabs for text (for more information, see the earlier section, "Adding Static Text to Forms").

Field names must conform to specific rules, as follows:

▶ They must be unique on a given form. For example, you cannot have two fields called Address on the same form. They can, however, be duplicated on different forms in the same database.

▶ They can be up to 32 characters long.

▶ They cannot begin with a number or contain spaces.

It is recommended that field names conform to the following guidelines and conventions:

▶ They should not begin with $ or @ because Notes uses these symbols in hidden fields and in functions; the likelihood that you will duplicate a name that Notes is already using is greater if you use names beginning with these characters.

▶ Do not use any of the following reserved names: SendTo, CopyTo, Sign, Encrypt, SaveOptions, MailFormat, or DeliveryPriority, Form field. These field names are expected to perform certain functions and might result in error if they do not.

▶ They should conform to initial-capitalization format (sometimes referred to as Hungarian notation or Camel notation), in which each new word in the field begins with an uppercase letter. This increases field name readability. For example, it is easier to understand a field name such as ManagersSpousesName than it is to understand Managersspousesname.

▶ They should be short (for ease of use) without being cryptic (for ease of understanding). There is no need to use the name Mnt when the addition of three more characters makes the name Amount readily understandable.

In the second line on the Basics tab are two fields bearing the label Type. These are the data type and the edit type. We will discuss the edit type first and then proceed to the data types.

Understanding Edit Types

Edit types enable you to define whether a field accepts direct user input or whether the value is computed by using a formula (see Figure 12.17). Having decided that, there are some refinements to computed types that enable you to define when the computations occur, how often, and whether the result of the computation is stored in the field or just displayed when the document is being viewed.

Figure 12.17
*The Field edit
type is chosen
from Field Proper-
ties Basics tab.*

Editable

If you choose the edit type Editable from the pull-down list, the
field is enabled for direct user input. This can be used for any
field in which it is desirable to elicit a value from a user.

Computed

If you choose the edit type Computed from the pull-down list, the
field is enabled for a computed value, as generated by the value
event in the field's design pane. The values for computed fields
are stored in the field, and the value is recomputed every time the
document is refreshed. This occurs manually if, when a document
is being edited, the user presses the F9 key or selects
View | Refresh. This also happens automatically when a document
is created and when it is saved.

Computed when Composed

If you choose the edit type Computed when Composed from the
pull-down list, the field is enabled for a computed value, as generated by the value event in the field's design pane. The values for
Computed when Composed fields are stored in the field but, unlike the Computed edit type, values for these fields are computed
only once, when the document is created.

Computed for Display

If you choose the edit type Computed for Display from the pull-
down list, the field is enabled for a Computed value, as generated by
the value event in the field's design pane. The values for Computed
for Display fields are not stored in the document, meaning that
this value only exists while the document is being viewed, and the

value cannot be accessed otherwise. This means that the field cannot be referenced from a view nor can it be obtained through the use of lookup functions like @DBLookup (for more information on @DBLookup, see Chapter 20). The value is recomputed every time the document is refreshed. This occurs manually if, when a document is being edited, the user presses the F9 key or selects View | Refresh. This also happens automatically when a document is created, opened, and saved.

Understanding Data Types

Field data types enable you to control what kind of information is valid to be input into a field. They also enable you to set formatting preferences, based on the type of field, and in some data types, enable certain special input methods. There are eight valid data types in Notes, all of which are available from the pull-down list on the Basics tab of the Properties for Field dialog box (see Figure 12.18). These are: Text, Time, Number, Keywords, Rich Text, Authors, Names, and Readers.

Figure 12.18

The Field data type is chosen from the Field Properties Basics tab.

Text

The Text data type is one of the most flexible. It enables the input of any type of information up to 15KB in size. There are no properties available for data types of text that have not already been discussed.

Time

The Time data type enables the entry and processing of date and time information. It enables the entry of any valid date or time (see Figure 12.19).

Figure 12.19

*The Time data
type.*

Note

Lotus Notes is compatible with dates outside the twentieth
century, either prior to or after; however, the default century is
the twentieth. As a result, any date entered with a year having
only two specified digits is interpreted as 19xx; for example,
98 is interpreted as 1998. Moreover, if a four-digit year in the
twentieth century is entered, it is displayed with a two-digit
year—1998 becomes 98. If, however, a four-digit year in any
other century is entered, Notes preserves the full four digits for
accuracy of interpretation—1860 remains 1860, and 2001
remains 2001.

The Time data type includes some properties on the Basics tab for
displaying dates and times. The Show pull-down list enables you to
control how much of the date is displayed. When dates are entered, they are saved to the second that the date was entered.
Therefore, you have the option of displaying the date and time,
just the date, just the time, or the words Today or Yesterday in place
of the date, if it is today or was yesterday, and the time.

Note

The words Today, Yesterday, and Tomorrow can be used as substitutes for actual dates in any date entry field. These words will
be translated into the appropriate date at document refresh time.

The Date Format pull-down list enables you to choose the format
of a displayed date. You can choose to have the month and day,
the month and year, or the month, day, and year appear.

The Time Format pull-down list enables you to choose the format
of a displayed time. You can choose to have the hour and minute,
or the hour, minute, and second appear.

The Time Zone pull-down list enables you to choose how dates and times appear, given various time-zone parameters. You can enable times to automatically convert to the current time zone (as understood by Notes); if the time the date was input was in a different zone, you can have the time zone always display (as a character abbreviation), or you can have the time zone display only if the time zone in which the date was input was different than the current one.

Number

The Number data type enables the entry and processing of numeric information (including currency) (see Figure 12.20). Notes enables any numeric character to be entered into number fields, as well as plus and minus signs, scientific notation (E), and constant notation (e).

Figure 12.20

The Number data type.

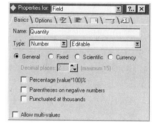

The Number data type includes some options for numeric formatting on the Basics tab of the Properties dialog box. There is a set of option buttons that enables you to specify the general format of the number to be displayed:

▶ General displays the number as entered.

▶ Fixed displays the number by using a fixed number of decimal places.

▶ Scientific displays the number by using scientific notation.

▶ Currency displays the number with a currency symbol.

If a display type other than General is selected, then you can indicate to how many decimal places the value should be rounded (rounding going up at 5).

Note

The value to which a number is rounded is what is actually stored in the field. This means that if the number of decimal places is changed later, decimal places removed by rounding will not be recovered.

If the Percentage (value*100)% check box is selected, the value entered is displayed as a percentage, having first multiplied the number by 100. For example, if the number .3 is entered, then the field displays the value 30%.

If the Parenthesis on negative numbers check box is selected, the value is shown in parentheses, if it is negative. For example, if the number -100 is entered, it displays as (100).

If the Punctuated at thousands check box is selected, the value is shown with commas at the thousand, million, billion marks and so on. For example, if the number 1435456 is entered, it displays as 1,435,456.

Keywords

The data type Keywords is special because it enables you to provide a user with a set of values from which to choose, rather than enabling any text value to be entered. In addition to enabling you to create a list, you can control how the list displays.

From the Choices pull-down list, you can choose from a variety of choice options. If you choose Enter Choices (One Per Line), in the box below, type in the valid choices; they are presented to the user in the format you desire. When typing in choices, simply enter the choice and press Enter to move to the next line (see Figure 12.21).

Figure 12.21

The Keywords data type.

Tip

Like the name for a form, sometimes the values presented in a keyword list are cumbersome to manipulate in formulas. Synonyms can be created to make programmatic access to the key-word values easier. These synonyms can be created by appending ¦ and the abbreviated choice to the keyword values. For example, if you have a keyword list that presents three invoice statuses, `Paid in Full`, `Balance Owing`, and `Really Overdue`, you can create synonyms for these choices to make formulaic manipulation of them easier. So, your keyword list might look like the following:

```
Paid in Full¦0

Balance Owing¦1

Really Overdue¦2
```

Now, when you use these values in formulas, rather than check for a value of Paid in Full, you can check for a value of 0. In fact, you must check for a value of 0 because as soon as a synonym is applied, it is the only value that is stored for the field; the other is simply a display value that Notes ignores when processing.

If you choose Use Formula For Choices, in the box below, you must enter a formula that generates a list of choices from which the user can choose. This is frequently accomplished by using an `@@DbColumn` formula (see Figure 12.22). For more information, see Chapter 20.

Figure 12.22

A Keywords data type with a formula, generating choices.

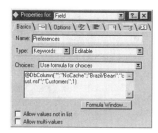

If you choose Use Address Dialog for Choices, the user has the option of bringing up a dialog box containing the names that are present in any of the public or personal address books to which he or she has access (see Figure 12.23). The check box Look Up Names As Each Character Is Entered, when selected, enables the user to type in the name required until a match for that name is located in an address book.

Figure 12.23

Use Address Dialog for Choices presents an address book dialog box.

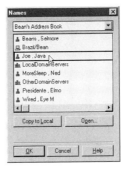

If you choose Use Access Control List for Choices, the user can bring up a dialog box that contains the entries in the ACL for the current database (see Figure 12.24). He or she can then choose a value for this field from the ACL entries present. Unlike address book dialog boxes, however, there is no option for type-ahead recognition of names.

Figure 12.24

Use Access Control List for choices.

If you choose Use View Dialog for Choices, you can present the user with a dialog box, displaying a view from any database to which you have access (see Figure 12.25). Selecting this option makes a number of other fields appear. You will be able to choose a database from a pull-down list that is generated from your workspace, so to get the lookup database you require, you must ensure that the database icon has been added to your workspace.

Figure 12.25

Use View Dialog for Choices.

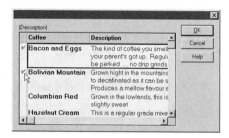

Next, you can choose a view from the database you have selected that will be presented to the user to choose a value from. In the Column # field, you must enter the column number on the view that corresponds to the information you want to be returned from the dialog box presented to the user. This column number is the number in the view design, not in the view display (for more information on this, see Chapter 20).

In all Choices types except Use View Dialog for Choices, you are given an additional check box, Allow Values Not In List, which, when selected, enables the user to type in values that are not in the list.

 Tip

Frequently, keywords are used when you have a limited number of choices and want to control the field value to one of those choices. Although this works in most cases, there are times when you can't provide an exhaustive list of choices. In that case, you can allow the user to enter his or her own values. In this way, when it is appropriate, you can give the user the ability to work outside the presented parameters. The other option is to present the user with a list of choices, none of which is correct, and ask him or her to choose. This only results in user frustration and manual work by you to increase the valid choices.

The Keywords data type includes an extra tab on the Properties dialog box that is not present with the other data types—the Display tab (see Figure 12.26). The Display tab page enables you to change the way the list of values is presented to the user. Having chosen either Enter Choices or Use Formula as the choice type, you can choose the presentation interface that you want to use to display the values. Three interfaces are available: dialog list, check box, and radio button. The dialog list interface presents a list of available values in a dialog box, which is brought up when the user clicks the down-arrow to the right of the field (the helper button) or presses the Enter key in the field.

Figure 12.26

The Display tab for the Keywords data type.

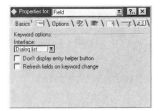

The check box interface presents the valid options as a series of check boxes (square boxes) in which the boxes can either be selected or deselected.

 Tip

Check boxes are typically used when a user can choose none or many of the choices available.

The radio button interface presents the valid options as a series of radio (or option) buttons (round buttons) in which only one of the buttons can be selected. As soon as you select a button, no option is available for turning off all the selections, only for changing the selection made.

 Tip

Radio buttons are usually used when a single choice is desired.

Both the check box and radio button interfaces have an option for the number of columns in which you want to present the values. If you specify multiple columns, Notes attempts to create the columns with an equal number of choices in each. In addition, you also can choose the frame type:

▶ 3D is a chiseled gray frame.

▶ Standard is white.

▶ None results in no frame around the choices.

The dialog list interface causes the check box Don't Display Entry Helper Button to appear. When selected, this check box causes the down-arrow that normally appears next to Keywords fields with this interface not to appear.

 Tip

In Notes 3.x, there was not even an option to show Helper buttons, and users were in the dark about whether a field was a keyword or not. In Notes 4.x, it is the default to display the Helper button. It is not recommended that you turn the Helper button off because it is difficult for users to know that they have a keyword list from which to choose.

In all Keywords types, the check box Refresh Fields On Keyword Change is present. When selected, this check box causes the field values on the document to be refreshed whenever a choice is made in the Keywords field. This is often desirable when calculations are made on the form that relate to the choices made in the Keywords field. For example, a manager field is populated, based on the department that is selected in a Keywords field. If the department changes, the new manager's name should be displayed to avoid confusion.

Rich Text

The rich text data type is the most flexible, as far as the user is concerned. Rich text fields enable special object insertion and manipulation, as well as the capability for the user to choose the format of the information displayed in the field.

A rich text field enables you to allow your users to enter a wide variety of information types, as well as do some fairly advanced customization. The rich text field type enables the entry of document links, attachments, OLE objects, sections, buttons, popups, and tables by the user. In addition, unlike all the other data types, with the rich text field, the user does not have to leave the text as you formatted it. The formats for text (including all the font formatting) are defaults from which the user can deviate by selecting the text and choosing new properties.

One major drawback of rich text fields is that their information is basically non-manipulatable in formulas nor viewable in views.

Names

The Names data type is used for the input and display of hierarchical names (see Figure 12.27). Lotus Notes user names, when inserted into text fields, appear in fully distinguished format and are saved in a format like this: CN=Java Joe/O=Bean. This kind of format is not readily understandable and is not the way people are used to seeing names. By using the data type of Names, you can input names in distinguished format (or have calculations produce names in that format) and have the names appear in abbreviated format—for example, Java Joe/Bean. This data type, therefore, gives you the ability to preserve the standard Notes naming scheme while enabling automatic conversion of those names to a readily understandable, abbreviated format.

Figure 12.27

The Names data type.

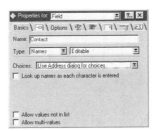

In addition to the automatic formatting of Lotus Notes names, the Names data type enables the option of some of the Keywords input formats when you choose an editable type. Like a Keywords data type, Names data types have a choices pull-down list, enabling the input of names by using address dialogs, Access Control List dialogs, and view dialogs for names choices. This makes it easy to provide users with the ability to select names for any field in which the data should be a Lotus Notes name—a manager, a list of company attendees at a meeting, or the content of a SendTo field (see Chapter 20).

If you choose a Choice option other than None from the pull-down list, a Display tab appears, enabling you to choose whether or not you want to see an entry Helper button displayed next to the field to alert the user that choices are available for the field through a dialog box.

Authors

Fields of type Authors are a twist on the Names type. Authors fields function exactly the same as Names fields, in terms of their data input and storage capacity; however, they have a special function—to enable you to control who is allowed to modify a document after it has been created. If one or more names are present in a field with data type authors, only those people will be allowed to edit the document after it has been created, provided that those people have author access to the database (for more information, see Chapter 24).

Readers

Like Authors fields, Reader fields function the same as Names fields in terms of data input and capacity. Like Authors fields, however, they also have a special function in a Notes document—to enable you to control who has the ability to see and read a document after it has been created. If one or more names are present in a field of type Readers, only the people listed can see the document after it has been created. This means that no matter what someone's level of access in the ACL, if they are not listed in the Readers field, they will not be able to see the document (for more information, see Chapter 24).

The job of the application developer is to decide what the layout of a form is to be, including both text and fields, and then to determine which field types are best suited both to the data that is being input into the fields, as well as the control that needs to be exercised over that data. Proper choice of field types enables you to maximize both functionality and control over the data being input.

Creating Response Forms

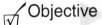Objective

As was mentioned in the section entitled "Form Types and Relationships," forms in Notes are often related in a Document/Response/Response-to-Response hierarchy. The designation of a document as type Response indicates that it must be created in relation to a document of type Document and that it cannot exist without such a relationship. The creation of Response forms is as simple as creating a form and, in its properties, indicates that it is of type Response or Response to Response.

After the Response forms are created, you frequently will want to inherit information from the parent to the response at the time of Response document creation. This is done by selecting the Formulas Inherit Values from Selected Documents or Inherit Entire Selected Document into Rich Text Field check boxes on the Defaults tab of the Response form's Properties dialog box (see the section, "Using the Defaults Tab"). After this is done, create fields that are computed, containing formulas that name fields on the parent document (see Chapter 13). This triggers the inheritance and pulls information from the parent to the response.

Note

The relationship between one specific form and another specific form is never made. Forms simply have types; they do not have explicit relationships to other forms. For example, if you have two forms of type document in your database—Fruits and Vegetables—you have the ability to use both of these forms to create documents of type Document. You might then have a single form of type Response, Evaluation. That Response form can be used to create a Response document to any of the type Document documents. There is no property that indicates that the Evaluation form responds to

continues

the Fruits form or to the Vegetables form; the form type property Response simply indicates that it must respond to a document of type Document. The actual relationship is made between the documents created with these forms, and that relationship is established at the time of document creation, not at the time of form creation.

Having seen the theory behind the creation of forms, the lab will help you apply it to a design task.

Exercises

You are an application developer for the Bean Coffee Company. In this lab, you will create a form for the input of customer information in their customer database. This database is available on your CD-ROM and should be copied to your default Notes data directory. The lab file is called cust12.nsf, and its title is Chapter 12 Customers. When you copy the file, make sure you remove the read-only attribute, or you will not be able to modify the database.

Exercise 12.1

1. Select File | Database | Open and select the database called Chapter 12 Customers from the pull-down list of local databases. Click the Open button to add the database to your workspace and open the standard view.

2. From the Create menu, choose Design, Form.

3. In the form builder window (the one on top), click your right mouse button and choose Form Properties from the menu that appears (see Figure 12.28).

Figure 12.28

The Properties for Form dialog box.

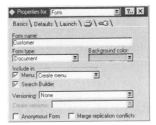

4. In the Form Name field, type Customer and from the Background color field, choose a light brown.

5. Click the tab called Defaults and select the Default Database Form check box. Close the Form Properties by clicking the Close Window button.

6. Position your insertion point on the top line of the form and from the Text menu, choose Text properties (see Figure 12.29).

continues

Exercise 12.1 Continued

Figure 12.29

Set the initial text properties.

7. Choose the following text properties:

   Font: Helv

   Size: 24

   Style: Bold and Underline

   Text Color: Dark Red

8. Click the Paragraph tab and choose the Center Alignment button from the top line (second from the left). Close the Text Properties dialog box by clicking the Close Window button.

9. Type Customer Entry and press Enter twice.

10. Open the Text properties and adjust the properties so that future text is left aligned, Helv, 14pt, Bold, and Dark Red. Close the Text Properties dialog box.

11. Type Customer: and then, from the Create menu, choose Field.

12. On the Basics tab of the Properties for Field dialog box, enter the following information:

   Name: Customer

   Type: Text, Editable

   On the Font tab, ensure that the style is Plain. Close the Properties for Field dialog box.

13. Press the spacebar a few times to move away from the field you just created and then type Country:. From the Create menu, choose Field.

    The properties for the field you just created are: Name: Country, Type: Keywords, Editable, Font Style: Plain.

14. On the Basics tab, enter the following in the choices field: U.S.A. (press Enter), Canada (see Figure 12.30). Close the Field Properties dialog box by clicking the Close Window button.

Figure 12.30

The Country keywords choices.

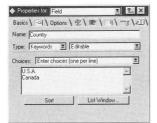

15. Enter information on the following lines, as per Table 12.1.

Table 12.1

Form Field Entry Characteristics		
Form line	Entry type	Properties
5	Text	Address:
5	Field	Name: Address; Type: Text, Editable; Font Style: Plain
7	Text	City:
7	Field	Name: City; Type: Text, Editable; Font Style: Plain
9	Text	State/Province:
9	Field	Name: Region; Type: Text, Editable; Font Style: Plain
9	Text	Zip/Postal Code:

continues

Table 12.1 Continued

Form line	Entry type	Properties
9	Field	Name: Code; Type: Text; Editable; Font Style: Plain
11	Text	Contact E-mail:
11		Name: Email; Type: Text; Editable; Font Style: Plain
13		Payment Terms:
13		Name: Terms; Type: Keywords; Editable; Font Style: Plain Choices: Net 30¦30 Net 45¦45 Net 60¦60
15		Author
15		Name: Author; Type: Author, Computed when Composed; Font Size: 10; Font Style: Plain; Text Color: Dark Green

16. Save the form and close it, returning to the standard view.

17. Test your form by choosing the Create Customer menu, and entering a customer name with information (make up a customer or enter information for yourself). Save the document and close.

18. Click the view called Customers at the top of the standard view to see the customer you just created.

Exercise 12.2

You want to create a response form in which you allow the entry of a customer's coffee preference, one per document. The challenge is to create a form called Preferences¦Coffee, which is of type Response. That form will include a field called Customer, with appropriate text that is of type Text and Editable. It will also contain a field called `PreferredCoffee`, which is an editable `Keywords` field with the choices being Domestic, Domestic Decaffeinated, Colombian, and Brazilian. Display the choices using radio buttons.

The answer to the challenge exercise is found in a form called `ChallengeAnswer` in the `cust12.nsf` database. You will be able to view your customers and their preferences by using the Customer Preferences view.

Review Questions

1. Goldilocks has a form that, in its properties, has the name `Accounting\Create Invoice¦Invoice`. What is the entry the user sees under the Create menu, what is the synonym, and what is the cascaded submenu?

    a. Create menu: `Accounting`; Synonym: `Create Invoice`; Submenu: `Invoice`

    b. Create menu: `Create Invoice`; Synonym: `Invoice`; Submenu: `Accounting`

    c. Create menu: `Invoice`; Synonym: `Accounting`; Submenu: `Create Invoice`

    d. Create menu: `Accounting`; Synonym: `Invoice`; Submenu: `Create Invoice`

2. Which of the following is not a Notes data type?

    a. Names

    b. Keywords

    c. Response

    d. Text

3. Cinderella creates a form of type Document called `Customers` and a form of type Response called `Contacts`. What is the relationship between these forms?

    a. There is no inherent relationship between forms.

    b. `Customers` is the parent form, whereas `Contacts` is the child.

    c. Contacts is the parent form, whereas Customers is the child.

    d. You must select a Customer in a view before you can create a Contact.

4. What are the four edit types for fields?

    a. Editable, Computed, Computed when Composed, and Computed for Display

    b. Editable, Computed, Computed when Disposed, and Display Only

    c. Full Control, Write, Read, and No Access

    d. Modify, Calculate, Calculate Once Only, and Show Value

5. What is the maximum number of characters in a field name?

    a. 64

    b. 255

    c. 32

    d. 15

6. Hansel wants documents created with a certain form to open automatically in edit mode if the users opening them have the ability to edit. How can he do this?

    a. Select the check box Automatically Enable Edit Mode in the Defaults tab of the Document's properties.

    b. Right-click the documents and choose Open in Edit Mode from the menu that appears.

    c. This cannot happen automatically.

    d. Select the check box Automatically Enable Edit Mode in the Defaults tab of the Form's properties.

7. Where can you set up a header and footer to print on a document when sent to a printer?

    a. From File | Page Setup

    b. From File | Print

    c. From the Printers tab in the Form Properties

    d. From the Defaults tab in the Form Properties

8. What do document types Response to Response respond to?

    a. Documents

    b. Documents and Responses

    c. Responses

    d. Documents, Responses, and Response to Responses

9. Goldilocks created a form and in its properties selected Default Database Form. What are the implications of what she has done?

    a. None. This is a Notes 3.*x* feature that is no longer used.

    b. Documents always open by using this form.

    c. When a document was created with a form not in this database, it opens by using this form.

    d. Documents in this database are always created by using this form.

10. Snow White opens a response form and, in a pane at the bottom of her screen, the parent document is displayed. What feature is enabled?

    a. Formulas inherit values from selected documents

    b. Show context pane

    c. Automatically enable edit mode

    d. Present mail send dialog

11. Which of the following is not a characteristic of rich text fields?

   a. Users can choose the text format of a rich text field.

   b. Users can insert attachments into rich text fields.

   c. Users can display rich text fields in views.

   d. Users can insert tables into rich text fields.

12. What is the difference between field data type and field edit type?

   a. Field data type is a document property, and field edit type is a form property.

   b. Field data type indicates what information is valid for a field, and field edit type indicates how information is entered into a field.

   c. Field data type is a form property, and field edit type is a document property.

   d. Field edit type indicates what information is valid for a field, and field data type indicates how information is entered into a field.

13. Which of the following are symbols with which you should not begin fields?

   a. * and #

   b. ! and ^

   c. % and +

   d. $ and @

14. Horace enters a date with a year of 2001 and wants Notes to understand that this is not in the twentieth century. How should he enter the year?

   a. 01

   b. 2001

     c. ~01

     d. \01

Review Answers

1. D. In a form name, the portion before a \ is the menu item that appears in the Create menu. The portion after the \ and before the ¦ is the submenu and the portion after the ¦ is the synonym by which you will refer to the form. For more information, please refer to "Using the Basics Tab."

2. C. Response is a document type, not a data type. For more information, please refer to "Understanding Data Types."

3. A. There is no inherent relationship between forms. Relationships are created between documents at the time of document creation. The most we can say is that a document of type Response must be created after selecting a document of type Document. For more information, please refer to "Using the Basics Tab."

4. A. Notes includes four edit types: three are computed and require formulas, and one is editable and requires data input by a user. For more information, please refer to "Understanding Edit Types."

5. C. The maximum number of characters in a field name is 32. For more information, please refer to "Adding Fields to Forms."

6. D. He must select the check box Automatically Enable Edit Mode in the Defaults tab of the form's properties. For more information, please refer to "Using the Defaults Tab."

7. C. The only place you can set up headers and footers for a document is in the Printing tab of the form that created the document. For more information, please refer to "Using the Printing Tab."

8. D. Response-to-Response documents are multipurpose and can respond to any of the document types. For more information, please refer to "Using the Basics Tab."

9. C. Documents and forms work together to display information. If a document is being opened in a database other than the one in which it was created, however, it is possible that the form it requires is not present. If this is the case, the form used to display the document information is the default form for that database. For more information, please refer to "Using the Defaults Tab."

10. B. She is seeing a context pane with the document's parent displayed. This is enabled through the Show Context Pane property in the Defaults tab for the form used to display the document. For more information, please refer to "Using the Defaults Tab."

11. C. Although rich text fields have many advantages, one of the disadvantages is that the data content in them cannot be displayed in views. For more information, please refer to "Rich Text."

12. B. A field data type indicates what kind of information is valid for a field, whereas a field edit type indicates how information is entered into a field. For more information, please refer to "Understanding Edit Types" and "Understanding Data Types."

13. D. Although you can begin your fields with these characters, Notes uses both to indicate special names. @ is the first character in most functions, and $ is the first character in many internal fields. By using field names with either of these initial symbols, you run the risk of duplicating field names already used by Notes. For more information, please refer to "Adding Fields to Forms."

14. B. Notes is compatible with non-twentieth century dates, but it defaults to the twentieth century, and all two-digit dates are assumed to begin with 19. To enter a twenty-first-century date, Horace must type 2001 as the year. For more information, please refer to "Time."

Answers to Test Yourself Questions at Beginning of Chapter

1. A form name synonym is a name used to aid programmatic access to a form. Only developers use this name, which is transparent to users, who see the display name instead. Synonyms are created as part of the structure of a form name and are the portion of the name following a |. For more information, refer to "Using the Basics Tab."

2. Response documents are used to respond to document documents. In a discussion, a response document is used to make the initial reply to a main topic. In other contexts, responses can be documents that contain follow-up information for a certain object type; for example, a type Document document can be a customer, while a response can be a contact for that customer. For more information, refer to "Using the Basics Tab."

3. There are eight field data types: text, time, number, keywords, rich text, authors, names, and readers. For more information, refer to "Understanding Data Types."

4. Static text serves to annotate and label a form. It indicates form use and title and provides labels for fields so that users know what information goes where. For more information, refer to "Adding Static Text to Forms."

5. Forms provide the initial framework for creating documents. After a document is created, forms provide the framework for opening the document either to read or edit. For more information, refer to "Designing and Creating Forms."

Chapter 13

Introduction to Formulas

This chapter will introduce you to the following objectives:

Objectives

- ▶ Understanding formulas
- ▶ Using formulas in fields
- ▶ Using @ functions

Test Yourself! Before reading this chapter, test yourself to determine how much study time you will need to devote to this section.

1. What are the main components of a formula and what function does each perform?

2. What are the four edit types for fields and what four events are most commonly modified by using formulas?

3. What is the @If function, its use, and syntax?

4. What combination of functions can be used to determine the common name of the current Notes user?

5. How can @Success and @Failure be used with @If functions?

Answers are located at the end of the chapter...

Formulas are symbolic representations of calculations that you want to evaluate or processes that you want to invoke. They can perform simple tasks, such as adding two numbers, or complex ones, such as retrieving a list of values from a view to populate a keyword list. Formulas are found almost everywhere in Notes. They can be used to create view data, populate default field values, and create computed values. In addition, formulas are used for validating or modifying data that is input. You can also use formulas as the mechanism to conditionally hide form and view elements and to invoke commands at the click of a button.

Understanding Formulas

Formulas are symbolic representations of calculations you want to perform—work you want to do. They have specific constructions, or syntax, and specific component parts. Formulas can be as simple as a field name or some text in quotation marks or can be many lines long, performing complex calculations.

Formulas basically consist of any or all of the following components: constants, variables, operators, keywords, and functions.

Constants in Formulas

A constant is a value that is inserted into a formula and, as its name implies, always remains the same. Constants can be text, numbers, or dates. A text constant might be a name, a color, or a phrase; any combination of characters or numbers can be a text constant.

Text constants are always represented in formulas by characters enclosed in quotation marks. For example, "It is cold outside" is a constant, a phrase enclosed in quotation marks. The reason it is called a constant is that its value is typed into the formula and it is not going to change. It cannot be changed unless a developer changes the content between the quotation marks.

All characters are valid inside text constants; however, some characters require special handling because they themselves are special characters. The characters " (double quote) and \ (back slash) are examples. If, for example, you want to create a text constant containing the phrase `"He said, "Stop!""`, then you need special processing for the word "Stop!" because you want to include the quotation marks as part of the string. You use the \ character to indicate that characters which are normally interpreted as delimiters are instead interpreted as text characters. A \ in a text string is an indicator that what follows is a character in the string and should not be interpreted as anything else. In the preceding example, to create a text constant, you type `"He said, \"Stop!\""`.

If, for example, you want to place the path to a file on your hard drive in a text constant, you would have problems because the constant contains the \ character, (`"C:\Notes\Data\db.nsf"`) and is displayed as `"C:NotesDatadb.nsf"`. To remedy this situation, place two \\ characters where you had one before; the first \ indicates that the second is a character in the string and not a special character. To make your constant display as `"C:\Notes\Data\db.nsf"`, you use the constant `"C:\\Notes\\Data\\db.nsf"`.

A number can also be a constant and is indicated by using the number itself. For example, the formula 2 + 3 adds two numeric constants, 2 and 3. Notes also accepts special mathematical symbols in constants, such as the minus sign (–), the decimal point (.), and the scientific notation symbol (E).

A date can also be a constant. If you want to make reference to a specific date in a formula, you place the date you want to make a constant in square brackets ([]). For example, if you want to refer to New Year's day in 1998, you place the date in numeric date format (mm/dd/yy) in square brackets, [01/01/98]. Notes accepts a variety of date and time formats as constants: Times without am or pm are interpreted as 24-hour times ([5:30]); times with am or pm are interpreted as 12-hour times ([5:30PM]); dates without years are interpreted as the current year ([12/05]); dates with two-digit years are interpreted as 20th century years ([12/05/97]); dates with four-digit years are interpreted as using the full year ([12/05/2010]); and any combination of a valid date and time format is valid ([12/05/2001 5:30 pm]).

Variables in Formulas

In many cases, you want to represent a changing value in a formula, such as the value in a field. These changing values are reevaluated every time the formula is recomputed and may have different values every time the value is reevaluated. These changing values are called *variables*. Variables are names that hold values. The most common variable in Notes is the field. *Fields* contain values that change or might change, depending on the circumstance. A formula might contain a constant name, such as `Billy the Kid`, or a formula might contain a variable, such as a field called `Outlaw`. This field is not presented in quotation marks because then it would be a constant. Instead, it simply stands by itself as its name, `Outlaw`. When a formula with a variable is computed, Notes interprets the variable as the constant, which is the current value contained in the variable. On one document, the variable `Outlaw` might evaluate to `Billy the Kid` and on another, to `Josey Wales`. In fact, if the field is edited, on one day it might evaluate to one value in a document and on another, another value; that is the nature of variables.

Another kind of variable is not a field name, but a name that you create yourself for temporarily holding a value while you do another calculation. This is called a temporary variable. For more information on temporary variables, see Chapter 18, "Advanced Formulas Part I."

Operators in Formulas

A simple formula can be a constant or a variable by itself. For example, to create a formula that calculates the current value of the Outlaw field, you can simply use the field itself as the formula, `Outlaw`. However, it is often helpful to use a number of values together to produce a result. One way of doing this is to use operators-special symbols that combine values in predefined ways.

The two kinds of operators in Notes are calculation operators, which perform mathematical operations on numbers or, in the case of plus (+), concatenate values on text, and logical operators, which perform comparison operations.

Note A special operator, the colon (:), is used for list concatenation. Lists are discussed in Chapter 18.

Calculation Operators

The valid mathematical operators are multiply (*), divide (/), add (+), and subtract (−). These operators all can be used to mathematically manipulate numeric values, such as in the formula 3 + 4 or in the formula Qty * Price (where the variables Qty and Price are expected to represent numeric values).

In addition to mathematical operations, two of these operators can also manipulate text and time. The add operator can be used to join two text values together, commonly known as concatenation. For example, to take the name John and join it to the name Smith you can use the add operator as follows: John + Smith. The result of this is JohnSmith. If this particular result is not desired because you want a space between the values, simply concatenate a space between the two names, John + + Smith to produce John Smith.

You can use the subtract operator to determine the length of time between two dates or times. If you want to know how much time passed between 5:00 am and 7:32 pm or how much time passed between 01/01/98 and 03/02/98, then you can use the subtraction operator as follows: [7:32 pm] − [5:00 am], or [03/02/98] − [01/01/98], or even, DueDate − SubmitDate (if you have variables containing two dates).

Tip All date subtractions result in a number representing the number of seconds that separate the two times or dates. This means that if you want to determine how many days separate two dates, you must divide the result by 86,400 (the number of seconds in a day).

A date that does not contain a time component is assumed to contain the time 00:00:00 (12:00 a.m. and no seconds).

Comparison Operators

You use comparison operators to compare two values for equality or nonequality or to determine whether one value is larger than another. In addition, comparison operators are also used to combine other comparisons to determine whether a number of things or only some things are present.

The valid comparison operators are equal to (=), not equal to (<>, ><, !=, =!), greater than (>), less than (<), greater than or equal to (>=, =>), less than or equal to (<=, =<), not (!), and (&), and or (|).

Formulas that use comparison operators are often interpreted as questions when spoken. The formula FavoriteColor = "Red" is read as "Is the value of the variable called FavoriteColor equal to Red?" or simply "Is FavoriteColor Red?"

The result of a formula using a comparison operator is a boolean value, that is, it is either True (1) or False (0). In the preceding example, FavoriteColor = "Red", the answer is either True (in which case, the variable FavoriteColor does contain the value "Red") or the answer is False (in which case, it does not). By their nature, comparison formulas cannot evaluate to any other values.

Sometimes it is necessary to combine more than one comparison formula to determine an answer of greater scope. For example, if I want to determine whether I should write a Lotus Certification exam, I have three separate questions to ask. First, am I prepared for the exam? Second, do I have the time to take it? Third, do I have the money to pay for it? If any of these are false, then I will not be able to take the exam. It is only when all of these are true that I will be able to take the exam. This example and others like it require the use of a more complex comparison operator, such as and (&), or (|), or not (!). The use of the and operator asks, "Are all of the comparisons that I am considering true?" If the answer is "Yes," then the final result is True; otherwise, the answer is False. In my example, the formula looks like this:

```
Prepared = "Yes" & Time = "Yes" & Money = "Yes"
```

The result of the formula can only be True if all the separate conditions are satisfied; that is the nature of the "and" operator.

In some cases, it is not an all-or-nothing prospect, so you can use the "or" operator to check your conditions. If taking your exam depends only on paying for it, then you can ask two questions. First, do I have sufficient funds to pay for it? Second, will someone else pay for it? In this case, you only have to meet one of the two conditions to be able to take the exam; that is, only one must be True for the question, "Can I take the exam" to be True. The formula for this appears as follows:

```
SufficientPersonalFunds = "Yes" | SufficientExternalFunds = "Yes"
```

If either is true, then the statement if True. Only when they are both false is the statement False.

The final comparison operator is "not." The "not" operator does not ask a question; it simply takes the result of another condition and reverses its value. This reversing of value is sometimes beneficial in processing questions in the order you desire. The "not" operator, when applied to a True value, results in a False value and vice versa.

The Assignment Operator

The assignment operator (:=) is used to assign a value to a variable. Unlike (=), which could be read "is equal to?", the assignment operator could be read "is assigned the value of". Therefore, the following formula could be read as "Manager is assigned the value of "Brian"":

```
Manager := "Brian"
```

Care must be taken when using the assignment operator because it must follow the first variable in a Notes statement as shown in the preceding example. This restriction means that you cannot use the assignment operator as part of the result of an @If function (see "Using Logical Operation with @If" later in this chapter).

@ Functions in Formulas

Although in some cases you can construct useful formulas by combining constants or variables with operators, there are many occasions where the result you want is too complex for you to obtain simply with those tools. For instance, if you have a text value, such as "red," and want to make it appear as "RED," there is no combination of operators and constants or variables that allow you to do that. This is where @ functions come in. @ functions (pronounced "at-functions") are, for lack of better terminology, "black boxes" into which you put values and out of which come values changed in some way. The values that you put into an @ function are called parameters (or sometimes arguments), and what comes out of the other end is results.

@ functions, which are system defined and built in to Notes, are available to perform a wide variety of tasks. These tasks are described in greater detail in the section "Using @ functions" later in this chapter.

Keywords in Formulas

Keywords are special reserved words that fall at the beginning of a formula line and have specific meaning to Notes. Specific keywords that you need to be aware of are SELECT, FIELD, ENVIRONMENT, DEFAULT, and REM.

Note   Be sure not to confuse the term keywords with the field data type of keywords. They are separate in concept and in use.

Keywords are used to issue special directives in Notes formulas and to indicate special status to objects that follow in those formulas.

SELECT

The SELECT keyword is used in selection formulas to indicate that what follows is a criteria for determining what documents should be processed by using an agent or displayed by using a view. For example, in a View Selection formula, the following formula will choose the documents that satisfy the criteria, in this case, if they have been created by using a form called "Coffee":

```
SELECT Form = "Coffee"
```

For more information on view selection formulas, see Chapter 14, "Creating Views."

FIELD

You use the FIELD keyword in a Notes formula to indicate that the word which follows represents a field on the form being processed. FIELD can be used either to set a field to a certain value or to create a new field. If the field named exists already, then the keyword indicates that the value should be changed to whatever you specify. If the field does not exist, then a new field is created with the value that you specify. For example, the following formula sets the Color field to the text value "Red" if the field exists and, if not, creates a field for that document called Color and assigns it a value of "Red":

```
FIELD Color := "Red"
```

Note

> If you use the FIELD keyword to create a new field, this field does not show up on any forms, but it is available to be used in any formulas and you can reference it as you do any other field in your document. It cannot be edited unless you place it on a form and its data type is the data type of the last value assigned to it.

ENVIRONMENT

The keyword ENVIRONMENT is used to set environment variables. Environment variables are variables that exist outside the scope of the current field, document, and database. They are stored in the current workstation's Notes.ini file and, therefore, are available to any Notes application that runs on that workstation. Environment variables are handy to store global information for a database or profile information for the user of a workstation. For example, if you want to store the name of a user's department for later use in a database, you could prompt for the value and then set an environment variable:

```
ENVIRONMENT Department := EnteredDept
```

This variable could then be retrieved by using an @Environment function. For more information on environment variables, see Chapter 19, "Advanced Formulas Part II."

REM

The keyword REM is used to indicate that the line that follows in a formula is a comment and is not to be processed or checked for correct syntax. REM statements are used to document formulas when they are multilined and perhaps complex to interpret. The correct use of REM includes the keyword at the beginning of a line followed by text in quotation marks. A REM statement might look like this:

```
REM "What follows is a series of statements required to process";
REM "the current user's input information"
```

For more information on multiline formulas, see Chapter 18, "Advanced Formulas Part I."

Using Formulas in Fields

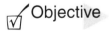Objective

Formulas are used in a number of places in Notes: views, actions, agents, selection, and forms. This section illustrates the operation of formulas by applying them in computations involving fields on forms.

When a field is created on a form, it is assigned one of four edit types:

- ▶ Editable

- ▶ Computed

> ▶ Computed when composed

> ▶ Computed for display

Each type has certain formula events associated with it. Formula events are distinct points in the life of the field where you can control what happens to the field through the use of formulas.

You can identify field events when a form design is edited and a field is selected. At the bottom of the design window is the design pane (see Figure 13.1), which contains definitions for all the field events.

Figure 13.1

The design pane is used to enter formulas for form events.

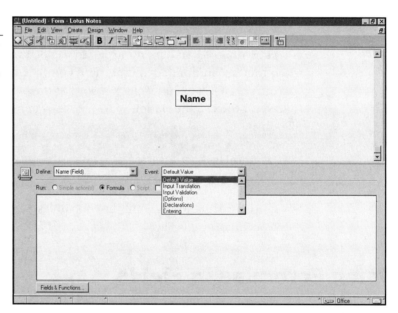

The design pane consists of four parts:

> ▶ The Define pull-down list, where the selected field's name appears

> ▶ The Event pull-down list, where you can select the events available for the defined choice

> ▶ The Run option group with a large area underneath in which you can type simple events, formulas, or Lotus Script code

▶ The buttons on the bottom, which produce dialog boxes where you can choose the functions, fields, or commands that you want to execute

The events available for a specific field depend on the edit type of the field. The type of code you are allowed to use depends on the event you are choosing. Some of the event types allow entry of both formula and script code; others allow only script. I will discuss formula code for four events: value, default value, input translation, and input validation.

As mentioned in earlier, the four edit types for fields are editable, computed, computed when composed, and computed for display. Each of these types has different events that can be controlled through the use of formulas. Editable fields, which take input directly from users, have three events that I will discuss:

▶ Default value

▶ Input translation

▶ Input validation

All of the computed types have a single event, the value event. The value event controls the computed value for the field.

The default value event is computed when the document is created. It allows you to generate a value that will become the default for the field. Because the field is editable, the user has the ability to change the value to something else; however, if he or she chooses, the default value can remain the permanent value.

The input translation event is calculated when the document is saved or refreshed. Its purpose is to take a value that is entered into a field and to modify it in some way, usually to make it conform to some standard format. For example, you can write a formula to convert all the alphabetic characters entered into a field to uppercase or a formula to convert a ten-digit phone number, such as 3125551212, to a (xxx) xxx-xxxx format, such as (312) 555-1212.

The input validation event is calculated after the input translation event. Its purpose is to ensure that a field value conforms to criteria as defined by the developer. For example, validation could confirm that a value was entered into a field.

Computed fields have only one event that I will discuss here, the value event. Computed fields do not allow for any user input; therefore, the primary way of getting a value into computed fields is usually through a formula in the value event. The effect of this formula and the frequency with which it is recalculated depend on the computed type. The "computed when composed" value event acts in much the same way as the "editable" default value event; they are calculated when the document is created and then are not calculated again. This ensures that once a value is placed into a computed when composed field, it is never changed again by the formula. For example, you might want to populate a field with the name of the person who is creating the current document. This calculation is done only at time of creation, for if it were done each time the document were edited, the original editor's name would be overwritten with the name of the person editing the document.

Computed value events are calculated when the document is created and then recalculated when the document is saved or refreshed while being edited. These kinds of fields have values that can change frequently because of being recalculated many times. Computed fields contain information that may change and therefore need to be updated.

Computed for display value events are calculated when the document is created, when the document is opened for editing or reading, when the document is saved, and when it is refreshed while being edited or read. Unlike computed fields, computed for display fields do not store their values permanently in the document. These field values are computed but are only available while the form is open. Outside an open form, the formulas are not computed and the values cease to exist.

When creating formulas for fields, it is important to remember that a value must be generated by the formula that is appropriate for the field. If the data type is numeric, then the formula must generate a numeric value; if the data type is text, then the formula must generate a text value. The value that is given to the field is the result of the formula.

Note

> The line that returns the value generated by the formula is called the main expression. This main expression must be the last thing the formula calculates before it is finished processing and returns the value. (For more information on main expressions, see Chapter 18.)

These formulas could simply be the name of another field, placed by itself. The result takes the value for the field mentioned in the formula and places it into the field for which the event is generated. Another formula might add two numbers together or do a calculation based on the value of two fields. For example, a formula for a field called Total might take the value of a field called Quantity and multiply it by the value of a field called Price:

```
Quantity * Price
```

This formula, when placed in the value event of a field called Total, would have the effect of producing a number that is the product of the two field values. It is important that the produced value is valid for the data type of the field into which it is placed.

Using @ Functions

Objective

@ functions are one way to increase the power of your formulas. Sometimes what you need to do with a formula goes beyond simple mathematical manipulation or value comparison. When that is the case, you can turn to @ functions to perform operations that are not possible with the simple operators.

Regardless of their purpose, all @ functions have certain characteristics in common. They all have a name that distinguishes them from other @ functions, such as @Uppercase or @If. They all have a set of parameters (or arguments) that they use to perform their calculation. These parameters may be different in number and require different data types for each @ function. For example, the @ function @Uppercase has one parameter, the string that you want converted to uppercase, whereas the @Left function has two parameters, the string that you want the left-hand characters of and a number representing the number of characters from the left you want to return. These parameters, if required, are always enclosed in parentheses and are always separated from each other by semicolons (;). Finally, all @ functions return a value of a predefined type. For example, the following formula produces a text string containing the leftmost character of the variable called name:

```
@Left(Name;1)
```

If the name is Walter, the function returns the letter W. In this example, the name of the function is @Left, the number of parameters is two, the data types of the parameters are Text for the first one and Number for the second, and the data type of the result is Text.

Some functions have more than one format and, therefore, more than one set of possible parameters. The @Left function is one such function. As an alternative to the preceding format (or syntax), you could also use the function as follows:

```
@Left(Name;" ")
```

In this case, the second parameter is not numeric but is text. This syntax produces a text string, which is the leftmost characters up to the first space. The second parameter represents the character that ends the search.

@ functions can be categorized by the kind of function they perform and the type of data on which they perform it. I cannot provide an exhaustive discussion of all the @ functions here, but I discuss a number of the common ones so that you get an idea of what kinds of @ functions you might be required to know for an exam. The categories that I examine are string manipulation, logical operations, date/time operations, arithmetic operations, data conversion functions, and special functions (a group of miscellaneous functions).

Using String Manipulation

String manipulation functions operate on text values or create new text values out of old ones. Some string manipulation functions of note are @ProperCase, @Trim, @Length, @Left, and @NewLine.

@Left

The @Left function returns a string that is a certain number of characters from the left of a string passed to the function. @Left has two syntaxes:

```
@Left(String;NumberofCharacters)
```

```
@Left(String;Delimiter)
```

In the first form, a string and a number are passed to the function, and the result is a string representing the leftmost NumberofCharacters characters. The following example returns the string "That m":

```
@Left("That mouse is red!";6)
```

In the second form, two strings are passed to the function, and the result is a third string that represents the leftmost characters of the first string up to, but not including, the first occurrence of the second string. The following example returns the string "That":

```
@Left("That mouse is red!";" ")
```

@Length

The @Length function returns a number that is the total length, in characters, of the string passed to it. The syntax is

```
@Length(String)
```

The following example returns the number 18:

```
@Length("That mouse is red!")
```

@NewLine

The `@NewLine` function returns a newline character. It takes no parameters and is used just as displayed. It is used in character strings where you want to cause the string to be multilined. The following example creates a three-line text string.

```
Name + @Newline + Address + @NewLine + City + ", " + Region
```

@ProperCase

The `@ProperCase` function returns a text string that is the string passed into the function modified so that each word has an initial capital letter. Its syntax is

```
@ProperCase(String)
```

The following formula results in the text string `"Lotus Notes Exam Guide"`.

```
@ProperCase("lotus notes exam guide")
```

 Note

> It is important to note that the function is really misnamed and might be properly called `@InitialCaps` instead. This is because the function does not discriminate in changing a word's case, sometimes resulting in incorrect constructions. For example, although the phrase, "Winnie the Pooh" should remain as shown, the `@ProperCase` function converts the initial character in "the" to a capital letter. The result is "Winnie The Pooh," which, in English, is structurally incorrect.

@Trim

The `@Trim` function takes a passed text string and returns a string that is the original minus redundant spaces. Redundant spaces are leading, trailing, or multiple spaces in a string. The syntax is

```
@Trim(String)
```

The following formula results in the string `"Bob is a snail catcher"`:

```
@Trim("  Bob is   a  snail  catcher    ")
```

Using Logical Operation with `@If`

Logical operation functions are used to perform conditional processing based on criteria usually evaluated using comparison operators. The logical operation function in the Notes formula language is `@If`.

The `@If` function uses a comparison operation to determine which of at least two operations should be executed. The `@If` function takes anywhere between 3 and 99 parameters, as long as the number is odd; such as 3, 5, 7, and so on.

The basic syntax of `@If` is

```
@If(Condition; Statement if condition is true; Statement if
condition is false)
```

An extended version of this syntax includes any of 48 additional condition/statement-if-condition-is-true pairs. This results in a formula such as the following:

```
@If(Color="Red";"Stop";Color="Yellow";"Slow down";
➥Color="Green";"Go! Go! Go!"; "Huh?")
```

In this example, three pairs of condition/statement-if-condition-is-true pairs result in the function returning "Stop" if the value of the variable Color is "Red," "Slow down" if it is "Yellow," and "Go! Go! Go!" if it is "Green." The final parameter is the result of the `@If` statement if all of the previous conditions are false; the function returns "Huh?" in that case.

The syntax can also be extended by nesting one `@If` function in another. In such a scenario, a second `@If` statement is put into the function in place of the true or false statements. This might result in the following formula:

```
@IF(Color="Red";@If(Brakes="Good";"Stop";"Barrel through");"Go!
Go! Go!")
```

In this case, the second `@If` is nested in the first and asks an additional question after it has been determined that the color is `"Red"`. The result if the condition is not `"Red"` is presented after the second `@If` has been completely checked.

Tip

Nested `@If` statements can sometimes be difficult to decipher at a later date, and it is recommended that you use them only when absolutely necessary. In the preceding example, the formula could have been made more readable (albeit a little longer) by phrasing it as follows:

```
@If(Color="Red" & Brakes="Good";"Stop";Color="Red" &
➥Brakes!="Good";"Barrel through";"Go! Go! Go!")
```

The `@If` function is essential whenever you want to present different formula results depending on certain predefined conditions.

Using Date/Time Operations

Date/time functions are used to manipulate dates and times. In Notes, date/times are eight-byte floating-point values. The integer part represents a serial day counted from the date January 1, 100 AD. The fractional part represents the time as a fraction of a day, measured from midnight on the preceding day. These functions either produce, adjust, or interpret dates and times. The date/time functions I examine are `@Created`, `@Adjust`, `@Today`, `@Tomorrow`, `@Yesterday`, `@Now`, `@Month`, and `@Weekday`.

@Created

The `@Created` function returns a time value that represents the date and time the current document was created. This function takes no parameters and its syntax is indicated as follows:

`@Created`

The value for `@Created` is always constant for the same document because the created date is recorded internally in the document by Notes and does not change once the document has been created.

@Adjust

The @Adjust function takes a date/time and six numeric parameters and returns a time that is adjusted either forward or backward by any combination of years, months, days, hours, minutes, and seconds. The syntax of @Adjust is as follows:

```
@Adjust(Time;Years;Months;Days;Hours;Minutes;Seconds)
```

For example, an @Adjust function can compute a due date from an invoice date by adding 30 days to it. Such a formula would look like

```
@Adjust(InvoiceDate;0;0;30;0;0;0)
```

Each of the numeric parameters must be supplied, regardless of whether it is used. If it is not used, the parameter takes a zero. You can use negative numbers to adjust a time backward in time.

 Note

@Adjust works from seconds up to years as it computes the adjusted value. This has implications for the computed value. For example, if you adjust the date March 28, 1997 by one month and four days, the four days are added first (moving you to April 1, 1997) and then one month is added (moving you to May 1, 1997).

@Today

The @Today function returns a date/time representing the current date. This function takes no parameters and its syntax is

```
@Today
```

In a field formula, @Today takes its value from the client computer's system clock, whereas in a view formula, @Today takes its value from the computer on which the database is resident (server or local workstation). The value returned by @Today contains only a date component and no time.

Note

> The use of time-based formulas like @Today in view selection or column formulas can have adverse effects on views because the value is almost constantly being reevaluated. This causes the refresh indicator to always stay on. For more information, see Chapter 14.

@Tomorrow

The @Tomorrow function returns a date/time representing tomorrow's date. This function takes no parameters and its syntax is

@Tomorrow

In a field formula, @Tomorrow calculates its value from the client computer's system clock, whereas in a view formula, @Tomorrow calculates its value from the computer on which the database is resident (server or local workstation). The value returned by @Tomorrow contains only a date component and no time.

@Yesterday

The @Yesterday function returns a date/time representing yesterday's date. This function takes no parameters and its syntax is

@Yesterday

In a field formula, @Yesterday calculates its value from the client computer's system clock, whereas in a view formula, @Yesterday calculates its value from the computer on which the database is resident (server or local workstation). The value returned by @Yesterday contains only a date component and no time.

@Now

The @Now function returns a date/time representing the current date and time. This function takes no parameters and its syntax is

@Now

In a field formula, @Now takes its value from the client computer's system clock, whereas in a view formula, @Now takes its value from the computer on which the database is resident (server or local workstation). The value returned by @Now contains both a date and a time component.

@Month

When passed a date/time value, the @Month function returns a number representing the month of the date. This number is a value between 1 and 12. The syntax of @Month is as follows:

@Month(Date)

This might be used in a formula to compute the month of today's date:

@Month(@Today)

If today were November 7, 1997, the preceding formula would result in the number 11 being returned.

@Weekday

When passed a date/time value, the @Weekday function returns a number representing the day of the week on which the date falls. This number is a value between 1 and 7 where 1 represents Sunday and 7 represents Saturday. The syntax is as follows:

@Weekday(Date)

This might be used in a formula to compute the weekday of a date:

@Weekday([12/25/97)

In this case, because Christmas 1997 falls on a Thursday, the result is the number 5.

Arithmetic Operations

Arithmetic operations are used for complex mathematical manipulation of numbers. These operations can perform comparison, rounding, or adding numeric series. The arithmetic operations that I discuss are @Max, @Min, @Round, and @Sum.

@Max

The @Max function accepts two numeric values and returns the number that is the larger of the two. The syntax of @Max is as follows:

```
@Max(Number1;Number2)
```

If you want to create a formula that returns the larger value of either the lowest price you are willing to take for the sale of your car or the offer that a potential buyer has made, you might write a formula as follows:

```
@Max(AskingPrice;OfferedPrice)
```

If the buyer offered $50 and your lowest price is $75, then the function returns $75; if the buyer offered $100, then the function returns $100.

 Note

If the numbers passed into the function are lists, then the result is a list representing the pair-wise comparison of the values of each list. If the function is passed the lists 10:20:30 and 25:15:10, the result is 25:20:30. For more information on lists, see Chapter 18.

@Min

The @Min function accepts two numeric values and returns the number that is the smaller of the two. The syntax of @Min is as follows:

```
@Min(Number1;Number2)
```

If you want to create a formula that returns the smaller value of either your age or the number 30, you might write a formula as follows:

```
@Min(CurentAge;30)
```

If you are 18 years old, the function returns 18; if you are 40, the function returns 30.

 Note

> If the numbers passed into the function are lists, then the result is a list representing the pair-wise comparison of the values of each list. If the function is passed the lists 10:20:30 and 25:15:10, the result is 10:15:10. For more information on lists, see Chapter 18.

@Round

The @Round function accepts a number and either returns the number rounded to the nearest whole number or, if provided with an additional numeric parameter, rounds to the nearest multiple of the additional parameter. The @Round function always rounds up if the choice is ambiguous; for example, when passed the number 10.5, @Round rounds up to 11. The syntaxes for @Round are

```
@Round(Number)
@Round(Number;Factor)
```

In the first syntax, the result is the number rounded to the nearest whole number, so the value 10.4 rounds to 10 and 11.5 rounds to 12. In the second syntax, the result is the number rounded to the nearest multiple of the factor. For example, the number 123, when @Round is provided with a factor of 10, is rounded to 120.

 Note

> The factor provided could be a decimal number, in which case @Round rounds to the nearest multiple of that decimal value. If you round 123.09 with the factor 0.1, the result is 123.1, the nearest multiple of 0.1.
>
> Negative numbers in the number parameter result in the rounded number being negative; however, a negative factor has no impact on the end result. In essence, the rounding is done on a positive number with a positive factor and then the sign of the number is applied to the result.

@Sum

The @Sum function returns the sum of any number of numeric parameters passed to it. These parameters could be single values or lists.

The syntax of the @Sum function is as follows:

```
@Sum(Number1;Number2;Number3;...;Numberx)
```

x is any number.

The result of the preceding line is the sum of all the numbers listed.

Note

@Sum requires that all the parameters are numeric. If any of them are variables that do not contain a value, they are interpreted as a NULL (a text value) and the function returns with an error condition.

If the parameters are numeric lists, the @Sum function adds all the elements of all the lists to produce its result. For more information on lists, see Chapter 18.

Using Data Conversion Functions

Data conversion functions are used to convert data of one type to another. For example, you can convert a text value to a number or a numeric value to a text value. This is often necessary because many formulas require that the data types of combined values all be the same. The data conversion functions that I examine are @Text, @TexttoNumber, and @TexttoTime.

@Text

The @Text function takes a date/time or number and returns the equivalent text value. An optional additional parameter enables you to include a code that lets you control the format of the time or number value when converted to text.

The syntaxes for @Text are as follows:

```
@Text(NumberorTime)
@Text(NumberorTime;"formatcode")
```

The first syntax returns the date/time or number formatted using default settings: Numbers return in general format and date/time return in the default short date format as set in your operating system settings. For example, a number 124.5 is returned as the text value "124.5", a number 124.50 is returned as "124.5", and the number 1.5E+6 is returned as "1500000."

The second syntax returns the date/time or number formatted as indicated by the formatting codes passed as the second parameter. These codes, which are text values separated by commas presented in quotation marks, are any combination of the codes listed in Table 13.1.

Table 13.1

Formatting codes for @Text.

Data type	Category	Codes	Display what?
Date/Time	Date	D0	Year, month, and day
		D1	Month and day, year if not current
		D2	Month and day
		D3	Year and month
	Time	T0	Hour, minute, and second
		T1	Hour and minute
	Zone	Z0	Always convert time to local zone
		Z1	Display zone if not same as local
		Z2	Always display time zone

continues

Table 13.1 Continued

Data type	Category	Codes	Display what?
	Portion	S0	Date only
		S1	Time only
		S2	Date and time
		S3	Date, time, today or yesterday
Number	n/a	G	General format
		F	Fixed format
		S	Scientific format
		C	Currency format
		%	Percentage format
		(	Parentheses around negatives
		Number	Number of decimal places

When a date/time value is formatted by using date/time formats, you must be aware of certain things. First, by default, both the date and the time appear if the value contains both. Second, the date/time formats are divided into four groups of codes. You can only choose one from each to combine the formats together as a single, non-delimited text string in quotation marks. Third, dates are always displayed using the short date format defined in your operating system. Fourth, if you want to display only date or only time, use one of the Sx formats. (This format will override any formats that indicate a preference for the portion eliminated by the Sx format.)

For example, the function `@Text(@Now)` produces 11/09/97 01:36:15 PM, `@Text(@Now;"D2")` produces 11/09 01:36:15 PM, and `@Text(@Now;"D2S0")` produces 11/09.

When a number is formatted by using numeric formats, you must be aware of certain things:

▶ First, by default, @Text produces a number in a general format.

▶ Second, any of the alphabetic codes used by itself will produce its result with two decimal places, except "G", which ignores decimal place codes.

▶ Third, you can use as many of the formats as you like, but if one code contradicts another, the one that is farthest to the right will take precedence. The codes can be strung together or separated using commas as a delimiter. The string must be enclosed in quotation marks.

▶ Fourth, the result of displaying a fixed number of decimal places is a number rounded up to the number of decimal places indicated.

For example, @Text(10.653) produces "10.653", @Text(10.653;"F2") produces "10.65", @Text(10.652;"C0") produces "$11", and @Text(10.653;"F2C3S1") produces "1.1E+01" (the result of the last code in the list overriding the others).

Note

The date/time formats only work for date/times and generate error messages if used with numbers. The same will happen if numeric formats are used with date/times.

@TexttoNumber

The @TexttoNumber function returns the numeric representation of a text value. The syntax is as follows:

@TexttoNumber(TextValue)

The text value can contain any of the valid numeric symbols (numbers, numeric punctuation, E, and e). If it contains non-numeric values, then the conversion results in an error unless the initial values of the text value are numeric. For example, the string "-134.34" is converted to the number -134.34, and the string "123AB" is converted to the number 123. The strings "AB123" and "One" both result in errors.

@TexttoTime

The @TexttoTime function returns the date/time representation of a text value. The syntax is as follows:

```
@TexttoTime(TextValue)
```

The text value can contain valid date and time combinations, date/time ranges, or the text strings Today, Tomorrow, or Yesterday. For example, if passed 12/25/97, @TexttoTime converts the string to a valid date/time value, and if passed Today, the function returns today's date. If passed A Week from Thursday or 12/42/97, an error condition results because neither are convertible to a date/time value.

Using Special Functions

The special functions category is used to group functions that represent a miscellany of different special-interest functions. These include functions for determining the name of the current Notes user, determining if a value is text or a number, and returning values if error conditions arise. The special functions I examine are @Username, @Name, @AllChildren, @AllDescendants, @IsResponseDoc, @IsNewDoc, @IsText, @IsNumber, @Failure, and @Success.

@UserName

Taking no parameters, the @UserName function returns the fully distinguished name contained in the ID that is currently active on the workstation or server requesting formula execution. The syntax of the function is

```
@UserName
```

For example, if Java Joe/Bean is the current user, the following line returns Java Joe/Bean:

```
@UserName
```

@Name

The @Name function takes a fully distinguished name and, using an action parameter, returns some portion of the name in the format that you choose. The syntax of @Name is as follows:

@Name([action];NotesName)

A variety of action parameters (all enclosed in square brackets) allow you to modify the name that is passed to the function. For example, the action [CN] returns the common name portion of an ID. Some of the common actions you will use are listed in Table 13.2.

Table 13.2

Actions for @Name

Action Parameter	Returned Value
[Abbreviate]	Returns a name with the component labels removed; CN=Java Joe/O=Bean becomes Java Joe/Bean.
[C]	Returns the country component of a name; CN=Java Joe/O=Bean/C=US becomes US.
[CN]	Returns the common name component of a name; CN=Java Joe/O=Bean/C=US becomes Java Joe.
[O]	Returns the organization component of a name; CN=Java Joe/O=Bean/C=US becomes Bean.
[OUn]	Returns the *n*th organizational unit of a name where the count begins from the rightmost organizational unit and progresses to the left; [OU2] of CN=Java Joe/OU=Production/OU=Brazil/O=Bean becomes Production.

The @Name function is useful for abbreviating names in fields as well as in views and can be combined with other functions to increase functionality. The following example returns the common name of the currently active user ID:

@Name([CN];@UserName)

@AllChildren

You can use the @AllChildren function in selection formulas to return all the responses of documents matching a specific criteria—that is, one level of descendants. The @AllChildren function takes no parameters but must be used in a specific way in a selection criteria. The syntax of its use is as follows:

```
SELECT selectionformula | @AllChildren
```

For example, to return all the documents that have the value "Red" in their color field and all the responses to those documents, you could use a formula such as

```
SELECT Color = "Red" | @AllChildren
```

@AllDescendants

You can use the @AllDescendants function in selection formulas to return all descendants (responses and response to responses) of documents matching a specific criteria. The @AllDescendants function takes no parameters but must be used in a specific way in a selection criteria. The syntax of its use is as follows:

```
SELECT selectionformula | @AllDescendants
```

For example, to return all the documents that have the value "Red" in their color field and all the responses and response to responses to those documents, you could use a formula such as

```
SELECT Color = "Red" | @AllDescendants
```

@IsResponseDoc

The @IsResponseDoc function takes no parameters and returns a boolean value (1 or 0) to indicate if the current document is a response document (created using a form of type Response or Response to response). It is used as the condition in a @If statement to determine an operation to perform based on whether the document is a response:

```
@If(@IsResponseDoc;Statement if true;Statement if false)
```

Note   This function returns a 0 if used in a response document that has not been saved yet.

@IsNewDoc

The @IsNewDoc function takes no parameters and returns a boolean value (1 or 0) to indicate if the current document is being created and has not been saved yet. It is used as the condition in a @If statement to determine an operation to perform based on whether the document has been saved since it was created:

```
@If(@IsNewDoc;Statement if true;Statement if false)
```

@IsText

The @IsText function takes a single parameter and evaluates if the type of the value passed is text. If it is, it returns a boolean 1, and if it is not, it returns a boolean 0. The syntax is

```
@IsText(Value)
```

This function is useful for determining the type of a value before doing processing, assuming that it is type text. Using this function can ensure that you catch errors before Notes returns a runtime error to your application.

@IsNumber

The @IsNumber function takes a single parameter and evaluates if the type of the value passed is numeric. If it is, it returns a boolean 1, and if it is not, it returns a boolean 0. The syntax is as follows:

```
@IsNumber(Value)
```

This function is useful for determining the type of a value before doing processing, assuming that it is type number. For example, you might want to check that a value a user entered is numeric before trying to perform a mathematical computation with it.

@Failure

Designed for use in input validation formulas, @Failure displays a dialog box containing the message you provide as the single parameter. The syntax of @Failure is as follows:

```
@Failure(message)
```

@Failure is typically used in the false condition of an @If function when the condition determines whether a value input into an editable field is valid. For example, if an editable field requires a value be entered into it, then the following @If/@Failure combination checks for the value and reports an error condition when the user attempts to save the document. If the validation fails, you do not allow the user to save and exit the document.

```
@If(Name!=NULL;@Success;@Failure("You must enter a name")
```

 Note

@Failure is designed for use in input validation formulas. If you use the @Failure function elsewhere, a dialog box is not produced. Instead, the message is returned to the field executing the function.

@Success

Designed for use in input validation formulas, @Success indicates that a condition was met and returns a 1, a true value. @Success takes no parameters and its syntax is as shown as follows:

```
@Success
```

@Success is typically used in the true condition of an @If function when the condition determines if a value input into an editable field is valid. For example, if an editable field requires that a value is entered into it, the following @If/@Success combination checks for an error condition. If none exists, the function allows the document to be saved and exited:

```
@If(Name!=NULL;@Success;@Failure("You must enter a name")
```

Note

@Success is designed for use in input validation formulas. If you use the @Success function elsewhere, a dialog box is not produced. Instead, the number 1 is returned to the field executing the function.

Having examined formula forms, some contexts in which formulas are used, and some @ functions, you can now tackle a lab to put the theory you learned into practice.

Exercises

As an enhancement to the Customers database that you have been working with, in this lab you will add some formulas to validate data and to pass information from your documents to your responses. To be more specific, you will add validation to the Customer field to ensure that it is not left NULL; you will add a default value to the Country field so that it starts out with "U.S.A."; and you will add a new field called CreateDate, which will compute the date the document was created. In addition, on the response form, you will enable inheritance and then get the value for the Customer field from the Customer field on the document to which it is responding. This database is available on your CD-ROM and should be copied to your default Notes data directory. The lab file is called cust13.nsf and its title is Chapter 13 Customers. Be sure that when you copy the file, you remove the read-only attribute or you will not be able to modify the database.

Exercise 13.1

1. From the File menu, choose Database|Open and select the database called Chapter 13 Customers from the pull-down list of local databases. Click the Open button to add the database to your workspace and open the standard view.

2. If the design category is not expanded, click the twistie to the left to expand and then click the forms view to show the forms on the right.

3. Double-click the form called Customer to edit its design.

4. Click the Customer field to display its events in the design pane at the bottom of the display. Change to the "Input Validation" event by clicking the down arrow to the right of the label Event: and choosing that event from the list (see Figure 13.2).

5. Click into the design pane and type the following formula:

   ```
   @If(Customer != NULL;@Success;@Failure("Please enter a
   ➥customer")
   ```

Figure 13.4

*The input transla-
tion for the Re-
gion field.*

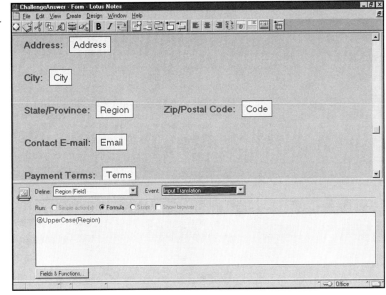

10. Change to the "Input Validation" event for the Region field
    by clicking the down arrow to the right of the label "Event:"
    and choosing that event from the list (see Figure 13.5).

Figure 13.5

*The input valida-
tion for the Re-
gion field.*

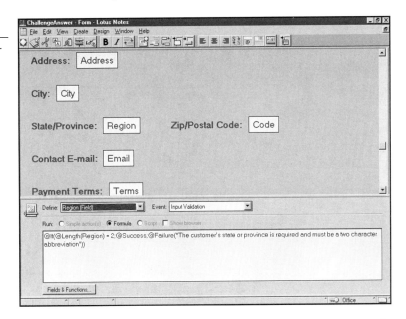

continues

11. Click into the design pane and type the following formula:

```
@If(@Length(Region) = 2;@Success;@Failure
➤("The customer's state or province is required
➤and must be a two character abbreviation"))
```

Click the green check mark on the left of the design pane to check your syntax. If you get an error, check what you typed against the preceding formula and repair the error.

This checks to see if the length of the value the user typed is two characters. If it is not, then he or she either typed too many characters (such as the whole name) or typed too few characters (such as not typing anything at all). The failure message takes both scenarios into consideration as it issues a generic error message.

12. Scroll down to the bottom of the form and click to the right of the author field to position your insertion point to its right.

13. Press the space bar a few times to move away from the author field and type Create Date: and then, from the Create menu, choose Field (see Figure 13.6).

Figure 13.6

The properties for the CreateDate field.

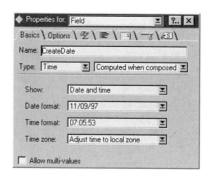

14. The properties for the field you just created are Name: CreateDate; Type: Time, Computed when Composed; Font Style: Plain.

15. Close the Properties for Field dialog box by clicking the close window button.

16. Because you just exited from the properties for the Create-Date field, its events should be present in the design pane. Change to the "Value" event by clicking the down arrow to the right of the label "Event:" and choosing that event from the list (see Figure 13.7).

Figure 13.7

The value formula for the CreateDate *field.*

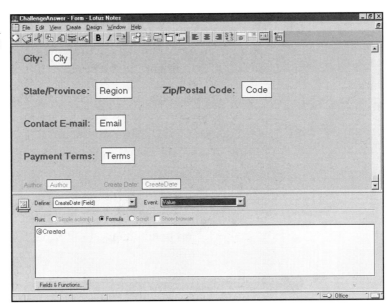

17. Click into the design pane and type the following formula:

    @Created

    Click the green check mark on the left of the design pane to check your syntax. If you get an error, check what you typed against the preceding formula and repair the error.

    This formula obtains the date the document was created and places it into the value of the field.

18. From the Design menu, choose Test form and click "Yes" when prompted to save the form.

continues

19. Click into the address field and type an address. Then from the File menu, choose Save. A dialog box appears telling you that you have to enter a customer name (that's your @Failure function working). Click the OK button to confirm the message.

20. Click into the customer field and type a customer name.

21. From the File menu, choose Save. You should get a message telling you that you need to enter a value into the city field. Click OK to confirm the message.

22. In the City field, type "New York". From the File menu, choose Save. You should get a message telling you that you need to enter a value into the region field. Click the OK button to confirm the message.

23. In the State/Province field, type "New York". From the File menu, choose Save. You should get the error message again, but when you click the OK button, notice that the value "New York" has been changed to "NEW YORK"; that's @UpperCase working.

24. Remove "New York" from the State/Province field and type "ny". From the File menu, choose Save. This time, the document should save properly and exit to the design of your form.

25. Save the form and close it, returning to the standard view.

26. Double-click the Preferences form to edit its design.

27. Right-click in the form builder window and choose Form Properties from the menu that appears.

28. Click the defaults tab in the Properties for form dialog box and select the checkbox next to "Formulas inherit values from selected document" (see Figure 13.8). This will allow you to get the customer name from the document we are responding to instead of typing it again.

Figure 13.8

Enable form inheritance in the form properties dialog box.

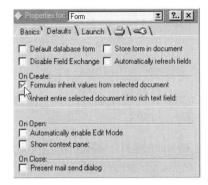

29. Close the properties dialog box by clicking the close window button.

30. Double-click the customer field to display its properties. Change its type from Editable to Computed when composed and close its properties by clicking the close window button.

31. Change to the "Value" event for the Customer field by clicking the down arrow to the right of the label "Event:" and choosing that event from the list.

32. Click into the design pane and type the following formula

    ```
    Customer
    ```

    Click the green check mark on the left of the design pane to check your syntax. If you get an error, check what you typed against the preceding formula and repair the error.

    This reference to Customer takes the value from the customer field on the document you are responding to and places it into this computed field.

33. Save the form and exit to the Standard view.

34. Click the "Customers" view to display the list of customers (including the customer you saved in Step 24).

35. Click the name of the customer you created and, from the Create menu, choose Preferences.

continues

Exercise 13.1 Continued

36. When the response document appears, it should have the customer name already filled in. Choose a preferred coffee type from the radio buttons. Save and close the document.

Exercise 13.2

You now need to complete the validation and default values for the rest of the fields on your two forms. The challenge follows:

1. On the Customer form, ensure that the Address, City, and Code fields are not NULL when the user saves the document. Also ensure that the Terms field defaults to Net 45.

   Hint: The Terms field is a keywords field and the keywords use synonyms. Values entered are the synonym, and that is what you need to default to.

2. On the Preferences form, add a DateCreated field with the same properties and formulas as you created in Steps 13–17 in the first exercise.

The answer to the challenge exercises are found in forms called ChallengeAnswer and ChallengeResponse in the cust13.nsf database. You can view your customers and their preferences by using the Customer Preferences View.

Review Questions

1. Of the following, which is not a valid formula component?

   a. alias

   b. constant

   c. variable

   d. operator

2. What is the purpose of the REM keyword?

    a. Creates a reminder with a alarm in your formula

    b. Issues a remote command

    c. Creates a remark, which is not processed

    d. Calculates a remainder

3. If a FIELD keyword is used in a formula and the field name associated with the keyword does not refer to a field on the current document, what is the result?

    a. A runtime error occurs and the application stops.

    b. A new field is created on the document.

    c. A new field is created on the form.

    d. The command is ignored.

4. Reginald creates a formula that looks like this:

```
FirstName + LastName
```

where the values of FirstName and LastName are "William" and "Shakespeare". What is the result of the formula?

    a. WilliamShakespeare

    b. William Shakespeare

    c. 0

    d. An error when Notes tries to add the two text strings together

5. What is the area in which formulas are entered into form events?

    a. The programming pane

    b. The field

    c. The design pane

    d. The form builder window

6. When are Computed for Display fields recalculated?

    a. Only when the document is opened and edited

    b. When the document is opened for reading or editing

    c. When the document is saved

    d. When the document is opened, saved, or refreshed

7. Bruce creates the following formula:

```
@Left("Batman and Robin";" ")
```

What does it return?

    a. Bat

    b. Batman

    c. Nothing; the syntax is incorrect

    d. Robin

8. What does the @Trim function do?

    a. It removes redundant spaces in a text string.

    b. It removes half of the characters in a text string.

    c. It removes characters on the right based on the value of a parameter passed to the function.

    d. It removes characters on the left based on the value of a parameter passed to the function.

9. How many parameters does an @If function take?

    a. 3

    b. Any number

    c. Any number up to 99

    d. Any odd number up to 99

10. What is the difference between the `@Today` and the `@Now` functions?

    a. `@Now` produces the current date only; `@Today` produces date and time.

    b. `@Now` produces the current time only; `@Today` produces the current date only.

    c. `@Today` produces the current date and time; `@Now` produces only the current date.

    d. `@Today` produces only the current date; `@Now` produces the current date and time.

11. Which function will convert a number or a date/time value to a text string?

    a. `@Text`

    b. `@Convert`

    c. `@NumberorTimetoText`

    d. `@NumConv`

12. Julia's Notes name is Julia Froggley/Production/Brazil/Bean. She is using Notes and the following formula runs in an application she is using:

    `@Name([OU2];@UserName)`

    What is the result of the formula?

    a. Julia Froggley

    b. Bean

    c. Production

    d. Brazil

13. When does the function @IsNewDoc return a "True" value?

    a. When a document is first created and then saved

    b. When a document is opened for editing after being created and saved

    c. When a saved document is edited and modified but not yet saved again

    d. When a document is first created and not yet saved

14. In what kind of event are the @Success and @Failure functions designed to be used?

    a. Field default value

    b. Field value

    c. Field input validation

    d. Field input translation

Review Answers

1. A. Aliases are names that application developers see but users do not. It is appropriate to use the name of a alias in a formula, but it is not a formula component; it is simply a value. For more information, refer to the section titled "Understanding Formulas."

2. C. REM is a keyword that indicates that the line it is on is a remark and should not be checked for syntax nor be processed. The information on the line must be enclosed in quotation marks. For more information, refer to the section titled "REM."

3. B. If the field does not exist on the current document, it is created, but only for that document; it is not placed on the form that created it. For more information, refer to the section titled "SELECT."

4. A. The operator, "+" when used with text values, concatenates (joins) the values together. Because there are no spaces concatenated between the first and last names, the result is the two names joined together as one continuous name. For more information, refer to the section titled "Mathematical Operators."

5. C. The forms design environment consists of three panes, the form builder window, the actions pane, and the design pane. The design pane is used to enter formulas for form events. For more information, refer to the section titled "Using Formulas in Fields."

6. D. Computed for display fields are calculated when the document is originally created, when it is saved, when it is opened in either read or edit mode, and whenever a refresh happens (either invoked manually by the user or by some form process). For more information, refer to the section titled "Using Formulas in Fields."

7. B. The syntax used in this version of @Left returns the characters to the left of the first occurrence of the second parameter—in this case, the characters to the left of the first space. For more information, refer to the section titled "@Left."

8. A. @Trim is used to remove leading, trailing, or duplicate spaces in a text string, all of which are redundant. For more information, refer to the section titled "@Trim."

9. D. The @If function is constructed around pairs of conditions with operations if the condition is true. If no conditions are true, then a single false operation is performed. The maximum number of parameters in an @If function is 99, but the total number must be odd (even pairs plus 1). For more information, refer to the section titled "@If."

10. D. @Today only returns the current date, whereas @Now produces both the date and the time. For more information, refer to the sections titled "@Today" and "@Now."

11. A. The @Text function converts either a number or a date to a text value. In addition, a second parameter can be used to control the format of the resulting string. For more information, refer to the section titled "@Text."

12. C. The @UserName function returns Julia's fully distinguished name. The @Name function with the initial [OU2] parameter returns the second organizational unit of her name—in this case, O = Bean, OU1 = Brazil, OU2 = Production, and CN = Julia Froggley. For more information, refer to the section titled "@Name."

13. D. The function @IsNewDoc is designed to inform you whether the document is new and not yet saved. Once the document has been saved, @IsNewDoc returns a false value. For more information, refer to the section titled "@IsNewDoc."

14. C. These functions are designed to be used when validating data. In field input validation, @Success does nothing and @Failure produces an error dialog box. In all other contexts, both @Success and @Failure return values, but no dialog boxes are produced. For more information, refer to the section titled "@Success" and "@Failure."

Answers to Test Yourself Questions at Beginning of Chapter

1. The main components of a formula are constants, variables, operators, keywords, and functions. Constants are constant values, such as "Red" or the number 10. Variables are either temporary or field names and hold values that might change from one formula execution to another. Operators perform calculations on constants, variables, or the results of @ functions, or they perform comparisons of values. Keywords are special words that perform special functions or indicate special handling to be done with the information that follows them. Finally, functions are "black boxes" that are designed to perform specific calculations, take values in the form of parameters, and produce some kind of result. For more information, refer to the section titled "Understanding Formulas" and its subsections.

2. The four edit types for fields are editable, computed, computed when composed, and computed for display. The four events most commonly modified using formulas are default value, input translation, input validation, and value. For more information, refer to the section titled "Formulas in Fields."

3. The @If function is a logical operation function designed to take a condition, evaluate its value (true or false), and then execute an operation. Its syntax is as follows:

```
@If(condition; trueresult; falseresult).
```

The syntax can be extended in that up to 48 pairs of conditions and true results can be present, in addition to the single false result. For more information, refer to the section titled "@If."

4. The functions @UserName and @Name can be used as follows:

```
@Name([CN];@UserName)
```

For more information, refer to the sections titled "@UserName" and "@Name."

5. In the context of a field input validation, @Success and @Failure can be used to pass or reject validation as a result of a test for valid data in the field. @Success allows the validation to continue; @Failure produces an error message indicating the validation failed:

```
@If(Color != NULL;@Success;@Failure("You must enter a color")
```

For more information, refer to the sections titled "@Success" and "@Failure."

Chapter 14

Creating Views

Objectives

▶ Planning views

▶ Understanding view types

▶ Creating a view

▶ Creating a folder

Test Yourself! Before reading this chapter, test yourself to determine how much study time you will need to devote to this section.

1. What is the purpose of the Show Responses Only property for a View column?

2. What is the function of the view selection formula?

3. What are the three view types and their unique characteristics?

4. What are the three ways of defining the contents of a View column?

5. What is the difference between a folder and a view?

Answers are located at the end of the chapter...

For users to effectively use a Notes database, they first must be able to tell what is in it. Views are like tables of contents to your databases, showing enough information for users to tell if a specific document is of interest, or to generally know what documents are in a database. As an application developer you must be able to build views that are needed by the user community at large. You also may have to educate certain users to build views themselves.

Planning Views

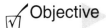

As mentioned earlier, views are like tables of contents to your databases. They can be used to present information about some or all of the documents present in your databases. This information can be summaries of document information, or enough information to let users decide whether they want to open a document to investigate its contents further. Every database has at least one view, and some have many. Regardless of how many there are in a database, they are essential to knowing what is present.

As with forms, doing some preliminary design work before committing anything to Notes is good practice. A sketch on paper is often useful in determining what is needed in a view and what can be left out. A number of diagnostic questions are also helpful to enable you to determine what features to implement:

- ▶ Should everyone be able to use this view or only me?

- ▶ Should all documents display or only a subset?

- ▶ Should documents be sorted or categorized? If so, by which field values?

- ▶ Should unread markers display?

- ▶ What should display in each column: a field or a formula value?

▶ Should response documents be indented underneath their parents? What information should display for my responses?

▶ Should statistics display for the view?

▶ Should any special shortcut features be included?

After these questions have been answered, creation of the view itself is fairly elementary.

Understanding View Types

 One of the first diagnostic questions asked when creating a view is, "Who needs access to this view?" The answer to this question determines which view type you want to create. There are three types of views: shared, private, and shared-personal on first use. Each of these views has a different purpose.

 It is very important to decide which kind of view you are creating before you begin the creation process because after a view has been created using a specific type, you cannot change it to another. You need to know this for the exam because the contrast between shared and private views is very important.

Shared Views

Shared views are stored in a database. By default, all users who have access to the database have access to the shared views. These views contain information that is of general interest to everyone who uses a certain database, and therefore are available to everyone.

 There are security features that can make a shared view unavailable to certain users. This is called the View Access list and is discussed at length in Chapter 23, "Securing Applications."

To create a shared view, you must have permission to create shared folders/views in the database ACL; this is automatically given to those with Designer access and can optionally be given to those with Editor access.

Private Views

Private views are created by individual users of a database. These views are stored locally on their workstation in the DESKTOP.DSK file. Therefore, private views are only accessible to the person who created them, and only on the machine on which they were created (unless the DESKTOP.DSK has been copied to another machine). Private views are created by an individual who has certain needs that are not requirements of all users, which would generally clutter the shared design of the database and cause undue work for the database's application developer.

To create a private view, you must have permission to create personal folders/views in the database ACL; this is automatically given to those with Designer access and can optionally be given to those with Reader or higher access.

Shared-Personal on First Use Views

Shared-personal on first use views are are created as shared views, but become private views once a user first uses them. As with a shared view, these views are stored as part of the design of the database on the server, meaning that anyone can get initial access to it. Like private views, however, shared-personal on first use views become views that are stored locally on a user's workstation.

A developer can use shared-personal on first use views to create a generic view that can be distributed to all users, and then be changed by those users to conform to their specifications. They increase efficiency because the design is built once, and minimal training is necessary to help the users modify the view to their specifications.

As with shared views, you must have permission to create shared folders/views in the database ACL to create a shared-personal on first use view. This permission is automatically given to those with Designer access and can optionally be given to those with Editor access.

Creating a View

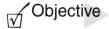 Objective ▶ Every Notes database must have at least one view. When a database is created, a view is created called *Untitled*. This view has only one column and shows the number of each document in the view (a number that Notes maintains automatically for the documents).

The created view can be modified to be your primary or default view. In addition to that view, you may want to create new views and have them display a variety of documents and fields.

Creating a New View

To create a new view, complete the following steps:

1. Open the database by double-clicking its icon on your workspace.

2. From the Create menu, choose View, and the Create View dialog box appears (see Figure 14.1).

Figure 14.1

The Create View dialog box enables you to set the initial parameters for the view.

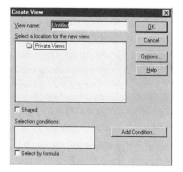

3. Type a name in the View Name field. This name is what the users will see in the navigation pane for the database. It should describe the function of the view.

4. Choose a view type by selecting the Shared if you want the view to be shared checkbox, or leave it unchecked if you want the view to be private.

If you select the Shared checkbox, another checkbox appears so that you can select if you want the view to be shared-personal on first use (see Figure 14.2).

Figure 14.2

The Create View dialog box for a shared view.

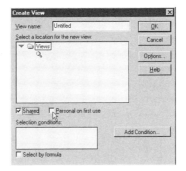

5. In the Select A Location For The New View box, click on the place where you want the view to appear in the list of views. If your view is shared, you see a list of yellow shared views to choose; if your view is private, you see a list of gray views. By selecting either the Private Views view (form personal views) or the Views view (for shared views), you ensure that your new view is displayed in the first column of the view list. If you choose any of the existing view names, your new view appears as a subview under the view you choose, and a twistie appears next to its parent to indicate that view can be expanded to show its subviews.

6. If you want to make this view display only a subset of the total documents in this database, you can enter a selection condition. Selection conditions can be entered either by using the search builder tool (by clicking on the Add Condition button) or by selecting the Select By Formula checkbox and entering a formula that begins with the keyword SELECT (for more information on SELECT, see Chapter 13, "Introduction to Formulas").

7. If you want this view to be created to look the same as a view that already exists (for example, you want to pattern the columns and look of the view after another one), you can click the Options button, choose a view to inherit the design from (in essence, the view template) in the Options dialog box, and click the OK button (see Figure 14.3).

Figure 14.3

The Options dialog box enables you to define design inheritance.

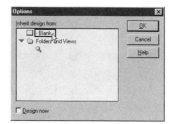

8. If you want to move straight from the creation of the view to designing the view, select the Design Now checkbox and click the OK button in the Options dialog box.

9. Click the OK button to complete the view creation and initial design.

Of all the parameters and values set in the procedure, all can be changed after the view has been created except the view type (shared, private, or shared-personal on first use) and the view template. Setting the rest of the parameters is discussed at length in the following sections.

Now that you have created view, you may want to modify its design. If you selected the Design Now checkbox in the preceding procedure, the view design environment appears, enabling you to modify the design.

Entering the View Design Environment

The view design environment is the place in which changes to view design are made. To enter the view design environment from the navigation pane, complete the following steps:

1. Expand the design section by clicking its twistie.

2. Select View to display a list of views on the right side.

3. Double-click the view that you want to edit in the view list.

This environment consists of three panes, although usually only two show: two panes on the top and one on the bottom (see Figure 14.4). Each of these panes can be independently resized to allow for design in any of the three areas. On the top is the View Builder window, which is the area in which the view design actually occurs. This area is like a sketch pad on which you create your view's final look.

Figure 14.4

The view design environment with all three panes showing.

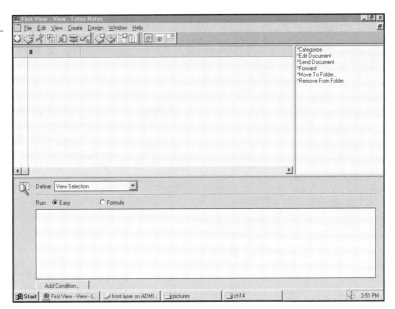

On the bottom is the design pane, which is the area in which column contents and view events are defined. If you need this area to be larger or smaller, resize it by dragging its top border up or down. Its top border is the thick line that divides this pane from the View Builder window.

The final pane is usually hidden. Its left border can be seen on the right side of the View Builder window, just to the right of the View Builder window's vertical scrollbar. You can open this pane by either dragging the border to the left with your mouse, or by selecting View|Action Pane. This pane shows a list of Actions that have been defined for this view, either by default, or by a developer (for more information, see Chapter 15, "Creating Actions and Hotspots").

View Properties

As with other Notes objects, views have properties that define their characteristics. You can see and set these properties for a view by bringing up the Properties For View dialog box. Click with your right mouse button on any blank area in the View Builder window and choose View Properties from the menu that appears to bring up this dialog box. This Properties dialog box is divided into tabs: Basics; Options; Style; Advanced (the one with the beanie on it); and Security (the one with the key on it) (see Figure 14.5).

Figure 14.5

The Properties For View dialog box enables you to set view properties.

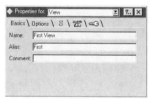

The Basics Tab

The Basics tab contains fields for information relating to the basic definition of the view: its name, alias, and comments. The view name is what users will see in the views list in the navigation pane. This name can be up to 64 characters long (or 129 if you cascade to more than one level).

You can create cascaded views (either in the view list or in the view menu) by creating a name that includes one or more backslashes (\) (see Figure 14.6). Each backslash indicates that a new category is to be created, which can be expanded or collapsed using a twistie that will be present next to it. Cascading your menus increases the name of your view up to 129 characters.

Figure 14.6

*Cascaded
views created
from the names*
Management\
Accounting
and Management\
Production.

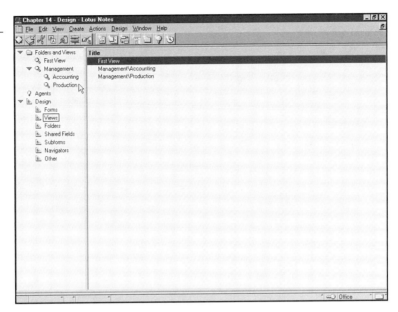

Note

There is no limit to the number of cascades you can do as long as you do not exceed the total number of name characters. If you cascade too many times, however, you are unable to expand the final categories because there is no horizontal scrolling allowed on the left side of the navigation pane.

If you choose to cascade to more than one level, you are able to expand the levels in the Standard view; however, only one additional level is allowed in the View menu.

The cascaded groups can either be categories that do not actually represent views, or they can be views themselves. If you create a view called Management and create another view called Management\Invoices, for example, you get a cascade effect, but both are valid views. On the other hand, if you create a view called Management\Invoices and Management does not already exist, clicking the Management option in the navigation pane simply expands or collapses it; it does not display a Management view.

The alias is a name you use to programmatically refer to this view. This additional text makes long view names easy to handle because you never have to actually refer to them that way in formulas. The alias is usually short and concise, while the actual name of the view is usually verbose and descriptive.

 Note

Once you assign an alias name, that is the name you must refer to the view by in all programmatic interaction with Notes. The other name is simply for the users, and Notes does not recognize or respond to it in formulas.

 Tip

Sometimes you may want to create views that are hidden (that is, they do not show up anywhere on a user's workstation). These views are typically used as places to do lookups in formulas using the @DBColumn and @DBLookup functions (for more information on these functions, see Chapter 19, "Advanced Formulas, Part II"). To make a view hidden, simply enclose its name (the part before the alias) in parentheses.

The Comment field is where you can type free-form comments documenting your reason for creating the view. These comments are stored in a hidden view field called $Comment and are only available to designers who look on this tab of the properties or at the design properties from the navigation pane.

The Options Tab

The Options tab enables you to set default characteristics for the view (see Figure 14.7).

Figure 14.7

The View Options tab.

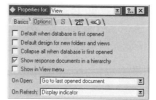

By selecting the Default When Database Is First Opened option, you can ensure that this view is the one opened the first time the database is opened. This is not to say that this will be the view that is presented every time the database is opened; however, because some database properties may override the launch property, On Database Open will override this if it is set to Restore As Last Viewed By User.

Note

The view that had the Default When Database Is First Opened checkbox set last is the one that becomes the default view when first opened.

By selecting the Default Design For New Folders And Views checkbox, you can ensure that every created view uses this view as its template unless the view creator goes to the create options and chooses another one (see the section titled "Creating a View").

Note

The view that had the Default Design for New Folders and Views checkbox set last becomes the default design for new views.

By selecting the Collapse All When Database Is First Opened checkbox, you can ensure that all categorized columns are initially collapsed when the view is first opened. As with the Default When Database Is First Opened checkbox, this setting can be overridden with the database property Restore As Last Viewed By User.

By selecting the Show Response Documents in a Hierarchy checkbox, you can ensure that all Response and Response to Response documents display indented under their parents instead of in a vertical column. This checkbox is selected by default for ease of view interpretation and is usually left that way.

By selecting the Show In View checkbox, you can ensure that this view appears as a choice at the bottom of the View menu. This means that the view is accessible not only from the navigation pane, but also from the View menu.

The On Open: field is a pull-down list of three choices, which allows you to indicate which document a user should be placed on when he chooses this view. If you choose Go To Last Opened Document, which is the default, the user is placed on the last document he opened. If you choose Go To Top Row, the user is taken to the first document in the view. If you choose Go To Bottom Row, the user is taken to the last document in the view.

The On Refresh field is a pull-down list of four choices, which allows you to indicate how the user should be informed of new documents being present in the view when the view index is refreshed (see the discussion on view indexes in the following section, "The Advanced Tab"). The following are the available options:

▶ If you choose Display Indicator, which is the default, then when the index is refreshed, a refresh indicator (a clockwise pointing blue arrow) appears in the upper-left corner of the view. The user must click the arrow, press the F9 key, or choose View | Refresh to make new changes appear in the view.

▶ If you choose Refresh Display, the documents displayed in the view are automatically refreshed every time the view index is refreshed; the refresh indicator does not display.

▶ If you choose Refresh Display From Top Row, the documents displayed in the view are automatically refreshed from the top row to the bottom row every time the view index is refreshed; the refresh indicator does not display.

▶ If you choose Refresh Display From Bottom Row, the documents displayed in the view are automatically refreshed from the bottom row to the top row every time the view index is refreshed; the refresh indicator does not display.

 Note

Refreshing the display automatically can affect performance because a large database that is being updated frequently executes a time-consuming refresh frequently. Users notice this process because the display pauses for a short time as it is refreshed. If you choose the manual refresh feature, refresh does not happen automatically, but a user can choose a convenient time to refresh.

The Style Tab

You use the Style tab to change the presentation style of the view and its aesthetic appearance (see Figure 14.8). Pull-down menus are available to change the colors of the background, column totals (if you choose to total numeric columns), rows that have not been read, and, if you want, a color for alternate rows.

Figure 14.8

The View Style tab.

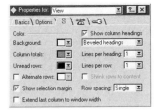

 Note

If you select the Alternate Rows checkbox, odd-numbered rows (1, 3, 5,...) are the color indicated in the Background field, and even-numbered rows (2, 4, 6,...) are the color specified as the alternate row color.

By selecting the Show Selection margin, you can ensure that the selection margin (the column that displays just to the left of the documents in a view) displays. This feature is turned on by default, but if you want, you can turn it off by deselecting this checkbox.

 Note

From a user's perspective, when the Show Selection Margin checkbox is deselected for a view, the selection margin is not present when looking at documents in that view. However, if a user desires to select multiple documents (to print, for example), he can Shift+click a document to make the selection margin appear. The margin remains visible after that until all of the documents are deselected (their check marks are removed), at which time the selection margin again disappears.

The Extend Last Column To Window Width checkbox enables you to ensure that the last column in the view is as large as possible by having Notes automatically extend it to the width of its window.

The Show Column Headings checkbox enables you to turn the headings on and off for the View columns. These headings normally show up at the top of each column and contain text that you specify to identify the contents of a column. If desired, you may turn off the column headings by deselecting this checkbox (it is selected by default). If column headings are selected to show, you also have a pull-down menu below the checkbox that enables you to indicate how you want the headings to appear. Beveled headings are slightly raised gray boxes with borders around them, and simple headings are a single white row.

The Lines Per Heading pull-down list enables you to choose how many lines deep a heading will be (anywhere from one to five lines). This option enables you to place a lot of text in a heading without necessarily making the column really wide. In so doing you sacrifice a bit of depth to ensure that you are not sacrificing too much view width.

The Lines Per Row pull-down list enables you to choose how many lines deep a row will be (anywhere from one to nine lines). This option enables you to display a lot of information in a column without having to sacrifice much of your view's width.

If you choose a value other than one from the Lines Per Row pull-down list, you are also able to select the Shrink Rows To Content checkbox. When selected, this checkbox ensures that if a row is set to display three lines, but only has two lines of information, it is reduced to two lines to conserve view depth.

 Tip

> If you specify Shrink Rows To Content, selecting Alternate Rows and choosing a color for alternate rows is good practice. Because the number of lines in a row is not constant, users may be confused as to where one document ends and another begins. By changing colors for alternating documents, you can reduce confusion.

The Row Spacing pull-down list enables you to specify the amount of white space placed between rows. The amount of whitespace increases as you switch from Single to Double.

The Advanced Tab

The Advanced tab enables you to configure advanced properties for index update frequency, index discard frequency, the display of unread markers, and adjusting of the forms with which documents display (see Figure 14.9).

Figure 14.9

The View Advanced tab.

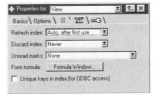

The first two pull-down lists on the Advanced tab present view indexes: Refresh Index and Discard Index. A *view index* is an internal list that Notes keeps, indicating which documents should be displayed in the view (this is not to be confused with a full-text index, which is a searching tool built from the contents of the documents in a view).

The Refresh Index pull-down list enables you to indicate how often the view index is to be rebuilt. The difference between the choices is one of speed versus accuracy. The following options are available:

▶ Auto, After First Use—If you choose this option, the index is not updated until the view's first use. The first time a view is used, it may take some time to display all the documents because the index is being built at that time.

▶ Automatic—If you choose this option, the view is rebuilt incrementally every time a change is made to a document being referenced in the view. This ensures that the view is always up-to-date, and because the view is updated whenever a change is made, there is no long initialization time the first time the view is opened.

▶ Manual—If you choose this option, the index is never refreshed unless manually asked for by the user (by clicking the refresh indicator or choosing View | Refresh). For databases that are large and updated frequently, this may be the best option because it avoids the constant and time-consuming update process every time a change is made to a document in the view. The view does not necessarily show all the documents and their current information, however, until the view index is updated.

▶ Auto, At Most Every—This option is a compromise between Automatic and Manual. It ensures that the view is updated on a regular basis and also ensures that it is not updated more frequently than you specify. This timing is indicated by entering a value into the Hours field, which appears to the left of the choice you've made. The hour value enables you to indicate that, if necessary, the index be refreshed at the interval specified, but never more than once during the interval. Therefore, when a change is made to a document displayed in a view, Notes checks to see whether an update has been made in the last x hours. If it has, the index is not updated; if it has not, the index is updated.

The Discard Index pull-down list enables you to control how often the view index is re-created. Changing this setting is primarily done to save space. The following options are available:

▶ Never—If you choose this option from this pull-down list, the index is always preserved and amended to account for any necessary changes. This ensures speed of view opening, but also takes up space on the Notes machine on which the view is kept.

▶ After Each Use—If you choose this option, the index is discarded after you close the view. This removes the index from the server and releases that disk space to be used elsewhere. Although this option is frugal with space, it is not so with time. A large database whose index is discarded after every use may take several minutes to open because it must re-create its index every time it is accessed.

Note

Regardless of the Discard Index option, the index is not actually immediately discarded. The removal of the index is done by a server task called UPDALL, which is scheduled (by default) to run at 2:00 a.m. every morning. If you close the view at 3:00 p.m., the index is not actually discarded until 2:00 a.m. the next morning.

▶ If Inactive For—If you choose this option, you are given a field in which to type a number of days. If a view has not been accessed for the number of days you specify, then the next time the UPDALL tasks runs on the server, the view index is removed (see the preceding note).

The Unread Marks pull-down list enables you to control whether stars appear in the selection margin next to documents that a particular user has not opened yet. The following options are available:

▶ None—If you select this option from the list, no unread markers are displayed. This choice makes for fast view display because the unread information does not need to be recalculated; however, it offers the least functionality because it does not enable a user to see at a glance which documents she has not read.

 Note

An unread list is maintained for every user. Therefore, if Mary opens a document, it does not affect the unread status of that document for Brad.

▶ Unread Documents Only—If you select this option, unread markers are placed next to each document in the view that has not yet been read by the current user. This is not quite like Standard (Compute In Hierarchy), which also displays unread markers next to collapsed sections in a view that contains unread documents in them. Standard unread display takes the longest time to open because the computation of where to place unread markers is the most complex;

however, it allows for the most functionality because a user cannot only see which documents he has not read, but also which collapsed categories he might be interested in investigating further due to their unread documents.

The Form Formula field enables you to control how documents listed in this view appear when opened. Normally, unless a form is stored with the document, when a document is opened, it displays using the form that was used to create it (this as indicated in the internal field, Form). If you want to have documents display differently when opened in one view rather than from another, a form formula can be created. This form formula must evaluate to the name of a form in the current database. If a form is not stored with a document, and then a form formula is specified, the documents are opened using the form to which the formula evaluates. Only if neither of the two conditions mentioned are present does the form open using the form name stored in the Form field. Form Formula fields are very powerful because they enable you to display part or all of a document based on certain conditions evaluated at the time the document is being opened.

The Security Tab

The Security tab contains a checkbox, and a list box that enables you to specify which users or groups are allowed to see documents using this view (see Figure 14.10). For a more complete description of view access lists, see Chapter 23.

Figure 14.10

The View Security tab.

After you specify the view properties, you must build the view by adding columns and defining what information should display in them.

View Columns

Each column in a view has certain properties and configurations that enable it to display specific information in a particular way. You must consider how many columns of information you want to display, what information should display in each, whether that data is from a field or from a formula calculation, and what the format of that information should be.

Each column has a header that distinguishes it from the other columns in the view. An existing column can be selected by clicking once on its header. You can edit an existing column's properties by double-clicking its column header. After a column has been selected, a new column could be inserted either before or after the last column. A selected column also can be deleted.

A new view column can either be inserted in front of a selected column or appended after the last column. To insert a column in front of an existing column, follow these steps:

1. Select the existing column by clicking its header once.

2. From the Create menu, choose Insert New Column.

To append a column after the last column, choose Append New Column from the Create menu.

After a column has been created, you can modify it using the Properties For Column dialog box. Column properties enable you to define how a column appears, its title, size, how it is sorted and categorized, and how different data types are formatted. These characteristics are modified in the Properties for Column dialog box (see Figure 14.11). In addition, the definition for what information displays in the column needs to be set. You can do this in the design pane at the bottom of the view design environment.

Figure 14.11

The Properties for Column dialog box enables you to define column properties.

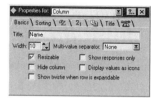

The Properties for Column dialog box is divided into seven tabs: Basics, Sorting, Font, Number, Date-time, Title, and Advanced. The following sections cover each of these tabs.

The Basics Tab

The Basics tab enables you to specify identification and basic column properties. If you want, you can put a title at the top of the column. You enter this title in the Title field on this page. You can place a maximum of 80 characters in this field; however, the title appears truncated if the width does not allow Notes to display the whole title.

The Width field enables you to set the default width for the column. This width, which defaults to 10, has a theoretical size of tens of thousands of characters; however, that is much more than you would ever use. This width determines how wide the column is, but a user can change the width if you allow the column to be resized.

Note

The width that you set is the width of the column every time you open the view. Although a user can change the width of a column, that width is always reset back to the original width when the view is closed and reopened.

The multivalue separator enables you to indicate how you want fields containing lists to be delimited (for more information on lists, see Chapter 18, "Advanced Formulas, Part I"). You can separate multiple values with a space, a comma, a semicolon, or a new line.

The Resizable checkbox enables you to indicate whether a user should be allowed to modify the size of the column while looking at it in the view. By default this checkbox is selected, but if you deselect it, the column is not resizable, and its header appears without a delimiting line to its right.

The Hide Column checkbox enables you to make this column hidden in the view. You can use it in computations and for sorting without displaying the information. You may want to show documents in a view sorted by the date they were created, for example, without the clutter of actually showing the date-created column. You could make this column hidden by selecting this checkbox.

The Show Twistie When Row Is Expandable checkbox can be used to turn the displaying of twisties on and off. With this checkbox selected, whenever a document with a value in this column has a child document, it displays a twistie to enable the users to expand or collapse the document to show its children. This can also be used to indicate when a category has documents under it.

Note

Using the Show Twistie When Row Is Expandable checkbox for all documents that may have a child document under them at any time is a good idea. The twistie shows up only if there are child documents. When they do, users are instantly able to see that these documents exist and are able to expand the parent to see them. It is only necessary to have a twistie for one column on a particular row, however, and that column is normally the one farthest to the left. If your view displays the fields Name, Address, and City, for example, and there are child documents for the documents displaying this information, you want to set this property only for the Name field, but not for the others.

The Show Responses Only checkbox enables you to create a column that appears and shows information only when the document for which its information displays is a response document. Frequently, the fields present on response documents are not the same as the fields present on main documents. Placing all the possible combinations of main document and response document fields in a view can mean a lot of wasted space because many of the columns only display values when there is a response document. To reduce the impact of displaying response documents, you can designate one of your columns as a Responses Only column. This column is normally placed just to the left of the column displaying the document information under which you want your response information to be indented.

 Tip

Responses Only columns display information the full width of your view starting from wherever you place the column. If you designate more than one column as being responses only, only the first column will show because it covers up all the Responses Only columns to the right. To overcome the limitation of having only one column dedicated to response information, create a formula that concatenates a number of response document fields together and displays the result of this formula in the Responses Only column.

The Display Values As Icons checkbox enables you to translate any numeric values appearing in this column into icons by using a table of icons. There are 170 icons available, so the number displayed in this column should be between 1 and 170 (any value outside that range does not display anything). Whatever number is displayed in this column is translated through the table to present an icon (see Figure 14.12).

 Tip

Icons are useful when you want to give pictorial information about the status of a document. You can use them to indicate acceptance or rejection of an item or to indicate the secrecy of a document. You can even use them to indicate if a document has an attachment (as in your Notes mail file).

Figure 14.12

The icon transla-tion table; a num-ber is translated into the corre-sponding icon here.

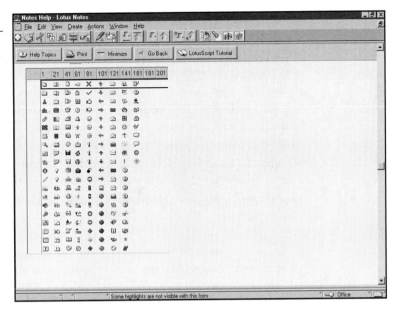

Figure 14.12

The icon transla-tion table; a num-ber is translated into the corre-sponding icon here.

The Sorting Tab

The Sorting tab enables you to define if and how a column is sort-ed, as well as if and how summary information is to be displayed (see Figure 14.13).

Figure 14.13

The View Column Sorting tab.

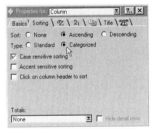

You can choose to sort any column. By selecting the Ascending or Descending radio button, you can sort in either direction.

You can choose to categorize a column. In conjunction with an ascending or descending sort, you can choose either standard or categorized sorting. Categorized sorting differs from standard sorting in that the values being categorized appear on a line by themselves and appear only once for the group of documents that have a common value. For example, if your view consists of the columns Company and Contact Name, and you want to sort by company, you can either sort it standard or categorized. If you sort it standard, you put pairings of companies and contacts on individual rows. If you categorize, however, you get a row that contains nothing but a company name, and underneath that row you get a list of all the contacts who have that company in common; the company name would not be repeated. If you then couple this categorization with the Show Twistie When Row Is Expandable checkbox, you can present each company name as an expandable category, the contacts of which a user can choose to view or not.

The Case Sensitive Sorting checkbox enables you to indicate whether two values that are identical in characters are to be sorted based on character case. If you select this checkbox, two column values that are the same except in case are sorted by lowercase first and then uppercase; otherwise, documents are presented in the order in which they were entered.

Note

Case-sensitive sorting does not mean that all of the documents with lowercase letters appear first, followed by all documents with uppercase letters. Instead, this has an effect only if the characters differ in their case (for example, dog appears before DOG, which appears before doug, which appears before Doug).

The Accent Sensitive Sorting checkbox enables you to indicate whether two values that are identical in characters are to be sorted based on accents on one or more of the characters. If you select this checkbox, then two column values that are the same except in accent are sorted based on the priority of their accents; otherwise, documents are presented in the order in which they were entered.

By selecting the Click On Column Header To Sort checkbox, you can allow users to dynamically change the way a view sorts (see Figure 14.14). In many instances it is valuable for users to be able to sort in a way that cannot be permanently part of a view. To allow this, a different view can be created for each need; however, that takes a lot of development time and may result in many views being present in a database, all of which are identical except for the way the columns sort. Another way to allow this is to give the users the ability to sort by a certain column by clicking the header of that column. By selecting this checkbox, a pull-down list appears that enables you to define sorting order as being enabled by clicking the column header. The choices available in the pull-down list are ascending, descending, both, and change to view.

Figure 14.14

The View Column Sorting tab with column header sort enabled.

If you choose either ascending or descending, the user is able to turn sorting on and off with successive clicks on the column heading. If you choose Both, the user is able to cycle through ascending, descending, and no sorting with successive clicks on the column heading. Evidence of dynamic sort enablement is in an up-arrow, a down-arrow, or both being present on the right side of the column header.

When you select the Click On Column Header To Sort checkbox, another the Secondary Sort Column checkbox appears. By selecting this checkbox, you have the option of choosing another column in the view that acts as a secondary sort column when you sort by the column whose header you clicked. You can also choose how that sorting is to happen (ascending or descending) by choosing from the pull-down list that appears.

If you choose Change To View from the Click On Column Header To Sort pull-down list, you are presented with another pull-down list that enables you to choose a view in the current database (see

Figure 14.15). This selection enables you to let the user move to another view through a click on the column header. An option like this is handy when users are frequently moving from one view to another, and you want to easily allow that movement. Evidence of being able to move to another view through a click on a column header is a small round arrow on the right side of the column header.

Under the Totals label is a pull-down list that enables you to allow simple statistical reporting for the documents in a view. If you choose one of the options here, you are also able to select the Hide Detail Rows checkbox, which suppresses the display for that column and displays only the statistics.

Note

When this chapter mentions *documents*, it is referring to the technical definition (that is, these statistics are not available for responses or responses to responses).

The Total choice results in a subtotal for each category (if categories exist in the view) and a grand total for the numeric column in which you enable this feature. The Average Per Document choice calculates an average for each category based on the sum of the values in the category divided by the total number of documents, and calculates a final average at the end of the view based on the sum of all the values in the column divided by the total number of documents in the column.

The Average Per Sub-category choice calculates an average for each category based on the sum of the values in the category divided by the total number of documents and calculates a final average at the end of the view based on the sum of all the values in the column divided by the total number of categories in the view.

The Percent Of Parent Category choice calculates a total for each category, and then expresses that total as a percentage of the total for all the documents in the column. It then displays 100 percent as the column total.

The Percent Of All Documents choice is supposed to calculate a total for each category, and then expresses that total as a percentage of the total for all the documents in the column, as well as calculating and displaying each document value as a percentage of the total value for the category in which it is found. However, the actual result is always the same as the Percent Of Parent Category.

The Font Tab

The Font tab enables you to change the display characteristics for the text appearing in a column (see Figure 14.16). Changing the display for one or more columns to set them apart from the rest of the data in the view is very handy. Perhaps this is a category that you want to emphasize or a numeric column with totals. This tab enables you to set the font face, point size, text style, text color, and column justification. If you click the Apply To All button, all the text for all the columns is set to the font characteristics displayed here.

Figure 14.16

The View Column Font tab.

The Numbers Tab

The Numbers tab enables you to adjust how the numbers in a column display (these settings have no effect on non-numeric column values) (see Figure 14.17). You can set the number type (general, fixed, scientific, or currency), the number of decimal places (for all but general numbers), whether you want the number displayed as a percentage, how negative numbers are to display (with or without parentheses), and whether numbers should have comma punctuation at thousands.

Figure 14.17

The View Column Numbers tab.

The Date-Time Tab

The Date-Time tab enables you to adjust how the dates and times in a column display (these settings have no effect on non-date-time column values) (see Figure 14.18). You can set what date-time information should be displayed, how dates should display, how times should display, and when, if ever, time zones should display.

Figure 14.18

The View Column Date-Time tab.

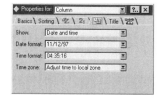

The Title Tab

The Title tab enables you to change the display characteristics for the text appearing in the title of a column (see Figure 14.19). You may choose to accentuate one or more columns by changing their heading font characteristics, or you may want to change all the headings from the default font. This tab enables you to set the font face, point size, text style, text color, and column title justification. If you click the Apply To All button, all the text for all the column titles is set to the font characteristics displayed here.

The Advanced Tab

The Advanced tab enables you to set how access can be granted to values in this column through the use of LotusScript (see Figure 14.20). As the warning on the tab indicates, it is unwise to change the value displayed here because Script formulas may already have this name coded into them.

Figure 14.19

The View Column Title tab.

Now that you have seen how to define the properties for a column, you need to consider defining its contents (that is, what information to display in the column.

Figure 14.20

The View Column Advanced tab.

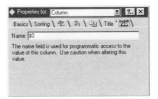

Defining Column Contents

You define column content in the design pane of the view design environment. This design pane is at the bottom of the screen. The design pane consists of three parts, the first of which is the Define pull-down list that enables you to define an element of the view. The second is the Display options, which let you choose what kind of value displays (simple function, field, or formula). Finally, the large white area is the place where you choose a function or field or define a formula for the column value.

The Define pull-down list enables you to choose the element that you are going to define. These elements consist of the view selection formula (View Selection), which defines the way in which documents are chosen or rejected for inclusion in this view, the names of the columns (*column name* (column)), and actions (*actionName* (action)) (see Figure 14.21).

Figure 14.21

The Define pull-down list enables you to choose which part of the view you are modifying.

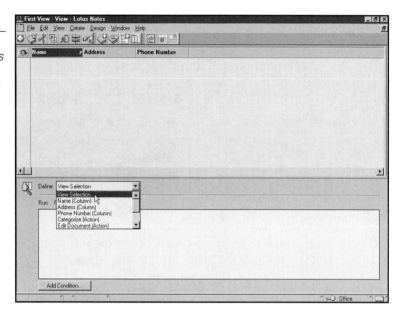

When you open a view to edit the design, the View Selection always appears. If you want to define a column, you can either click its header, or you can choose its name from the Define list.

Once you have chosen a column to define, you must then choose between three display types: simple function, field, or formula.

Simple Function Display

Simple functions are internal Notes processes that obtain values from internal variables or computations (see Figure 14.22). Some notable examples are summarized in Table 14.1. A simple function can be assigned to a column as follows:

1. Select the column you want to assign the value to by clicking its title once.

2. In the design pane, choose Simple function. If a message appears telling you that you will lose whatever display method was formerly present in the column, click the Yes button.

3. Choose the simple function you want from the list presented.

Figure 14.22

Choose a simple function from the list presented.

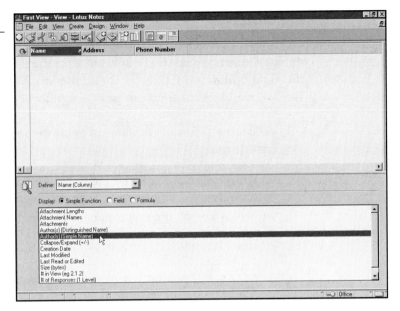

Table 14.1

Some simple functions.

Function Name	Value Displayed
Attachments	The number 1 if there are attachments on this document, and the number 0 if there are not.
Author(s) (Distinguished Name)	The fully distinguished names of all the people who are listed in any fields of type Authors in this document.
Author(s) (Simple Name)	The common names of all the people who are listed in any fields of type Authors in this document.
Creation Date	The date this document was created.
Last Modified	The date this document was last modified.
# of Responses (1 Level)	The number of direct responses to this document that are present.
# of Responses (All Level)	The total number of responses to this document that are present at any level.

Field Display

Field displays are displayed values that are obtained from fields in database documents. The field list that appears when you select the Field option is the total list for all the forms in this database (see Figure 14.23). A field can be assigned to a column as follows:

1. Select the column you want to assign the value to by clicking its title once.

2. In the design pane, choose Field. If a message appears telling you that you will lose whatever display method was formerly present in the column, click the Yes button.

3. Choose the field you want to display from the list presented.

Figure 14.23

Choose a field from the list presented.

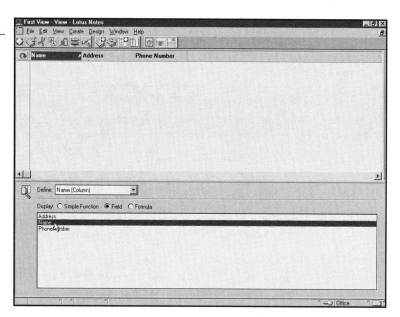

Formula Display

In some cases there is not a simple function or a field that displays the value you want to see in a particular column. In this case, you may have to create a formula that results in the value you want to display. For example, in a Response Only column, you may want to display a set of concatenated text values. This can be done by creating a formula that performs the concatenation and returns the value to the column. For example, in the following formula,

```
TextValue1 + TextValue2 + TextValue3
```

the text values may be field names or text strings in quotation marks (for more information on formulas in Notes, see Chapters 13, 18, and 19).

If you are creating a formula and need a list of available functions or fields, you can display a list of either and then copy and paste the correct text. This list can be displayed by clicking the Fields & Functions button, and then choosing either category from the options presented (see Figure 14.24). When you locate the field or function you want, you can then select it and click the Paste button to have the text pasted into your formula.

Figure 14.24

The Fields and Functions dialog box is useful for finding field and function names.

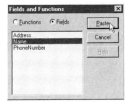

Note   Some functions cannot be used in view columns because of limitations on their functionality. For example, you cannot use functions that require user input (like @Prompt) because that is not possible in the context of a view. For more information, see the appropriate documentation for the function you are using.

Defining View Selection Formulas

A view selection formula defines what documents are present in your view. In the absence of a selection formula, Notes displays all the documents in your database without discrimination. That is not always the desired result, however, as many times you may want one or more views that display only a subset of the total documents. For example, you have a customer database that includes customers from a variety of locations. You want to be able to view only the customers from a certain city (Kalamazoo, for example). In that case, you would create a selection formula that enables only documents that contained the word Kalamazoo in the City field to be displayed.

 Tip

For a response document to display in a view that has the property Show Responses in a hierarchy set, its parent must also display. Therefore, in such a view, if you create a selection formula that chooses only response documents, no documents are displayed in the view. Instead, create a selection formula that selects parent documents and include the display of their children by using the function `@AllChildren` or `@AllDescendants`, such as the following:

```
SELECT City = "Kalamazoo" ¦ @AllChildren
```

To define a view selection formula, you must first choose View Selection in the Define list in the design pane of the view design environment (see Figure 14.25). Having selected that option, you are then presented with two Run choices: Easy and Formula.

Figure 14.25

Defining the View Selection Formula.

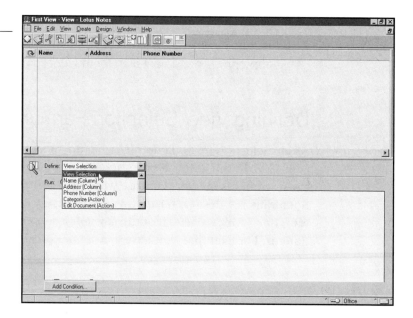

Easy Run Conditions

The Easy option enables you to choose one or more conditions from a Search Builder dialog box. The Search Builder can be invoked by clicking the Add Condition button at the bottom of the design pane (see Figure 14.26).

Figure 14.26

The Search Builder dialog box.

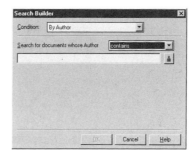

The Search Builder enables you to choose a condition type from the pull-down list, and then define the specification for the conditions. The conditions are By Author, By Date, By Field, By Form, and By Form Used. The options are described as follows:

▶ If you select the By Author condition, you are able to choose if the author is or is not one or more people, as defined by the list you type or by the people you select from the address book you choose.

▶ If you select the By Date condition, you are able to choose either to search By Date Created or By Date Modified. Then you can choose from a number of operators to determine what the relationship between the date you enter and either the modified or created date (see Figure 14.27). For example, you create a condition in which you ask for those documents whose modified date is before a certain date, or after a certain date, or more than some specified number of days ago.

▶ If you select the By Field condition, you are able to choose the field that you want to compare against, choose an operator to do the comparison, and finally enter a value to compare (see Figure 14.28). The operators change depending on the data type of the field (for example, numeric fields give you operators for greater than, less than, and equal to, whereas text fields give you only contains or does not contain).

Figure 14.27

The Search Builder, By Date.

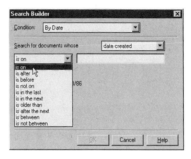

Figure 14.28

The Search Builder, By Field.

▶ If you select the By Form condition, you are able to choose a form from the database (see Figure 14.29). Then by filling values into the sample form, you can create a condition where a document must match all the values for the fields into which you entered values to be included in the view.

Figure 14.29

The Search Builder, By Form.

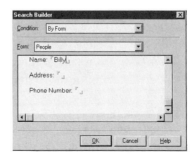

▶ If you select the By Form Used condition, you can choose one or more forms from the database by selecting from the form list presented, and documents are selected only if they were created using one of the forms selected (see Figure 14.30). This comparison is made against the form in each document.

Figure 14.30

The Search Builder, By Form Used.

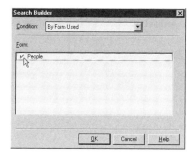

After you define the search condition, click the OK button in the Search Builder dialog box. Multiple conditions can be defined by clicking the Add Condition button to invoke the dialog box over and over. Each of these conditions are separated by the keyword AND, which indicates that for any document to be listed in the view, it must conform to all of the conditions in all the searches you built. If you want, you can click into the text area in the design pane and change the ANDs to ORs to include any document that fulfills any of the conditions.

After a condition is defined, you can modify it by double-clicking its gray definition area. You can also delete conditions by clicking its definition once, and then pressing the Delete key.

Formula Run Conditions

If an easy condition is not flexible enough to perform the kind of selection that you require, you must write a selection formula instead. Selection formulas may be simple or complex. Whatever their structure, they must end with a main expression beginning with the keyword SELECT. For example, if you want to create a formula that selects all the documents whose color field contains the value `"Red"` and whose Manager field contains the name `"Bud"` in it, and you also want all the response documents for those documents, you create a selection formula like this:

```
SELECT (Color = "Red" & Manager = "Bud") ¦ @AllChildren
```

In that formula, the first check is for documents that contain the correct color and manager. After those documents are found, then all of the children associated with them are also selected.

> **Note** If you create a view selection using a simple function and then click the Formula Run option, you see how it looks in the formula language.

Views are only one type of structured document display available to you. The other type is folders, a view with a user-selectable set of documents in it.

Understanding the Creation of Folders

The planning, types, and definition of folders are virtually identical to that of views. What sets a folder apart from a view is the set of documents contained in it. With views, the set of documents displayed is dependent on a selection condition, which by default is all documents. A user cannot add documents to a view nor remove documents from a view except by adding and removing documents from the database. With folders, the set of documents is empty by default, and documents can be placed into a folder only by manually dragging them in.

> **Note** Views and folders are simply different ways of seeing documents: They are not different copies of the documents. Selecting and deleting a document from a view or from a folder has the same effect: It removes the document from the database. This phenomenon tends to confuse many users who drag documents into a folder, and then are surprised when they

delete the document from the folder, and it is gone from the database. You can prevent this effect by instructing users to select the document in the folder, and then select Actions | Remove from Folder instead of selecting it and pressing the Delete key.

When deciding whether a view or a folder is appropriate in a certain circumstance, the question to ask is, "Can I determine through a formula or simple function which documents should display in this list?" If the answer is yes, create a view; if the answer is no, create a folder. If you have a customer database and want to display all the customers from Toronto, for example, the answer to the question is yes, as long as the City field contains the value Toronto, then the document should display. If you want a listing of all of the customers you want to call tomorrow, however, you need to create a folder because the selection is based on a number of factors, including your gut feelings which, of course, cannot be defined in a formula. As a result, what you need is a folder to which you can drag all those customers whom you want to call tomorrow.

Creating a Folder

Like views, folders can be shared, private, and shared-personal on first use. Shared folders contain information that whomever is interacting with the folder has placed into it, and the results are seen by everyone. Folders have design and properties just like views, and the specifications are identical (with the exception of the Security tab, which includes specification for who is allowed to modify the contents in addition to who may use the folder). In fact, the only thing that folders do not have that views have are selection criteria, since folders have contents selected by the users, not by a formula. To create a folder, follow these steps:

1. Open the database by double-clicking its icon on your workspace.

2. From the Create menu, choose Folder, and the Create Folder dialog box appears (see Figure 14.31).

Figure 14.31

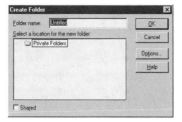

The Create Folder dialog box enables you to set the initial parameters for the folder.

3. Type a name in the Folder Name field. This name is what the users see in the navigation pane for the database; it should describe the function of the folder.

4. Choose a folder type by selecting the Shared checkbox if you want the folder to be shared, or leave it unchecked if you want the folder to be private.

Note ▶ If you select the Shared checkbox, another checkbox appears so that you can select whether you want the folder to be shared-personal on first use (see Figure 14.32).

Figure 14.32

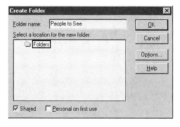

The Create Folder dialog box for a shared folder.

5. In the Select A Location For The New Folder box, click the place where you want the folder to appear in the list of folders. If your folder is shared, you see a list of yellow shared folders to choose, and if your folder is private, you see a list of gray folders. By selecting either the Private Folders folder (from personal folders) or the Folders folder (for shared folders), you ensure that your new folder is displayed in the first column of the folder list. If you choose any of the

existing folder names, your new folder appears as a subfolder under the folder you choose, and a twistie appears next to its parent to indicate that folder expand to show its subfolders.

6. If you want this folder to be created looking the same as a folder or a view that already exists (that is, you want to pattern the columns and feel of the folder after another folder or view), you can click the Options button and choose a folder or view to inherit the design from in the Options dialog box and click the OK button (see Figure 14.33).

Figure 14.33

The Options dialog box enables you to define design inheritance.

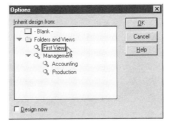

7. If you want to move straight from the creation of the folder to designing the folder, select the Design Now checkbox in the Options dialog box and click the OK button.

8. Click the OK button to complete the folder creation and initial design.

All the parameters and values set in the preceding procedure can be changed after the folder has been created except the folder type (shared, private, or shared-personal on first use) and the folder or view to inherit from.

Entering the Folder Design Environment

Now that the folder has been created, you may want to modify its design. If you selected the Design Now checkbox in the preceding procedure, the folder design environment appears, enabling you to modify the design.

To enter the folder design environment from the navigation pane, follow these steps:

1. Expand the design section by clicking its twistie.

2. Select the Folder view to display a list of folders on the right side.

3. Double-click the folder you want to edit in the folder list.

Now that you have seen the theory of creating views and folders, you can do the exercises to put some of that theory into practice.

Exercises

As an enhancement to the Customers database you have been working with, in this lab you add some views to allow the users to see the documents in a number of different ways. You create an All Customers view to show customer and preference information, and then you add a By Country view to display customer information categorized by country. The database you use for this lab is available on your CD-ROM and should be copied to your default Notes data directory. The lab file is called cust14.nsf, and its title is Chapter 14 Customers. Be sure that when you copy the file, you remove the read-only attribute, or you will not be able to modify the database.

Exercise 14.1

1. Select File | Database | Open and select the database called Chapter 14 Customers from the pull-down list of local databases. Click the Open button to add the database to your workspace and open the Standard view.

2. If the design category is not expanded, click the twistie to the left of it to expand, and then click the Views view to show the views on the right.

3. From the Create menu, choose View to display the Create View dialog box (see Figure 14.34).

Figure 14.34

The Create View dialog box for the All Customers view.

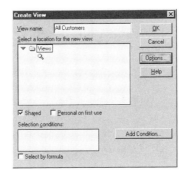

4. In the View name field, type All Customers.

continues

Exercise 14.1   Continued

---

5. Select the Shared checkbox and click the View folder to indicate that this view is to be in the first hierarchical level of views.

6. Click the Options button and then click the Blank choice in the Inherit design from box. Click the OK button to return to the Create View dialog box.

7. Click OK to return to the navigation pane.

8. In the list of views on the right, double-click the All Customers view to edit its design.

9. There is one column pre-defined in this view, and its title contains a number sign (#). Double-click this column header to edit its properties (see Figure 14.35).

Figure 14.35

Edit the properties for the first column.

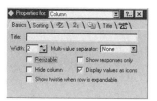

10. Delete any characters from the Title field, set the width field to 2, select the Display Values as Icons checkbox, and deselect the checkbox labeled Resizable checkbox. Click the Close Window button to close the column properties.

11. In the design pane, click the Display option called Formula (see Figure 14.36), remove the contents of the formula window, and type the following:

```
@If(Premium = "Yes"; 158;0)
```

This creates a column that displays a handshake symbol for all premium customers.

12. Click the header of the column you just created, and from the Create menu, choose Append New Column and double-click on the column heading that appears.

Figure 14.36

Enter the formula to compute the icon number to display.

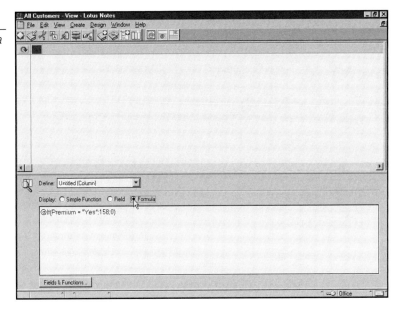

13. Reduce the width of the column to 1, deselect the Resizable checkbox, and select the Show Responses Only checkbox (see Figure 14.37). Click the Close Window button to close the column properties.

Figure 14.37

Edit the properties for the second column.

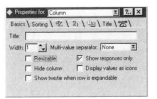

14. In the design pane, click the Display option called Formula, remove the contents of the formula window, and type the following:

```
"Prefers: " + PreferredCoffee + "in quantities of " + @Text
➥(PreferredQty) + " lbs. -- by"+@Name([CN];Author)
```

This displays the customer's preferred coffee and how much he usually orders. Because this information comes only from

continues

Exercise 14.1 Continued

response documents, the Show Responses Only checkbox is selected.

15. Click the header of the column you just created, and from the Create menu, choose Append New Column and double-click on the column heading that appears (see Figure 14.38).

Figure 14.38

Edit the properties for the Customer column.

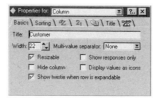

16. In the title field, type Customer and set the width to 22.

17. Ensure the Resizable checkbox is selected and select the Show Twistie When Row Is Expandable checkbox. Click the Close button to close the column properties.

18. In the design pane, click the Display option called Field, and click the Yes button when the Warning dialog box appears.

19. From the field list that appears in the formula window, select Customer.

20. In the middle of the view builder pane, click with your right mouse button and choose View properties from the menu that appears.

21. Click the Options tab and select the Default When Database Is First Opened checkbox (see Figure 14.39).

Figure 14.39

Edit the View properties.

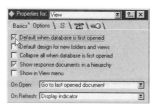

22. Click the Style tab (the one with the *S* on it) and choose a light color from the Background pull-down list.

23. Click the Close Window button and then save and close the view to return to the navigation pane.

24. Click the All Customers view at the top of the view list (on the left side) to view the results of your work (see Figure 14.40).

Figure 14.40

The final result: the All Customers view.

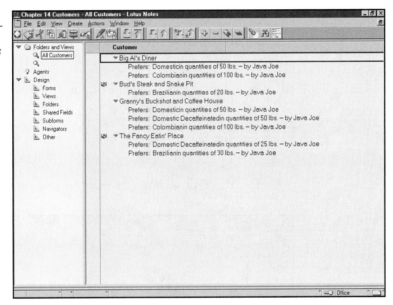

Exercise 14.2

1. Click the Views view to show the views on the right.

2. From the Create menu, choose View to display the Create View dialog box.

3. In the View name field, type By Country.

4. Select the Shared checkbox and click the View folder to indicate that this view is to be in the first hierarchical level of views.

continues

Exercise 14.2 Continued

5. Click the Options button and then click the Blank in the Inherit design from box. Click the OK button to return to the Create View dialog box.

6. Click OK to return to the navigation pane.

7. In the list of views on the right, double-click the By Country view to edit its design.

8. There is one column predefined in this view, and its title contains a number sign (#). Double-click this column header to edit its properties.

9. Remove all the characters from the Title field and set the width to 1.

10. Select the Show Twistie When Row Is Expandable checkbox.

11. Click the Sorting tab, select the Sort option Ascending, and select the Type option Categorized (see Figure 14.41).

Figure 14.41

Edit the properties for the Country column.

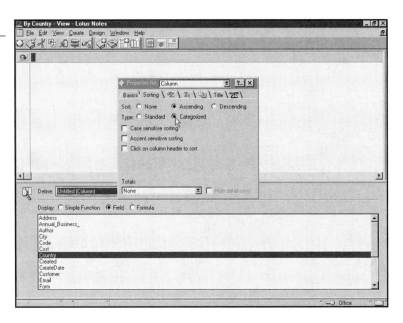

12. Click the Font tab, select 12 from the Size column, Bold from the Style column, and dark blue from the Text color pull-down menu. Click Close Window to close the dialog box.

13. In the design pane, click the Display option called Field and click Yes when the Warning dialog box appears.

14. From the field list that appears in the Formula window, select Country.

15. Click the header of the column you just created, and from the Create menu, choose Append New Column, and double-click the column heading that appears.

16. In the title field, type Customer and set the width to 22.

17. Click the Sorting tab, select the Click On Column Header To Sort checkbox, and leave the default value of Ascending in the Sort Direction box to its right (see Figure 14.42). Click the Close Window button to close the dialog box.

Figure 14.42

Edit the properties for the Customer column.

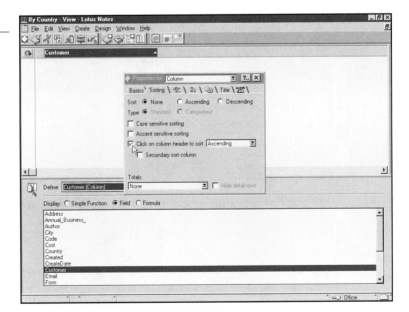

continues

18. In the design pane, click the Display option called Field and click the Yes button when the Warning dialog box appears.

19. From the field list that appears in the Formula window, select Customer.

20. Click the header of the column you just created, and from the Create menu, choose Append New Column, and double-click on the column heading that appears.

21. In the title field, type Address and set the width to 13. Click the Close Window button to close the dialog box.

22. In the design pane, click the Display option called Field and click the Yes button when the Warning dialog box appears.

23. From the field list that appears in the Formula window, select Address.

24. Click the header of the column you just created, and from the Create menu, choose Append New Column, and double-click on the column heading that appears.

25. In the title field, type Location. Click the Close Window button to close the dialog box.

26. In the design pane, click the Display option called Formula, remove the current contents in the Formula window, and type the following:

```
City + ", " + Region
```

27. In the middle of the view builder pane, click with your right mouse button and choose View Properties from the menu that appears.

28. Click the Style tab (the one with the *S* on it) and choose a light color from the Background pull-down list.

29. Click the Close Window button.

30. In the design pane, choose View Selection from the Define pull-down list and choose Formula from the Run options.

31. In the Formula window replace the contents with the following:

    ```
    SELECT Form = "Customer"
    ```

32. Save and close the view to return to the navigation pane.

33. In the views list on the right side, click the (*Untitled*) view to select it, and press the Delete key (confirming that you want to delete this now redundant view).

34. Click the By Country view at the top of the view list (on the left side) to view the results of your work (see Figure 14.43).

Figure 14.43

The final result: the By Country view.

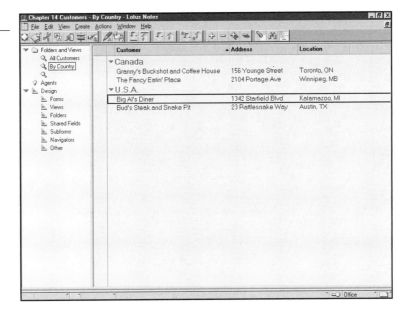

Exercise 14.3

It has been suggested that you need separate views for each of the countries in which you have customers. The challenge is this: Using the above exercises as general procedural guidelines to create two new views: one to display U.S. customers, and another to display Canadian customers. These views are to look exactly like the By Country view with the exception that the Country column

continues

(which is redundant here) should not be present. The first view should be called By Country\Canada and the second should be called By Country\U.S.A. This ensures that both cascade under the By Country view that you just created. Use selection formulas that select by a value in the Country field for each view instead of selecting by form, which the By Country view does.

The answers to this challenging exercise are found in the view category called ChallengeAnswer.

Review Questions

1. Walter wants to create a view that everyone using his database can see and use. Which view type should he create?

    a. Private

    b. Personal

    c. Shared

    d. Shared-personal on first use

2. Alphonse has created a private view. Where will he find the view property to change this view to a shared view?

    a. There is no such property.

    b. In the View properties.

    c. In the Database properties.

    d. In the properties for the first view column.

3. Edwina wants to restrict the documents displayed in her view to show only those that she created. Which view property will enable her to do this?

    a. There is no such property.

    b. The view selection formula.

    c. The view display formula.

    d. The view subset formula.

4. Clive creates a view and gives it the name Managers\People. What displays when he looks in the Create menu?

    a. The word People with a black arrow pointing to the left.

    b. The word Managers with a black arrow pointing down.

    c. The phrase "Managers, People."

    d. The word Managers with a black arrow pointing to the right.

5. Which property will William set for his view to ensure that he is informed when new documents are present in the view, but he has the choice of when to display them?

    a. Display indicator

    b. Refresh display from top row

    c. Refresh display from bottom row

    d. Refresh display

6. Samantha creates a view and sets the background color to blue and the alternate row color to yellow. What is the effect when she looks at the view?

    a. Column colors alternate between blue and yellow.

    b. Row colors alternate between blue and yellow.

    c. Column and row colors alternate between blue and yellow.

    d. This is not a release 4 feature.

7. What is the effect of discarding the view index?

   a. You won't be able to see any documents in the view.

   b. If the database is large, it may take several minutes to open the view again.

   c. There is no significant effect.

   d. None; the index cannot be discarded.

8. In what major way does a folder differ from a view?

   a. Folders can't be shared.

   b. Folders don't have columns.

   c. Folders don't have selection formulas.

   d. Folders are not yellow.

9. Nancy has created a view with two columns having the Show Responses Only property set. However, only one of these columns is displayed. What has she done wrong?

   a. She should change the color of the second column to highlight it.

   b. She should alternate between response columns and regular columns.

   c. She cannot display more than one response column due to view design considerations.

   d. She should sort by the first response column.

10. Martin wants to display an icon in the first column of his view. What does he need to do to ensure that this happens?

   a. He should ensure that his column has the Show Values As Icons property set.

   b. He should ensure that he has a column formula that uses the @Icon function to display the icon.

    c. He should ensure that he has a column formula that produces a desired icon number and that his column has the Show Values As Icons property set.

    d. He should ensure that he has a column formula that uses the `@Icon` function to display the icon and that his column has the Show Values As Icons property set.

11. Helen wants to display a subset of documents along with all their responses and response to responses. Which of the following would work?

    a. `SELECT DocumentCriteria & @AllChildren`

    b. `SELECT DocumentCriteria ¦ @AllChildren`

    c. `SELECT DocumentCriteria & @AllDescendants`

    d. `SELECT DocumentCriteria ¦ @AllDescendants`

12. Which feature is available to create selection criteria without the use of formulas?

    a. The Selection wizard

    b. The Search Builder

    c. The full-text indexer

    d. The viewer manager

13. Edgar needs to create a way for the users of his database to collect random documents and put them into a list. Which feature is available to provide this functionality?

    a. Subforms

    b. Views

    c. Directories

    d. Folders

14. Andrew wants to ensure that users always know when a document has responses. Which column property should he set?

    a. Show responses only

    b. Hide column

    c. Show twistie when row is expandable

    d. Categorize by a response field

Review Answers

1. C. Only the shared view enables all users to use it. Shared-personal on first use does not actually enable its users to use the view, only to create a personal copy of it. For more information, please refer to the section titled "Understanding View Types" and its subsections.

2. A. Once a view has been created as a certain type, it cannot be changed. There is no property to affect the change that Alphonse wants. Instead he must create a new view using his original as the design basis. For more information, please refer to the section titled "Understanding View Types."

3. B. View selection formulas enable you to specify that you want to see either some or all of the documents in a database in a specific view. For more information, please refer to the sections titled "Understanding the Creation of Views" and "Defining View Selection Formulas."

4. D. What Clive has created is a cascading menu. The text before the first backslash is displayed in the Create menu, while the text following becomes a submenu indicated with a black arrow pointing to the right. For more information, please refer to the section titled "The Basics Tab."

5. A. All of the Refresh display choices listed automatically refresh the view without William having any control. However, the Display indicator tells him and enables him to refresh at his convenience. For more information, please refer to the section titled "The Options Tab."

6. B. The colors she specified alternate from document to document and from row to row. For more information, please refer to the section titled "The Style Tab."

7. B. Discarding the view index is sometimes done to conserve space on the hard drive of the server. However, this index needs to be rebuilt the next time the view is opened. In the case of a large database, this may take several minutes. For more information, please refer to the section titled "The Advanced Tab."

8. C. Because folders contain documents placed there by users, they do not have selection formulas. For more information, please refer to the section titled "Understanding the Creation of Folders."

9. C. Due to constraints in view design, Nancy may display only one response column. The second and following will be overwritten by the first, and therefore will not be displayed. For more information, please refer to the section titled "The Basics Tab."

10. C. He needs to ensure that he created a column formula that generates a numeric value corresponding to the icon he wants to display and that his column has the Show Values As Icons parameter set. For more information, please refer to the section titled "The Basics Tab."

11. D. In addition to her document criteria (which will select all the main documents), she must also include OR (|) @AllDescendants. This ensures that the responses and response to responses of the selected documents also are displayed in her view. For more information, please refer to the section titled "Defining View Selection Formulas."

12. B. The Search Builder enables you to specify selection criteria that Notes interprets. You do not need to create a formula; in effect, Notes creates it for you. For more information, please refer to the section titled "Easy Run Conditions."

13. D. Views allow for the selection of documents based on a formula. Only folders enable users to pick documents at

random. For more information, please refer to the section titled "Understanding the Creation of Folders."

14. C. By using twisties, Andrew can be certain that his users know when responses exist. Otherwise, if document categories are collapsed, they may not be aware that unseen responses exist. For more information, please refer to the section titled "The Basics Tab."

Answers to Test Yourself Questions at Beginning of Chapter

1. The purpose of Show Responses Only is to create a column solely for the purposes of displaying response document information. Because this information is not always present and frequently not seen with the same importance as document information, it is important to keep it from cluttering your views. This can be done by displaying it outside of the context of the document fields in a Show Responses Only column. For more information, refer to the section titled "The Basics Tab."

2. The view selection formula enables you to specify that a view should display only a subset of the total documents in a view. This enables you to create special purpose views that only display certain documents. For more information, please refer to the sections titled "Creating a View" and "Defining View Selection Formulas."

3. The three view types are shared, private, and shared-personal on first use. Shared views can be seen and used by the user community at large and are stored with the design of the database. Private views can be used only by the person who created them and are stored on the user's workstation. Shared-personal on first use enables a designer to create view templates which, on first use, become Private views, which are stored on a user's workstation. For more information, refer to the section titled "Understanding View Types."

4. The three ways of defining view column contents are function, field, and formula. Simple functions are built into Notes and provide common view data features. Fields display field information. Formulas display information based on the result of the formula you create. For more information, refer to the section titled "Defining Column Contents."

5. A folder differs from a view primarily in that a folder contains information that users select at random from a document list, whereas a view contains documents selected through the use of a selection formula. Folders do not have selection formulas. For more information, refer to the section titled "Understanding the Creation of Folders."

15

Creating Actions and Hotspots

This chapter will introduce you to the following objectives:

 Objectives

- ▶ Introducing actions and hotspots
- ▶ @Commands
- ▶ Execution events
- ▶ Creating form and view actions
- ▶ Creating hotspots

Test Yourself! Before reading this chapter, test yourself to determine how much study time you will need to devote to this section.

1. What are the three types of execution events for actions and hotspots?

2. What is the difference between an action and a hotspot?

3. What is the primary function of the @Command?

4. What are the two types of actions?

5. What are the two types of hotspots that execute functions?

Answers are located at the end of the chapter...

Essential to creating good databases is the ability to automate and simplify certain tasks. One of the ways to do this is to provide users with buttons that are well-labeled and obvious. These buttons should execute commands and formulas that would take more effort and database understanding than most users want to apply. These buttons are called *actions* and *hotspots*.

Introducing Actions and Hotspots

 Objective

Increasing user friendliness is one of the objectives of application development. Giving a user the ability to click a button to get a job done or to invoke a command that normally would take a menu option (which he or she might not even be able to find) increases the usability of your databases. Actions and hotspots provide this kind of usability.

Actions are form and view buttons that are located in a line just below the smart icon set and just above the form or view itself. This line, which is only visible when an action is present, is called the *action bar*.

Hotspots are areas on a form or navigator that a user can click to invoke a command or formula. The hotspots that you encounter in this chapter are buttons. To fully understand what an action or a hotspot can do, you must first learn some of the things that can run when initiated by a click action. The click results can be initiated by one of three categories of commands: simple actions, formulas, and Lotus Script. Because script is beyond the scope of the AD1 and AD2 exams, it is not discussed here.

Understanding Execution Events

The click of an action button or hotspot can invoke the execution of three different kinds of events: simple actions, formulas, and Lotus Script. Simple actions are predefined commands that are supplied by Notes whose execution you invoke by asking that a certain action be performed. Formulas support any of the Notes functions and formula commands, and, as you will see in this chapter, formulas are frequently used to execute @Command functions. Lotus Script is a high-level language based on the Basic language that performs powerful commands that you create in a structured programming environment. Neither the AD1 nor AD2 exams cover any Lotus Script topics.

Using Simple Actions

Simple actions are predefined in Lotus Notes and may be added with a click on the Add Action button. The following are the simple actions that are available in actions and hotspots (this list is also discussed in the context of agents in Chapter 21, "Creating Agents"):

▶ Copy to Database will copy the selected documents to a database that you choose.

▶ Copy to Folder will copy the selected documents to a folder in the current database.

▶ Delete from Database will delete the selected documents from the current database.

▶ Mark Document Read/Unread will add or remove unread markers from the selected documents.

▶ Modify fields will modify the fields you choose by either replacing or appending to the existing value the field that you type.

▶ Modify Fields by Form allows you to use the graphical design of the form you choose to decide which fields should be changed and what their new values will be.

▶ Move to/Remove from Folder allows you to add or remove selected documents to or from the folder you specify.

▶ Reply to Sender allows you to create a reply to a mailed-in document, which is automatically sent. This reply can include the body text of your choice and can also include the full text of the document to which you are replying.

▶ Run Agent allows you to trigger the execution of an agent.

> ► Send Mail Message allows you to compose and send a mail message to specified recipients, with the subject of your choice and any body information you care to include. In addition, this mail message can also contain the full text of the selected document or a document link to that document.
>
> ► Send Newsletter Summary allows for the creation of a mailed newsletter that contains summaries of the selected documents. This summary can be mailed to any recipients and can contain any subject or body. In addition, the newsletter can summarize the documents using information from any view in the database.
>
> ► @ Function Formula allows you to execute a Lotus Notes @ Function that might create a new document, update selected documents, or select other documents.

 Tip   You can add any number of simple actions to an agent. These actions are executed in the order they are listed. You can delete an action as you delete standard text (selecting and deleting) and modify an action by double-clicking the action and modifying the action criteria. Simple actions may not be combined with functions or Lotus Script.

Using @Commands

Although most formula constructions can be executed from an action or hotspot, you will frequently want to execute functions such as those provided from Notes menus. These functions can be executed through the use of a special class of functions called @Commands. Although all @Commands require parameters, they are unique in that all @Commands require a first parameter that defines which function is being executed. The syntax of a typical @Command is as follows:

```
@Command([NameofCommand];par2;par3;par4;. . .)
```

Each @Command can be identified through the use of its command name, and that name is always provided as the first parameter, enclosed in square brackets ([ ]). As with other functions, some @Commands take other parameters that include information which the @Command needs to do its processing; others take no parameters in addition to the command name.

 Tip

> For the most part, @Commands are used to execute menu functions, such as invoking a spell check in a document. To maintain compatibility with previous versions of Notes, the @Command names remained constant. This might cause problems when learning them because the menu structure and names have not remained constant through each new release of Notes. For example, the menu item in Notes release 4 that you use to create a new document once forms are created is the Create menu. However, in Notes release 3, that menu was called Compose. As a result, the @Command for executing the call to create a new document is @Command([Compose];FormName), not @Command([Create];FormName).
>
> Be sure that you not only remember just what the function is supposed to do, but that you also pay close attention to the name. If you rely on your knowledge of Notes release 4 menus to help you remember @Command names, you might be disappointed on the exam.

There are two classes of @Commands: @Commands and @PostedCommands. @Commands are the preferred class used in Notes release 4; @PostedCommands are provided to ensure compatibility with Notes release 3. In a multiline formula block, you may have included @Commands (for information on multiline formulas, see Chapter 18, "Advanced Formulas Part I"). For example, if you want to set a field to a certain value, spell check the document, and then save it, you may have create a formula block as follows:

```
@Command([ToolsSpellCheck]);
FIELD CheckDate := @Today;
@Command([FileSave])
```

In Notes release 4, this block executes as it is written; a spell check is initiated, the value of the CheckDate is set to today's date, and then the document is saved. However, in Notes release 3, all @Commands were executed after all other processing, no matter where they fell in the actual code. As a result, in Notes release 3, the order of execution is different; the value of CheckDate is set to today's date, the spell check is initiated, and finally the document is saved. To preserve this order and ensure that formulas from release 3 still execute the same when compiled in a release 4 environment, the @PostedCommand was introduced; @PostedCommands always execute at the end of the formula, regardless of their position. When re-lease 3 formulas are brought into release 4, all the @Commands are converted to @PostedCommands, which preserves their execution order.

 Tip

It is not recommended that you use @PostedCommands because they are only included in the syntax of release 4 to provide the same functionality as was present in release 3. If you want an @Command to execute at the end of a formula, it should be placed where you want it to execute; this prevents confusion at debug time. However, you might be asked questions about the execution of @PostedCommands on the exam, and you might also encounter them when you debug formulas.

 Note

Some @Commands always execute after all other processing, even when you use them in Notes release 4. These commands are FileCloseWindow, FileDatabaseDelete, FileExit, NavigateNext, NavigateNextMain, NavigateNextSelected, NavigateNextUnread, NavigatePrev, NavigatePrevMain, NavigatePrevSelected, NavigatePrevUnread, ToolsRunBackgroundMacros, ToolsRunMacro, ViewChange, and ViewSwitchForm.

What follows are some of the more popular commands, both in application development as well as on the exams.

[Compose]

Compose is used to create a new document from a specified form. You use such a command when giving your users a convenient one-click method of beginning the creation of a new document. The syntax of Compose is as follows:

@Command([Compose];server:Database;Form)

This command takes two additional parameters; a list containing the name of the server and database (each in quotation marks and separated by a colon) in which the form is contained and the name of the form you want to use to create the new document. If the server is the local machine or the database is the currently active database, you can leave the server portion null ("" or NULL). The server name should be the fully distinguished name (not just the common name) and the database name is either the name of the database relative to the default Notes data directory or the full pathname (either Coffee.nsf or C:\Notesdatabases\Coffee.nsf).

 Tip

> Remember that if you need to specify a pathname in quotation marks, you must use two backslashes in order to represent one. If you want to specify the path C:\NotesDatabases\Coffee.nsf, you must use the text string "C:\\NotesDatabases\\Coffee.nsf".

If both the server and database portions are NULL, that whole parameter can be removed. The form is either the name or the synonym of the form. For example, if the form is called Main Topic | Main, then you can use either Main Topic or Main in specifying the form (the name is not case-sensitive).

 Note

> This command creates a document in the database in which the form is located, not in the database from which the @Command is executed.

As an example, if you want to create a new document in a discussion database called coffee.nsf, which is located on a server called Brazil/Bean, using a form called Main Topic, then the syntax of the command is

```
@Command([Compose];"Brazil/Bean":"coffee.nsf";"Main Topic")
```

[FileCloseWindow]

FileCloseWindow takes no additional parameters and is used to close the currently active window. It is one of the @Commands that is not executed until the end of a formula block regardless of its position within the block. The syntax is

```
@Command([FileCloseWindow])
```

 Tip   If the window you are closing is a document window, you might want to ensure that the document has been saved before you execute this command. To do this, run a @Command ([FileSave]) before executing the @Command([FileCloseWindow]). If changes remain unsaved, the user is prompted to save as usual.

[FileExit]

FileExit takes no additional parameters and is used to exit from Notes. It is one of the @Commands that is not executed until the end of a formula block regardless of its position within the block. The syntax is

```
@Command([FileExit])
```

[FilePrint]

FilePrint takes two syntaxes, one with no additional parameters and one that takes parameters. Both syntaxes are used to print either from a view or from a form. The one with no additional parameters displays the File Print dialog box and executes the print once you click OK in the dialog box. The syntax is

```
@Command([FilePrint])
```

The one that takes parameters can be used to fully execute a print statement by specifying the print options that you desire. The syntax is

```
@Command([FilePrint];numcopies;fromPage;toPage;draft;
➥printView;formName;pageBreak;resetPages)
```

If you specify any of the parameters, you must specify values for all of them, even if the values are only NULL (""). The parameters are described as follows:

- ▶ The numCopies parameter allows you to indicate the number of copies of the document you want to print. If you specify a number as this parameter, that number of copies is printed; NULL indicates one copy.

- ▶ The fromPage parameter allows you to indicate the page where you want to begin printing. If you specify a number as this parameter, printing begins with that page; NULL indicates page one.

- ▶ The toPage parameter allows you to indicate the last page of the printout. If you specify a number as this parameter, printing ends with that page; NULL indicates the last page.

- ▶ The draft keyword allows you to indicate whether you want the document to print in draft mode. The word draft (without quotation marks around it) indicates that the printing should be done in draft mode; NULL indicates regular printing.

- ▶ The printView keyword allows you to indicate that the view displayed and not the document selected should be printed. The word printView (without quotation marks around it) indicates that you want the current view to be printed; NULL indicates that the currently selected documents should be printed. In an open document, this parameter is ignored.

▶ The `formName` parameter allows you to indicate a form from the current database to use to print the documents. In the absence of this parameter, the documents are printed using the form indicated in the form field for each document. This parameter is ignored in open documents.

▶ The `pageBreak` keyword indicates how multiple documents should be separated. If `NULL` or the word `pageBreak` (without quotation marks around it) is specified, then each new document begins on a new page. The word `line` (without quotation marks around it) indicates that a blank line should separate the documents. This parameter is ignored in open documents.

▶ The `resetPages` keyword allows you to indicate whether the page numbers should be reset at the beginning of each new document if you are printing multiple documents in a view. If the word `resetPages` (without quotation marks around it) is specified here, then as each new document begins, the page numbers are reset to 1. If `NULL` is specified as this parameter, then numbering continues incrementally with each new page, regardless of whether a new document begins.

For example, if you want to print all the currently open documents using regular print density and using the form that was used to create it, you could use the following statement:

```
@Command([FilePrint];1;NULL;NULL;NULL;NULL;NULL;NULL;NULL)
```

 Tip

An exception to the rule about specifying all parameters is if parameters at the end of the parameter list are NULL. NULL parameters at the end of the parameter list can be omitted without Notes generating a syntax error. Therefore, the preceding example could be shortened to

```
@Command([FilePrint];1)
```

[FileSave]

FileSave takes no additional parameters and is used to save the currently open Notes document or the currently open design element, such as form, view, and so on, in design mode. The syntax is

```
@Command([FileSave])
```

[OpenNavigator]

OpenNavigator takes two parameters and is used to open a navigator in the current database. (For more information on navigators, see Chapter 16, "Finalizing the Database.") The syntax is

```
@Command([OpenNavigator];navigatorName;alone)
```

The navigatorName parameter is used to specify the name of the navigator that you want to open; it must be present in the current database. The alone parameter is set to either NULL (in which case it can be omitted) or to "1". A "1" in the second parameter indicates that the navigator should be opened in its own window, unaccompanied by a view.

For example, if you want to open the navigator called "MainMenu" in its own window, the command looks like this:

```
@Command([OpenNavigator];"MainMenu";"1")
```

[ToolsSpellCheck]

ToolsSpellCheck takes no additional parameters and is used to check the spelling of the current document, provided that it is opened for editing. The syntax is

```
@Command([ToolsSpellCheck])
```

Tip

Because this command only works when a document is in edit mode, you might want to couple its execution with the command @Command([EditDocument]). For example:

```
@Command([EditDocument]);
@Command([ToolsSpellCheck])
```

Alternatively, you could use @IsDocBeingEdited to create a hide formula for the action or hotspot you are using to invoke this command so that the button is not available unless the user is already in edit mode.

[EditDocument]

EditDocument can be used either with or without an additional parameter. Its syntax is

```
@Command([EditDocument;mode)
```

When used without the mode parameter, this command changes the mode of the current document from read mode to edit mode or from edit mode to read mode, toggling back and forth.

The mode parameter either takes the value "1" or "0" and moves you to edit mode ("1") or read mode ("0"). For example, if you want to ensure that you end up in edit mode regardless of which mode you are in when the command is executed, use the following form:

```
@Command([EditDocument];"1")
```

 Note

This command cannot override the normal security present in the document. If a user does not have permission to manually enter edit mode for a certain document, then this command will not allow him to do so programmatically.

[Execute]

Execute can be used to execute an external program from Notes. This command takes two parameters, one of which is optional in the following syntax:

@Command([Execute];PathOfApplication;PathOfInitialFile)

When given only the path of the application you want to run, Notes starts that application. When given the path of a file, then Notes runs the application and opens the file you indicate.

Remember that when you specify pathnames, they must be in quotation marks and as a result, each backslash (\\) must be represented by two backslashes.

Notes will only execute the application on the local machine, and the Execute cannot be used to start applications on other machines or on a Notes server.

For example, if you want to launch the Paint program from a Windows 95 workstation running Notes, you can use the following formula:

@Command([Execute];"C:\\Windows\\pbrush.exe")

Now that you have seen some of the actions and commands that can be executed, look at some of the places where these can be executed. The first place is in form and view actions.

Understanding Form and View Actions

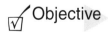

Form and view actions are created in forms and views. Once created, they are placed in the Actions menu, in an action bar, or in both. The action bar is located just above the form or view and just below the smart icon set. Actions in action bars take the form of buttons with identifying text and, optionally, with identifying icons. These buttons provide single-click invocation of the formula associated with them.

Using System Actions

Certain actions are present on every view and form by default and cannot be removed. These are system actions. System actions display in the Actions menu and not in the action bar, but you can include them in the action bar or remove them from the Actions menu if you want. These actions, which are identified by asterisks (*) in an actions list, are Categorize, Edit Document, Send Document, Forward, Move to Folder, and Remove from Folder.

The Categorize action is used to manipulate categories for documents using specific techniques. For this action to be effective, the database must contain a field called Categorize and the view in which the action is available must be categorized by that field.

The Edit Document action is used to edit the current document. If this action is present in a view, the document opens for reading and the mode is then changed to edit. This action cannot override a user's normal access to a document by allowing a reader to edit a document.

The Send Document action is used to send documents to the location indicated in the SendTo field. If a document does not have a SendTo field, this action fails with an error message. For more information on SendTo fields, see Chapter 19, "Advanced Formulas Part II."

The Forward action is used to forward a document to any valid mail address. When this action is clicked, the selected document is placed into the body of a mail message and the user can address the message.

The Move to Folder action gives a user the capability to place the current document in a folder of his or her choice. A dialog box appears and the user can choose a folder from the folders available. If the folder does not exist, a new folder can be created at that point.

The Remove from Folder action removes a currently selected document from a folder. If a document is not selected, this action has no effect.

To view system actions, follow these steps:

1. Open the view or form in which you want to see the system actions.

2. Open the Action pane in the form or view builder window by selecting View | Action Pane (see Figure 15.1).

Figure 15.1

All forms and views have the default system actions.

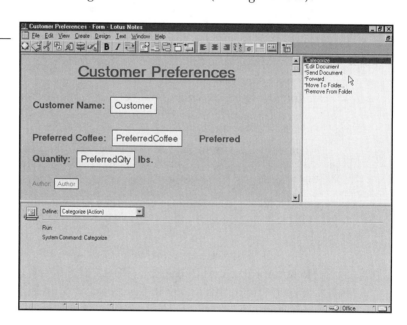

Creating Form Actions

You can use form actions to issue any command or action that is appropriate for a document. This includes, but is not limited to, changing from read to edit mode, printing the current document, generating a response to the current document, saving and exiting from the current document, checking the spelling of the current document, and even performing field value assignment and modification.

To create an action in a form, follow these steps:

1. Open the design of the form where you want to place the action.

2. From the Create menu, choose Action. At this point, the Properties for Action dialog box, shown in Figure 15.2, appears, and if it is not already showing, the Action pane will appear on the right side of the Form Builder window.

Figure 15.2

The Properties for Action dialog box allows you to set action properties.

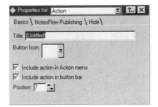

3. Set the desired properties in the Properties for Action dialog box (see the section titled "Action Properties" later in this chapter).

4. Assign an execution event by clicking in the Design pane (at the bottom of the screen), choosing the run type, and entering the formula or simple action in the Formula window.

Creating View Actions

You can use view actions to issue any command or action that is appropriate for a view. This includes, but is not limited to, printing the current document or view, creating a new document or response with a database form, editing the selected document, and switching to a new navigator.

To create an action in a view, follow this procedure:

1. Open the design of the view where you want to place the action.

2. From the Create menu, choose Action. At this point, the Properties for Action dialog box appears, and if it is not

already showing, the Action pane appears on the right side of the View Builder window.

3. Set the properties in the Properties for Action dialog box (see the section "Action Properties" later in this chapter).

4. Assign an execution event by clicking the Design pane (at the bottom of the screen), choosing the run type, and entering the formula or simple action desired in the Formula window.

Once an action has been created, you will want to modify its properties to control the name associated with it, the icon on the button, its position on the action bar (if it displays), and its hide characteristics.

Action Properties

The Properties for Action dialog box consists of three tabs:

▶ Basics

▶ NotesFlow Publishing

▶ Hide

You can display these properties either by creating a new action (they are displayed automatically) or by double-clicking the desired action in the actions list in the Action pane (which can be viewed by selecting View | Action Pane in either a view or a folder).

Of the three tabs, only two are relevant to the AD1 and AD2 exams: Basics and Hide. The third, NotesFlow Publishing, contains only advanced data exchange fields, which are used to exchange information between Notes and data exchange–enabled applications.

The Basics page begins with the action title. This title is displayed on the action button when it is visible and is also displayed in the Actions menu if the appropriate check box is selected. If no title is entered, (Untitled) appears on the actions bar and in the Actions menu.

Below the title is a pull-down list that allows you to choose an icon to place on the action button. This is optional, and if you do not choose one, the button simply contains the action's title.

The Include Action in Action Menu check box allows you to display the action in the Action menu and enable its execution from there (see Figure 15.3). If selected, the action will appear in the menu. The default is for the check box to be selected.

Figure 15.3

The Actions menu with system and user-defined actions present.

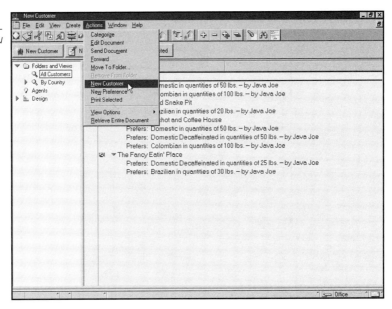

The Include Action in Button Bar check box allows you to display the action in the action bar (see Figure 15.4). If this check box is not selected, the action does not display in the action bar.

The Position field allows you to set the relative position of the action in either the menu or the action bar. I say relative because the position only indicates where the button or menu option appears if all the previous buttons also appear. If the position is 7, then the action appears seventh but only if the first six appear as well. If none of the previous numbered actions are set to appear, then the action appears first in the list.

The Hide tab allows you to control under which circumstances the action appears (see Figure 15.5). For forms, four checkboxes allow you to specify if the action should appear when previewed or opened and in read or edit mode. For views, none of these check boxes appear. If you select any of those checkboxes, then the action will not appear under those circumstances.

Figure 15.4

An action bar for a view showing user-defined actions.

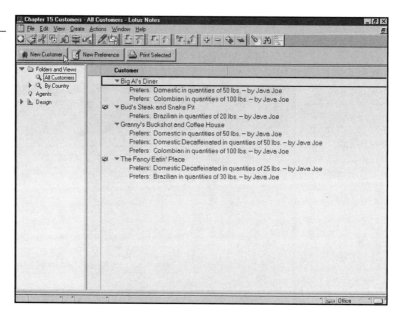

Figure 15.5

The Hide tab for a form action button allows you to define when the action is visible on the form.

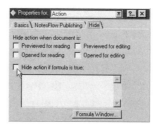

For both forms and views (see Figure 15.6), there is a Formula window that you can use to specify a complex condition under which the action should be hidden.

Figure 15.6

The Hide tab for a view action button allows you to define when the action is visible in the view.

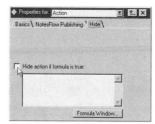

To specify this, select Hide Action If Formula Is True and then type a formula that evaluates to either a true or false result. For example, to get a button to appear only when the day of the week is Monday, you can use the following formula in the Formula window:

```
@Weekday(@Today) = 2
```

Note

> The refresh of the action bar when actions are hidden does not always work as expected. In some instances, actions do not disappear until a manual refresh of a view or document is done (the user presses F9). In other instances, the action bar remains even after all the action buttons have disappeared.

Understanding Hotspots

Objective

Hotspots are areas on documents or navigators that, when clicked, execute a simple action, a formula, or Lotus Script (for more information on navigators, see Chapter 16). Hotspots are different from actions in that they appear in the body of a form or navigator, not at the top, and they are not available in views. Two kinds of hotspots are relevant to this discussion: buttons hotspots and action hotspots.

Creating Button Hotspots

Buttons hotspots are gray buttons (with or without text on then) that you can place on a form for the purpose of adding functionality to a document. These buttons can be created anywhere on a form, including in a layout region (for more information on layout regions, see Chapter 20, "Layout Regions and Subforms").

To create a button hotspot, follow these steps:

1. Open the design of the form where you want to place the button.

2. Position your insertion point at the place you want to have the button inserted.

3. From the Create menu, choose Hotspot | Button.

4. Assign properties as desired (see Figure 15.7); the Properties for Button dialog box appears when the button is created. The only properties that differ from those of text are on the interface tab (the first one). Enter a label that will appear on the button (or leave it blank to create a blank button). Enter a button width. This width is either the width of the text in the button (if the Wrap Text check box is not selected) or it is a preset width (if the Wrap Text check box is selected). Select the Wrap Text check box if you want to have the button appear multiple lines high and be a fixed width.

Figure 15.7

The Properties for Button dialog box allows you to define button properties.

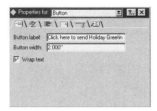

5. Create a formula or use a simple action to define what the button does.

Creating Action Hotspots

An action hotspot is an area of a form that can be clicked to perform the action of your choice. This area could be text, a graphic, a section, a table, or almost anything as long as it does not contain another hotspot. Action hotspots are more flexible than button hotspots in that they do not have a fixed appearance but can perform the same functions.

To create an action hotspot, follow these steps:

1. Open the design of the form where you want to place the button.

2. Select the part of your form that you want to convert to an action hotspot by clicking and dragging over it with your mouse.

3. From the Create menu, choose Hotspot | Action Hotspot.

4. Assign properties as desired (see Figure 15.8); the Properties for Action Hotspot dialog box appears when the button is created. The only property that differs from those of text are on the interface tab (the first one). By selecting the Show Border Around Hotspot check box, you can identify the hotspot for a user by adding a green border around it. If you do not select this check box, your users might only know of the presence of the hotspot when they happen to click it.

Figure 15.8

The Properties for Hotspot Button dialog box allows you to define button properties.

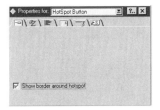

5. Create a formula or use a simple action to define what the button does.

Note   If you make a field part of an action hotspot, every time a user clicks the field, the action is performed. However, if the user tabs into the field, then the action is not performed.

Exercises

To further enhance the Customers database and make it a little more user friendly, you are going to add some user conveniences in the form of actions. On the Customer form, you will add two actions: one to check the spelling on the document and another to save the document and exit back to the view. On the All Customers view, you will add three actions: one to create a new customer, one to create a customer preference, and one to print the documents selected in the view. The database you will use for this lab is available on your CD-ROM and should be copied to your default Notes data directory. The lab file is called cust15.nsf and its title is Chapter 15 Customers. Be sure that when you copy the file, you remove the read-only attribute or you will not be able to modify the database.

Exercise 15.1

1. From the File menu, choose Database|Open and select the database called Chapter 15 Customers from the pull-down list of local databases. Click the Open button to add the database to your workspace and open the navigation pane.

2. If the design category is not expanded, click the twistie to the left of it to expand and then click the forms view to show the forms on the right.

3. Double-click the form called Customer to open the design of the customer form.

4. From the View menu, choose Action Pane to open the Action pane. Note that there are currently no actions except system actions (those with asterisks beside them).

5. From the Create menu, choose Action; the Properties for Action dialog box appears (see Figure 15.9).

6. In the title field, type Check Spelling.

7. Click the down arrow beside the Button Icon field and click the icon with the red check mark over the piece of paper (third row, eleventh column).

Figure 15.9

Define the Check Spelling action.

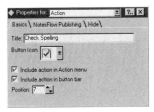

8. Click the Hide tab and select the check boxes Previewed for Reading and Opened for Reading. This will ensure that the only people who can try to check spelling are those who can put the document into edit mode.

9. Click the formula window of the Design pane (at the bottom of the screen) and type the following formula:

```
@Command([ToolsSpellCheck])
```

10. Click the Close Window button in the Properties for Action dialog box.

11. From the Create menu, choose Action; the Properties for Action dialog box appears (see Figure 15.10).

Figure 15.10

Define the Save and Exit action.

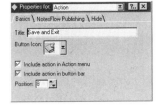

12. In the title field, type `Save and Exit`.

13. Click the down arrow beside the Button Icon field and click the icon with the green arrow pointing into the blue book (tenth row, tenth column).

14. Click in the Formula window of the Design pane (at the bottom of the screen) and type the following formula:

```
@Command([FileSave]);
@Command([FileCloseWindow])
```

continues

Exercise 15.1   Continued

15. Click the Close Window button in the Properties for Action dialog box.

16. Save the form and close it.

17. Click the All Customers view to display the current customers.

18. Double-click the customer called Big Al's Diner to open it in read mode; the only button present should be the Save and Exit button.

19. Press Ctrl+E to enter edit mode; the field brackets should appear around the editable field, and the Check Spelling button should appear.

20. Click the Check Spelling button to check the spelling, click Skip whenever a word is flagged, and then click the OK button when the spell check is complete.

21. Click the Save and Exit button to exit back to the view.

Exercise 15.2

1. From the design section, choose Views to show the views on the right.

2. Double-click the view All Customers to open the design of the All Customers view.

3. From the View menu, choose Action Pane to open the Action pane. Note that there are currently no actions except system actions (those with asterisks beside them).

4. From the Create menu, choose Action; the Properties for Action dialog box appears (see Figure 15.11).

5. In the title field, type New Customer.

6. Click the down arrow beside the Button Icon field and click the icon with the group of people and the starburst (third row, eighth column).

Figure 15.11

Define the New Customer action.

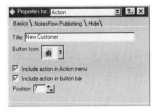

7. Click the Formula window of the Design pane (at the bottom of the screen) and type the following formula:

   `@Command([Compose];"Customer")`

8. Click the Close Window button in the Properties for Action dialog box.

9. From the Create menu, choose Action; the Properties for Action dialog box appears (see Figure 15.12).

Figure 15.12

Define the New Preference action.

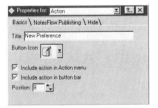

10. In the title field, type `New Preference`.

11. Click the down arrow beside the Button Icon field and click the icon with the pencil writing on the paper (third row, sixth column).

12. Click the Formula window of the Design pane (at the bottom of the screen) and type the following formula:

    `@Command([Compose];"Coffee")`

13. Click the Close Window button in the Properties for Action dialog box.

14. From the Create menu, choose Action; the Properties for Action dialog box appears (see Figure 15.13).

continues

Exercise 15.2 Continued

Figure 15.13

Define the Print Selected action.

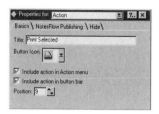

15. In the title field, type `Print Selected`.

16. Click the down arrow beside the Button Icon field and click the icon with the printer on it (ninth row, third column).

17. Click the Formula window of the Design pane (at the bottom of the screen) and type the following formula:

```
@Command([FilePrint];1)
```

18. Click the Close Window button in the Properties for Action dialog box.

19. Save the view and close it.

20. Click the All Customers view to display the current customers (the three actions you created should display).

21. Click the New Customer button; a new Customer Entry document should appear. Fill it in or exit.

22. Click the customer called `Bud's Steak and Snake Pit` and then click the New Preference button; a new Customer Preferences document should appear. Fill it in or exit.

23. If you have a printer enabled for your workstation, click in the selection margin to the left of two or three documents in the view (that should place checkmarks beside each of the documents selected) and click the Print Selected button. The documents should print without your intervention.

Exercise 15.3

Your user community is asking for more actions. The challenge is to create two more actions on the Customer form, one to print the current document and the other to create a new preferences document.

The answers to this challenge exercise are found in the form called `ChallengeAnswer`.

Review Questions

1. What is the place where form and view actions appear to a user?

   a. The action bar

   b. The button bar

   c. The smart icon bar

   d. The toolbar

2. What is the place where form and view actions appear to a designer?

   a. The button bar

   b. The action builder area

   c. The Action pane

   d. The place of pain

3. Which of the following is not a type of event that can be executed from an action?

   a. Simple action

   b. Lotus Script

   c. Formula

   d. Simple command

4. Which pair of characteristics identifies all @Commands?

    a. They all execute menu commands and are all identified with syntax beginning with @Command.

    b. They are all identified with syntax beginning with @Command and the first parameter is always the command in square brackets.

    c. They all execute menu commands and all have a first parameter of the command in square brackets.

    d. They are all identified with syntax beginning with @Command and they all have only one parameter, the command name.

5. Carla created the following formula:

```
@Command([FileSave]);
@Command([FileCloseWindow]);
FIELD Color = "Red"
```

Will her formula preserve the change to the color field?

    a. Yes

    b. No

6. Walter is using @Command([Compose]) to create a new document. The form he is using to create the document is his local workstation, is called NewDoc, and is in a database called Documents.nsf. He has an action on a form called DifferentDoc in the same database. Which of the following syntaxes will work?

    a. @Command([Compose];"":"Documents.nsf";"NewDoc")

    b. @Command([Compose];"":"";"NewDoc")

    c. @Command([Compose];"NewDoc")

    d. All of the above

7. Patricia created a hotspot button on a form and executed the following formula:

`@Command([FilePrint])`

What will be the result when a user clicks the button?

   a. The current document will be printed.

   b. A print dialog box will appear.

   c. Nothing will happen.

   d. An error message will appear.

8. Barney creates an action on his form that uses `@Command ([ToolsSpellCheck])`. He gets complaints from his users that the button works only sometimes. What is the most likely cause of his problem?

   a. The users are clicking the wrong button.

   b. The command is really `@Command([EditCheckSpelling])`.

   c. This command must be executed from a view, not from a form.

   d. Some users are executing it while in edit mode and others while in read mode.

9. Wanda wants to create a view action that will edit the currently selected document. What is the easiest way to do this?

   a. Enable the system action Edit Document for the view.

   b. Create an action, call it "Edit Document," and use the formula `@Command([EditDocument])`.

   c. Create an action, call it "Edit Document," and use the formula `@Command([EditDocument];"1")`.

   d. She can't do this from a view; she must create a form action instead.

10. Carl created a view action and sets the position property to 6. Where does the action appear in the action bar?

   a. Always in position 6 (about two-thirds of the way from the left)

   b. At the left side of the action bar

   c. At most at position 6, depending on how many other displayed actions have lower numbers

   d. At the right side of the action bar

11. Anne wants to click a graphic of her dog and run a program called `c:\bark.exe`. How can she do this?

   a. Without Lotus Script, she can't.

   b. Paste the graphic onto her form, select it, create an action hotspot, and use the function `@Command ([Execute];"c:\bark.exe")` to run the program.

   c. Paste the graphic onto her form, select it, create a button, and use the function `@Command ([Execute];"c:\bark.exe")` to run the program.

   d. Paste the graphic onto her form, select it, create an action hotspot, and use the function `@Command ([Execute];"c:\\bark.exe")` to run the program.

Review Answers

1. A. The action bar appears just below the smart icon set and just above either the document or the view that the user is viewing. This bar appears as long as at least one action is displayed for that form or view. For more information, refer to the section titled "Introducing Actions and Hotspots."

2. C. The Action pane is a normally hidden area to the right of either the View Builder pane or the Form Builder pane. You can open it by selecting View|Action Pane while designing a form or view. For more information, refer to the section titled "Understanding Form and View Actions."

3. D. The three execution types are simple action (for system defined actions), formula, and Lotus Script. For more information, refer to the section titled "Execution Events."

4. B. @Commands frequently have more than one parameter and do not always execute menu commands. Even those that do most frequently execute Notes release 3 menu commands, not Notes release 4. For more information, refer to "@Commands."

5. B. Some @Commands execute where they are placed in a multi-line formula; others always execute at the end. In this case, there is a combination of the two. @Command([FileSave]) executes where it is placed; @Command([FileCloseWindow]) executes at the end of the formula. This means that the document will be saved, the Color field will be changed, and then the document will attempt to close. On closing, you are prompted to save the document. For more information, refer to the sections titled "[FileSave]" and "[FileCloseWindow]."

6. D. When the location of the form's database is both local and the same as the database executing the @Command, the server and database parameters are optional. As a result, any of the forms listed will work. For more information, refer to the section titled "[Compose]."

7. B. She needs at least one additional parameter for the print to happen without her intervention (for example, she could have added ;1 to indicate that she wanted one copy printed). [FilePrint] without parameters always produces a print dialog box. For more information, refer to the section titled "[FilePrint]."

8. D. The most common cause of spell check failure results from users not being in edit mode when the spell check is invoked. He could have prevented this by hiding the action when the documents are in read mode and only allowing it to be seen when it would be effective. For more information, refer to the section titled "[ToolsSpellCheck]."

9. A. It is always preferable to use a predefined action rather than create a function. In this case, an action exists to edit the document, and therefore, Wanda should do this. For more information, refer to the section titled "Using System Actions."

10. C. The position number for an action is always relative to the presence of other actions. If other actions are enabled to display and they have smaller numbers, then his action appears to their right. However, if his is the only action, or if his action has the smallest number, then that action appears at the far left side. At most, this action will be in the sixth position on the bar. For more information, refer to the section titled "Action Properties."

11. D. The correct answer combines both a knowledge of correct terminology as well as correct syntax and an understanding of Notes text strings. The correct object to create is an action hotspot, which can be used to provide single-click execution of a simple action, formula, or Lotus Script event on any selected object on a form. The @Command can be used to execute an external program; however, to indicate its path, you must use double backslashes to prevent Notes from ignoring the backslashes altogether. For more information, refer to the section titled "Creating Action Hotspots" and "[Execute]."

Answers to Test Yourself Questions at Beginning of Chapter

1. Actions and hotspots execute three different kinds of events: simple actions, formulas, and Lotus Script. Simple actions are system-defined events whose function cannot be modified. Formulas use the Notes formula language (including field names, constants, and @ functions) to perform complex commands. Lotus Script is a structured programming language that provides the most powerful execution ability in Notes but that also requires the most experience to use correctly. For more information, refer to "Understanding Execution Events."

2. The primary difference between actions and hotspots is that actions appear only on the action bar and in the Actions menu and can be present both for forms and views, whereas hotspots are not available on views and appear in the body of forms and navigators. For more information, refer to "Introducing Actions and Hotspots."

3. The primary function of the @Command is to execute system events, most of which are available through the Notes menu. For more information, refer to "@Commands."

4. The two types of actions are view actions and form actions. They are really only different in where they are placed (either on a view or a form) and not by function or creation method. For more information, refer to "Understanding Form and View Actions."

5. The two types of hotspots that execute functions are button hotspots and action hotspots. These are different in their visual appearance; button hotspots are always gray and appear raised from the form, whereas action hotspots can be created from text, graphics, fields, and other form objects. For more information, refer to "Understanding Hotspots."

Chapter 16

Finalizing the Database

This chapter will introduce you to the following objectives:

 Objectives

▶ Creating navigators

▶ Creating a Database icon

▶ Understanding database properties

▶ Implementing security

Test Yourself! Before reading this chapter, test yourself to determine how much study time you will need to devote to this section.

1. What is a graphical navigator and how does it differ from the Folders navigator?

2. Where is the Database icon stored and how can it be modified?

3. What technique can be used to inform users of every new change to a database using built-in database properties?

4. How can you get your graphical navigator to launch every time a database is opened?

5. What is the ACL and what are the levels of access?

Answers are located at the end of the chapter...

Finalizing the database before releasing it to your user community is as important as all of the design processes that have gone before. Some of this process is cosmetic, and some of it is functional. The cosmetics are essential because the initial appeal your application has to your users largely determines how eager they will be to use it. If the application is not visually appealing and not easily usable, people will find every excuse not to use it. The functional parts ensure that the ability to see and modify data is only in the hands of those who need it. This chapter discusses the finalizing process.

Creating Navigators

Objective

Navigators are the road maps to your databases. They let your users know which views are available, which documents they can create, and which agents they can run. Every database comes with a navigator called Folders (see Figure 16.1). This navigator is part of the navigation pane that comes up when you initially create a database, and unless you build other navigators, is the one that your users see. This navigator displays on the left of the navigation pane; on the right side is the content of the view that is selected in the Folders navigator. This navigator includes the special views categorized under the heading Design, which a designer uses to access the design class of database elements (forms, views, and so on).

Figure 16.1

*The standard
Folders navigator.*

The Folders
navigator

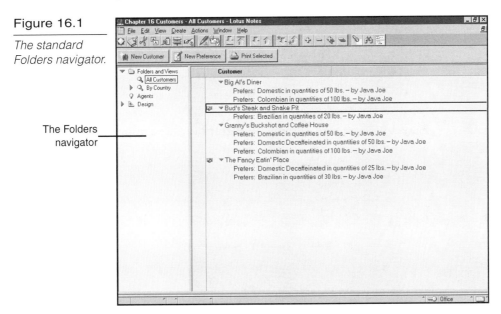

The Folders navigator is not always the best way to display the capabilities of the database to the user community. Outside of actions on your views, for example, your users must use menu navigation to locate the forms to create new documents, and in the case of a database with many views, the lists on the left side can get long and cumbersome to work with. Because of this, Notes gives you the ability to create new navigators—graphical navigators.

Working with Graphical Navigators

A *graphical navigator* is a navigator you create that introduces the user to the capabilities of and the elements in your database through the use of graphics and hotspots that invoke various utilities. Instead of choosing a specific view name to see a list of all the customers in Kalamazoo, for example, a user may be given the opportunity to click that city on a Michigan map. Instead of going to the Create menu (or even to an action button) to create a new customer, there may be a button on the map of Michigan that says "Click Here to Add A New Customer." Through the use of a graphical presentation, users can be made to feel more comfortable with the database and make the process of learning a lot quicker and easier.

A graphical navigator consists of many kinds of elements: the background, hotspots, shapes, text boxes, and so on. The background can be plain, a solid color, or it can be a graphic image you can paste in from outside Notes. If you use a graphic image, it can be in any format; as long as you can copy it to the clipboard, you can paste it onto your navigator. The inserted objects, which serve to annotate and provide clickable areas to invoke formula action, are then laid over the graphic at the appropriate spots.

To create a graphical navigator, perform the following steps:

1. Open the database by double-clicking its icon on your workspace.

2. Select Create I Design, Navigator.

Now that the navigator has been created, you need to add the appropriate background and hotspots to it; but first, you must understand the navigator design environment.

Using the Navigator Design Environment

The *navigator design environment* is what comes up when you initially create a navigator, or if one already exists, it displays when you double-click a navigator in the navigators list in the navigation pane (see Figure 16.2). This environment consists of two panes: one on the top and one on the bottom. Each of these panes can be independently resized to allow for design in either of the areas. On the top is the navigator builder window, which is the area where the navigator design actually occurs. This area is like a sketch pad on which you create your navigator's final look.

Figure 16.2

The navigator design environment.

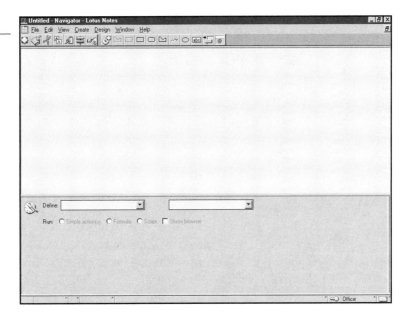

On the bottom is the design pane, which is the area where actions for hotspots are defined. If you need this area to be larger or smaller, it can be resized by dragging its top border up or down. Its top border is the thick horizontal line that divides this pane from the form builder window.

Understanding Navigator Properties

Like other Notes objects, navigators' properties define their characteristics. These properties can be seen and set for a navigator by bringing up the Properties for Navigator dialog box. This dialog box can be brought up by clicking with your right mouse button on any blank area in the navigator builder window and choosing Navigator Properties from the menu that appears. This properties dialog box is divided into two tabs: Basics and Grid (see Figure 16.3).

Figure 16.3

The Properties for Navigator dialog box enables you to set navigator properties.

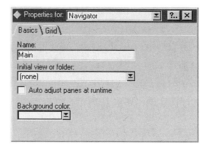

Using the Basics Tab

The Basics tab contains fields for information relating to the basic definition of the navigator. This includes name, the initial view or folder associated with this navigator, automatic adjustment of pane widths, and the background color.

The navigator name is the name the users see in any menu system, and which you see when you look at a list of navigators from the navigation pane. Navigator names can be as long as 64 characters, with the option of 64 more characters if you specify an alias. Like forms and views, navigator names can be cascaded for ease of location in the menu system. These cascades can be created by inserting a backslash in the appropriate place in the navigator name (for a more complete description of cascading and names, see Chapter 14, "Creating Views").

Note Navigators can be accessed via View|Choose Show; the available views appear at the bottom of that submenu. If no graphical navigators have been created, the only one present will be the Folders navigator.

The pull-down list labeled Initial View Or Folder enables you to specify which view should be paired with this navigator when it is displayed. The default is None, which means that whichever view is currently showing when this navigator displays continues to show. The pull-down list shows all the views that are currently defined in this database and any of them could be paired with the navigator. If this is done, the chosen view also displays when the navigator displays.

Note

This view or folder is only the default. Once the navigator displays, any of the other views can then be moved, providing that there is a mechanism in the navigator for doing so.

By selecting the Auto Adjust Panes At Runtime check box, you can ensure that the whole navigator shows when it displays. Some navigators even have graphics. Without this check box selected, the navigator has the same amount of room as the last one was given, which may be too much or too little to show it effectively. If you select this check box, the display pane is resized to fit the navigator when it displays.

The Background Color pull-down list gives you the opportunity to choose a color to display in the navigator's background. Like the background of a form, this should not be so bright that it is an irritation to your users (remember that they may be using this navigator a lot).

Note

If you are going to place a graphic on the background of the navigator, this background color may never show. To be safe, however, you may want to choose a color that is aesthetically compatible with your graphic.

Using the Grid Tab

The Grid tab enables you to define the design environment by providing selection for snapping to a background grid and for defining the size of that grid.

The grid is used to align objects you create and drag around on the navigator. Since there is no alignment feature, Notes gives you a set of invisible lines that all objects attach themselves to when created. This attachment is called *snapping to*, and if you select the Snap to Grid check box, this feature becomes enabled. To allow for more or less space between these grid lines, you can adjust the number in the Grid Size field. This number can vary between 2 and 16. The larger the number, the more space between the grid lines, and the less fine the position adjustments you make for your objects.

Placing Objects on the Navigator

Designing navigators is about placing objects on them that enhance their visual appeal or provide places to click that perform functions. Sometimes, if you want, visually appealing objects also execute functions. All objects, once placed onto the navigator, can be set up to execute a command when clicked.

Inserting Graphic Backgrounds

A graphic background is designed to take the place of the color background, which is available in the navigator by default. Any kind of graphic can be made the background of the navigator, providing that you can copy it to the clipboard; Notes requires that the graphic be in the clipboard before it can be inserted into the navigator. These graphics may be pictures, sets of nicely designed buttons, company logos, maps, or anything else to increase the usability of the navigator.

 Tip

The more detail and background is present on the graphic, the less object creation you must do in the navigator itself. If you have a bitmap of a map of a region in which your customers are located, for example, you are best off using that, rather than trying to create such a thing using the objects available to you in the navigator design environment.

To insert a graphic background into your navigator, perform the following steps:

1. From whatever graphic program is suitable, copy the graphic to the operating system clipboard.

2. From the Create menu, choose Graphic Background (see Figure 16.4).

Figure 16.4

An example of a graphic background.

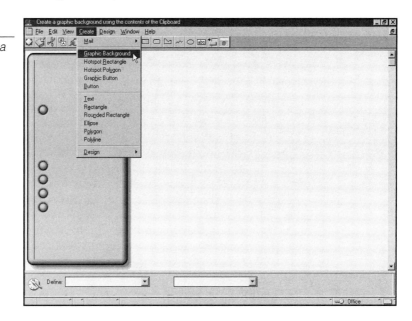

Note

Once the graphic has been inserted onto the navigator, it cannot be modified, nor can its position on the navigator be changed. If you need to modify the appearance (size or content) of the navigator, it must be changed from the source file, removed from the navigator, and then reinserted.

To remove a graphic background from a navigator, perform the following steps:

1. From the Design menu, choose Remove Graphic Background.

2. Now that your background is established, add other objects to your navigator.

If the graphic you added is complete enough, all you must do is add hotspots for executing commands; otherwise, you may have to add other graphic objects to increase user understanding of the navigator.

Inserting Hotspots

Hotspots are areas on your navigator that a user can click to execute some sort of command. Hotspots are normally invisible, but can be made to appear when the user passes his or her mouse pointer over or clicks them. Because they are normally invisible, hotspots are usually placed over graphic images or other navigator objects that the user would know to click—the image of a button, for example. Two kinds of hotspots are available:

▶ Hotspot rectangles—Use these when you want to highlight a square or rectangular object.

▶ Hotspot polygons—Use these when you want to highlight an irregularly shaped object (such as the outline of a map).

To insert a rectangular hotspot, do the following:

1. Select Create | Hotspot Rectangle.

2. Position your mouse pointer where the upper-left corner of the hotspot is to be. You will be able to reposition and resize the hotspot when the operation is complete.

3. Click and drag the rectangle to the size desired.

 Tip

If you press the Shift key while dragging the hotspot, the rectangle will be perfectly square. Be sure to release your mouse button before you release the Shift key.

To insert an irregularly shaped hotspot, do the following:

1. Select Create | Hotspot Polygon.

2. Position your mouse pointer where you want to construct the polygon.

3. Click and release your mouse button. At each point where a corner is to begin, click the mouse button; an anchor will be placed there.

4. To complete the polygon, double-click at the end point. When you double-click, a line from your end point to the starting point will be drawn.

Note   A polygon can have an unlimited number of segments.

After your hotspot has been created, a Properties for Hotspot Rectangle or Hotspot Polygon dialog box will appear (see Figure 16.5). These identical dialog boxes contain two tabs: Basics and HiLite.

Figure 16.5

*A Hotspot Proper-
ties dialog box
with the Basics
tab showing.*

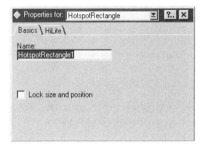

The Basics tab allows you to name the hotspot (for programmatic manipulation) and to lock its size and position. When selected, the Lock Size and Position check box prevents you from acciden-tally moving or resizing the hotspot.

The HiLite tab allows you to define when the border of the hotspot will appear to a user (see Figure 16.6). When selected, the Highlight When Touched check box causes the hotspot to appear with the characteristics you define when the user's mouse pointer touches the hotspot. The Highlight When Clicked check box causes the hotspot to appear with the characteristics you define when the hotspot is clicked by the user. The pull-down menus associated with Highlight Outline Width and Highlight Outline Color appear only when one of these check boxes has been select-ed. These pull-down menus allow you to define the characteristics of the hotspot's outline. The Make Default for Hotspots button causes the characteristics you define for this hotspot to become the default characteristics for all new hotspots created on this navigator. Clicking this button does not alter existing hotspots.

Figure 16.6

*A Hotspot Proper-
ties dialog box
with the HiLite tab
showing.*

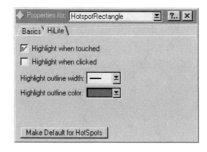

Inserting Graphic Buttons

Graphic buttons are graphics that act as buttons. To create a graphic button, you must first have the graphic in the operating system's clipboard. The graphic is treated as an object on your navigator that can be clicked to engage some function. To insert a graphic button, do the following:

1. From whatever graphic program is suitable, copy the graphic to the operating system clipboard.

2. Select Create | Graphic Button.

Note

As with a graphic background, the size and content of a graphic button cannot be changed after it has been inserted. However, unlike with a graphic background, you can change the position of the button at any time.

After your hotspot has been created, the Properties For Graphic Button dialog box will appear. This dialog box mirrors the Properties for Hotspot Rectangle dialog box in form and function (refer to Figures 16.5 and 16.6). Refer to the section titled "Inserting Hotspots" to review the properties of these dialog boxes.

Inserting Buttons

Buttons in Lotus Notes are standard Windows 3D buttons. They are rectangular in shape and appear raised from the surface of the navigator. Buttons can have text printed on them or they can be blank. To insert a button, do the following:

1. Select Create | Button.

2. Position your mouse pointer at the place where the upper-left corner of the button is to begin. You can reposition and resize the button when the operation is complete.

3. Click and drag the button to the size desired.

 Tip

> If you press the Shift key while dragging, the button will be perfectly square. Be sure to release the mouse button before you release the Shift key.

After your button has been created, a Properties for Button dialog box will appear (see Figure 16.7). This dialog box contains four tabs:

▶ Basics—This tab is the same for buttons as for hotspots except that it contains a Caption field, which allows you to insert text that will be displayed on the face of the button.

▶ Font—This tab allows you to define the font for any text placed in the Caption field on the Basics tab (see Figure 16.8). After you have defined the text characteristics, click the Make Default for Buttons button if you want all future buttons on this navigator to have these font characteristics.

▶ Presentation—This tab enables you to change the button's color, bevel width (this adjusts how high the button appears to be), and outline color (see Figure 16.9). After you have defined the presentation characteristics, click the Make Default for Buttons button if you want all future buttons on this navigator to have these characteristics.

▶ HiLite—This HiLite tab is the same as for the one for hotspots (refer to Figure 16.6). Refer to the section titled "Inserting Hotspots" for more information.

Figure 16.7

A Properties for Button dialog box with the Basics tab showing.

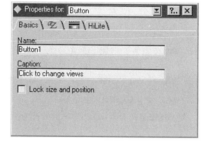

Figure 16.8

A Properties for Button dialog box with the Font tab showing.

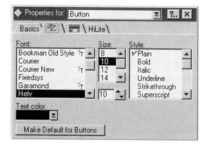

Figure 16.9

A Properties for Button dialog box with the Presentation tab showing.

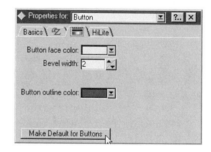

Inserting Text Boxes

Text boxes on a navigator are used primarily to insert static, annotational text. As with other objects, the text can have an action associated with clicking it. Text is not simply inserted onto the navigator as it is on a form; instead, it is inserted into an object called a *text box*. This object is self-contained and can be dragged around and resized. To insert a text box, do the following:

1. Select Create | Text.

2. Position your mouse pointer where the upper-left corner of the text box is to begin. You can reposition and resize the text box when the operation is complete.

3. Click and drag the text box to the size desired.

 Tip

If you press the Shift key while dragging the text box, the box will be perfectly square. Be sure to release your mouse button before you release the Shift key.

After your text box has been created, a Properties for Text dialog box appears. This dialog box contains four tabs:

▶ Basics—This Basics tab is the same as the one for hotspots, except that there is more room to insert text for the text box content (refer to the section titled "Inserting Hotspots" and to Figure 16.7).

▶ Font—This Font tab is the same as the one for buttons (refer to the section titled "Inserting Buttons" and to Figure 16.8).

▶ Presentation—This tab is unique to text boxes; it includes properties for the width and color of the box outline as well as for the fill color of the box (see Figure 16.10).

▶ HiLite—This HiLite tab is the same as the one for hotspots (refer to the section titled "Inserting Hotspots" and to Figure 16.6).

Figure 16.10

A Properties for Text dialog box with the Presentation tab showing.

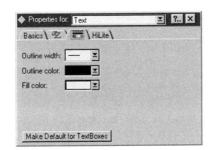

Tip

If you want your text to appear as though it is not contained in a box, make the outline and fill colors the same color as the background on which the text will be placed. These characteristics can be found on the Presentation tab of the Properties dialog box.

Inserting Shapes

Notes provides a number of shapes that can be used to provide backgrounds or buttons on which users can click. Shapes differ from hotspots in that they always appear; they are never invisible (unless the fill and border are the same color as the background on which they are created). The available shapes are rectangle, rounded rectangle, ellipse, and polygon. To insert a rectangle, rounded rectangle, or ellipse, do the following:

1. Select Create | Rectangle/Rounded Rectangle/Ellipse.

2. Position your mouse pointer where the upper-left corner of the shape is to begin. You can reposition and resize the shape when the operation is complete.

3. Click and drag the shape to the size desired.

 Tip

If you press the Shift key while dragging the shape, the shape will be perfectly proportioned. Rectangles and rounded rectangles will be perfect squares; ellipses will be perfect circles. Be sure to release your mouse button before you release the Shift key.

To insert a polygon, do the following:

1. Select Create | Polygon.

2. Position your mouse pointer where you want to begin constructing the polygon.

3. Click and release your mouse button. At each point where a corner is to begin, click your mouse button to place an anchor.

4. To complete the polygon, double-click the end point. When you double-click, a line from your final point to the first point will be drawn to complete the border of the polygon.

Note   Remember: A polygon can have an unlimited number of segments.

After your shape has been created, a Properties for Rectangle, Rounded Rectangle, Ellipse, or Polygon dialog box will appear. This dialog box contains four familiar tabs:

▶ Basics—This Basics tab is the same as the one for hotspots (refer to "Inserting Hotspots" and to Figure 16.7).

▶ Font—This Font tab is the same as the one for buttons (refer to "Inserting Buttons" and to Figure 16.8).

▶ Presentation—This Presentation tab is the same as the one for text boxes (refer to "Inserting Text Boxes" and to Figure 16.10).

▶ HiLite—This HiLite tab is the same as the one for hotspots (refer to "Inserting Hotspots" and to Figure 16.6).

Inserting Polylines

It is sometimes convenient to be able to draw one or more lines on your navigator. These lines are created in the same way as polygons, except that they are not expected to close when they are complete (that is, no line will be automatically generated to enclose an object). To insert a polyline, do the following:

1. Select Create | Polyline.

2. Position your mouse pointer where you want to begin constructing the polyline.

3. Click and release your mouse pointer. At each point where a new segment is to begin, click your mouse button to place an anchor.

4. To complete the polyline, double-click at the end.

Note | A polyline can have an unlimited number of segments.

After your polyline is created, a Properties for Polyline dialog box appears. This dialog box contains three familiar tabs:

▶ Basics—This Basics tab is the same as the one for hotspots (refer to Figure 16.6).

▶ Presentation—This Presentation tab is the same as the one for polygons, except there is no option for changing the fill color (see Figure 16.11).

▶ HiLite—This HiLite tab is the same as the one for hotspots (refer to Figure 16.7).

Figure 16.11

A Properties for Polyline dialog box with the Presentation tab showing.

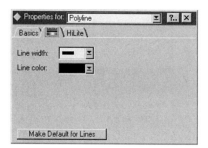

Assigning Actions to Navigator Objects

All navigator objects, with the exception of graphic backgrounds, can be associated with actions; when a user clicks a navigator object, that object can be made to perform some operation. What an object does when clicked is specified in the Design pane of the navigator (at the bottom of the navigator design environment). When you select an object in the navigator Builder window, the definition for that object appears, and its name appears in the field next to the Define label.

You can choose from three kinds of run categories when deciding what an object should do when clicked:

- ▶ Simple action

- ▶ Formula

- ▶ Script

Because the AD1 and AD2 exams don't deal with Script, I will discuss only the simple action and formula categories here.

Run Simple Action

A simple action is an executable, system-defined event. Selecting the Simple Action radio button invokes the Action field, which you can use to choose the kind of action you want to perform. The categories, as shown in Figure 16.12, are

- ▶ Open Another Navigator—Choosing this option invokes a pull-down menu, from which you can choose another navigator to open. This is useful if you want users to be able to move from one graphic image to another—for example, move to more detailed maps as they navigate a country looking for places and customers. You can choose only from navigators that already exist in this database.

- ▶ Open a View—Choosing this option invokes a View pull-down menu, from which you can choose another view to open. This does not cause the navigator to change; it only changes what view is displayed on the right side of the navigator. This is useful if you want to give your users access to more than one view without having to go back to the Folders navigator.

- ▶ Alias a Folder—If you choose this option, this object becomes, in essence, the folder of your choice. If the user clicks the object, the folder list will appear on the right of the navigator. If a user drags a document onto the object, that document will become part of the folder contents.

- ▶ Open a Link—If you choose Open a Link, this object will open a specified document, view, or database link when clicked. After you've chosen this action, a button labeled

Paste Link will appear. The expectation is that you have a link to a document, view, or database in the clipboard; a click on the Paste Link button will associate a click of this button with that link. If you do not have a link available, you will have to get one before this option will function.

Figure 16.12

The Navigator design pane with the Simple Actions list showing.

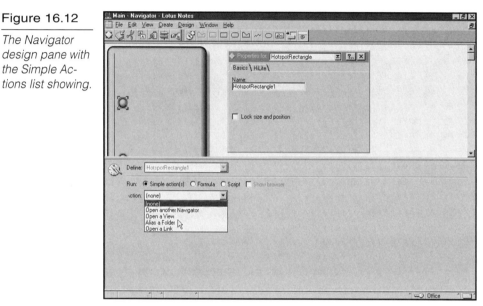

Run Formula

If you choose Formula from the run option buttons, you will be able to define a formula, which is executed when the object is clicked. For more information about formula construction, refer to Chapters 13, "Introduction to Formulas," 15, "Creating Actions and Hotspots," 18, "Advanced Formulas, Part I," and 19, "Advanced Formulas, Part II."

Note

Due to Notes limitations, some functions do not operate properly when executed from a navigator. A notable example: You cannot use the @Command([Compose]) function to create a Response or Response-to-Response document. For unknown reasons, a click on a navigator hotspot causes Notes to lose all record of any document selection in a view. As a result, if you try this kind of function, you will get an error indicating that no main document is selected.

Manipulating Navigator Objects

Navigator objects can be moved around and, with the exception of graphic buttons, can be resized. In addition, properties can be changed after they are assigned, and objects can be deleted. To change the size of an object, do the following:

1. Click the object once to select it, and then place your pointer on any of the black squares that appear around it.

2. Click and drag a square; the object will resize accordingly (see Figure 16.13).

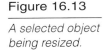

Figure 16.13

A selected object being resized.

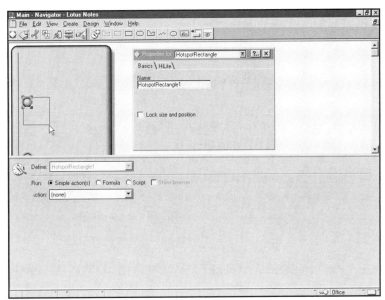

To change the position of an object, place your pointer in the middle of the object and click and drag; the object will move to the position you drag it to. To reorder objects that are piled on top of each other, do the following:

1. Click the object in the object pile that you want to reposition.

2. If you want to place the object on the top of the pile, select Design I Bring to Front.

3. If you want to place the object on the bottom of the pile, select Design | Send to Back.

To invoke the Properties dialog box for the object, double-click the object. To delete an object, click the object once to select it, then press the Delete key.

After you have finished the design of your navigator, you can save and close it to return to the Folders view. To see the navigator in action, select View | Show, then choose the name of the navigator you just created. To return to the Folders view, select View | Show | Folders.

You might want the navigator to appear automatically when the database is opened. To do this, you must set a database property. This and other database properties are discussed in the section titled "Database Properties."

Understanding the Database Icon

The Database icon is one of the first things users see after they add the database to their workspace. The purpose of the icon is to provide quick information about the database and the function it performs. This is a big task for a 32 by 32 pixel image!

Every database that is created has an icon, even if it is only the default Notes icon (three people standing together). There is no need to create the default icon, but you might want to modify it using the tools available in Notes or by copying another image from the clipboard into the icon. To modify the icon, you first must edit it:

1. Open the database by double-clicking its icon on your workspace.

2. If the Design category is not expanded, click the twistie, then click the Other view to show the miscellaneous elements on the right.

3. Double-click the element called Icon to edit its design.

The Design Icon dialog box, shown in Figure 16.4, is where changes to the Database icon are made. This design environment consists of six sections:

▶ The tool buttons

▶ The mode buttons

▶ The Icon Builder window

▶ The color palette

▶ The preview area

▶ The command buttons

Figure 16.14

The Design Icon dialog box enables you to change the appearance of the icon.

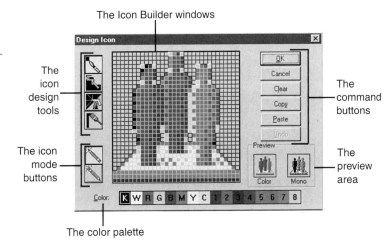

The Icon Builder windows

The icon design tools

The icon mode buttons

The color palette

The command buttons

The preview area

Using the Icon Design Tools

The icon design tools are found in a column in the upper-left corner of the Design Icon dialog box. These buttons consist of the following:

▶ Paintbrush—This tool is used to color with the current color one pixel at a time. Use this tool by clicking the center area (the Icon Builder window) of the square you want to modify.

▶ Roller—This tool is used to color over areas joined horizontally or vertically that are all the same color. If you click a square, all other squares of the same color that touch horizontally or vertically are changed to the active color. The only squares that are not altered are those that are a different color, those that do not touch the selected square, and those that touch corner-to-corner instead of side-to-side.

▶ Spray—This tool is like the roller, except that alterable squares include same-color squares that touch corner-to-corner with the square clicked.

▶ Line—This tool draws a line that is one square wide in the direction you are moving when you start to drag. If you begin in a square and click and drag to the right, you will be able to modify only the line in that horizontal plane. To change to a vertical line, release your mouse button and start again.

Using the Icon Mode Buttons

The mode buttons, located in the lower-left corner of the Design Icon window, are used to switch between draw and erase mode. The top button puts you into draw mode, where what you do gets drawn with the currently selected color. The bottom button puts you into erase mode, where everything you click gets cleared to allow the background color to come through; this background color will usually be gray.

Using the Icon Builder Window

The Icon Builder window is the center part of the screen where the design happens. This window is divided into 1,024 squares called *pixels*. The color of each of these pixels can be changed using the tools to the left of this window.

Using the Color Palette

Using the color palette, you can change the current active color. The active color is the one employed when you use the drawing tools. To change the active color, click the box representing the color you want to use.

Using the Preview Area

The preview area, located in the bottom-right of the Design Icon dialog box, is where you can see how the icon will look when it is finished. This is helpful because the large view is deceptive; in this view, the icon either looks better or (more frequently) worse than it really is. Monitor your progress using the preview area to see how your changes will be perceived.

Using the Command Buttons

Use the command buttons to issue design commands:

▶ Click the OK button to exit and save the changes you have made.

▶ Click the Cancel button to exit and dispose of all changes you have made in this editing session.

▶ Click the Clear button to start with a clean slate.

▶ Click the Copy button to copy the contents of the Icon Builder window to the operating system clipboard (this will allow you to paste it elsewhere in the future). This is useful for copying the icon from one database to another.

▶ Click the Paste button to copy the contents of the clipboard over the current contents of the Icon Builder window.

▶ Click the Undo button to undo the effect of the last change you made, be it a modification of a single pixel or a spray of a large area.

Note

Although the Paste button will copy from the clipboard to the Icon Builder window, it can copy only as much material as there is space for. Remember when copying that the icon can only be 40×40 pixels. If the image you are pasting is larger than that, you will get only the top-left corner of the image.

Understanding Database Properties

Like other Notes objects, databases have properties. Some of these are appropriate to look at in the context of finalizing the database; others are discussed in other places in this book or not at all because they do not relate to AD1 or AD2 exams or clarify other concepts.

To view database properties from your workspace, right-click the database you want to see the properties for and choose Database Properties from the menu that appears. The database properties are divided into six tabs:

- Basics

- Information

- Printing

- Design

- Launch

- Full Text

For the purposes of this discussion, I will examine certain properties of the Basics and Launch tabs.

Using the Basics Tab

The Basics tab, shown in Figure 16.15, can be used to alter information specified when the database was created, including the database title and local encryption method (refer to Chapter 11, "Introduction to Application Development Components"). For example, if the name of the database is no longer suitable, you can change this property in the Title field.

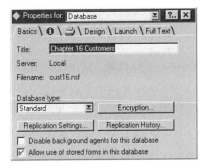

Using the Launch Tab

The Launch tab allows you to define two things: what happens when the database is opened, and when the About Database document is displayed (see Figure 16.16).

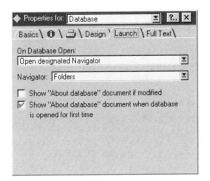

The On Database Open pull-down menu lists actions that can be taken when the database is opened by a user. The default for this list is Restore as Last Viewed by User, in which case the database will appear to the user as it did the last time he or she exited it. The navigator and view that he or she was last using will be displayed. The other options are as follows:

▶ Open About Database Document—If this option is chosen, the About Database document will be opened every time any user opens the database. For more information about the About Database document, see Chapter 17, "Creating Application Documentation."

▸ Open Designated Navigator—If this option is chosen, the display of an additional pull-down list allows you to choose from a list of the navigators available in this database. When a user opens the database, the navigator chosen will come up automatically. If the navigator has a view associated with it, that view will be displayed as well.

▸ Open Designated Navigator in Its Own Window—If this option is chosen, the display of an additional pull-down list allows you to choose from a list of the navigators available in this database. When a user opens the database, the navigator chosen will automatically come up, but it will appear without a view; instead, the navigator will cover the whole open window. This is useful when one or more of your navigators is simply a menu designed to provide the user with database choices but not to display information.

▸ Launch First Attachment in About Database—If this option is chosen, Notes will find and launch the first attachment in the About Database document.

In the case of all these choices, except Open About Database Document and Launch First Attachment in About Database, you can select two check boxes:

▸ Show About Database Document If Modified—If you select this check box, the About Database document will appear to users every time they open the database if that document has been modified since the last time they opened it. The About Database document is used to provide general information about the database. If there is new information about the database or if new features have been implemented and documented, it might be helpful to so inform users.

▸ Show About Database Document When Database Is Opened for the First Time—If you select this check box, the About Database document will be presented the first time a user opens a database.

Note   If you select the first check box, you cannot deselect the
second.

Implementing Security

Objective   The security inherent in Notes is one of its big selling features;
people like Notes because it can be made secure. One of the jobs
of the application developer is to consider and inform people
about levels of access to the databases they create. The application
development exams do not expect you to be a system administrator, but they do expect you to have working knowledge of database
security (at least at the Access Control List level for the AD1 exam).
That means you will need to know where the ACL is, how to look at
it, what the levels of access are, what these levels allow you to do,
and how to add people or groups to the ACL for a database.

Note   Other techniques can be used to build security into Notes
applications. Some of these are discussed in Chapter 23,
"Securing Applications."

The ACL is the first level of database security users must pass to
get to data in your database (prior to that, they had to get to the
server on which the database was held). The ACL is where the
database examines the user's ID file to determine whether access
should be given and at what level. The manager of a database has
the power to give or take away access to people or groups. That
access comes in a variety of grades, or levels, each of which grants
a certain level of access within the database.

Using the ACL Dialog Box

To manipulate the ACL, you must first open the Access Control
List dialog box, where all access levels are assigned. Each database
has its own ACL, so you can grant access to each person in your
organization for each database separately and at different levels.

To open the ACL dialog box from your workspace, right-click the database whose ACL you want to see and select Access Control from the menu that appears (see Figure 16.17).

Figure 16.17

The Access Control List dialog box allows access-level changes for the database.

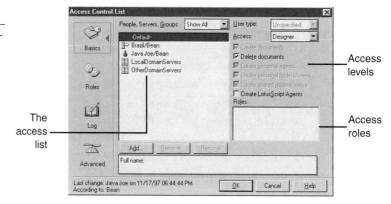

The access list

Access levels

Access roles

The ACL dialog box is divided into four tabs, each identified by an icon on the left side of the box. This discussion covers only the first tab, Basics, which is divided into three sections:

▶ The center column allows you to see the people and groups who have been assigned access levels.

▶ The upper-right section allows you to see the access level and refinements given to the person or group currently selected.

▶ The roles box, which is present in the lower-right area (for more information about roles, see Chapter 23, "Securing Applications").

Each person or group whose access needs to be controlled for this ACL is added to the ACL. At this point, a level of access is granted to allow those people to do what they need to do in the database, but no more.

Supporting ACL Levels

Notes supports seven access levels (shown in Figure 16.18) with six refinements that can be made to the default access. These levels are

► no access

► depositor

► reader

► author

► editor

► designer

► manager

Figure 16.18

The Access Control List dialog box with the access levels showing.

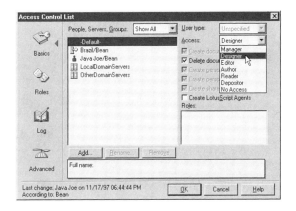

The refinements, which you can implement by selecting or deselecting check boxes below the access level, are

► Create Documents

► Delete Documents

► Create Personal Agents

► Create Personal Folders/Views

► Create Shared Folders/Views

► Create LotusScript Agents

Not all of these refinements can be added or taken away from all levels of access. Some levels cannot have certain rights removed, whereas others cannot have certain rights added.

No Access Privileges

Users with no access–level privileges to a database cannot put that database on their workspace. Any attempts to do so produce a message saying that they have insufficient access to add the database and the task is complete. This level is given to people who have no need at all for the data in the database.

 Note

If users add a database to their workspace and then have their access downgraded to no access, the Database icon will not be removed. However, attempts to access the database will produce a message indicating that they no longer have sufficient access rights to open it.

Depositor Privileges

Depositor access enables users to add documents to a database, but not read or modify those or any other documents. Depositor access is like the access you have to a ballot box when you vote in an election. You are given a card, you fill it in; after it is dropped in the slot, you cannot retrieve it, nor can you look at what anyone else has done. Users with depositor-level access have the Create Documents refinement, and that cannot be taken away. However, depositors cannot be given any of the other refined rights.

Reader Privileges

Reader access enables users to look at any documents in the database. Like someone who goes to a library, users can scan a list of all the reading material (through the use of one or more views) and if they see something they like, they can open the document to read it. However, they cannot create new or modify existing documents. This level of access is often given to reference databases such as policies and procedures manuals. Readers can be granted the ability to create personal agents, create personal folders/views, and create LotusScipt agents.

Author Privileges

The default definition of an author is someone who can create new documents, read all documents, and edit their own documents. Authors also frequently have the right to delete what they create. Like the author of a book, authors in a database can create new documents and modify what they create; however, when it comes to other peoples' material, authors are only readers. Authors can have the following rights granted or taken away:

- ▶ Create Documents

- ▶ Delete Documents

- ▶ Create Personal Agents

- ▶ Create Personal Folders/Views

- ▶ Create LotusScript Agents

The only right that cannot be granted is the right to create shared folders/views.

 Note   As mentioned in Chapter 12, "Creating Forms," an author's ability to modify a document after it has been created depends not only on the ACL settings or refinements; he or she must also be listed in an Authors field on the document he or she is trying to modify.

Editor Privileges

The default definition of an editor is someone who can create documents and modify anyone's documents. Like book editors, editors in databases have a global author right that allows them to change what anyone has done in any document. Editors are required in environments where depositors are creating documents because depositors cannot change documents they've created. Editors can be granted all refinements and cannot be denied the Create Documents right.

Designer Privileges

Users with designer-level privileges can change database design. They are the application developers, the ones who modify forms, shared views, agents, and navigators. Designers have the abilities of editors with the additional ability to modify the structure of the database. Every database should have at least one designer to maintain it after it has been created. Designers are granted all refinements, and can be denied only the Delete Documents and Create LotusScript Agents refinements.

Manager Privileges

Database managers have complete control over the database. They have the same abilities as designers, and therefore can look at and edit all documents as well as look at and modify design. In addition, managers can change ACL levels, and can delete the database from within Notes (via File|Database|Delete). A database must have at least one manager to maintain the ACL levels on an ongoing basis.

Managers have all rights, and only their ability to delete documents can be removed. Even that, however, is only a safety feature, for a manager can restore his or her ability to delete at any time. This feature ensures that the manager cannot accidentally delete documents.

Maintaining the ACL

The ACL contains three kinds of entries:

- Individuals (servers or people)
- Groups (servers, people, or mixed)
- Default

There is usually a group called LocalDomainServers that frequently has manager access. This allows servers that are part of your Notes domain to perform administrative tasks, such as replication, on the database. It is a good idea to leave the LocalDomainServers group in the ACL with a level of manager unless it is decided in conjunction with a systems administrator that changing the level or removing the group is a good idea. All other groups and individuals are optional.

 Caution

LocalDomainServers is necessary for the proper replication of databases. Unless you have explicitly listed the servers that are to replicate a specific database, do not remove LocalDomainServers; otherwise, replication might not happen.

The default entry is always present and cannot be removed. This group is assigned the access level that anyone trying to access the database who is not listed either individually or as part of a group should get. Frequently this level is reader or, in high-security environments, no access. It is very dangerous to provide access higher than reader; if you do, anyone will be able to create documents or worse (depending on the level of access granted to default).

Creating and Using Groups

The use of groups is the preferred way of granting access to the database. Groups, which are lists of people or servers, are kept in an address book that Notes consults every time access to a database is attempted. Groups are the preferred way of granting access because they make it easier to implement changes. For example, if you add 20 individuals to 20 databases and grant them the same level of access without using groups, you will have to type 400 entries. If individuals need to be added or removed, you will have to go to the ACLs of all 20 databases to make the change. But if that list of 20 people had been placed into a group and the group placed into the ACL of each of the 20 databases, then only 20 entries would have to be made, and any changes would need to occur only in one place.

A group needs to be created in an address book that must be accessible from the location of the database. That means that if a database is on a local workstation, the group could be in a Personal Address Book or the Public Address Book. If the database is on a server, the group must be present on an address book on the server (usually the Public Address Book).

To create a group in the Public Address Book, you must have at least author-level access with the role GroupCreator. If you do not have such access, you will have to get the manager of the PAB to give you that access or have someone else maintain the groups for you.

To create a group in an address book, do the following:

1. On your workspace, double-click the address book in which you want to create the group. The default view will appear.

2. Click the Groups view to see a list of existing groups.

It is a good idea to make sure there is not already a group containing the same list of people as the one you are about to create. There is no reason to create a second group if one already exists.

3. Click the Add Group action button to add a new group; a Group document will appear (see Figure 16.19).

Figure 16.19

The Group document allows you to define an address book group.

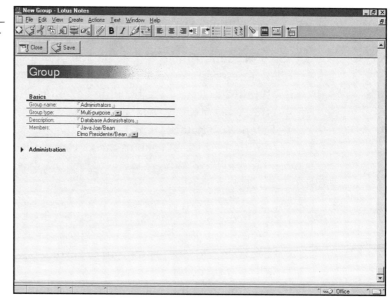

4. In the Group Name field, enter a name that describes the purpose of the group and that you can use later to identify it.

5. For an Access Control List group, either leave the group type as multipurpose or select Access Control List Only from the dialog box that appears when you click the down arrow.

6. If desired, type a description of the purpose of this group in the Description field. This description will appear in the list of groups for this address book and will help you identify its purpose later.

7. Type the names of the members of the group in the Members field, or click the down-arrow to invoke an Address dialog box from which you can choose the names of the people in your group.

8. Save the group and exit from the document as well as from the database.

Adding People or Groups to a Database ACL

Adding people or groups to your ACL involves getting their names into the ACL and assigning their names an access level.

Note

When adding people or servers individually to the ACL, you maintain the best security by using the fully distinguished name instead of the common name. If you assign access to only a common name (for example, `Java Joe`) instead of to the fully distinguished name (for example, `Java Joe/Sales/Columbia/Bean`), you are granting access to any person or server with that common name. If you use the fully distinguished name, you ensure that only the person or server you have in mind is the one with that level of access.

To add a person or group to a database ACL, do the following:

1. From your workspace, right-click the database whose ACL you want to see and choose Access Control from the menu that appears.

2. On the Basics tab for the ACL, click the Add button.

3. In the Add User dialog box, type the name of a person, server, or group to which you want to grant access and click the OK button to update the ACL (see Figure 16.20). If you need to use the address book to select the people, servers, or groups to add, click the Address Book button (the button with the head on it), add your users, and then click the OK button to update the ACL.

Figure 16.20

The Add User dialog box allows you to add a person, server, or group to the ACL.

 Tip

By using the Address Book button, you can add more than one entry at one time. The Add User dialog box enables you to add only one person, server, or group at one time.

4. For each person, server, or group that you added, click the ACL entry and then choose a user type from the User Type pull-down list to the right.

 Note

The user types are Unspecified, Person, Server, Mixed Group, Person Group, and Server Group. By choosing a type that is appropriate for the ACL entry, you increase security by ensuring that people using server IDs cannot function with the levels of access assigned to servers and to also ensure that groups cannot be created with the same names as people to gain the person's access level.

5. For each person, server, or group that you added, click the ACL entry and then choose a level of access from the Access pull-down list to the right.

6. If desired, select or deselect the ACL level refinements for that person, server, or group.

7. Click the OK button to make the ACL changes permanent and exit the Access Control List dialog box.

Note

It may happen that a person listed individually in an ACL is also part of a group or groups in the ACL. If the same level of access is not assigned to each, the following rules apply:

▶ If an individual is listed in the ACL and is also part of a group listed, the individual level of access always takes precedent over the group level, even if the individual level is lower.

▶ If a person is included in two groups, both of which are listed in the ACL, the person gets the highest level of access assigned to either group.

Removing People or Groups from a Database ACL

As part of ongoing security maintenance, certain people or groups might need to be removed from the ACL. When this happens, the people or servers will revert to the default access level unless they are included elsewhere in the ACL. To remove a person or group from a database ACL, do the following:

1. From your workspace, right-click the database whose ACL you want to see and choose Access Control from the menu that appears.

2. On the Basics tab, click the person or group you want to remove from the Access list.

3. Click the Remove button.

4. Click the OK button to make the ACL changes permanent and exit the Access Control List dialog box.

Exercises

To finalize this phase of database development, you are asked to add a graphical navigator that opens automatically when the customer database is opened. In addition, you need to create a group in the Public Address book and add it to the ACL, giving it (and its listed people) manager access to the database. The database you will use for this lab is available on the CD-ROM accompanying this book, and should be copied from it to your default Notes data directory. As well, you'll find a file called nav.bmp, which you will use to create the graphical navigator. The lab file is called cust16.nsf and its title is Chapter 16 Customers. Be sure that when you copy the file, you remove the read-only attribute or you will not be able to modify the database.

Exercise 16.1

1. Select File | Database | Open and select the Chapter 16 Customers database from the pull-down list of local databases. Click the Open button to add the database to your workspace and open the Standard view.

2. If the design category is not expanded, click the twistie, and then click the Navigators view to show the navigators on the right; this view contains only the answer to the challenge question.

3. Select Create | Design | Navigator.

4. Right-click in the middle of the Navigator Builder pane (the one on the top) and choose Navigator Properties from the pull-down menu. This invokes the dialog shown in Figure 16.21.

5. On the Basics tab of the Properties for Navigator dialog, type Main into the Title field, choose All Customers from the Initial View or Folders list, and select the Auto Adjust Panes at Runtime check box. Click the Close Window button to close the Properties for Navigator dialog box.

6. Start a graphics program and open the file nav.bmp, which you copied onto your hard drive in preparation for this lab.

Figure 16.21

The properties for the Main navigator.

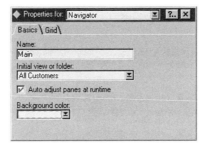

Note

If you are using Windows 95 or Windows NT 4.0, you can start the Paint program by selecting Start I Programs I Accessories I Paint. Open the file by selecting File I Open and navigating to the place where you copied the bitmap image.

7. In your graphics program, select the entire graphic and copy it to the clipboard.

Note

If you are using Paint as your graphics editor, select Edit I Select All, then select Edit I Copy.

8. Switch back to Lotus Notes; the navigator design environment should return.

9. Select Create I Graphic Background; the image you just copied should be pasted on the left side of the navigator (see Figure 16.22).

10. Select Create I Text. Starting near the top-left corner of the graphic, drag out a box like the one shown in Figure 16.23.

11. On the Basics tab of the Properties for Text dialog, type Bean Inc. in the title field. On the Font tab, choose the font size 24, the style Bold, and the color dark red. On the Presentation tab, choose the outline color light gray and the fill color light gray (this will make the box invisible but the text visible). Close the Properties dialog box by clicking the Close Window button.

continues

Exercise 16.1 Continued

Figure 16.22

The navigator with the graphic background inserted.

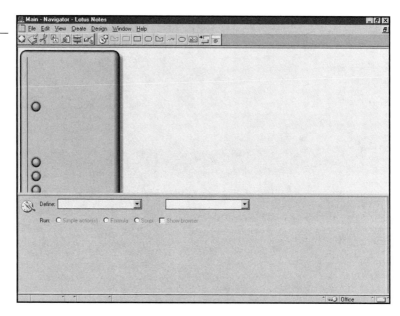

Figure 16.23

The navigator with the first text box inserted.

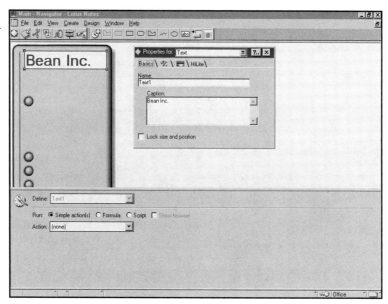

12. Select Create | Text and then, starting underneath the text box you just created, drag out a box like the one shown in Figure 16.24.

Figure 16.24

*The navigator
with the second
text box inserted.*

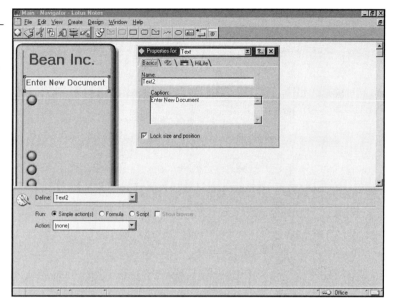

13. On the Basics tab of the Properties for Text dialog, type
    Enter New Document in the title field. On the Font tab, choose
    a font size of 12, the style Bold, and the color dark red. On
    the Presentation tab, select the outline color light gray
    and the fill color light gray (this will make the box invisible
    but the text visible). Close the Properties dialog box by click-
    ing the Close Window button.

14. Click the text box you just created (the resizing handles
    should be showing the corners) and, from the Edit menu,
    choose Copy. Then select Edit I Paste.

15. Drag the text box with the Enter New Document label into the
    open space below the first two buttons. Because this is a
    copy, the original should remain intact.

16. Double-click the text box you just dragged to open its prop-
    erties and replace the caption with the text Views (see Figure
    16.25). Close the Properties dialog box by clicking the Close
    Window button.

continues

Exercise 16.1   Continued

Figure 16.25

The text box you copied is now modified.

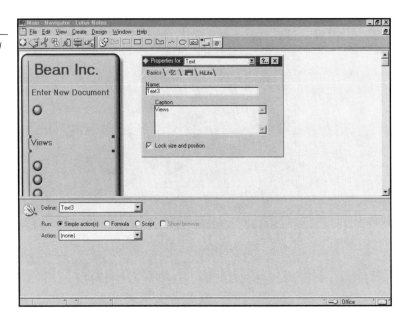

17. Using the same techniques, create text boxes so that your navigator looks like the one shown in Figure 16.26. The font characteristics are as follows:

   ▶ Size: 10

   ▶ Style: Plain

   ▶ Color: Black

   When you are finished, make sure the Properties dialog boxes are closed.

18. Select Create | Button; then, starting below the last text you created, drag a button out so that your navigator looks like the one shown in Figure 16.27.

19. In the Properties for Button dialog box, enter Exit this database in the Caption field and on the Presentation tab, choose a lighter shade of gray from the Button Face color palette. Close the Properties dialog box by clicking the Close Window button.

Figure 16.26

The navigator with the text labels complete.

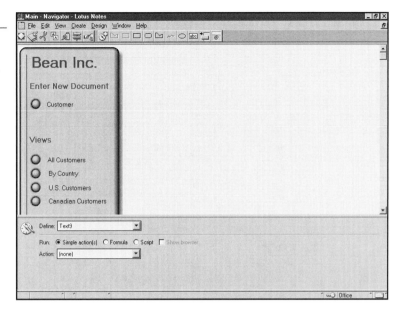

Figure 16.27

Add a button at the bottom of the navigator.

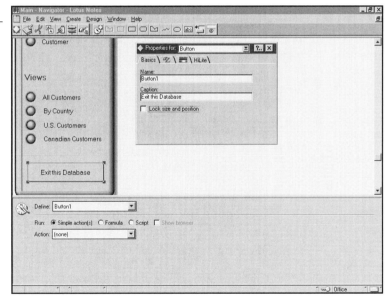

20. Select Create | Hotspot Rectangle and, starting in the upper-left corner of the top button of the background graphic, drag a rectangle that covers the whole button (see Figure 16.28).

continues

Exercise 16.1 Continued

Figure 16.28

A hotspot rectangle covers the first graphic button.

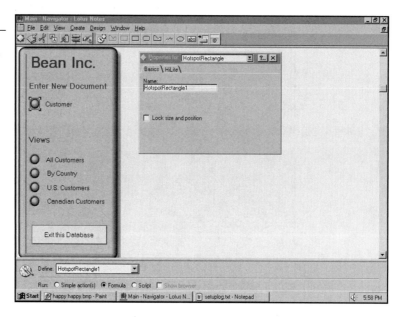

21. In the Properties for Hotspot Rectangle dialog box, click the HiLite tab and deselect the Highlight When Touched check box. This will ensure that users don't see that you have a hotspot that isn't the same shape as the button. The mere presence of the button should be enough to indicate that it should be clicked. Close the Properties dialog box by clicking the Close Window button.

22. Make a copy of the hotspot for each of the buttons by clicking it, choosing Edit I Copy, Edit I Paste, and then dragging the new copies onto their respective buttons. When you finish, the navigator should look like the one shown in Figure 16.29.

23. Click the hotspot to the left of the Customer label; handles should appear around it.

24. In the Design pane, click the Formula run option and, in the Formula window, type the following (see Figure 16.30):

```
@Command([Compose];"Customer")
```

Figure 16.29

The navigator with all the hotspots added.

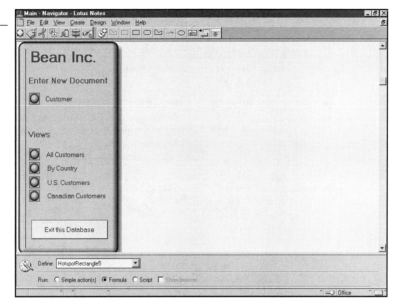

Figure 16.30

Create a run formula for the hotspot.

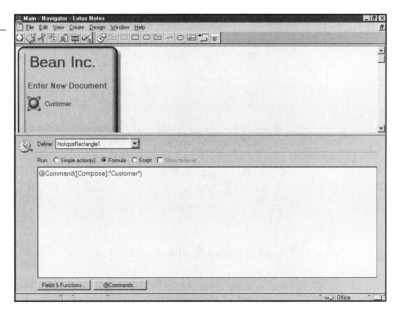

25. Click the hotspot to the left of the All Customers label; handles should appear around it.

continues

Exercise 16.1 Continued

26. In the Design pane, click the Simple Action run option, choose Open a View from the Action pull-down list, and choose All Customers from the pull-down list that appears to the left (see Figure 16.31).

Figure 16.31

Define a simple action to switch to the All Customers view.

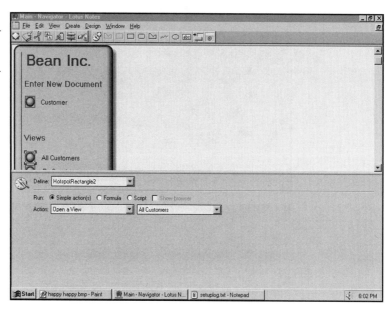

27. Click the button labeled `Exit This Database`.

28. In the Design pane, click the Formula run option and type the following in the Formula window:

```
@Command([FileCloseWindow])
```

29. Save the navigator and close to exit to the standard navigator.

30. Select View | Show | Main; the navigator should appear. Click the Customer button and a new Customer document should appear. Close the document.

31. Click the Exit This Database button to return to the workspace.

Exercise 16.2

1. Right-click the Chapter 16 Customers icon on your workspace and choose Database Properties from the menu that appears.

2. Click the Launch tab and, from the On Database Open pull-down list, choose Open Designated Navigator. From the Navigator pull-down menu, choose Main (see Figure 16.32).

Figure 16.32

The Properties for Database dialog box showing the Launch tab.

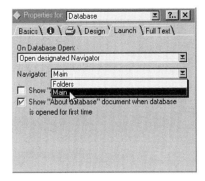

3. Close the Properties for Database dialog by clicking the Close Window button.

4. Double-click the Database icon. The database should open and display the navigator.

Exercise 16.3

1. Click the Exit This Database button to exit to the workspace.

2. Right-click the Chapter 16 Customers icon on your workspace and choose Access Control from the menu that appears.

 Note For the purposes of this exercise, you are assuming that a group called *Administrators* has already been created. Because you did not actually create this group, the group will not function, but you can see how the process works.

continues

Exercise 16.3 Continued

3. Click the Add button and, in the Add User dialog box, type Administrators (see Figure 16.33). Click the OK button to add the new group.

Figure 16.33

Add the Administrators group with the Add User dialog box.

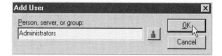

4. From the User Type pull-down list, choose Person Group and, from the Access pull-down list, choose Manager (see Figure 16.34).

Figure 16.34

Change the ACL setting for the Administrators group to manager.

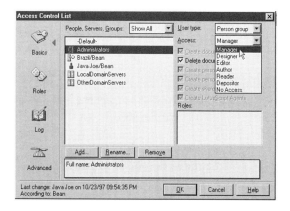

5. Click the OK button to complete the ACL change.

Exercise 16.4

You need to complete the modifications of the navigator. Your challenge is to add actions to all the remaining hotspots to allow your users to select any of the buttons and have them function. The answer to this exercise is found in a navigator called ChallengeAnswer.

Review Questions

1. Margaret wants to insert a graphic into the background of her navigator. What graphic format does Notes support for this?

   a. BMP

   b. PCX

   c. WPM

   d. Anything she can get into the clipboard

2. Of the following navigator objects, which cannot have an action associated with it?

   a. Polyline

   b. Background graphic

   c. Rectangular hotspot

   d. Ellipse

3. Brian wants to change the icon for his database. Under which design category is it located?

   a. Folders

   b. Views

   c. Other

   d. Pictures

4. Arnold copies a bitmap into the clipboard and then pastes it into his icon. How much of the image gets transferred to the icon?

   a. Regardless of its size, the whole picture gets transferred

   b. Only the upper-left 32×32 pixels

   c. Only the upper-left 60×60 pixels

   d. Only the upper-right 40×40 pixels

5. Juanita wants to ensure that her navigator opens every time a user opens her database. How can she ensure this happens?

   a. By choosing Open Designated Navigator in the On Database Open field on the Launch tab of the Properties for Database dialog box, and then choosing her database from the list.

   b. By choosing the Open About Database Document option in the On Database Open field on the Launch tab of the Properties for Database dialog.

6. Wilma has a graphical navigator that automatically appears when the database opens. How can she return to the Folders navigator without changing the database properties?

   a. With the Ctrl+Alt+Delete key combination

   b. With the Ctrl+Esc key combination

   c. Via File | Switch Navigators

   d. Via View | Show | Folders

7. Barney has created a navigator that he wants to open automatically when his database opens. It is a complete navigation system and he does not want a view to show with it. How can he accomplish this?

   a. By selecting File | Tools | User Preferences and picking the navigator name.

   b. By choosing Open Designated Navigator in Its Own Window from the Launch tab on the Properties for Database dialog box.

   c. By choosing Open Designated Navigator in Its Own Window from the Basics tab in the Properties for Database dialog box.

   d. By choosing Open Designated Navigator, and then choosing None from the Navigator pull-down list in the Properties for Database dialog box.

8. Fred wants to modify a form in a database on a Notes server. What is the minimum ACL level he needs to perform this action?

    a. Reader

    b. Author

    c. Designer

    d. Manager

9. Roger opens a database and, having double-clicked a document, chooses Edit Document from the Actions menu but nothing happens. What ACL level would make this happen for all documents?

    a. Reader

    b. Author

    c. Designer

    d. Manager

10. Wendy opens a database and, having double-clicked a document, chooses Edit Document from the Actions menu but nothing happens. What ACL level would make this happen for only some documents?

    a. Reader

    b. Author

    c. Designer

    d. Manager

11. Brad wants to give 20 people the same ACL level. What solution provides the easiest long-term maintenance?

    a. Create a group containing all the users and add it to the ACL with the appropriate access level.

    b. Add each user to the ACL individually, select them all, and change their access levels to the same level.

c. Add each user to the ACL individually and change each access level.

d. You cannot give more than one user the same level of access in the ACL.

12. Betty is a database manager and so is Perry. Betty wants to change Perry's access so that he cannot create new documents without removing his manager access. How can she do this?

a. Add Perry to the ACL a second time and give him reader access.

b. Deselect the Create Documents refinement check box.

c. Add a group containing Perry to the ACL and give it only reader access.

d. Betty cannot do this without changing Perry's access level.

13. On a navigator, what is the difference between a hotspot and a shape?

a. A hotspot always shows; a shape shows only sometimes.

b. A shape always shows; a hotspot shows only sometimes.

c. A shape can cause actions to execute; an action cannot.

d. A hotspot can cause actions to execute; a shape cannot.

Review Answers

1. D. Graphics are inserted into navigators via the clipboard. If you can get a graphic into the clipboard, you can get it into your navigator, regardless of what format it starts in. For more information, refer to the section titled "Inserting Graphic Backgrounds."

2. B. Of the navigator elements listed, the only one that cannot have an action associated with it is the background graphic.

All other elements that you can place on a navigator can be assigned actions. For more information, refer to the section titled "Assigning Actions to Navigator Objects."

3. C. The Other category contains the icon as well as the About Database and Using Database documents. For more information, refer to the section titled "Understanding the Database Icon."

4. B. The graphic area for an icon is only 32×32 pixels. As a result, any graphic you paste into an icon will have all area removed except for the upper-left 32×32 pixels. For more information, refer to the section titled "Using the Command Buttons."

5. A. To make this happen, Juanita must change the database property that controls what happens when the database is opened. This property, Open Designated Navigator, is located on the Launch tab. By choosing the specific navigator she wants, she will ensure that that navigator opens every time. For more information, refer to the section titled "Using the Launch Tab."

6. D. Selecting View|Show displays a list of available navigators. By choosing Folders from the list, she will return to the Standard Folders view. For more information, refer to the section titled "Manipulating Navigator Objects."

7. B. Barney wants to open the navigator by itself. This property is set on the Launch tab of the Properties for Database dialog. By choosing Open Designated Navigator in its Own Window, he can ensure that a view does not accompany the navigator he chooses when the database is opened. For more information, refer to "Using the Launch Tab."

8. C. To modify forms on shared databases, you must have at least designer-level access. An editor could be given the ability to create or modify shared folders/views, but no other shared components can be created or modified by anyone with less than designer-level access. For more information, refer to the section titled "Designer Privileges."

9. A. The only case in which this would always happen is if Roger has reader access. For more information, refer to the section titled "Reader Privileges."

10. B. If Wendy has author access and she is trying to edit a document for which she is not listed in the Author field, she will not be able to edit that document. However, if she is listed, she will be able to edit the document. For more information, refer to the section titled "Author Privileges."

11. A. The best long-term maintenance solution is provided through a group that is added to the ACL and assigned permissions. This affords easy changes of access levels to all the members of the group and also allows for the easy insertion of new people at that level through a change in group membership. The one downside is that any member of a group who needs a different access level will need to be added separately. For more information, refer to the section titled "Maintaining the ACL."

12. D. Most of the access levels can have refinements made to them to add or remove certain capabilities. Managers can be denied the Delete Documents refinement but not the Create Documents refinement. Perry's access level would have to be changed from manager to author before the Create Documents capability could be removed. For more information, refer to the section titled "Manager Privileges."

13. B. Shapes always show; hotspots can be made to appear, but by default, they do not show. For more information, refer to the sections "Inserting Hotspots" and "Inserting Shapes."

Answers to Test Yourself Questions at Beginning of Chapter

1. A graphical navigator is a navigator that you create yourself as an alternative to the Folders navigator. Its features, and what distinguishes it from the Folders navigator, are customized graphical backgrounds and objects that you can configure to perform actions, such as run formulas or simple actions. For more information, refer to the section titled "Creating Navigators."

2. The icon for a database is stored in the database's design. The icon can be viewed by navigating to the Design category in the Standard view, choosing Other, and then double-clicking the Icon option on the right side. From there, a Design window appears in which the icon can be modified. For more information, refer to the section titled "Understanding the Database Icon."

3. On the Launch tab of the Properties for Database dialog box is a Show About Database Document if Modified check box. If you select this check box and then modify the About Database document to reflect changes every time the database is modified, this document will appear every time new features are added to the database. For more information, refer to the section titled "Using the Launch Tab."

4. On the Launch tab of the Properties for Database dialog is an On Database Open pull-down list. If you choose Open Designated Navigator from this list and choose a navigator, you will ensure that that navigator is displayed every time the database is opened. For more information, refer to the section titled "Using the Launch Tab."

5. The ACL, or Access Control List, is where levels of access to a database are set. These levels of access control the baseline access that individuals or groups have in the database. These levels can be refined to be more restrictive through the use of ACL refinements or other database elements and properties. The levels of access are no access, depositor, reader, author, editor, designer, and manager. For more information, refer to the sections titled "Implementing Security" and "Supporting ACL Levels."

Chapter 17

Creating Application Documentation

This chapter will introduce you to the following objectives:

 Objectives

- ▶ Developing database-level documentation
- ▶ Developing form-level documentation
- ▶ Developing field-level documentation

Test Yourself! Before reading this chapter, test yourself to determine how much study time you will need to devote to this section.

1. What kinds of database-level documentation are provided with each Notes database?

2. What are some examples of tools that you can use to create form-level documentation?

3. How can you easily provide users with field-level documentation?

Answers are located at the end of the chapter...

Although developing database documentation is an important step of the application development process, it is a step that many developers overlook. In the rush to create applications, the time to create good documentation is often not allocated. Nonetheless, there are many ways that good documentation can be created with minimal design effort.

Developing Database-Level Documentation

 Objective

Database documentation is the highest level of documentation. The purpose of this documentation is to explain the workings of the entire database, and the documentation is available to all who use the database. Although the base design for database-level documentation is implemented at database creation, you must populate the documentation to use or reference it. This base documentation comes in the form of two special documents:

- ▶ The About Database document

- ▶ The Using Database document

The About Database and Using Database Documents

The About Database and Using Database documents are blank sheets when first opened, but can include many standard rich-text features:

- ▶ Attachments

- ▶ Graphics

- ▶ Document, view, and database links

- ▶ Sections

- ▶ Tables

- ▶ OLE objects

- ▶ Various hotspots

Although it lacks a rigidly defined function, the About Database document is intended to provide a forum for discussion about the general purpose of the database, what kind of people would use it, and its general structure. On the other hand, the Using Database document is intended to give you a place to create specific user documentation, including detailed descriptions of views, documents, fields, field contents, navigators, and any other information about the database that is relevant and should be documented.

Both of these documents are available to all database users, and should be developed to such an extent that all users can take advantage of the information found in them. To edit the About Database and Using Database documents, do the following:

1. Open the database by double-clicking its icon on your workspace.

2. If the Design category is not expanded, click the twistie on the left, and then click the Other view to display the icon, the Using Database document, and the About Database document on the right.

3. Double-click either the Using Database document or the About Database document to edit it.

After you create the database-level documentation, you will want to tell your users how they can access it. You might also want to provide automatic methods of presenting the documents to the users.

Giving Users Access to the Database Documentation

There are a variety of ways to give users access to the database-level documentation that you create in the About Database and Using Database documents. The About Database document can be configured to appear when the database is first opened, every time the database is opened, or every time the document has been modified. These options are set as part of the database properties (for more information, refer to Chapter 16, "Finalizing the

Database"). By using these options, you can ensure that every user has had the opportunity to see the About Database document. Furthermore, by enabling the About Database document to appear every time its content has changed, you can deliver up-to-date design changes through messages placed at its beginning. This will expose each user to new changes in the database every time they are made—provided, of course, that you update the About Database document.

In addition to automatically making the About Database document appear, the user can also make either document appear manually through the use of the Help menu. To make the About Database or Using Database document to appear manually, users can do the following:

1. Open the database by double-clicking its icon on their workspace.

2. From the Help menu (shown in Figure 17.1) select About This Database (to see the About Database document) or Using This Database (to see the Using Database document).

3. Press the Esc key to close the document when finished.

You can also make the About Database and Using Database documents appear through the use of the following commands (these commands require no parameters):

```
@Command([HelpAboutDatabase])
```

```
@Command([HelpUsingDatabase])
```

These functions could be invoked through the use of a navigator hotspot or an Action button.

After database-level documentation has been completed, you might consider adding documentation at a form level on a form-by-form basis.

Figure 17.1

The About Database and Using Database documents can be accessed from the Help menu.

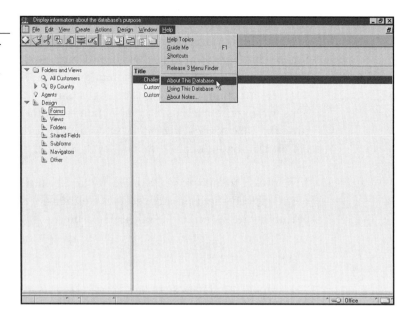

Developing Form-Level Documentation

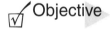 **Objective**

The second kind of documentation is form-level documentation. This includes any kind of documentation intended to make a form more usable and to allow users to quickly obtain information about certain tasks. Although no specific tool or document is designed exclusively to provide this kind of documentation, a number of tools and techniques effectively provide this form of documentation and help. These can be used to annotate your forms for easier understanding and use:

▶ Document, view, and database links

▶ Link hotspots

▶ Text and formula pop-ups

Working with Links

In Notes, links are connections you can make to documents, views, or databases. In the context of document-level documentation, links can provide quick access to Notes documents, views, or databases that contain detailed documentation, procedure manuals, or simple user-interface help. For example, if you create a Notes database that contains documents with detailed information about specific forms or fields, you can include a link in each form to provide the user with an easy way to double-click and bring that help up on his or her screen. To create a document link, do the following:

1. From the workspace, double-click the icon for the database that contains the document to which you want to link.

2. Click a view that will show you the document you want to link to and click the document to select it.

3. Select Edit|Copy as Link|Document Link.

4. Return to the workspace.

5. Double-click the icon for the database containing the form into which you want to place the link.

6. If the Design category is not already expanded, click the twistie and select the Form view.

7. Double-click the form into which you want to place the document link.

8. Click the form in the place you want to insert the document link. You might want to add static text at this point (for example, <--Double-click for help).

9. Select Edit | Paste to paste the document link onto the form (see Figure 17.2).

10. Save the form and close it.

To create a view link, do the following:

1. From the workspace, double-click the icon for the database that contains the view to which you want to link.

2. Click the view to which you want to link.

3. Select Edit|Copy as Link|View Link.

4. Return to the workspace.

5. Double-click the icon for the database containing the form into which you want to place the link.

6. If the Design category is not already expanded, click the twistie and select the Form view.

7. Double-click the form into which you want to place the link.

8. Click the form in the place you want to insert the link. You might want to add static text at this point.

9. Select Edit | Paste to paste link onto the form.

10. Save the form and close it.

Figure 17.2

An example of an inserted document link.

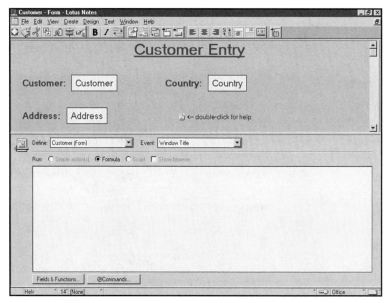

To create a database link, do the following:

1. From the workspace, click the icon for the database to which you want to link.

2. Select Edit | Copy as Link | Database Link.

3. Return to the workspace.

4. Double-click the icon for the database containing the form into which you want to place the link.

5. If the Design category is not already expanded, click the twistie and select the Form view.

6. Double-click the form into which you want to place the link.

7. Click the form in the place you want to insert the link. You might want to add static text at this point.

8. Select Edit | Paste to paste the link onto the form.

9. Save the form and close it.

Each of these procedures produces an icon that is placed on the form. If a user clicks a link in a document and holds his or her mouse button down, the path to the link is displayed in a small white text box. If any of these links is double-clicked, the source of the link (document, view, or database) will be displayed. When the user exits from the liked object, he or she will return to the document from which the link was initiated.

To delete a link, do the following.

1. Select the link on the form on which it was inserted.

2. Press the Delete key on your keyboard.

Working with Link Hotspots

Link hotspots are a twist on the links mentioned previously. With regular document, view, and database links, users double-click a small icon to follow the link; with link hotspots, a selected area of the form (usually text or graphic) becomes the clickable area. To create a link hotspot, do the following:

1. From the workspace, double-click the icon for the database that contains the document to which you want to link.

2. Click a view that will show you the document to which you want to link, and then click the document to select it.

3. Select Edit | Copy as Link | Document Link, View Link, or Database Link, depending on your needs.

4. Return to the workspace.

5. Double-click the icon for the database containing the form into which you want to place the link.

6. If the Design category is not already expanded, click the twistie and select the Form view.

7. Double-click the form into which you want to place the link.

8. Select the area of the form that you want to turn into a link (text, graphics, and so on).

9. Select Create | Hotspot | Link Hotspot; a green box will appear around the area you selected. If you leave the border around the hotspot, users creating or editing a document will see the box on which to double-click. If you do not want the hotspot box to appear around the selected area, right-click the box, choose HotSpot Properties from the menu, deselect the Show Border Around the Hotspot check box, and then click the Close Window button to close the properties.

10. Save the form and close it.

Whether the border shows or not, these links offer the same features as the links described previously; a single-click and hold displays the path to the linked object, and a double-click displays the source of the link. When the user closes the linked object, he or she will be returned to the original document.

To modify the properties, do the following:

1. Click the area of the form where the link hotspot is located to invoke a Hotspot menu.

2. From the Hotspot menu, choose Hotspot Properties. Make changes as necessary.

To remove a link hotspot, do the following:

1. Click the hotspot on the form; a Hotspot menu will appear.

2. From the Hotspot menu, choose Remove Hotspot.

Working with Text Pop-ups

Unlike a link, which displays information outside of a form, a text pop-up is an annotation that is present in the form. The purpose of a pop-up is to provide annotations that users can access by clicking and holding their mouse on an area of a form. When users do this, they invoke a small annotation box that provides a word, phrase, or full description of a field or procedure. When the user releases the mouse button, the annotation disappears. To create a text pop-up, do the following:

1. From the workspace, double-click the icon for the database containing the form into which you want to place the text pop-up.

2. If the Design category is not already expanded, click the twistie and select the Form view.

3. Double-click the form onto which you want to place the text pop-up.

4. Select the area of the form you want to turn into a text pop-up (text, graphics, and so on).

5. Select Create | Hotspot | Text Pop-up; a green box will appear around the area you selected and the Properties for Hotspot Pop-up dialog box will appear.

6. Click the Pop-up Text field and type (or copy and paste) the text you want displayed when the form area you selected is clicked. This field, shown in Figure 17.3, holds 1,002 characters.

7. If you do not want the green box to show around the area that activates the pop-up, deselect the Show Border Around Hotspot checkbox.

Figure 17.3

The Properties for Hotspot Pop-up dialog box with text entered.

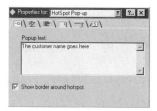

8. Click the Close Window button to close the properties and then save and close the form.

If you leave the border around the text pop-up, users creating or editing a document will see the box on which to click. Whether the border shows or not, the text typed into the Pop-up Text field will be displayed in a pop-up box when a user clicks and holds on the pop-up area. When the user releases the mouse button, the pop-up will disappear (see Figure 17.4).

Figure 17.4

An example of a text pop-up.

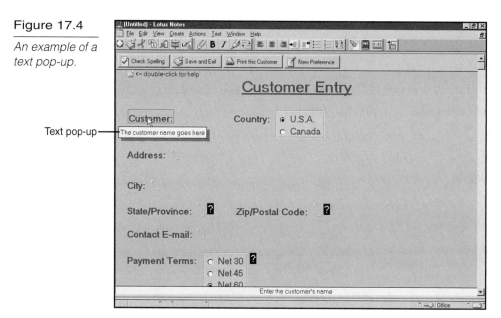

To modify the pop-up properties, do the following:

1. Click the area of the form where the text pop-up is located; a Hotspot menu will appear.

2. From the Hotspot menu, choose Hotspot Properties.

To remove a text pop-up:

1. On the form, click the area of the form where a text pop-up is located; a Hotspot menu will appear.

2. From the Hotspot menu, choose Remove Hotspot.

Working with Formula Pop-ups

A formula pop-up is just like a text pop-up except that rather than displaying static text, a formula is used to create the pop-up text. This type of pop-up is very flexible; what is displayed can change from person to person or from field value to field value. For example, what a user types into one field could depend on the value typed in another field. In such a case, the help provided can vary through the use of an @If statement.

Note

The only thing a formula can be made to do in a formula pop-up is to return a value to be displayed. You cannot use functions like @Prompt, @Dialog, or @PickList to display dialog boxes. The formula also cannot be made to produce other effects outside its direct scope (for example, a formula cannot change the value of fields).

To create a formula pop-up, do the following:

1. From the workspace, double-click the icon for the database containing the form on which you want to place the formula pop-up.

2. If the Design category is not already expanded, click the twistie and select the Form view.

3. Double-click the form on which you want to place the formula pop-up.

4. Select the area of the form you want to turn into a formula pop-up (text, graphics, and so on).

5. Select Create | Hotspot | Formula Pop-up; a green box will appear around the area you selected and the Properties for HotSpot Formula Pop-up dialog box will appear.

6. Click the formula window at the bottom of the dialog box and type a formula that will produce a value to be displayed in the pop-up window (see Figure 17.5). For example, you could enter the following formula to produce two different messages depending on the value of the Country field:

```
@If(Country = "U.S.A.";"A U.S. zip code appears as a 5 digit
➥numeric zip code, e.g., 11111";Country = "Canada";"A
➥Canadian postal code appears as a 7 digit alphanumeric,
➥e.g. T5J 1B6);"No country entered yet")
```

Figure 17.5

A sample formula for a formula pop-up.

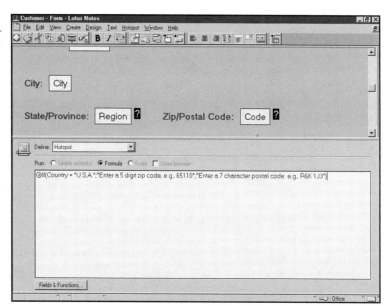

7. If you do not want the green box to show around the area that activates the pop-up, deselect the Show Border Around Hotspot checkbox in the Properties for HotSpot Pop-up dialog box.

8. Click the Close Window button to close the properties and then save and close the form.

If you left the border around the formula pop-up, users creating or editing a document will see the box on which to click. Whether the border shows or not, the result of the formula typed into the pop-up's formula window will be displayed in a pop-up box when a user clicks and holds on the pop-up area. When the user releases the mouse button, the pop-up will disappear.

 Tip

The calculation of the pop-up text operates on the same principle as a computed field. If the conditions on the document change such that the text should also change, the document must be refreshed for the pop-up text to appear changed. You might want to enable the Automatically Refresh Fields form property or the Refresh Fields on Keyword Change keyword field property to ensure that the pop-up text refreshes when conditions in your document change.

To modify the formula pop-up properties, do the following:

1. Click the area of the form where the formula pop-up is located; a Hotspot menu will appear.

2. From the Hotspot menu, choose Hotspot Properties.

To modify the formula pop-up formula, do the following:

1. In the Design pane, select Hotspot from the Define pull-down list; the formula will appear in the Formula window. If more than one formula pop-up is defined on this form, you might have to choose each one until you find the correct one.

2. Change the formula as desired.

To remove a formula pop-up, do the following:

1. Click somewhere in the formula pop-up on the form; a Hotspot menu will appear.

2. From the Hotspot menu, choose Remove Hotspot.

Developing Field-Level Documentation

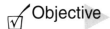 **Objective** Field-level documentation, the final level of documentation, is provided for the properties for each field. This documentation comes in the form of field comments, which are presented at the bottom of the user's screen as he or she types information into a form (see Figure 17.6). This feature can be turned on or off by the user.

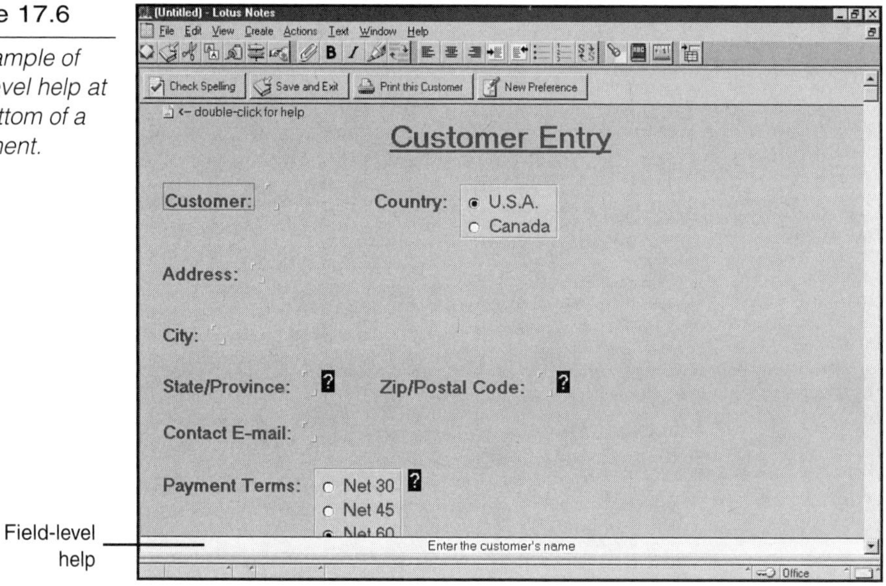

Figure 17.6

An example of field-level help at the bottom of a document.

Field-level help

![Screenshot of the Lotus Notes Customer Entry form showing fields for Customer, Country (U.S.A./Canada), Address, City, State/Province, Zip/Postal Code, Contact E-mail, and Payment Terms (Net 30/Net 45/Net 60). At the bottom is the field-level help text "Enter the customer's name".]

To create field-level documentation, do the following:

1. From the Standard view, expand the Design category by clicking its twistie and click the Forms view to list the forms on the right.

2. Double-click the form name on which the field to be documented is present to open the form's design.

3. Double-click the field for which you want to provide help to display the Properties for Field dialog box.

4. Click the Options tab and, in the Help Description field, type a phrase that will tell a user what kind of information to type in the field or what the format should be (see Figure 17.7).

Figure 17.7

The Properties for Field dialog box with the Options tab showing.

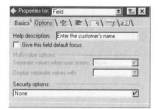

5. Click the Close Window button to close the properties and save and close the form. This returns you to the Standard view.

Showing this field-level documentation is the default for any user, but there might be occasions when a user might not want this help to show. Likewise, there might be times when, after turning it off, a user wants to re-enable this documentation. To enable or disable the display of field-level documentation, do the following:

1. Create or open a document in Edit mode.

2. Select View|Show|Field Help.

Note   The menu choice just mentioned is a toggle, meaning that if field help is enabled, the menu choice will be disabled, and if field help is disabled, the menu choice will be enabled.

Exercises

Now that design has been completed on this database, documentation must be finished. You must ensure that database-level, document-level, and field-level documentation have been added to this database. To accomplish this, add some text to the About Database and Using Database documents and add hotspots in the graphical navigator to display them. You will also add a document link and some pop-ups to the customer form to allow the user to click (or double-click) for more information while filling in the form. In addition, you will complete the form by adding field-level documentation. The databases you will use for this lab are available on the CD-ROM accompanying this book, and should be copied from it to your default Notes data directory. Use the file question.bmp to create some of the pop-ups on your form. The lab files are called cust17.nsf and doc17.nsf, and their titles are Chapter 17 Customers and Chapter 17 Documentation. Be sure that when you copy the files, you remove their read-only attributes or you will not be able to modify the databases.

Exercise 17.1

1. Select File | Database | Open and select the Chapter 17 Documentation database from the pull-down list of local databases. Click the Add Icon button to add the database to your workspace. Select the Chapter 17 Customers database from the list of databases and click the Open button. When the database opens, the graphical navigator will appear.

2. Click the Switch to Folders Navigator button at the bottom of the navigator to switch to the folders navigator. If the design category is not expanded, click the twistie to the left of it to expand, and then click Other.

3. Double-click the Using Database document to open it. The document is currently blank.

4. Type the following:

   This is the Using Database document. I will add text to fully describe the use of the database. I may also paste graphics here to enhance the understandability of what I am saying. In addition, I may add attachments allowing you to run videos or onscreen demonstrations. I may also add tables, document links, and so on to make this document a fully functional help tool.

5. Save and close this document.

6. Double-click the About Database document to open it. The document is currently blank.

7. Type the following text:

This is the About Database document. I will add text to describe the purpose of this database and the kinds of people who will use it. I may add comments on the company's strategic plan regarding the use of Lotus Notes and the place of this database in it. As with the Using Database document, I may add pictures, video, tables, document links, and so on, to make this document something my users will feel is helpful when using this database.

8. Save and close the document.

9. Click the Navigators view and double-click the Main navigator on the right side.

10. Scroll to the bottom of the navigator; you will find two buttons with labels on them indicating that they open the About and Using documents.

11. From the Create menu, choose Hotspot Rectangle and, starting in the upper-left corner of the About button, drag a rectangle that covers the whole button (see Figure 17.8).

12. In the Properties for Hotspot Rectangle dialog box, select the Lock Size and Position check box on the Basics tab. Click the HiLite tab and deselect the Highlight When Touched check box. This will ensure that users don't see that you have a hotspot that isn't the same shape as the button; the mere presence of the button should be enough to indicate that it should be clicked. Close the Properties dialog box by clicking the Close Window button.

continues

Exercise 17.1   Continued

Figure 17.8

Add the hotspots to activate the About and Using documents.

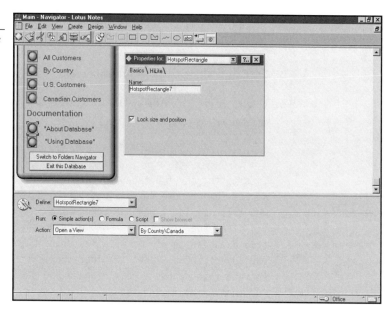

13. Repeat steps 11 and 12 to create a hotspot for the Using button.

14. Click the hotspot for the About Database label to display its definition in the Design pane at the bottom of the navigator.

15. Click Formula from the run options and type the following in the Formula window:

    ```
    @Command([HelpAboutDatabase])
    ```

16. Click the hotspot for the Using Database label to display its definition in the Design pane at the bottom of the navigator.

17. Click Formula from the run options and type the following in the Formula window:

    ```
    @Command([HelpUsingDatabase])
    ```

18. Save, and close the navigator.

19. Test the navigator by selecting View | Show | Main to display the navigator and click the About button at the bottom. When the document appears, press the Esc key to return to the navigator and repeat the procedure with the Using button. Click the Switch to Folders Navigator button when finished.

Exercise 17.2

1. Close the Customers database and return to the workspace.

2. Double-click the Chapter 17 Documentation icon to open that database; the Documents view will open and a single document called Customer Form will appear on the right side.

3. Click the Customer Form document to select it, and then select Edit | Copy As Link | Document Link.

4. Close the database to return to the workspace.

5. Double-click the Chapter 17 Customers icon to open that database and click the Switch to Folders Navigator button at the bottom of the navigator.

6. Expand the design category by clicking the twistie and click the Forms view to list the forms on the right.

7. Double-click Customer Form to edit its design.

8. Select Edit | Paste; this pastes the document link you just made into the upper-left corner of this form. To the right of the document link, type the following text (see Figure 17.9):

   ```
   <-- double-click for help
   ```

9. Scroll down on the form and position your insertion point just to the right of the Region field. Select File | Import. Navigate on your hard drive to the place where you copied the question.bmp file and double-click it to import the graphic onto your form (Figure 17.10 shows the completed pop-up).

continues

Exercise 17.2 Continued

Figure 17.9

Create the document link and use text to identify its purpose.

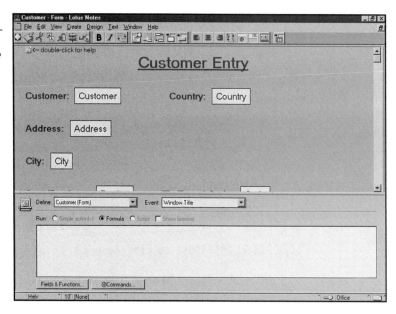

Figure 17.10

The completed formula pop-up for the Region field.

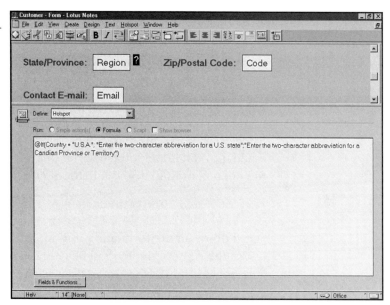

10. Place your pointer to the right of the graphic you just created and drag from right to left over it until it is highlighted. Select Create | Hotspot | Formula Pop-up.

11. On the Properties dialog box, deselect the Show Border Around Hotspot checkbox and then click the Close Window button.

12. Click the Formula window at the bottom of the screen and type the following:

```
@If(Country = "U.S.A.";"Enter the two-character abbreviation
➡for a U.S. state";"Enter the two-character abbreviation for
➡a Canadian Province or Territory")
```

13. Click to the right of the Code field, then select File | Import. Navigate on your hard drive to the place where you copied the question.bmp file and double-click it to import the graphic onto your form.

14. Place your pointer to the right of the graphic you just created and drag from right to left over it until it is highlighted. Select Create | Hotspot | Formula Pop-up (Figure 17.11 shows the completed pop-up).

Figure 17.11

The completed formula pop-up for the Code field.

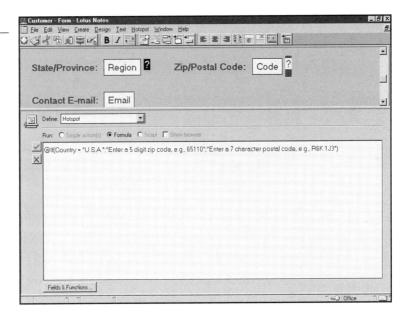

15. On the Properties dialog box that appears, deselect the Show Border Around Hotspot checkbox, and then click the Close Window button.

continues

---

16. Click the Formula window at the bottom of the screen and type the following:

    ```
    @If(Country = "U.S.A.";"enter a 5 digit zip code, e.g.,
    ➡65110";"Enter a 7 character postal code, e.g., R6K 1J3")
    ```

17. Scroll down and click to the right of the Terms field. Select `File | Import`. Navigate on your hard drive to the place where you copied the `question.bmp` file and double-click it to import the graphic onto your form (Figure 17.12 shows the completed pop-up).

Figure 17.12

The completed formula pop-up for the Terms field.

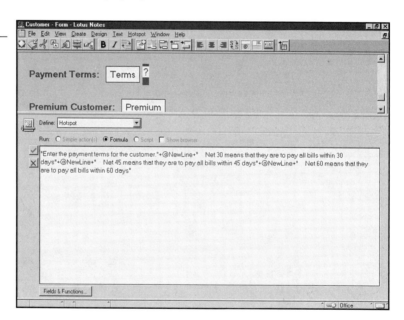

18. Place your pointer to the right of the graphic you just created and drag from right to left over it until it is highlighted. Select `Create | Hotspot | Formula Pop-up`.

19. On the Properties dialog box that appears, deselect the Show Border Around Hotspot checkbox, and then click the Close Window button.

20. Click the Formula window at the bottom of the screen and type the following:

    ```
    "Enter the payment terms for the customer." + @NewLine+" Net 30
    ➥means that they are to pay all bills within 30 days"+@New-
    ➥Line+" Net 45 means that they are to pay all bills within 45
    ➥days"+@NewLine+" Net 60 means that they are to pay all
    ➥bills within 60 days"
    ```

21. Scroll down and click to the right of the Premium field. Select File | Import. Navigate on your hard drive to the place where you copied the question.bmp file and double-click it to import the graphic onto your form (Figure 17.13 shows the pop-up).

Figure 17.13

The text pop-up for the Premium field.

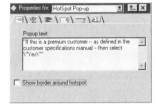

22. Place your pointer to the right of the graphic you just created and drag from right to left over it until it is highlighted. Select Create | Hotspot | Text Pop-up.

23. On the Properties dialog box that appears, deselect the Show Border Around Hotspot checkbox; in the pop-up text field, type the following:

    ```
    "If this is a premium customer — as defined in the customer
    ➥specifications manual — then select \"Yes\""
    ```

24. Close the Properties dialog box by clicking the Close Window button.

Exercise 17.3

1. Scroll up to the top of the form and double-click the Customer field to display its Properties dialog box.

continues

---

2. Click the Options tab and, in the Help Description field, type the following (see Figure 17.14):

```
Enter the customer's name
```

Figure 17.14

The field-level help for the Customer field.

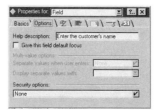

3. Close the dialog box by clicking the Close Window button.

4. Double-click the Country field to display its Properties dialog box, then click the Options tab. In the Help Description field, type the following:

```
Select the country from the radio options.
```

5. Click the Close Window button to close the Properties dialog box. Save the form and exit to the Standard view.

6. Click the All Customers view to display a list of customers. Double-click the customer Big Al's Diner to open the document; you will be in read mode.

7. Double-click the document link in the upper-left corner to invoke the Help document for this form. Press the Esc key to return to the form.

8. Scroll down on the document, and then click and hold each question mark to display its pop-up.

9. Select Actions | Edit Document to enter edit mode.

10. Change the country from U.S.A. to Canada and then click and hold the question mark next to the Code field. Note that the text has changed according to the formula.

11. Close the document to return to the Standard view.

Review Questions

1. Warren wants to provide users of his database with a summary of the purpose of the database and what kind of people will use it. Which built-in document is intended for this purpose?

    a. The Explaining Database document

    b. The About Database document

    c. The Using Database document

    d. The Releasing the Database document

2. Which of the following is not a valid link type?

    a. Notes link

    b. Document link

    c. View link

    d. Database link

3. Ingrid wants to create a pop-up that contains a different message depending on the circumstances under which it is clicked. What kind of object should she insert?

    a. A text pop-up

    b. A graphic pop-up

    c. A variable pop-up

    d. A formula pop-up

4. What field property is available to provide help when a user clicks a field?

    a. Help Description

    b. Field Description

    c. Field Title

    d. Description Help

5. If a border is displayed around a pop-up, what color is it?

    a. Yellow

    b. Blue

    c. Brown

    d. Green

6. What function is available to invoke the display of the About Database document from a hotspot or action button?

    a. `@Command([ShowAboutDoc])`

    b. `@Command([HelpAboutDocument])`

    c. `@Command([HelpAboutDoc])`

    d. `@Command([WhatAboutMe])`

Review Answers

1. B. The intent of the About Database document is to provide an overview of the function of the database and the kinds of people who would normally use it. For more information, refer to the section titled "The About Database and Using Database Documents."

2. A. A document link links you to a Notes document; a view link links you to a Notes view; a database link links you to a Notes database. For more information, refer to the section titled "Working with Links."

3. D. A formula pop-up displays a message based on the result of a formula. If the conditions change, the result of the formula could change, as could the displayed message. For more information, refer to the section titled "Working with Formula Pop-ups."

4. A. The Help Description field is found on the Options tab of the Field Properties dialog box, and displays a message at the bottom of a user's screen when data is being entered into a document field. For more information, refer to the section titled "Developing Field-Level Documentation."

5. D. The border around a hotspot, if it is showing, is always green. For more information, refer to the section titled "Working with Link Hotspots."

6. B. The function is `@Command([HelpAboutDocument])`. To display the Using Database document, the function is `@Command([HelpUsingDocument])`. For more information, refer to the section titled "Giving Users Access to the Database Documentation."

Answers to Test Yourself Questions at Beginning of Chapter

1. Two kinds of database-level documentation are provided with each Notes database. These come in the form of documents called About Database and Using Database. They can be accessed from the Design category in the Standard view by selecting the Other view. For more information, refer to the section titled "The About Database and Using Database Documents."

2. A variety of tools can be used to create form-level documentation. Some of the ones discussed in this chapter are document links, view Links, database links, link hotspots, text pop-ups, and formula pop-ups. For more information, refer to the section titled "Developing Form-Level Documentation."

3. You can provide field-level documentation by adding text to the Help Description field property. This property is available for every field, and can be accessed from the Options tab. For more information, refer to the section titled "Developing Field-Level Documentation."

Chapter

18

Advanced
Formulas Part I

This chapter introduces you to the following objectives:

 Objectives

▶ Using multiline formulas

▶ Using list manipulation

▶ Getting user input

Test Yourself! Before reading this chapter, test yourself to determine how much study time you will need to devote to this section.

1. How does the term *main expression* relate to multiline formulas and what is the implication of not having a main expression?

2. What is a list? What is the name of the function designed to convert a list to a string? What is the name of the function designed to convert a string to a list?

3. Why do you need to take care when adding a new number or date to a list that may not have any values?

4. What is the basic function of the @Prompt? What are the nine forms of the @Prompt dialog box?

5. What two functions can @PickList perform?

Answers are located at the end of the chapter...

Many formula types and techniques are not introduced to a novice Lotus Notes developer. These formulas and techniques are essential for developing good applications and for increasing the user-friendliness of your applications.

Using Multiline Formulas

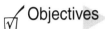 Objectives

The most basic Lotus Notes formulas are a single line. They ask a simple question or produce a result with a minimum of processing. For example, a field may have a default value that is inserted through the use of a piece of static text.

There are many cases where a single line does not perform all the operations necessary. In some cases a single line may be impossible to debug because of its complexity. In other cases a number of steps may need to execute in order to complete a task.

Using Temporary Variables

Up until this point, all formulas that have been discussed used one of two sources for information: static values (numbers, dates, or text) and field values. Temporary variables are names that do not relate to field names, but they can be used to temporarily store values until they are needed in the formula window in which you defined them.

You use a single statement to define and assign values to temporary variables. Like fields, they have a datatype, but the datatype is not formally assigned. Rather, the datatype is assigned based on the value you assign to the temporary variable.

An example of an assignment statement is:

```
Temp := "A Name"
```

In this statement, the temporary variable, Temp, is assigned the value of the text string "A Name". In so doing you have implicitly made the variable Temp a type Text. The implicit declaration can be reassigned if you assign, in another statement, the value of 1—a number—to the variable. The type of variable then changes to numeric.

Temporary variables can be assigned values using the assignment := operator or using the @Set statement. If on a line by itself, the program uses the := operator to assign a type. If in the context of an @If statement, you must use the @Set function to assign the value, as shown in the following example:

```
@If(Color = "Blue"; @Set("Temp";"Eyes");@Set("Temp";"Hair")
```

The preceding statement uses an @If function, and @Set assigns a value of "Eyes" to the variable Temp if the Color field (or temporary variable) has the value "Blue", and @Set assigns Temp to "Hair" if the color is other than "Blue".

 Note   To use the @Set function, you must first assign a value to the temporary value that you reference by using the := operator. If no value is desired for the variable, simply assign it the value NULL.

Using Multiline Formulas to Create Complex Computations

One of the uses for multiline formulas is to create complex computations. For example, if an action requires you to save a document and exit Notes, a multiline formula is required. The form of a multiline formula is that each separate function is written as though it were solitary, and a semicolon (;) is used to delimit the functions. The following listing is an example:

```
@Command([FileSave]);
@Command([FileExit])
```

 Note   You do not have to place multiline formulas on multiple lines. It is easier to read them, however, if each new function begins on a new line, and creating multiple lines is the commonly used convention.

Any number of calculations may be placed together in a single formula. You must remember to include, however, what Notes refers to as a main expression. A main expression returns a value back to the field, column, or button that invoked the formula. Notes considers the last line of any multiline formula to be the main expression, and that line must return a value, even if the returned value is the current value of the field, or a NULL. For example, you want to create a button that increments a field by 3. When the code is produced—despite the fact that you do not actually want to return a value to the button (what you really want to do is add to a field)—you must still return something in the form of a main expression. You might be tempted to write code that looks like the following:

```
FIELD Quantity := Quantity+3
```

In that case, you are given an error like the one shown in Figure 18.1.

Figure 18.1

An error message that indicates a formula error.

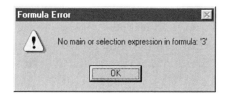

Instead, you must write a formula that does what you desire, but then add another line to return some value, in this case a NULL, to the button:

```
FIELD Quantity := Quantity+3;
NULL
```

Using Multiline Formulas to Increase Formula Readability

Not everything in Notes programming has to do with functionality. In some cases, you prevent confusion in the future when you, or another designer, looks at the code that you have written. For example, you want to prompt the user for input—using the user's common name to increase comfort—and make a decision whether or not to save the current document based on the user's response. To do this you could write code, as follows:

```
@If(@Prompt([YesNo];"Save?";"Do you want me to save this document
"+@Name([CN];@UserName)+"?");@Command([FileSave];NULL)
```

This code, however, is very difficult to read and would be difficult to interpret later. Instead, you might want to use multiple lines and temporary variables to increase the readability, as follows:

```
CurrentUser := @Name([CN];@UserName);
Response := @Prompt([YesNo];"Save?";"Do you want me to save this
➥document "+CurrentUser+"?");
@If(Response;@Command[FileSave];NULL)
```

Exiting out of Multiline Formulas

At times it is beneficial to exit out of a multiline formula without completing all the steps. For example, you have a multiline formula that should be executed only if the value of a certain field is not NULL. If it is NULL, you do not want to complete any of the lines of the formula. The @Return function enables you to prematurely exit out of a formula, and if desired, return a value. The syntax is simple:

```
@Return(Value)
```

The following function, when executed, immediately terminates processing the formula in which it is executed if the field name is NULL:

```
@If(Field := NULL;@Return(NULL);Statement1);
Statement 2;
Statement 3
```

In the preceding example, if the value of the field is NULL, the @Return is executed and a NULL value is returned. If it is not NULL, statement 1 is executed as the else portion of the @If and processing proceeds through statements 2 and 3. If not for the @Return, Statements 2 and 3 would have been processed no matter what the value of field.

Caution   You must take care when using the `@Return` function. If a formula calculating the value of a field contains an `@Return` that is executed, whatever the `@Return` returns (a `NULL` or a value) is placed into the field, possibly overwriting a value that was previously there.

Using List Manipulation

A list is a field that contains multiple values. In many programming languages (including Lotus Script), these kinds of structures would be defined as arrays.

Lists are useful because they eliminate the need to have multiple fields that all contain the same kind of value; some that are filled and others that are not filled because you are not sure how many slots you will need to hold the information. For example, you want to create a list of people to invite to a meeting. You could decide that only five people will ever be invited and then create five fields: `INVITEE1`, `INVITEE2`, and so on. This is either wasteful or limiting, however. It is wasteful in cases where you invite less than five people because you have a number of extra fields that you are not using. It is limiting in those cases where you want to invite ten people but find that you cannot because you do not have enough spaces in which to put all their names. A list can solve the problem because it enables you to place as many values as you want into the field without having to create space for them beforehand.

Lists can be created either by direct user input into a field designated as allowing multivalues, or programmatically through the use of a button, action, agent, or field formula, which assigns a value, or appends a value, to a field.

Lists are displayed in fields or in view columns as multiple values delimited by a variety of separators including the following: commas, semicolons, new lines, or blank lines.

Using List Functions

A number of functions are designed specifically for manipulating lists. Table 18.1 describes these functions.

Table 18.1

List Functions.

@ Function	Description
@Contains	Looks for one string within another (including a list) and returns 1 if it is found or 0 if it is not.
@Elements(list)	Counts the number of elements in a list and returns that value.
@Explode	Converts a string or date range into a list and returns that list.
@Implode	Converts a list into a string and returns that string.
@IsMember	Looks to see if a value or list is contained within another list and returns 1 if it is and 0 if it is not.
@IsNotMember	Looks to see if a value or list is not contained within another list and returns 1 if it is not and 0 if it is.
@Keywords	Looks to see which elements in one list are contained in another list and returns a list of all contained elements.
@Member	Looks for the presence of an item in a list and returns 0 if it is not found, or a number between 1 and n, where n is the number of elements in the list, if it is found.
@Replace	Given a destination list and two source lists, replaces all occurrences of the first source list with the corresponding elements of the second source list in the destination list.
@Subset	Returns the first or last x number of elements of a source list.

@ Function	Description
@Unique	Without parameters, returns a unique, random text value, provided with a list, returns a list with all the repeated values removed.

The @Contains Function

The @Contains function is not specific to lists but can be used with them. @Contains does a simple text search for one string within another by using the following syntax:

```
@Contains(String;Substring)
```

The function returns a Boolean value; a 1 if the statement is true, a 0 if the statement is false.

The string, the substring, or both can be lists. Here are some examples:

```
@Contains("Red":"Blue":"Yellow":"Pink";Substring)
```

If the substring is "Red", the result is true, because the text is contained in at least one of the elements of the list. If the substring is "Green", the result is false, because the text is not contained in any of the elements of the list:

```
@Contains(Sting;"Sam":"Bill":"Ed":"Norman")
```

If the string is "Edward was a king", the result is true because one of the elements of the list is found in the string (the list produces the effect of a logical OR). If the string is "Norm eats worms", the result is false because none of the elements of the list is contained in the string; in order for this to be true, the string would have to be "Norman eats worms". If the string itself is a list ("Sam for president":"Kyle is a maniac":"Harry loves Notes"), as long as one of the elements in the substring is contained in any of the elements of the string, the result is true; otherwise, the result is false.

The @Elements Function

When a list is passed, the @Elements function counts the number of items in that list and returns a number. If the list is NULL, the function returns the number 0. For example, the following returns the number 4:

```
@Elements("Red":"Yellow":"Black":"White")
```

The @Explode Function

The @Explode function takes a string or range of dates and converts it into a list. It takes two basic syntaxes:

```
@Explode(DateRange)
```

```
@Explode(String;Separator;includeEmpties)
```

In the first syntax, when the function is passed a range of dates in the format [12/15/97-12/25/97], the function creates a list of dates from the beginning to the end of the range. In this case, the function creates a list of each individual day from December 15, 1997 to December 25, 1997; 11 elements in all.

Note

In the date range syntax, it is imperative that the date be passed as a constant date surrounded by square brackets ([ ]) and not a string surrounded by quotation marks (" ").

In the second syntax, the function must be passed, at minimum, a string. The separator and the flag, includeEmpties, are optional parameters. When passed a string alone, the function returns a list that is each word delimited by a space, a comma, or a semicolon. The following is an example:

```
@Explode("In my opinion, this is a great book; my opinion being
biased")
```

The preceding example returns the following list:

```
"In":"my":"opinion":"this":"is":"a":"great":"book":"my":"opinion":"being":
➡"biased"
```

The optional parameter separator is used to override the default text delimiter, which includes a space, a comma, and a semicolon. If you include a character or characters in quotation marks, the list will be built using those characters as the delimiters. The following is an example:

```
@Explode("In my opinion, this is a great book; my opinion being
biased";";")
```

The preceding returns the following two-element list because only the character semicolon (;) indicates the start of a new list element:

```
"In my opinion, this is a great book":"my opinion being biased"
```

The optional flag [includeEmpties] causes a NULL list element to be created if two list item delimiters are found together in the text string. In other cases, two adjacent delimiters are treated as one. The following is an example:

```
@Explode("Blue Green,,Red Orange";includeEmpties)
```

The preceding returns the following list:

```
"Blue":"Green":"":"Red":"Orange"
```

The following is another example, which returns a different list:

```
@Explode("Blue Green,,Red Orange")
```

The preceding returns the following list and ignores the two adjacent commas:

```
"Blue":"Green":"Red":"Orange"
```

The @Implode Function

The @Implode function takes a text list and converts it to a text string and, optionally, inserts the delimiter of your choice into the text string. The syntax is as follows:

```
@Implode(TextList;Delimiter)
```

The parameter Delimiter is optional. If you omit it, a space delimits the text values. This particular example returns the string `"The list is: Red, Blue, Green"`, as follows:

```
"The list is: "+@Implode("Red":"Blue":"Green";", ")
```

The string `"The list is: the color Red, the color Blue, the color Green"` is returned by the following example:

```
"The list is: the color "+@Implode("Red":"Blue":"Green";", the color "
```

The @IsMember Function

The @IsMember function checks whether string or string-list is contained in another list. The syntax is as follows:

```
@IsMember(String;List)
```

The result of the function is a *Boolean* value—1 if the string is a member of the list and 0 if it is not. Unlike the @Contains function, the string must be an entire element, not simply a portion of a list element, and the comparison is case sensitive. If the string itself is a list, the function returns back a 1 only if all the elements of the first list are elements of the second list; however, the order of the elements does not matter.

The following example returns a 1 because the string `"Red"` is contained in the list:

```
@IsMember("Red";"Blue":"Green":"Red")
```

The result, however, is a 0 if the string had been `"red"` or if the string had been simply `"R"`.

The following example returns 1 because both the elements of the first list are elements in the second list:

```
@IsMember("Red":"Blue";"Blue":"Green":"Yellow":"Red")
```

However, if the second list did not contain `"Red"`, the result would be 0.

The @IsNotMember Function

The @IsNotMember function checks to see whether a string or string-list is not contained in another list. The syntax is as follows:

```
@IsNotMember(String;List)
```

The result of the function is a Boolean value—1 if the string is not a member of the list and 0 if it is. Like the @IsMember function the comparison is case sensitive. If the string itself is a list, the function returns back a 1 only if all the elements of the first list are not elements of the second list.

The following example returns a 0 because the string "Red" is contained in the list:

```
@IsNotMember("Red";"Blue":"Green":"Red")
```

The result would be 1, however, if the string had been "red" or if the string had simply been "R".

The following example returns 0 because both the elements of the first list are elements in the second list:

```
@IsNotMember("Red":"Blue";"Blue":"Green":"Yellow":"Red")
```

If the second list did not contain "Red", however, the result would be 1.

 Note

The function @IsNotMember is not simply !@IsMember. In order for @IsMember to be true, all the elements of the first parameter must be present in the second. That means that for !@IsMember to be true, all that we require is that one of the elements of the first parameter not be present. On the other hand, in order for @IsNotMember to be true, none of the elements of the first parameter can be present in the second. Because !@IsMember requires only one of the first not to be present in order to be true, it, therefore, is not identical to @IsNotMember.

Ensure you use the proper function to produce the result that you want, and that you thoroughly check your logic before releasing functions into production.

The @Keywords Function

The @Keywords function compares two lists and returns a list of those items in the second list that are found in the first; if no items are found, the function returns a NULL string. The syntax is as follows:

```
@Keywords(List1;List2;separator)
```

The first and second list are required, but the separator is an optional parameter. When used without the separator parameter, the function parses all the words in all the elements of the first list, using the delimiters, ?!;:[](){}<>, and a space to separate words. A list then returns indicating which of the elements in the second list are found in the parsed list of words. The comparison is case sensitive.

For example, when given a set of newspaper headlines in a list, you want to find out whether the words *book*, *Lotus*, or *shoe* are found in any of them. You could write a function as follows:

```
@Keywords(List1;"book":"Lotus":"shoe")
```

If the first list consists of the headlines "Lotus offers free upgrades to Notes 5.0":"New Lotus Notes Exam Guide released":"Shoe Sale at Ed's Shoes", the function returns the list "Lotus".

If you want to control how the first list is parsed, include a third parameter; a string consisting of the delimiters that you want to use. The following example searches for the words *One*, *Two*, and *Three* in the list provided; however, these words are found only if surrounded by commas. The following is an example:

```
@Keywords(List1;"One":"Two":"Three";",")
```

If the first list consists of the phrases "Three counting words are One, Four, and Six":"Three more are One,Two,Five", the result is the list "Two" because, of all the occurrences of the words One, Two, and Three, only one consists of a number, Two, surrounded by commas. The others have the words bordered by spaces on at least one side.

Note   If you include more than one character in your delimeter string—for example ., ",.:,"—all are used as delimiters.

The @Member Function

The @Member function finds the position of a text value in a text list and returns back a number indicating the position in which the value was found(a 0 if the value was not found). The following example searches for the text string "One" in the list and returns back the number 1—the position at which the string was found in the list:

```
@Member("One";"One":"Two":"Three")
```

The @Replace Function

The @Replace function finds a value in a list and replaces it with another value.

This function works with the following three lists:

- ▶ A list in which the value is to be replaced

- ▶ A list of values to replace

- ▶ A list of values to replace with

The values in the second list are paired with corresponding values in the third list. A search is done in the first list for all occurrences of the elements in the second list, and if found, the elements are replaced with the paired values from the third list. The result is a list consisting of the elements of the first list after the replacement has been done. For example, the following produces the list "1":"2":"3":"Four":"Five":

```
@Replace("One":"Two":"Three":"Four":"Five";"One":"Two":"Three";
➥"1":"2":"3")
```

It does not matter in what order the second list is: all values will still be replaced. If no values from the second list are found in the first list, the list will return unchanged.

The @Subset Function

The @Subset function returns a number of elements of a list counting either from the left or the right.

Using the following syntax, the function returns the leftmost *n* elements from the source list if *n* is positive and the rightmost *n* elements from the source list if *n* is negative:

```
@Subset(SourceList;n)
```

The following example returns the list
`"Calgary":"Winnipeg":"Toronto":`

```
@Subset("Calgary":"Winnipeg":"Toronto":"New
York":"Boston":"Orlando";3)
```

The following function returns the list `"Boston":"Orlando":`

```
@Subset("Calgary":"Winnipeg":"Toronto":"New
York":"Boston":"Orlando";-2)
```

The @Unique Function

The @Unique function trims duplicate elements out of a list and returns a list that contains all the unique elements of that list.

Using the following syntax, the function returns a list of all the unique elements found in the list, stripping out any duplicates:

```
@Unique(List)
```

The following example returns the list
`"Calgary":"Winnipeg":"New York":"Toronto":"Vancouver":"Boston":`

```
@Unique("Calgary":"Winnipeg":"New
York":"Toronto":"Vancouver":"New York":"Boston")
```

This function is case sensitive, so an element called `"Shoe"` will not be removed if an element called `"shoe"` already exists.

The @Unique function also has another syntax, which consists of the function with no argument. If used in this way, the function returns a unique random string value.

Using List Operations and Operators

Lists can have many of the same operations performed on them as regular text, number, or date fields. However, many of the results are considerably different with lists than they are with single-value fields.

There are two kinds of operations with lists:

▶ Pair-wise

▶ Permuted

These two kinds of operations apply to all the calculation (* / + -) and comparison (> < >= <= = !=) operators used with lists; however, the calculation and comparison operators are all preceded by an * when performing permuted operations (** */ *+ *- *> *< *>= *<= *= *!=).

Pair-wise List Operations

Pair-wise operations treat two lists as pairs of elements—element 1 in list 1 paired with element 1 in list 2, and so on. In pair-wise operations, whatever operator is used is applied to each pair, and the result is a single list item. If there isn't an equal number of elements in each list, the extra elements in the larger list are paired with the last element in the smaller list. As a result, the number of elements in the resulting list is always equal to the number of elements in the largest initial list. The following is an example:

```
1:2:3:4+1:2:3:4
```

The preceding results in a list `2:4:6:8` because each element in the first list was added to its corresponding element in the second list. However, the following example produces different results:

```
1:2:3:4+1:2
```

There are no corresponding third and fourth elements in the second list, so the third and fourth elements are added to the last element—the second—of the first list, which results in the list 2:4:5:6.

Permuted List Operations

Permuted list operations treat each element in two lists as though they should be paired with each element in the other list. As in mathematical permutations, the result of permuted combinations of lists is a list that contains the number of elements in list 1 times the number of elements in list 2. For example, a list with 3 elements is added to a list with 4 elements by using a permuted addition operation, and the result is a list with 3*4=12 elements. The following is an example:

```
1:2:3*+1:2:3:4
```

The preceding results in a list 2:3:4:5:3:4:5:6:4:5:6:7 because each element in the first list was added to each element in the second list (for example, 1+1, 1+2, 1+3, 1+4, 2+1, 2+2, and so on).

List Calculation Operators

The calculation operators that work with lists are as follows: * / + - ** */ *+ *-. All these serve to produce the same results as with single-value numbers, dates, and strings except that the values of lists (either operated on pair-wise or permuted) are being combined instead of single values. Mathematical computations are performed with * / + - (and the permuted counterparts) on numeric lists and concatenation is performed with + and *+ on text lists.

List Comparison Operators

The comparison operators that work with lists are as follows: > < >= <= = != *> *< *>= *<= *= *!=. These operators produce similar results to those seen with single-value numbers, dates, and strings. The difference, however, is in the breadth of the comparison. When the comparison x=y is done with single-values, the answer is true only if the value for x is identical to the value to y. On the other hand, when x and y are lists, this pair-wise comparison checks each element in the first list against its counterpart in the second list, and the result is true if any of the pairs are the same. The following is an example:

```
1:2:3=4:2:5
```

The preceding results in a true value because the second pair is equal (for example, 2=2), even though the other pairs are not. If, however, the statement were as follows:

```
2:1:3=4:2:5
```

The value would be false in the preceding example because no pair is equal.

As with computed pairings, if the two lists do not have the same number of values, the extra values in the longer list are compared to the last value in the shorter list.

When a permuted comparison, such as x*=y is done, the statement is true if any of the permuted pairings are true. Therefore, the following example is true:

```
2:1:3*=4:2:5
```

The result is true because all that is necessary is that one of the permuted comparisons be true. The permuted comparisons in this case are the following: 2=4, 2=2, 2=5, 1=4, 1=2, 1=5, 3=4, 3=2, and 3=5. Because one of those comparisons, 2=2, is true, the statement is true.

This type of logic is used with all pair-wise and permuted list comparisons.

Order of Precedence and Lists

You must take care when using operators in the context of lists. The list operator (:) takes precedence over all other operators, sometimes resulting in unexpected results. The following formula is an example:

```
1:2:-3:4+10:20:30:40
```

You might expect the result to be the list 11:22:27:44, with each element being added to its counterpart, and the third pairing being, in effect, 30-3=27. However, because the list concatenation takes precedence over the minus sign on the third element of the first list, the third and fourth elements are concatenated to each other, and then the minus is applied, which makes both the third and fourth elements negative. The result is the list 11:22:27:36. To prevent this from happening, parentheses must be placed around the first list's third element, as follows:

```
1:2:(-3):4+10:20:30:40
```

Then the expected result, 11:22:27:44, is produced.

Adding Elements to a List

New elements can be added easily to a list if the new element is to be added to the front, or to the back. This is done using the following syntax:

```
ColorList:"Red" or
"Blue":ColorList
```

You must take care when adding new items to a list that has not been initialized. In the case of concatenating a new text value to a NULL list, the first element of the list is NULL, whereas the second is the element just added. This can be overcome by applying an @Trim function to the new list, which has the effect of removing the NULL list items.

```
@Trim(List:"Red")
```

The case of concatenating a date or a number to an uninitialized list causes more severe problems. Because an uninitialized list has a NULL value in all cases, you get an error about incompatible data types if you attempt to concatenate a new date or number value onto the NULL list. To overcome this, when adding new date or number values to a list, always check to see whether the list is NULL first, and if it is, make the new value the list instead of concatenating the value.

Note   Adding a list of different data types always causes problems. Notes requires that operations like list concatenation always be done with the same data types. You get errors if you try to add a text element to a numeric or date list, as well.

Here is an example of logic you can use to add a new number to a numeric list if you don't know whether it contains any values:

```
NumberList := @If(NumberList =
➥NULL;NewNumber;NumberList:NewNumber)
```

Inserting values into a list is a little more complex because it requires that the list be split into two pieces: the new element attached to the end of the first piece, and then the second piece attached to the end of the new list. To accomplish this, you can use the @Subset function, as follows:

```
SizeofList := @Elements(OriginalList);
PositionToInsert := 5;
FirstPiece := @Subset(OriginalList;PositionToInsert);
SecondPiece := @SubSet(OriginalList;-(SizeofList-
➥PositionToInsert));
NewList := FirstPiece:NewElement:SecondPiece;
OriginalList := NewList
```

Using the @Elements function, you calculate the total size of the original list and place it into the temporary variable, SizeofList. You then set PositionToInsert to a value indicating where in the list you want to place the new value; normally you perform a calculation, such as using @Member to determine this position. Then use the @Subset function along with the PositionToInsert value to set the FirstPiece variable to be the first set of list elements. Use the SizeofList—PositionToInsert to get the number of elements left over after the first list segment has been removed. When made negative, this causes the @Subset function to take those elements from the right side of the list. Now you finish by putting the pieces back together; you concatenate the FirstPiece, the NewElement, and the SecondPiece to create a NewList, which you then use to replace the value of the OriginalList.

Getting User Input

In a typical Notes environment, editable fields on forms gather user input. However, there are many other ways to prompt users for input, some of which are easier and more user friendly than the simple editable field.

The @Prompt Function

The @Prompt function produces a dialog box that either displays information or gathers information from the user and passes it back to a field or variable within a formula.

The syntax of the @Prompt function is as follows:

```
@Prompt([BoxStyle]:[NoSort];title;prompt;defaultChoice;ChoiceList)
```

The [BoxStyle] parameter indicates which kinds of buttons will be present and how the user will indicate values to pass back to the function, if any are required. Box styles are entered in the form of particular codes in square brackets ([]). The valid box styles are as follows:

- ▶ [OK]

- ▶ [YesNo]

- ▶ [YesNoCancel]

- ▶ [OKCancelEdit]

- ▶ [OKCancelList]

- ▶ [OKCancelCombo]

- ▶ [OKCancelEditCombo]

- ▶ [OKCancelListMult]

- ▶ [Password]

The optional parameter [NoSort] is used only for styles containing lists of values. When present, it is added to the box style as the second element of a two-element list. If not present, the list of values from which the user will choose is sorted alphabetically. If included, the list of values will appear as you enter it into the formula or as it is generated from another function.

Title is a required parameter that displays a text title at the top of the dialog box. This title can be static text or a computed value, and it can be NULL if no title is desired.

Prompt is a required parameter that displays a message in the body of the dialog box, usually asking a question or displaying a message. This message may be NULL if no body message is desired.

DefaultChoice is an optional parameter used only for styles requiring a user to type in a text value or choose from a list. This choice is the value displayed in a text box or the option from a list that is chosen by default. This value is selected if the user simply clicks the OK button without taking any other action.

ChoiceList is an optional parameter used only for styles that display choices to the user, either as a list or a combo box. This choice list can either be hard-coded into the formula or can be the result of another function's calculation, such as an @DBColumn function.

The [OK] Box Style

The [OK] box style produces a dialog box designed to display information to a user without any interaction except to exit the box by clicking the OK button. When clicked, the OK button returns a value of 1 (true) to the @Prompt function. Pressing the ESC key also returns a value of 1. The statement

```
@Prompt([OK];"Shopping";"Bring home milk and eggs")
```

produces the dialog box shown in Figure 18.2.

Figure 18.2

An example of a dialog box produced by the [OK] *box style.*

The [YesNo] Box Style

The [YesNo] box style produces a dialog box designed to display information to a user and elicit a yes or no response to the question. This is done by producing a statement and two buttons, Yes and No. The @Prompt function returns a value of 1 (True) if the Yes button is clicked and 0 if the No button is clicked. The button with focus is always the Yes button. This is the only one of the @Prompt types in which pressing the Esc key has no effect at all; to exit the dialog box, one of the buttons must be pressed. The statement

```
Result := @Prompt([YesNo];"Exit";"Do you want to exit Notes?")
```

produces the dialog box shown in Figure 18.3, and the variable result is set to either 1 or 0.

Figure 18.3

An example of a dialog box produced by the [YesNo] *box style.*

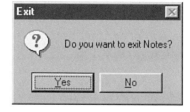

The [YesNoCancel] Box Style

The [YesNoCancel] box style produces a dialog box designed to display information to a user, elicit a yes or no response to the question, and at the same time enable a complete cancellation of the request. This is done by producing a statement and three buttons: Yes, No, and Cancel. The @Prompt function returns a value of 1 (True) if the Yes button is clicked, 0 if the No button is clicked, and -1 if the Cancel button is clicked or the Esc key is pressed.

The button with focus is always the Yes button. The following statement produces the dialog box shown in Figure 18.4, and the variable result is set to either 1, 0, or -1:

```
Result := @Prompt([YesNoCancel];"Save?";"Do you want to save when
exiting?")
```

Figure 18.4

An example of a dialog box produced by the [YesNoCancel] *box style.*

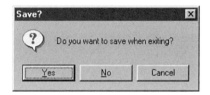

The [OKCancelEdit] Box Style

The [OKCancelEdit] box style produces a dialog box designed to display information to a user and to elicit a response in the form of a typed word or phrase. This is done by producing a statement, two buttons (OK and Cancel), and an edit box in which the user can type a response. The parameter DefaultValue is required for this @Prompt type; however, if you do not want to use the default value, simply make the parameter value NULL (""). The @Prompt function returns the value typed into the edit box when the OK button is clicked, and returns nothing if the Cancel button is clicked or the Esc key is pressed. In fact, if Cancel is clicked or Esc is pressed, all processing halts in the formula in which the @Prompt appears (for example, Esc and Cancel cannot be trapped with this function by checking for a NULL result). The following statement produces the dialog box shown in Figure 18.5, and the variable result is set to the text the user typed into the edit box:

```
Result := @Prompt([OKCancelEdit];"Name";"Enter your name";NULL)
```

Figure 18.5

An example of a dialog box produced by the [OKCancelEdit] *box style.*

Tip

There is a roundabout way to trap for a user canceling out of a dialog box such as this one. Because the only way that processing of the formula in which the @Prompt is found will continue is if the user enters a value in the edit box, you can set a field value if a value was entered. Then, in some other formula, you can check for the value of the field, and if it is NULL you know that the user pressed Esc or Cancel to exit. The code might look like this:

```
Result := @Prompt([OKCancelEdit];"Name";"Enter your
name";NULL);FIELD Name := Result
```

The [OKCancelList] Box Style

The [OKCancelList] box style produces a dialog box designed to display information to a user and to elicit a response in the form of a selection from a presented list. This is done by producing a statement, two buttons (OK and Cancel), and a list box from which the user can select a single response. The parameter DefaultValue is required for this @Prompt type; however, if you do not want to use the default value, simply make the parameter value NULL (""). The parameter ChoiceList is also required for this @Prompt type. The list of values can either be typed in list form or can be the result of a formula (for example, @DBColumn). By default, the list of values is sorted alphabetically; however, if you include the [NoSort] flag, the list is presented in the order it appears in the list.

This @Prompt function returns the value selected in the list box if the OK button is clicked and returns nothing if the Cancel button is clicked or the Esc key is pressed. In fact, if Cancel is clicked or Esc is pressed, all processing halts in the formula in which the @Prompt appears (Esc and Cancel cannot be trapped with this function by checking for a NULL result). The following statement produces the dialog box shown in Figure 18.6, and the variable result is set to the value the user selected from the list:

```
Result := @Prompt([OKCancelList];"Color";"Choose a color from the
➥list";NULL;"Red":"Orange":"Green":"Blue")
```

Figure 18.6

An example of a dialog box produced by the [OKCancelList] *box style.*

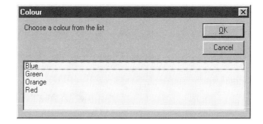

The [OKCancelCombo] Box Style

The [OKCancelCombo] box style produces a dialog box designed to display information to a user and to elicit a response in the form of a selection from a drop-down list. This is done by producing a statement, two buttons (OK and Cancel), and a drop-down list from which the user can select a single response. The parameter DefaultValue is required for this @Prompt type and is usually specified; however, if you do not want to use the default value, make the parameter value NULL (""). The parameter ChoiceList is also required for this @Prompt type. The list of values can either be typed in list form, or can be the result of a formula (for example, @DBColumn). By default, the list of values is sorted alphabetically; however, if you include the [NoSort] flag, the list is presented in the order it appears in the list.

This @Prompt function returns the value selected from the drop-down list if the OK button is clicked and returns nothing if the Cancel button is clicked or the Esc key is pressed. In fact, if Cancel is clicked or Esc is pressed, all processing halts in the formula in which the @Prompt appears (Esc and Cancel cannot be trapped with this function by checking for a NULL result). The following statement produces the dialog box shown in Figure 18.7, and the variable result is set to the value the user selected from the drop-down list:

```
Result := @Prompt([OKCancelCombo];"Color";"Choose a color from
➥the list";"Red";"Red":"Orange":"Green":"Blue")
```

Figure 18.7

An example of a dialog box produced by the [OKCancelCombo] box style.

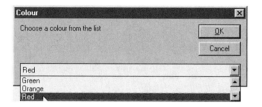

The [OKCancelEditCombo] Box Style

The [OKCancelEditCombo] box style produces a dialog box designed to display information to a user and to elicit a response in the form of a selection from a drop-down list or a value typed into the edit box. This is done by producing a statement, two buttons (OK and Cancel), and a drop-down list from which the user can select a single response contained in an edit box in which the user can also type in a response not found in the list. The parameter DefaultValue is required for this @Prompt type; however, if you do not want to use the default value, simply make the parameter value NULL (""). The parameter ChoiceList is also required for this @Prompt type. The list of values can either be typed in list form or can be the result of a formula (for example, @DBColumn). By default, the list of values is sorted alphabetically; however, if you include the [NoSort] flag, the list is presented in the order it appears in the list.

This @Prompt function returns the value selected from the drop-down list or typed into the edit box if the OK button is clicked, and it returns nothing if the Cancel button is clicked or the Esc key is pressed. In fact, if Cancel is clicked or Esc is pressed, all processing halts in the formula in which the @Prompt appears (Esc and Cancel cannot be trapped with this function by checking for a NULL result). The following statement produces the dialog box shown in Figure 18.8, and the variable result is set to the value the user selected from the drop-down list or typed into the edit box:

```
Result := @Prompt([OKCancelEditCombo];"Color";"Choose a color
➥from the list or enter your own";NULL;"Red":"Orange":"Green":
➥"Blue")
```

Figure 18.8

An example of a dialog box produced by the [OKCancelEdit-Combo] box style.

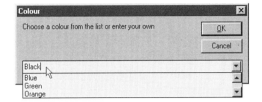

The [OKCancelListMult] Box Style

The [OKCancelListMult] box style produces a dialog box designed to display information to a user and to elicit a response in the form of a selection of one or more values from a presented list. This is done by producing a statement, two buttons (OK and Cancel), and a list box from which the user can select one or more values. The parameter DefaultValue is required for this @Prompt type; however, if you do not want to use the default value, simply make the parameter value NULL (""). The parameter ChoiceList is also required for this @Prompt type. The list of values can either be typed in list form, or it can be the result of a formula (for example, @DBColumn). By default, the list of values is sorted alphabetically; however, if you include the [NoSort] flag, the list is presented in the order it appears in the list.

This @Prompt function returns a list of the values selected in the list box if the OK button is clicked, and returns nothing if the Cancel button is clicked or the Esc key is pressed. In fact, if Cancel is clicked or Esc is pressed, all processing halts in the formula in which the @Prompt appears (Esc and Cancel cannot be trapped with this function by checking for a NULL result). The following statement produces the dialog box shown in Figure 18.9, and the variable result is a list of the values the user selected from the list:

```
Result := @Prompt([OKCancelListMult];"Color";"Choose one or more
➥colors from the list";NULL;"Red":"Orange":"Green":"Blue")
```

Figure 18.9

An example of a dialog box produced by the [OKCancelList-Mult] box style.

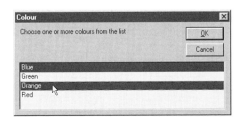

The [Password] Box Style

The [Password] box style produces a dialog box designed to request a secret password in the form of a typed word or phrase. This is done by producing a statement, two buttons (OK and Cancel), and an edit box in which the user can type the password. Typing into the edit box does not produce the characters typed, but instead, a random number of Xs are produced for each character typed. The @Prompt function returns the password typed into the edit box if the OK button is clicked, and it returns nothing if the Cancel button is clicked or the Esc key is pressed. In fact, if Cancel is clicked or Esc is pressed, all processing halts in the formula in which the @Prompt appears (Esc and Cancel cannot be trapped with this function by checking for a NULL result). The following statement produces the dialog box shown in Figure 18.10, and the variable result is set to the password the user typed into the edit box:

```
Result := @Prompt([Password];"Shhhh";"This is a secret document,
➥enter the password")
```

Figure 18.10

An example of a dialog box produced by the [Password] box style.

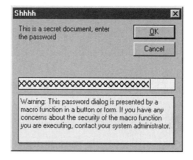

Note

The value entered in this type of box is not secure. It is simply masked by X characters. What is passed back to the function, and what is stored if you choose to put it into a field, is stored as text.

The @DialogBox Function

The @DialogBox function is designed to display the values in a document using a form that appears in a dialog box. This function has the effect of making the entry of information more "Windows-like" than normal Notes document entry. The @DialogBox function is often used for entering profile information or for entering information into logical sections in a document (see Figure 18.11).

Figure 18.11

Values displayed in a document using a form that appears in a dialog box.

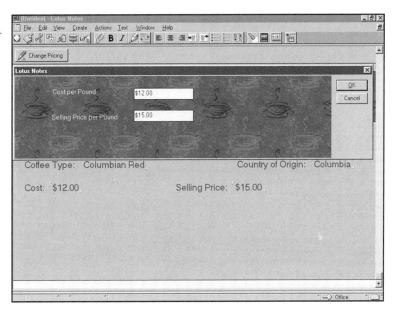

The syntax of the @DialogBox function is as follows:

```
@DialogBox(form;[AutoVertFit]:[AutoHorzFit])
```

At minimum, the name of the form display in the dialog box is necessary. This must be a form in the current database because no additional fields are available to indicate which server/database combination is to be used. The optional flag list of [AutoVertFit]: [AutoHorzFit] is used to resize the dialog box to the size of the first layout region on the form. If these flags are used, only the first layout region on the form displays, even if there are fields outside of layout regions or on other layout regions.

Note

Due to a "feature" in Notes, if a second layout region exists on the form to be displayed in the dialog box, a user will be able to tab off of the first layout region and onto the second, even when the auto fit flags are set. If the user has some knowledge of the underlying regions, she could actually enter information into the fields. In order to prevent confusion through inadvertent tabbing out of the first layout region, it is recommended that you use only one layout region in forms that display using the @DialogBox function.

When @DialogBox is invoked, it presents a form in a dialog box and populates its fields with the values in the matching field names from the document currently displayed. When an entry is made in the dialog box, these field values are passed into the corresponding fields on the open document, provided that the underlying document is in edit mode and that the user has the ability to modify the fields in question.

If there are fields in the dialog box not present in the underlying document, @DialogBox creates those fields in the document, even if they are not displayed on any form.

The @DialogBox function is one of many ways to update the values of a field without giving the user direct editor access to the fields. It is most effective when triggered from actions or from manual agents. You must remember, however, that if the underlying document is open, that document must be in edit mode to receive the changes. If you trigger the @DialogBox function from a view action or agent, all that is necessary for document update is that you have sufficient rights to modify the document; when the dialog box opens and you modify the field values, the corresponding field values are changed in the underlying document.

To use the @DialogBox Function to update computed fields, follow these steps:

1. Create the form to be used to display document information (the main form) and populate it with the required fields (see Figure 18.12).

Figure 18.12

Create the main form from which to execute the @DialogBox function.

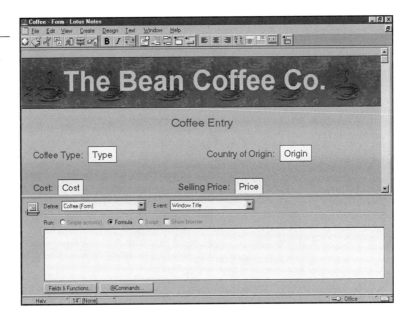

2. Create the form to be displayed in the dialog box (the secondary form), create a layout region on it, and populate that region with fields bearing the same names as the computed fields to be updated on the main form (see Figure 18.13).

Figure 18.13

Create the form to be displayed in the dialog box.

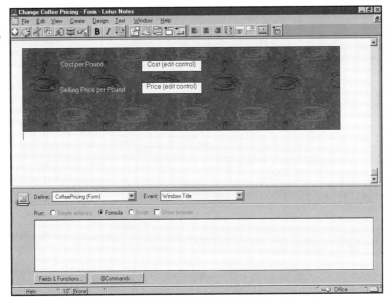

3. Create an action (or some other trigger) on the main form, which uses the @DialogBox function to display the secondary form (see Figure 18.14). Use a formula such as the following:

```
@DialogBox("Secondary";[AutoVertFit]:[AutoHorzFit])
```

When the user clicks the action, the dialog box appears as in Figure 18.14.

Figure 18.14

The @DialogBox function is used to display the form in a dialog box.

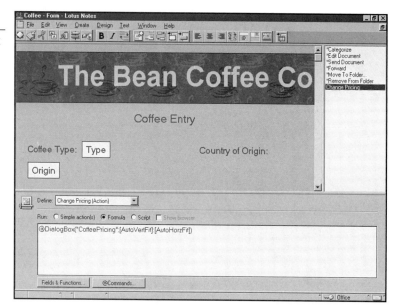

The @PickList Function

The @PickList function enables you to display a view, which in turn enables a user to obtain a value from one or more documents in that view. This could be used to choose people from the accessible address book, parts from a stock list, or books from a library. The @PickList function allows for the display of many fields in a database because it is displaying what a view displays. This enables the user to better understand what he is choosing; it is not simply a code. In addition, the @PickList function can also be used to display an address dialog box from which to select people.

Note

For a user to access a view using `@PickList`, she must have at least `reader` access to the database in which the view is contained.

Displaying a View

The `@PickList` function can be used to display a view in a dialog box. The syntax for that form of the function is as follows:

```
@PickList([Custom];server:database;view;title;prompt;column)
```

This syntax enables you to display a view in a dialog box, from which a user can choose one or more documents (see Figure 18.15).

Figure 18.15

Selecting from a dialog box produced by an `@PickList` *function.*

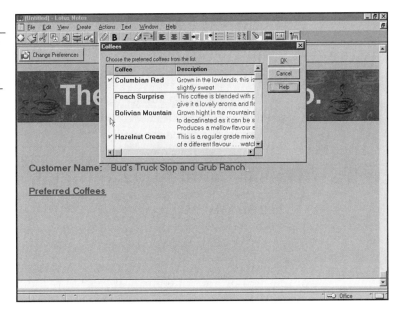

The first parameter is required, and the [Custom] value indicates that this form of `@PickList` is to display a view in a dialog box.

The second parameter consists of two optional values: server and database. This indicates the location of the view display in the dialog box. If the database being referenced is the currently open database, or if the database being referenced is on the local work-station, you do not have to specify the server name; otherwise, indicate the server name using its fully distinguished name in quotation marks (for example, `"Brazil/Bean"`). If the database being referenced is the currently open one, you do not have to specify its name; otherwise, you must indicate the location of the database on the server you specified. If the database is located in the default data directory (frequently `c:\notes\data`), you can simply indicate the database's filename in quotation marks (`"database.nsf"`); otherwise, indicate either the path relative to the default Notes directory or the complete path including the drive letter and all intervening directories (`\accounting\database.nsf` or `c:\accounting\database.nsf`).

Note

> Because the database name must be in quotes, you must use the proper syntax when referring to the database path. Because Notes recognizes the \ character as a delimiter, you must precede it by another \ to indicate that you actually want to include the \ and not use it as a delimiter. This would mean that the path `c:\accounting\database.nsf`, when placed into quotation marks, would look like this: `"c:\\accounting\\database.nsf"`.

If the database to which you are referring is the currently open one, this whole parameter can be replaced by NULL (`""`).

The third parameter is the name of the view you want to display in the dialog box. The name you specify must be in quotation marks, and it must be either the alias of the view (as specified in the view properties) or the full name of the view (including all cascading menus).

The fourth parameter is a title to be displayed at the top of the View dialog box.

The fifth parameter is a prompt to be displayed near the top of the dialog box, just above the view.

The sixth and final parameter is the column in the view containing the value to be returned by the @PickList. When you count the columns, you must determine the number that you count in Design view because all columns, whether they display or not, are counted by Notes. If the first column is hidden, the first displayed column is the second column.

The following is an example of how to use @PickList to return a list of values to a field:

You have created a multivalued text field called PreferredCoffee on a form. You want to obtain a list of coffees that your customers prefer to purchase. This list is to come from the Description view in a database called referenc.nsf. This view consists of two columns: the first is a coffee name (the value you want to return), and the second is the description. The form on which you are executing the @PickList is not in the same database as the Referenced view; however, they are both on the Brazil server. The following procedure would produce a dialog box for a user from which he could choose one or more coffees:

1. In the properties for the PreferredCoffee field on your form, ensure that the field type is text and that it is multivalued (see Figure 18.16).

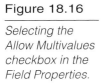

Figure 18.16

Selecting the Allow Multivalues checkbox in the Field Properties.

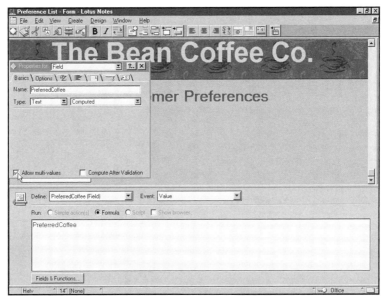

2. Create a trigger for the input of information (for example, a button on the form or an action).

3. In the button that you created, type the following formula:

```
FIELD PreferredCoffee := @PickList([Custom];"Brazil/Bean":
➥"Referenc.nsf";"Description";"Coffees";"Choose the
➥preferred coffees from the list";1)
```

When the user clicks the button, a dialog box appears with choices from the Description view (see Figure 18.17).

Figure 18.17

A @PickList formula to display the Description view in a dialog box.

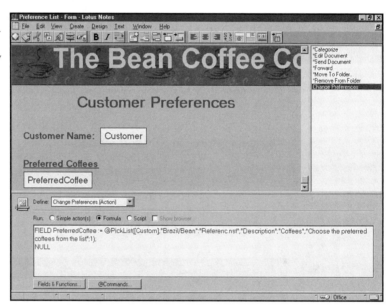

Displaying the Address Dialog Box

The @PickList function can be used to display the Address dialog box, either one that multiple people can be chosen from or a single-choice dialog box. The syntax for that form of the function is as follows:

```
@PickList([Name]:[Single])
```

This syntax enables you to display either the Address dialog box, enabling you to choose one or more people from any, or all, accessible address books, or a single Address dialog box from which a user can choose a single name from any accessible address book.

This form of @PickList has only one parameter and a list of two flags, the first being required, the second optional. The [Name] flag is required because it distinguishes this form of @PickList from the first. The second flag, if present, indicates that the user will be able to return only one value from the dialog box; otherwise, the user can return multiple values.

The two variations of this syntax produce dialog boxes with appearances such as those in Figures 19.18 and 19.19.

Figure 18.18

An address dialog box enables you to choose one or more people from an address book.

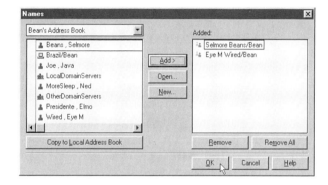

Figure 18.19

A single address dialog box enables you to choose a single person from an address book.

Exercises

On your CD-ROM there are two databases you need for this lab. Copy order18.nsf and ref18.nsf to your Notes data folder (ensuring you remove the read-only attribute from the files) and add the databases titled Chapter 18 Orders and Chapter 18 Reference to your workspace.

In the Chapter 18 Orders database, there is a form called Preference List, which is incomplete. The intent of this form is to enable you to enter a customer's name, the coffees that the customer usually buys, and the quantity that is usually shipped.

This lab takes you through the process of adding a list of preferred coffees (taken from a view list), along with the quantity usually ordered (obtained from a dialog box).

Here are some important objects you need to reference:

▶ Database 1: Filename: orders18.nsf; Title: Chapter 18 Orders

▶ Database 2: Filename: ref18.nsf; Title: Chapter 18 Reference

▶ Form to modify: Database: orders18.nsf; Name: Preference List

▶ View to reference: Database: ref18.nsf; Name: (Description); Alias: Description

Exercise 18.1

1. Open the Chapter 18 Orders database, and in the forms list, double-click the Preference List form to edit its design.

2. Navigate down to the bottom of the form, just below the Customer field.

3. From the Create menu select Table and accept the default table size of 2×2. You will use this table to house the lists you are creating for coffee type and quantity.

4. In the first row of the first column, type the label `Coffee`; in the cell to its right, type the label `Qty` (see Figure 18.20).

Figure 18.20

The first row of the table contains heading information.

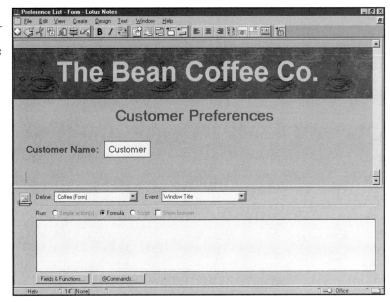

5. In the second row, first column, create a field called `PreferredCoffee`. Ensure that it is a text field, that it is computed, and that it enables multiple values (see Figure 18.21).

Figure 18.21

The properties for the `Preferred Coffee` field, which allows multiple values.

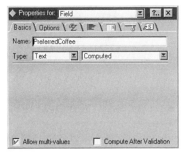

6. In the Properties for Field dialog box, go to the Options tab and choose New Line from the Display separate values with pull-down list (see Figure 18.22).

continues

Exercise 18.1 Continued

Figure 18.22

Display separate values in this field with a new line.

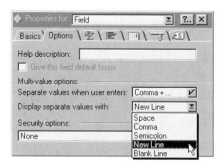

7. In the Design window, set the formula for the value event for PreferredCoffee to PreferredCoffee (see Figure 18.23).

Figure 18.23

Make the computed field equal to its own value; it changes only through a click of the button.

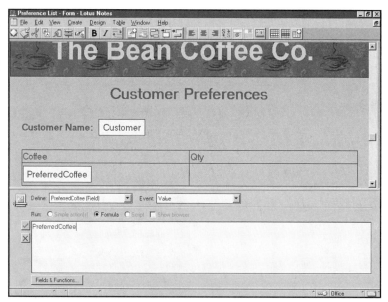

8. In the second row of the second column, create a field called PreferredQty. Make it a number field and allow multiple values. Go to the Options tab and choose New Line from the Display Separate Values With pull-down list.

9. In the Design window, set the formula for the value event for PreferredQty to PreferredQty.

10. Above the table you just created, create a button by clicking at the spot you want the button to appear and selecting

Create | HotSpot | Button. Add the text `Add a Coffee` to the Button Label field and close the Properties for Button dialog box (see Figure 18.24).

Figure 18.24

The button you create will activates a formula used to add a new line to the table.

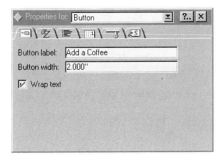

11. In the Design window for the button, type the following code (feel free to leave out the REM statements—they are for your benefit):

```
REM "Using a temporary variable, get a value from the";
REM "description view";
Coffees := @PickList([Custom];"":"ref18.nsf";"Description";
➥"Coffees";"Choose a coffee from the list";1);
REM "We can only process one new coffee at a time. If none";
REM "was entered, we want to exit, if more than one was";
REM "entered, we want to get the first one from the list";
REM "and discard the rest. We do this by using the";
REM "@Subset function to get only the first element from";
REM "the Coffees list";
@If(Coffees = NULL; @Return(NULL);@Set("Coffees";
➥@Subset(Coffees;1)));
REM "Now that we have a single value, we need to get the";
REM "qty required for that value, we'll use @Prompt";
Result := @Prompt([OKCancelEdit];"Qty";"Enter the qty";
➥desired of "+Coffees;NULL);
REM "We want to set the value of Qty using @Set, but Qty";
REM "has to have a value first";
Qty := 0;
```

continues

Exercise 18.1 Continued

```
REM "The @Prompt above has returned a text value, we want";
REM "to convert it to a number to add to our PreferredQty";
REM "field but only if it isn't NULL; that will cause an";
REM "error";
@If(Result = NULL;@Set("Qty";0);@Set("Qty";
➥@TexttoNumber(Result)));
REM "Let's add the new coffee and the new quantity to the";
REM "appropriate fields. Because we don't know if this is";
REM "the first time we have entered values in these fields";
REM "we need to find out whether the fields are currently";
REM "NULL and process accordingly. The @Trim function,";
REM "when used on a list, will remove the NULL elements.";
FIELD PreferredCoffee := @Trim(PreferredCoffee:Coffees);
FIELD PreferredQty := @If(PreferredQty = NULL;
➥Qty;PreferredQty:Qty)
```

12. Test the form by selecting Design | Test and adding a number of preferred coffees using the button, and then save and exit the form.

Exercise 18.2

There are a number of limitations to the preceding design. One is that once an element has been added, it can't be removed. The challenge is this:

1. Create a button that prompts the user for the number of the coffee she wants to remove (its position in the PreferredCof-fee field).

2. When the number is entered, echo a confirmation by presenting a dialog box that asks for confirmation using the name of the coffee requested, not the position.

3. Remove the coffee and its associated quantity from the list.

Use the functions `@Prompt` and `@Subset`. The answer to the challenge is in a form called ChallengeAnswer, which is found in the `orders18.nsf` database.

Review Questions

1. How is the datatype of a temporary variable set?

   a. It is set through the variable properties.

   b. Datatype is a nonsense term when applied to temporary variables.

   c. It is set by the datatype of the last value assigned to it.

   d. It is declared at the top of the formula window.

2. How do you set the value of a temporary variable in an `@If` function?

   a. Using the assignment operator (`:=`)

   b. Using the `@Set` function

   c. Using the `@Value` function

   d. Using the `@ChangeValue` function

3. What symbol is used to delimit multiple lines in a multiline formula?

   a. Comma

   b. Colon

   c. Period

   d. Semicolon

4. What is an advantage of using lists?

   a. You can keep better track of the groceries you need to buy.

   b. You can store multiple discrete values in the same field.

c. You can store text and numeric values in the same field.

d. You don't have to use keywords anymore.

5. What does the @Explode function do?

    a. It converts a string or date into a list.

    b. It populates multiple fields using a list.

    c. It is not a Notes function.

    d. It converts a list to a string.

6. What is the difference between a positive and a negative second parameter in an @Subset function?

    a. None.

    b. A positive value takes elements from the right, and a negative value takes elements from the left.

    c. A positive value takes elements from the top, and a negative value takes elements from the bottom.

    d. A positive value takes elements from the left, and a negative value takes elements from the right.

7. Given the list "Red":"Green":"Yellow":"Blue", which function would you use to change "Green" to "Pink" and "Blue" to "Black"?

    a. @Member

    b. @Subset

    c. @Replace

    d. @Trim

8. What is the difference between permuted and pair-wise list operations?

    a. Pair-wise combines each element in one list with its corresponding element in another, and permuted combines each element in one list with the first element of the other.

    b. Permuted combines each element in one list with its corresponding element in another, and pair-wise combines each element in one list with all the elements in another.

    c. Pair-wise combines the first element of one list with the last element of the other into the center of both lists, and permuted starts from the center and works outward.

    d. Permuted combines each element in one list with all the elements in the other, and pair-wise combines each element in one list with its corresponding element in the other.

9. Which of the @Prompt types does not enable you to exit using the Esc key?

    a. [OK]

    b. [YesNo]

    c. [Password]

    d. [OKCancelList]

10. What effect do the flags [AutoHorzFit] and [AutoVertFit] have in an @DialogBox function?

    a. They cause the entire form to display in the dialog box.

    b. They cause the dialog box to expand to the size of the screen.

    c. They cause the dialog box to shrink to the size of the first layout region.

    d. They cause the dialog box to appear in the upper-right corner of your screen.

11. An @DialogBox function presents a form with a field called Name, with a document with a Field called Name already open. What is the effect of changing the value of the Name field in the dialog box?

    a. There is no effect.

    b. The value of the document's Name field is also changed.

    c. The field is passed out to an environment variable.

    d. The value of the document's Name field is changed if the document is in edit mode.

12. What kind of access does a user need to have to a view to see values appear in an @PickList dialog box?

    a. depositor

    b. manager

    c. reader

    d. author

13. What do the two types of @PickList syntax result in?

    a. A dialog box containing a view and a dialog box containing an address list

    b. A dialog box containing a form and a dialog box containing a view

    c. A dialog box containing a view and a dialog box containing a layout region

    d. A dialog box containing a graphic and a dialog box containing an address list

14. If an @PickList function is drawing from a view having the same server/database combination as the form in which it is being executed, what do you need to place in the second parameter in the @PickList function?

    a. [Custom]

    b. The dialog box title

    c. Server:Database

    d. NULL

Review Answers

1. C. Temporary variables do not have any inherent data type. Once they have a value assigned, however, they act as though the type of the value is their type. For more information, please refer to the section titled "Using Temporary Variables."

2. B. You can use the `:=` operator only when the variable name begins a line, but in an `@If` function, that is not possible. So, you must use the `@Set` function. For more information, please refer to the section titled "Using Temporary Variables."

3. D. Semicolons are the standard delimiter in Notes, and are used to delimit multiple lines in a formula. For more information, please refer to the section titled "Using Multiline Formulas to Create Complex Calculations."

4. B. Lists are designed to allow for multiple values of the same datatype to be stored in a single field. That eliminates the need for many fields, which may or may not be needed to store the values, thereby increasing design efficiency. For more information, please refer to the section titled "Using List Manipulation."

5. D. `@Explode` is designed to convert a list to a string for convenient display of list information. For more information, please refer to the sections titled "List Functions" and "The `@Explode` Function."

6. D. The `@Subset` function returns a list of a certain number of elements of another list. The last parameter indicates how many elements, positive values indicating X elements starting from the left, and negative values indicating X elements starting from the right. For more information, please refer to the section titled "The `@Subset` Function."

7. C. The `@Replace` function takes a pair of lists and substitutes each value in the first list, which is found in a third list, with the corresponding element in the second list. For more information, please refer to the sections titled "Using List Functions" and "The `@Replace` Function."

8. D. Pair-wise combines each list element in one list with a single element in another. Permuted combines each element in one list with each element in another. For more information, please refer to the sections titled "Pair-Wise List Operations" and "Permuted List Operations."

9. B. Only the [YesNo] type allows you to prevent Esc from exiting the dialog box. For more information, please refer to the section titled "The [YesNo] Box Style."

10. C. The flags cause the dialog box to shrink to the size of the first layout region. This makes the dialog box look cleaner. It will eliminate non-layout region fields from the dialog box, however, if they are present. For more information, please refer to the section titled "The @DialogBox Function."

11. D. If a field in the dialog box is also present in the open document, the document's field is updated as long as the document is in edit mode. Documents that are opened for reading are never modified by @DialogBox. For more information, please refer to the section titled "The @DialogBox Function."

12. C. To see anything in a view, you must have at least reader access to a database. So, to see information that a view-based function produces, you must also have at least reader access to that view. For more information, please refer to the section titled "The @PickList Function."

13. A. A pick list can either be a dialog box that contains a view or an address dialog box. The determination is made by the initial parameter; if it is [Custom] a view will be displayed, and if it is [Name] an address dialog box will be displayed. For more information, please refer to the sections titled "The @PickList Function," "Display a View," and "Display an Address Dialog Box."

14. D. When referring to the currently open database, NULL is used to indicate current server and current database. For more information, please refer to the section titled "Display a View."

Answers to Test Yourself Questions at Beginning of Chapter

1. The main expression of a multiline formula is the line that returns a value back to the calling object (button, field, action, and so on). Notes requires that all formulas have a main expression, either in the form of returning a value or a selected list. For more information, refer to the section titled "Using Multiline Formulas to Create Complex Computations."

2. A list is a single variable or field that contains multiple discrete values that can be manipulated separately. These values must all have the same datatype.

   The function for converting a list to a string is called @Implode, and the function for converting a string to a list is called @Explode. For more information, refer to the sections titled "Using List Functions," "The @Explode Function," and "The @Implode Function."

3. Lists that do not have values assigned to them are NULL by default. If you concatenate a number or a date to a NULL list, an incompatible datatype error generates because you are trying to combine a text value with a non-text value. It is helpful in these cases to check the list for a NULL value before you concatenate new values to it. For more information, refer to the section titled "Adding Elements to a List."

4. @Prompts are designed to produce dialog boxes that give information and/or ask for user input. The nine forms of @Prompt are [OK], [YesNo], [YesNoCancel] [OKCancelEdit], [OKCancelList], [OKCancelCombo], [OKCancelEditCombo], [OKCancelListMult], and [Password]. For more information, refer to the section titled "The @Prompt Function."

5. @PickList can either display a view in a dialog box, allowing a user to choose one or more values to return, or it can display an address dialog box, allowing a user to choose one or more people from any address book to which he has access. For more information, refer to the sections titled "The @PickList Function," "Displaying a View," and "Displaying an Address Dialog Box."

Chapter 19

Advanced Formulas Part II

This chapter introduces you to the following objectives:

 Objectives

▶ Database lookups

▶ Environment variables

▶ Mail-enabling applications

Test Yourself! Before reading this chapter, test yourself to determine how much study time you will need to devote to this section.

1. How does @DBColumn differ from @DBLookup?

2. What are environment variables and where are they stored?

3. What is the difference in function between @MailSend with and without parameters?

4. What field is required on any form that uses a parameterless mail-send method?

Answers are located at the end of the chapter...

Two important skills an application developer needs are the ability to obtain information from sources outside the current document and the ability to use the mail router to deliver information from one database to another. This chapter will introduce you to

▶ Getting information from Notes databases through the use of @DBColumn and @DBLookup

▶ Saving and retrieving user information using environment variables

▶ Using the router to move information by mail-enabling forms

Understanding Database Lookups

 Objective

It is handy to go outside of the current document in order to obtain information. This information may be a lookup to another document to obtain a description for a code entered, or it may be a list of values from a view to use in a keyword list.

The @DBColumn Function

The @DBColumn function is used to generate a list of values from a specific view in a specified database on a specified server. This is useful because it can be used to create a keyword list dynamically through the use of a formula instead of having to hard-code in an ever-changing list of values. The syntax of @DBColumn is as follows:

```
@DBColumn(class:"NoCache";server:database;view;ColumnNumber)
```

The first parameter consists of a list of two optional values. The class indicates the type of lookup being done and distinguishes lookups into Notes views from lookups into non-Notes (ODBC) databases. In order to indicate a lookup in a Notes view, either specify NULL ("") or "Notes". The rest of the syntax described in this chapter assumes a Notes class. The exam does not expect knowledge of the ODBC class.

"NoCache" is also optional and indicates that you would like Notes to rebuild the list of values every time the list is required. This is compared with a scenario where you would like the values cached to have the same values used over and over again. The benefits of caching are that the lookup is faster the second and successive times; however, if the source changes, you will not see those changes. Regardless of your caching request, the cache is only persistent in a single Notes session and is discarded when your session ends. If this element is left NULL, then the list values will be automatically cached.

The second parameter consists of two optional values, server and database. This indicates the location of the view from which you want to pull the list of values. If the server is the same as the place from which the @DBColumn is being run, you do not have to specify the server name. Otherwise, indicate the server name using its fully distinguished name in quotation marks, for example, "Server1/Bean". If the database is also the same as the place from which the @DBColumn is being run, its name can also be left out. Otherwise, you must indicate the location of the database on the server. If the database is located in the default data directory (frequently C:\Notes\Data), you can simply indicate the database's file name in quotation marks ("database.nsf"). Otherwise, indicate either the path relative to the default Notes directory or the complete path including the drive letter and all intervening directories (\accounting\database.nsf) or (C:\accounting\database.nsf).

Note

Because the database name must be in quotes, you must be careful that you use the proper syntax when referring to the database path. Because Notes sees the \ character as a delimiter, you must be sure to precede it by another \ to indicate that you actually want to include the \ and not use it as a delimiter. This would mean that the path C:\accounting\ database.nsf, when placed in quotation marks, would appear as "C:\\accounting\\database.nsf".

Tip
> If there are multiple replicas of the database in which the view is found, you may not want all the lookups to go to a single, hard-coded server/database. You can have Notes seek out the "closest" replica by specifying the replica ID of the database instead of specifying the server and database name. This means that instead of indicating the location of the view as `"Server1/Bean":"Database.nsf"`, you would use `"8625652B:0056A4A8"`, which is that database's ID as found in the database properties (right-click the icon for the database on your workspace and navigate to the Information tab).

If you do not need to specify either the server or database name, you can replace the whole parameter with `NULL` (`""`).

The third parameter is the name of the view from which you want to obtain the list of values. The name that you specify must be in quotation marks and must be either the alias of the view (as specified in the view properties) or the full name of the view (including all cascading menus).

The final parameter is the number of the column in the view from which you will be pulling the list of values. Notes uses a particular methodology for determining the column number, and therefore, you must follow the same methodology when determining what column you want to refer to. To determine the column number do the following:

1. Look at the view's design (see Figure 19.1) and count to your referenced column from left to right (this includes all columns, whether they actually display when the user sees the view or not).

2. Remove 1 from your count for every column that contains a constant value: a text string, a number, or a constant date.

3. Remove 1 from your count for every column that contains a formula consisting only of one of the following functions: `@DocChildren`, `@DocDescendants`, `@DocLevel`, `@DocNumber`, `@DocParent`, `@DocParentNumber`, `@DocSiblings`, `@IsCategory`, or `@IsExpandable`.

Figure 19.1

Count the columns in the view but be sure you include those that the user may not see.

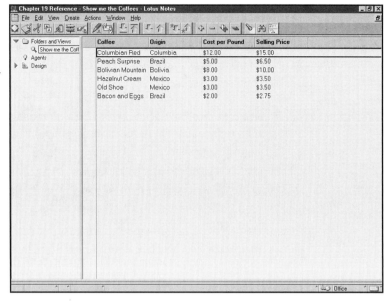

The following is an example of how to use @DBColumn to get a list of values for a keyword list.

You have created a field called Coffee on a form and it is a keyword list. You want to obtain a list of coffees from a database called referenc.nsf that has a view called CoffeeLookup, which has been created. This CoffeeLookup view consists of a single column containing the coffee description. Although your form is not in the reference database, it is on the same server. The following procedure would allow you to get a keyword list from the view:

1. In the properties for the Coffee field on your form, ensure that the field type is keyword and that the Choices field indicates you are going to use a formula to generate the choices (see Figure 19.2).

Figure 19.2

A formula to obtain keyword choices using @DBColumn.

2. In the Formula window, type in the following formula:

```
@DBColumn("":"NoCache";"":"database.nsf";"CoffeeLookup";1)
```

There are two limitations of `@DBColumn` that you will need to be aware of. First, the function can only return 64KB of information. If your lists are larger than that, you will have to use Lotus Script to produce those lists.

Second, in order for a user to access a list from a keyword field, that user must have at least `reader` access to the view from which the list is being generated.

Having seen how to obtain a list of information from a view using `@DBColumn`, let's now examine `@DBLookup`, which is a function to obtain document information by using a document key in a view.

The `@DBLookup` Function

The `@DBLookup` function allows you to get document information given the key to the document as found in a database view. There are two acceptable syntaxes for `@DBLookup`:

```
@DBLookup(class:"NoCache";server:database;view;key;FieldName)
```

```
@DBLookup(class:"NoCache";server:database;view;key;columnNumber)
```

As with the `@DBColumn` function, the first parameter of `@DBLookup` consists of a list of two optional values. The `class` indicates the type of lookup being done and distinguishes lookups into Notes views from lookups into non-Notes (ODBC) databases. In order to indicate a lookup into a Notes view, either specify `NULL ("")` or `"Notes"`. The rest of the syntax assumes a Notes class.

The `"NoCache"` element is also optional and indicates that you would like Notes to rebuild the list of values every time the list is required. This is set against a scenario where you would like the values cached to have the same values used over and over again. The benefits of caching are that the lookup is faster the second and successive times; however, if the source changes, you will not see those changes. Regardless of your caching request, the cache is only persistent in a single Notes session and is discarded when your session ends. If this element is left `NULL`, then the list values will be automatically cached.

The second parameter consists of two optional values, `server` and `database`. This indicates the location of the view from which you want to pull the list of lookup keys. If the server is the same as the place from which the `@DBLookup` is being run, you do not have to specify the server name. Otherwise, indicate the server name using its fully distinguished name in quotation marks, for example, `"Server1/Bean"`. If the database is also the same as the place from which the `@DBLookup` is being run, its name can also be left out. Otherwise, you must indicate the location of the database on the server. If the database is located in the default data directory (frequently `C:\Notes\Data`), you can simply indicate the database's file name in quotation marks: `"database.nsf"`. Otherwise, indicate either the path relative to the default notes directory or the complete path including the drive letter and all intervening directories (`\accounting\database.nsf` or `C:\accounting\database.nsf`). If you do not need to specify either the server or database name, you can replace the whole parameter with `NULL` (`""`).

The third parameter is the name of the view from which you want to obtain the list of keys. The name that you specify must be in quotation marks and must be either the alias of the view (as specified in the view properties) or the full name of the view (including all cascading menus).

The fourth parameter is the key to the document from which you want to get information. This key must be a value located in the first sorted column of the view indicated in the third parameter.

The last (fifth) parameter can be one of two values. In the first syntax, it is the name of the field on the keyed document that the function is to return. The case of the field name does not matter, but you must be sure to match punctuation exactly.

In the second syntax, the last parameter is the column number in the view specified in the third parameter, which contains the value that you want to return. Notes uses a particular methodology for determining the column number, and therefore, you must follow the same methodology when determining what column you want to refer to. Determine the column number as you did in the section of this chapter titled "The @DBColumn Function."

The following is an example of how to use @DBLookup to get a value from a document given a key to that document.

You have created a field called Coffee on a form and it is a keyword list. You obtain a list of coffee codes by using an @DBColumn, but after the user has chosen the code, you want to display the description for the coffee on the form. You have created a Computed for Display field on your form called CoffeeDescription. There is a list of coffees in a database called referenc.nsf, in a view called CoffeeLookup. This view contains two columns: The first is a sorted column of coffee codes; the second contains their corresponding descriptions. Although your form is not in the reference database, it is on the same server. The following procedure would enable you to get a description from the view:

1. In the properties for the CoffeeDescription field on your form (see Figure 19.3), ensure that the field type is Text and that it is Computed for Display.

Figure 19.3

Ensure that this field is computed for display.

2. In the Formula window for the CoffeeDescription field, type in the following formula:

```
@DBLookup("":"NoCache";"":"database.nsf";"CoffeeLookup";Coffee;2)
```

This formula will look up the value in the Coffee field on the current document in the CoffeeLookup view from the database.nsf database and return the corresponding value from the second column of that view.

Note In order for a user to access the view that contains the document key, that user must have at least reader access to it.

Although it is fast and easy to obtain information from views and documents and to prompt for user input, sometimes you require specific information about users that cannot be obtained from either views or documents. Getting this information can be tedious through fields and prompts, especially when it is required in a number of different places in your applications. Environment variables provide a possible solution to this problem.

Understanding Environment Variables

 **Objective** Certain information remains constant for a certain user: his name, department, location, and so on. This information is often required in applications as a way of identifying or categorizing document information. As with any pieces of data, these things can be prompted for. However, if a user has to enter the same information over and over again in each new document he produces, it can create frustration, not to mention the potential to make mistakes in entry. Environment variables are variables that sit outside the context of any of your databases or forms that can be used to hold information that remains constant. Defined and recalled from the Notes.ini file on each local machine, these variables can be used to store information once, and then that information can be recalled whenever it is necessary. If you design a form to define and save this information, that form can also be used to modify the information should it ever change.

 Note There are two downsides to environment variables. The first is that because they are stored in the Notes.ini file, they are workstation specific and not user specific. If a user moves from one workstation to another, the information does not move. As a result, they are best used in environments where users are always at a fixed machine. Second, the information is not secure. Anyone with the ability to edit the Notes.ini file can see and modify the variable information.

In order to use environment variables, they first have to be defined and assigned values.

Defining Environment Variables

Because environment variables exist outside the scope of any particular form or database, they cannot simply be defined by placing them onto a form as is the case with fields. Instead, they are defined using special functions and keywords that reference them in their own context: the Notes.ini file.

Because environment variables exist in a file on a local workstation, they are generally used only in contexts where a single user would be using a single workstation. If more than one user used a certain workstation, the environment variables would reflect information from the person using the station the last time the variables were assigned values. If these were variables such as Name, Company, and Birthday, the information would be incorrect for all but one person.

Environment variables are often prompted for in forms that ask for personal information in a database, or through the use of @Prompts where a series of questions are asked when initiated through the click of an action or a button hotspot on a form. These values are then written out to the Notes.ini file and used whenever one of the saved values is needed. Sometimes, an application will check first to see whether the variables have been set, and if they have not, the application will stop processing to retrieve the information either from a document field or directly from the user. These values will then be written to the Notes.ini so that they will not have to be prompted for in the future.

In the Notes.ini file, an environment variable exists as a single line that looks like this:

```
$Variablename = value
```

Environment variables can be defined using a number of functions and syntaxes. These include @Environment, @SetEnvironment, and the keyword ENVIRONMENT.

The @Environment Function

The @Environment function has two syntaxes: one for assigning a value to an environment variable, and the other for retrieving an environment variable's value. The syntax for assigning or defining an environment variable is as follows:

```
@Environment("Variablename";value)
```

In this syntax, the variable name must be in quotation marks, or must be a variable that has been assigned the value that you want to be the environment variable name. The most likely of the two is usually a static name, provided in quotation marks (such as "Name"). For example, if you want to create an environment variable called Name in the Notes.ini file, you can use the syntax:

```
@Environment("Name";"Bob")
```

 Tip

If you have more than one person using the same workstation and want to save multiple instances of a variable (Name or Department, for example), you can use a combination of variable and static text to form the variable name. If you create a variable name by concatenating part or all of the user's common name using the @Name function, you can concatenate that variable text with static text such as "Department". This would ensure that the name of the variable was unique for each person who was using that workstation. For example, if you want to set a department name to a department that a user enters, you might use the syntax:

```
@Environment("Department";@Prompt([OkCancelEdit];
➥"Department";"Enter your department";NULL))
```

However, if 10 different people used the same workstation at different times, you would want to track each of their departments. You can do this by attaching the first name of their user name to the word department to create a unique field; that is, instead of a field called Department, call it BobDepartment using the following syntax:

```
@Environment(@Left(@Name([CN];@UserName);" ")+"Department";
➥@Prompt([OkCancelEdit];"Department";"Enter your
➥department";NULL)
```

When entered, Notes takes the variable name that you use and attaches a dollar sign ($) to the beginning of it. Notes then checks the Notes.ini file to see whether that variable name exists. If it does, the value indicated in the formula is assigned to the variable. If the variable does not exist, Notes creates it, assigning the initial value to the value indicated in the formula.

The second syntax is for retrieving environment information and looks like this:

```
@Environment("VariableName")
```

As with the first syntax, the variable name must be in quotation marks, and to return a value, the variable name must be present in the Notes.ini file, otherwise, a NULL value is returned. For example, if you want to obtain the value for the "Department" variable for a specific workstation, you can use a formula such as:

```
@Environment("Department")
```

The @SetEnvironment Function

The syntax for @SetEnvironment is the same as for @Environment except that it can only be used to assign values to environment variables and cannot be used to retrieve them. The syntax is

```
@SetEnvironment("Variablename";value)
```

For more information on how the function works, see the preceding section, "The @Environment Function."

The ENVIRONMENT Keyword

Like other keywords in Notes, the ENVIRONMENT keyword indicates that what follows it has special significance. In this case, the keyword ENVIRONMENT indicates that the word following it is to be used as an environment variable name. In the ENVIRONMENT syntax, assignments are done using the assignment symbol (:=), as follows:

```
ENVIRONMENT Department := "Accounting"
```

Although this keyword works almost the same as the functions previously mentioned, there are some significant differences that make this a less preferred method of variable assignment than either of the @ functions.

There are some drawbacks to using the keyword syntax for assigning values to environment variables, which, in many cases, make it the least preferred of the options. First, as with any keyword, it can be used only at the beginning of a formula line. That means that you cannot use the keyword as a result clause in an @If statement.

Second, because the name of the variable is set and not in quotation marks, you cannot generate variable names on the fly like the previous example in the section titled "The @Environment Function."

Now that you have seen how to declare and assign values to environment variables, you will learn how to retrieve and use the values saved in them.

Using Environment Variables

In order to use an environment variable's value, that value must first be obtained from the Notes.ini file. Unlike declaring and assigning a value to an environment variable, where there are many ways to accomplish that task, there is only one way to retrieve an environment variable: using @Environment. The syntax for retrieving a value is

```
@Environment("VariableName")
```

The result of such a function can then be assigned to a temporary variable, to a field, or can be used in an @If statement to determine which course of action to take in a particular event. For example, use of an environment variable can be as simple as storing user information and then populating field values with it. It can also be as complex as using the value in a management field to determine which subform to insert into a new document: the one with management information in it, or the one with accounting information in it (see Chapter 20, "Layout Regions and Subforms").

The bottom line in environment variables is that they provide you with a place to store user-specific information that can be used as a shortcut to obtain that information many times in the future.

Mail-Enabling Applications

Objective

As Notes applications get more and more complex, it is often desirable to split the data into multiple databases. However, it is not always feasible, or desirable, to use @DBColumn and @DBLookup to pull information from one database to another. In many cases, what would be desirable is to have certain documents begin in one database and then be moved to another. For example, an employee survey is created and sent to all the people in a company. When this survey is filled in, it would be desirable to have it mailed back to a database where the information can be analyzed.

Mail-enabling applications is an efficient way to allow documents to be moved from one physical location to another. To fully understand this process, you must first know something about the Notes mail router.

Using the Mail Router

The Notes mail router is a process that runs on most Lotus Notes servers. It is designed to move documents from one database to another through the use of addresses, usually obtained in the Public Address Book. When asked to deliver a document, the router looks to the document's information regarding destination and checks the Public Address Book to see where the physical location of that destination is. If it can find the location, the router moves the document from the current source location to the destination. If the destination is on another server, the router simply passes the document on to the destination's server and allows the router from that server to complete the process.

If the destination's address cannot be found in the Public Address Book, one of two things will happen. If the Notes system is enabled for communication to other systems (for example, the Internet), it will send the message out to that external system. If the Notes system is not enabled for external communication, an error condition will be returned indicating that the destination could not be found.

So, in order for the router to successfully deliver documents from one database to another, it must first find the destination in the Public Address Book.

Mail-Enabling Destinations (Databases)

Many mail destinations are pre-enabled for the reception of mail. For example, all of the personal Notes mail databases that users in an organization use are enabled for mail reception when they are created. However, when you build applications and want to have the router deliver documents into those databases, it needs an address by which to locate the mail destinations. These addresses, like the addresses used to deliver electronic Notes mail, are found in the Public Address Book. However, unlike your personal mail, which is identified through a Person document with your name on it, database destinations are identified through the use of Mail-In Database documents. These documents specify the filename of the database and what server they are located on.

Without a Mail-In Database document in the Public Address Book, the router will be unable to locate the destination for the documents that you are sending, and your application will fail. Therefore, it is important that you understand how these are created.

To create a Mail-In Database document in the Public Address Book:

1. Ensure that you create the database that you want to mail to, and identify what its filename is and what server it is on.

2. Ensure that you have proper permissions to create Mail-In Database documents in the Public Address Book. You may have to get your server administrator to give you author access to the Public Address Book or have him complete the Mail-In Database document–creation process for you.

3. Open the Public Address Book and, in the Navigation pane, expand the servers section by clicking the twistie to the left of it, the select the Mail-In Databases subsection.

4. Click the Add Mail-In Database action button to have a new Mail-In Database document appear (see Figure 19.4).

Figure 19.4

A sample Mail-In Database document.

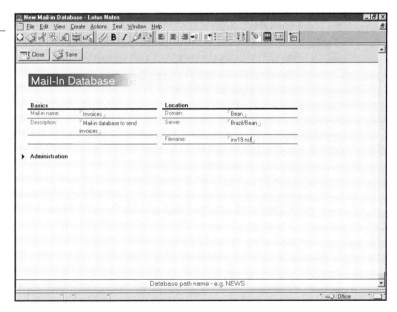

5. In the Mail-In Name field, type the name that you want to specify when you want to send documents to this database. The name can be anything, but to prevent confusion, it should meaningfully describe the function of the database.

6. In the Description field, type a phrase that describes the purpose of this Mail-In Database.

7. In the Domain field, type the name of the Notes domain that this database is a part of. Usually, this will be the same as the one you are in. Contact your system administrator if you are unsure of this.

8. In the Server field, type in the fully distinguished name of the server on which the database resides; for example, `Brazil/Bean`.

9. In the Filename field, type the name of the database file. This can either be the database name relative to the default Notes directory (frequently `C:\Notes\Data`) or the full path if the database is not found in the default Notes directory tree. The name must include the extension, for example, `invoices.nsf`. If the database is in a subdirectory of the default Notes directory, indicate that by prefixing the database name with the name of the directory in which it is found beginning from the first one under the default Notes directory. For example, if the database is found in the path `C:\Notes\Data\accounting`, the name will be specified as `accounting\invoices.nsf`.

10. Save the document and close it; then close the Public Address Book.

Now that you have enabled a database to mail to, you have to enable the documents you want to mail by adding fields or formulas to the forms that create them.

Mail-Enabling Sources (Forms)

Mailing documents doesn't just happen all by itself. It requires that the forms that create these documents be prepared in advance. This may include any combination of special functions, such as `@MailSend`, invoked automatically or through actions, and special reserved fields, such as `SendTo`, that Notes looks to when determining to send parameters.

For example, when you decide that a scheduled agent needs to run on your invoice file every day and check for overdue invoices, sending mail to remind the customers to pay, Notes needs to know three things:

▶ That it should send mail

▶ Who it should send to

▶ What the parameters for sending are (such as whether the document should be signed or encrypted)

Reserved Words for Mail Send

In all but one of the mail sending techniques, values are required to provide information regarding where to send the document, and what parameters should be included in the send (for example, sign, encrypt, and so on). This information is usually provided through the use of reserved fields on the mail-enabled form. These fields can all be populated in the usual ways; they can either have values input directly by a user in an editable field, or they can have values calculated in a computed field. Reserved fields are specific names that have been predefined as having a certain function. When fields with these names appear on forms, Notes assumes you are using them a specific way and Notes assumes that they will have certain kinds of values. If you use any of the fields in Table 19.1 for the purposes other than what they were intended, or if you populate the fields with invalid values, you may get errors.

Table 19.1

Reserved Mail Fields.

Field name	Values	Field function
MailOptions	1, 0	If set to 1, the document currently being edited will be mailed to the address in the SendTo field on document save.
SaveOptions	1, 0	If set to 1, the document currently being edited will be saved when it is mailed.

continues

Table 19.1 Continued

Field name	Values	Field function
Sign	1, 0	If set to 1, the document currently being edited will be signed when it is mailed.
Encrypt	1, 0	If set to 1, the document currently being edited will be encrypted when it is mailed.
SendTo	Any name that the router can deliver to	Used to obtain the address of the primary destination(s) of the document to be mailed. This field is required for all functions and mailing methods other than @MailSend with parameters.
CopyTo	Any name that the router can deliver to	Used to obtain the address of the CC destination(s) of the document to be mailed.
BlindCopyTo	Any name that the router can deliver to	Used to obtain the address of the BCC destination(s) of the document to be mailed.
DeliveryPriority	L, N, H	Determines the priority of the send. L = low, N = normal, H = high.
DeliveryReport	B, C, T, N	Specifies under what circumstances a delivery report should be returned to the sender. B = on delivery failure, C = on failure and success, T = trace route to destination, N = no reports.
ReturnReceipt	1, 0	If set to 1, the sender will get a message indicating when the document sent is opened for the first time.

Now that you have seen the reserved fields, let's turn to the actual mechanisms for mail-enabling forms.

Mail-Enabling by Using Form Properties

The first and easiest way to mail-enable a form is to change the properties of the form to prompt a user, on document save, as to whether he wants to mail the document. This method requires that there be a SendTo field (either computed or editable) that has the name of the document's destination. To mail-enable a form using form properties:

1. Create the form to be mail-enabled and edit its design.

2. Create a field called SendTo on the form; if it is a computed field, you may want to hide it on the form.

3. Right-click a blank area of the form, and select Form Properties from the menu that appears.

4. Navigate to the Defaults tab in the Properties for Form dialog box.

5. Check the Present Mail Dialog Box check box in the On Close section (see Figure 19.5).

Figure 19.5

Select the Present Mail Dialog Box check box to mail-enable the form.

6. Close the Properties for Form dialog box by clicking the Close Window button, and then save and exit the form.

After the form has been created and mail-enabled, every time a document is modified and closed, you will be prompted for the action to take (see Figure 19.6).

Figure 19.6

Closing the document produces a Mail Specifications dialog box.

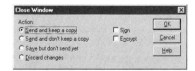

Note

> If you have a MailOptions field on your form, that field will over-ride any choices made in the dialog box appearing from the Present Mail Dialog Box form property. This may be quite con-fusing to users and, therefore, it is not recommended that you have both enabled.

Mail-Enabling Using Reserved Fields Only

Mail-enabling a form does not require property changes in the form, nor does it require user intervention of any kind. In fact, through the use of reserved fields, you can mail-enable a form without using any special mailing functions at all.

In Table 19.1, you were shown the reserved fields that Notes as-sumes will be used for mailing. They can be combined on a form to mail-enable that form.

The minimum information that Notes needs to route a document to a destination is that the document should be mailed and where that document should go. This information can be provided through the use of a MailOptions field and a SendTo field. The two possible values for MailOptions are 1 and 0. This field can either have its value computed, or, if user input is required, can be edit-able.

Tip

> Because Notes wants to see only the values 1 or 0 in the MailOptions field, and because the meaning of these values may be rather obscure to users, you may want to make the MailOptions field a keyword list with values you provided:
>
> Send this document¦1
>
> Don't send this document¦0
>
> This will ensure that the user can choose only one or the other option, and that he or she can choose from meaningful En-glish phrases, not obscure Notes Boolean values. However, by using an alias for the values, you can ensure that Notes can correctly interpret the users' choices.

The SendTo field can also be either editable or computed and can also contain multiple values for delivery to multiple destinations.

 Tip

If your SendTo field is to be editable, you may want to put some controls over what information is entered in it. Because the router will deliver only to valid addresses, the process will fail if the addresses input are incorrect. You can get around this problem by making the field type Names: Editable, and then indicate that you want to use the Address dialog for choices. If the field does not allow multiple values, the user can select a single person, group, or Mail-In Database from the dialog box when he or she requests that the dialog box appear. If the field does allow multiple values, the user can select multiple destinations from the address book when it appears.

If there is a possibility that the sender might want to send this document to a non-Notes destination (that is, through some sort of gateway), you will have to enable them to allow values not in the list (another field property).

In addition to the two required fields, you may also use any of the other reserved mail fields (refer to Table 19.1) to enhance the send. These include CopyTo and BlindCopyTo, Sign, Encrypt, DeliveryPriority, DeliveryReport, and ReturnReceipt. As with SendTo and MailOptions, these fields may all be either computer or editable, and you can use the techniques outlined in the tips for those fields to restrict the ability of the users to enter invalid choices into the fields.

When forms have been mail-enabled using a MailOptions field, the documents produced will be mailed every time a change is made to the document and the document is saved or exited.

It may not always be desirable to have documents mailed simply by filling in fields. You may want specific triggers to activate mail send. If so, you will want to send mail using the special function Notes has for mailing: @MailSend.

Mail-Enabling Using @MailSend Without Parameters

If you want to send a document using a field formula, an action or hotspot button, or in an agent, you will need to use the @MailSend function.

Used without parameters, the @MailSend function looks to the document for a value in the SendTo field and sends the document to that destination. Without a SendTo field, @MailSend without parameters will fail. The syntax of @MailSend without parameters is

@MailSend

If present, @MailSend will also take advantage of all the other reserved mailing fields; simply add them to the form you want to mail-enable and populate them with values (refer to Table 19.1). The function will abide by the parameters that you have set up.

 Note

The function @Command([MailSend]) performs exactly the same function as @MailSend without parameters. It also uses the values of the reserved mailing fields (refer to Table 19.1) to augment its sending characteristics.

Sometimes, you may prefer not to route the current document to another database, but actually send a Notes mail message as part of your document processing. If that is the case, use @MailSend with parameters.

Sending Notes Mail Memos Using @MailSend with Parameters

If you want to make sending a Notes mail memo a part of the processing of a document, you can use the @MailSend function with parameters. When used this way, @MailSend composes mail and sends it to the destination of your choice, including external Internet mail if your system is configured to allow that.

Sending mail can be very beneficial when you want to alert a person of the arrival of a new document in a database that he is interested in, or when you want to inform someone of the status of a document, for example, informing a customer that his invoice is overdue.

The syntax of @MailSend with parameters is

`@MailSend(SendTo;CCTo;BCCTo;Subject;BodyComment;BodyFields;[flags])`

The SendTo parameter might be a single value or a list of values that represent the destination(s) to which you want the message sent. This value can be a text string, typed into the parameter, or it can refer to a field on the form in which the function is being executed. For example, you can place a person's name into the parameter Java Joe/Bean, or you can place that person's name into a SendTo field on the form and then simply reference the value through the field name SendTo. This parameter is required.

The CCTo parameter may be a single value or a list of values representing the carbon copy destination that you want the message sent to. As with SendTo, the value can be a text string or a reference to a form field. This parameter is optional but if not desired, it must be replaced with a NULL value (either the word NULL or the NULL string, "").

The BCCTo parameter may be a single value or a list of values representing the blind carbon copy destination that you want the message sent to. As with SendTo, the value can be a text string or a reference to a form field. This parameter is optional but if not desired, it must be replaced with a NULL value (either the word NULL or the NULL string "").

The Subject parameter is a text string representing the value you want placed into the Subject field on the message being sent. It is optional, but if not desired, it must be replaced with a NULL value.

The BodyComment parameter is a text string that will be placed as introductory information at the beginning of the body of the message being sent. It is optional, but if not desired, must be replaced with a NULL value.

The BodyFields parameter is a list of @ functions, static text, or field names on the document from which the @MailSend function is being executed, whose contents are to be concatenated in the body of the message being sent. These values must be identified by concatenating them as text strings enclosed in quotation marks. For example, to include the text from the fields called Name, Address, and PhoneNumber, you would place into this parameter the string "Name":"Address":"PhoneNumber". To add static text or functions, add those values to the list (for example, "PhoneNumber":@NewLine:" Double-click the link to open —>"). This parameter is optional, but if not desired, it must be replaced with a NULL value.

The flags parameter is a list of optional processing flags, concatenated together and enclosed in square brackets. The valid flags are as follows:

▶ [Sign] will sign the message from the user or server initiating the mail send.

▶ [Encrypt] will encrypt the message with the public key of the recipient.

▶ [PriorityHigh] delivers the message at high priority, [PriorityNormal] delivers the message at normal priority, and [PriorityLow] delivers the message at low priority.

▶ [ReturnReceipt] ensures that a return message is sent to the sender when the message is opened by the recipient.

▶ [DeliveryReportConfirmed] ensures that a return message is sent to the sender if the message is successfully or unsuccessfully delivered to the recipient.

▶ [IncludeDocLink] will create a document link to the document that is being processed or edited when the @MailSend is triggered and will place that document link into the body of the message being created.

The default values for these flags, in the case where any or all are not provided, are as follows: no signing, no encryption, deliver at normal priority, no return receipt, delivery receipt only on delivery failure, and don't include doclink to source.

This parameter is optional and should be replaced with a NULL value if no deviation from default is required.

Now that you have sent a document or mail message to a destination, you have to consider whether that document will be readable at the destination.

Ensuring That Document Information Is Accessible at the Destination

When the document arrives at its destination, Notes needs to display that document in the database in which it is found. As part of Notes' internal processing when a document is created, it populates a field called *form* that it uses to determine what form it should use to display the information in the document. When you ask to open a document, Notes looks at the form field, gets the form layout, and then displays the document by merging the document information with the form layout. However, this process breaks down if the form is not present in the place where the document is being opened.

Because mail-enabling applications is all about transferring information from one database to another by using the router, it is assumed that documents will frequently be viewed in databases other than the one they were created in. In order to view the information properly, there has to be an appropriate form in the destination database, for example, the form that is indicated in a document's form field.

If the form field's contents are not the name of a form found in the destination database, then Notes will seek out the default form for the database and display the information using that form. Before doing that, however, Notes will generate an error message (see Figure 19.7) to tell you that the form that it wanted to display the information could not be found and it had to use the default form for that database.

Figure 19.7

An error will be generated if Notes cannot locate the form indicated in the document.

When you use @MailSend with parameters, however, the process does not create a form field for the mail memo. As a result, you will never see the error message appear when you open a message produced in this way.

In order to overcome the lack of a source form in a destination database, the following techniques are suggested:

1. Copy the source form into all the databases to which the document will be mailed.

2. Change the name of the form in the sent document to a form in the destination database when the document arrives in the new database.

3. Save the source form as part of the document and then send it, thus making the form available with the document wherever it arrives.

Although each of these techniques will be effective to allow document information to be viewed properly at any destination, there are plusses and minuses to each.

If you copy the source form into each destination database, you create two problems. First, you will have to take up space in each database to save the new form. Second, you will have the additional maintenance of adding that form to each database that you want to mail to and of having to update the form in each of those databases when it changes in the source. If, however, you link all your form designs to the same form template, you can alleviate some of the maintenance (see Chapter 22, "Maintaining Application Designs"). This option takes the least sophisticated processing but is a very "brute-force" solution.

If you change the name of the form field in the document when it arrives in the new database, you can get around the problem of having to have the source form resident in each new database. This change can be accomplished quite easily through the use of an agent, triggered by incoming mail and running a simple action, which changes the form field to the value of your choice (see Chapter 21, "Creating Agents"). However, like copying the form in the first solution, you will still have to ensure that there is some kind of form capable of displaying the information that you require, even if it is not exactly the same form as the source database. Moreover, you will have to set up the agent and the destination form in every new database that you want to mail to.

You have, as your last option, the choice of simply saving the form definition as part of the data in the document. When done, this bypasses all of the form-and-document–relatedness problems. Because the document and the form are never separated, as is usually the case, when you have the document, you always have the form that you need to display it. This solution can be accomplished by changing one property on the form that produces the document.

To enable a form to save the form with each document it produces:

1. Open the form to edit its design.

2. Right-click any blank area of the form, and choose Form Properties from the menu that appears.

3. Navigate to the Defaults tab in the Properties for Form dialog box.

4. Check the box next to the Store Form in Document property.

5. Close the Properties for Form dialog box, and save and close the form.

The only drawback to this method of ensuring that document data appears in the destination database is that each document will take up much more space. Because the full definition of the form is saved with each new document, the space requirement can be enormous.

Exercises

On your CD-ROM, there are three databases that you need for this lab. Copy inv19.nsf, ref19.nsf, and cust19.nsf to your Notes data folder (ensuring you remove the read-only attribute from the files) and add the databases titled Chapter 19 Invoices, Chapter 19 Reference, and Chapter 19 Customers to your workspace.

In the Chapter 19 Orders database, there is a form called Invoice that is incomplete. The intent of this form is to allow you to enter an invoice with multiple line items for a specific customer. Then, when the invoice is complete, you can send the invoice to that customer.

When you add a new line item to the invoice, you are given a list of coffees to choose from, and then you are prompted for the quantity and the price. At that point, the total is calculated.

This lab takes you through the process of modifying the Add a Coffee button so that as soon as the coffee is chosen and a quantity is entered, @DBLookup will get the price from the reference database. In addition, you will add an action that will send the invoice to the mail address of your choice.

Here are some important objects you will need to reference:

- ▶ Database 1: Filename: inv19.nsf; Title: Chapter 19 Invoices

- ▶ Database 2: Filename: ref19.nsf; Title: Chapter 19 Reference

- ▶ Database 3:Filename: cust19.nsf; Title: Chapter 19 Customers

- ▶ Form to modify: Database: inv19.nsf; Name: Invoice

- ▶ View to reference: Database: ref19.nsf; Name: (Description); Alias: Description

- ▶ View to reference: Database: cust19.nsf; Name: (E-Mail Addresses); Alias: EMail

Exercise 19.1

1. Open the Chapter 19 Invoices database and in the forms list,
   double-click the Invoice form to edit its design.

2. Navigate down to the Add a Coffee button and click it to
   display its formula in the Design pane at the bottom of the
   screen.

3. Select and remove the lines that are highlighted in Figure
   19.8. This removes the prompt and the code necessary to
   process that prompt.

Figure 19.8

*Remove the lines
highlighted here.*

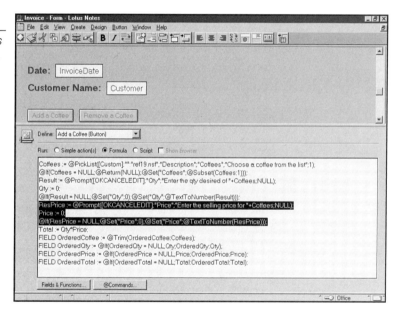

4. Position your insertion point at the end of the line that begins
   @If(Result = NULL...), press Enter, and add the following line:

   ```
   Price :=@DBLookup("":"NoCache";"":"ref19.nsf";"Description";
   ➥Coffees;3);
   ```

   This will result in a lookup in the Description view of the
   Reference database, returning the value in the third column
   corresponding to the row that has the value of the Coffee
   field in the first sorted column (in our case, the selling price
   for that coffee).

5. From the Create menu, choose Action.

6. To create an action to mail the invoice, type `Mail Invoice` in the Title field, choose the icon indicated in Figure 19.9, and close the Properties for Action dialog box by clicking the Close Window button.

Figure 19.9

Define the action properties as shown here.

7. Click the Design pane for the action, and type the following code (feel free to leave out the REM statements; they are for your benefit):

```
REM "Using the value of the Customer field as a key, use
@DBLookup to look into";
REM "the Email view in the cust19.nsf database, and bring
back the second";
REM "column value . . . the Email address of the customer";
Recipient :=
@DBLookup("":"NoCache";"":"cust19.nsf";"EMail";Customer;2);
REM "Since we are sending the invoice, we should save it at
this point";
@Command([FileSave]);
REM "Send a mail message to the Email address we got from
the @DBLookup above,";
REM "do not specifiy CC or BCC recipients. In the subject
simply tell the";
REM "recipient we want payment. In the body, indicate how
much was ordered and";
REM "on what day and then when it should be paid. The calcu-
lation for payment";
REM "is a simple @Adjust of the invoice date — date plus 30
days";
@MailSend(Recipient;NULL;NULL;"Please pay this invoice (Net
30)";"You ordered a
➥total of "+@Text(InvoiceTotal;"C2")+ " worth of goods on
```

```
➡"+@Text(InvoiceDate;"S0")+"; please remit by
➡"+@Text(@Adjust(InvoiceDate;0;0;30;0;0;0);"S0")+".";NULL;NULL);
REM "Now that we are done we should close the invoice.";
@Command([FileCloseWindow])
```

8. Save and close the form.

9. You can test your form by creating a new customer in the Chapter 19 Customer database (be sure you fill in an e-mail address) and then creating a new invoice, specifying the customer you just created. When you enter new line items, you should get prices and totals calculating automatically (the total owing will not calculate unless you save or refresh manually; press F9). When you click the Mail Invoice action, a notice of invoice will be mailed to the e-mail address you specified if you are working in an environment with a Notes server capable of doing mail routing.

Exercise 19.2

One of the frustrations of this design is that you have to type in the customer's name. The challenge is to change the type of the CustomerName field on the Invoices form to Keywords and then create a formula that will do a lookup into the customer database (cust19.nsf) to get a list of customers to choose from on data entry.

The answer to the challenge is in a form called ChallengeAnswer found in the inv19.nsf database.

Review Questions

1. Romeo wants to save a value in an environment variable. Which of following will not work?

   a. @PutEnvironment("Manager";"Bazyl")

   b. @SetEnvironment("Manager";"Bazyl")

   c. @Environment("Manager";"Bazyl")

   d. ENVIRONMENT Manager := "Bazyl"

2. Juliet is trying to retrieve a value from a view using @DBLookup, however, her syntax is incorrect and her function will not work. Given her function:

```
Colour := @DBLookup("":"NoCache";"Brazil/
➥Bean";"Hair.nsf";"HairLookup";HairColour;2)
```

what is the problem?

   a. She has specified the name of the server incorrectly.

   b. She needs to put the name of the key in quotation marks.

   c. The server/database combination should be a list with a colon (:) separating them.

   d. The term "NoCache" is not a valid @DBLookup parameter.

3. Guildenstern has created an environment variable using the formula

```
@Environment("FavoriteFruit";"Chocolate")
```

What will the line in the Notes.ini look like if he were to examine it?

   a. `FavoriteFruit=Chocolate`

   b. `$FavoriteFruit=Chocolate`

   c. `FavoriteFruit="Chocolate"`

   d. `FavoriteFruit$=Chocolate`

4. Rosencrantz has mail-enabled a form using the form property On Close Present Mail Send Dialog. He also has an editable keyword list field called MailOptions in which a user can choose 1 or 0. A user chooses 1 in the MailOptions field and then, when prompted to save and send the message, chooses Save But Don't Send Yet in the Close Window dialog box on document exit. What is the result?

   a. The document is saved and not sent.

   b. The document is sent and not saved.

c. The document is sent and saved.

d. The document is neither sent nor saved.

5. The `SendTo` field is not essential to the proper functioning of which of the following?

a. `@MailSend` with parameters

b. `MailOptions="1"` reserved field

c. `@MailSend` without parameters

d. The form property On Close Present Mail Send Dialog

6. Polonius wants to send an invoice into an archive database using the mail router. What must he set up in the Public Address Book in order for this to be successful?

a. A Cluster document

b. A Person document

c. A Programs document

d. A Mail-In Database document

7. Ophelia wants to use `@MailSend` with parameters to inform accounts receivable that a new invoice has been generated. She wants to include a document link to the invoice in the mail memo she is generating. What flag does she use to accomplish this?

a. `[SendDocLink]`

b. `[GenDocLink]`

c. `[IncludeDocLink]`

d. `[LinktoDoc]`

8. Mr. Lear sends a document into a database using the mail router. However, all users who attempt to open these documents get the following message: `Can't Locate Form: Invoice.`

How can he prevent this from happening without adverse side effects?

   a. He can create an agent in the destination database, triggered on incoming mail, that will change the form name from `Invoice` to a form name that exists in that database.

   b. He can make the form field editable in his source database and let the users change the form field before it is sent.

   c. He can stop sending documents to the destination database.

   d. He can create an agent in the source database, triggered on mail send that will change the form name from `Invoice` to a form name that exists in the destination database.

9. Which function is useful in creating dynamic lists for keyword fields based on lookups to other databases?

   a. `@DBLookup`

   b. `@PickList`

   c. `@DBColumn`

   d. `@Prompt`

10. Which of the following is not a Notes reserved field for mail processing?

   a. `SendTo`

   b. `Envelope`

   c. `Sign`

   d. `SaveOptions`

11. Puck creates an @DBColumn and wants to ensure that the same server is not always being hit with requests for view information. How can he ensure that the "closest" replica is used by any user?

    a. He cannot do this.

    b. He can specify the server name as Random.

    c. He can specify the server/database combination using the database's replica ID.

    d. He can create a Mail-In Database for view requests.

12. William has created an @DBColumn that looks into the third column of a view to retrieve a value; however, he continually gets back what he sees as the second column data. What is he not taking into account?

    a. The bending of linear space when counting view columns.

    b. That Notes counts view columns from right to left.

    c. That sorted columns are never counted.

    d. That hidden columns are counted.

13. Richard wants to create a document that mails itself without any user intervention. Can this be done?

    a. Yes

    b. No

14. Oscar creates an action that uses an @MailSend without parameters. He wants the document he is sending to be signed. How can he do this?

    a. @MailSend without parameters does not have this option.

    b. Create a Sign field on the form and assign it the value 1.

    c. Create a Sign field on the form and assign it the value 2.

      d. Assign the form the On Close Sign the Document property.

Review Answers

1. A. The function `@PutEnvironment` does not exist. All the other forms are valid ways of setting and updating environment variables. For more information, refer to the sections titled "Defining Environment Variables," "The `@Environment` Function," "The `@SetEnvironment` Function," and "The `ENVIRONMENT` Keyword."

2. C. Looking closely at her code, you will see that she has mistakenly created two parameters out of the server/database combination. These are actually to be two elements of a list, joined by a colon. For more information, refer to the section titled "The `@DBLookup` Function."

3. B. When written to the `Notes.ini` file, environment variables appear with a $ preceding them. For more information, refer to the section titled "Defining Environment Variables."

4. C. The reserved field `MailOptions` will override the On Close Present Mail Send Dialog form property. So, despite the fact that the user did not ask to send the document, it was sent anyway. For more information, refer to the section titled "Mail-Enabling Using Form Properties."

5. A. All of these require the `SendTo` field to indicate the destination except `@MailSend` with parameters. The `@MailSend` with parameters function has the destination as one of its parameters. However, it is the convention to place a hidden `SendTo` field on the form anyway and to make reference to the `SendTo` field when specifying the destination of an `@MailSend` with parameters function. For more information, refer to the section titled "Sending Notes Mail Memos Using `@MailSend` with Parameters."

6. D. In order to successfully route mail to any destination, it must have an entry in the Public Address Book (unless it is being routed through a gateway). The appropriate document for a database is a Mail-In Database document. For

more information, refer to the section titled "Mail-Enabling Destinations (Databases)."

7. C. To include a document link in the body of a message, include the flag [IncludeDocLink]. For more information, refer to the section titled "Sending Notes Mail Memos Using @MailSend with Parameters."

8. A. The option with the fewest side effects is to change the name of the form as it enters the new database. This can be accomplished through the use of an agent, which is triggered when new mail arrives in the database. Of course, this will only be the case if the form whose name you use in the destination database has the fields that were present on the old form. If this is the case, this option is preferable to storing the form with the document as it avoids the overhead of having the form present with every document. For more information, refer to the section titled "Ensuring That Document Information Is Accessible at the Destination."

9. C. @DBLookup will only return a single value. @Picklist will return a number of values, but those values will populate the keyword list and then the user will have to choose again. The user does double work every time. First, he chooses the items in the keyword list manually; then he chooses the value he wants from the keyword list. @Prompt will also return a value, but again, to the keyword list, not to the field. Only @DBColumn will return a list of values suitable to choose from in a keyword list. For more information, refer to the sections titled "The @DBColumn Function" and "The @DBLookup Function." You may reference @PickList and @Prompt in Chapter 18, "Advanced Formulas Part I."

10. B. Envelope is not a reserved word whereas SendTo, Sign, and SaveOptions are fields that Notes assumes have particular meaning and values. For more information, refer to the section titled "Reserved Words for Mail Send."

11. C. By providing the replica ID of the database in which he wants to look, Notes will search for the one nearest to the environment in which the information is being asked for. If there are multiple servers with replicas of this database, the spread of requests should be relatively even across all of

them if the user communities for each server use the database about the same amount. For more information, refer to the section titled "The `@DBColumn` Function."

12. D. There are specific rules for determining the number of a column in a view that you need to specify to Notes to get specific information from that view. Of the four choices, the only one that is a factor that Notes counts columns in the design, not in what the user sees. William probably counted the columns in the view that a user sees and did not go into the view's design to see if there were hidden columns. For more information, refer to the section titled "The `@DBColumn` Function."

13. A. There are a number of ways to create mail without user intervention. Richard can create a number of reserved mail fields, including `MailOptions` and `SendTo`, that have computed values. He can also create `@If` statements in computed fields to trigger `@MailSend` with or without parameters. These are only a few of the ways to do what he wants. For more information, refer to the sections titled "Mail-Enabling Using Reserved Fields Only," "Mail-Enabling Using `@MailSend` Without Parameters," and "Sending Notes Mail Memos Using `@MailSend` with Parameters."

14. B. `@MailSend` respects all reserved mail fields that are on a document. Therefore, if Oscar creates a field called `Sign` (which is a reserved mail field) and assigns it the value of 1, the document will be signed when mailed. For more information, refer to the sections titled "Mail-Enabling Using `@MailSend` Without Parameters" and "Reserved Words for Mail Send."

Answers to Test Yourself Questions at Beginning of Chapter

1. The main difference between @DBColumn and @DBLookup is that @DBColumn is designed to return a list of values from the view specified in the function's parameters, and @DBLookup is designed to return a single value based on a document key. For more information, refer to "The @DBColumn Function" and "The @DBLookup Function."

2. An environment variable is a workstation-specific variable designed to hold user profile information, such as department, manager, or favorite fruit, as well as general-purpose global variables that need to be saved outside of the context of any specific field or formula. Environment variables are stored in the Notes.ini file on a local workstation. For more information, refer to "Environment Variables" and "Defining Environment Variables."

3. The @MailSend function is designed to use the mail router to send documents from one database to another. @MailSend without parameters will send a copy of the current document to the destination of your choice depending on the value of the SendTo field on that document. @MailSend with parameters will send a Notes mail memo to the destination of your choice. In one case, both the destination and the document being sent are user/application-developer determined. In the other case, only the destination is configurable; the document is not. For more information, refer to "Mail-Enabling Using @MailSend Without Parameters" and "Sending Notes Mail Memos Using @MailSend with Parameters."

4. In all mail-send circumstances, the destination of the document must be specified. In all but @MailSend with parameters, there is no facility inherent in the structure of the calling entity to obtain the destination so the presence of a reserved field, SendTo, must be present in the document being sent to indicate the destination. For more information, refer to "Reserved Words for Mail Send," "Mail-Enabling by Using Form Properties," Mail-Enabling Using Reserved Words Only," and Mail-Enabling Using @MailSend Without Parameters."

C h a p t e r 20

Layout Regions
and Subforms

This chapter introduces you to the following objectives:

 Objectives

▶ Create and format layout regions

▶ Create and insert subforms

▶ Insert subforms using formulas

Test Yourself! Before reading this chapter, test yourself to determine how much study time you will need to devote to this section.

1. What is a layout region and how does it differ from a regular form area?

2. How can using subforms increase design efficiency?

3. What does it mean to insert a subform based on a formula and what is the result?

Answers are located at the end of the chapter...

Design efficiency and aesthetic appeal are two things that become more important as the applications you create grow in size and in user base. You have two important tools to help increase design efficiency: layout regions and subforms; one of the fortunate side effects of layout regions is that some features not only increase efficiency but also increase aesthetic appeal and functionality as well.

Creating and Formatting Layout Regions

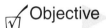

Layout regions are areas on your forms where you can easily insert and move design elements. In the regular form environment, the positions of fields and text are restricted; they must attach to the sides of the form or to other pieces of text or fields, and they must stay within the structure of their paragraphs. In a layout region, fields and text float around in a predefined area, and you can drag the fields and text wherever you choose—sometimes overlapping other objects and sometimes sitting alone in one spot.

Layout regions are very nice to work with because you can easily drag objects to different places, instead of having to cut and paste. Furthermore, some features are available only in layout regions—for example, some extra display types for keyword fields.

Creating a Layout Region

A layout region is like any other element on a form. You insert the layout region at a particular place by moving your insertion point to that place. At that point, select Create|Layout Region, New Layout Region, and a rectangle appears on your screen (see Figure 20.1).

Layout regions always begin as the same size, but you can make them larger or smaller as you desire.

Figure 20.1

A layout region is an element you insert on a form.

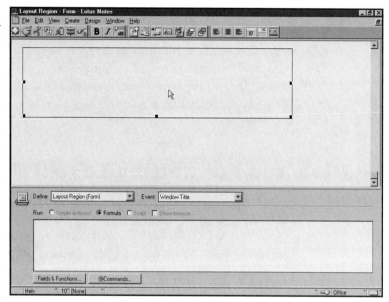

When you create the layout region, it is selected, and you can tell that because the layout region has resizing handles (little black squares) around the outer edges. To work with the layout region, it has to be selected; that way Notes understands that any objects you create are to be placed within the region.

If you place your pointer on any of the resizing handles, your pointer changes to a double-headed arrow. This indicates that you can change the size of the region. By clicking and dragging on any of the resizing handles, you can make the region wider, narrower, higher, or shorter. If you click outside the layout region, it is deselected, but you can reselect it by clicking anywhere inside the region or on its border.

Like other Notes form elements, layout regions have properties. If you right-click the layout region and choose Layout Properties from the menu that appears, the Properties for Layout dialog box displays. On the Basics tab of this dialog box, you can change the size of the region using numbers of inches, rather than dragging the resizing handles with your mouse. The field labeled Left is the distance that the layout region begins from the left-hand side of the form (see Figure 20.2).

Figure 20.2

The Properties for Layout dialog box enables you to define the basic layout properties.

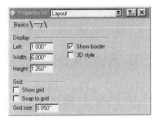

Check boxes are on the Basics tab for turning the border on and off and for making it appear with a 3D style, which essentially displays the region with a gray background, like a standard Windows dialog box.

To make object placement and alignment easier, you can use the grid check boxes. One check box turns on and off a grid, giving you reference points inside the region. The other check box enables the Snap to Grid feature. If enabled, this feature ensures that when an object is created in the layout region, the object is attached to one of the fixed points on the grid, which makes it easier to align one object with another. Finally, the field labeled Grid Size enables you to choose the size of the grid—the larger the number in the field, the farther apart the grid markers will be (see Figure 20.3).

Figure 20.3

Showing the grid makes it easier to align objects in your layout region.

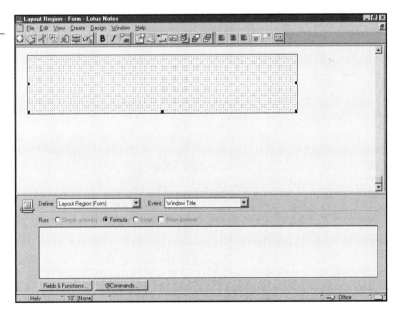

Hiding characteristics are also available for the layout region; they are on the second tab in the Properties dialog box. The layout region is treated like one large paragraph for the purposes of hiding. If any of the hiding characteristics are selected, the whole layout region will be hidden.

Inserting and Manipulating Fields on Layout Regions

Like other areas on a Notes form, you can create fields inside layout regions. Unlike other areas, these fields become moveable objects, which you can click and drag from place to place inside the layout region. To create a field in a layout region, complete the following steps:

1. Ensure that the layout region is selected.

2. From the Create menu, choose Field, or alternatively, click the Create Field button on the smart Icons bar.

3. Drag the field from the middle of the layout region to the place where you want it.

4. Double-click the new field to display the Properties for Field dialog box (see Figure 20.4).

Figure 20.4

A new field inserted into a layout region with its properties showing.

The properties for fields in layout regions are almost the same as for fields in text areas on your form, but there are two notable exceptions: First, you cannot choose field type rich text inside a layout region because these areas do not support any rich text features. In fact, you cannot insert into the layout region any of the notable rich text features, including attachments, doclinks, tables, and sections. Second, whereas with fields in text areas, only keyword lists have option properties tabs to enable you to choose the presentation interface, all fields in a layout region have such a tab (see Figure 20.5).

Figure 20.5

All fields in layout regions have presentation tabs, enabling you to define the presentation style.

These properties enable you to choose how the field appears and what its size is. For all data types, the lower section of this page contains the layout options. The layout options enable you to change the size and position of the field inside the layout region. The fields labeled Left and Top enable you to specify where, relative to the top-left corner of the layout region, the top-left corner of the field will be. If the numbers are 2 and 1 (left and top, respectively), the top-left corner of the field will be 2 inches from the left of the region and 1 inch from the left. The fields labeled Width and Height control the dimensions of the field.

For all field types except keywords, this top section of the Display tab contains edit control options. These options enable you to modify how information appears in the field and whether the region has a border and a scrollbar. Unlike other form fields, layout region fields have fixed sizes and do not grow with the amount of text entered. Selecting the Multiline check box ensures that text inside the field wraps when it is too big to fit inside the box; however, if the height of the box is too small, not all the lines are visible after entry is complete. If you select the check box labeled Scroll Bar, a scrollbar is made available to scroll through multiple lines of text in the field.

For the keywords data type, the top section of the Display tab is the keywords interface. In text regions on your form, keywords can be presented as one of dialog list, check box, or radio button.

In layout regions, the dialog list interface is replaced with either a list box or a combo box (see Figure 20.6).

Figure 20.6

The interface choices for key-words have been changed in layout regions.

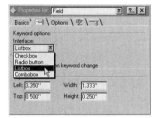

These two interfaces are much like the standard Windows list box and combo box objects. A list box is a list from which you choose, and a combo box is an editable field with a pull-down list from which you can choose that disappears after you make your selection.

In all other ways, fields act exactly the same in a layout region as in other areas on a form.

 Note

If you create a field outside of a layout region, you can cut and paste it into the region, preserving all its characteristics, as long as it is not a rich-text field, and as long as it is not a key-words field with a dialog list interface. The reverse, however, is not true. If you select and cut a field from a layout region and then try and paste it into another area on your form, the field is pasted surrounded by a new layout region.

Inserting Text Boxes on Layout Regions

Unlike text in text regions on your forms, text in layout regions must be contained within text boxes. These text boxes are objects, just like fields, and you can drag them and define properties for them. To create a text box and place text within it, complete the following steps:

1. Ensure that the layout region is selected.

2. Select Create|Layout Region Text or alternatively, click the Create Textbox button on the toolbar.

3. Drag the text box from the middle of the layout region to the place where you want it.

4. Double-click the text box to display the Properties for Control dialog box.

Because text is placed inside a text box object, text in layout regions has properties that are accessed in very different ways from text region text. Two sections are on the Display tab (see Figure 20.7); the first is for static text options, and the other is for layout options.

Figure 20.7

The Text Properties dialog box enables you to add text and modify the box.

The static text options enable you to choose how the text you type is aligned within the confines of the text box and whether the text is to be centered vertically inside the text box. Should the box be higher than the lines of text displayed in it? The Text field is used to type the static text, which appears inside the text box.

As with field objects, the layout options control where in the layout region the text box is located and how large the object will be.

As with text in a text region, the Style tab (AZ icon) is used to change the font face, size, color, and style of the text . However, with text boxes, you have an additional option: the Transparent check box. By default, text boxes are transparent, meaning that they have no apparent borders and show the color or pattern of the form through them. If you choose to deselect this check box, a field appears to its right enabling you to choose the background color for the text box (see Figure 20.8).

Figure 20.8

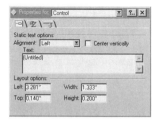

Selecting the Transparent check box enables the background color of the layout region to show through the region.

Inserting Graphics in Layout Regions

You can also insert graphic objects into layout regions. To insert a graphic into a layout region, you must first copy it to the Windows clipboard. This means that you can insert a graphic of any format into a Notes layout region, as long as some facility exists outside of Notes to select the graphic and copy it; you cannot directly import a graphic into a layout region.

When inserted, a graphic becomes a graphic object in the layout region. Like a field object or a text box, you can drag it within the confines of the layout region to reposition the graphic object, and it has properties which you can set.

To insert a graphic into a layout region, complete the following steps:

1. Select a graphic in an application outside of Notes and copy it to the clipboard.

2. Within Notes, ensure that the layout region is selected.

3. Select Create|Layout Region Graphic.

4. Drag the graphic object from the middle of the layout region to the place where you want it.

5. Double-click the graphic to bring up the Properties for Control dialog box (see Figure 20.9).

Figure 20.9

A graphic inserted into a layout region with its Properties dialog box showing.

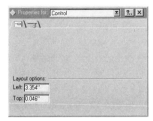

Unlike a field or a text box, the properties of a graphic object allow only for the repositioning of the object, not for the resizing of it. This means that the size of the graphic when copied into the clipboard is the size that it remains in the layout region. If the layout region is not large enough to accommodate the graphic, the layout region will be resized to be as large as the graphic. If a graphic is smaller than the layout region, the graphic appears in the middle of the layout region, just as all other objects appear when you first create them. The layout region then can be resized to be as small as, but no smaller than, the graphic object.

Inserting Hotspot Buttons on Layout Regions

You can create two kinds of buttons in a layout region: a standard hotspot button and a graphic button. Both kinds of buttons are created as button objects, and you can move them within the layout region just as you move other objects. Complete the following steps to create a hotspot button:

1. Ensure that the layout region is selected.

2. Select Create|Hotspot Button or alternatively, click the Create Hotspot button on the toolbar.

3. Drag the button from the middle of the layout region to the place where you want it.

4. Double-click the button to display the Properties for Button dialog box (see Figure 20.10).

Figure 20.10

The Properties for Button dialog box enables you to set the button text and layout.

As with hotspot buttons created in text regions on forms, hotspot buttons in layout regions can have text displayed in them, or they can be plain gray. On the Display tab of the Properties for Button dialog box, you can type text into the Button Label field to have text appear in the button. If you select the Wrap Text check box, the button always stays the fixed width specified in the Button Width field. This causes the button to increase in height if the label cannot display in the width provided. If you do not select the Wrap Text check box, the button stays one line high but increases in length as the amount of text increases.

As with other layout region objects, hotspot buttons are set in a particular position within the layout region, which you can specify in the buttons' properties. To create a graphic button, complete the following steps:

1. Select a graphic in an application outside of Notes and copy it to the clipboard.

2. Within Notes, ensure that the layout region is selected.

3. From the Create menu, choose Layout Region, then click the Graphic button. Alternatively, click the Create Graphic button on the toolbar.

4. Drag the button from the middle of the layout region to the place where you want it.

5. Double-click the button to display the Properties for Control dialog box (see Figure 20.11).

Unlike a hotspot button, a graphic button cannot contain a text label. However, its uniqueness is that you create it from a graphic that has been copied to the clipboard. As a result, the button can appear as any design or picture that you want, with a specific function or action that is triggered by a user's click on that graphic.

Figure 20.11

Figure 20.11

A graphic button is a graphic object that can be clicked to perform an action you specify.

The properties for a graphic button include only the hiding properties and the position of the button within the layout region.

Working with Multiple Objects in a Layout Region

Because layout regions are areas of object manipulation, and because you can position these objects at any place within the layout region, certain design tools are provided and techniques are recommended for working with these objects.

When two or more objects overlap, it is often convenient to take one of those objects and place it at the bottom of the stack or to take one object and move it to the top. This might occur after you place a number of fields and text boxes in a layout region and then decide to add a graphic background to the region. If the graphic is the full size of the layout region and if you insert it last, the graphic covers up all the other objects. You then want to move the graphic behind all the other objects. To move an object to the front or back of an object stack, do the following:

1. In the layout region, click the object you want to move.

2. From the Design menu, choose Bring to Front to bring the object to the top of the stack, or choose Send to Back to send the object to the bottom of the stack.

In a text region on a form, when you want certain fields to appear under certain circumstances and then disappear under others (for example, one field appears when you are editing a document and does not appear when you are not), you can change the hide-when properties for the paragraph in which the field is found.

This makes the entire contents of the line disappear when the condition is met and appear when it is not met. In layout regions, this process is not as simple because the objects are not part of lines, they are entities in their own right. If you want one field to show under one circumstance and have another field show in the same place under another circumstance, you must appropriately set their hide-when properties and then move the objects so that they overlap each other.

To have one field appear in edit mode and other appear in the same place in read mode, complete the following steps:

1. Create the fields in the layout region (I refer to them as field X and field Y; X shows in edit mode, Y shows in read mode).

2. Double-click field X to display the Properties for Field dialog box and navigate to the Hide-When tab (the one with the blind on it).

3. Select the Previewed For Reading and Opened For Reading check boxes to hide the field in all read circumstances.

4. Close the field properties by clicking the Close Window button.

5. Double-click field Y to display the Properties for Field dialog box and navigate to the Hide-When tab.

6. Select the Previewed For Editing and Opened For Editing check boxes to hide the field in all edit circumstances.

7. Close the field properties by clicking the Close Window button.

8. Drag field X to the place where both fields are to display in your layout region.

9. Drag field Y to cover field X.

Note   Unlike with text regions, the lines in layout regions do not disappear even when all the objects on that line are hidden. You invariably end up with blank spaces in your layout region when objects disappear.

Because the layout region itself is an object in the text region of the form, it has hiding properties. You can set the complete layout region to appear and disappear under certain circumstances, either through predefined check boxes or through the processing of a formula. To enable the hide properties of a layout region, do the following:

1. Select the layout region by clicking it.

2. Right-click anywhere in the layout region and choose Layout Properties from the menu that appears. This displays the Properties for Layout dialog box.

3. Navigate to the Hide-When tab and select the check boxes necessary to enable the desired check boxes and/or write a hide formula.

4. Close the layout properties by clicking the Close Window button.

Layout regions increase design efficiency in one way, by making the placement and movement of fields, text, buttons, and graphics easy for a developer. Note, however, that because of their complexity, they do add to the time it takes a document to open. Subforms also increase design efficiency by enabling you to share groups of design components between forms.

Creating and Inserting Subforms

Subforms are groups of form elements that are saved together for the purpose of inserting the group in more than one place in a database. A subform may be as simple as a standard header and footer, or may be as complex as the body of a form, which needs to be reproduced in many places in your database.

Subforms can contain any elements that you normally can place onto a form, including fields, text, layout regions, tables, sections, document links, attachments, actions, hotspots, and even other subforms. A subform makes design more streamlined by creating certain groups of elements once and then using those groups over and over again.

Creating a Subform

To insert a subform into a form, you must first create a subform. As with forms, it is best to sketch the layout for the subform before you begin creating it in Lotus Notes. In your sketch, include the position of all the design elements that are to be placed on it. Then, when you are sure of how the layout will look, begin committing it to electronic form. Complete the following steps to create a subform:

1. Design the subform on paper.

2. Open the database in which you want to create the subform and select Create|Design Subform.

3. Right-click and choose Subform Properties to display the Properties for Subform dialog box (see Figure 20.12).

Figure 20.12

The Properties for Subform dialog box.

4. Enter a meaningful name for the subform and add an alias if you desire (for example, A new subform|subform).

5. The three check boxes control who is allowed to see this subform and from where. When selected, the check box Include in Insert Subform Dialog enables you to manually

insert a subform in a form (by selecting Create, Insert Subform) and to have the subform appear in the dialog box
listing subforms to insert. When selected, the check box
Include in Insert Form Dialog causes a dialog box to appear
when a new form is created, asking which of the subforms
with this check box selected you want to insert into the new
form. Finally, when selected, the Hide Subform from R3
Users ensures that if a subform is inserted into a form, its
contents does not display to Notes release 3.*x* users. Use this
feature when a subform contains features that were not available until release 4.*x*.

6. Close the Subform Properties dialog box by clicking the
   Close Window button.

7. Add fields, text, and other elements as you would in a regular form.

8. Save the subform and close to return to the database design.

Having created a subform, you can now view the list of all subforms from the database's standard navigator by expanding the
design section and selecting subform. After a subform has been
created, the next step is to insert it into a form.

Manually Inserting a Subform

After you create a subform, you need to insert it into a form to
perform any function. By inserting the subform into a form, you
make all the elements of the subform part of the form. That
means you must ensure that no field names on the main form
have been duplicated in the subform or the duplicate names in
the subform will be changed to name_1 to make them unique. To
insert a subform into a form, complete the following steps:

1. Create the form into which you want to insert the subform
   and open its design.

2. Position your insertion point at the place in the form where you want the subform to be inserted.

3. From the Create menu, choose Insert Subform and then choose the name of the subform that you want to insert (see Figure 20.13).

Figure 20.13

The Insert Subform dialog box enables you to indicate which subform to insert in a form.

Note

You cannot insert the same subform into a form more than once. If you try to insert a subform that has already been inserted on a form, you get an error message indicating that it is already present on the form and no additional action is taken.

4. Save the form design and close it.

Manually inserting a subform is only one way to insert it into a form. You can also insert the form through the use of a formula.

Inserting a Subform Using a Formula

In some cases, the subform that is to be inserted into a form cannot be known until a document is being created from the form. For example, if you have a form that asks for customer information, you may want to choose between form formats so that state and zip code are inserted when the customer is from the United States and province and postal code are inserted when the customer is from Canada. You could create two identical forms and have the user choose which he or she wants to create, or you could create one form with a formula in it that determines which subform to insert (either the U.S. or the Canadian) at the time of document creation.

Complete the following steps to insert a subform based on a formula:

1. Create the form into which you want to insert the subforms and open its design.

2. Position your insertion point at the place in the form where you want one of the subforms to be inserted.

3. From the Create menu, choose Insert Subform and then, from the Insert Subform dialog box, select the Insert Subform Based on Formula check box and click the OK button (see Figure 20.14).

Figure 20.14

Selecting the Insert Subform Based on Formula check box enables you to write a formula to compute what subform should be inserted.

4. In the design pane for Define Computed (Subform), type a formula that results in one of the names of the subforms to be inserted (see Figure 20.15); for example, if the two subforms are Customer and Employee, the result of the formula must be either Customer and Employee or no subform will be inserted.

 Tip

The calculation for the insertion of the subform happens before any of the editable fields on the form can be filled by the user. That means the criteria for insertion into the form must be in place before the user has a chance to input any values. Computed field values are calculated in the order in which they appear on the form; if two computed fields are above the subform, they are calculated and then the calculation for the name of the subform is done. That means the only values you have to work with when computing which subform to insert are environment

continues

variables, computed fields that appear above the subform, and the subform formula itself.

You may want to use an `@Prompt` in the subform insertion formula to ask the user what subform to insert or at least for some value with which you can determine the subform to insert.

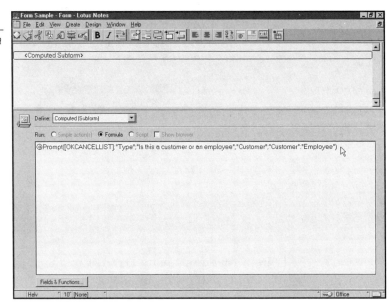

Figure 20.15

You must create a formula that re-sults in the name of one of the subforms in your database.

5. Save the form design and close it.

By using computed subforms, you have the flexibility of building a generic form that is made specific when the document is created. Subforms also ensure that if new subforms are necessary—for example, a subform to insert the geographical information for Mexico—they can easily be inserted simply by changing the insertion formula on the form.

Editing a Subform

After a subform has been created, it can be modified from two places. First, you can edit its design by double clicking the subform's name in the subforms list, which is obtained by selecting the subform view in the design section of the standard view.

Second, you can also edit a subform's design by double-clicking the subform placeholder in the form in which it has been inserted. When you are editing a form, the places where subforms are inserted are indicated with boxes surrounding them when they are clicked. At the point when a subform is clicked, a message appears in the design area saying, You may edit the contents of this subform by double-clicking it. If you double-click the place where the subform has been inserted, you edit the design of the subform (see Figure 20.16).

Figure 20.16

By double-clicking the subform on the form, you can edit the subform in its own design window.

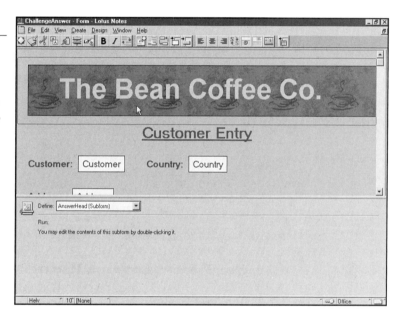

Note

One of the advantages of inserting subforms into forms is that when the subform is changed, the change is automatically made in all the forms in which the subform has been inserted. This means that the design of a subform has to be changed only in one place and not in each of the individual forms. Moreover, the change to the subform is also automatically made in all the documents created with the forms in which that subform is inserted.

Exercises

Three databases you need for this lab are on your CD-ROM . Copy inv20.nsf, ref20.nsf, cust20.nsf, and Bean.bmp to your Notes data folder (ensuring you remove the read-only attribute from the files) and add the databases titled Chapter 20 Invoices, Chapter 20 Reference, and Chapter 20 Customers to your workspace.

In the Chapter 20 Customers database, a form called Customer is incomplete. The intent of this form is to enable you to enter customer information for the Bean organization. Right now, the address is incomplete because you need to provide a way to have either the state and zip code fields appear or the province and postal code fields appear, depending on whether a customer is from the U.S. or Canada. In addition, you want to create a standard header in a subform that includes a layout region containing the company's trademark graphic.

This lab takes you through the process of creating three subforms: two to be inserted using a formula and one to be statically inserted into the form.

Here are some important objects you need to reference:

▶ Database: Filename: cust20.nsf; Title: Chapter 20 Customers

▶ Form to modify: Invoice

▶ Subforms to create: Canada; U.S.A.; Header

▶ Graphic: Bean.bmp

Exercise 20.1

1. Open the Chapter 20 Customers database and, from the Create menu, choose Design I Subform.

2. From the Create menu, choose Layout Region I New Layout Region.

3. Start the Paint program or some other graphics editor. If you are using Windows 95, click the Start button, and from the Start menu select Programs I Accessories I Paint.

4. Open the graphic `Bean.bmp`, which you copied to your `Notes\Data` folder.

5. Select the whole graphic (in Paint, from the Edit menu, choose Select All) and then copy it to the clipboard (in Paint, from the Edit menu, choose Copy).

6. Close the graphics program by clicking the Close Window button and return to Notes.

7. With the layout region still selected, select Create | Layout Region, Graphic to paste the graphic into the layout region.

8. Drag the graphic into the upper-left corner of the layout region.

9. Select the layout region by clicking inside it (anywhere but on the graphic), and then resize it using the resizing handle on the bottom so that it is the same height as the graphic (see Figure 20.17).

Figure 20.17

Drag up the bottom resizing handle to make the layout region the same size as the graphic.

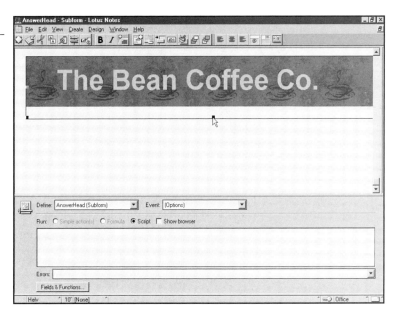

10. Right-click the subform and choose Subform Properties from the menu that appears.

continues

11. In the Name box, type `Header` and close the Subform Properties dialog box by clicking the Close Window button.

12. Save the subform and close it, returning to the standard view.

13. From the Create menu, choose Design|Subform (the completed subform looks like Figure 20.18).

Figure 20.18

The completed U.S.A. subform.

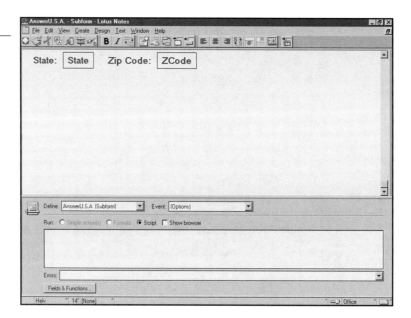

14. From the Text menu, choose Text Properties and change the font face to Helv, 14pt, Bold, Dark Red. Close the Text Properties dialog box.

15. Type `State:` and turn off bolding.

16. From the Create menu, choose Field and set the field properties as follows, and close the Field Properties dialog box by clicking the Close Window button:

    `Name: State; Type: Text; Editable`

17. After inserting a few spaces, turn bolding back on and type `Zip Code:` and then turn bolding back off.

18. From the Create menu, choose Field and set the field properties as follows and then close the Field Properties dialog box by clicking the close window button:

    `Name: ZCode; Type: Text, Editable`

19. Right-click the subform and choose Subform Properties from the menu that appears.

20. In the name box, type `U.S.A.` and close the properties dialog box by clicking the Close Window button.

21. Save the subform and close it, returning to the standard view.

22. Following steps 13–21, create a subform called Canada that contains the text `Province:` followed by a field called Province, followed by the text `Postal Code:`, and followed by a field called Postal Code (see Figure 20.19).

Figure 20.19

The completed Canada subform.

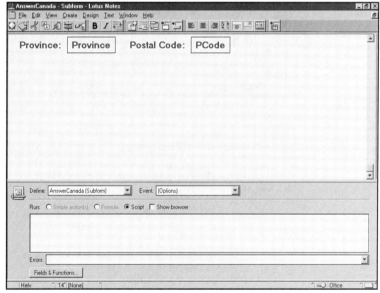

23. From the standard view, expand the design section and click the Forms view to display a list of forms; double-click `Customer` to edit it.

24. When you enter the form's design, your insertion point should be to the right of the title Customer Entry. From the

continues

Exercise 20.1 Continued

Create menu, choose Insert Subform, select Header from
the list of subforms to insert, and click the OK button to
insert the subform (see Figure 20.20).

Figure 20.20

*Select the
Header subform
from the
subforms list*

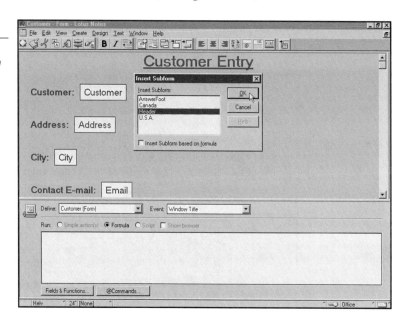

25. Select the text `Customer Entry` and from the Text menu,
    choose Align Paragraph|Center to center the text.

26. Double-click the Country field to display its properties and
    change the field type from Editable to Computed when
    Composed. In the design area for the value event, type the
    following formula (see Figure 20.21):

    ```
    @Prompt([OKCancelList];"Country";"Choose the country in which
    ➡this customer is based";"U.S.A.";"Canada":"U.S.A.")
    ```

Figure 20.21

*The Country field
contains a formula
that enables the
user to choose a
country; this value
is used to insert
the subform.*

27. Close the field properties by clicking the Close Window button.

28. Scroll down in the form design and click below the City field to position your insertion point to insert the computed subform.

29. From the Create menu, choose Insert Subform and select the Insert Subform Based on Formula check box, clicking the OK button to complete the selection (see Figure 20.22).

Figure 20.22

Insert Subform Based on Formula check box.

30. In the design area, type the following formula to define the computed subform:

```
Country
```

31. Test the form by saving it and, from the Design menu, choose Test Form. You should be able to select either U.S.A. or Canada from the country list and the appropriate fields should appear; the result of inserting one or the other subforms.

Exercise 20.2

You have no Authors fields on any of your forms, and you want to put both the author and the date into a subform called Footer and insert it into your Customer form. The challenge is to create a subform called Footer that contains fields called Author and CreateDate—both Computed when Composed fields—with appropriate accompanying text and to insert that subform at the bottom of the Customer form.

The answer to the challenge is in a form called ChallengeAnswer, which you find in the cust20.nsf database that also includes the forms AnswerHead, AnswerFoot, AnswerU.S.A., and AnswerCanada.

Review Questions

1. Which of the following is not a valid object in a layout region?

   a. Text box

   b. Keyword field

   c. Table

   d. Graphic button

2. Nelly is inserting a computed subform in a form. In the design pane she types Fruit into the formula window. What subform is inserted into the form?

   a. The subform called Fruit.

   b. The subform which has the same name as the value of the Fruit field.

   c. The subform called Banana.

   d. The subform which has the same name as the value of the Banana field.

3. Tina has inserted a keywords field in a layout region. Which of the following is not a valid display format for this field?

   a. Combo box

   b. List box

   c. Dialog list

   d. Radio button

4. Kim wants to create a button in a layout region that has the graphic of a happy face on it. How can she do this?

   a. She cannot create such a button in a layout region.

   b. She can create a hotspot and overlay a graphic on it.

   c. She can create a graphic and overlay a hotspot on it.

   d. She can create a graphic button using a happy face graphic.

5. Paul creates a subform with a field called Manager and inserts it into a form that already has a field called Manager. What will be the result?

   a. The form ends up with two fields called Manager.

   b. The original Manager field disappears from the form, leaving only the one from the subform.

   c. Both Manager fields remain, but Paul is unable to save the form without first deleting the subform.

   d. The Manager field on the subform changes to Manager_1.

6. Janna inserts a graphic into a layout region, and it covers up all the other objects that were already there. How can she rearrange the objects so that the fields and text appear on top of the graphic?

   a. Click the graphic and from the Design menu, choose Send to Back.

   b. Delete the graphic, create a new layout region, paste the graphic on the layout region, and cut and paste the text and fields into the new region.

   c. Drag the graphic off the layout region, select the layout region and from the Design menu, lift the corner, and then slide the graphic under the layout region.

   d. Delete all the objects in the layout region and starting from the graphic, recreate them.

7. Of the following, which can be copied and pasted from a text region to a layout region?

   a. Static text

   b. Subforms

   c. Fields

   d. Sections

Part II   Application Development

8. Rose creates a subform, and in its properties, she selects the Include in Insert Form Dialog box check box. What is the result when she creates her next form?

    a. The subform is automatically inserted into the form at the top.

    b. This check box has no effect on form creation.

    c. The subform is automatically inserted at the bottom of the form when it is saved.

    d. The Insert Subform dialog box appears with the subform as one of its choices.

9. Debbie creates a layout region and then inserts a graphic. However, when she tries to make the layout region smaller, she cannot. Why?

    a. Layout regions containing graphics cannot be resized.

    b. Layout regions containing graphics cannot be made smaller than the default size.

    c. Layout regions containing graphics cannot be made smaller than the graphic.

    d. Layout regions cannot be resized.

10. Carole clicks the 3D property for a layout region. What is the result?

    a. When she puts on red and green classes, the layout region floats in the air.

    b. The layout region is displayed with a gray background.

    c. The objects on the layout region appear stacked like blocks on the region.

    d. There is no result; this is a Notes 3.*x* feature.

11. What tool is available to aid in the alignment of objects in a layout region?

    a. Rulers

    b. Segment marks

    c. Rastors

    d. Grid lines

12. Jeanne wants to create a subform containing actions, computed fields, graphics, sections, and static text. Can she create such a subform in Notes 4.*x*?

    a. Yes

    b. No

13. Tami creates a subform that contains a layout region. In the layout region, she wants to display a keyword field in edit mode and a text (computed for display) field in read mode. How can she do this?

    a. Create the two fields in the layout region, appropriately set their hide-when properties, and drag one over the top of the other.

    b. Create two fields in the layout region, appropriately set their hide-when properties, and put them on different lines in the region.

    c. Create two fields side-by-side in a text region, appropriately set their hide-when properties, and copy and paste them into the layout region.

    d. You cannot do this in a layout region.

14. Ron has inserted a subform into a form and is now editing the form. He wants to modify the subform. What is the easiest way to get to the design of the subform?

    a. Close the form and edit the subform.

    b. Use the Window menu to move back to the standard view and double-click the subform.

    c. Scroll down to the subform and double-click it on the form.

    d. From the Edit menu, choose Subform.

Review Answers

1. C. Layout regions cannot contain any rich-text features, including rich-text fields, sections, document links, attachments, or tables. For more information, refer to the section titled "Inserting and Manipulating Fields on Layout Regions."

2. B. The subform that is inserted as the result of the formula. Because this formula is simply the name of a field, the subform is whatever is in the Fruit field when the subform is inserted onto the form. For more information, refer to the section titled "Inserting a Subform Using a Formula."

3. C. In moving to layout regions, the keywords field gets two new display types: combo box and list box, but it loses the dialog list. For more information, refer to the section titled "Inserting and Manipulating Fields on Layout Regions."

4. D. By copying a graphic to the clipboard, Kim can create a button from that graphic by choosing Layout Region|Graphic Button from the Create menu. For more information, refer to the section titled "Inserting Hotspot Buttons on Layout Regions."

5. D. Because the fields on a subform become fields on the form in which it has been inserted, you cannot have duplicate names. To repair this problem, Notes renames the subform field(s) by placing an _1 after each duplicated field. For more information, refer to the section titled "Manually Inserting a Subform."

6. A. You can send an object to the bottom of the object pile by selecting it and then choosing Send to Back from the Design menu. For more information, refer to the section titled "Working with Multiple Objects in a Layout Region."

7. C. Of these, only fields can be copied from a text region to a layout region. For more information, refer to the section titled "Inserting and Manipulating Fields on Layout Regions."

8. D. This property prompts you to insert the subform when any new form is created. If more than one subform has this property, more than one appears in the Insert Subform dialog box that is presented. For more information, refer to the section titled "Creating a Subform."

9. C. Graphics in layout regions cannot be resized. Therefore, a layout region cannot be made smaller than the graphic contained in it. For more information, refer to the section titled "Inserting Graphics in Layout Regions."

10. B. 3D in layout regions always refers to the standard gray windows background, not to a raised appearance. For more information, refer to the section titled "Creating a Layout Region."

11. D. The tool is called grid lines and can be turned on from the properties of the layout region. For more information, refer to the section titled "Creating a Layout Region."

12. A. All the features available in a regular form are also available in a subform including all the features listed. For more information, refer to the section titled "Creating and Inserting Subforms."

13. A. Because each object on a layout region has its own properties, Tami can simply set the appropriate properties for each field and then drag one on top of the other. For more information, refer to the section titled "Working with Multiple Objects in a Layout Region."

14. C. The design of a subform inserted into a form can be accessed by double-clicking the place where the subform is inserted. For more information, refer to the section titled "Editing a Subform."

Answers to Test Yourself Questions at Beginning of Chapter

1. A layout region is an area on a form in which elements that are inserted can be easily moved by dragging them and which contains layout features unavailable elsewhere on a form. The difference between layout regions and other form areas is that the objects you create (text boxes, fields, graphics, hotspot buttons, and buttons) can be dragged to the position where you want them independent of the line on which they began. These objects can overlap each other, as well. Other differences are that keyword fields have extra display attributes, while losing the dialog list display type. In addition, layout regions cannot hold rich-text fields or any rich-text features, such as tables, sections, doclinks, or attachments. For more information, refer to "Creating and Formatting Layout Regions."

2. Subforms are groups of design elements that are saved together and then inserted as a group into another form. These subforms can contain any elements that a regular form can contain, including fields, text, graphics, tables, attachments, and actions. With subforms you increase design efficiency because you need to create a particular subform needs only once and then it can be inserted over and over again (as with a standard form header or footer). In addition, when a subform is changed, those changes are automatically reflected in all the forms that contain that subform. For more information, refer to "Creating and Inserting Subforms."

3. Inserting a subform based on a formula means that you decide at the time a document is created which subform is to be included in the form on which the document is based. This means that, based on certain field values or questions asked of the user, any of a number of subforms can be inserted into a form. The resulting documents, which each are created from the same form, can look radically different. For more information, refer to "Inserting a Subform Using a Formula."

Chapter 21

Creating Agents

This chapter introduces you to the following objectives:

 Objectives

- ▶ Planning agents

- ▶ Creating shared or personal agents

- ▶ Attaching an agent to an action

- ▶ Running an agent with another agent

Test Yourself! Before reading this chapter, test yourself to determine how much study time you will need to devote to this section.

1. How are scheduled agents distinguished from manual agents?

2. What are the available types of agent triggers?

3. What are the three main categories of actions that an agent can perform, and how do these actions compare in efficiency?

4. What is the difference between a personal and a shared agent? Can you convert one to the other?

5. How can an agent be triggered from an action?

6. How can an agent be hidden from nondesigners?

7. How can an agent be run from another agent?

Answers are located at the end of the chapter...

Understanding Agents

An *agent* is a process that works on your behalf. Generally, this is work that could be done manually but, because of its complex nature, frequent repetition, or timing, is something that would be best left to an automated process. Agents can be created in a database to perform any task that you could do normally, and, in some cases, perform non-Notes tasks, such as file I/O.

Notes databases do not need agents; however, agents often increase the usability of the databases in which they are created. The secret to developing and building agents in Notes is to understand the business process that the database is trying to mimic and to understand the steps that go into making that process complete. Without a clear understanding of the process and the steps, which a user is required to perform to do his or her job, automation at the agent level is either impossible or useless.

After the processes for automation have been identified, agents can be created that ensure that these processes are done at the right time and follow a consistent set of steps to completion. Triggers can then be created, setting the agent into motion. These triggers might include activation from a menu, at the click of a button or action, following the receipt of mail or the creation of a new document, or on a predetermined schedule.

Agents can be created to perform simple, predefined Lotus Notes tasks (such as moving a document into a folder, or changing the value of a field), simple Notes function procedures (such as copying a document to another database or prompting for the input of information), or complex Lotus Script procedures (such as attaching a file and mailing it to a certain destination).

Planning Agents

Before creating an agent in Notes, you should determine the following:

- ▶ How to identify the agent (its name)

- ▶ When the agent should run

- ▶ Which documents the agent processes

- ▶ What action the agent performs

The *how* variable is important because it enables you to designate a meaningful name that will be used to identify the agent later for the purposes of manual execution or for modification. The *when* variable enables you to determine the event to trigger it. This variable is basically divided into two main categories:

- ▶ Manual triggers involve any event that requires direct interaction with a database view or menu to activate. This interaction might include running an event from the Actions menu or the Agents list, or pasting documents into the database.

- ▶ Scheduled triggers are those that do not necessarily require direct intervention by a user. This type of trigger can occur upon creation or modification of documents, upon arrival of mail, or on a schedule.

The *which* variable enables you to implement selected criteria for the agent to process documents. Certain triggers include built-in selection criteria; however, by using the search builder or a SELECT formula, you can narrow the search.

The *what* is the core of the agent; this variable defines the agent's function. Any one of these three types of functions can be associated with the agent:

- ▶ A simple built-in Notes action (such as moving a document to a folder)

- ▶ A Notes function formula (such as changing the value of a field based on the results of an @If function)

- ▶ A Lotus Script procedure (such as attaching or detaching a file in a document)

As an example, the sections in the agent creation dialog box cor-
respond to the major questions in the design process (see Figure
21.1):

- ► How—Name field

- ► When—Trigger for the agent

- ► Which—Selection criteria for the agent

- ► What—Action the agent should perform

Figure 21.1

*The agent
creation dialog
box.*

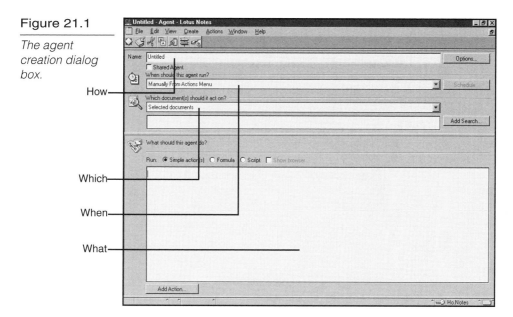

Now that you understand the questions to be answered, you are
ready to begin working with agents.

Working with Agents

Agents are grouped into one of these two main categories:

- ► Accessibility mode (shared or private)—This is determined
  by whether the agent is shared. *Shared* agents can be used by
  anyone who has access to the database; *private* (nonshared)
  agents can be used only by the person who created it.

▶ Processing mode (scheduled or manual)—This is determined by the mechanism by which the agent is triggered. You do not directly set the processing mode; Notes sets the mode for you, based on the trigger:

　▶ Scheduled processes are activated automatically by events that are usually out of the control of a user (such as time schedules).

　▶ Manual processes are the direct result of user intervention in a database (such as the manual activation of an agent).

Understanding the Types of Agents

The combination of the two main categories allows for four types of agents:

▶ Private manual

▶ Private scheduled

▶ Shared manual

▶ Shared scheduled

Private Manual Agents

A *private manual agent* is created and used by only one person and requires the user's direct intervention to run. A user can create private manual agents in a database—they are stored in the user's `desktop.dsk` file. Execution of these agents cannot be directly controlled by a server administrator. You must have at least Reader access to the database to create and use these agent types.

An example of a private manual agent is an agent designed to take selected clients in a contact database and move them into a private folder in response to the user's selection from the Action menu.

Private Scheduled Agents

A *private scheduled agent* is created and used by only one person but does not require direct intervention by a user to activate. A user can create private scheduled agents in a database; these agents are stored in the user's `desktop.dsk` file. Execution of these agents can be directly controlled by a server administrator.

An example of a private scheduled agent is one that a manager might create to e-mail himself every time a new document is created in a database relating to a specific project that he is overseeing.

Shared Manual Agents

You must have `designer`- or `manager-level` access to the database to create a *shared manual agent*. These agents can be used by any number of users and are stored in the server database. Execution of these agents cannot be directly controlled by a server administrator.

An example of a shared manual agent is one that changes the status of a suggestion document from Open to Rejected at the click of a button. Because many people might need to use this agent, it must be shared to allow global access.

Shared Scheduled Agents

You must have `designer`- or `manager-level` access to the database to create a *shared scheduled agent*. These agents are stored on the server database. Execution of these agents can be directly controlled by a server administrator.

An example of a shared scheduled agent is one that periodically searches through a database and archives documents greater than a certain age. Because the agent needs to be accessible on every replica of the database, it is created as a shared agent and therefore is stored in the database on the server.

 Tip

After you have defined whether an agent is shared or private, you cannot change this property. Instead, you must create a new agent and specify the desired type.

Copying an Existing Agent

In some cases, you will want to create an agent very similar to one that already exists. Rather than creating an agent from scratch, you can simply copy the existing one. To copy an existing agent, complete the following steps:

1. Open the database in which the agent you want to copy is located. It can be copied into the same database or into another database.

2. On the navigation pane, click Agents.

3. In the View pane, select the agent you want to copy (see Figure 21.2).

Figure 21.2

Select the agent from within the View pane.

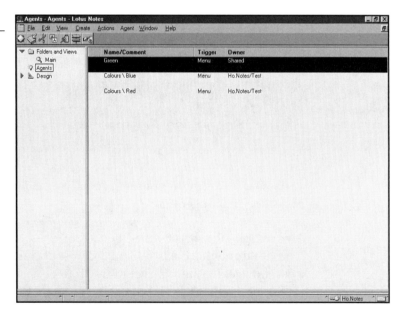

4. Choose Edit | Copy to copy the agent to the clipboard.

5. Open the database in which you want the new agent to be created.

6. On the navigation pane, click Agents.

7. Click on the View pane, then choose Edit | Paste to copy the contents of the clipboard. The new agent is created.

If you are copying an agent into the same database, the agent is pasted into the same list of agents but is renamed by changing the agent name to `Copy of` *agentname*. This can be renamed by editing the agent.

Creating a New Agent

If you do not already have an agent similar to the one that you need, you will have to create a new agent from scratch. To create a new agent, complete the following steps:

1. Open the database to display the navigation pane (refer to Figure 21.2).

2. Choose Agent from the Create menu.

3. Change the agent name from `Untitled` to the name of your choice (see Figure 21.3). This chosen name will appear in the Actions menu (if you use the Manually from Actions Menu trigger) and in the Agents list.

Figure 21.3

The Agent dialog box is displayed.

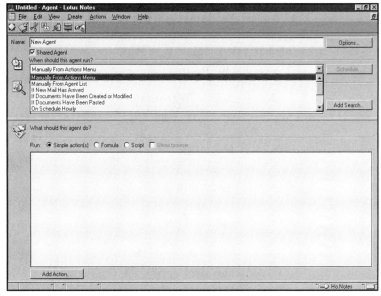

Tip

Agents that are triggered manually from the Actions menu will have their names show up in that menu. You can create cascading menus of agents in the menu by using backslashes (\) in the agents's names.

4. If you want to create an agent available to all users, select the Shared Agent check box. This will be available only if you have designer or manager access to the database. (Private agents are the default type.) You must select this check box before the agent is saved; you cannot change this property after the agent has been saved.

5. Clicking the Options button enables you to select as many as three execution options. These options are as follows:

   ▶ Use the agent's selection criteria in the search bar.

   ▶ Permanently store highlights from a search in the document once the agent has finished processing it.

   ▶ Allow use of this agent by people who have only been designated as public readers and writers in the ACL.

6. Select a trigger type from the When Should This Agent Run? drop-down options:

   ▶ Manually from Actions Menu—This option enables you to run the agent from the Actions menu. Agents listed will appear at the top of the Actions menu when listed from a view, and at the bottom of the menu when listed from any other database location. These agents are divided into two groups by a horizontal line: The agents listed above the line are shared, and the agents listed below the line are personal.

   ▶ Manually from Agent List—This option enables you to run the agent from the list of agents produced from the Agents list in the navigation pane. This list is available only to those people with designer or manager access. The implication is that these agents are hidden to the average user; therefore the agent name is indicated with the standard hidden syntax (parentheses around the name).

- ▶ If New Mail Has Arrived—This option enables you to designate this as a scheduled agent, running only when mail is delivered into the database.

- ▶ If Documents Have Been Created or Modified—This option enables you to designate this a scheduled agent, running only when new documents are created in the database, or when existing ones are modified.

- ▶ If Documents Have Been Pasted—This option enables you to have the agent triggered by the pasting of documents, either from the database in which the agent is running, or from elsewhere.

- ▶ On Schedule Hourly (Daily, Weekly, Monthly, or Never)—This option enables you to designate this a scheduled agent, running at specific intervals of time. If one of these trigger types is chosen, the Schedule button will be enabled to allow you to set schedule parameters. These parameters include the intervals at which to run the agent, the start and stop times and dates for execution, the option to disable the agent on weekends, and the server on which to execute the agent.

Note Scheduled agents that have a workstation designated as the server on which to run will never execute. Workstations do not have agent managers; therefore, no trigger for scheduled execution time can be generated.

Note The schedule option Never is included for compatibility with Notes release 3 and is not intended for use in release 4.*x*.

7. If you want to be more specific about when you schedule your event, click the Schedule button. The Schedule dialog box appears (see Figure 21.4). When you finish with the scheduling specifics, click OK to return to the Agent dialog box.

Figure 21.4

The Schedule dialog box.

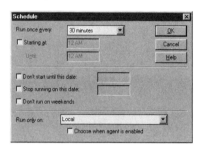

8. Select the main category of documents the agent should act upon from the Which Document(s) Should It Act Upon? drop-down options. The categories change as the trigger changes and are summarized in Figure 21.5.

Note

The selection type of Run Once will not run interactively through all the selected documents as the others will; instead, it is designed for a single execution.

9. Enter a more specific search criteria, if desired. This criteria could be a formula created with a select statement or using the Search Builder, or invoked by clicking the Add Search button (refer to Figure 21.3). The Search Builder dialog box appears (see Figure 21.6). When finished with the specific search criteria, click the OK button to return to the Agent dialog box.

10. Enter the action that the agent should perform in the What Should This Agent Do? section. This action can be in the form of a simple action, a formula, or a Lotus Script, chosen from the Run option buttons in the Agent dialog box.

Figure 21.5

*Selection
categories by
trigger type.*

Trigger Type					
	Manually from menu	On mail arrival	On doc creation	On doc pasting	On schedule
All documents in database	X				X
All new and modified docs since last run	X				X
All unread in a view	X				
All docs in a view	X				
Selected documents	X				
Run once	X				
New mail docs		X			
New modified docs			X		
New pasted docs				X	

(Left vertical label: **Available Selection**)

Figure 21.6

*The Search
Builder dialog
box.*

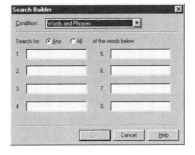

 Tip   Speed of execution reduces as you move from simple actions, through formulas, to Lotus Script. If the desired result can be obtained using a simple action, always use a simple action. If the desired result can be obtained using a formula, always choose a formula over Lotus Script.

Simple actions are predefined in Lotus Notes and can be added to an agent with a click on the Add Action button (refer to Figure 21.3). The following are the simple actions available in the Action drop-down list in the Add Action dialog box (see Figure 21.7):

▶ Copy to Database—Copies the selected documents to a database that you choose.

▶ Copy to Folder—Copies the selected documents to a folder in the current database.

▶ Delete from Database—Deletes the selected documents from the current database.

▶ Mark Document Read/Unread—Adds or removes unread markers from the selected documents.

▶ Modify Field—Modifies the selected field to replace or append to the existing value in the field of the selected documents. This action is chosen in Figure 21.7.

Figure 21.7

The Add Action dialog box.

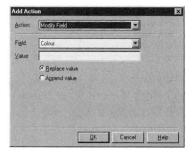

▶ Modify Fields by Form—Enables you to use the graphical design of your chosen form to determine which fields should be changed and what their values will be changed to for the selected documents.

▶ Move to/Remove from Folder—Enables you to add or remove selected documents to or from the folder you specify.

▶ Reply to Sender—Enables you to create a reply to a mailed-in document that is automatically sent. This reply can include the body text of your choice and can also include the full text of the document to which you are replying.

- ▶ Run Agent—Enables you to trigger the execution of one agent from within another.

- ▶ Send Mail Message—Enables you to compose and send a mail message to specified recipients, with the subject of your choice, and containing any body information that you want to include. In addition, this mail message can contain the full text of a selected document or a document link to that document.

- ▶ Send Newsletter Summary—Allows for the creation of a mailed newsletter that contains summaries of the selected documents. This summary can be mailed to any recipient(s) and can contain any subject or body. In addition, the newsletter can summarize the documents by using information from any view in the database.

- ▶ @ Function Formula—Enables you to execute a Lotus Notes @ function that can create a new document, update selected documents, or select other documents.

 Tip

Any number of simple actions can be added to an agent. These actions will be executed in the order in which they are listed. Actions can be deleted as one would delete standard text (selecting and deleting) and can be modified by double-clicking on the action and modifying the action criteria. Simple actions cannot be combined with @ functions or Lotus Script.

After you have filled in all the fields in the agent definition, you can exit and save. You will want to test the agent to see whether it actually performs the way you think it should before releasing it into a live environment.

Viewing the Design and Modifying an Agent

The design of a personal agent can be viewed and modified by the owner of that agent. The design of a shared agent can be viewed and modified by anyone with either designer or manager access to the database.

The design of an agent can be viewed and modified as follows:

1. Open the database to display the navigation pane (refer to Figure 21.2).

2. Select Agents in the standard navigator and double-click the agent to modify it in the View pane.

3. Modify the design of the agent as desired, saving the modifications upon exit.

Understanding Agent Permissions and Execution

The execution of agents can include the following restrictions (see Figure 21.8):

▶ Lack of ACL permissions to create agents—The database manager can restrict the permissions of users with reader, author, or editor access so that they can create neither personal (script or non-script) agents. The manager can also restrict the permissions of users with designer access so that they cannot create Lotus Script agents. This would be evidenced in an error message and a lack of ability to save an agent.

▶ Lack of ACL permissions to execute agents—An agent cannot be created to perform functions that you cannot do manually at a workstation. Therefore, if you have only Reader access to a database, you cannot create an agent that will create, modify, or delete documents in that database. Agents will run; however, the desired results will not come about.

▶ Server execution restrictions—System administrators often restrict who can execute certain types of scheduled agents (see Figure 21.9).

Figure 21.8

The Access Control List options.

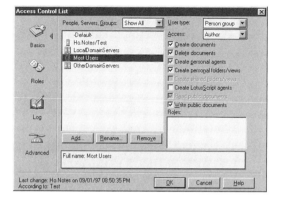

Figure 21.9

An example of some assigned agent restrictions.

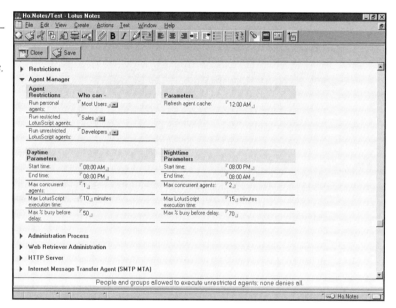

When you have made your choices in the Access Control List dialog box, select the OK button to enter these restrictions into the server document. The restrictions fall into three categories:

▶ Personal agents are classified as any scheduled agents that use only simple actions or Notes @ functions to obtain their desired results.

▶ Restricted Lotus Script agents are any agents that use Lotus Script but do not perform system maintenance or file I/O.

▶ Unrestricted Lotus Script agents are any agents that use Lotus Script to perform system maintenance or file I/O.

The default execution permissions are as follows: Everyone can execute personal agents but no one can execute any sort of Lotus Script agent. Lack of execution privileges are evidenced by an error message upon exiting or saving an agent, which indicates that you cannot enable this agent because you do not have the proper privileges to execute it.

In the process of debugging an agent that does not seem to be performing as expected or does not seem to be running at all, refer to the preceding for helpful checks. If none of these restrictions or permissions apply in your circumstance, then your trouble could be a logic or selection problem preventing the agent from running properly.

Running Agents

An agent must be invoked in order for it to do any good. A scheduled agent is run when its trigger happens; this is an event beyond the control of the creator of the agent. A manual agent runs when it is called for. What follows are some of the common ways to run an agent manually.

Running Agents Manually

There are two ways to run agents manually: through the Actions menu, and in the Agents list. To run an agent through the Actions menu, complete the following steps:

1. Open the database where the agent you want to run is located.

2. From the Actions menu, select the agent to run from the list appearing in the menu.

To run an agent from the Agents list, complete the following steps:

1. Open the database in which the agent you want to copy is located. It can be copied into the same database or into another database.

2. On the navigation pane, click on Agents (refer to Figure 21.2).

3. In the View pane, select the agent you want to run.

4. Choose Run from the Actions menu, or right-click the agent and choose Run from the pop-up list.

For either manual Run type, the same rules apply: you will only see those agents that are shared or that you created. You might not, however, be able to run all agents from the Agents list; agents that are shared are not accessible from that list unless you have at least designer access to the database.

Running Agents from Actions

Agents can be executed from an action, either in a form or a view. Actions can be created on both forms and views as follows:

1. Create the agent to be activated via an action.

2. On the navigation pane, expand the Design view and select either Forms or Views.

3. In the View pane, double-click the form or view on which you want to create the action.

4. In Design mode on the form or view, open the Actions pane either by choosing View | Action Pane, or by double-clicking (or dragging) the Action pane border.

5. Create (using Create | Action) or edit (double-click the action already present in the Action pane) the action that will activate the agent.

6. Choose the Simple Action(s) option button from the Run list in the Edit pane and click Add Action at the bottom (see Figure 21.10).

7. From the Action drop-down list, choose Run Agent, and from the Agent list, choose the agent to run.

Figure 21.10

The Add Action dialog box enables you to run an agent from an action.

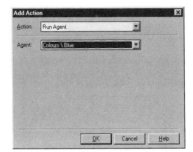

To run an agent attached to an action, complete the following steps:

1. Open the view or document that contains the action.

2. Click the action to activate the agent.

Actions are a very good way to run an agent when you want to control who can access that agent and when. Because actions can be shown or hidden under different circumstances, access to an agent can be enabled or disabled, giving access to these powerful tools only to those who need them, and only in circumstances in which the tools are needed.

Running Agents from Other Agents

Agents may be nested inside other agents. In this way, the execution of one agent can be part of the execution of another, or the execution of one of a number of agents can be controlled by a conditional statement, such as @If. To run an agent from within another agent, complete the following steps:

1. In the development section of the agent, choose Simple Action(s) as the control type, and click the Add Action button.

2. From the Add Action dialog box, choose Run Agent from the Action list and choose the agent desired (refer to Figure 21.10).

Note

Any number of agents can be run in sequence by agent execution actions. These agents can also be interspersed with other simple actions.

Another way to run an agent from within another agent is as follows:

1. Create an agent with the Run Once option (@Commands may be used) chosen in the Which Document(s) Should It Act On? field (refer to Figure 21.1).

2. Choose the Formula radio button from the Run list in the Edit pane and compose a formula including the following command, in which "agentname" is the name of the agent enclosed in quotation marks:

```
@Command([ToolsRunMacro];"agentname")
```

Tip

A number of agents can be run using a conditional statement. For example, to run an agent to run another agent based on the value of a field, use the following command:

```
@If(Type="Book";@Command([ToolsRunMacro];"ChangeAuthor");
➡@Command([ToolsRunMacro];"ChangeColor"))
```

By combining one agent with another, you can keep from executing the same code from more than one place. Simply create generic agents and run them from other agents as the need arises.

Exercises

On your CD-ROM are three databases that you need for this lab. Copy inv21.nsf, cust21.nsf, and ref21.nsf to your Notes Data folder (ensure that you remove the read-only attribute from the files) and add the databases titled Chapter 21 Customers, Chapter 21 Invoices, and Chapter 21 Reference to your workspace.

This set of databases represents a customer-invoicing application and it currently functions—to a point. However, you now will add some automation in the form of agents. Create a scheduled agent that, running every day, locates the past due invoices. After you locate these invoices, look up the e-mail addresses of each of the late-paying customers and send a past-due notice.

Note

This lab assumes that you are working in a context with a mail-routing server. In order for the mail-routing portion of this agent lab to function, you must be able to send mail. If you cannot, then replace the @MailSend function with an @Prompt that displays the message that would have been sent.

Here are some important objects you need to reference:

▶ Database 1—Filename: cust21.nsf; title: Chapter 21 Customers

▶ Database 2—Filename: ref21.nsf; title: Chapter 21 Reference

▶ Database 3—Filename: inv21.nsf; title: Chapter 21 Invoices

Exercise 21.1

1. Open the Chapter 21 Orders database and, from the Create menu, choose Agent (see Figure 21.11).

2. In the Name field, type Overdue Daily and then click the check box below it to make it shared.

3. You want this agent to run every morning at 5:00, so, from the When Should This Agent Run on Local? field, choose the On Schedule Daily option.

Figure 21.11

Choosing the agent.

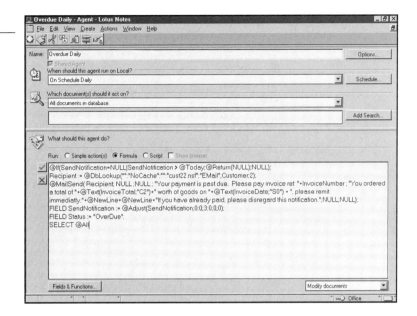

4. Click the Schedule button. The Schedule dialog box appears (refer to Figure 21.4). In the Starting At field, type 5 AM and then click OK to exit.

5. In the What Documents Should It Act On? field, choose All Documents in Database.

6. In the What Should the Agent Do? field, first ensure that Formula is selected as the run type. In the Design pane, type the following code (feel free to leave out the REM statements, which are for your benefit only):

```
REM "Since we have chosen all documents to process, the";
REM "first thing we need to do is to ensure that we only";
REM "actually report on those documents that need to be";
REM "reported on. The field SendNotification on the";
REM "Invoice form has a field called SendNotification,";
REM "which is a date. At first it is set to the due date";
REM "but after this agent runs, it gets incremented";
REM "by three days. When the invoice finally gets paid,";
REM "this field is set to NULL. So, we skip over";
REM "documents that we do not want to process by checking";
REM "to see whether the SendNotification is NULL, ie.,';
REM "the invoice is paid, or whether it is greater than";
```

continues

Exercise 21.1:   Continued

```
REM "today, ie., we will notify them sometime in the;
REM "future.";
@If(SendNotification=NULL¦SendNotification > @Today;@Return
➥(NULL);NULL);
REM "On the invoice form, we have the customer name. Using";
REM "@DBLookup, we look into a hidden view called Email in";
REM "the customer database and return the second column";
REM "value for that document; the customer contact's e-mail";
REM "address. We will use this address when we send mail.";
Recipient := @DBLookup("";"NoCache";"":"cust23.nsf";EMail";
➥Customer;2);
REM "Use the @MailSend function to send a message to the";
REM "e-mail address you just obtained.";
@MailSend(Recipient;NULL;NULL;"Your payment is past due.
Please pay invoice ref: "+InvoiceNumber;"You ordered a
➥total of "+@Text(InvoiceTotal;"C2")+" worth of goods on
➥"+@Text(InvoiceDate;"S0")+". Please remit immediately."
➥+@NewLine+@NewLine+"If you have already made this
➥payment, please disregard this notice.";NULL;NULL);
REM "Add 3 days to the SendNotification and set the Status";
REM "field to overdue.";
FIELD SendNotification :=
➥@Adjust(SendNotification;0;0;3;0;0;0);
FIELD Status := "OverDue";
REM "We need a main statement; this will do the trick";
SELECT @All
```

7. Exit the agent and save it.

8. Open the cust21.nsf database and change the e-mail addresses of your customers to addresses to which your mail router is capable of delivering. You can use either internal Notes addresses or external Internet addresses.

9. If you are not running this agent on a server, you will not be able to test the scheduling. However, you can test the agent's operation by right-clicking it in the Agent list and choosing Run. The agent should cycle through the documents and Return a message reading that the operation completed successfully.

Exercise 21.2

Agents often are created to test applications. In the case at hand, because you have no manual control over the SendNotification, there really is no way to be sure that the agent you just built is actually working. The first challenge is this:

1. Create an agent to run on selected documents in the Invoice database and set the SendNotification field to be equal to today's date.

2. Test that your agent worked by running the first agent. You should receive a list of all the invoices that you selected when running the agent.

The second challenge is as follows:

1. Create an agent called Unpaid Monthly, which runs in the inv21.nsf database on the first day of each month at some time early in the morning. This agent must check the status fields of all documents and if a field indicates that an invoice has not been paid, a newsletter needs to be compiled and mailed to you. The newsletter should use the Unpaid Invoices view to summarize the invoice information.

2. Test your agent by running it manually.

The answer to the challenge is in two agents, Challenge1 and Challenge2, in the inv21.nsf database.

Review Questions

1. Alexander has created a personal agent and now wants to change it to be a shared agent. What must he do?

   a. Edit the agent and set the shared check box.

   b. Make a copy of the agent and set the shared check box.

   c. Write a Lotus Script program to reset the shared field.

   d. Create a new agent with the same formula and make it shared.

2. Emma has created an agent to change the Color field of all pasted documents in a database to blue. The agent does not seem to work, however, even though she knows that documents exist that the agent should process. Which of the following might be the cause?

   a. She does not have permission to run scheduled agents on the server.

   b. She has selection criteria in the agent that eliminates the documents that she wants to process.

   c. She has specified an incorrect action.

   d. Any of the above.

3. Which run type executes the fastest and most efficiently?

   a. Simple action

   b. Formula

   c. Lotus Script

   d. Chisel and hammer

4. To create a shared agent, what access do you need to a database?

   a. reader

   b. depositor

    c. president

    d. designer

5. Where are private agents stored?

    a. In the default Notes directory

    b. In a server IDX file

    c. In the user's `desktop.dsk`

    d. In a PVI workstation file

6. Noah wants to scan a database every morning and have a summary of all the new documents e-mailed to him. What is the best way to accomplish this?

    a. He can't do this with an agent.

    b. Noah must create a manually triggered personal agent to process all the documents, and write a Lotus Script program to search through the documents, compile a report, and send it to him.

    c. He must create a manually triggered shared agent to process all new documents, and he must use a simple action to create a newsletter that his assistant runs every morning.

    d. He needs to create a personal agent that is triggered on schedule (daily at 5:00 a.m.), and enable it to run on a server, process all new documents, and use a simple action to send him a newsletter summary.

7. Debra is a Notes r3.*x* programmer who has never used Notes r4.*x*. What term will she use to refer to agents?

    a. Processors

    b. Agents

    c. Macros

    d. Sidekicks

8. Which of the following major selection types is available when running a time scheduled agent?

    a. All unread documents in view

    b. Selected documents

    c. All documents in database

    d. Newly received mail documents

9. Which agent types can a server administrator prevent a user from executing?

    a. Any agent run manually

    b. Any scheduled agent

    c. Any shared agent

    d. Any personal agent

10. Egbert has reader access to a database. Which of the following will his personal agent be able to do?

    a. Readers cannot create personal agents.

    b. It can modify all documents.

    c. It can create new documents.

    d. It can move documents to a folder.

11. Zach needs an agent in a workflow database. He already has an agent in a discussion database that does exactly what he wants the new one to do. Can he copy the agent from one database to another?

    a. Yes

    b. No

12. Boris is a Notes developer who has an agent that can change the status of a request document to Rejected and then move the document to an archived database. What is the most intuitive way to present this agent to his users?

    a. Have the users select the document(s) to be processed in a view and then run the agent from the Actions menu.

    b. Have the users select the documents one at a time and run the agent from the Agents list.

    c. Have the users make the change manually without using the agent at all.

    d. Create an action called Reject in the Main view, and then have the users select the document(s) to be processed and click the Reject button.

13. Nicholas has a library of agents from another database. After copying the appropriate agents to his new database, can he create an agent that will execute the appropriate agent based on the value of a field in a document?

    a. Yes

    b. No

14. Jackson has created a number of shared agents and specified that they can be run manually from the Agents list. Who will be able to see these agents in the list?

    a. Readers

    b. Authors

    c. Anonymous users

    d. Designers

Review Answers

1. D. After you set the shared or private attribute of an agent and save it you cannot change it back. To change it, Alexander must create a new agent with the same functionality and make it shared. For more information, refer to the section titled "Creating a New Agent."

2. D. All of these things could be problems. If Emma does not have permission to run scheduled agents, she cannot have her agent triggered on Paste. If she is using incorrect selection criteria, she could be filtering out the very documents she wants to modify. And, of course, there is the possibility that her agent really doesn't perform the correct action to do what she wants it to do. For more information, refer to the sections titled "Creating a New Agent" and "Understanding Agent Permissions and Execution."

3. A. The more precompiling that comes with the process, the faster the process will run. Simple actions run fastest, functions next, and finally Lotus Script. This is not to say that you should never use Lotus Script—simply avoid it unless you cannot accomplish your task by using a simple action or a function. For more information, refer to the section titled "Creating a New Agent."

4. D. To create a shared component on a server-based database (this includes agents) you must have designer access. For more information, refer to the section titled "Creating a New Agent."

5. C. All private components, including agents, are stored in the desktop.dsk file on the user's workstation. For more information, refer to the sections titled "Private Manual Agents" and "Private Scheduled Agents."

6. D. The best way to use an agent in this case is to have it scheduled, rather than having to manually activate it; this ensures that the agent gets run periodically. The simple action will then create the summary and mail the document. For more information, refer to the section titled "Creating a New Agent."

7. C. In release 3 of Notes, agents were referred to as macros and many developers still call them that.

8. C. Because scheduled agents are not triggered by direct user intervention, they can process neither selected documents nor documents in views. As well, because the agent is specifically time-scheduled, it cannot process newly received mail

documents; that would be on an incoming mail agent. The agent must process all the documents in the database. The other option for this type of agent is to process all documents added or modified since the last run. For more information, refer to the section titled "Creating a New Agent," especially Figure 21.5.

9. B. Server administrators have control only over scheduled agents, not over manually triggered agents. For more information, refer to the sections titled "Private Scheduled Agents" and "Shared Scheduled Agents."

10. D. Because Egbert does not have the ability to modify documents, and because his agent cannot have more power than he does, his agent can only move documents to folders. For more information, refer to the section titled "Understanding Agent Permissions and Execution."

11. A. As with most design components, agents can be copied from one database to another. For more information, refer to the section titled "Copying an Existing Agent."

12. D. The most intuitive solutions are those that put the solution directly before the user. Having to run and agent from a menu or from an agent list is not a good way to accomplish this. Rather, create an action that can be used after the document or documents have been selected. For more information, refer to the sections titled "Creating a New Agent" and "Running Agents from Actions."

13. A. Nicholas can either include a selection in his agent to choose the documents to process or can use an @If command to ask the question and then execute the agent using an @Command. For more information, refer to the sections titled "Creating a New Agent" and "Running Agents from Actions."

14. D. The only people for whom shared agents are available from the Agents list are those with designer access. For more information, refer to the section titled "Creating a New Agent."

Answers to Test Yourself Questions at Beginning of Chapter

1. Scheduled and manual agents are distinguished by their triggers. In essence, a manual agent runs through the direct action of a user, such as the click of a button or the selection of the agent from a menu. Scheduled agents run as a result of system events or timings, such as the arrival of mail in a database or the arrival of a specified time. Scheduled and manual agents are also distinguished by how much control a system administrator can exercise over their execution. Manual agents cannot be controlled by a system administrator; the execution of scheduled agents, however, can be completely controlled by a system administrator. For more information, refer to the sections titled "The Types of Agents" and "Permissions and Execution."

2. There are 10 types of agent triggers:

   ▶ Manually from Actions Menu
   ▶ Manually from Agent List
   ▶ If New Mail Has Arrived
   ▶ If Documents Have Been Created or Modified
   ▶ If Documents Have Been Pasted
   ▶ On Schedule Hourly
   ▶ On Schedule Daily
   ▶ On Schedule Weekly
   ▶ On Schedule Monthly
   ▶ On Schedule Never

   For more information, refer to the section titled "Creating a New Agent."

3. Agents can perform actions in three categories. In order of efficiency, these are simple actions, formula actions, and Lotus Script actions. The more precompiling that has been done on an action, the more efficiently it runs. For more information, refer to the section titled "Creating a New Agent."

4. A personal agent is created and stored locally on a user's workstation. This agent can execute any kind of action but can be accessed only by the person who created it. A shared agent is created as part of a database's design. The shared agent can be accessed by anyone to whom the designer gives access but can be modified only by a designer or manager. After it is created, an agent cannot be converted to another type; rather, another agent must be created in a different type but with the same functionality. For more information, refer to the section titled "The Types of Agents."

5. An agent can be triggered from an action through the simple action Run Agent. For more information, refer to the section titled "Running Agents from Actions."

6. The simplest way to hide an agent from nondesigners is to make it triggered manually from the Agent list. Shared agents in the Agent list are visible only to designers; therefore, any user with `editor` or lower access to the database is not able to view the agent and cannot run it unless some other triggering mechanism such as an action triggers it. For more information, refer to the section titled "Creating a New Agent."

7. An agent can run another agent through the use of a simple action: Run Agent. For more information, refer to the section titled "Running Agents from Other Agents."

Chapter 22

Maintaining Application Designs

This chapter will introduce you to the following objectives:

 Objectives

- ▶ Creating and understanding database templates
- ▶ Understanding and implementing the design-update process
- ▶ Refreshing the database design manually
- ▶ Replacing the database design

Test Yourself! Before reading this chapter, test yourself to determine how much study time you will need to devote to this section.

1. What is the significance of the NTF file type?

2. How is a template created and used?

3. What are the two ways to update the design of a database from a template?

4. How can you enable a single database to inherit design elements from more than one template?

5. How can you change the template from which a database refreshes and refresh the design all in one command?

6. How can the design of a database be completely hidden from all users of that database?

7. What is a good methodology for designing and distributing ongoing database changes into a live database?

Answers are located at the end of the chapter...

In a controlled design environment, applications are maintained in such a way that the application's designer can make as many changes as possible with the least amount of work, and the process of changes to the database is transparent to the user community. This chapter is designed to help you understand the most efficient way of maintaining your applications as you make ongoing changes to their design.

Understanding Database Templates

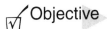 A *template* is a source of design elements for a database. It contains the definition for the database and is consulted for updates when the database needs to change.

A template can hold the complete design for a single database or a number of databases, or a subset of design elements for one or more databases.

The designation of template is not dependent on the file extension (although the .ntf extension has been designated for Notes templates); rather, template is a functional definition, indicating that one database (.nsf or .ntf) is the source of design elements for another database.

Understanding the NTF File Type

The NTF file type is called a template but, if not designated as such in the properties for the database, does not function as a template. That said, however, it is best to create NTF files to act as templates because this use will make administration of the templates easier.

The creation of an NTF file is the same as the creation of a regular NSF file, with the exception of its designated extension.

To create an NTF file from scratch or from a template, complete the following steps:

1. Select File | Database | New.

2. In the New Database dialog box (see Figure 22.1), fill in the field appropriately; however, when you fill in the database name, instead of ending it with an .nsf extension, end it with an .ntf extension. At this point, however, the database is not a template—it is simply a database with an .ntf extension.

Figure 22.1

The New Database dialog box.

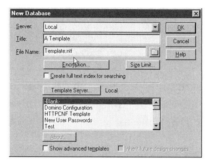

To create an NTF file by copying another database or template, complete the following steps:

1. On your workspace, place an icon for the database to be copied. Select the icon.

2. Select File | Database | New Copy.

3. In the Copy Database dialog box (see Figure 22.2), fill in the fields appropriately; however, when you fill in the database name, instead of ending it with an .nsf extension, end it with an .ntf extension. This database will become a template when you change its properties to make it so; right now it's just a database with an .ntf extension.

Figure 22.2

The Copy Data-base dialog box.

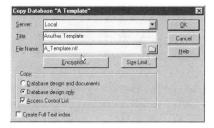

Creating a Template

Because a template is not a file structure or an object, per se, but rather the way to use an object, you might wonder how a template is created. Well, it isn't created. Instead, a database that already exists is enabled to act as a template, and a separate database is linked to the original database (see Figure 22.3).

Figure 22.3

Linking a data-base to a tem-plate.

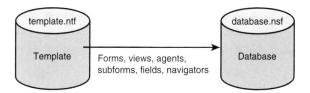

The process of enabling and linking is the template creation process. After the two databases are linked, you are ready to perform ongoing maintenance of design from a single point, your template. To enable a database as a template, complete the following steps:

1. Place the database (`.nsf` or `.ntf`) on your workspace as an icon.

2. Right-click the database design and choose Database Properties.

3. Choose the Design tab at the top of the Properties for Database dialog box.

4. Click the Database Is a Template check box (see Figure 22.4), and fill in a template name (*alias*) for the template.

Figure 22.4

Selecting the database design properties.

Note

The alias is the only name that Notes will recognize in the linking process. When you link a database to this template, you will link via the template name, not the filename or the title. Therefore, it is very important that you remember what the name is or you will not be able to easily find it.

5. Close the database properties by clicking the Close Window button.

Now that you have enabled the database to act as a template, you must link another database to it to complete the process. There are two ways to do this: You can link them (or enable inheritance) upon the creation of the second database or you can assign the link after the database is created.

Note

You can enable inheritance at creation time only if the template has an .ntf extension. If the template does not have an .ntf extension, you cannot see it in the new database dialog box and must manually enable inheritance later.

To link at database creation, complete the following steps:

1. Select File | Database | New.

2. In the New Database dialog box, fill in the Title and File Name fields as desired.

3. Choose the template to link to from the list of templates.

4. Ensure that the Inherit Future Design Changes check box is checked (see Figure 22.5).

Figure 22.5

Choosing to inherit future design changes upon database creation.

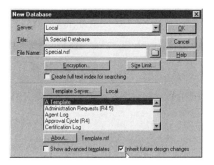

5. Complete the creation process.

Note

Linking upon database creation is possible only if two criteria are met. The template must have been created using an `.ntf` extension. This enables the template to show up in the templates list. The template also must have been enabled as a template in its properties. This enables the template to have its future design changes propagated to the new database.

To link after the database already exists, complete the following steps:

1. From the workspace, right-click the database icon of the database that is to inherit changes from a template, then choose Database Properties.

2. Choose the Design tab at the top of the Properties for Database dialog box.

3. Click the Inherit Design from Template check box (see Figure 22.6) and fill in the name (alias) of the template to inherit from.

Figure 22.6

Linking to a template from an existing database using the template name.

Note

You must use the alias name of the template here. Notes will not recognize the template filename or title.

4. Close the database properties by clicking on the Close Window button.

Now that you have linked your databases to templates, the next step is to ensure that those databases are refreshed with new template updates.

Updating the Design of a Database

Objective

After a database has been linked to a template, the database design can be controlled through either an automatic or a manual refresh procedure. The result of either procedure updates the database with any design changes made to the template so that ongoing changes can be distributed easily. These procedures are discussed in the following sections.

Using the Automatic Process

The normal distribution of changes is accomplished automatically through the use of a server process called DESIGN. This process, which is typically scheduled to run at 1:00 a.m. each morning, compiles a list of all databases that are linked to templates and then updates them to conform to the designs of their templates. The trigger of this process appears in the Notes.ini file on the server that includes the DESIGN process in a SERVERTASKSAT line. The trigger is as follows:

```
SERVERTASKSAT1=CATALOG,DESIGN
```

For this process to work, the template to which each database refers must be locally present on each server. This is done by replicating the template onto every server that has a database referring to it. In addition, the template must be in the default Notes data directory (usually `C:\NOTES\DATA`) or in a subdirectory of the default.

If the server is running the `DESIGN` process on a regular schedule, no more intervention is necessary on the part of the designer after the changes to the templates are placed onto a server.

Using the Manual Process

In some cases it is necessary or more convenient to update the design of a database from its template at a time other than that normally scheduled by the server. This situation could occur when an update to the database must be distributed immediately, or if the template does not normally replicate with a ser-ver, such as when the template changes are on a local workstation.

Two methods are available for initiating the refresh process manually. The `DESIGN` process can be started on the server through the use of the command `LOAD DESIGN`. This initiates `DESIGN`, which processes all the databases and templates on the server. The command is entered as follows at the server console:

```
LOAD DESIGN
```

A specific database also can be refreshed through the use of a process initiated through a menu choice. In this case, only the database selected is refreshed and all others wait until the regularly scheduled update time. To manually refresh a single database, complete the following steps:

1. Select the database to be refreshed on the workspace.

2. Select File | Database | Refresh Design.

3. When prompted for the location of the server containing the template to refresh from (see the Refresh Database Design dialog box in Figure 22.7), choose one from the pull-down list or type in the appropriate server name.

Figure 22.7

The Refresh Database Design dialog box.

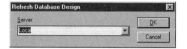

**Note**   Unlike DESIGN process, this process does not require that you refresh from the server on which the destination database is held. You can choose to update from a template held on another server or on the local workstation, if that is appropriate.

4. When warned that the process will update design elements, click the Yes button to continue the refresh.

You are now familiar with how to ensure that a database design is dependent on a template; however, in some cases you might want to limit the scope of the changes to include only certain design elements.

Controlling the Scope of Design Updates

Objective   When a database is enabled to inherit its design from a template, most of its design elements are flagged as receiving updates. These design elements include forms, views, agents, navigators, shared fields, and the database properties. Some elements are, by default, not changed by design refresh. These elements include the icon, the ACL, and the database title.

All the elements of a database can be flagged to accept or reject changes from a design refresh. If a certain form has been customized and changing the customization by a design refresh is not desired, then that form can be designated as not accepting design changes. At the same time, if the icon should change as the icon in the template changes, the form can be enabled for accepting design changes.

When a refresh is initiated, whether manually or on schedule, the refresh properties for each element are checked. Any that are enabled for design refresh are updated, and any that are not are left alone. To enable or disable the update of an element's design, complete the following steps:

1. Open the database and navigate to the navigation pane.

2. Expand the design section to show the list of element views.

3. Select the element type from the list to show the elements of that kind for the database (for example, forms).

4. In the list of elements, select the one whose properties you want to modify.

5. Select Edit | Properties to display the Properties dialog box.

Note

The dialog box that appears when calling for form properties from the forms list is not the same as the dialog box that appears when calling for form properties while editing the form's design. Be sure you are getting the properties you want by calling for them in the right context.

6. Choose the Design tab at the top of the Properties dialog box (see Figure 22.8).

Figure 22.8

The Properties for the Design Document enable you to choose whether you enable or disable inheritance.

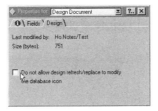

7. To enable design inheritance, ensure that the Do Not Allow Design Refresh/Replace to Modify check box is not checked. To disable inheritance, ensure that it is checked.

8. Exit the properties by clicking the Close Window button.

Note Design elements that are created in the destination database but not present in the template are, by default, disabled for inheritance. This ensures they are not removed when the design is refreshed.

Sometimes design refresh involves more than obtaining some or all of a database design from a single template. The following section discusses inheriting design into a database from multiple templates.

Inheriting the Design from Multiple Templates

In some cases it may be advantageous to inherit design elements from more than one template (see Figure 22.9). A view may come from one source, and a form may come from another source. This may be simply a matter of convenient coincidence, or designed as a developer's component library.

Figure 22.9

Inheriting the design from multiple templates.

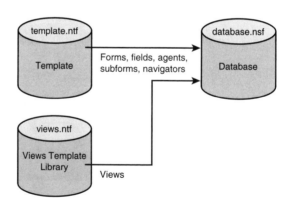

When a database is enabled to inherit from a template, all design elements that do not have their Do Not Allow Design Replace/ Refresh to Modify the Database Icon check box checked inherit design changes from the template. If in addition to checking the box, however, you also indicate the design element should inherit its design from a specific template, this indication overrides the inheritance set up at the database level.

To enable inheritance from multiple templates, complete the following steps:

1. Enable inheritance for the database from the template that contains the most design elements to be refreshed.

2. Ensure that the Do Not Allow Design Refresh/Replace to Modify check box is cleared so that all design elements can be updated by any template.

For each element that is to inherit from an alternate template, also complete these steps:

1. From the Design view, select the element and then select Edit | Properties.

2. Choose the Design tab on the Properties dialog box (see Figure 22.10).

Figure 22.10

The Design Document properties enable you to choose the design template to inherit from.

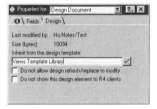

3. Enter the name of the template to inherit from in the Inherit from the Design Template field.

4. Ensure that the Do Not Allow Design Replace/Refresh to Modify the Database Icon check box is cleared.

5. Close the Properties dialog box by clicking the Close Window button.

For ongoing updates to a database design, the refresh process is sufficient. In some cases, however, changes are significant enough to warrant a complete template change. The following section discusses database design replacement.

Replacing the Database Design

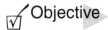Objective
A database design is replaced when a complete changeover in design is required on a specific database. This may occur when a major update to a database has been completed, and the template on which the new design is stored is different from the original one.

An example of a need for such a replacement is when a server is upgraded from Lotus Notes 4.0 to Lotus Notes 4.5. In this upgrade, among other things, the design for the mail database completely changes. This overhaul was done in a new template, Std45Mail (mail45.ntf). When the server was upgraded, however, each individual's mail database was not automatically converted to the new template. So, each user's mail database was still pointing to the old template, Std4Mail (mail4.ntf). For the new features of mail to be used, the design of the mail databases needed to be replaced, not simply refreshed (see Figure 22.11).

Figure 22.11

Replacing the database design.

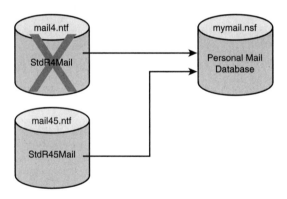

Replacing the database design has the effect of completing the following, automated steps:

1. Remove all database elements not present in the new template that do not have their Do Not Allow Design Refresh/Replace to Modify check box checked, and that do not have a template name in their Inherit Design from Template field.

2. Add all database elements present in the new template.

3. Update all database elements with the same name as an element in the template that do not have their Do Not Allow Design Refresh/Replace to Modify check box checked, and that do not have a template name in their Inherit from the Design Template field.

4. Replace the current contents of the Inherit from the Design Template field in the Properties for Database dialog box if the template is a design template and if you choose to inherit changes in the future.

Replacing a database design has no effect on the following elements:

▶ Any design element that has its Do Not Allow Design Refresh/Replace to Modify check box checked.

▶ Any design element that does not have its Do Not Allow Design Refresh/Replace to Modify the Database Icon check box checked and has a template name in the Inherit from the Design Template field.

To replace a database design, complete the following steps:

1. Select the database whose design is to be replaced from the workspace.

2. Select File | Database | Replace Design.

3. From the Replace Database Design dialog box, choose the server on which the template to replace with is located by clicking the Template Server button and choosing the server from the list produced.

4. Choose a template from the list of templates presented in the Replace Database Design dialog box (see Figure 22.12).

 Tip   If the template desired is not present in the list, perhaps it is an advanced template. Select the Show Advanced Templates check box to see more templates.

Figure 22.12

Choose from the list of templates available.

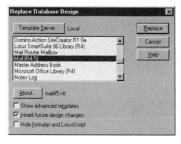

5. If desired and available, check the Inherit Future Design Changes check box. This ensures that the template chosen is the design template for the database and will refresh the database with design changes when available.

6. Click the Replace button to initiate design replacement. When warned that the process will update design elements, click the Yes button to continue.

7. Observe the dialog box indicating the status of the design replacement (see Figure 22.13).

Figure 22.13

You can see that the database design is being replaced.

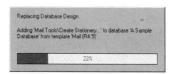

Replace design has one feature that enables application designers to protect their intellectual property: the ability to remove all the design components from a database. The following section discusses hiding these components.

Hiding Database Design Using Replace Design

In some cases it is desirable to have the design of a database completely hidden from all users. Unfortunately, the default ACL levels give designers and managers the ability to view and change the database design. In addition, any user with at least reader access may replicate or copy a database to his or her local workstation.

On this copy, that user has manager access, giving the user complete access to the database design.

As a developer, you may not always want your design and design methodology available to all users. This may especially be so if you are a developer creating Notes applications for third-party retail. You simply do not want anyone with the databases to be able to reverse-engineer your design.

Using the replace design feature, you can create databases that function normally, but that do not give any user, no matter what ACL level he or she has, the ability to see or modify the database design.

To hide database design, complete the following steps:

1. Select the database on your workspace that is to have its design hidden.

2. Select File | Database | Replace Design.

3. From the Replace Database Design dialog box, choose the server on which the template to replace with is located.

4. Choose a template from the list of templates presented in the Replace Database Design dialog box.

5. If desired and available, check the Inherit Future Design Changes check box. This ensures that the chosen template is the design template for the database and will refresh the database with design changes when available.

6. Check the Hide Formulas and Lotus Script check box.

7. Click the Replace button to initiate design replacement. When warned that the process will update design elements, click the Yes button to continue.

8. Observe the dialog box indicating the status of the design replacement.

Keep in mind that once a database has had its design removed, that design cannot be reestablished by replacing the design without the Hide Formulas and Lotus Script checkbox checked.

Additionally, no one can access shared agents from the Agents list. Any agent access must be through the Actions menu or through buttons and other automation.

Using a Suggested Design and Distribution Methodology

To make the most efficient use of templates and reduce the disruption to your user community, I suggest the following as a procedure in the ongoing process of design (see Figure 22.14).

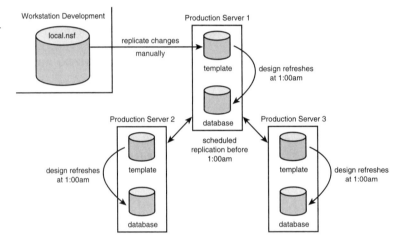

Figure 22.14

Updating a production database and its replicas.

1. Do the original database design on your local workstation. This ensures that no users can inadvertently gain access to your unfinished and untested database and become alarmed at its lack of functionality.

2. Before you consider your design complete, ensure that you have enabled it to be a template.

3. Once the design is complete, replicate the database to the server as an NTF file.

4. If your template is an NTF file, create a new database based on that file by selecting File | Database | New. Ensure that the Enable Future Design Changes check box is checked.

5. Replicate the new database and its template to all the servers that will act as hosts for this database.

 Tip

The smoothest design update operation comes from having a replica of both the database and its template on all servers. Although design updates propagate to all replicas of the database through the replication process (even if only one replica of the template exists), a warning message appears on every server that has a replica of the database when the design process runs at 1:00 a.m. This warning indicates that the template for the database cannot be found. In order to prevent confusion over this, it is good idea to have the template replicated as well as the database.

6. New changes to the database should be done and tested on your local workstation, just as the initial design was. This ensures that your users are insulated from the changes you make until you are sure they work properly.

7. When new changes are to be implemented, replicate these changes from your workstation to the template on the server. These changes will be distributed when the DESIGN task runs that night. If it is necessary to implement the changes right away, manually refresh the design.

 Note

For this process to work smoothly in a multiserver environment, your server administrator should ensure that your templates are replicating before DESIGN starts at 1:00 a.m. That way, when the design process is initiated, all replicas of the database are updated with the latest template design.

Exercises

On your CD-ROM there are three databases needed for this lab. Copy inv22.nsf, cust22.nsf, and ref22.nsf to your Notes data folder (ensuring you remove the read-only attribute from the files), and add the databases titled Chapter 22 Customers, Chapter 22 Invoices, and Chapter 22 Reference to your workspace.

This set of databases represents a customer invoicing application. As a developer, you are ready to release this application to your user community, and you want to follow good design and maintenance practices. To facilitate this, you are going to create templates from the databases, and then build new databases using these templates as the design foundation.

Exercise 22.1

1. Select the Chapter 22 Invoices database on your workspace and select File | Database | New Copy (see Figure 22.15).

Note

If you have a server on which to work, you might want to make this more realistic by choosing Database | New Replica and placing the template and the database you will create based on that template on the server. This would be the procedure you would follow in a production environment; however, the steps assume you have only a local Notes workstation.

Figure 22.15

The Copy Database dialog box.

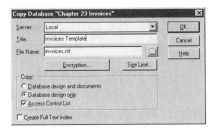

2. Leave the server name as Local, and type Invoices Template in the Title field and Invoices.ntf in the File Name field.

3. From the Copy options, choose Database design only and select OK to initiate database creation.

4. From the workspace, right-click on the database you just created, choose Properties from the menu, and navigate to the Design tab of the Properties for Database dialog box (see Figure 22.16).

Figure 22.16

The Design tab of the database design properties.

5. Select the Database Is a Template check box and type `Invoices` in the Template Name field.

6. Clear the Show in 'Open Database' dialog check box to ensure that users do not inadvertently add this template to their workspaces.

7. Click the Close Window button to exit from the dialog box.

8. Select File | Database | New (see Figure 22.17).

Figure 22.17

The New Database dialog box.

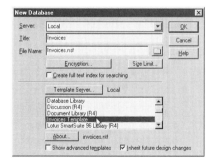

9. Leave the server name as `Local`, and type `Invoices` in the Title field and `Invoices.nsf` in the File Name field.

10. From the list of templates at the bottom of the dialog box, locate and click Invoices Template.

11. Ensure that the Inherit Future Design Changes check box is selected and click the OK button to create the database. Exit the new database when it opens automatically.

12. Open the Invoices Template database, expand the design section in the navigator, and click Forms to see the forms list.

13. Double-click the Invoice form to edit its design.

14. On the form, click the DueDate field to display its design pane at the bottom of the window. Change all occurrences of `cust22.nsf` to `customer.nsf`.

15. Select View | Action Pane to display the form's actions and click the action called Mail Invoice to display its design pane. Change all occurrences of `cust22.nsf` to `customer.nsf`.

16. Click the Add a Coffee button to display its design pane and change all occurrences of `ref22.nsf` to `referenc.nsf`.

17. Save and close the form to return to the navigator.

18. Click Agents in the navigator to display the Agents list.

19. Double-click the Overdue Daily agent to edit its design.

20. In the Run pane, change all occurrences of `cust22.nsf` to `customer.nsf`.

21. Save and close the agent.

22. Exit the database and return to the workspace.

23. Select the Invoices database on your workspace, select File | Database | Refresh Design and click the OK button when the Refresh Database Design dialog box appears. This selects your local workstation as the location for the design template.

24. Click Yes when informed that design elements in your database may be modified by this process.

25. When the process completes (disk activity stops), open the `Invoices` database and confirm that the process worked by editing the design of the Invoice form and examining the fields, buttons, and action you modified in the template. All occurrences of `Chapter 22` databases should have been replaced.

26. Close the `Invoices` database and return to your workspace.

Exercise 22.2

Perform the same procedure on the Chapter 22 Customers and Chapter 22 References databases. Create templates called Customers Template (customer.ntf) and Reference Template (referenc.ntf), and from them create databases called Customers (customer.nsf) and Reference (referenc.nsf). Then modify the templates to reflect the new filenames in the field lookups. When you are done modifying, refresh the database designs.

Review Questions

1. Colleen has a database configured to accept design updates from a template. She wants to ensure that the icon in the database will change as the icon in the template changes. How does she accomplish this?

   a. This happens by default.

   b. Navigate to the properties of the icon and ensure that the Do Not Allow Design Refresh/Replace to Modify check box is not selected.

   c. You cannot have the icon in a database refresh with a change in the template.

   d. Navigate to the properties of the icon and ensure that the Do Not Allow Design Refresh/Replace to Modify check box is selected and that the template name is listed in the Inherit Design from Template field.

2. What causes a template to appear in the templates list in the Create New Database dialog box?

   a. An .nsf file extension.

   b. Selecting the Database Is a Template check box in the Properties for Database dialog box.

   c. All databases appear in this list.

   d. An .ntf file extension.

3. Angela wants to create a template from which she can re-fresh a database. Of the following, which is the most impor-tant step?

    a. Create a database with an .ntf extension.

    b. Create a database using a template for its design.

    c. Select the Database Is a Template check box in the database properties and give it a template name.

    d. Create the database on a server.

4. Victoria wants her database to refresh when a specific tem-plate is changed. What name must she place into the Inherit from the Design Template field in the properties of her data-base?

    a. The filename of the template relative to the default notes directory

    b. Her name

    c. The title of the template

    d. The name of the template as entered into the template's Database Is a Template field

5. Alexander wants to ensure that users of his applications can-not reverse-engineer them by accessing his formula and Lo-tus Script. How does he do this?

    a. Create his database and replace the design from a tem-plate with the Hide Formulas and Lotus Script option chosen.

    b. Give the users only reader access to the database.

    c. Provide only databases and not templates to the users.

    d. Make them promise not to reverse-engineer them.

6. Renee created a new form in her mail database. How can she ensure that the design process will not remove this form?

    a. Enable the Do Not Allow Design Replace/Refresh to Modify property for the form.

    b. She cannot prevent the design process from removing this form.

    c. Her form is protected from being removed by default.

    d. Insert a layout region in the form and make it read-only.

7. Which server process refreshes the design of databases from their associated templates?

    a. EVENT

    b. DESIGN

    c. SMTPMTA

    d. WEB

8. Emma wants to advise her system administrator when to schedule replication of her templates to ensure that the DESIGN process will update her databases correctly on all replicas. If the system administrator has not changed the default time that design runs, when must all replications be complete?

    a. 5:00 a.m.

    b. 3:00 a.m.

    c. 1:00 a.m.

    d. 7:00 a.m.

9. Debra has made changes to a design template, which must be incorporated into a database immediately. What is the least disruptive way to do this?

    a. Manually run the DESIGN process on the server.

    b. Edit the design of the database and make all the necessary changes.

c. After selecting the database on her workspace, select File | Database | Refresh Design.

d. Shut down the server and initiate the DESIGN process.

10. Noah has just upgraded his server and users from Lotus Notes 4.1 to Lotus Notes 4.5. How can he give his users access to the new calendar and scheduling features in their mail databases?

a. The installation of the Notes 4.5 server software ensures this will happen automatically.

b. Run the FIXMAIL server process.

c. Run the server process DESIGN manually or wait for it to run at 1:00 a.m.

d. Replace the design of each mailfile with the new STD45MAIL template.

11. Albert has modified the Memo form in his mail database to include a new field. How does he ensure that these changes will not be wiped out when the DESIGN process runs?

a. Modify the properties of the form to disable modification by refresh or replace.

b. No manual changes are ever wiped out by the DESIGN process.

c. Replace the design of his mail database and then make the modification to the memo form.

d. Set up a mail design block on his workstation.

12. Lori has created a new database that has its design refreshed by a template. However, she wants to get the design of her main view from a view library, which is in a template called VIEWLIB. How can she do this?

a. Lori cannot have a view refresh from one template while everything else refreshed from another.

    b. She needs to create a refresh selection formula for the database reading `SELECT DESIGN = "TEMPLATE" & VIEW = "VIEWLIB"`.

    c. She needs to refresh her database against the `VIEWLIB` template.

    d. She needs to change the design properties for the view to inherit from the design template `VIEWLIB`.

13. Len wants to create a database from an NTF database that is designated a design template. What is the most efficient way to enable design refresh from that template?

    a. Create the database, then from the workspace go to the database design properties, choose Inherit Design from Template, and enter the template name in the field.

    b. On the new database dialog box, choose the template name and select the Inherit Future Design Changes check box.

    c. Design refresh will be enabled by default given these parameters.

    d. There is no easy way to enable design refresh under these circumstances.

14. Polly manually replaced the design of a database with the design of a template. Which design elements have been replaced?

    a. All design elements are replaced.

    b. All design elements except the database icon are replaced.

    c. Only the database icon is replaced.

    d. All design elements except those that have the Do Not Allow Design Replace/Refresh to Modify the Database Icon property or did not inherit their design from the former design template will have been replaced.

Review Answers

1. B. Individual elements can be configured to be updated by the template provided that they do not have the Do Not Allow Design Refresh/Replace to Modify check box selected. By deselecting this check box, you can ensure that the icon will be modified. For more information, refer to section titled "Controlling the Scope of Design Updates."

2. D. Although an .ntf extension does not make a database a template, it does enable it to appear in the list of templates when you create a new database. For more information, refer to the section titled "Creating a Template."

3. C. The most important thing in creating a template is that it is configured as a template in its properties and that it has a name that can be referred to when configuring a database to have its design refreshed from that template. For more information, refer to the section titled "Creating a Template."

4. D. The name entered must be the template name specified in the database properties of the template, not the title of the template or the filename. For more information, refer to the section titled "Creating a Template."

5. A. To prevent reverse engineering, design elements must be hidden. To do this, Alexander can replace the design, indicating that formulas and script should be hidden in the process. For more information, refer to the section titled "Hiding Database Design Using Replace."

6. C. By DEFAULT, any new forms or views added to a database are exempt from being removed by the refresh process. For more information, refer to the section titled "Controlling the Scope of Design Updates."

7. B. The DESIGN process, normally scheduled to run on each server at 1:00 a.m., is responsible for updating database design. For more information, refer to the section titled "Using the Automatic Process."

8. C. In order for DESIGN to complete its job properly, all template changes must be replicated to the servers by the time the DESIGN process is scheduled to run; at 1:00 a.m. For more information, refer to the section titled "Using the Automatic Process."

9. C. The Refresh Design menu ensures that the design of the database is enabled without having to shut down the server or invoke design on the server. Invoking design on the server would update all databases, and that may not be a desirable thing. For more information, refer to the sections titled "Using the Manual Process" and "Using the Automatic Process."

10. D. Because the upgrade necessitated the change from one mail template to another, he must replace the design of each mail template with the new one, STD45MAIL. For more information, refer to the section titled "Replacing the Database Design."

11. A. In order to ensure that changes to his form are preserved, he must disable modification by refresh or replace. This is done in the form properties and applies to all changes in that form. For more information, refer to the section titled "Controlling the Scope of Design Updates."

12. D. Lori wants to update some components from one template and others from another. When she indicated that her database was to be refreshed by a template, that indicated all elements in that database. However, if she changes the refresh properties for the view that she wants updated from the view library to update from that template, then she can have most elements refresh from one template and the view update from the other. For more information, refer to the section titled "Controlling the Scope of Design Updates."

13. B. He can enable this when the database is being created by selecting the template to create based on and then selecting the Inherit Future Design Changes check box. For more information, refer to the section titled "Creating a Template."

14. D. Replace will replace those only elements that have permission to change; that is, all the elements that were refreshed by the previous template. Elements that are exempt from that are those that have the Do Not Allow Design Replace/Refresh to Modify check box selected and those that are being refreshed by templates other than the one being replaced. For more information, refer to the section titled "Replacing the Database Design."

Answers to Test Yourself Questions at Beginning of Chapter

1. Use of the NTF file type ensures that a template will appear in a list of templates in the New Database dialog box. For more information, refer to the section titled "Creating a Template."

2. Templates are created in the same way as a regular database. They may or may not have .ntf extensions. To use a template you must enable the database as a template and give it a template alias, and enable another database to inherit design changes from that alias. For more information, refer to the section titled "Creating a Template."

3. A database's design can be updated (refreshed) either manually or automatically once enabling design change inheritance. The manual process is to select File | Database | Refresh Design. The automatic process is to wait for the nightly run of the DESIGN process on the server. For more information, refer to the section titled "Updating the Design of a Database."

4. A database can be enabled to inherit design from more than one template by changing the design properties for each element to inherit design. When the design properties for a database are set to inherit design, all the design elements also inherit design from the template. However, if a particular design element's properties indicate inheritance from a different template, those properties will override the database properties. For more information, refer to the section titled "Inheriting the Design from Multiple Templates."

5. You can enable a database to inherit design changes from a different template and have that design refreshed by selecting File | Database | Replace Design. This is used when a wholesale change of design for a database is required, such as in the case of a version release of software that radically changes the design of a database. For more information, refer to the section titled "Replacing the Database Design."

6. Database design can be completely removed, and therefore hidden from all users of that database by using the Replace Design menu and indicating that the replace should hide formulas and Lotus Script. This strips all design permanently from the database. For more information, refer to the section titled "Hiding Database Design Using Replace Design."

7. A good methodology for implementing and changing live databases is as follows: do your design locally and replicate those design changes to a server-based template. Have the live database inherit design changes from the template. New design changes are done locally, insulating the template from any change until manual replication is done. Once the template has been changed, the DESIGN process will take care of updating the live database. For more information, refer to the section titled "A Suggested Design and Distribution Methodology."

Chapter 23

Securing
Applications

This chapter introduces you to the following objectives:

- ▶ Creating and using roles

- ▶ Using view and form access lists

- ▶ Using Readers and Authors fields

- ▶ Using electronic signatures

- ▶ Using field-level encryption

Test Yourself! Before reading this chapter, test yourself to determine how much study time you will need to devote to this section.

1. What are roles and how are they used?

2. What do view and form access lists do?

3. What are the purposes of Readers and Authors fields on forms?

4. What are two ways to implement signing on a form?

5. What does encryption do and where can encryption keys be obtained?

Answers are located at the end of the chapter...

Lotus Notes has a number of security features. Many are controlled at the server by the system administrator. The control of access to individual databases and the design and data elements within them, however, are the responsibility of the application developer.

Using good techniques, a developer can control which users access which design elements, such as forms, views, agents, and so on. A developer also can build in user access to control the ability for users to modify documents, read documents, and even read certain fields in documents.

A developer can also control the verification of field modification through the use of electronic signatures.

Creating and Using Roles

Objective   In many cases, the use of certain design elements needs to be restricted to a person or a certain group of people. Although this is an important concept in itself, equally important are the tools for implementing such restriction. The lists that control access to design elements within a Lotus Notes database rely on groups to make maintenance and administration easier, just as an ACL does. This tool is referred to as a *role*.

Defining User Roles

User roles are jobs or statuses defined within the context of a single database. A company may have certain groups of people who are given certain responsibilities based on a grouping (managers, for example). A Notes database may also have certain groups of people defined as having certain roles, and therefore are given the ability to do certain things.

The role of the same name may have different connotations from database to database, just as the term *manager* may from company to company. No specific abilities are built into a role name: It is simply a tool used to grant or restrict access to forms, views, actions, and so on.

Here is an example before you look at the creation and use of roles. One may define the role of "shoe-wearer" as one who is able to create documents relating to the tracking of clients. As you can see, there is no inherent meaning in the term "shoe-wearer," it is simply an arbitrary term I chose to use. Of course, it would make more intuitive sense to use a role name that had some inherent meaning. As you begin to grasp the concept, begin to realize that the powers of a role are defined by you, the developer. They are not imposed from within the structure of Notes itself.

Creating Roles

Roles are created in the Access Control List (ACL). Once created, these roles may be used to grant access to certain functions in the Notes database. Once these functions are defined, individuals or groups are assigned to one or more roles in the ACL.

To create a role, complete the following steps:

1. From the workspace, right-click the database icon in which you want to create the role and choose Access Control.

2. Select Roles on the left side of the ACL dialog box.

3. Click the Add button and identify the role by assigning it a meaningful name (see Figure 23.1).

Figure 23.1

The Add Role dialog box enables you to create a role.

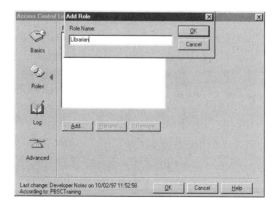

Note   The name of the role appears enclosed in square brackets. From this point forward, the role needs to be referred to enclosed in those brackets. If you typed Librarian, for example, the role would appear and have to be referenced as [Librarian].

4. Click OK to exit the ACL or Add to add another role.

Now that you have created a new role, you need to know how to assign roles to users and groups.

Assigning Roles to Users and Groups

Roles are assigned to users and groups or even servers. This assignment is done in the ACL of the database in which the roles were defined. In order to assign a user or group to a role, they must first be given access to the database by adding them to the ACL. Once they are added, users and groups may have roles associated with them.

To assign a role to a user or a group, complete the following steps:

1. From the workspace, right-click the database icon in which you want to create the role and choose Access Control.

2. Add the appropriate users and groups to the ACL and give them some access if they have not already been added.

3. Select the user or group to assign to the role and then click the role to which they are to be assigned (see Figure 23.2).

4. Exit the ACL when finished.

After creating the roles and assigned users and groups to them, you need to use them to enforce security in your database.

Using Roles

Roles can be accessed and used in a number of different ways. The fundamental purpose for roles, however, is to group permissions into a specific name, which can be assigned to a group, person, or server. As you will see in the following sections, roles can be used to control access to views, forms, and sections. Roles can also be used to control hiding and viewing of certain design elements, such as form text, fields, and sections, as well as actions on views and forms (see Figure 23.2).

Figure 23.2

The Access Control List dialog box enables you to assign roles.

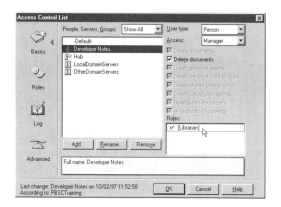

Although the other forms of access will be discussed later (see the section titled "View and Form Access Lists"), this is an appropriate time to discuss the use of roles in hiding properties for form elements and actions.

Through the use of the hide-when properties, a design element may be hidden under a certain circumstance. The presence of a user name, for example, can be one of those circumstances. If you want a field, section, piece of text, or action to appear or disappear based on the role of [Librarian] being assigned to the current user, you may use the following formula (see Figure 23.3):

```
@Member("[Librarian]";@UserRoles)=0
```

Figure 23.3

The Properties for Action dialog box enables you to specify an action to hide if a particular formula is true.

In this example, the @Member function determines if a text string (in this case "[Librarian]") is present in a list. The list is generated by the @UserRoles function, which creates a list of all the roles to which the current Notes user is assigned. The @Member function returns the number 0 if the text is not present in the list, and a number denoting what position the text is found in the list if it is in the list. In this case, if the role of [Librarian] is not found, the formula will return a 0 and the element (for example, Action button) will be hidden; otherwise, it will show.

Using View and Form Access Lists

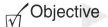 Objective

A developer can exercise control over who is allowed to use views and forms. This control is maintained through the use of access lists found in the properties of these objects. This control is essential to ensure that certain users are not able to use specific views, forms, or documents created with these forms.

Using View Access Lists

View access lists are designed to enable access to a specific view in a database. Whereas naming a view with parenthesis, for example (Lookup), makes a view hidden to all but application developers, a view access list can make a view hidden to certain people and visible to others. This enables the creation of views, which contain information that should not be seen by everyone with reader access to the database.

 Note

Of course, simply denying a user access to a certain view does not deny access to the information in that view. Any user with reader access can, by default, create a new view that mimics the function of the view to which he has been denied access.

The view access list is a property of the view and can be modified while editing the view's design. The access list, by default, allows all users who have reader access or higher to use the view.

However, you can reduce this to specific people or groups listed in the ACL, or assign specific roles to the use of the view.

When a user is restricted from using a certain view, it neither shows up in the list of views, nor does it appear in the View menu for that user, even if its other properties indicate that it should.

The interaction of ACL permissions and view access lists is an example of a case where lowest permissions are the overriding ones. Granting access to a user in a view access list cannot give that user more permission than she had originally, but it can restrict what that user's normal access permissions are. If Bob has no access to a database, for example, he cannot access any portion of that database. His name could be placed in the view access list; however, this would not grant him permission to the database, and therefore would not grant him access to the view.

As another example, Jeannette has manager access to the database. Normally, this would give her complete access to all portions of the database. This would include the ability to use all views and modify the design of all shared components. If she is denied access to a view through noninclusion in a view access list, however, she can neither use the view to see documents, nor can she see the view to modify it in the design view list.

To modify a view access list, complete the following steps:

1. Navigate to the navigation pane in the database and expand the views list in the design section.

2. Double-click the view to be modified.

3. Right-click the view and choose View Properties to display the Properties for View dialog box (see Figure 23.4).

4. Navigate to the Security tab (the one with the Key icon).

5. Deselect the All Readers And Above check box indicating that all entries in the ACL, with at least reader access, can use this view.

Figure 23.4

The Security tab of the Properties for View dialog box enables you to restrict access to the view.

6. Select the users, groups, servers, or roles allowed to access this view by clicking on each in turn. If the user or server is not listed in the box, use the address tool (the button with the head on it) to access an address book and choose from there.

7. Exit from the Properties for View dialog box and the design of the view.

Using Form Access Lists

Much like view access lists, form access lists are designed to allow selective access to specific forms in the database. Where form access differs from view access, however, is in its scope. With views there is only the ability to allow or disallow use of the view itself; that option is available with forms. There are also other database elements that are connected with forms: the documents that are created from these forms. You can control read access to a form (who can read documents with this form) and create access to the form (who can create documents with this form).

Using form access lists, you can control not only access to the forms themselves, but also to the entire set of documents created from these forms. Also those two controls are independent, so you can make access to a form very restricted while at the same time making access to the documents very loose. Or you also can make both accesses very restricted or very loose.

The form access list is a property of the form and can be modified when editing the design of the form. The access list, by default, allows all users who have reader access or higher to view documents created from the form, and allows all users with author access or higher to use the form to create documents. You can reduce these to specific people or groups listed in the ACL, or assign specific roles to the use of a form or its documents.

Note

Form access lists are not complete security against the use of documents created with a specific form. When allowing or disallowing access, Notes checks the internal field, Form, in the document. There are three ways to overcome the security created by the use of a form access list. First, a user can create a document with another form, and then rename the form field to the name of the restricted form. Second, a user can create a local replica of the database, create new documents in it, and then replicate the new documents into the server database. Finally, a user can create documents in another database with a form called by the same name, and then paste the documents from one database into another.

When a form's use is restricted to not allow a user access, it neither shows up in the Create menu, nor can the user access it programmatically, as with a @Command([Compose]) statement.

The interaction of ACL permissions with form access lists is the same as with views. Granting access to a user in a form access list can only restrict that user's ACL access. It can never grant access that the ACL would not allow.

To modify a form access list, complete the following steps:

1. Navigate to the standard view in the database and expand the forms list in the design section.

2. Double-click the form to be modified.

3. Right-click the form and choose Form Properties to display the Properties for Form dialog box (see Figure 23.5).

4. Navigate to the Security tab (the one with the Key icon).

5. Deselect the All Readers And Above check box, indicating that all entries in the ACL with at least `reader` access can read documents created with this form.

Figure 23.5

The Security tab of the Properties for Form dialog box enables you to restrict access to the form and its documents.

6. Select the users, groups, servers, or roles allowed to access documents created with this form by clicking on each in turn. If the user or server is not listed in the box, use the address tool to access an address book and choose from there.

7. Deselect the All Authors And Above check box, indicating that all entries in the ACL with at least `author` access can create documents with this form.

8. Select the users, groups, servers, or roles allowed to create documents with this form, clicking on each in turn. If the user or server is not listed in the box, use the address tool to access an address book and choose from there.

9. Exit the Properties dialog box and the design of the form.

As you have seen, the access lists enable you to control access to views, forms, and documents. The following section introduces you to techniques for controlling access to specific documents on a document-by-document basis.

Using Readers and Authors Fields

 Objective

Readers and Authors fields on your form enable you or your users to control access to documents. Just as with access lists, these fields do not allow more access to documents than an ACL would allow, but they do restrict edit or read access to documents.

Using Authors Fields

To edit a document, a user must have one of the following:

▶ An ACL level of editor or higher or

▶ An ACL level of author with the current user's name in a field with an Authors type.

When a Notes document is created, Notes does not automatically store a list of who is allowed to edit that document in the future. All it tracks is who has edited it. Therefore, author access does not automatically grant a user the rights to modify the documents that he or she has created. To have that access, a form must contain a field with an Authors type.

Note

An Authors field having no names present indicates that no users with Author access in the ACL can access that document after it has been created.

When a user tries to enter edit mode in a document, Notes checks two things:

▶ Whether the user has editor access

▶ Whether the user's name is present in an Authors field on the document

If the user has editor or higher access in the ACL, Notes does not do the second check; editors have automatic edit access to all documents.

A document may have more than one Authors field. If that is the case, the cumulative list of all authors identified on all Authors fields is created and checked when a user tries to edit a document.

An Authors field, like any other field, may either be editable or computed. If the field is editable, the list of authors may be adjusted by anyone with the ability to edit the document. If the field is computed, the form designer can create a field that computes the authors.

 Tip

> There is an inherent danger with editable Authors fields: an author removing her own name from the Authors field, and thereby removing ability to edit the document in the future. This danger can be removed by creating a computed field on the form that is populated with the creator's name (using @UserName), in addition to an editable field. In this way, regardless of what is done to the editable field, the original author does not have authorial ability removed.

To create an Authors field, complete the following steps:

1. Edit the design of the form on which you want to place the Authors field.

2. Position the insertion point at the place at which you want to create the field, and select Create | Field.

3. When the Properties for Field dialog box appears, give the field a name not already used on the form and choose Authors from the Type pull-down list (see Figure 23.6).

4. Choose Editable or one of the computed types from the other list.

5. If the field is computed, or if it is editable and you want to populate the field with the creator's name, click the design pane (at the bottom of the form window), and after choosing the Value or Default Value event, type *@UserName* as the formula.

Having learned to restrict edit access to a document through the use of Authors fields, you now turn to restricting access to restricting view (read) access to documents using Readers fields.

Figure 23.6

The Basics tab of the Properties for Field dialog box enables you to choose the Creator field type.

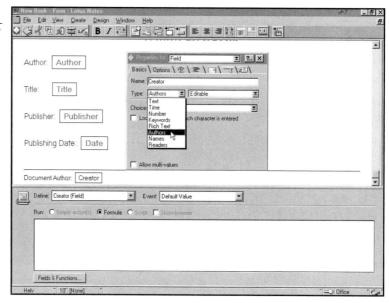

Using Readers fields

The ability to see a document in a view is dependent on two things:

▶ An ACL level of reader or higher

▶ The presence of the current user's name in a Readers field if one exists for the document and has names in the field

Whereas a view access list prevents a user from seeing the view at all, a Readers field permits a user to see documents only where he or she is listed as a reader.

Like Authors fields, Readers fields can be either editable or computed. If these fields are editable, any user who can edit the document will be able to populate the field; if computed, you will need to write a formula, which automatically populates the field with the user or users to be able to see the document in a view.

Readers fields have an effect only if there is data in them. A blank Readers field allows anyone to see the document who has reader access to a view in which the document shows up. Once any data is in the Readers field, only those people whose names appear in the field, or who belong to a group or role that is in the field, will be able to see the document in a view. This is the case even when the field has a name, which is not a valid entry in any address book. If a space is inadvertently placed in the field, it removes all access to every user.

Note

In a Readers field, unlike an Authors field, no name present means that all users can read that document once it has been created.

Like Authors fields, there may be more than one Readers field on a document. The sum total of all the names in all the Readers fields becomes the list of users who can read the document.

Note

The Authors field is considered to be a Readers field as well. So, even if the Readers field does not contain a user's name, if his name is in an Authors field on the document, he will be able to read the document. Authorship always implies readership.

The effect of a Readers field is so powerful that it can restrict the access of anyone to a document, regardless of her ACL access level. Even a user who has manager access to a database will be unable to see the document in any view if she is not listed in the Readers field or in a group or role that is.

A Readers field can also have replication implications. If Barry creates a document on the client database on Server1 and names Edward as a reader, Edward will be able to see the document if he looks at the database on Server1. However, let's say Edward accesses the client database on a replica, which is on Server2. If Server1 and Server2 are not listed in the Readers field of the document, then the document will not be replicated, and Edward will not be able to view the document. Therefore, it is good practice to include a hidden Readers field, which is computed to have the group LocalDomainServers as its member. This way, the document will replicate to all servers, and all users listed in an editable Readers field will be able to view the document.

To create a Readers field, complete the following steps:

1. Edit the form design on which you want to place the Readers field.

2. Position the insertion point at the place at which you want to create the field and select Create | Field.

3. When the Properties for Field dialog box appears, give the field a name not already used on the form and choose Readers from the Type pull-down list (see Figure 23.7).

Figure 23.7

The Basics tab of the Properties for Field dialog box enables you to choose the Readers field type.

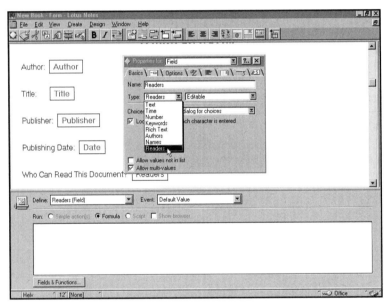

4. Choose Editable or one of the computed types from the other list.

5. If the field is computed, or if it is editable and you want to populate the field with a name or group, click the design pane (at the bottom of the form window), and after choosing the Value or Default Value event, type the population formula.

Having seen how to restrict access to documents, both at an editing level as well as at a viewing level, you now turn to validating authenticity of document information by signing.

Using Electronic Signatures

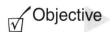 Just as in the world of pen-and-paper office routines, Lotus Notes applications need tools for ensuring the validity of information, especially when more than one user has access to sensitive document fields. *Signing* is the tool that Notes uses to ensure validity.

Signing, which can be applied to whole documents or to specific sections within documents, is a process by which a user's ID is used to create a shell around certain information. This shell carries the name of the user who signed and can be used to verify who changed data in a document, or that data was changed without a signature being attached (the information may not be trustworthy). Modification of the field after someone has signed it causes the signature to be broken, thereby invalidating it and making the veracity of the signed information suspect.

Implementing Signing

Signing can be implemented at the document level or at the section level. At the document level, one or more fields are enabled to trigger signing, and the document must be enabled to be mailed. At the section level, one or more fields are enabled to trigger signing, and these fields are placed into access-controlled sections.

At the document level, only one signature can exist. Any change by any editor to any signed field therefore causes the document to be re-signed by that user.

At the section level, each section can have a signature associated with it. Therefore, a change in field data in a section only re-signs that section. All other signatures remain intact.

To enable a form for document-level signing, complete the following steps:

1. Create the field or fields to contain signed data.

2. Double-click each signed field to access its Properties dialog box.

3. Click the Options tab, expand the Security options field list, and choose Sign If Mailed or Saved in Section (see Figure 23.8).

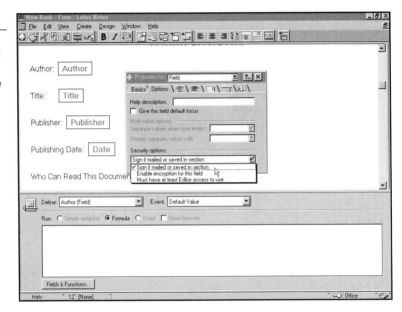

4. Enable the form for document mailing and include an option to sign the document (see Chapter 19, "Advanced Formulas Part II").

To enable a form for section-level signing, complete the following steps:

1. Create the field or fields to contain signed data.

2. Double-click each signed field to access its Properties dialog box.

3. Click the Options tab, expand the Security options field list, and choose Sign If Mailed or Saved in Section.

4. Create one or more access-controlled sections containing the fields, which will be signed. Complete this by selecting the fields to include in the section, selecting Create | Section | Controlled Access, and setting the appropriate section properties.

Note   It is not recommended that you enable a SendTo field for signing. During mail routing, Notes updates this field, and as a result, it will be re-signed.

Having enabled fields for signing, you now need to verify that a signature has been preserved in a document or section, which the following section describes.

Signing Results

Successful signing and verification occurs when a document is signed by an editor, and then can be verified as unchanged since the signing. This verification is possible because the algorithm for signing takes into account both the private key of the signer, as well as the values of the fields that triggered the signing.

A signature is not verified if the fields included in the signature have been changed by an editor since the last editing session (for example, another user has run an agent to modify the fields without entering edit mode on the documents), or the signature cannot be verified because it was created by an untrusted user (for example, a person from another Notes organization for whom there is no cross certificate in the Public Name and Address book).

The visible signs of signing vary with the type, or scope, of the signature (see Figures 23.9 and 23.10). Documents signed at the document level display a message in the status bar at the bottom of the reader's screen to indicate whether a signature is present, and if that signature could be verified.

Documents signed at the section level have message in the title of the section to indicate that the signature was verified.

If the signature could not be verified, a pop-up message appears, indicating that the contents of the section cannot be trusted because the signature could not be verified (see Figure 23.11).

Figure 23.9

An example of a document signed at the document level.

Figure 23.10

An example of a document signed at the section level.

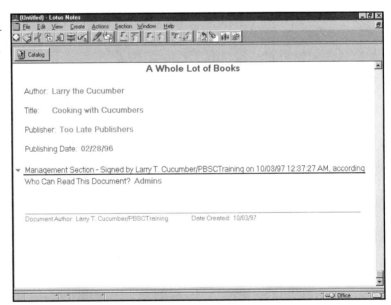

Using Field-Level Encryption

 Objective

Encryption is used in Notes to hide field information from all users without special keys. Like placing valuables behind a locked door and giving only trusted people access to the keys, encryption

locks valuable information and only allows certain people access
to it.

Figure 23.11

*An example of a
pop-up message
if the signature
could not be
verified.*

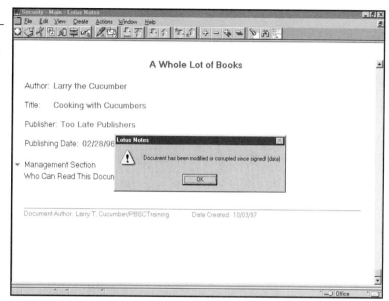

Note

Unlike access lists and Readers fields, encryption is not an
all-or-nothing access to a document. A user may have access
to read and even edit most of a document. Encryption enables
the securing of certain fields on that document so that even
editors without the keys cannot see or modify the field data.

Notes supports two kinds of encryption: single-key and dual-key.
Both single-key and dual-key encryption can be used by a developer for *field-level* encryption.

Dual-key encryption uses a mathematically related pair of keys to
encrypt and decrypt. A public key is available to everyone and
used to encrypt. The other, a private key, is available only to
the user for whom the encrypted information has been created
and is used to decrypt. This is how Notes encrypts mail when you
enable encryption in the delivery options.

Single-key encryption generates a secret key and adds it to a user's
ID. This single key is used both for encryption as well as

decryption, and every user who wants to either encrypt data using it or decrypt data encrypted with it must have the key in their user ID. This means that to encrypt or decrypt information, a user must either create a key or be one of a group to whom the key has been given.

Creating and Distributing Single-Key Encryption Keys

In single-key encryption, all users who need to encrypt or decrypt data must have the same encryption key incorporated into their Notes IDs. In dual-key encryption, all the keys necessary for encryption are available in the public address book, and all the decryption keys are available in each user's ID.

After secret single keys are created, they can be distributed through e-mail or on a disk.

Creating a Secret Encryption Key

To create a secret encryption key, complete the following steps:

1. Select File | Tools | User ID to display the User ID dialog box (see Figure 23.12).

2. Navigate to the encryption section by clicking the Encryption button on the left.

Figure 23.12

The encryption portion of the User ID dialog box enables you to create and distribute encryption keys.

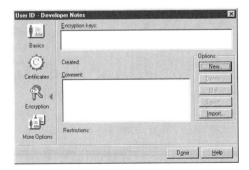

3. Click the Add button to display the Add Encryption Key dialog box (see Figure 23.13).

4. Enter an encryption key name, the encryption type (North American or International), and a comment about the key (optional).

Figure 23.13

A key is named and described in the Add Encryption Key dialog box.

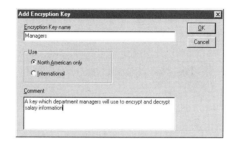

5. Click OK to save the key.

Distributing a Secret Encryption Key Using E-Mail

To distribute a secret encryption key using e-mail complete the following steps:

1. Select File | Tools | User ID to display the User ID dialog box.

2. Navigate to the encryption section by clicking the Encryption button on the left.

3. Select the key you want to mail to another user from the list of keys at the top of the dialog box.

4. Click the Mail button to display the Mail Address Encryption Key dialog box (see Figure 23.14).

Figure 23.14

Addressing a memo to deliver an encryption key.

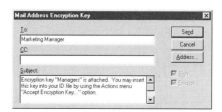

5. Enter a name or names to send the key to and click Send to send the mail.

6. When the dialog box appears asking whether you want to allow the recipient(s) to send the key to others, answer based on the control you want over the key (see Figure 23.15). If you allow recipients to send the key to others, you have no control over who ends up with it. One of the recipients may decide to forward the key to all the employees in your company, thus making the key completely useless as a device for restricting field access only to certain people.

Figure 23.15

Allow only those people you trust to have the key.

 Tip

A key that allows its recipient to send to others may quickly become so widely distributed that it loses its effectiveness; a key that everyone has is really no key at all. Use discretion when sending a key that you allow the recipients to send to others.

Distributing a Secret Encryption Key Using a Disk

To distribute a secret encryption key using a disk or network, complete the following steps:

1. Select File | Tools | User ID to display the User ID dialog box.

2. Navigate to the encryption section by clicking the Encryption button on the left.

3. Select the key you want to export to a file from the list of keys at the top of the dialog box.

4. Click the Export button to display the User ID Encryption Key Export dialog box (see Figure 23.16).

5. If you want, apply a password to the use of the key.

Figure 23.16

*Select the access
options you want
for the encryption
key in the User ID
Encryption Key
Export dialog
box.*

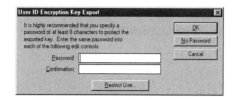

Note

If no password is applied to the key, anyone who gains access to the key file on a disk or on another storage medium will be able to import it into his Notes ID.

6. If you want to ensure that only a specific person can import the key into his Notes ID, click the Restrict Use button to display the Encryption Key Restrictions dialog box, and enter either a person's distinguished or common name (see Figure 23.17).

Figure 23.17

*Allow only those
people you trust
to have the key.*

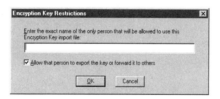

Note

You may also indicate here whether the recipient may distribute this key to others by leaving the check box selected or by clearing it.

7. If you chose not to apply a password, click the No Password button to export. If you applied a password, click OK to export.

8. When the Specify File for Exported Key dialog box appears, navigate to the appropriate place. Give the key a meaningful name and click Save. The key has a .key extension when exported unless you specify otherwise.

Now that the keys have been distributed either by mail or by disk, the recipients have to incorporate them into their user IDs for the keys to be used.

Incorporating a Single Encryption Key Using E-Mail

To incorporate a secret encryption key into your user ID from e-mail, complete the following steps:

1. Once you have received a key by e-mail, open the mail item containing the key.

2. Select Actions | Accept Encryption Key to display the Accept Encryption Key dialog box (see Figure 23.18).

3. If you want, enter a comment about the key.

4. Click the Accept button to incorporate this key into your user ID.

Figure 23.18

Click the Accept button in the Accept Encryption Key dialog box to incorporate the key into your user ID.

Incorporating a Secret Encryption Key Using Import

To incorporate a secret encryption key using import, complete the following steps:

1. Having received a file containing an encryption key, select File | Tools | User ID to display the User ID dialog box.

2. Navigate to the encryption section by clicking the Encryption button on the left.

3. Click the Import button to display the Specify File Containing the Key dialog box and navigate to the key's location.

4. Click the Open button to display the Accept Encryption Key dialog box.

5. If you want, enter a comment about the key.

6. Click the Accept button to incorporate this key into your user ID.

Creating and distributing keys is only a precursor to the actual security implementation, which is using field-level encryption to control access to data in fields.

Using Encryption Keys

Field-level encryption can be implemented in two ways: a form can be enabled to automatically encrypt fields using one or more keys, or it can be enabled to allow a user to manually encrypt using the key or keys of his choice. By enabling a form for encryption, you do not actually encrypt the form: you allow the form to encrypt the encryptable fields, hence the term field-level encryption. In all cases, you must have at least one field enabled for encryption to do this.

Enabling a Field for Encryption

To enable a field for encryption, complete the following steps:

1. Edit the form.

2. Create the field(s) you want to encrypt.

3. In the Properties for Field dialog box, navigate to the Options tab.

4. In the Security Options field, choose Enable Encryption for This Field from the pull-down list (see Figure 23.19).

5. Close the Properties for Field dialog box.

Figure 23.19

The Options tab of the Properties for Field dialog box allows you to enable a field for encryption.

Enabling a Form for Automatic Secret Key Encryption

To enable a form for automatic secret key encryption, complete the following steps:

1. Edit the form.

2. Enable the desired field(s) for encryption.

3. Right-click the form and choose Properties to display the Properties for Form dialog box.

4. Navigate to the Security properties (the tab with the key on it).

5. In the Default Encryption Keys field, choose the key or keys you wish to encrypt with the encryption-enabled fields with on document save (see Figure 23.20).

Figure 23.20

The Security tab of the Properties for Form dialog box enables you to select one or more keys to enable field-level encryption.

6. Close the Properties for Form dialog box.

Enabling a Form for Automatic Dual-Key Encryption

To enable a form for automatic dual-key encryption, complete the following steps:

1. Edit the form.

2. Enable the desired field(s) for encryption.

3. Enable the form for document mailing and include an option to sign the document (see Chapter 19).

 Note
Notes can use only dual-key encryption for specified document recipients that have public keys. If the recipient is a mail-in database or an Internet e-mail recipient, no encryption will occur.

If at least one field is enabled for encryption on a form but automatic encryption is not enabled, the form is enabled for manual user encryption.

Using Manual Encryption

The keys defined by the developer of an application (the defaults) do not have to be the keys an actual author uses to encrypt. In some cases, an author may choose to remove some or all of the encryption keys, or may even choose to replace the default keys with new keys. Of course, the documents created will have fields that are accessible only by those with the new keys.

Manually encrypting with specific keys can be done during the creation of a document, or afterwards by modifying the document properties.

To manually encrypt a document, complete the following steps:

1. At creation, select Edit | Properties and navigate to Form properties when the Properties dialog box displays.

Alternatively, in a view, right-click the document to be modified and choose Document Properties from the quick menu.

2. Click the Security tab to move to the security properties for the document.

3. Choose one or more Secret Encryption Keys (single-key) and/or Public Encryption keys (dual-key).

4. Close the Properties for Document dialog box.

Encryption Effects

There are a variety of effects when creating forms with automatic encryption and encrypting documents with one or more keys:

▶ Encrypted fields do not appear in views or in document field values (found in document properties), even to those people who have the proper keys.

▶ If a field is encrypted with more than one key, any user with at least one of those keys can see the encrypted information.

▶ If a document is encrypted, users with at least reader access are still able to open the document, but no users regardless of access are able to edit any fields on the document without at least one of the encryption keys.

▶ If a user who does not have all the default encryption keys tries to create and save a document, he will be prevented from doing so because he is unable to provide the appropriate keys to encrypt.

▶ Any author, either at creation or afterward, may modify the encryption keys used to encrypt his or her document. If that author chooses, he may remove encryption altogether or change the keys so that fewer than the default number are being used, or a key or keys other than the defaults are used.

▶ If a form is created using a certain key as the default and documents are created using these default keys, modification of the form to include different keys does not cause previously created documents to re-encrypt using the new keys. This is the case even if the document is edited and changed.

▶ Encryptable fields appear surrounded with red field markers (instead of the default gray) when documents containing them are created or edited.

As already mentioned, field-level encryption allows for selective hiding of important information. By creating, distributing, and then using keys to encrypt fields, you can be sure that sensitive data is kept secret.

Exercises

On your CD-ROM there are three databases you need for this exercise. Copy `inv23.nsf`, `cust23.nsf`, `ref23.nsf`, `joe.id`, and `selmore.id` to your Notes data folder (ensuring you remove the read-only attribute from the files) and add the databases titled `Chapter 23 Customers`, `Chapter 23 Invoices`, and `Chapter 23 Reference` to your workspace.

This set of databases represents a customer invoicing application that works, up to a point. You have decided to add some security to the database by implementing a signed section and field-level encryption, as well as some view-access restrictions.

Here are some important objects you need to reference:

▶ Database 1: Filename: `cust23.nsf`; Title: `Chapter 23 Customers`

▶ Database 2: Filename: `ref23.nsf`; Title: `Chapter 23 Reference`

▶ Database 3: Filename: `inv23.nsf`; Title: `Chapter 23 Invoices`

▶ User ID 1: `joe.id`—used to create an encryption key

▶ User ID 2: `selmore.id`—used to test encryption

Exercise 23.1

1. Select File | Tools | Switch ID. Navigate to the `Notes\Data` folder and select `joe.id` (the password is `lotusnotes`).

2. Select File | Tools | User ID to display the User ID dialog box.

3. Navigate to the Encryption tab by clicking the keys on the left of the dialog box.

4. Click the New button in the options section on the right of the dialog box to invoke the Add Encryption Key dialog box.

5. Type `Management` in the Encryption Key name field and click OK to create the key (see Figure 23.21).

Figure 23.21

The Add Encryption Key dialog box.

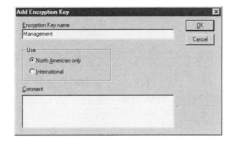

6. Click Done to exit the User ID dialog box.

7. Open the Chapter 23 Customers database, expand the design section in the navigator, and click Forms to see the forms list.

8. Double-click the customer form to edit its design.

9. Scroll to the bottom of the form and create a new line below the Terms field.

10. Create a line consisting of the following:

    ```
    Text: "Annual Business"; Field: AnnualBusiness;
    ➥Text: "Our Percent"; Field: OurPercent.
    ```

    The specifics of the fields are as follows:

    AnnualBusiness: Number, editable, currency, two decimals, Enable Encryption for This Field (as found on the Options tab in the Security pull-down list)

    OurPercent: Number, editable, fixed, no decimals, percentage, Enable Encryption for This Field

11. Select the text Payment Terms along with the Terms field.

12. From the Create menu, select Section | Controlled Access to create a section.

13. In the properties for the Form Section dialog box, enter the title Accounting and exit the dialog box by clicking the Close button (see Figure 23.22).

continues

Exercise 23.1   Continued

Figure 23.22

After entering Accounting *in the Title field.*

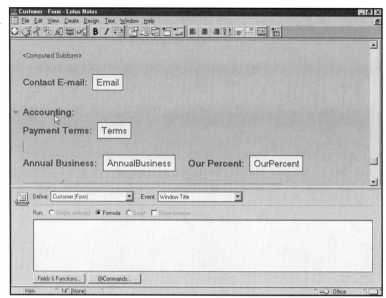

14. Double-click the Terms field to display its properties dialog box and navigate to the Options tab.

15. Click the security options field to produce the pull-down list, select Sign If Mailed Or Saved in Section, and close the Properties dialog box by clicking the Close button.

16. Select the text and fields in the Annual Business line you just created, and select Create | Section | Controlled Access to create a section.

17. In the properties for the Form Section dialog box, enter Management in the Title field and close the dialog box by clicking the Close button (see Figure 23.23).

18. Right-click any blank area of the form and choose Form Properties from the menu that appears.

19. Click the Security tab to display the form's security properties.

20. Click in the Default Encryption Keys field and select the Management key from the pull-down list (see Figure 23.23).

Figure 23.23

After entering
Management into
the Title field.

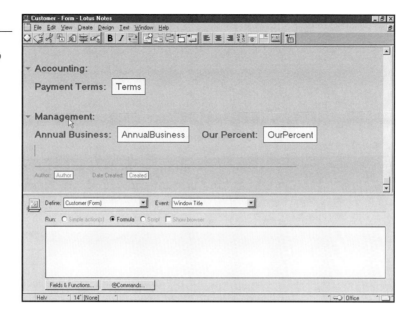

Figure 23.24

Selecting the
Management key
from the Default
Encryption Keys
field.

21. Close the dialog box by clicking the Close button.

22. Save the form and close it.

23. Test the changes you made by creating a new customer, fill-
    ing in the fields, and closing the new document. Close the
    database, switch to selmore.id (password is lotusnotes), and
    re-open the database, opening the customer you just created.
    The encrypted fields should not be visible, and the signing
    message should appear.

23. Switch back to the joe.id user ID.

25. Close the document and the database and return to your
    workspace.

continues

26. Click with your right mouse button on the Chapter 23 Invoices database and choose Access Control from the menu that appears.

27. Navigate to the Roles tab by clicking the masks on the left side of the dialog box.

28. Click the New button at the bottom of the roles section, enter AR in the role name field, and click OK to exit (see Figure 23.25).

Figure 23.25

The Access Control List dialog box.

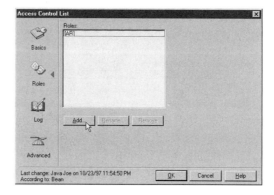

29. Navigate to the Basics tab by clicking the book and key on the left side of the dialog box.

30. Select Java Joe from the list of users in the center column of the ACL and then click the role [AR] in the roles box at the bottom right (a check mark should appear to the left of the [AR] role).

Figure 23.26

Select Java Joe/Bean from the list of users and assign the [AR] role.

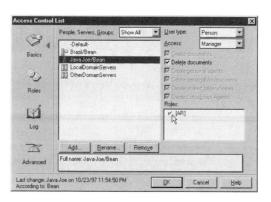

31. Click OK to exit the dialog box and return to the workspace.

32. Open the Chapter 23 Invoices database, expand the design section in the navigator, and click Forms to see the forms list.

33. Double-click the Invoice form to edit its design.

34. From the View menu, choose Action Pane to enable you to see the list of actions created for this form.

35. Double-click the Mail Invoice Action to display its properties.

36. Navigate to the Hide button and append the following code to the code that is already present in the Hide Action If Formula Is True field:

```
¦@Member([AR];@UserRoles)=0
```

37. Close the properties for the action by clicking the Close button and repeat steps 35 and 36 for the actions Change Invoice Number and Invoice Paid.

38. Save and close the form.

39. Your changes can be tested by creating a new invoice (the actions should all appear when the form is open), closing the database, switching to the selmore.id user ID, opening the database, and opening the invoice you created. Because Selmore isn't a member of the role [AR], you should not be able to see the actions, even if you enter edit mode.

Exercise 23.2

Adjust the properties for the Create a New Invoice action in the Invoices view of the Chapter 23 Invoices database so that only people in the role [AR] can see the action and test it by switching between joe.id and selmore.id.

Review Questions

1. Dion has placed Maresa's name into a Readers field on a document, which he created. Maresa, who usually gains access to the database on a different replica from Dion, cannot see the document, even after replication has occurred. What is the problem?

   a. Maresa has only reader access to the database; she needs author to see this document.

   b. Maresa is looking in the wrong view.

   c. LocalDomainServers has not been placed into a Readers field, so the document doesn't get replicated.

   d. The Readers field is not editable on the document.

2. What is the difference between the role [Manager] and the ACL level manager?

   a. There is no difference.

   b. The ACL level manager has predefined abilities in a Notes database; the role has abilities defined by a developer.

   c. The role [Manager] has predefined abilities in a Notes database; the ACL level has abilities defined by a developer.

   d. The ACL level manager can be assigned to anyone in the Public Address Book; the role can only be assigned to ACL levels of designer.

3. When a form is enabled for encryption, what information is encrypted?

   a. All the fields on the form

   b. The user's public key

    c. The Public Address Book

    d. The fields enabled for encryption

4. Rene has no secret encryption keys. She creates a document, and when she tries to save it, she is told that she does not have the required key to save it. What can she do to save the document?

    a. She cannot save the document under any circumstances.

    b. She can edit the properties of the document and remove the default keys, and then save the document.

    c. She can delete the information from the encryptable fields.

    d. She can use the Actions | Remove Keys menu, and then save the document.

5. Under what circumstances can multiple signatures exist on a document?

    a. When the form is enabled for multiple document signatures.

    b. When the Authors field indicates multiple authors.

    c. You can never have multiple signatures on a document.

    d. When multiple Controlled Access sections exist on the document and contain signed fields.

6. Clyde mail-enables a form with encrypted fields. He sends the document to a mail-in database, indicated in a `SendTo` field. With what key will the document be encrypted?

    a. The document cannot be encrypted as the mail-in database has no public key.

    b. The document will be encrypted with Clyde's public key.

    c. The document will be encrypted with the certified ID.

    d. The document will be encrypted with a floating secret key, held in the keys document in the Public Address Book.

7. A document has Readers and Authors fields, which are populated with names. Who can see the document in a view?

    a. Everyone in the Readers and Authors fields

    b. Only those in the Readers field

    c. Only those in the Authors field

    d. Everyone with reader or higher access in the ACL

8. Alexander opens a document in a database. A dialog box appears with the message, Document has been modified or corrupted since signed. What may have happened to the document?

    a. The document was signed by another user, and he is the first one to open it.

    b. The document was created by one user, and then edited and saved by another.

    c. Someone created an agent to modify a signed field on the document.

    d. The document was encrypted with a key he does not have.

9. Brian has author access to a database. He creates a document and saves it. When he tries to edit the document again, however, he finds that he cannot. Which of the following would cause that phenomenon?

    a. He has only reader access to the database.

    b. He does not have the proper encryption keys.

    c. He is not listed in the Authors field in the document.

d. He is not listed in the Readers field in the document.

10. At what levels can signing be implemented on a form?

 a. Document and Controlled Access section

 b. Action and field

 c. Field and layout region

 d. Form and document

11. What must happen to a document for automatic encryption using a public key to work?

 a. The document must be saved.

 b. The document must be signed.

 c. The document must have an Authors field.

 d. The document must be mailed.

12. A document was encrypted using two keys. Henry and Eleanor each have one of the keys, and Victoria has both. Who will be able to read the encrypted fields?

 a. Only Victoria

 b. Henry and Eleanor, but not Victoria

 c. All three of them

 d. None of them

13. Rosie wants to ensure that only users who have the role [Librarian] can access a certain view in her database. How can she accomplish this?

 a. Modify the view read access list in the view properties to allow only the [Librarian] role to use the view.

 b. Make the view hidden.

    c. Create an agent to remove the Readers field from all the documents.

    d. Assign reader access to the [Librarian] role in the database ACL.

14. What color are the brackets surrounding an encrypted field when the document is in edit mode?

    a. Yellow

    b. Black

    c. Green

    d. Red

Review Answers

1. C. Servers are restricted by Readers fields the same way as users are. If a server's name does not show up in a Readers field, the server cannot see the document, and therefore cannot replicate it. Maresa would be able to see the document on Dion's server, but not on her own. For more information, please refer to the section titled "Using Readers fields."

2. B. ACL levels are defined as components of Notes. Roles, on the other hand, are created by an application developer. Therefore, ACL levels have inherent properties, whereas roles have only the properties assigned them in the design of the database in which they are found. For more information, please refer to the section titled "Defining User Roles."

3. D. Field-level encryption is a two-step process. First, fields are enabled for encryption, and then encryption keys are applied to the form, thus encrypting the fields. Since it is at the field level that the encryption is enabled, it is only the fields themselves that are encrypted, not the whole form. For more information, please refer to the section titled "Using Encryption Keys."

4. B. Automatic field-level encryption can be overridden by an author at document creation by changing the document properties to remove the default keys. For more information, please refer to the section titled "Using Manual Encryption."

5. D. Two kinds of signing are possible: One is at the document level (this may only have one signature), and the other is at the section level (there can be one signature per section). Multiple signatures are possible if you have more than one signed controlled-access section on your document. For more information, please refer to "Implementing Signing."

6. A. Mail encryption is, by definition, dual-key encryption. To encrypt in a dual-key encryption environment, you must be able to obtain the public key for the recipient from the Public Address Book. Because mail-in databases do not have public keys, the document cannot be encrypted in this way. For more information, please refer to the section titled "Enabling a Form for Automatic Dual-Key Encryption."

7. A. Document viewing is controlled by who is a reader. Both Authors and Readers fields function as Readers fields, and the effect is cumulative. Therefore, anyone whose name is listed in either the Authors or the Readers fields is able to read the document. For more information, please refer to the section titled "Using Readers fields."

8. C. Signing indicates information integrity (the information has not been modified by anyone since it was last opened and saved). An agent making modifications to a signed field would violate the integrity without resigning the document, and therefore Alexander would receive that message. For more information, please refer to the section titled "Signing Results."

9. C. Anyone with `author` access to a database has default permissions to create documents; Brian demonstrated that that is true. However, it is the presence of a user's name in an Authors field that allows that user to edit the document once

it has been created. Since Brian cannot edit the document, you must assume that there is no Authors field or that his name is not in it. For more information, please refer to the section titled "Using Authors Fields."

10. A. Signing can be implemented for the whole document, or it can be implemented for each controlled-access section. For more information, please refer to the section titled "Implementing Signing."

11. D. Automatic public key encryption (dual-key) requires mailing in order to function. If a document is not mailed, it can be manually field-level encrypted using either a single-key or a dual-key scheme. For more information, please refer to the sections titled "Enabling a Form for Automatic Dual-Key Encryption" and "Using Manual Encryption."

12. C. In order to decrypt a field, all that is required is the presence of one of the keys used to encrypt it. Since each of the three has at least one of the encryption keys, all can read the information in the fields. For more information, please refer to the section titled "Encryption Effects."

13. A. Hiding the view makes the view inaccessible to all users. Removing the Readers field influences the accessibility of the documents but does not influence the ability for users to use a particular view. A role cannot have an access level assigned to it (only people, servers, and groups). A view access list can be used with a role to accomplish the result that Rosie wants. For more information, please refer to the section titled "Using View Access Lists."

14. D. Encrypted fields are indicated with red brackets instead of the default black ones on a document. For more information, please refer to the section titled "Encryption Effects."

Answers to Test Yourself Questions at Beginning of Chapter

1. A role is a designer-created grouping of users and permissions in a database. Roles can be used to restrict access to forms, views, buttons, sections, and so on to certain individuals. They can also be used in hide-when formulas to ensure that only certain people can see elements on forms. Roles are created in the database ACL, and their uses are defined in the database design. For more information, refer to the section titled "Creating and Using Roles."

2. View and form access lists control who is allowed to view and use these design elements. A view access list controls who may use a specific view and who may access that view's design. A form access list controls who may use a specific form and who may access the documents created by that form. Neither of these access lists are true security as there are a variety of ways of circumventing the restrictions. For more information, refer to the sections titled "Using View Access Lists" and "Using Form Access Lists."

3. Readers fields on a form enable control of who is allowed to see the documents created with that form. Through the use of editable Readers fields, a designer can give a user the ability to restrict view of that document to only particular people. Authors fields on a form enable control of who can edit a document after it has been created. Through the use of an editable Authors field, a designer can give the user the ability to expand the list of authors to include other people or groups. For more information, refer to the section titled "Using Readers and Authors fields."

4. Signing can be implemented either at the document level or at the section level. For either, at least one field must be enabled for signing by indicating in the security options property that the field should be signed if mailed or saved in a section. At the document level, the document must have the signing flag enabled and the document must be mailed. At the section level, a section must be created as an access-controlled section, and the signed field must be included in it. For more information, refer to the section titled "Using Electronic Signatures."

5. Encryption scrambles the information in a field using an encryption key. This information can then only be viewed by someone with the proper key. Keys can be obtained either from someone who manually creates and distributes them or from the Public Address Book. For more information, refer to the section titled "Using Field Level Encryption."

24

Troubleshooting Application Development Problems

This chapter will introduce you to the following objectives:

 Objectives

- ▶ Troubleshooting databases and templates
- ▶ Troubleshooting forms
- ▶ Troubleshooting fields
- ▶ Troubleshooting views
- ▶ Troubleshooting formulas
- ▶ Troubleshooting subforms
- ▶ Troubleshooting agents
- ▶ Troubleshooting security

Test Yourself! Before reading this chapter, test yourself to determine how much study time you will need to devote to this section.

1. Why are troubleshooting skills important in application development and the certification process?

The answer is located at the end of the chapter...

Troubleshooting is an essential part of an application developer's skill set. Because few people always get things right the first time, troubleshooting is a skill that we all must have. Troubleshooting, simply put, is the ability to see a problem, logically or intuitively find its root, and then fix it. This chapter will introduce you to some of the most common sources of error in application development and will show you what causes them and how to fix them.

Troubleshooting: This Chapter and the Exams

Although it is not likely that you will be asked questions directly related to troubleshooting ("What tool would you use to troubleshoot?"), many of the application development questions will require that you have some troubleshooting skills ("Bart used the following syntax in his formula. What is wrong with it?"). Any troubleshooting skills you acquire will help you remember to do things well in the first place.

In this chapter, I have tried to provide a sampling of the kinds of problems you might encounter when you apply concepts you have learned in Part II, "Application Development." You have already seen and resolved some of the problems in this chapter; you will be seeing other problems here for the first time. You might notice that this chapter contains few quiz questions (the pre-chapter quiz asks only one). This is because most of the questions will be asked during the course of the chapter.

Troubleshooting Databases and Templates

☑ Objective   The following problems relate to databases and templates:

- ▶ Insufficient rights to create a database

- ▶ Template not available

- ▶ Incorrect template extension

▶ Incorrect form-modification practices

▶ Incorrect database design inheritance

Insufficient Rights to Create a Database

Problem: You select File | Database | New. You fill in the server name (Brazil/Bean) and the database name (NewDB.nsf). When you click the OK button to create it, you get the message shown in Figure 24.1.

Figure 24.1

This error message results from you having insufficient rights to create a database.

Reason & Solution: You have not been given permission to create new databases on the Brazil server. This user right is controlled by a document for the server in question and is maintained in the Public Address book. If the Restrictions section in this document contains names or groups in the Create New Databases field but yours is not represented, you will not be able to create new databases on that server. Talk to the server administrator to get your name added to this field (either as an individual or as part of a group). For more information on creating new databases, refer to Chapter 11, "Introduction to Application Development Components."

Template Not Available

Problem: You want to create a new database from a template, but the template you want to use cannot be found in the list in the New Database dialog box.

Reason & Solution: Either the template you are looking for does not exist, or it does not exist in the place you are looking. You could select the Show Advanced Templates check box under the Templates list to see the advanced templates; you could also try changing template servers to locate the template on another Notes machine.

It might be that the template you are looking for is present but does not have an .ntf extension; the only templates that appear in the template list are those with .ntf extensions. If this is the case, you might want to create a new copy of the template and rename it with the appropriate extension. For more information about creating databases from templates, refer to Chapter 11.

Incorrect Template Extension

Problem: You created a database and, on the Design tab of the Properties for Database dialog box, you selected the Database Is a Template check box and typed a name in the Template Name field. But when you go to create a new database, this template does not appear in the list of templates for the server on which it is present.

Reason & Solution: The list of templates shown in the New Database dialog box is simply a list of the databases with an .ntf extension. Your database probably has an .nsf extension. To fix this problem, create a new copy of the database with an .ntf extension. For more information about creating templates, refer to Chapter 22, "Maintaining Application Designs."

Incorrect Form-Modification Practices

Problem: When you edit a form in a database, the message shown in Figure 24.2 appears. Having made the modification you desire, you exit the form. When you edit the form the next day, the changes you made are gone.

Figure 24.2

This error message results from incorrect form-modification practices.

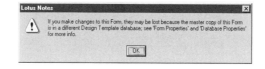

Reason & Solution: The initial message indicates that the changed database is linked to a design template; that is, on the Design tab of the Properties of Database dialog box, the Inherit Design from Template check box is selected, and a template name is present. When the DESIGN process runs on the server and updates the database with the differences from its template, your changes are seen as differences between the template and the database that need to be removed.

To solve this problem, deselect the Inherit Design from Template check box in the Properties of Database dialog to prevent the design from being updated, or deselect the check box in the Properties for Element dialog to prevent that element from being updated. If this is not desirable, change the template instead of changing the database. For more information about design inheritance, refer to Chapter 22.

Incorrect Database Design Inheritance

Problem: Although you have created links between a database and a design template using the database properties of each, one form does not update in the database when you change it on the template.

Reason & Solution: The properties of each database element can be set to override the database design inheritance. In this case, the design properties for the form in question have been changed so that it does not inherit design changes or it inherits design changes from a template other than the one you changed. You can fix this problem by adjusting the design properties for the form. For more information on selective design inheritance, refer to Chapter 22.

Troubleshooting Forms

The following issues relate to form problems:

▶ Form name changes

▶ Document inheritance

▶ Incorrect use of form type

Form Name Changes

Problem: You change the name of a form from `Build A New Customer` to `Create A New Customer` because the database users asked that you change the menu name they use to create a new document. As a result, when users try to edit documents created before the change, they get the message shown in Figure 24.3. Afterward, the document seems to open, but certain fields do not display and the format is wrong.

Figure 24.3

This error message is the result of changing a form's name after documents have been created.

Reason & Solution: When a document is created using a specific form, a field called Form appears on the document to record the form used to create it. This field is consulted every time the document is opened so that Notes knows what form to use to display the field values. Because you changed the form name, you have made it impossible for Notes to know which form displays the document correctly. In this case, Notes uses the default form to display the document.

To fix this problem, change the name of the form so that it uses an alias. This alias will ensure that the form name remains constant even if the name used to access it changes. Then create an agent that executes a simple action to change the name of the Form field on each relevant document to the name of the form alias. For more information about the relationship between a form and a document, refer to Chapter 12, "Creating Forms."

Document Inheritance

Problem: You created a Response form and want the value in the Customer field on the document to be inherited into the Customer field on the Response form. But whenever you create a new Response document, the Customer field is blank.

Reason & Solution: There could be a number of things happening here. Of course, there is always the possibility that the Customer fields on the documents have no values in them. However, there are a few more likely reasons. First, you might not have enabled the Response form to inherit values. First, on the Defaults tab of the Properties for Form dialog box, the Formulas Inherit Values from Selected Documents check box must be selected for inheritance to work. Second, the Customer field on the Response form must be of the data type Computed when Composed or Editable Default Value, and the formula for that field should be Customer to ensure that the value for the Customer field in the document is inherited into the Customer field in the Response form. For more information about inheriting field values, refer to Chapter 12.

Incorrect Use of Form Type

Problem: You create a form to allow users to generate responses, but when you create a Responses Only view column to display values from the documents produced from that form, these values are not displayed.

Reason & Solution: One reason that happens might be that you have neglected to set the form type to Response. If it is still of type Document, its fields will not display in a Responses Only column. Another reason this information does not appear might be that the Show Response Documents in a Hierarchy view property is not selected, which prevents the Responses Only column from showing. Or it could be that a selection formula that excludes Response documents is present in the view. For more information about form types, refer to Chapter 12.

Troubleshooting Fields

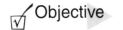 Objective The following problems relate to fields:

- ▶ Incorrect field types

- ▶ Incorrect interpretation of keyword aliases

▶ Incorrect use of rich-text fields

▶ Incorrect use of field edit types

Incorrect Field Types

Problem: You create a field to hold the author's name on a document, make it of the data type Computed when Composed, and add the formula `@UserName` to compute it. When documents are created, the names appear as `CN=Java Joe/O=Bean` instead of as `Java Joe/Bean`.

Reason & Solution: The field type is Text instead of Authors. Authors, Names, and Readers fields appear on forms in abbreviated format even though they are stored in canonical format; Text fields, however, always appear in canonical format. For more information about field data types, refer to Chapter 12.

Incorrect Interpretation of Keyword Aliases

Problem: You have created a Keywords field called `Coffee` and typed values using numeric synonyms (aliases) to identify the values. You create the following formula, but no matter what value you choose, you always get `Domestic` as the result:

```
@If(Coffee = 1;"Columbian";Coffee = 2; "Brazilian";"Domestic")
```

Reason & Solution: Synonyms for keywords are always treated as text values. As a result, the formula will never find the value 1 or 2; instead, the values are `"1"` and `"2"`. This means that the last value will always be the result, and `Domestic` will always be returned. Change your formula as follows, and it will work as you expect:

```
@If(Coffee = "1";"Columbian";Coffee = "2";
"Brazilian";"Domestic")
```

For more information about keywords and their aliases, refer to Chapter 12.

Incorrect Use of Rich-Text Fields

Problem: You create a field in which you allow users to add attachments and format text according to their specifications. You create a view and put this field into a view column, but the values never appear even though you know there are values in the field.

Reason & Solution: The specifications for this field indicate that it is rich text. Rich-text values will not display in view columns. For more information about rich-text fields, refer to Chapter 12.

Incorrect Use of Field Edit Types

Problem: Bill, who has `author` access to a database, creates a document and is able to edit that document after it has been created. Norris, who has `editor` access, edits Bill's document; now Bill can't edit it any more.

Reason & Solution: The form used to create the document has the Authors field as data type Computed using the following formula:

```
@UserName
```

As a result, with every successful edit, the field is being set to the name of the current user. When Norris edited the document, he became the author, and now Bill can't edit it. Change the data type of the field to Computed when Composed, and this problem will no longer happen. For more information about field edit types, refer to Chapter 12.

Troubleshooting Views

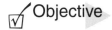 Objective   The following problems relate to views:

- ▶ Incorrect use of a view selection formula
- ▶ Incorrect use of a hidden column
- ▶ Incorrect use of view categorization

▶ Incorrect use of a default view design

▶ Incorrect use of personal views

▶ Incorrect display of the Time value in a view

Incorrect Use of View Selection Formula

Problem: A view has a selection formula of

```
SELECT City = "Kansas City"
```

When the view is displayed, it does not display any Response documents.

Reason & Solution: It is probable that the Response documents do not contain a City field. As a result, the selection formula filters these documents out when selecting the ones that display (the main documents only). Modify the formula to include responses to the main documents with either of the following:

```
SELECT City = "Kansas City" ¦ @AllChildren
```

```
SELECT City = "Kansas City" ¦ @AllDescendants
```

For more information about selecting Response documents in views, refer to Chapters 13, "Introduction to Formulas," and 14, "Creating Views."

Incorrect Use of a Hidden Column

Problem: You create a column in a view. When you are designing the view, you see values in the column when you refresh it. However, when the database users use this view, the column does not appear at all.

Reason & Solution: You have made the column hidden through the Hidden check box on the Basics properties tab of the column. This hidden column will appear to you in design, but not to users. Deselect the Hidden check box, and the column will appear properly. For more information, refer to Chapter 14.

Incorrect Use of View Categorization

Problem: You create a view that shows the value of the Customer and ContactName fields from the Customer form. You have sorted the documents by the Customer field, which is displayed in the first column of the view. When you look at the view, all the Customer values appear with twisties, even though there are no responses to any of them, and the ContactName always appears on the line below.

Reason & Solution: In addition to sorting by the Customer field, you have categorized by that field. This causes that field to appear in its own row, with other document information displayed in the row below. To fix this problem, remove the categorization from the view column. For more information, refer to Chapter 14.

Incorrect Use of a Default View Design

Problem: You create multiple views in a database, but all views subsequent to the first appear with the same design as the first.

Reason & Solution: You have made the first view the default for the design, and in the Create View dialog box, you did not select the Options button to move the design from the Blank view. As a result, every view assumes the design of the first view. You can solve this problem by choosing the Blank view from the Options dialog box when creating new views. For more information about default views, refer to Chapter 14.

Incorrect Use of Personal Views

Problem: You create views on your server-based database, but none of the users can see them.

Reason & Solution: When creating these views, you did not select the Shared check box on the Create View dialog box. As a result, each of these views is personal and cannot be seen or used by anyone but you. In the future, select the Shared check box to create shared views. You can also create new views that use these personal views as defaults for design, so you don't have to re-create the whole view. For more information about personal and shared views, refer to Chapter 14.

Incorrect Display of a Time Value in a View

Problem: You have a view that displays a column consisting of the following formula:

```
(DueDate-@Today)/86400
```

The column displays the correct information, but the refresh indicator always appears, even after it has been clicked.

Reason & Solution: The @Today value is being constantly updated as the time changes. Therefore, Notes perceives the views as in constant need of refreshment. You can prevent this problem by changing your formula to

```
(DueDate-@TexttoTime("Today"))/86400
```

The date in this formula is now a static value, and the refresh indicator will no longer appear; however, the view will be updated every time it is opened. For more information about displaying date-time values, refer to Chapter 13.

Troubleshooting Formulas

Objective   The following problems relate to formulas:

> ▶ Incorrect mode for function operation

> ▶ Incorrect formula syntax

> ▶ Incorrect function references

> ▶ Incorrect mixing of data types

> ▶ Incomplete setup for @MailSend

> ▶ Incorrect mail address

▶ Incorrect technique for list append

▶ Incorrect function context

Incorrect Mode for Function Operation

Problem: You have an action that uses the following formula to check the spelling on a document:

```
@Command([ToolsSpellCheck])
```

Your users complain that it does not work, even on documents with spelling errors.

Reason & Solution: Your users are trying to use this action when they are in read mode instead of edit mode. As a result, the function does nothing; users assume your code has a bug. You can solve this problem by ensuring that the action appears only when users are in edit mode. To do this, select the Hide tab in the properties for the action, and then select the Previewed for Reading and Opened for Reading check boxes. For more information about read and write mode in conjunction with certain functions, refer to Chapter 15, "Creating Actions and Hotspots."

Incorrect Formula Syntax

Problem: You created a hotspot button on a form whose purpose is to modify a field value when clicked. The following formula is created for the button:

```
@Adjust(DueDate;0;0;30;0;0;0);
NULL
```

When you click the button in edit mode, the DueDate field is not modified.

Reason & Solution: The button formula is returning a value to the button and not to the field. To modify the field, you must use an assignment statement like the following:

```
FIELD Duedate := @Adjust(DueDate;0;0;30;0;0;0);
NULL
```

For more information about function syntax, refer to Chapters 13, 15, 18, and 19.

Problem: You create a formula to return the first three characters of a string that has been passed in. You type the following into the Formula window:

```
@Lft(Name;3)
```

When you try to exit the Formula window, you get the following message:

```
Unknown @Function: '@Lft'
```

Reason & Solution: You spelled the function name incorrectly. Function names are not case-sensitive, but they must be complete and accurate. You can solve this problem and others like it by double-checking the names of the functions you type in your formulas. For more information about function names, refer to Chapters 13, 15, 18, and 19.

Problem: You create a formula designed to adjust the date by six days. You type the following in the Formula window:

```
@Adjust(Date;0;0;6;0;0)
```

When you try to exit the Formula window, you get the following message:

```
Insufficient arguments for @Function: ')'
```

Reason & Solution: You have not provided the correct number of parameters to the function. Each function has not only a name, but also a definition for required parameters. In some functions, you can leave NULL parameters out, but this is not the case for all. You can fix this problem by adding the correct number of parameters. For more information about function parameters, refer to Chapters 13, 15, 18, and 19.

Problem: You create a formula designed to adjust a date by six days and to place that value into a field. You type the following formula in the Formula window:

```
FIELD Date := @Adjust(Date;0;0;6;0;0;0)
```

When you try to exit the Formula window, you get the following message:

```
No main or selection expression in formula ')'
```

Reason & Solution: A formula must either return a value to the place from which it was called or select documents. These statements must be the last thing the formula does. This formula has no main expression because the formula does not return a value to the field or function that called it; it simply produces a result in another field. To repair the problem, add a semicolon to the end, and on the next line, type NULL:

```
FIELD Date := @Adjust(Date;0;0;6;0;0;0);
NULL
```

For more information about main expressions in formulas, refer to Chapter 18, "Advanced Formulas, Part I."

Problem: You create a formula designed to adjust a date by six days and to place that value in a field. Realizing that you must supply a main expression, you create the following code:

```
FIELD Date := @Adjust(Date;0;0;6;0;0;0)
NULL
```

When you try to exit the Formula window, you get the following message:

```
An operator or semicolon was expected but none was encountered:
'NULL'
```

Reason & Solution: You have missed a semicolon in your formula. This mistake could be anywhere in the formula; in this case, you have neglected to end your first statement with a semicolon. In any multistatement formula, each statement (except the last one) must end in a semicolon to distinguish it from the next one. For more information about multiline formulas, refer to Chapter 18.

Problem: Cliff creates a formula to set a field value depending on the result of an @If statement as follows:

```
@If(Color = "Red";FIELD Eyes := "Green";FIELD Eyes := "Blue")
```

When he tries to exit the Formula window, he receives the following message:

```
Missing semicolon: 'FIELD'
```

Reason & Solution: He cannot use the FIELD keyword in this syntax because it must appear at the beginning of a line; the error reflects the fact that Notes expects FIELD to begin a new statement and is confused about the syntax. Cliff should use the following syntax:

```
FIELD Eyes := @If(Color := "Red";"Green";"Blue")
```

For more information about the FIELD keyword, refer to Chapter 13.

Incorrect Function References

Problem: You create a keyword field called Coffee and, for its choices, you create the following formula:

```
@DBColumn("":"NoCache";"Norman/Bean":"Reference.nsf";"Coffee";1)
```

When you test the form, you click the helper button next to the Coffee field and one of the following (or nothing at all) appears in the Keywords dialog box:

```
Unable to find path to server
```

```
Server error: File does not exist
```

```
A view of that name cannot be found in the specified database
```

Reason & Solution: The first message indicates that the server you specified in the formula could not be located. In this case, the server `Norman/Bean` either does not exist or cannot be found on the network.

The second message indicates that the server could be found but that the database was not present. Either the database called `Reference.nsf` does not exist on that server or it does not exist in the default Notes data path.

The third message indicates that the server and database were found but that the view name you used does not exist. Perhaps you spelled the name incorrectly.

If no values appear in the list but no error message is generated, either a column of the number specified does not exist or the column does not have any values in it to return. For more information about references in `@DBColumn` and `@DBLookup` functions, refer to Chapter 19, "Advanced Formulas Part II."

Incorrect Mixing of Data Types

Problem: You are attempting to create a summary field for a document. This field will be used to provide a value for inheritance from a response. The Summary field is computed using the following formula:

```
"The user named " + Author + ", who has an annual salary of " +
➥Salary + "created this document on " + CreateDate
```

Whenever the value is inherited into a response, the value appears as

```
ERROR: Incorrect data type for operator or @Function: Text
expected
```

Reason & Solution: You are mixing data types in the same formula. To concatenate these values, you must convert the `Salary` (number) and the `CreateDate` (Time) to text using the `@Text` function.

A functioning formula might look like this:

```
"The user named " + Author + ", who has an annual salary of " +
➡@Text(Salary;"C0") + "created this document on " +
@Text(CreateDate;"S0")
```

For more information about converting data types, refer to Chapter 13.

Incomplete Setup for @MailSend

Problem: You create an action on a form that is designed to send the document being edited into a mail-in database. The following formula is associated with the action:

```
@MailSend
```

When you test the form and click the button, the following message appears:

```
No 'SendTo' field in document. Use 'Forward' on the 'Actions'
menu instead.
```

Reason & Solution: When used without parameters, the @MailSend function relies on the presence of a field called SendTo, which has the name of the destination of the mail. In this case, you have failed to put a SendTo field on the form, and the function cannot operate as desired. To fix this problem, place a SendTo field on the form and either compute its value or have the user enter it. For more information about the @MailSend function, refer to Chapter 19, "Advanced Formulas Part II."

Incorrect Mail Address

Problem: You create an action on a form that is designed to send the document being edited into a mail-in database. The following formula is associated with the action:

```
@MailSend
```

When you test the form and click the button, the following message appears:

```
DestinationDB not found in any Address Book. Choose OK to skip;
Cancel to stop.
```

Reason & Solution: You have correctly placed a SendTo field on the form that the function is using to determine the mail destination. However, the value in the field is not a valid mailing address. In the SendTo field, you must have the name of a person, group, or mail-in database that is present in one of the address books the server can see. To solve this problem, ensure that a correct name is placed in the field. If this field is editable, give the users an Address Book dialog box to choose from when addressing. For more information about mail addresses, refer to Chapter 19.

Incorrect Technique for List Append

Problem: You add a number to a list using the following formula:

```
NumberList := NumberList + NewNumber
```

You get the following error message at runtime:

```
ERROR: Incorrect data type for operator or @Function: Text
expected
```

Reason & Solution: The NumberList variable has not been initialized and, therefore, contains a NULL value. NULL is considered by Notes to be text; therefore, you are adding a number value to a text list, which is an unacceptable mixing of data types. A solution is to use an @If command to check the current value of the list and assign it the value of the NewNumber if it is NULL:

```
NumberList := @If(NumberList =
NULL;NewNumber;NumberList:NewNumber)
```

Alternatively, you can give the NumberList variable the default value of 0. For more information about list manipulation, refer to Chapter 18.

Incorrect Function Context

Problem: You create a view column and, in its formula, use the `@Prompt` function to produce its value. When you look at the view, no values appear in the column and you are not prompted for them.

Reason & Solution: Some functions are designed to work only in certain circumstances. `@Prompt` cannot be used in a view column formula; therefore, it returns no values to the column. For more information about function contexts, refer to Chapters 13, 15, 18, and 19.

Problem: You create a navigator button to compose a response to a document selected in a view. When you select a document and click the button, you get this message:

```
No document is selected; please select a document to respond to.
```

Reason & Solution: You cannot create a response using a navigator action. When you click the navigator button, the document selected in the view loses the focus and Notes does not realize it was selected. You can solve this problem by using a view action instead. For more information about creating responses using navigator actions, refer to Chapter 16, "Finalizing the Database."

Troubleshooting Subforms

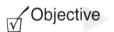Objective   The following problems relate to subforms:

- ▶ Incorrect formula for subform insertion

- ▶ Incorrect subform field names

Incorrect Formula for Subform Insertion

Problem: You have created a form; on this form, you have created a formula to insert a computed subform. However, neither of the subforms you want inserted gets inserted.

Reason & Solution: To insert a subform, your formula must generate the name of the subform to insert. Check the logic in your formula to ensure that the subform names are being generated by the formula, and that the names are spelled correctly. For more information about computed subforms, refer to Chapter 20, "Layout Regions and Subforms."

Incorrect Subform Field Names

Problem: When you insert a subform called MiddlePart into a main form, the following message appears and the field called Description ends up as Description_1 on your subform.

```
Error, the form and the subform MiddlePart both have a field
entitled Description
```

Reason & Solution: You can only have one occurrence of a field name on a form. When you inserted the subform into the main form, its fields became part of the form. You have a field called Description on your form as well as on your subform. To allow you to insert the subform, Notes changes the duplicate field names on the subform to the same name with a _1 on the end. You can prevent this problem from happening by naming the fields on your subform with names that you do not use on your forms. For more information about subform field names, refer to Chapter 20.

Troubleshooting Agent Problems

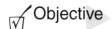 The following problems relate to agents:

- ▶ Incorrect agent execution rights
- ▶ Insufficient agent creation rights
- ▶ Incorrect agent selection formula

Incorrect Agent Execution Rights

Problem: You create an agent with an If New Mail Has Arrived trigger. Even though mail is arriving in the database, this agent never runs.

Reason & Solution: You probably have incorrect permissions on the server to run scheduled agents. This permission is set up in the Server document for the server on which you want to run this agent. The Agent Manager field in the Server document contains three permission fields: Run Personal Agents, Run Restricted Lotus Script Agents, and Run Unrestricted Lotus Script Agents. If your agent contains no Lotus Script code, your name must be in the list of names or groups in the Run Personal Agents field. If your agent contains Lotus Script, your name must be in one of the Lotus Script agent fields. The default for the Run Personal Agents field is to allow everyone, so if the field is set to NULL, you will have permission to run this agent. For more information about background agent execution rights, refer to Chapter 21, "Creating Agents."

Insufficient Agent Creation Rights

Problem: You open a database and select Create | Agent to create a new agent. When you do this, the following message appears; you are prevented from creating a new agent:

```
You are not authorized to use agents in this database
```

Reason & Solution: You do not have sufficient rights in the database ACL to create agents. The ACL has two access-level refinements: Create Personal Agents and Create Lotus Script Agents. The access levels of editor, author, and reader can either be allowed to or prevented from creating agents by selecting or deselecting the first refinement. If the check box is deselected, you get the error message when you try to create an agent. To solve this problem, get the database manager to give you the ability to create personal agents. For more information about rights to create agents, refer to Chapter 21.

Incorrect Agent Selection Formula

Problem: You create an agent that runs but does not modify all the documents it should.

Reason & Solution: If the agent runs and modifies some documents but not others, the problem is probably with your selection formula. The selection formula determines which documents should be processed. To solve the problem, check your selection formula logic to ensure that all the documents you want to modify are selected to be modified. For more information about document-selection formulas in agents, refer to Chapter 21.

Troubleshooting Security

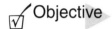

The following problems relate to security:

- ▶ Incorrect use of Readers field

- ▶ Incorrect use of Authors field

- ▶ Insufficient user rights

- ▶ Incomplete encryption key distribution

- ▶ Inadequate ACL rights

Incorrect Use of the Readers Field

Problem: Mary uses a form that allows her to add people to a Readers list to restrict who can view the completed documents. Mary creates a new document and places Bob's name in the Readers field, but Bob can't see the document in the database unless he views it from Mary's machine, which is in another building.

Reason & Solution: Because Bob and Mary work in different buildings, they probably work with different replicas of the database. For the servers to transmit this document, they must be able to see it in their replica. If the servers' names are not in the Readers field, Bob's server will not receive it. He can, however, see the document when he goes to Mary's workstation because that replica contains the document. This problem can be solved by adding an extra hidden and computed Readers field on the form that is automatically populated with the value LocalDomainServers. This value ensures that all servers will be able to see the documents created and to replicate them and update changes as well. For more information about Readers fields, refer to Chapters 12 and 23.

Incorrect Use of Authors Field

Problem: Maurice has author access to a database. He creates a document, but when he goes to edit it, he is prevented from doing so.

Reason & Solution: There is no Authors field in the document, or if there is, his name is not in it. You can solve this problem by creating an Authors field on the form and using a formula (such as @UserName) to populate its value with the name of the creator. For more information about Authors fields, refer to Chapters 12 and 23.

Insufficient User Rights

Problem: Some users complain that they cannot create documents in a database.

Reason & Solution: The inability of users to create documents could be caused by a number of factors. You could check their ACL level to ensure that they have at least author access. In addition, you might check the Form Access list for the form they want to use to create the documents to ensure that they have permission to use that form. This Form Access list is found on the Security tab of the Properties for Form dialog box. For more information about ACLs, refer to Chapter 16. For more information about Form Access Lists, refer to Chapter 23.

Incomplete Encryption Key Distribution

Problem: A user complains that when he opens a document, he cannot see the value in a certain field, while the person in the adjoining office can.

Reason & Solution: The field is probably encrypted, and he does not have the key to decrypt the field and view the value. Either explain that he is not allowed to see that information or supply him with the key via e-mail or diskette. For more information about encryption keys, refer to Chapter 23.

Inadequate ACL Rights

Problem: In setting up the ACL for a database you have created, you find that you need a group to simplify the access administration. However, when you go to create a new group in the Public Address Book, you receive following error message:

```
You are not authorized to add Group documents to this database.
```

Reason & Solution: You do not have sufficient access or do not have the GroupCreators role in the Public Address book. If your server administrator will not give you the access level or role membership you require, you can create your own roles in your database to substitute for the access restrictions you are trying to create. For more information about creating Public Address Book groups, refer to Chapter 16. For more information about database roles, refer to Chapter 23.

Troubleshooting Miscellaneous Issues

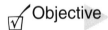 The following problems relate to miscellaneous issues:

- ▶ About Database document not initialized
- ▶ Incomplete setup for mail reception
- ▶ Incorrect use of environment variables

About Database Document Not Initialized

Problem: You associate the following function with a hotspot in a navigator to enable users to click the navigator to invoke the About Database document:

```
@Command([HelpAboutDatabase])
```

When your users click the button, they get the following message; even so, you know that you cannot have deleted the document from the database:

```
No Help-About document is available for this database
```

Reason & Solution: The document is present in the database but is not initialized; that is, you have not typed any text or inserted any objects into it. Even a single character typed into the document will initialize it and prevent this error from appearing. For more information about the About Database document, refer to Chapter 17, "Creating Application Documentation."

Incomplete Setup for Mail Reception

Problem: You create an action that mails a document into another database. When the document arrives, users trying to open the document are given the following message before the document opens:

```
Cannot locate form: Main Topic
```

Reason & Solution: When the document was created, its form was called Main Topic; that form name was placed in a field in the document called Form. This field is being used to determine what form should be used to display the document's contents. However, in the new database, this form does not exist, so the error message appears before the document opens with the default database form.

There are a number of ways to prevent this problem from happening. First, you could store the form in the document in the original database; that way, when the document is sent, it already has its form. Second, you could copy the form from the original database into the destination, thereby ensuring that the form is present when the document is opened. Third, you could devise a way to the change the form name in the document to refer to a form in the destination database; for example, create an agent that is triggered by mail arriving and that modifies the form field. For more information about the effects of mailing documents into databases, refer to Chapter 19.

Incorrect Use of Environment Variables

Problem: While Bob was using Notes on his workstation, a function he was working with stored his manager's name in an environment variable. This variable consistently obtained his manager's name until Bob was transferred to a department on another floor of the building; now his manager's name never shows up when it should.

Reason & Solution: It is likely that Bob got a new computer when he was transferred and he left his environment settings on his old computer. Because environment variables are stored in the Notes.ini file, they do not move as the user moves from machine to machine. Ensure that the formulas displaying the environment variables check to see whether those variables have been set. If not, you could use @Prompt to make sure the variables are populated. For more information about environment variables, refer to Chapter 19.

Exercises

This lab centers around troubleshooting and fixing a broken database. The instructions will simply tell you how to find the problems; it is your job to fix them. The lab files are called `brokecst.nsf`, `brokeref.nsf`, and `brokeinv.nsf`, and their titles are Broken Customers, Broken Invoices, and Broken Reference. Be sure that when you copy the files, you remove their read-only attribute or you will not be able to modify the databases.

1. From your workspace, double-click the Broken Reference icon. An error message immediately appears. Troubleshoot and fix this problem. *Hint: database properties.*

2. From your workspace, double-click the Broken Reference icon. In the list of coffees presented on the right, double-click Bolivian Mountain. Click the action Check Spelling, and an error will appear. Select Actions | Edit Document; the Check Spelling button is gone. Troubleshoot and fix this problem.

3. From your workspace, double-click the Broken Customers icon. Click the Customer Preferences view. Notice the error appearing in the Response documents. Troubleshoot and fix this problem.

4. From your workspace, double-click the Broken Customers icon. Click the Customer Preferences view. Double-click the preference list for the first customer; an error message will appear about the form not being found. Troubleshoot and fix this problem. *Hint: Check the document properties to find the correct form name.*

5. From your workspace, double-click the Broken Customers icon. Click the Customer Preferences view. Create a new preference document for the company Granny's Buckshot and Coffee House by selecting that document in the view and clicking the Add Preferences action. When the new document appears, the customer name is not present in the field; it should be. Troubleshoot and fix this problem.

6. From your workspace, double-click the `Broken Customers` icon. Click the Customer Preferences view. Create a new customer by clicking the Add Customer action. When the new document appears, a prompt will ask you which country your customer is from. Choose the default and click OK. The Province and Postal Code fields for Canadian customers do not appear. Troubleshoot and fix this problem.

7. From your workspace, double-click the `Broken Invoices` icon. Click the Invoices view. Create a new invoice by clicking the Create a New Invoice action. When the new document appears, click the helper button next to the Customer field. A dialog box appears, but an error message is in it. Troubleshoot and fix this problem.

8. From your workspace, double-click the `Broken Invoices` icon. Click the Invoices view. Create a new invoice by clicking the Create a New Invoice action. When the new document appears, select a customer from the pull-down list, and then click the Add a Coffee button. Select a coffee from the list presented, then enter a quantity. An error message appears in the table. Troubleshoot and fix this problem.

9. From your workspace, double-click the `Broken Invoices` icon. Click the Invoices view. The view should show a final column called Total, but does not. Troubleshoot and fix this problem.

10. From your workspace, double-click the `Broken Invoices` icon. Click the Overdue Invoices view. The view should display all invoices that are overdue, but does not. Troubleshoot and fix this problem.

Solutions to the Exercises

1. This error occurs because an attempt is being made to open an uninitialized About Database document. When this document has not been modified from `NULL`, it is considered to be not present in the database. This means that any reference to it will result in an error. You can fix the problem by changing the database properties as shown in Figure 24.4.

Figure 24.4

Adjust the data-base properties to not open the About Database document every time the database is opened.

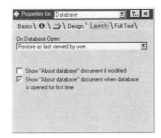

2. This error occurs because you are allowing the Check Spelling button to be clicked in read mode. To make the problem worse, incorrect use of hiding characteristics makes the button appear in read mode and not in edit mode. To fix the problem, edit the design of the Coffee form. In the Actions pane on that form is an action called Check Spelling; double-click this action to modify the properties. Change the Hide tab so it looks like the one in Figure 24.5.

Figure 24.5

Modify the hiding properties of the Check Spelling action.

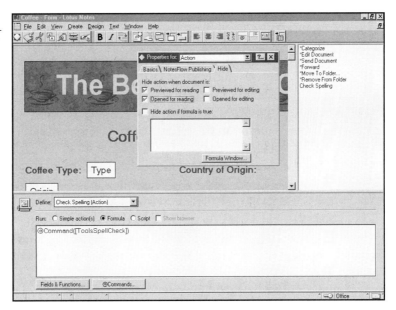

3. This error occurs because of an incorrect concatenation statement. An attempt was made to concatenate a number to a text string, resulting in the error message shown. To correct this problem, edit the design of the Customer Preferences view and, in the formula for the response

column (the first one), change the reference to the PreferredQty field to be modified by the @Text function, as
shown in Figure 24.6.

Figure 24.6

*Modify the for-
mula to use @Text
to convert a num-
ber to text.*

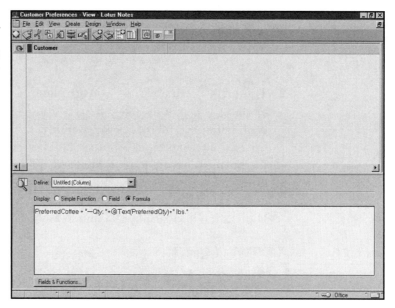

4. This error occurred because the form name of the
   Preference List form was changed after documents were
   added to the database. The alias was removed, so the existing
   documents could not find their creating form to display. Fix
   this problem by adding the alias back onto the form (see
   Figure 24.7); the alias name (Coffee) could have been located by right-clicking any of the documents that would not
   open, choosing Document Properties from the menu that
   appeared, navigating to the Fields tab, and then scrolling
   down to find the Form field and its value of Coffee.

5. This problem occurs because the response wants to inherit
   the value for the customer name from the parent document,
   but cannot because it is not enabled to. You can fix this
   problem by editing the Preference List form and selecting
   the Formulas Inherit Values from Selected Document check
   box on the Defaults tab of its properties (see Figure 24.8).

Figure 24.7

Add the alias back to the form name.

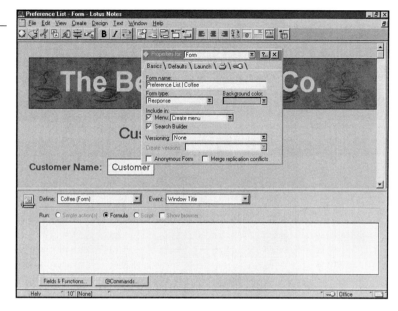

Figure 24.8

Select the Formulas Inherit Values from Selected Document check box.

6. This problem occurs because the list of countries does not include the proper form name to be inserted as a subform. The formula for inserting the subform relies on the Country field to supply the subform name, so if the Country field does not contain the proper values, the subform will not be inserted. In this case, a typographical error caused the value chosen to be an incorrect subform name. You can fix this problem by editing the Customer form and clicking the Country field. In the Formula window, fix the spelling of Canada for the default as well as in the choices list (see Figure 24.9).

Figure 24.9

Correct the spelling of Canada in the formula.

Make sure spelling is correct

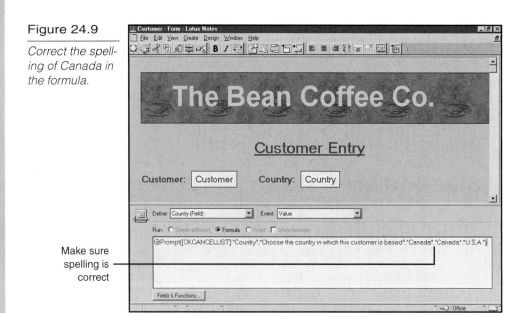

7. This problem occurs because the database being referenced in the @DBColumn formula is incorrectly identified. As a result, the @DBColumn fails and there is nothing but an error message in the dialog box that is supposed to show the Customer choices. You can fix this problem by editing the Invoice form and double-clicking the Customer field. In the properties dialog box that appears, adjust the formula so it appears like the one shown in Figure 24.10.

Figure 24.10

Correct the database name in the @DBColumn formula.

Database name

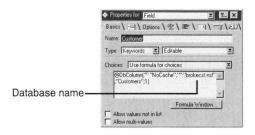

8. This problem occurs because a numeric value is being concatenated to a NULL (text) string. As a result, a mismatch in data types occurs and the error results. You can fix this problem by editing the Invoice form and clicking the Add a Coffee button. In the Formula window, adjust the statement dealing with OrderedQty so that it checks for a NULL value before adding to the list (see Figure 24.11).

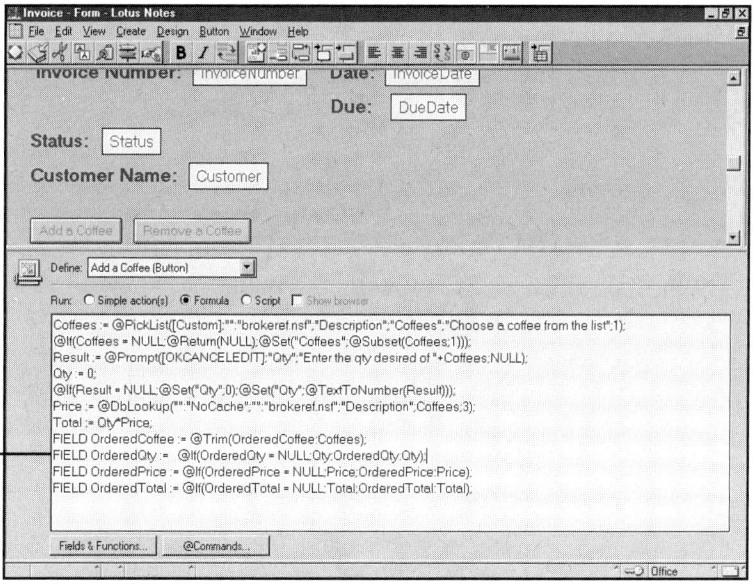

Figure 24.11

Change the statement so the formula checks for a NULL value in the field before appending a numeric value to it.

Checking for NULL

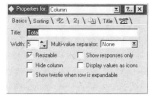

9. This problem occurs because the Total column was hidden by mistake. It would have appeared in the view design, but does not appear to a user. To fix this problem, edit the Invoices view and double-click the Total column. Deselect the Hide Column checkbox to ensure that it appears under all circumstances (see Figure 24.12).

Figure 24.12

Deselect the Hide Column checkbox for the Total column.

10. This problem occurs because the selection formula for the view is incorrect. In this case, the formula checks only for invoices whose due dates are today, not today or less. This problem can be fixed by editing the Overdue Invoices view and adjusting the view selection formula to appear as shown in Figure 24.13.

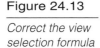
Figure 24.13

*Correct the view
selection formula
as shown.*

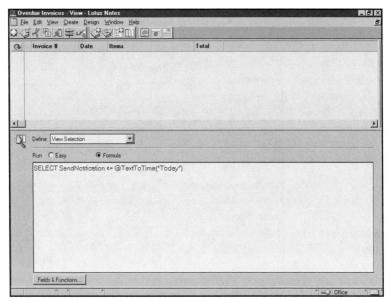

Review Questions

1. Farley wants to create a new database on the Brazil/Bean server, but every time he completes the New Database dialog box specifying Brazil/Bean as the server, he gets the message You are not authorized to create new databases on this server: Brazil/Bean *xxxxx*.nsf. Why does the creation fail?

   a. You are not allowed to create a database directly on the server; instead, you should create it locally and replicate to the server.

   b. The server Brazil/Bean does not exist.

   c. Farley has not been given permission to create new databases in the Server document for Brazil/Bean in the Public Address Book.

   d. Farley is disconnected from the network.

2. Sandra modifies the Memo form in her mail database to include some new fields. When she tests the form everything works fine, but the next day when she sends mail, the new fields are missing. What is the problem?

a. Sandra does not have sufficient access in the ACL of her mail database to make lasting changes.

b. Sandra's mail database is inheriting its design from a template; during the night, the DESIGN process reverted her mail database design back to that of the template.

c. Sandra modified a local copy of her mail database.

d. By default, changes to mail databases last for only three hours and are removed automatically.

3. Janna created a view in the server-based database she is designing, but no one can see this view but her. What is the problem?

a. Janna created a personal view and therefore only she can see and use it.

b. All views can be seen only by the person who created them.

c. Janna does not have designer access in the ACL, and shared views created by a non-designers cannot be seen by anyone but the creator.

d. Janna created the view while she was using the server, so the database was local to her at the time and the view was not shared.

4. Tami creates an agent that transfers mail to a folder when it arrives in her mail database. When she selects mail and manually executes the agent, it works; but the trigger does not seem to make the agent run. What is the problem?

a. Tami does not have sufficient rights on the server to run background agents.

b. Tami does not have sufficient ACL rights to create agents.

c. Tami does not have access to the server on which her mail database is stored.

d. The agent is running; Tami is just looking in the wrong place for the results.

5. Jeanne creates a document in which she places Joanne's name as the sole reader. Joanne, who lives in another city, comes to town and realizes, when accessing the database, that the document is present. When she goes home, however, she cannot find the document in her database. What is the problem?

a. The Hide characteristics for the document are set to not display the document in Joanne's city.

b. Joanne's server is not listed as a reader, so the document is not replicated to that server.

c. The contents of the Readers field conflict with the contents of the Authors field, so Joanne can't see the document at home.

d. Joanne must be overlooking the document at home, as this cannot happen.

6. Arnold and Brutus have reader access to a database. When Arnold opens documents, he sees the contents of the Price field; when Brutus opens the documents, he sees the field label, but not the field contents, and he can't see the values in views either. Why is this happening?

a. No values are in the Price field when Brutus opens the documents.

b. A bug in the application prevents Brutus from seeing the values.

c. A Hide characteristic is set to prevent Brutus from seeing the field value.

d. The field is encrypted; Arnold has the key, but Brutus does not.

Review Answers

1. C. The message Farley is getting indicates that he is finding the server but that there is something wrong with his permission to create new databases. This permission is assigned in the Server document for the server on which he is trying to create the database (Brazil/Bean). This Server document is located in the Public Address book for Farley's organization. For more information, refer to the section titled "Insufficient Rights to Create a Database."

2. B. Because Sandra made the changes and tested her database, you know that she had sufficient rights to do what she did. Forms changing back to previous versions is a sure sign that a template refresh is involved. In this case, the mail database design is being refreshed from a template by the DESIGN process on Sandra's home server. As a result, any changes she makes will be removed from the database design unless she removes the inheritance property from the database or from the database design element she wants to change. For more information, refer to the section titled "Incorrect Form-Modification Practices."

3. A. Because Janna is working with a server-based database, she is capable of creating views visible to anyone who accesses the database. Because other users cannot see the view, you can only assume that she has created a personal view instead of a shared view. It is possible that there is a view access list as well, but given the information you have, you would not expect that to be the case. For more information, refer to the section titled "Incorrect Use of Personal Views."

4. A. Tami tested the agent by running it manually; this proves that the agent is capable of doing what she wants it to do. However, because it is not being triggered, the likely problem is that she does not have the correct access on the server to run background agents, which is what an agent triggered by mail arriving is. She should check with her server administrator to determine whether she can run background agents,

and have that ability added if it is not present. For more information, refer to the section titled "Incorrect Agent Execution Rights."

5. B. Because Jeanne and Joanne live in different cities, it is safe to assume that they work from different replicas of the same database. The presence of a document in one replica and its absence in another is a sure clue that replication is not working. Because there is an editable Readers field on the document, it is likely that the servers are not being included as readers of the document. As a result, one or more servers cannot see the document, and it is not being replicated. Joanne can see the document when she looks on Jeanne's replica, but not on her own. For more information, refer to the section titled "Incorrect Use of the Readers Field."

6. D. Arnold can see the field value in all circumstances; Brutus cannot see the field value in any circumstances. This is probably because there is encryption on the field and Brutus does not have the key. Many design techniques can prevent the field from not being present on a form to Brutus, but encryption is the most likely cause if Brutus cannot see it in views either. To give Brutus access, give him the encryption key. For more information, refer to the section titled "Incomplete Encryption Key Distribution."

Answer to Test Yourself Question at Beginning of Chapter

1. Troubleshooting skills are important for application development in general as well as for certification in specific. Good troubleshooting skills not only enable you to easily diagnose and repair database problems, they make it more likely that you will get the design right the first time. Because you are always looking for design flaws, you can spot them as you are designing instead of repairing them when your user community complains. For exams, troubleshooting skills are essential because many the questions relate directly to problems for which you need to find a resolution; troubleshooting skills are essential for this.

Appendix

Using TestPrep Software

The *CLP Training Guide: Lotus Notes* CD-ROM enables you to prepare for and take practice tests using a collection of exclusive TestPrep test engines. The TestPrep software simulates the CLP exams; it provides you with a method of evaluating your knowledge of the exam material and reinforces the information. TestPrep is not intended to function as a single source of preparation, but rather as a review of information and a set of practice tests to help increase the likelihood of success when you take the actual exam. The CD-ROM also includes two other learning aids: TestPrep study cards and TestPrep flash cards. These software programs will be explained in the following sections.

Getting Started

To get started, perform the following steps:

1. Put the CD into the CD-ROM drive. After a moment, you see a setup dialog box asking you if you are ready to proceed. Click OK.

2. You are then prompted for the location of the directory in which the program can install a small log file. Choose the default or type the name of the drive and directory where you would like it to go, then click OK.

3. The next prompt asks for a Start Menu name. If you like the default name, click OK. If not, type the name you would like to use.

Setup is now complete. For an overview of the CD contents, double-click the CD-ROM Contents icon.

Instructions on Using the TestPrep Software

TestPrep software consists of three applications:

▶ Practice exams help you review information specific to each test's objectives. This application is in multiple-choice format.

▶ Study cards serve as a study aid organized around the specific exam objectives. This application is in multiple-choice format.

▶ Flash cards require responses to open-ended questions, testing your knowledge of the material at a level that is deeper than that of recognition memory.

To start the software, begin from the overview of the CD contents. The left window provides you with options to obtain further information about any of the TestPrep applications. Simply click an icon and a listing of related topics will appear below it. Clicking an application name brings up more detailed information for that application in the right window.

To launch the application you want to use, follow the instructions in the right window. In the Explorer window that opens on the left, double-click the application's icon.

Using TestPrep Practice Exams

The practice exams interface is simple and straightforward. To begin taking a practice exam, do the following:

1. Double-click the TestPrep icon.

2. Click the Next button to see a disclaimer and copyright screen. Read the information and click TestPrep's Start button.

3. A notice appears indicating that the program is randomly selecting questions for the practice exam from the exam. They are selected from a larger corpus of 150–300 questions. The random selection of questions from the database takes some time to retrieve. Don't reboot; your machine is not hung.

4. After the questions have been selected, the first test item appears.

Notice that this window has several important features:

▶ The question number is located at the top-left corner of the window in the control bar.

▶ The Mark check box, which enables you to mark any exam item as one you would like to return to later, is located below the question number.

▶ The total time remaining in the exam can be found across the screen from the Mark check box.

▶ The test question is located in a colored section. Directly below the test question, in the white area, are response choices.

▶ Immediately below the response choices are instructions about how to respond, including the number of responses required. You will notice that question items requiring a single response have radio buttons. Items requiring multiple responses have check boxes.

 Note

Some questions and some responses do not appear on the screen in their entirety. You will recognize these because a scrollbar appears to the right of the question item or response. Use the scrollbar to reveal the rest of the question or response item.

▶ The buttons at the bottom of a window enable you to move back to a previous test item, proceed to the next test item, or exit TestPrep practice exams.

Some items require you to examine additional information, referred to as *exhibits*. These screens typically include graphs, diagrams, or other types of visual information needed to respond to the test question. Exhibits can be accessed by clicking the Exhibit button, also located at the bottom of the window.

After you complete the practice test by moving through all the test questions for your exam, you arrive at a summary screen titled Item Review. This window enables you to see all the question numbers, your response(s) to each item, any questions you have marked, and any left incomplete. The buttons at the bottom of the screen enable you to review all of the marked items and incomplete items in numeric order.

If you want to review a specific marked or incomplete item, simply type the desired item number in the box at the lower-right corner of the window and click the Review Item button. This takes you to that particular item. After you review the item, you can respond to the question. Notice that this window also offers the Next and Previous options. You can also select the Item Review button to return to the Item Review window.

Note

If you exceed the time allotted for the test, you do not have the opportunity to review any marked or incomplete items. The program will move on to the next screen.

After you complete your review of the practice test questions, click the Grade Now button to find out how you did. An examination score report is generated for your practice test; this report provides you with the required score for this particular certification exam, your score on the practice test, and a grade. The report also breaks down your performance on the practice test by the specific objectives for the exam. Click the Print button to print the results of your performance.

You also have the option of reviewing those items that you answered incorrectly. Click the Show Me What I Missed button to receive a summary of those items. Print this information if you need further practice or review; the printouts can be used to guide your use of study cards and flash cards.

Using TestPrep Study Cards

To start the study cards software, do the following:

1. From the overview of the CD contents, click the Study Cards icon to see a list of topics. Clicking Study Cards brings up more detailed information for this application in the right window.

2. To launch the study cards, follow the instructions in the right window and click on the "hot" word, Explorer.

3. In the window that opens on the left, double-click the Study Card icon. After a moment, you see an initial screen similar to the one for practice exams.

4. Click the Next button to see the first study cards.

The interface for study cards is very similar to that of practice exams. However, you have several important options that enable you to prepare for an exam. The study cards material is organized using the specific objectives for each exam. You can opt to receive questions on all the objectives or use the check boxes to select coverage of a limited set of objectives. For example, if you have already completed a practice exam and your score report indicates that you need work on Create forms, you can choose to cover only the Create forms objectives for your study cards session.

You can also specify how many questions are presented by typing the number you desire in the Number of Questions field at the right of the screen. You can specify how much time you will be allotted for a review by typing the number of minutes into the Time Limit field immediately. Click the Start Test button, and the study cards program randomly selects the indicated number of questions from the question database. A dialog box informs you that this process could take some time.

Respond to the questions in the same manner as you did to practice exam questions. Radio buttons signal that a single answer is required; check boxes indicate that multiple answers are expected.

Notice the menu options at the top of the window. File pulls down to allow you an exit from the program. Edit allows you to use the copy function and even copy questions to the Windows clipboard. Should you feel the urge to take some notes on a particular question, the Options pull-down menu offers you that choice. When you pull it down, choose Open Notes to open Notepad. Options also allows you to start over with another exam.

This application provides you with immediate feedback as to whether you answered the question correctly. Click the Show Answers button to see the correct answer(s) highlighted on the screen. The study cards program also includes Item Review, Score Report, and Show Me What I Missed features, which are essentially the same as those in practice exams.

Using TestPrep Flash Cards

Flash cards offer a third way to use the exam question database. The flash cards do not offer you multiple-choice answers; instead, they require you to respond in a short-answer/essay format. The idea behind flash cards is to help you learn the material well enough to respond with the correct answers in your own words, rather than just by recognizing the correct answer. If you have the depth of knowledge to answer questions without prompting, you will certainly be prepared to pass a multiple-choice exam.

Flash cards are started in the same fashion as practice exams and study cards:

1. Double-click the Flash Cards icon to see the opening screen.

2. Click Next, and the first Flash Card screen will appear.

3. Flash cards can be chosen by the various objectives, just as with study cards. Select the objectives you want to cover, the

number of questions you want, and the amount of time you want to restrict yourself to.

4. Click the Start Test button to start the flash cards session; you see a dialog box notifying you that questions are being selected.

5. The flash cards appear in an interface similar to that of practice exams and study cards. Notice, however, that although a question is presented, no possible answers appear.

6. Type your answer in the white space below the question.

7. Compare your answer to the correct answer by clicking the Show Answers button. You can also use the Show Reference button in the same manner as with study cards.

The pull-down menus provide nearly the same functionality as they do in study cards, except that you'll find a Paste option on the Edit menu instead of a Copy Question option. Flash cards provide simple feedback. They do not include an Item Review or Score Report. They are intended to provide you with an alternative way to assess your level of knowledge that will encourage you to learn the information more thoroughly than through other methods.

I n d e x

D

Restrictions section, Server document, 209
Results database, Log Events view, 387
@Return function, 756
returning
  lists
    @Explode function, 760-761
    @Keywords function, 764-765
    @Unique function, 766-767
  strings
    @Implode function, 761-762
    @IsMember function, 762
    @IsNotMember function, 763
  values
    @PickList function, 787-788
    from incomplete formulas, 756
    main expressions, 755
[ReturnReceipt] flag, 828
ReturnReceipt field, 822
rich text, placing in layout regions, 850
Rich Text data type fields, 500-501
rich-text fields, 996
rights
  to administrators, assigning, 27
  agents
    creation rights, 1009
    execution rights problems, 1008-1009
  problems
    ACL (Access Control List) rights, 1012
    with users, 1011
  to create databases, 990
  see privileges

roles
  ACLs, Public Address Book, 222
  GroupCreator, 222
  GroupModifier, 222
  NetCreator, 222
  NetModifier, 222
  ServerCreator, 222
  ServerModifier, 222
  UserCreator, 222
  UserModifier, 223
roles (security), 943-947
  assigning to users/groups, 945
  creating, 944-945
  defining, 943-944
  hiding form properties, 945-947
@Round function, 541

ROUTE AT ONCE IF connection, 187
Route At Once If field, 170
Route at Once If/Routing Cost field, 131
Route console command, 72
Route through field, 144
Router program, 76
router tasks
  mail, 162-163
  paths, 163
routers
  domains, communicating between, 342-343
  Server Connection document, 172
Routing Cost field, 171
RSA cryptosystem, 191-193
running
  agents, 896-899
    from actions, 897-898
    from agents, 898-899
    manually, 896-897
    permissions, 894-896
  formulas, 682
  simple actions, 681-682

S

safe copies, certificates, 317-318
Sample Billing view, 386
SaveOptions field, 821
saving documents, 640
scheduled agents
  private, 884-885
  shared, 885
scheduled triggers, agents, 882
SCOS (Single Copy Object Store), *see* mail, shared
scrollbars, inserting in fields, 851
Search Builder dialog box, 605
search formulas, views, easy run conditions, 605-607
secret encryption keys, 962-963
  distributing, 963-966
  enabling forms for, 968
  incorporating into user ID, 966-967
security, 22, 943
  access lists
    forms, 949-951
    views, 947-949
  ACLs (Access Control Lists), 691-692

T

W-X-Y-Z

A V I A C O M   S E R V I C E

The Information SuperLibrary™

Bookstore

Search

What's New

Reference Desk

Software Library

Newsletter

Company Overviews

Yellow Pages

Internet Starter Kit

HTML Workshop

Win a Free T-Shirt!

Macmillan Computer Publishing

Site Map

Talk to Us

CHECK OUT THE BOOKS IN THIS LIBRARY.

You'll find thousands of shareware files and over 1,600 computer books designed for both technowizards and technophobes. You can browse through 700 sample chapters, get the latest news on the Net, and find just about anything using our massive search directories.

All Macmillan Computer Publishing books are available at your local bookstore.

We're open 24 hours a day, 365 days a year.

You don't need a card.

We don't charge fines.

And you can be as **LOUD** as you want.

The Information SuperLibrary
http://www.mcp.com/mcp/   ftp.mcp.com

MACMILLAN COMPUTER PUBLISHING USA

A VIACOM COMPANY

Technical Support:

If you need assistance with the information in this book or with a CD/Disk accompanying the book, please access the Knowledge Base on our Web site at **http://www.superlibrary.com/general/support**. Our most Frequently Asked Questions are answered there. If you do not find the answer to your questions on our Web site, you may contact Macmillan Technical Support **(317) 581-3833** or e-mail us at **support@mcp.com**.

Getting Started with the CD-ROM

This page provides instructions for getting started with the CD-ROM.

Windows 95/NT Installation

Insert the CD-ROM into your CD-ROM drive. If autoplay is enabled on your machine, the CD-ROM setup program automatically starts the first time you insert the CD-ROM.

If setup does not run automatically, perform the following steps:

1. From the Start menu, select Programs | Windows Explorer.

2. Select your CD-ROM drive under My Computer.

3. Double-click `SETUP.EXE` in the Contents list.

4. Follow the onscreen instructions that appear.

Setup adds an icon named CD-ROM Contents to a program group for the book. To explore the CD-ROM, double-click the CD-ROM Contents icon.

License Agreement

This software is copyrighted and all rights are reserved by the publisher and its licensers. Your are licensed to use this software on a single computer. You may copy the software for backup or archival purposes only. Making copies of this software for any other purpose is a violation of United States copyright laws. THIS SOFTWARE IS SOLD AS IS, WITHOUT WARRANTY OF ANY KIND, EITHER EXPRESSED OR IMPLIED, INCLUDING BUT NOT LIMITED TO THE IMPLIED WARRANTIES OF MERCHANTABILITY AND FITNESS FOR A PARTICULAR PURPOSE. Neither the publisher nor its licensers, dealers, or distributors assumes any liability for any alleged or actual damages arising from the use of this software. (Some states do not allow exclusion of implied warranties, so the exclusion may not apply to you.)

The entire contents of this CD-ROM and the compilation of the software are copyrighted and protected by United States copyright laws. The individual programs on this disc are copyrighted by the authors or owners of each program.